English-Metric Conversion

		Inches	Millimeters	TEMPERATURE	
				Fahrenheit	Centigrade
1 meter = 39.370 inches		1	25	32	0
1 sq. mile = 2.59 sq. kilometers		2	51	40	4.4
1 sq. kilometer = .386 sq. mile		3	76	45	7.2
1 pound = 454 grams		4	102	50	10.0
1 kilogram = 2.205 pounds		5	127	55	12.8
1 inch = 2.540 centimeters		6	152	60	15.6
1 foot = .305 meter		7	178	65	18.3
1 yard = .848 meter		8	203	70	21.1
1 centimeter = .394 inch		9	229	75	23.9
1 meter = 1.094 yards		10	254	80	26.7
		11	279	85	29.4
		12	305	90	32.2
		13	330	95	35.0
		14	356	100	37.8
		15	381		
		16	406		
		17	432		
		18	457		
		19	483		
		20	508		
		25	635		

INLAND FISHES
of CALIFORNIA

INLAND FISHES
of CALIFORNIA

by PETER B. MOYLE

Illustrated by
ALAN MARCIOCHI
and
CHRIS van DYCK

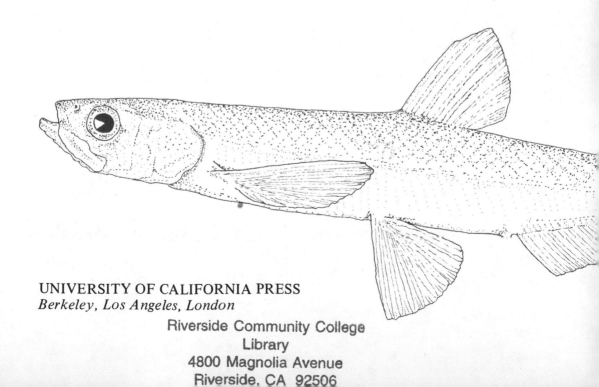

UNIVERSITY OF CALIFORNIA PRESS
Berkeley, Los Angeles, London

University of California Press
Berkeley and Los Angeles, California

University of California Press, Ltd.
London, England

ISBN 0-520-02975-5
Library of Congress Catalog Card Number: 75-3776
Printed in the United States of America

Contents

Acknowledgments

This book would not have been possible without the willing help of many people. J. Phillip Bartholomew made the initial contacts which indicated that the book was both possible and needed. Without this stimulus, the project would probably have been delayed several years, if not completely. I was fortunate to have Alan Marciochi and Chris Van Dyck as illustrators. Both of them worked cheerfully and skillfully to make the drawings as accurate as possible. My colleague on the University of California, Davis, fisheries faculty, Hiram W. Li, has been a source of many ideas and arguments and contributed many unpublished behavioral observations. Stephen J. Nicola has been a ready source of information on native fishes. Carl L. Hubbs contributed much pertinent information from his vast experience with California fishes, while Laura Hubbs helped make my brief stay with them both productive and enjoyable. Hiram Li, Stephen Nicola, Robert R. Miller, and Carl Hubbs critically reviewed much of the manuscript. Bruce Bachen served as my research assistant while I was writing much of the book, and his high level of competence freed me from many tasks and worries that normally eat up my time. Grant Barnes of the University of California Press provided sound editorial advice and encouraged this project from its inception.

The following individuals contributed unpublished information or reviewed selected portions of the manuscript: Dean Ahrenholz, Donald Alley, James K. Andreasen, George Barlow, Roger A. Barnhart, J. Phillip Bartholomew, Jonathan N. Baskin, Robert Behnke, Carl E. Bond, Martin R. Brittan, Robert Brown, Ted Cavender, Mark Caywood, Glen P. Contreras, Sherburne F. Cook, Jr., Millard Coots, Almo Cordone, Louis Courtois, John Deinstadt, Lillian Dempster, David Dettman, Christopher Dewees, Julie Donnelly, Ralph E. Elston, Don C. Erman, Richard Flint, Eric R. Gerstung, David W. Greenfield, Bobby Greenlee, Richard Haas, Craig Harasek, William J. Hauser, Charles R. Hazel, Kaaren J. Hiscox, David Hoopaugh, Franklin G. Hoover, Michael H. Horn, Erland T. Juntunen, Kurt Kline, Glenn M. Kottcamp, Richard J. Kresja, James F. LaBounty, E. Fred Legner, Michael Lembeck, Don E. McAllister, Craig E. McDonald, Alan Marciochi, Michael Martin, Robert R. Miller, Lee W. Miller, John B. Moyle, Robert R. Nichols, John Norton, Ronald Pelzman, Leo Pinkas, Edwin P. Pister, Robert R. Rawstron, Norman Reimers, James A. St. Amant, Peter Schulz, John D. Simms, Gerald R. Smith, Jerry J. Smith, Jamie Sturgess, Thomas L. Taylor, Chris Van Dyck, David Vanicek, Daniel Varoujean, Charles E. Vicker, Vadim D. Vladykov, Charles E. von Geldern, Jr., James White, and Paul A. Zellmer.

The task of producing a readable manuscript from my handwriting and typing was accomplished by Paula Buchignani, Donna Courtois, Josie Latiker, Maggi Trull, and Louisa Ruedas.

This book is dedicated to those people who have done the most to shape my ideas and attitudes: my parents, John B. and Evelyn W. Moyle, both aquatic biologists, who gave me most of my education; my wife Marilyn, who gave birth to our two children, Petrea and Noah, while the book was in preparation and yet managed to put up with the long hours I was away, mentally or physically, while working on the manuscript; James C. Underhill, my major professor while I was a graduate student at the University of Minnesota, who stimulated my interest in native fishes; Carl L. Hubbs, who has provided continuous encouragement for my studies of California fishes; and my good friends and colleagues, Richard Haas and Hiram Li, at Fresno and Davis, respectively, who willingly provided comments, ideas, and encouragement when I needed them.

Introduction

This book was written to provide biologists, students, and amateur naturalists with a survey of the information available on the natural history, identification, and management of California's inland fishes. Special efforts have been made to point out gaps in our knowledge of the native fishes, in order to stimulate interest in them before more species become rare, endangered, or extinct.

The first three chapters on distribution and zoogeography, ecology, and change are meant to offer the reader an overview of the biology and status of the inland fish fauna, as well as to link together the individual life-history summaries that make up the bulk of the book. To make these chapters more readable, extensive literature citations have been omitted; interested readers will find most of the citations they need in the individual species accounts.

The keys to the fishes have been the most frustrating part of this book to write. They have gone through innumerable versions that have been tested by numerous undergraduate and graduate fisheries students, yet they are far from foolproof. The variability of many species is so great that some individual fish are bound to end up at the wrong end point. I urge key users, therefore, to exercise caution and carefully check identifications with the descriptions and drawings that are part of each species account.

Each species account is organized as follows:

COMMON NAME

Scientific name

   I. *Systematic notes (optional)*
  II. *Identification*
 III. *Names*
 IV. *Distribution*
  V. *Life History*
     A. Habitat
     B. Social behavior
     C. Feeding habits
     D. Age and growth
     E. Reproduction
     F. Early life history
 VI. *Status*
     A. Abundance
     B. Management
VII. *References*

Systematic notes. These are included only for species that have been the subject of recent systematic controversies or have an exceptionally confusing taxonomic history. They are used to summarize the problems and to point out areas where research is needed. Minor questions of name changes or long-settled taxonomic questions are usually mentioned in the "names" section of each species account.

Identification. This is not meant to be a complete species description but only an aid to identification. Terminology used is defined in the introductory chapters on structure and identification.

Names. Most common and scientific names used are from the American Fisheries Society 1970 *List of Common and Scientific Names of Fishes from the United States and Canada*. The main exceptions are species described or introduced since the publication of the list. Extensive synonymies of the scientific nomenclature are not given since such compilations are both tedious and largely redundant with other publications (which are usually cited). The space spent delving into the origins of the common and scientific names of each species simply reflects my fascination with the subject.

Distribution. These are descriptions of the world and California distributions of each species. Table 1 in the chapter on distribution and zoogeography is a species checklist by drainage system meant to supplement this description. Distributional maps are not included because the limits of distribution of each species are poorly known and are changing rapidly as the nature of California's aquatic habitats change. The last extensive surveys in the state were those of Cloudsley Rutter (1908) and J. O. Snyder (1908-1933). In a few years it may be possible to draw statewide distribution maps of the fishes, at least for the early 1970s. Distributional surveys have been completed or are underway by: (1) the author and his graduate students, of the San Joaquin, Pit, McCloud, Pajaro, Clear Lake, and various coastal drainage systems; (2) Stephen J. Nicola, Mark Caywood, and Michael Aceituno, of the lower Sacramento River system; (3) E. P. Pister and coworkers, of the Owens, Walker, and Amargosa drainage systems; (4) Carl L. Hubbs and Robert R. Miller, of the Great Basin; (5) David Koch and Glen Contreras, of the Lost River system; and (6) James Andreasen and Carl Bond, of the upper Klamath system. Other distributional information can probably be gleaned from the regional files of the Department of Fish and Game.

Life History. Much of the information on the life histories of California fishes is in unpublished theses and reports. This section should provide at least a partial key to those sources, as well as to the published literature. Life-history observations without documentation in the text are usually those of the author. Individuals looking for research topics should take note of the many gaps in the knowledge of most species, especially in relation to behavior. But, please, if you are going to undertake a life-history investigation, aim to have your results published in a scientific journal.

Status. This section has two purposes. The first is to state whether or not the species under discussion is threatened, declining, common, abundant, or expanding its range. The second is to be a place where I can state my opinions about management, value, and future of the species in California. I hope that some of these opinions will serve as working hypotheses for future research.

Distribution and Zoogeography

California is a fascinating place for the student of fish zoogeography and evolution. It contains all or part of six large drainage systems, each with its own endemic fish fauna: (1) the Klamath River system, (2) the Sacramento-San Joaquin system, (3) the Lahontan system, (4) the Death Valley system, (5) south coastal drainages, and (6) the Colorado River system. Each major system in turn is divided into two or more minor drainage systems, each with one or more endemic species or subspecies but otherwise faunistically similar (Fig. 1).

The number of genera and species confined to each drainage system, major and minor, is a good indicator of the degree and length of its isolation from other drainage systems (Tables 1, 2). In recent years, the fish fauna of each drainage system has been greatly augmented through the introduction of fish species from all over the world (Table 1). Since many of these exotic species are still expanding their ranges in California, mostly with the help of man, the fish lists for each drainage system (Table 2) are bound to keep changing. As introduced species spread and native fishes

Table 1
Number of endemic, resident and anadromous, marine euryhaline, and introduced species occurring in the major drainage systems of California

	Klamath	Sacramento-San Joaquin	Lahontan	Death Valley	So. Calif.	Colorado	All Calif.
Endemic spp.	6[1]	17[2]	5[3]	8[4]	2	6	25[5]
Native resident or anadromous spp.[6]	25	40	8	7	11	6	63
Native marine euryhaline spp.[7]	9	15	0	0	11	3	20
Introduced spp.[7]	17	36	14	22	30	25	49
Total spp.[7]	51	91	22	29	52	33	132

[1]Includes *Lampetra minima*, now extinct, but formerly found in Miller Lake, Oregon (Bond and Kahn, 1973).
[2]Includes redband trout (*Salmo sp.*)
[3]Includes *Eremichthys acros* and *Chasmistes cujus* found only outside of California.
[4]Includes three species of pupfish and killifish (*Cyprinodon* and *Empetrichthys*) found only in Nevada.
[5]Species confined to California but may be within more than one drainage system within the state. Also includes Sacramento-San Joaquin fishes found in Goose Lake drainage in Oregon.
[6]California only, including endemic species.
[7]California only.

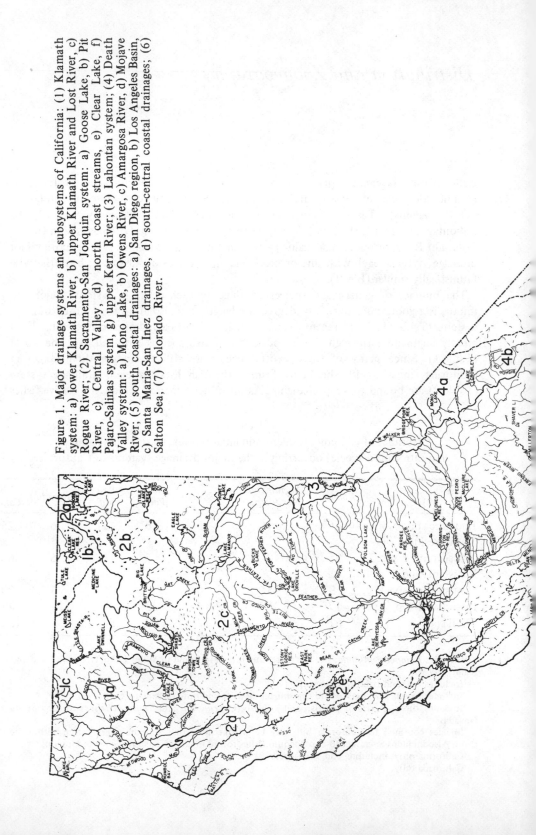

Figure 1. Major drainage systems and subsystems of California: (1) Klamath system: a) lower Klamath River, b) upper Klamath River and Lost River, c) Rogue River; (2) Sacramento-San Joaquin system: a) Goose Lake, b) Pit River, c) Central Valley, d) north coast streams, e) Clear Lake, f) Pajaro-Salinas system, g) upper Kern River; (3) Lahontan system; (4) Death Valley system: a) Mono Lake, b) Owens River, c) Amargosa River, d) Mojave River; (5) south coastal drainages: a) San Diego region, b) Los Angeles Basin, c) Santa Maria-San Inez drainages, d) south-central coastal drainages; (6) Salton Sea; (7) Colorado River.

COLORADO RIVER

7

DAMSBY LAKE

FORD LAKE

CADIZ LAKE

COLORADO RIVER

BRISTOL LAKE

DALE LAKE

AMERICAN CANAL

COACHELLA CANAL

E HIGHLINE CANAL

SALTON SEA

COLORADO RIVER AQUEDUCT

WHITEWATER RIVER

SODA LAKE

LAVA LAKE

TROY LAKE

BORREGO SINK

6

AMARGOSA RIVER

4c

AMARGOSA RIVER

MOJAVE RIVER

COYOTE LAKE

LUCERNE LAKE

4d

L. HENSHAW

SAN L. CAPITAN RES.

BORENA

5

5a

LOWER OTAY RES.

BARRETT L.C.

SEARLES LAKE

CHINA LAKE

KOSHA LAKE

ROGERS LAKE

LAKE ARROWHEAD

BIG BEAR L.

SAN JUS RA.

SAN DIEGO R.

DIEGO

SAN DIEGO AQUEDUCT

HODGES

OWENS LAKE

2g

KERN RIVER

LAKE ISABELLA

KERN RIVER

ROSAMOND LAKE

LAKE MATHEWS

RAILROAD CANYON RES.

ELSINORE LAKE

SANTA ANA RIVER

5b

KERN RIVER
NO. FORK
SO. FORK

KERN RIVER

KAWEAH RIVER

FRIANT KERN CANAL

HOMELAND CANAL

BUENA VISTA LAKE

BUENA VISTA SLOUGH

KINGS RIVER

TULARE LAKE

BOUQUET RES.

SANTA CLARA RIVER

SANTA MONICA BAY

SAN PEDRO BAY

SANTA CATALINA ISLAND

SAN CLEMENTE ISLAND

SAN JUAN RIVER

SALINAS RES.

5c

SANTA MARIA RIVER

SANTA YNEZ RIVER

SAN MIGUEL ISLAND

SANTA ROSA ISLAND

SANTA CRUZ ISLAND

ANACAPA ISLANDS

SAN NICOLAS ISLAND

SALINAS R.

NACI-MIENTO RES.

SAN ANTONIO RES.

5d

2f

MILES

KILOMETERS

0   10   30   50   70
0 10 3m 50 70 90

Table 2

Distributional checklist of the inland fishes of California by major drainage system.

N = native; I = introduced; O = occasional marine visitor; A = anadromous; E = extinct; R = rare; ? = status uncertain

Species	Klamath			Sacramento-San Joaquin							Lahontan	Death Valley				So. Calif.				Colorado	
	Lower	Upper	Rogue	Goose L.	Pit	Central Valley	Coast	Clear L.	Pajaro-Salinas	Kern		Mono L.	Owens	Amargosa	Mojave	San Diego	L.A. Basin	St. Maria-St. Inez	Coastal	Salton	Colo. R.
	1a	1b	1c	2a	2b	2c	2d	2e	2f	2g	3	4a	4b	4c	4d	5a	5b	5c	5d	6	7
Petromyzontidae																					
Pacific lamprey	NA	N	NA	N	—	NA	NA	NE	NA	—	—	—	—	—	—	—	NA	NA	NA	—	—
river lamprey	?	—	—	—	—	NA	NA	—	NA	—	—	—	—	—	—	—	—	—	—	—	—
Pacific brook lamprey	—	—	—	—	—	N	?	—	N	—	—	—	—	—	—	—	—	—	—	—	—
Pit-Klamath brook lamprey	—	N	—	N	N	—	—	—	—	—	—	—	—	—	—	—	—	—	—	—	—
Acipenseridae																					
white sturgeon	NA	—	—	—	—	NA	NA	—	—	—	—	—	—	—	—	—	—	—	—	—	—
green sturgeon	NA	—	—	—	—	NA	NA	—	—	—	—	—	—	—	—	—	—	—	—	R	—
Elopidae																					
machete	—	—	—	—	—	—	—	—	—	—	—	—	—	—	—	—	—	—	—	NE	O
Clupeidae																					
Pacific herring	O?	—	—	—	—	O	O	—	O	—	—	—	—	—	—	—	—	—	O?	—	—
American shad	IA	—	—	—	—	IA	IA	—	—	—	—	—	—	—	—	—	—	—	—	—	—
threadfin shad	—	—	—	—	—	I	?	—	I	—	—	—	—	—	—	I	I	I	I	I	I

Table 2 (continued)

Osmeridae																			
eulachon	NA	—	NA	—	—	—	—	—	—	—	—	—	—	—	—	—	—	—	—
delta smelt	I	—	—	—	—	N/I	—	—	—	—	—	—	—	—	—	—	—	—	—
surf smelt	O	—	O	O	—	O	O?	—	—	—	—	—	—	—	—	O	—	—	—
longfin smelt	O?	—	N	—	—	N	—	—	—	—	—	—	—	—	—	—	—	—	—
Salmonidae																			
mountain whitefish	—	—	—	—	—	—	—	—	N	—	—	—	—	—	—	—	—	—	—
pink salmon	NA	—	NA	NA	—	NA	—	—	—	—	—	—	—	—	—	OA	—	—	—
chum salmon	NA	—	NA	NA	—	NA	—	—	—	—	—	—	—	—	—	OA	—	—	—
coho salmon	NA	NA	NA/I	NA	—	NA/I	—	—	—	—	—	—	—	—	—	NA	—	—	—
chinook salmon	NA	NA	NA	NA	—	NA	—	—	—	—	—	—	—	—	—	NA	—	—	—
sockeye salmon	OA	OA	OA	OA	—	NA	—	—	—	—	—	—	—	—	—	OA	—	—	—
kokanee	I	—	I	—	—	I	—	—	—	I	—	—	—	—	—	—	—	—	—
brook trout	I	?	I	I	I	I	I	I	I	I	I	I	I	I	I	I	I	—	—
lake trout	—	—	—	—	—	—	—	—	I	—	—	—	—	—	—	—	—	—	—
interior Dolly Varden	NE?	—	NR	NR	—	NR	—	—	—	—	—	—	—	—	—	—	—	—	—
coast Dolly Varden	?	—	—	I	—	I	—	—	—	—	—	—	—	—	—	—	—	NE	—
cutthroat trout	N	N	N	?	—	N	—	—	—	—	—	—	—	—	—	—	—	—	—
brown trout	I	I	I	I	I	I	I	I	N	I	I	I	I	I	I	I	I	—	—
redband trout	—	NE?	NR	—	—	—	—	—	—	—	—	—	—	—	—	—	—	—	—
golden trout	N	—	N	I	—	I	—	—	—	—	—	—	—	—	—	N	—	—	—
rainbow trout	N	N	N	N	N	N	N?	N?	N	N	N	N	N	N	N	N	N	IE	IE
arctic grayling	I	—	—	I	—	I	—	—	—	—	—	—	—	—	—	—	—	I	—
Cyprinidae																			
carp	—	—	—	—	—	—	—	—	—	I?	—	I?	—	—	—	—	—	—	—
goldfish	—	—	—	—	—	—	—	—	—	I?	I?	—	—	—	—	—	—	—	—

Table 2 (continued)

Species	Klamath			Sacramento-San Joaquin							Lahontan	Death Valley				So. Calif.				Colorado	
	Lower	Upper	Rogue	Goose L.	Pit	Central Valley	Coast	Clear L.	Pajaro-Salinas	Kern	Lahontan	Mono L.	Owens	Amargosa	Mojave	San Diego	L.A. Basin	St. Maria–St. Inez	Coastal	Salton	Colo. R.
	1a	1b	1c	2a	2b	2c	2d	2e	2f	2g	3	4a	4b	4c	4d	5a	5b	5c	5d	6	7
tench	—	—	—	—	—	—	—	—	I	—	—	—	—	—	—	—	—	—	—	—	—
golden shiner	—	I	—	—	I	I	I	I	I	—	I?	—	—	—	—	I	I	I	I	I?	I
Sacramento blackfish	—	—	—	—	—	N	I	N	N	—	—	—	—	—	—	—	I?	—	—	—	—
hardhead	—	—	—	—	N	N	N	N	—	—	—	—	—	—	—	—	—	—	—	—	—
hitch	—	—	—	—	—	N	N	N	N	—	—	—	—	—	—	—	—	—	—	—	—
Sacramento squawfish	—	—	—	—	N	N	N	N	N	—	—	—	—	—	—	—	—	—	—	—	—
Colorado squawfish	—	—	—	—	—	—	—	—	—	—	—	—	—	—	—	—	—	—	—	NE	NE
bonytail	—	—	—	—	—	—	—	—	—	—	—	—	—	—	—	—	—	—	—	NE	NE
blue chub	(N)	N	—	—	—	—	—	—	—	—	—	—	—	—	—	—	—	—	—	NE	NE
tui chub	(N)	N	—	N	N/I	NE/I	—	—	—	—	N	—	N	—	N	—	—	—	—	—	—
arroyo chub	—	—	—	—	—	—	—	—	—	—	—	—	—	—	I	—	N	I	—	—	—
thicktail chub	—	—	—	—	—	NE	—	NE	—	—	—	—	—	—	—	—	—	—	—	—	—
Sacramento splittail	—	—	—	—	—	N	—	—	—	—	—	—	—	—	—	—	—	—	—	—	—
Clear Lake splittail	—	—	—	—	—	—	—	NR	—	—	—	—	—	—	—	—	—	—	—	—	—
California roach	—	—	—	N	N	N	N	N	N	—	—	—	—	—	—	—	N	—	—	—	—
speckled dace	N	N	N	N	N	N	N	—	N	—	N	—	N	N	—	—	—	I	I	—	—
Lahontan redside	—	—	—	—	—	I	—	—	—	—	N	—	—	—	—	—	—	—	—	—	—

Table 2 (continued)

	1	2	3	4	5	6	7	8	9	10	11	12	13	14	15	16	17	18	19	20	21	22	23	24	25	26
red shiner	—	—	—	—	—	—	—	—	—	—	—	—	—	—	I?	—	—	—	—	—	—	—	—	—	—	—
fathead minnow	—	—	—	—	—	—	—	—	—	I?	—	—	I	I	I	—	—	—	—	N	—	NR	NR	I	N	I
Catostomidae																										
bigmouth buffalo	—	—	I	—	—	—	—	—	—	—	—	—	—	—	—	—	—	—	—	—	—	—	—	—	—	—
Lost River sucker	—	—	—	—	—	—	—	—	—	—	—	—	—	NR	—	—	—	—	—	—	—	—	NR	—	(N)	—
shortnose sucker	—	—	—	—	—	—	—	—	—	—	—	—	—	—	—	—	—	—	—	—	—	—	NR	—	—	—
Santa Ana sucker	N	N	N	N	—	—	—	—	—	N?	—	—	—	—	—	—	—	—	—	—	—	—	—	—	—	—
mountain sucker	—	I	—	—	—	—	—	—	—	—	—	—	—	—	—	—	—	—	—	—	—	—	—	—	—	—
humpback sucker	NR	—	—	—	—	—	—	—	—	—	—	—	—	—	—	—	—	—	—	—	—	—	—	—	—	—
Klamath small-scale sucker	—	—	—	—	—	—	—	—	—	—	—	—	—	—	—	N	—	—	—	—	—	—	—	—	N	—
Modoc sucker	—	—	—	—	—	—	—	—	—	—	—	—	—	—	—	—	—	—	—	—	—	—	—	—	—	—
Tahoe sucker	—	—	I?	—	N	—	—	—	—	I?	—	—	—	—	—	N	—	—	—	—	—	—	—	—	—	—
Owens sucker	—	—	I?	—	N	I	—	—	—	—	—	—	—	—	—	—	—	—	—	—	—	—	—	—	—	—
Klamath large-scale sucker	—	—	—	—	I	—	—	—	—	—	—	—	—	—	—	—	—	—	—	—	—	—	—	—	—	—
Sacramento sucker	—	—	—	—	—	—	—	—	—	N	N	N	N	N	N	—	—	—	—	—	—	I?	—	—	(N)	—
Ictaluridae																										
blue catfish	—	—	I	I	—	I	—	—	—	—	—	—	—	—	—	—	—	—	—	—	—	—	—	—	—	—
channel catfish	I	I	I?	I?	I?	I	I?	—	I	I	I	I	I	I	I	—	—	—	—	—	—	—	—	—	—	—
white catfish	—	—	I	I	I	I	I	—	I	I	I	I	I	I	I	—	—	—	—	I	I	—	—	I	I	—
yellow bullhead	I	—	I?	I?	I?	I	I?	—	I	I	I	I	I	I	I	—	—	—	—	—	—	—	—	—	I	—
brown bullhead	I	I	I	I	I	I	I	—	I	I	I	I	I	I	I	—	—	—	—	I	I	—	—	I	I	—
black bullhead	I	I	I?	I?	I?	I	I?	—	I	I	I	I	I	I	I	—	—	—	—	—	—	—	—	—	—	—
flathead catfish	I	—	—	—	—	—	—	—	—	—	—	—	—	—	—	—	—	—	—	—	—	—	—	—	—	—
Cobitidae																										
Chinese weatherfish	—	—	I	—	—	—	—	—	—	—	—	—	—	—	—	—	—	—	—	—	—	—	—	—	—	—

Table 2 (continued)

Species	Klamath Lower 1a	Klamath Upper 1b	Klamath Rogue 1c	Sac.-S.J. Goose L. 2a	Sac.-S.J. Pit 2b	Sac.-S.J. Central Valley 2c	Sac.-S.J. Coast 2d	Sac.-S.J. Clear L. 2e	Sac.-S.J. Pajaro-Salinas 2f	Sac.-S.J. Kern 2g	Lahontan 3	D.V. Mono L. 4a	D.V. Owens 4b	D.V. Amargosa 4c	D.V. Mojave 4d	So.Cal. San Diego 5a	So.Cal. L.A. Basin 5b	So.Cal. St. Maria-St. Inez 5c	So.Cal. Coastal 5d	Colorado Salton 6	Colorado Colo. R. 7
Cyprinodontidae																					
rainwater killifish	—	—	—	—	—	I	—	—	—	—	—	—	—	—	—	—	I	—	—	—	—
Argentine pearlfish	—	—	—	—	—	—	—	—	—	—	—	—	—	—	—	—	I	—	—	—	—
Trinidad rivulus	—	—	—	—	—	—	—	—	—	—	—	—	—	—	—	—	—	—	—	I?	—
California killifish	—	—	—	—	—	—	O	—	O	—	—	—	—	—	—	N	N	N	N	—	—
desert pupfish	—	—	—	—	—	—	—	—	—	—	—	—	—	—	I	—	—	—	—	N	NR
Owens pupfish	—	—	—	—	—	—	—	—	—	—	—	—	NR	—	—	—	—	—	—	—	—
Amargosa pupfish	—	—	—	—	—	—	—	—	—	—	—	—	—	N	—	—	—	—	—	—	—
Salt Creek pupfish	—	—	—	—	—	—	—	—	—	—	—	—	—	N	—	—	—	—	—	—	—
Cottonball Marsh pupfish	—	—	—	—	—	—	—	—	—	—	—	—	—	N	—	—	—	—	—	—	—
Poeciliidae																					
mosquitofish	—	—	—	—	I	I	I	I	I	—	I	—	I	I	I	I	I	I	I	I	I
sailfin molly	—	—	—	—	—	—	—	—	—	—	—	—	—	—	—	—	—	—	—	I	—
shortfin molly	—	—	—	—	—	—	—	—	—	—	—	—	—	—	—	—	—	—	—	I	—
guppy	—	—	—	—	—	—	—	—	—	—	—	—	—	—	—	—	I?	—	—	—	—
variable platyfish	—	—	—	—	—	—	—	—	—	—	—	—	—	—	—	—	—	—	—	I?	I?
green swordtail	—	—	—	—	—	—	—	—	—	—	—	—	—	—	—	—	I?	—	—	—	—

Table 2 (continued)

Atherinidae																		
topsmelt	O	–	–	–	–	–	–	–	–	O	O	O	O	–	–	O	–	–
Mississippi silverside	–	–	–	–	–	–	–	–	–	–	–	–	–	–	–	–	–	–
Gasterosteidae																		
threespine stickleback	N	–	N	NR	N	N	–	I	N	N	N	N	N	–	–	N	–	–
Syngnathidae																		
bay pipefish	–	–	O	N	O	–	–	–	–	–	–	–	–	–	–	–	–	–
Percichthyidae																		
striped bass	–	–	I	I	I	O	–	–	–	I	–	I	–	I	–	I	–	I
white bass	–	–	–	–	O	–	–	–	–	–	–	–	–	–	–	–	–	–
Centrarchidae																		
Sacramento perch	–	–	NR	I?	NR	NR	I	NE	–	I	I	–	I	–	I	–	–	–
black crappie	–	?	–	–	I	NR	–	I	–	I	I	–	I	–	I	–	–	–
white crappie	–	–	I	–	I	I	–	I	–	I	I	–	I	–	I	–	–	–
warmouth	–	–	–	–	I	–	I?	I?	–	I	I	–	I	–	I	–	I?	–
green sunfish	I?	–	I	–	I	I	I?	I	I?	I	I	–	I	–	I	–	I?	–
bluegill	–	–	I	IE	–	I	–	–	–	I	I	–	I	–	I	–	–	–
pumpkinseed	–	–	I	I	IE	I	–	–	–	I	I	–	I	–	I	–	–	–
redear sunfish	–	–	I	–	I	I?	–	–	–	I	I	–	I	–	I	–	–	–
largemouth bass	–	–	I	I	I	I	–	–	–	I	I	–	I	–	I	–	–	–
spotted bass	–	–	I	–	I	–	–	–	I	I	I	–	I?	–	I?	–	–	–
smallmouth bass	–	–	I	I	I	IE	I?	I	I?	I	I	–	I?	–	I?	–	I?	–
redeye bass	–	–	–	I?	I	I	–	–	–	I	I	–	I	–	I	–	–	–
Percidae																		
yellow perch	I	–	–	–	IE	–	–	–	–	I	I	–	I	–	I	–	–	–
bigscale logperch	–	–	–	–	I	–	–	–	–	–	–	–	–	–	–	–	–	–

Table 2 (continued)

Species	Klamath			Sacramento-San Joaquin							Lahontan	Death Valley				So. Calif.				Colorado	
	Lower 1a	Upper 1b	Rogue 1c	Goose L. 2a	Pit 2b	Central Valley 2c	Coast 2d	Clear L. 2e	Pajaro-Salinas 2f	Kern 2g	3	Mono L. 4a	Owens 4b	Amargosa 4c	Mojave 4d	San Diego 5a	L.A. Basin 5b	St. Maria-St. Inez 5c	Coastal 5d	Salton 6	Colo. R. 7
Cichlidae																					
Mozambique mouthbrooder	—	—	—	—	—	—	—	—	—	—	—	—	—	—	—	—	—	—	—	I	I
Zill's cichlid	—	—	—	—	—	—	—	—	—	—	—	—	—	—	—	—	—	—	—	I	I
Embiotocidae																					
shiner perch	O	—	—	—	—	O	O	—	O	—	—	—	—	—	—	O	O	O	O	—	—
tule perch	—	—	—	—	N	N	N	N	NE	—	—	—	—	—	—	—	—	—	—	—	—
Mugilidae																					
striped mullet	—	—	—	—	—	—	—	—	—	—	—	—	—	—	—	O	—	—	—	O	N
Eleotridae																					
spotted sleeper	—	—	—	—	—	—	—	—	—	—	—	—	—	—	—	—	—	—	—	—	O
Gobiidae																					
tidewater goby	—	—	—	—	—	N	N	—	N	—	—	—	—	—	—	N	N	N	N	—	—
yellowfin goby	—	—	—	—	—	I	I	—	I	—	—	—	—	—	—	—	—	—	—	—	—
longjaw mudsucker	—	—	—	—	—	O	O	—	O	—	—	—	—	—	—	O	O	O	O	I	O
arrow goby	O	—	—	—	—	O	O	—	O	—	—	—	—	—	—	O	O	O	O	—	O
chameleon goby	—	—	—	—	—	?	—	—	—	—	—	—	—	—	—	—	?	—	—	—	—

Table 2 (continued)

	1	2	3	4	5	6	7	8	9	10	11	12	13	14	15	16	17	18	19	20	21
Pholidae																					
penpoint gunnel	?	—	—	—	—	—	—	—	?	—	—	—	—	—	—	—	—	—	—	—	—
saddleback gunnel	?	—	—	—	—	—	—	—	?	—	—	—	—	—	—	—	—	—	—	—	—
Cottidae																					
sharpnose sculpin	O	—	—	—	—	O	O	—	O	—	—	—	—	—	—	—	—	—	—	—	—
staghorn sculpin	N	—	—	—	—	N	N	—	N	—	—	—	—	—	—	N	N	N	N	—	—
rough sculpin	—	N	—	—	NR	—	—	—	—	—	—	—	—	—	—	—	—	—	—	—	—
slender sculpin	N	—	N?	—	—	—	—	—	—	—	—	—	—	—	—	—	—	—	—	—	—
coastrange sculpin	N	N	—	N	—	N	—	—	—	—	—	—	—	—	—	—	N	N	N	—	—
prickly sculpin	N	—	—	—	—	N	N	N	N	N	—	—	—	—	—	—	N	N	N	—	—
Pit sculpin	—	N	—	—	—	N?	—	—	—	—	—	—	—	—	—	—	—	—	—	—	—
marbled sculpin	N	N	—	—	—	N?	—	—	—	—	—	—	—	—	—	—	—	—	—	—	—
Piute sculpin	—	—	—	—	—	—	—	—	—	—	N	—	—	—	—	—	—	—	—	—	—
riffle sculpin	—	—	—	—	—	N	N	—	N	—	—	—	—	—	—	—	—	—	—	—	—
reticulate sculpin	—	—	N	—	—	—	—	—	—	—	—	—	—	—	—	—	—	—	—	—	—
Pleuronectidae																					
starry flounder	N	—	—	—	—	N	N	—	N	N	—	—	—	—	—	—	N	N	N	—	—
No. Native Spp.	29	12	10	7	14	47	35	13	30	3	9	0	4	4	1	11	14	15	17	4	10
No. Introduced Spp.	13	14	1	3	12	32	19	16	20	2	14	9	15	3	15	20	26	20	21	18	24
TOTAL NO. SPP.	42	26	11	10	26	79	54	29	50	5	23	9	19	7	16	31	40	35	38	22	34

become rare, extinct, or established in other drainage systems, the study of the zoogeography of native forms becomes, lamentably, more and more an exercise in past history, where ancient museum specimens and old field notes are more meaningful than populations of live fish. Nevertheless, the subject is still worth pursuing for the insights it can provide into the distributional patterns and speciation of the native fishes.

Any summary of the zoogeography of native California fishes is, in large part, a summary of the work of Robert R. Miller and Carl L. Hubbs, who have devoted an extraordinary amount of time and effort to the study of western freshwater fishes (Hubbs and Miller, 1948; Hubbs, Miller, and Hubbs, 1974; R. R. Miller, 1958, 1961, 1965).

KLAMATH RIVER SYSTEM

The Klamath River system has three distinct parts: (1) the upper Klamath River above Klamath Falls, including the Lost River; (2) the Klamath River below the falls, including the Trinity River; and (3) the Rogue River, with only a few tributary headwaters in California.

The distinctness of the fish faunas of the upper and lower Klamath River reflects that the connection between the two systems is geologically recent. They share only two fishes, Klamath speckled dace and marbled sculpin, mainly endemic to the Klamath system. The lower Klamath has only one species or subspecies of its own (Klamath smallscale sucker), while the upper Klamath has seven in California (Pit-Klamath brook lamprey, blue chub, Klamath tui chub, shortnose sucker, Klamath largescale sucker, Lost River sucker, and slender sculpin). The upper Klamath presumably once flowed into the Great Basin, because the closest relatives of Klamath tui chub, speckled dace, and shortnose sucker are found there. There is also evidence of at least headwater connections with the Pit River of the Sacramento-San Joaquin system. The Pit and Upper Klamath rivers share Pit-Klamath brook lamprey and marbled sculpin. In addition, the closest relative of the slender sculpin appears to be the rough sculpin of the Pit River (Robins and Miller, 1957). With the exception of the Pit River fishes and the Klamath largescale sucker, which appears to be close to both the Columbia largescale sucker, *Catostomus macrocheilus*, and the Sacramento sucker, the upper Klamath fish fauna shows few affinities to the fishes of either the Columbia system on the north or the main Sacramento-San Joaquin system on the south. This is surprising since the Columbia and Sacramento-San Joaquin faunas show some affinities to each other. In any case, the distinctness of the upper Klamath fish fauna indicates a long period of isolation from other faunas. The connection with the lower Klamath probably was created during one of the high rainfall eras of the Pleistocene. The water level of Klamath Lake then rose to a point where it could spill over a low divide into the lower Klamath River system, eventually eroding a permanent connection that would flow even when the lake level was low, as it is today. Until reservoirs were constructed on the lower Klamath River, upper Klamath fishes were unable to colonize the lower river because of the absence of suitable habitat, although individuals were occasionally washed into downstream areas.

The Rogue River can be considered allied to the lower Klamath system because it contains the one true freshwater fish endemic to the lower Klamath, the Klamath smallscale sucker. However, the Rogue has obviously never been an integral part of the Klamath system because it lacks other Klamath fishes, such as speckled dace and marbled sculpin, and contains reticulate sculpin, a species abundant in coastal streams further north.

SACRAMENTO-SAN JOAQUIN SYSTEM

The Sacramento-San Joaquin drainage system dominates central California (Fig. 1). Its large size, diverse habitats, and isolation from other systems have made it the center of freshwater-fish speciation in California. No fewer than seventeen species live solely in this system (Table 1). Many of these species are divided into subspecies, indicating that the Sacramento-San Joaquin system can itself be divided into distinct subsystems that have been at least partially isolated from each other: (1) Central Valley, (2) Goose Lake, (3) Pit River, (4) north coastal streams, (5) Clear Lake, (6) Pajaro-Salinas system, and (7) upper Kern River. The upper McCloud River, currently under investigation by the author, may also deserve recognition as a subsystem since it contains apparently distinctive redband trout and Dolly Varden.

The *Central Valley* is drained by the Sacramento and San Joaquin rivers. The Kern, Tule, Kaweah, and Kings rivers of the southern end of the San Joaquin Valley join with the San Joaquin River only during years of exceptionally high flows. It has been the center of speciation for the entire Sacramento-San Joaquin system because it is huge and centrally located, it contains a wide variety of habitats, and many of its essential features are ancient.

The precursor of the present valley was formed during the Pliocene period, which began 9 to 11 million years ago (Howard, 1967; Oakeshott, 1971). The ancestors of the present-day fishes presumably invaded during the middle of this epoch, 4 to 5 million years ago, when the predecessors of the Sierra Nevada and the coastal ranges had been eroded down to low hills. The renewal of mountain building at the end of the period isolated the system from its interior sources of freshwater fishes. These sources were streams that were part of the ancient Columbia River system, which seems to have been the center of fish evolution in western North America (R. R. Miller, 1965).

Despite their variety, the endemic Central Valley fishes show evidence of having a rather limited ancestry. There are two species (hardhead, Sacramento perch) whose closest relatives are late Pliocene fossils from Idaho (R. R. Miller, 1965; R. R. Miller and Smith, 1967), two species of marine ancestry (tule perch, Delta smelt), two species with close relatives outside the system (Sacramento sucker, Sacramento squawfish), and a cluster of distinctive minnows (splittail, hitch, Sacramento blackfish, California roach, thicktail chub). With the exception of the roach, the latter five species evolved in response to the varied lowland habitats of the system. This freshwater fauna is supplemented with a number of anadromous species (families Petromyzontidae, Acipenseridae, Salmonidae, Gasterosteidae), species of recent marine origin (families Cottidae, Osmeridae), and various marine fishes which can spend part of their life cycle in fresh water. Therefore, the number of species that were able to invade California from the interior prior to the rise of the Sierra Nevada was apparently small. Alternately, if the fossil record shows that a greater variety of forms invaded than the present fauna would indicate, only a small number of them were able to survive the harsh conditions that must have prevailed at various times in the Central Valley during the Pleistocene period.

Goose Lake is a large, shallow, alkaline lake on the California-Oregon border that apparently first appeared in the late Pleistocene period. In recent times it has overflowed through a low, marshy area at the southern end of the lake into the Pit River and then dried up almost completely (Pease, 1965). The lake and its tributary streams contain only six native species (dwarf Pacific lamprey, Sacramento sucker, tui chub, speckled dace, California roach, Pit sculpin). Redband trout (recorded as cutthroat by Snyder, 1908a) were apparently present in a number of the tributary systems. The sucker, tui chub, and roach have been described as belonging to Goose Lake subspecies or species, but they in fact seem to be very close to the forms found in the upper Pit River. Martin (1967) showed that Goose Lake suckers intergrade in their characteristics with Pit River suckers which in turn intergrade with Sacramento River suckers. This was probably also true of redband trout (R. Behnke, pers. comm.). Goose Lake, therefore, might better be treated as part of the Pit River system, rather than as an isolated basin.

The *Pit River* drains most of the northeastern corner of California, an area that was subject to intense mountain building and vulcanism during the Pliocene and Pleistocene periods. The heavy lava flows that created the desolate Devils Garden region repeatedly changed the face of the landscape. In the late Pliocene the upper Pit River drained north and west, into the upper Klamath River. At the beginning of the Pleistocene, however, this flow was dammed by the lava and a deep lake was created (a shallow lake was already present) which eventually spilled over through a gap in the Adin Mountains, joining the lower Pit River in Big Valley (Pease, 1965). The site of the lake (Lake Alturas) is now largely covered with basalt flows.

As a result of these dramatic changes in flow, the Pit River contains fishes derived from both the Klamath and Sacramento systems. The Sacramento fishes are all recent invaders that were able to get past the falls and rapids in the middle stretches of the river: Sacramento squawfish, hardhead, California roach, Sacramento sucker, speckled dace, and Pit sculpin. The Pit sculpin seems to be a recently evolved derivative of the riffle sculpin. The fishes whose ancestors inhabited the Klamath system are Pit-Klamath brook lamprey, marbled sculpin, and rough sculpin. The marbled sculpin of the Pit River is distinct from that of the Klamath system, and was originally described as a separate species (Rutter, 1908). The rough sculpin seems to be quite close to the slender sculpin of the Klamath. Both sculpins, however, give evidence of a long period of separation from the Klamath system. The relationships of two other species, the tui chub and the Modoc sucker, need to be investigated. The tui chub is probably closest to the Klamath tui chub but it may also have been derived from the *obesa* form of the nearby Lahontan system. The origin of the Modoc sucker is difficult to explain because it does not appear to have close relatives in either the upper

Klamath or Sacramento rivers. The possibility exists, however, that it was derived from the Tahoe sucker, the result of a tributary capture from the Lahontan system.

The *north coastal streams* drain the coast range from Tomales Bay north to the mouth of the Klamath River. Most of the streams are small and contain only fishes that can move readily through salt water, and so are of little zoogeographic interest. However, the Mad, Eel, Bear, Navarro, Gualala, and Russian rivers, as well as three tributaries to Tomales Bay (Walker, Papermill, and Olema creeks) all contain freshwater fishes derived from the Sacramento-San Joaquin River system.

The Mad, Eel, and Bear rivers, in Humboldt County, contain a subspecies of the Sacramento sucker (*Catostomus occidentalis humboldtianus*) which presumably entered the Eel River through capture of a headwater stream that originally flowed into the Sacramento River. The divide separating the two drainages is quite narrow in places, and may have been even easier to bridge when the coastal mountains were lower. California roach also are present in the Eel River. They were not noticed by Snyder (1908c) and they are now becoming increasingly common in the system, suggesting that they were recently introduced by man (Fite, 1973).

The Navarro River contains both California roach and Sacramento sucker, while the only true freshwater fish in the Gualala River is the roach. Taxonomic analysis indicates that these fishes were derived from Russian River populations, presumably through headwater captures in the geologically recent past (Snyder, 1908c; Murphy, 1948c).

One of the more interesting problems in California zoogeography is the origin of the fishes of the Russian River. It has been a topic of debate ever since Holway (1907) suggested that the river was the ancestral home of the entire Sacramento-San Joaquin fish fauna, an idea rejected almost immediately by Snyder (1908d). The Russian River is a coastal stream of special interest because it contains not only California roach and Sacramento suckers, but also Sacramento squawfish, hardhead, hitch, and tule perch. The tule perch is sufficiently different from other populations to be recognized as a subspecies (Hopkirk, 1973).

Two methods have been proposed that could result in the transfer of Sacramento-San Joaquin fishes into the Russian River: (1) through the Clear Lake basin and (2) through streams tributary to San Francisco Bay. Both hypotheses have much to recommend them and it is quite possible that both routes were used.

The transfer of fish from Clear Lake to the Russian River is favored by geological evidence. This evidence, explained in detail below, indicates that Clear Lake first drained into the Sacramento River via Cache Creek. Cache Creek was blocked by a lava flow, forcing the lake to spill over into Cold Creek, which flows into the Russian River. Cold Creek was then blocked by a landslide, and the drainage down Cache Creek was reopened.

The transfer of fishes to the Russian River through streams tributary to San Francisco Bay was possible because the saltwater flooding of the river valley that once existed where the bay is now was a geologically recent event. In addition, the surface waters of the bay may have had very low salinities during times when the Sacramento and San Joaquin rivers flood, permitting the passage of freshwater fishes. Getting the fish over the divide separating the two drainages presents little difficulty since, according to Murphy (1948c), even today there are only low divides between creeks flowing north and south in the Santa Rosa Valley (Copeland and Petaluma creeks, respectively) and in the Sonoma Valley (Santa Rosa and Sonoma creeks). Admittedly, the present-day creeks are all rather small and intermittent. However, there may also have been a number of San Francisco Bay tributary captures by the Russian River when the coastal hills rose during the Pleistocene (Wahrshaftig and Birman, 1965).

A close examination of the fish fauna supports the hypothesis that both routes were used. The California roach of the Russian River seems to be closer to the form in streams tributary to San Francisco Bay than it is to the form in the Clear Lake Basin (Murphy, 1948c), although the Russian River tule perch bears greater similarity to the Clear Lake form than to the Sacramento-San Joaquin form (Hopkirk, 1973). Hardhead are present in the Russian River, but absent from the Clear Lake Basin. Sacramento perch and Sacramento blackfish, once two of the most abundant species in Clear Lake, were absent from the Russian River until introduced by man, an indication that lack of suitable habitat was probably not a factor in keeping them from becoming established in more ancient times. All other true freshwater fishes in the Russian River are species adapted for stream living that could have entered the river through either route.

Clear Lake, the largest freshwater lake completely within California, occupies a small drainage basin in the Coast Range. Its outlet, Cache Creek, flows through a steep, narrow canyon and eventually joins the Sacramento River. Its native fish fauna is dominated by species otherwise found mainly in the quiet waters of the Central Valley floor. These fishes are incapable of moving up Cache Creek as it exists today, so they could only have entered the lake when the gradient between it and the valley floor was not so precipitous. The fishes present in the lake have thus been isolated from the main system for a long time, and a number of the fishes have diverged enough morphologically from the valley forms so that they have been recognized as separate species or subspecies: Clear Lake splittail, Clear Lake hitch, Clear Lake tule perch and, possibly, Clear Lake prickly sculpin (Hopkirk, 1973).

The series of geologic events that lead to the formation of Clear Lake and to the establishment of its fish fauna, and perhaps the fauna of the Russian River as well, is complex (Anderson, 1936; Hinds, 1952; Brice, 1953; Hodges, 1966; Swe and Dickinson, 1970; Hopkirk, 1973). In the early or middle Pleistocene (probably at least 100,000 years ago) when the Coast Range was much lower, the Clear Lake Basin was a valley connected by a low-gradient stream (Cache Creek or, possibly, Putah Creek) to the Sacramento system. The basin may also have drained via Cold Creek into the predecessor of the Russian River. The basin at this time presumably contained one or more small lakes which would provide suitable habitat for the invading Sacramento fishes. As the Coast Ranges rose higher, the gradient of Cache Creek increased, isolating the fishes in the basin. Tectonic activity, or perhaps the deposition of alluvial deposits from Scotts Creek, may also have blocked the outflow through Cold Creek (Hodges, 1966; Hopkirk, 1973). Meanwhile, faulting was causing the northwest portion of the basin to subside relative to the rest of the basin, resulting in the depression that now contains the main arm of Clear Lake. Volcanic activity in the middle and late Pleistocene, including that which created Mt. Konocti, further modified the lake basin. Most dramatic was the lava flow which blocked Cache Creek near its exit from the lake, raising the lake level and making Cold Creek the main lake outlet. This change may have permitted the Russian River to be colonized by some Clear Lake fishes. Finally, in the very late Pleistocene a landslide blocked Cold Creek, allowing the lake to spill over the Cache Creek lava flow, making Cache Creek the outlet once again.

The *Pajaro-Salinas* system consists of three major streams that flow into Monterey Bay: the Pajaro, Salinas, and San Lorenzo, Pajaro, and Salinas rivers. The Pajaro River has (or had in 1909) nearly the full complement of the true freshwater fishes characteristic of the Sacramento-San Joaquin system: Sacramento sucker, California roach, hitch, Sacramento blackfish, Sacramento squawfish, speckled dace, Sacramento perch, and tule perch. The only species missing are hardhead, splittail, and thicktail chub. The true freshwater fishes of the Salinas River are similar, except that the squawfish now present are probably the result of an introduction, since Snyder did not find any in his extensive collecting in 1909. The San Lorenzo River contains only suckers, roach, and dace. Of the fishes present in the Pajaro-Salinas system only the sucker and roach are well enough differentiated to justify calling them subspecies. The hitch was originally described as a separate species by Snyder (1913) but it does not seem to merit even subspecies rank, because Snyder's description was based in part on hybrids between the hitch and roach (Miller, 1945).

The nature of the fish fauna of the Pajaro-Salinas system indicates that it probably had two separate connections during the middle or late Pleistocene to the main Sacramento-San Joaquin system: (1) a headwater connection between the San Benito River (a tributary of the Pajaro) and the San Joaquin River system, and (2) a lowland connection between Coyote Creek and Llagas Creek (also a Pajaro tributary). The San Benito connection came earlier and permitted roach, suckers, and dace to enter the system (Murphy, 1948c). The main evidence for this early connection is (1) the degree of differentiation of the roach and sucker, compared to the other fishes, (2) their similarity to their counterparts in the San Joaquin system, and (3) the presence of populations of roach above impassable falls in the San Benito River (Murphy, 1948c). The other fishes native to the Pajaro-Salinas system are mainly lowland forms. They presumably entered by way of Coyote Creek, which now flows into San Francisco Bay. There is strong geological evidence that the upper portion of Coyote Creek has changed course several times in the past to flow into Llagas Creek (Branner, 1907). Coyote Creek also makes a plausible source for the lowland species because it contains (or did until recently) nearly a full complement of the Sacramento-San Joaquin fishes, despite having long since been cut off by salt water from the main system. The only unexplainable difference between the fish fauna of Coyote Creek and that of the Pajaro-Salinas system is the absence of the hardhead in the latter, since plenty of suitable hardhead habitat seems to exist.

From the Pajaro River, the freshwater fishes presumably spread to the Salinas and San Lorenzo rivers through lowland connections that existed when sea level was lower, or through estuarine connections, which have existed in historical times between the Pajaro and Salinas rivers when flooding makes the surface waters nearly fresh.

The *Upper Kern River* flows through a mountainous basin which contains the river and its tributaries above the present site of Isabella Reservoir. Only two species of fish are native to the basin, the Sacramento sucker and the endemic golden trout. The sucker is apparently a recent invader from the lower Kern River but the golden trout presumably became isolated in the upper Kern during the middle or late Pleistocene. One indication of the long isolation of the trout is that at least two subspecies within the basin can be recognized, *Salmo aguabonita aguabonita* from Golden Trout Creek and the south fork of the Kern River, and *S. a. whitei* from Little Kern River (Schreck and Behnke, 1971; Gold and Gall, in press). Another distinctive trout, found in the main Kern River, has also been placed in the golden trout complex, but is perhaps best considered as a subspecies of the rainbow trout (*S. gairdneri gilberti*).

The origin of the golden trout, and hence its relationships to other trout species, has been the subject of considerable debate in recent years. There are basically two schools of thought, one summarized by Miller (1972) and the other by Schreck and Behnke (1971). Miller's hypothesis is that the golden trout is derived from an ancestral form that entered the upper Kern via the San Joaquin River system when the mountains of the Sierra Nevada were somewhat lower. These trout were then isolated in the Kern River by glacial and geologic activity and the rainbow trout replaced (or evolved from) the ancestral form in the rest of the Sacramento-San Joaquin system. The redband trout complex of northern California may be representatives of this ancestral trout as well since they also seem to have survived in areas isolated by glaciation. The hypothesis of Schreck and Behnke is that the golden trout is derived from an ancestral trout that lived in the lower Colorado River system, one that also gave rise to the isolated Gila and Apache trouts (*S. gilae* and *S. apache*) of Arizona and New Mexico. This would require an invasion, presumably by tributary capture, over the east slope of the Sierras in the Owens Valley region. There presently are no native trout in the latter basin.

Unfortunately, neither hypothesis is supported by much hard evidence, particularly fossils. The systematic information from modern trouts can be used to support either hypothesis and proponents of both agree more such information is needed. Miller's hypothesis is the easiest to accept on the basis of geology. However, during the Pleistocene the region was subjected to much geologic change and to dramatic climatic fluctuations so that stream connections between the Kern Basin and the Colorado River system are certainly within the realm of possibility.

LAHONTAN SYSTEM

Lake Lahontan was an enormous body of water that once occupied much of the northwestern third of Nevada and the Honey Lake region of California. It existed in the Pleistocene during periods of heavy rainfall that coincided with advances of continental glaciers in more northern regions. The Lahontan system today consists of remnants of this lake (the largest being Pyramid Lake, Nevada), streams on the east side of the Sierra Nevada that once flowed into Lake Lahontan, the Lake Tahoe Basin, and Eagle Lake.

Although the Lahontan system is in the Great Basin and, due to its central location, has probably had connections in the past to most of the major drainage systems of the

West, its fishes indicate that the system has in fact been isolated for most of its history. Ten species of fish are native to the system, five of them endemic: Tahoe sucker, Lahontan redside, Piute sculpin, desert dace (*Eremichthys acros*), and cui-ui (*Chasmistes cujus*). The last four species are found only in Nevada. Of the five species with ranges that extend beyond the Lahontan system (speckled dace, tui chub, mountain sucker, mountain whitefish, cutthroat trout) only the whitefish does not seem to have a distinctive Lahontan form. Both the tui chub and the cutthroat trout have at least two forms each in the Lahontan system. The tui chubs present an interesting problem in speciation. The stream-adapted form (*Gila bicolor "obesa"*) and the lake-adapted form (*G. b. "pectinifer"*) coexist in Lake Tahoe and Pyramid Lake with little interbreeding, but they have apparently extensively hybridized in Eagle Lake (Hubbs, Miller, and Hubbs, 1974). The cutthroat trouts of the Lahontan system were originally described as at least six species and subspecies (La Rivers, 1962) but they have now been reduced to two subspecies, the wide-ranging Lahontan cutthroat trout (*Salmo clarki henshawi*) and the Piute cutthroat (*S. c. seleniris*). An undescribed form from the upper Humboldt River Basin in Nevada is yet to be named (R. Behnke, personal communication to R. R. Miller). The Piute cutthroat trout, which bears many independently evolved similarities to the golden trout of the upper Kern River Basin, arose in the isolated headwaters of Silver King Creek, Alpine County.

Adjacent to the main Lahontan Basin are a number of smaller basins, formerly containing lakes. Some of these basins have endemic species or subspecies derived from the Lahontan fish fauna. In Modoc County, the Cowhead Lake Basin has a distinctive tui chub subspecies and the Surprise Valley has a distinctive sucker species, both undescribed (C. L. Hubbs, pers. comm.). The Surprise Valley sucker lives in Wall Canyon Creek in Nevada but may occasionally be washed into California by floods.

DEATH VALLEY SYSTEM

Like the Lahontan system, the Death Valley system is an isolated part of the Great Basin that was dominated by pluvial lakes during the Pleistocene (Hubbs and Miller, 1948). At one time the three major streams in the system, the Owens, Amargosa, and Mojave rivers, drained ultimately into Lake Manly, which occupied the now dry floor of Death Valley. The presence of many other dry lake beds in the region today testifies that Lake Manly was just the largest of an interconnected series of lakes that were alternately full and dry as the climate and local topography changed with time. At the present time the three river basins are isolated from each other and each has its own endemic fishes, despite the fact that the Amargosa and Mojave rivers may still join each other on the floor of Lake Manly during years of heavy rainfall (C. L. Hubbs, pers. comm.). The Mojave River Basin has only one endemic form, the Mojave tui chub. The Owens River Basin has four endemics: the Owens tui chub, the Owens sucker, the Owens pupfish, and a distinctive speckled dace. The Amargosa River Basin, which includes Death Valley itself, has distinctive speckled dace and seven species of pupfish and killifish (*Cyprinodon* and *Empetrichthys* spp.), which are subdivided into at least ten subspecies.

The high degree of endemism in the system reflects both the long period it has been isolated from other systems and the harshness of the environment. In the Amargosa River Basin, the large number of pupfish species and subspecies results from the isolation of populations in warm springs and disrupted saline waters. Rapid evolution has been possible in these springs because of the small populations, the warm temperatures which permit several generations per year to be produced, and the uniqueness of the physical and chemical environment of each spring (Miller, 1961b). Because the pupfishes are of great interest to students of evolution, attempts have been made to determine the approximate length of time the populations have been isolated from each other. One of the most distinctive of the pupfishes, the Devil's Hole pupfish (*C. diabolis*) of the Ash Meadows region of Nevada, has been isolated for perhaps 100,000 years while the subspecies of the Amargosa pupfish in the same region have been isolated for about 25,000 years (Miller, 1961b). Under severe conditions speciation may be even more rapid. LaBounty and Deacon (1972) indicate that, in the extraordinarily harsh conditions of the Death Valley floor, the Cottonball Marsh pupfish evolved to the species level in less than 4,000 years.

Although the Death Valley system has been isolated for a long period of time, its fishes show that it has been connected to both the Lahontan system and to the Colorado River in the distant past. The ancestral pupfishes presumably entered the system from the precursor of the Colorado River at the end of the Pliocene, and the minnows and sucker entered from the Lahontan system at a later date, after the connection to the Colorado had been broken (Miller, 1958). The Lahontan connection presents some problems to the zoogeographer because the intervening Mono Lake Basin was fishless when first surveyed. The presence of fish bones overlain by volcanic ash in the basin, however, indicates that its fishes were wiped out by comparatively recent volcanic eruptions (C. L. Hubbs, pers. comm.). The absence of cutthroat trout and sculpins from the Owens Basin is somewhat puzzling, therefore, since suitable habitat for trout and sculpins exists in upper reaches of the Owens River and tributaries.

SOUTH COASTAL DRAINAGES

Only four species or subspecies of true freshwater fishes are native to the coastal streams of southern California: the arroyo chub, the speckled dace, the Santa Ana sucker, and the unarmored threespine stickleback. They originally lived in four streams on the Los Angeles Plain: the Santa Clara, Los Angeles, San Gabriel, and Santa Ana rivers (Culver and Hubbs, 1917). These drainages formerly were intermittently interconnected during years of high water (C. L. Hubbs, pers. comm.).

The origin of the sucker and minnows is a zoogeographic problem that needs to be resolved because their nearest relatives are now far removed geographically (Miller, 1958). Presumably the ancestors of the three species reached the coastal area shortly after it was uplifted in the early Pleistocene. The most likely route of entry was either through the ancient Colorado River, which may have had an outlet to the ocean in the region during the early Pleistocene (Smith, 1966), or through the ancient capture of a tributary to the lower Colorado River by the Santa Ana River (C. L. Hubbs, pers. comm.).

True freshwater fishes were absent from coastal streams north and south of the four rivers of the Los Angeles Plain prior to introductions by man, with the exception of the unarmored threespine stickleback in the Santa Clara River system and probably the arroyo chub in the Santa Margarita and San Luis Rey rivers. The population of speckled dace in San Luis Obispo Creek is a bit of an enigma. It is difficult to see from physiographic evidence how they could have become established there naturally yet, if they were brought there by man (presumably as bait), they must have been introduced prior to 1880, when D. S. Jordan first collected them from the creek (C. L. Hubbs, pers. comm.).

COLORADO RIVER SYSTEM

The Colorado River is of major interest to students of fish evolution and zoogeography in western North America because it drains much of the southwestern United States. It has served both as a highway to distribute fish species throughout the southwest and as a major center of fish evolution. The latter role has been possible because the system as we know it today consists of a number of separate drainage basins that were isolated from each other for long periods of time (Miller, 1958). In California, the lower Colorado River was the ultimate source of the ancestors of a number of species endemic to the Death Valley system and to southern California. It was home to only four native freshwater fishes (aside from the mullet and other marine visitors), the humpback sucker, the Colorado squawfish, the bonytail, and the desert pupfish, although many other native fishes normally found elsewhere in the lower Colorado drainage system, especially the Gila River in Arizona, undoubtedly washed into the California portion on occasion. It is most likely that the minnows and suckers of the lower Colorado evolved in upstream regions where other related species are also found.

Ecology

Most of California's freshwater fishes are highly adaptable. Both populations and individuals are capable of living under a surprisingly wide range of environmental conditions and interacting with many other species of fish. Each species has its environmental limits, however, and these limits define its habitat (or better, its fundamental niche as defined by Hutchinson, 1966). In actuality members of a species usually live well within the range of their environmental limits, in habitats that approach being optimal for survival, growth, and reproduction (realized niche). Optimal habitat requirements often change as a species passes from one stage of its life history to the next. The most extreme examples of this change occur in anadromous fishes like coho salmon and Pacific lamprey, which live as young in streams but as adults in the ocean. Most freshwater fishes exhibit similar, if more subtle, habitat changes during their life cycles. This means that to fully understand the ecological requirements of a fish species, the requirements for each stage of its life history have to be known.

Environmental factors that limit the distribution of a fish species are many, but some of the most important are: temperature, stream gradient and flow, dissolved oxygen, water chemistry, salinity, depth, cover, bottom type, barriers to movement, seasonal changes, presence of other fish species, invertebrate populations, and aquatic plant abundance. With the arrival of civilization, such factors as pollution, dams, dewatering of streams, canals connecting previously separated systems, and the introduction of exotic fishes, invertebrates, and plants have also become important determinants of fish distribution. Although some of the factors, such as temperature and stream gradient, exert a stronger influence on fish distribution than others, they all interact and the fish must respond to their concerted effect. Since different species of fish have different tolerances and preferences they react in different ways to a given set of environmental conditions. The result is environmental segregation on a broad scale (e.g., coldwater stream fishes vs. warmwater lake fishes) and niche segregation on a local scale.

Each geographical region of California has groups of species with similar environmental requirements. They occur together on a regular basis and interact to subdivide available habitats and their resources (niche segregation). Species that occur together on a regular basis have long been recognized as being part of distinct zones, each zone with its own physical, chemical, and biological characteristics. The idea of zonation of fishes was first studied systematically by Huet (1959) who attempted to classify the fish zones of European streams. He described four main zones: (1) the Trout Zone, dominated by brown trout in cold, high-gradient, headwater streams; (2) the Grayling

Zone, dominated by grayling and trout, but with a few fast-water minnows present as well, in cool, fairly fast, midelevation streams; (3) the Barbel Zone, dominated by stream cyprinids with a few fishes from the zones above and below, in slow, warmwater stretches of stream close to the valley floor; and (4) the Bream Zone, dominated by deep-bodied cyprinids and predatory fishes, such as pike and perch, in the warm, sluggish waters of the valley floor. The concept of zonation is useful mostly as a broad descriptive tool, since the exact composition of the fish fauna tends to vary from stream to stream as a result of minor environmental differences and accidents of distribution. Also, sharp boundaries between the zones are rare. The fish fauna changes gradually as the nature of each stream shifts from swift headwaters to slow river. The faunal change is generally less a replacement of one species by another than it is an addition of species as the habitat becomes more complex. For example, in Europe trout are found not only in the Trout Zone but also in the Grayling and Barbel zones.

Despite these limitations, zonation remains a handy way to describe the fish fauna of a region and its relationships to the different types of stream and lake habitats. In fact, fish zones can be described quantiatively, as has been shown for the fishes of the foothills above the San Joaquin Valley (Moyle and Nichols, 1973). There, 80 percent of the stream localities sampled had a fish fauna that could be assigned by computer to one of four fish associations (= zones). The following sections on the fish ecology of each major California drainage system will, therefore, attempt to describe the fish zones both as they were before civilization and as they are today. They will also, where possible, describe how the species that occur together in these zones subdivide the habitat and its resources.

SACRAMENTO-SAN JOAQUIN SYSTEM

Despite the enormous size of this system, fish zones are surprisingly similar in its various subsystems. The differences in fish fauna between subsystems indicate the presence of zoogeographical barriers. Hardhead, for example, apparently were never able to invade the Pajaro-Salinas subsystem nor were Sacramento blackfish able to invade the Russian River subsystem. Both systems seem to have suitable habitats for the missing species. Similarly, the slow-water fishes of the Central Valley (splittail, blackfish, Sacramento perch, tule perch) have been unable to get over the falls on the lower Pit River, although suitable habitats abound for them in its upper reaches. Nevertheless, throughout the Sacramento-San Joaquin system five fish zones can be recognized: (1) Rainbow Trout Zone, (2) California Roach Zone, (3) Squawfish-sucker-hardhead Zone, (4) Deep-bodied Fishes Zone, and (5) Estuarine Fishes Zone.

Rainbow Trout Zone. This zone is found in clear headwater streams where the stream gradient is high (usually a total drop of 3 m or more for every km of stream). The water is swift and permanent with more riffles than pools. The water is also cold, seldom exceeding 21°C, and is saturated with oxygen. The bottom material is predominately cobbles, boulders, and bedrock. The banks are well shaded and frequently undercut. Aquatic plants, submerged or emergent, are few except where the streams flow through boggy alpine meadows. The dominant native fish is rainbow trout but sculpin (usually riffle or Pit sculpin) and speckled dace are likely to be found in the lower portions of the zone. In some streams they may be joined by Sacramento sucker or California roach.

The Rainbow Trout Zone has also been greatly extended by man through the planting of fish in barren waters, the poisoning of marginal trout streams that normally contain mostly nongame species, and by the construction of dams which have cold, permanent outflows. Prior to the extensive planting programs of the late nineteenth and early twentieth centuries most streams and lakes of the high Sierras were fishless. The only major exceptions to this were the upper reaches of the Kern River where golden trout evolved and those tributaries to the Pit and McCloud rivers that contained redband trout. The Rainbow Trout Zone has now been extended, through planting, to include most of the streams and lakes of the Sierras. At lower elevations the zone, or at least the dominance of trout, has been extended downstream into sections normally inhabited by fishes of the Squawfish-sucker-hardhead Zone, through poisoning operations followed by planting of hatchery trout. These extensions normally last only a few years, after which the treatment has to be repeated if the artificially large trout populations are to be maintained. Rainbow trout habitat has also been created at low elevations by cold waters flowing from dams. Often these waters, due to their low temperatures and swift currents, naturally exclude native minnows and suckers without further intervention by man.

A further result of man's manipulation of the Rainbow Trout Zone has been an increase in the complexity of the fish community through the introduction of brook trout, brown trout, and golden trout into many of the streams. Golden trout seldom maintain populations when other trout species are present but brook, brown, and rainbow trout may coexist by living in slightly different places and adopting different feeding strategies. When all three species occur together, brook trout tend to be found in cold, springfed tributaries of the main stream, feeding equally on surface and bottom foods. Brown trout tend to be found in the pools of the main streams feeding mostly on bottom invertebrates and other fish, while rainbow trout are more apt to be in the riffles, feeding on surface insects and drift. Different breeding times and places may also help keep the species segregated. Whether or not the above relationships among the three species are stable is not really known. In some California streams, brown trout have become the most numerous species but this may be due to the greater vulnerability to angling of rainbow and brook trout.

When sculpin, speckled dace, and rainbow trout occur together, sculpin and speckled dace feed by picking invertebrates from the bottom, while rainbow trout feed primarily on drifting insects, terrestrial and aquatic (Li and Moyle, unpublished data). The trout also capture larger and faster prey than the other two species. Sculpin segregate from dace by picking larger invertebrates from rocks while dace browse on smaller forms. Sculpin also typically live and feed in swifter water than dace.

California Roach Zone. Streams characteristic of this zone are small warm tributaries to larger streams and flow through open foothill woodlands of oak and digger pine. In the San Joaquin Valley, these streams are located in a narrow altitudinal band in the foothills of the Sierra Nevada (Fig. 2). Since streams are usually intermittent during the summer, the fish are confined to stagnant pools that may exceed 30°C during the day. During winter and spring the streams are swift and subject to flooding. The main

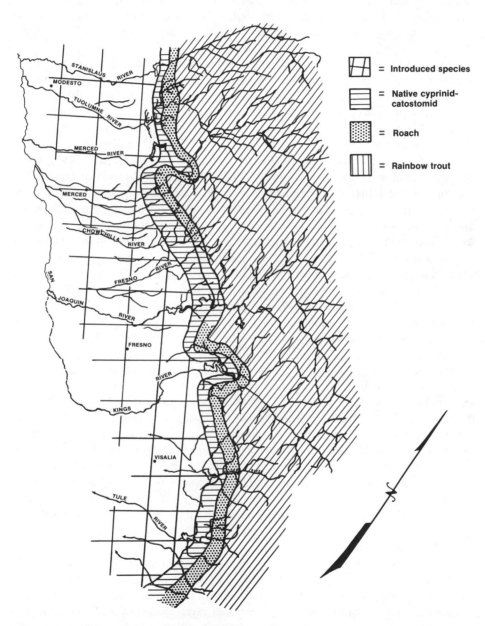

Figure 2. Fish zones of the San Joaquin River system, from Moyle and Nichols (1974).
The Introduced Fishes Zone is equivalent to the Deep-bodied Fishes Zone.

permanent native residents are California roach. Due to their small size and tolerance of low oxygen levels and high temperatures, they can survive where most other fishes cannot. In many areas, the Roach Zone is now dominated by green sunfish or, occasionally, fathead minnows. Green sunfish have apparently replaced California roach in some areas, such as tributaries to the upper San Joaquin and Fresno rivers (Fig. 2).

During the winter and spring, anadromous fishes, especially steelhead rainbow trout, may use these streams for spawning. The young fish generally move out into larger streams before the Roach Zone streams dry up. Sacramento suckers, squawfish, and other native minnows also commonly use these streams for spawning. If the pools are sufficiently large and deep, their young of the year will survive the summer in them.

Squawfish-sucker-hardhead Zone. Most of the streams inhabited by the fishes of this zone have average summer flows of 300 or more liters per second, deep rocky pools, and wide, shallow riffles (Moyle and Nichols, 1973). Some of the streams, however, may become intermittent in the summer or at least have such reduced flows that the fish are confined to the pools. Summer water temperatures typically exceed 20°C and fluctuate with air temperatures in smaller streams. In the Sierra foothill streams of the San Joaquin Valley the Squawfish-sucker-hardhead Zone occupies a narrow altitudinal range, from about 27 to 450 m above sea level (Fig. 2). The range appears to be much wider in streams of the Sacramento Valley foothills.

Sacramento squawfish and Sacramento suckers are usually the most abundant fishes in the zone. Hardhead are largely confined to the zone but their distribution is irregular. Where they are found, however, they are abundant. Other native fishes that may live here are tule perch, speckled dace, California roach, prickly sculpin, and rainbow trout. In recent years, introduced species (especially smallmouth bass, largemouth bass, green sunfish, mosquitofish, carp, white catfish, and channel catfish) have become increasingly common. In the San Joaquin Valley, the zone is sharply separated from the zones above and below it, largely because of low summer flows. In the more permanent streams of the Sacramento Valley, however, species replacement is not so much the rule as is species addition. Thus, rainbow trout live in the zone in the larger and colder streams. Many anadromous fishes (mainly chinook salmon, steelhead rainbow trout, white sturgeon, and Pacific lamprey) have major spawning grounds in the zone. Newly hatched salmon and sturgeon drift downstream into the Estuarine Zone but young steelhead spend a year or more in the streams. Pacific lamprey spend the entire five to seven years of the ammocoetes stage of their life cycle in muddy backwaters, migrating downstream only when they metamorphose into the predaceous adult stage.

How the native resident fishes of the zone subdivide its space and resources can be seen from their feeding relationships (Fig. 3) and from their distribution in each section of stream (Fig. 4). Large Sacramento suckers stay on the bottom in deep pools feeding on algae, detritus and associated small invertebrates. They may move into shallower or swifter water to feed at night. Juvenile suckers remain throughout the day and night in the shallow water of the stream edges, the smallest fish in the shallowest water.

Squawfish, like the suckers, are largely confined to pools or quiet stream edges.

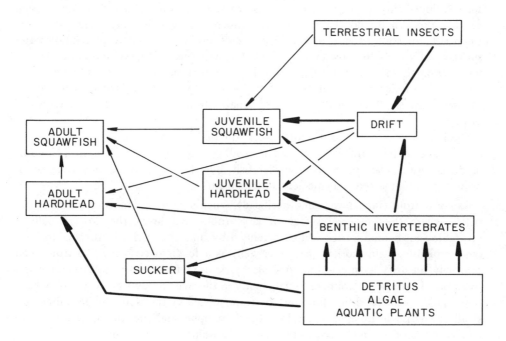

Figure 3. Diagrammatic representation of the feeding relationships of the dominant fishes in a Sierra Nevada foothill stream.

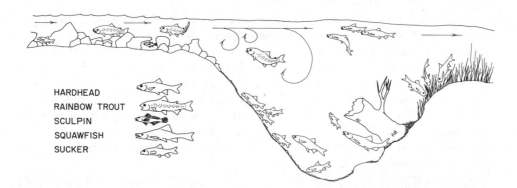

Figure 4. Cross-section of a stream in the upper reaches of the Squawfish-sucker-hardhead Zone.

Small squawfish feed mainly on terrestrial and aquatic insects which drift downstream on the water's surface. Small schools of 10 to 25 cm TL squawfish are thus commonly seen stationed close to the surface of pools, where the incoming current is slow enough so that the fish do not have to expend much energy swimming against it. Large squawfish, in contrast, are solitary hunters of other fish, mostly of minnows and suckers but also of their own young. They hide underneath large submerged rocks and logs during the day, capturing occasional fish with a sudden rush from cover. They come out to forage actively in the evening. Among the most frequently taken prey of squawfish are small hardhead which, like squawfish, mainly inhabit the quieter water of pools.

The hardhead poke about the bottom for aquatic insect larvae, occasionally rising to the surface to take drifting insects. The feeding habits of large (20+ cm TL) adult hardhead are similar to those of smaller fish, but they are more omnivorous, often browsing on submerged and emergent aquatic plants.

Rainbow trout (including young steelhead), when present, are most abundant in the riffles where they take advantage of large rocks that break the flow. Usually a favorable spot behind a rock will be defended by one trout against others of its kind (and probably against other species as well) as a feeding territory. The trout feed primarily on drifting insects but they also pick up a few bottom invertebrates and small fish. In the pools trout are found mostly in the swift headwaters where they have first chance at the food that floats in. Anything missed by the trout will be grabbed by small squawfish in quieter water. Like trout, sculpins and speckled dace are found mostly in the riffles and behave as they do in the Rainbow Trout Zone.

This description of habitat subdivision by the fishes is obviously an idealized picture of the interactions in undisturbed sections of stream that are largely without introduced fishes or heavy fishing pressure. The actual relationships among the species vary from place to place with the relative abundance of each species. The species of the zone also differ in other aspects of their life history and behavior, such as spawning times and places, larval habitat, seasonal movements, and daily rhythms in feeding, although these differences are poorly known.

Deep-bodied Fishes Zone. Before the Sacramento and San Joaquin rivers were reduced in flow and confined between levees, this zone occupied the warm, meandering waterways of the valley floor: sluggish river channels, oxbow and floodplain lakes, swamps, and sloughs. Its fishes also lived in Tulare and Buena Vista lakes of the San Joaquin Valley — huge, shallow lakes that filled each year with flood waters from the Kern, Tule, Kaweah, and Kings rivers, as well as various smaller streams. Today the zone exists mainly in the lower reaches of the larger streams and in the upper portions of the Delta. Even Tulare and Buena Vista lakes have been drained for farmland, although they reappear in exceptionally wet years when floods rush down the old river channels again.

The zone contained, and still does to a certain extent, a variety of habitat types ranging from stagnant backwaters and shallow tule beds to deep pools and long stretches of slow-moving river. The native fish fauna, as a consequence, was a varied mixture of true freshwater fishes, anadromous fishes, and fishes of marine origin.

Deep-bodied forms (Sacramento perch, hitch, thicktail chub, tule perch) predominated in the weedy backwaters while specialized but more streamlined minnows (blackfish, splittail) occupied the large stretches of open water. Large squawfish and suckers who moved down from their upstream spawning and nursery areas, also lived here in abundance. Anadromous salmon, steelhead, and sturgeon passed through the zone on their way upstream to spawn, but the juvenile fish, especially juvenile sturgeon, may have spent a year or more in the zone, feeding on the abundant invertebrates and small fish.

Today the nature of this zone has changed drastically. Even in the Delta, most of the water flows through man-modified channels and the once vast tule beds have been reduced to remnanants. The native fishes have either become extinct or have been reduced to a minor part of the fauna, living mostly in the least disturbed sloughs. The dominant fishes today are all introduced species: largemouth bass, white and black crappie, bluegill, threadfin shad, American shad, striped bass, logperch, white catfish, brown bullhead, carp, and goldfish. Other introduced species are present in lesser numbers. Not enough is known about the ecology of the native fishes nor about their precivilization habitats to make many worthwhile guesses about how the fishes subdivided the zone's space and resources. Today it hardly seems worthwhile even to devote much time to the interactions among the introduced species since if any stable associations have been established they are likely to be soon upset as the waters of this zone continue to change, and as other new species become established in them.

Estuarine Fishes Zone. This zone is in the lower reaches of the main rivers, in the region influenced daily by tides, through changes in current, temperature, and salinity. In the Delta, it merges imperceptibly with the Deep-bodied Fishes Zone. It contains some forms that live nowhere else in the system (delta smelt, longfin smelt), anadromous forms that may spend most of the adult portion of their life cycle there (white sturgeon, Pacific lamprey), marine forms that may spend the juvenile stages there (staghorn sculpin, shiner perch, starry flounder, jacksmelt, Pacific herring), and freshwater forms that can tolerate low salinities of 3 to 10 ppt. (tule perch, splittail). Most of these fishes live (or lived), directly or indirectly, off the superabundant crustaceans, especially oppossum shrimp (*Neomysis mercedis*), amphipods (*Corophium* spp.), and copepods. Today these crustaceans, along with some introduced forms, still support large fish populations, including those of the native fishes. However, the most abundant pelagic fish seems to be juvenile striped bass. Yellowfin gobies, recently accidentally introduced, are becoming an increasingly common bottom-living form.

Species segregation in the Estuarine Fishes Zone is not well understood but salinity preferences, feeding habits, and seasonal movements appear to play important roles. Delta smelt feed pelagically on copepods in the freshwater regions while longfin smelt feed pelagically on oppossum shrimp in the brackish areas. The ecology and feeding habits of juvenile striped bass appear to be similar to those of longfin smelt. Other plankton-feeding fishes (American shad, Pacific herring) only enter the zone on a seasonal basis while sturgeon, starry flounder, staghorn sculpin, and yellowfin goby are all bottom forms with different feeding strategies, although the native sculpin and introduced goby may be in direct competition with each other. All the marine forms tend to have seasonal peaks in abundance which usually depend on spawning times.

CLEAR LAKE

Clear Lake is the largest natural freshwater lake completely within California's borders. It has a surface area of about 17, 670 ha, an average depth of 8 m, and a maximum depth of 18 m. Because it is shallow and is regularly subjected to strong winds, Clear Lake does not thermally stratify in the summer for long periods of time. Instead, its low elevation (440 m) assures that its summer temperatures are uniformly warm (20 to 25°C) from top to bottom. The lake is highly productive and the high nutrient levels, even before the arrival of civilization to the basin, have probably always resulted in summer blooms of algae, causing the lake to belie its name. The eutrophic nature of Clear Lake has also led to large fish populations, although the total number of abundant species, even with introductions, has seldom exceeded seventeen.

There are three broad fish habitat zones in the lake: (1) the Shallow Water Zone, from shore down to the limits of rooted aquatic plant growth, probably seldom deeper than 4 m; (2) the Benthic Zone, consisting of the bottom below the limits of aquatic plant growth; and (3) the Open Water Zone, the water column away from shore, from the surface to the bottom. The native fishes that inhabited the three zones were basically lake-adapted variants of species that originally inhabited the Deep-bodied Fishes Zone of the main Sacramento-San Joaquin system.

The *Shallow Water Zone* was inhabited by large numbers of young-of-the-year hitch, Sacramento blackfish, and Clear Lake splittail. These "greenback minnows" greatly impressed early visitors to the lake with their abundance. Presumably these fish fed on small planktonic organisms or on invertebrates associated with the large beds of tules and aquatic plants. Not surprisingly, three of the other fish species that lived here were piscivores: Sacramento perch, squawfish, and thicktail chub. Each presumably had distinctive methods of capturing the abundant small fishes. One other common species in shallow water was the tule perch, which lived by picking small invertebrates off the aquatic plants and the bottom.

The *Benthic Zone*, although home to huge populations of midge larvae, was utilized extensively by only two species, the prickly sculpin (an invertebrate predator) and the Sacramento sucker (a grazer on algae, detritus, and invertebrates).

The *Open Water Zone* was inhabited by large schools of juvenile and adult hitch, splittail, and blackfish. The hitch and splittail fed on zooplankton and emerging midges, while the blackfish fed almost exclusively on phytoplankton.

Besides these year-round residents of the lake, early records indicate that anadromous steelhead rainbow trout and Pacific lamprey may have entered the lake through its outlet, Cache Creek, and then spawned in the lake's tributaries. Such migrations were halted by the construction of Rumsey Dam in 1914.

Today the native associations of fish for each zone have been largely replaced by associations of introduced species. At least thirteen introduced species are now established in the lake and only four of the native species are still maintaining large populations: hitch, blackfish, tule perch, and prickly sculpin. Although each introduced species has definite habitat preferences, too little is known about their ecology in Clear Lake to make reasonable speculations about their interactions. In addition, both the lake habitat and the species composition of its fish fauna are still changing. For example, the Mississippi silversides was introduced in 1967 and is now the most abundant fish species in the lake. In shallow water it has largely replaced the bluegill as the dominant fish, just as the bluegill apparently replaced the small minnows that were once so abundant there.

CENTRAL VALLEY RESERVOIRS

Ever since the white man settled in California, the rivers of its great Central Valley have been a source of both admiration and frustration: admiration for their abundant flows and potential for making the rich soils of the valley floor yield crops and frustration at their fluctuations from raging spring floods to quiet summer trickles. The response has been to build dams and store the water in reservoirs. The construction of dams, always a major activity in the Central Valley, gained momentum with the advent of the Central Valley Project in the 1940s. The project created most of the large reservoirs that now dominate the larger streams of the valley. Reservoirs have thus become one of the major fish habitats in the Sacramento-San Joaquin system. The nature of each reservoir and its fish fauna is determined by its elevation, size, location, and water quality. In general, reservoirs are much less productive per surface hectare than are lakes because their deep, steep-sloped basins and fluctuating water levels greatly limit habitat diversity. The reservoirs range from clear, oligotrophic, coldwater lakes at high elevations to turbid, eutrophic, warmwater impoundments at low elevations. Most of the reservoirs, and the largest, lie at midelevations in the foothills and have characteristics of both warmwater and coldwater impoundments. These are the only reservoirs that will be discussed in detail.

The midelevation reservoirs support a mixture of native fishes that lived in the streams prior to the construction of the dams and exotic fishes that were introduced by man. In many cases the native forms, particularly hardhead and squawfish, have become uncommon after an initial period of abundance. However, in a few reservoirs hitch or tui chubs, often initially introduced by man as forage for game fish, have become the most abundant species. Normally a variety of exotic species dominate the fish fauna. The exact species composition in each reservoir varies with the history of the introductions, but some species are now almost universal in their occurrence: bluegill, largemouth bass, carp, golden shiner, black crappie, brown bullhead, mosquitofish, and rainbow trout (hatchery strains). It is possible to divide the typical midelevation reservoir into four ecological zones, each with a more or less distinct fish assemblage: (1) the Littoral Zone, (2) the Epilimnetic Zone, (3) the Hypolimnetic Zone, and (4) the Deepwater Benthic Zone.

The *Littoral Zone* occurs along the edges, down to the depth of light penetration or to the upper limits of the thermocline, whichever comes first. It is the zone most severely affected by fluctuations in water level, since large areas may alternately be flooded or exposed in a relatively short period of time. Despite the fluctuations, large numbers of fish are found here. Bluegill, largemouth bass, and golden shiners (or, alternately, young tui chubs or hitch) live close to the water's surface near shore. Mosquitofish stay in the flooded grass in very shallow areas. Brown bullheads, white catfish, and carp stay close to the bottom. Black crappie cluster around submerged boulders and logs during the day, moving out into the open water to feed on plankton and fish in the evening. Reproduction is a problem for most of these species because a sudden drop in water level may expose a nest of eggs and a sudden rise can submerge it to unfavorable depths.

The *Epilimnetic Zone* occupies the well-lighted, well-oxygenated surface waters away from shore and above the thermocline. Its fish fauna is perhaps the most variable from reservoir to reservoir. Since its primary means of supporting fishes is its abundant zooplankton, it contains three main types of fish: (1) plankton-feeding larvae of Littoral Zone fishes, especially bluegill and other centrarchids; (2) plankton-feeding adult fishes; and (3) fishes that prey on the plankton feeders. The population biology of the planktonic larval fishes in reservoirs is poorly understood, but it is likely that large plankton-feeding fishes, notably threadfin shad, reduce their numbers through predation or through the reduction of zooplankton populations. Threadfin shad are perhaps the most common permanent plankton-feeding residents of the Epilimnetic Zone despite the fact that they were not introduced into the Central Valley until 1959. Other zooplankton grazers which may occupy this zone, mostly in reservoirs that lack threadfin shad, are hitch, tui chub, delta smelt (Japanese subspecies), Mississippi silversides, and American shad. Striped bass are assuming the role of chief epilimnetic predator in a number of reservoirs although their inability to spawn in most reservoirs means that they have to be planted on a regular basis. Fish from other zones also prey on epilimnetic fish, especially those that venture close to shore.

The *Hypolimnetic Zone* occupies the cold (less than 20°C) water below the thermocline in the deep reservoirs that stratify during the summer months. The main inhabitants are rainbow trout, which often enter the epilimnion in the evening or night to feed on whatever forage fish are most abundant. Kokanee salmon are also commonly present but they stay in the cold depths in the summer months feeding on zooplankton.

The *Deepwater Benthic Zone* is on the bottom, below the thermocline and usually below the limits of light penetration. It is the one zone in which native fishes, especially prickly sculpin and Sacramento sucker, may predominate. White and channel catfish also may live in this zone but they usually move up into the Littoral Zone to feed at night.

It should be emphasized that the fish zones described for reservoirs are present primarily during the summer months and even then they may be disrupted by extreme drawdowns of the reservoirs. Species also move freely among the zones, probably because of the instability of the habitat. In the winter, when low temperatures greatly reduce fish activity, zonation tends to disappear altogether.

COASTAL STREAMS

The streams that flow directly into the ocean without first entering a major river system are highly variable. They range from the warm, intermittent streams of southern California, including the Santa Ana River system, to the permanent, cold-flowing streams of the redwood region of the northern part of the state. Most of the streams vary seasonally in their flows, often from flooding torrents in the spring to quiet trickles in the summer. Most also have a high gradient and flow rapidly to the sea, although a few of the larger ones meander across flood plains in their lower reaches.

Despite variation in temperature regimes, flow, and locality, California's coastal streams are similar in the composition of their fish fauna, which consists largely of anadromous species and euryhaline freshwater and marine species. In addition, many streams contain true freshwater fishes (minnows and suckers) which have entered coastal drainages through the erosional capture of tributaries that formerly flowed into interior systems. Usually three intergrading fish zones may be recognized in coastal streams: (1) Resident Trout Zone, (2) Anadromous Fishes Zone, and (3) Intertidal Fishes Zone.

The *Resident Trout Zone* occupies the uppermost reaches of the streams, typically above natural barriers that halt upstream migration of anadromous fishes. The water is cold, swift, and well oxygenated with rocky riffles the predominant habitat type, much as in the Trout Zone of the Sacramento-San Joaquin system. Rainbow trout are the most common fish, although cutthroat may occur in a few streams in northern California. Frequently associated with the trout are California roach, speckled dace, and sculpin of various species (but usually riffle or prickly sculpin).

The *Anadromous Fishes Zone* exists as far upstream as the fishes can migrate and downstream to the regions influenced by tidal action. Although the water is also generally cold and fast flowing, pools become increasingly large and frequent as the streams approach the sea. Between the pools there are long stretches of shallow riffles over rock, gravel, or sand, which are used for spawning by coho salmon (and occasionally other species of salmon), rainbow trout (steelhead), and Pacific lampreys. The young salmon and trout usually spend a year or two in the streams before migrating to sea, but the ammocoetes of the lampreys live in the silty backwaters and stream edges for at least four to five years. This zone is also home to threespine stickleback and at least three species of sculpin (prickly, coastrange, and riffle). Sticklebacks and sculpins may complete their entire life cycle in the stream but they are also capable of migrating out into salt water for one or more life-history stages. If true freshwater fishes are present they will be most common in this zone, although the particular species present depends on the location of the stream. Thus, in streams of the Los Angeles Basin, Santa Ana sucker, arroyo chub, and speckled dace are (were) the only native, true freshwater fishes present. In streams flowing into San Francisco Bay, as well as in the Gualala, Navarro, and Eel rivers, the only true freshwater fishes present are California roach and, usually, Sacramento sucker.

The ecological relationships among the fishes of this zone are not well understood. They deserve close study since the zone produces much of the salmon and steelhead so important to the commercial and sport fisheries of the state. The fishes are also continually being threatened with stream dewatering for irrigation and stream perturbation through logging.

The *Intertidal Zone* is the section of stream influenced daily by the tides, which create reversing currents, fluctuating temperatures, and salinity gradients. In some streams, such as the Navarro River, the zone may be 4 to 5 km long, but more often than not it is less than 1 km in length, usually stopping at the first rocky riffle. The middle sections are generally slow moving and shallow, but occasionally have depths of 2 to 3 m. At the lower end there is almost invariably a lagoon behind wind-and-wave-piled sand bars. The stream bottom is mostly sand or mixed sand and silt.

The species most common here, although not necessarily all in one stream, are threespine stickleback, prickly sculpin, coastrange sculpin, riffle sculpin, staghorn sculpin, topsmelt, starry flounder, and tidewater goby. Other marine forms are frequently present as well. In each stream, species tend to segregate according to salinity tolerances, as illustrated by the fishes found in this zone of the Navarro River in August, 1973. Starry flounder, the sculpins, and threespine stickleback were common throughout the zone, from completely fresh water down to the mouth. Sacramento suckers disappeared before the salinity reached 1 ppt, although the largest concentration of adults observed in the river was located just above the reach of salt water. California roach dropped out at about 3 ppt, where shiner perch and topsmelt started to become common. At 9 to 10 ppt, bay pipefish suddenly appeared, living in beds of filamentous algae. Staghorn sculpins were also first found here. Closer to the ocean, at salinities of 23 to 28 ppt, staghorn sculpin, shiner perch, and bay pipefish were abundant and two marine species, penpoint gunnel and saddleback gunnel, made their appearances. Although no attempt was made to sample the lagoon just above the mouth, it presumably contained more marine and euryhaline fishes, together with any young salmonids that had recently moved downstream. In the spring, the lower reaches are used for spawning by marine fishes such as the Pacific herring and plainfin midshipman (*Porichthys notatus*). Although the fish species found in the Navarro River may not be typical of every coastal stream, a downstream change in species is typical of every stream with long enough lower reaches to possess a salinity gradient.

LOWER KLAMATH RIVER SYSTEM

The lower Klamath River system consists of the Klamath River below Klamath Falls, the Trinity River, and over 200 smaller tributary streams. The system is, on the basis of its physical characteristics and fish fauna, essentially a large coastal stream. Although it is second in size in California only to the Sacramento River, it lacks the warm, lowland habitat that has fostered the evolution of the more complex fauna of the Sacramento-San Joaquin system. Instead, it is a cold, fast-flowing, rocky-bottomed trout stream over most of its length. Also, the river's geological history has made its colonization by true freshwater fishes difficult. Thus, the fish fauna is dominated by anadromous forms: Pacific lamprey, threespine stickleback, green sturgeon, American shad (introduced), eulachon, chinook salmon, steelhead rainbow trout, and coastal cutthroat trout. Little is known about the ecology of the young of these species in the lower Klamath system although larval sturgeon, shad, and eulachon presumably are rather quickly washed into the estuary. The young salmonids spend anywhere from a few months to two years in the streams before moving out to sea.

In addition to the numbers of anadromous fishes in the system, there are also abundant species that spend all or most of their life cycle in fresh water: prickly sculpin, coastrange sculpin, marbled sculpin, threespine stickleback, brown trout (introduced), speckled dace, and Klamath smallscale sucker. The latter two species are the only "true" freshwater species native to the system. The construction of reservoirs on the main river and the gravel pits along its side have permitted the development of a warmwater fish fauna in recent years, a combination of introduced species (most notably yellow perch, pumpkinseed, largemouth bass, and brown bullhead), native species washed down from the upper Klamath River, and the original resident fishes.

The zones are as described for coastal streams: (1) a Resident Trout Zone in the upper reaches of the tributaries, (2) an Anadromous Fishes Zone in most of the main channels, and (3) an Intertidal Zone in the lower 5 to 6 km of river.

UPPER KLAMATH RIVER SYSTEM

The upper Klamath River system, which includes the Lost River, is ecologically and faunistically distinct from the lower Klamath system. This is due in part to the geologically recent connection between the two systems and in part to the natural, large, shallow lakes of the upper Klamath system (Upper and Lower Klamath lakes and Tule Lake) which have no counterparts in the lower Klamath River. The fish fauna is dominated by true freshwater fishes rather than by anadromous forms. Historically the upper limit of anadromous fish migration was Klamath Falls, Oregon, although the dams which created Copco Lake and Iron Gate Reservoir have pushed this limit down into California and, by the creation of the lakes, have extended downstream the habitat suitable for upper Klamath fishes.

Three species of upper Klamath fishes are primarily lake dwellers: the Klamath Lake sculpin (*Cottus princeps*, not yet recorded in California but it can be expected from Klamath River reservoirs), the shortnose sucker, and the Lost River sucker. The two suckers spawned in large numbers in the Lost and Klamath rivers but the young were quickly washed into the lakes, to assume the (presumably) plankton-feeding habits of the adults. Both species are now rather uncommon. Native fishes that are found in the streams as well as in the lakes are dwarf Pacific lamprey, rainbow trout, Klamath largescale sucker, blue chub, Klamath tui chub, speckled dace, and marbled sculpin. Both the lamprey and the trout are apparently holdovers from the time when anadromous fishes had access to the upper Klamath system, although the trout may have been introduced by man. The lamprey is a small version of the Pacific lamprey, with an adult stage adapted for living in large lakes and preying on large suckers and minnows. It apparently gave rise to the stream-dwelling but nonpredacious Pit-Klamath brook lamprey. The Klamath largescale sucker is the typical bottom-feeding sucker of the system but it apparently has never been very common. The blue chub and the tui chub are, and probably always have been, the most abundant fish in Klamath and Tule lakes. Just how the two rather similar species segregate ecologically is not clear, since they both are opportunistic omnivores. Blue chubs, however, will ascend farther up the small tributary streams than will tui chubs. Speckled dace and marbled sculpin are primarily stream dwellers but they will also live in the rocky-bottomed shallows of the lakes, where conditions are similar to riffle habitat. In recent years, introduced species have become more important in the system, especially in its more disrupted portions: Delta smelt (Japanese subspecies), yellow perch, and pumpkinseed in Copco and Iron Gate reservoirs, and Sacramento perch and brown bullhead in Clear Lake Reservoir on the Lost River. The ecology of the native and introduced fishes in the entire system is badly in need of study.

LAHONTAN SYSTEM

The streams of the Lahontan system rush down the steep eastern slope of the Sierra Nevada, slowing occasionally to meander through alpine meadows and eventually emptying into large lakes or desert sinks. The swift flows assure that water temperatures remain low enough to support trout even at low elevations. The lack of variety in stream habitat has limited the number of native fish species to eight which efficiently subdivide the resources available. Fish zones are hard to define (and will not be here) because, as the streams increase in size and habitat diversity from headwaters to lakes, fish species are added but seldom removed (Flittner, 1953; Gard and Flittner, 1974).

The headwaters usually contain only trout. Their range has been considerably extended by man above natural barriers. Lahontan and Piute cutthroat trout were the original headwater inhabitants but they have been largely replaced by introduced brook trout and, slightly lower down, by rainbow trout and brown trout. The first fish to join the trout as the streams flow downward are Piute sculpins. They feed on bottom invertebrates while the trout concentrate on invertebrate drift and small sculpins. Mountain suckers, mountain whitefish, and speckled dace become evident some distance downstream from the highest reach of the sculpins. The suckers are adapted for scraping diatoms, detritus, and small invertebrates from rocks in fast water, while the dace live by browing on small riffle insects. As the number and size of pools start to increase with the lengths of streams that meander through alpine meadows, fish which require slower moving water become abundant: Tahoe suckers, mountain whitefish, and Lahontan redsides. The exact role of these three species in the streams, especially their relationships to trout, needs more study. Apparently, Tahoe suckers are slow-water grazers on detritus, algae, and small invertebrates, whitefish are bottom feeders on large, active invertebrates, and redsides are opportunistic, invertebrate-feeding pool dwellers. In the lowest reaches of the streams, close to the lakes, tui chubs of the *obesa* type become common. They are omnivorous but feed mostly on bottom organisms. In these low reaches, trout, sculpin, speckled dace, and mountain sucker are most abundant in the riffles, while the other species dominate the pools.

LAKE TAHOE

Lake Tahoe is one of the largest high-mountain lakes in the world (surface area, 304 km²), remarkably deep (maximum 501 m; mean, 313 m), and clear (the bottom can be seen at a depth of 20 to 30 m). It is 36.4 km long, 20.9 km wide, and lies at an altitude of 1,899 m above sea level. The total area of the Lake Tahoe watershed, including the surface of the lake itself, is only 830 km². It drains through the Truckee River into Pyramid Lake, Nevada.

The native fishes are the same species that occur in Lahontan system streams, except that the lake-adapted *pectinifer* form of the tui chub is present along with the *obesa* form, and the stream-adapted mountain sucker is absent. The only major changes in the fish community wrought by man so far have been the replacement of Lahontan cutthroat trout with lake trout, rainbow trout, and brown trout and the addition of kokanee salmon. The cutthroat trout, once the support of a commercial fishery, is now extinct in the lake. Despite similarities between the fish fauna of Lake Tahoe and of Lahontan streams, ecological relationships among the species are somewhat different from those in the streams. This was first revealed by R. G. Miller (1951). Miller recognized three distinct fish associations or zones: (1) the Shallow Water Association, (2) the Deepwater Benthic Association, and (3) the Midwater Association. The feeding relationships among the fishes of the associations are presented in Figure 5.

The *Shallow Water Association* lives mostly in water less than 10 m deep, in rocky-bottomed areas. The association is composed of six species: speckled dace, Lahontan redside, Piute sculpin, Tahoe sucker, rainbow trout, and brown trout. Dace live among the rocks, swimming about in loose aggregations. They feed on small invertebrates such as small snails and blackfly larvae, that live on the surface of the rocks. They tend to hide during the day, becoming active at night. In contrast to dace, redsides are diurnal, surface oriented, and swim about in large schools. They feed equally on bottom, surface, and midwater invertebrates and are perhaps the most numerous fish in the lake. Piute sculpin live under the rocks during the day but come out to forage at night on the larger bottom invertebrates, especially midge and caddisfly larvae. Tahoe suckers are present mostly as juveniles (less than 10 cm TL). They are also most active at night, browsing on detritus, algae, and small invertebrates. They are the one species that seems to feed on a regular basis in the more exposed sandy-bottomed areas, as well as in the rocky areas. Rainbow trout and brown trout are the main predators on the other fishes of the association, moving in to forage in the evening. They capture mostly suckers and redsides, the two species most likely to be out in the open. Dace and sculpin form only a very small part of their diet (Fig. 5).

Besides these permanent inhabitants of shallow water, young of the year of most of the other species that live in the lake can be found here at one time or another. Large congregations of young-of-the-year fishes are especially likely to be found along marshy shores, where the emergent plants provide some measure of protection.

The *Deepwater Benthic Association* has two distinct types of habitat: thin beds of aquatic plants and plant-free areas. The aquatic plants, mostly *Chara*, filamentous algae, and aquatic moss, grow on the lower gradient slopes down to depths of about 150 m. Most of the plants are present between depths of 67 and 116 m, with the largest concentrations at 100 to 116 m (Frantz and Cordone, 1967). The plant-free habitat is in water deeper than 150 m, on steep-sloped areas at intermediate depths, and on sandy bottoms at depths of less than 33 m.

The fishes that make up this association are lake trout, Piute sculpin, the *obesa* form of the tui chub, large Tahoe sucker, and mountain whitefish. Lake trout mostly cruise about close to the bottom foraging among the aquatic plants as well as in the plant-free areas. Their usual prey are other deepwater fishes, in the following order of importance: Tahoe sucker, Piute sculpin, tui chub, and mountain whitefish. Suckers are probably the most important prey because they are large and almost continuously

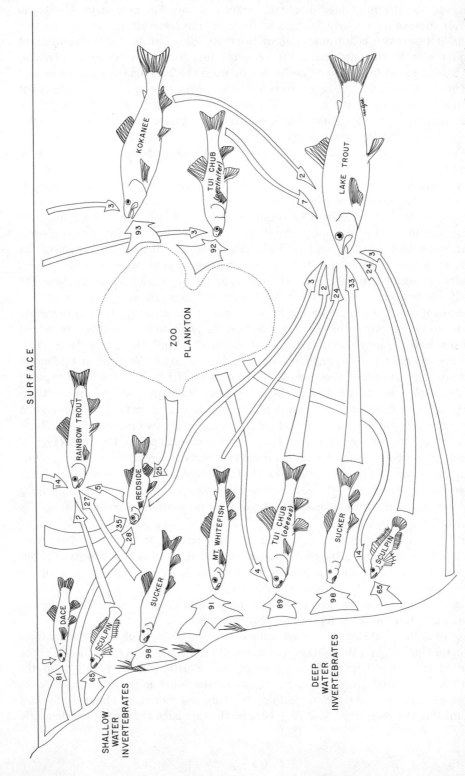

Figure 5. Feeding relationships of Lake Tahoe fishes, modified from R. G. Miller (1951). The numbers represent percent of the diet by volume. Kokanee data is from Cordone et al. (1971).

active, grazing the bottom in schools on algae, detritus, and invertebrates. Sculpins are abundant wherever they can capture detritus-feeding invertebrates (snails, amphipods, chironomid larvae) and each other. Some *obesa* chubs move into this association during the day, returning to shallower water (less than 15 m) at night. Their food is predominately snails which live in large numbers on the aquatic plants, although various bottom-dwelling invertebrates are also common in their diet. Mountain whitefish are also probably found in association with beds of aquatic plants, but they seldom venture into the deep, plant-free areas. Feeding is mostly during the day, on snails, dragonfly larvae, and other plant-dwelling or bottom-living invertebrates.

The *Midwater Association* consists of two plankton feeders (kokanee salmon and *pectinifer* tui chubs) and one predator (rainbow trout) that live in the open waters of the lake. The relationship between the recently introduced kokanee and the *pectinifer* chub needs to be explored in detail since they are both pelagic feeders on zooplankton, especially cladocerans (mostly *Daphnia pulex*) and copepods (*Epischura* and *Cyclops*). From what evidence is available, however, it does appear that the two species have slightly different habitats. Tui chubs seldom venture far from shore and appear to make regular, diurnal, vertical migrations, possibly following the diurnal migrations of zooplankton. They are found in the deep waters (but off the bottom) during the day, moving into the surface waters at night. This movement in part follows the contours of the bottom, since they are also found closer to shore at night than they are during the day. Kokanee, on the other hand, seem to be widely distributed in the open waters, remaining close to the surface continually except when the surface waters become too warm in August and September. During these months large schools of kokanee are found at depths of 15 to 40 m (Cordone et al. 1971). Rainbow trout are also widely distributed in the open waters of the lake, where they feed partially on plankton and partially on other fish, especially tui chubs. The trout commonly move into shallow water to feed on the abundant minnows during the evening.

EAGLE LAKE

Eagle Lake is the only large natural lake in California, besides Lake Tahoe, that contains Lahontan system fishes. The second largest freshwater lake completely within California (8900 ha), Eagle Lake is very alkaline (pH 8.4 to 9.6) and mostly less than 5 m deep, although it has a maximum depth of 23 m. It is fairly productive, supporting large beds of aquatic plants in shallow water. The surface waters usually reach 21°C in the summer and the lake freezes over in the winter. Strong winds usually prevent the development of a permanent, well-defined thermocline in the summer but the deep water nevertheless normally remains below 21°C.

Only five species of fish live in the lake: Eagle Lake trout (apparently a hybrid between native cutthroat and introduced rainbow), tui chubs, Tahoe sucker, Lahontan redsides, and speckled dace. The latter two species may have been introduced by bait fishermen since J. O. Snyder did not report any from the lake when he collected there in 1911. The redsides and dace inhabit the waters close to the surface. Large schools of young-of-the-year tui chubs are also found here. Large tui chubs live in the open waters of the lake, feeding on zooplankton, invertebrates that live on aquatic plants, and anything else of suitable size that moves. The chubs in turn are the main food of the trout, especially in the summer when high surface temperatures confine the trout to deep areas of the lake. The only species that shares the deep water with the trout is the Tahoe sucker which, apparently as a consequence of its bottom-dwelling habits, is seldom preyed upon by the trout.

At the present time, Eagle Lake trout populations are almost entirely maintained by hatchery plantings. The spawning fish are trapped as they run up Pine Creek, the lake's only permanent tributary. This operation is necessary because the flows of the creek have been greatly reduced by irrigation, making the survival of trout eggs and fry in the stream problematical.

DEATH VALLEY SYSTEM

There are three major components of the Death Valley system in California, each with its own native fish fauna: the Mojave River, the Amargosa River, and the Owens River. In addition there is the Mono Lake Basin which was fishless until recently.

The Mojave River originally contained only one species, the Mojave tui chub, now endangered. The river presently supports arroyo chubs, various introduced warmwater fishes, and trout in the headwaters. The Amargosa River, the springs that drain into it, and Salt Creek are the waterways of Death Valley itself. Salt Creek is home to Salt Creek pupfish while Cottonball Marsh pupfish inhabit the marsh into which the creek drains. The Amargosa River is home to Amargosa pupfish and all its subspecies that inhabit isolated springs, and to a distinctive form of speckled dace. The pupfish live in the pools of the streams or the warm springs, while the dace live in the outflows of a few of the springs.

The Owens River, with four coexisting species (Owens pupfish, Owens sucker, Owens tui chub, and speckled dace), has the most complex fish fauna of the three desert-stream systems. Unfortunately, the system was severely disrupted to supply water to Los Angeles long before any attempt was made to study the native fishes in detail, so the original fish interrelationships can only be guessed at. Dace seem to have been the dominant fish in the headwaters and in the riffles of the lower reaches, while pupfish inhabited the extensive marshy areas, feeding on mosquito larvae and other invertebrates. Suckers and tui chubs dominated slower moving, low-elevation sections of river, the suckers browsing on bottom algae, detritus, and invertebrates, and the tui chubs feeding opportunistically on the most abundant invertebrates.

Today the major feature of the system is Crowley Reservoir, which supports a good fishery for Sacramento perch, trout, and brown bullhead. It also contains large populations of Owens suckers and tui chubs. The chubs seem to be hybrids between Lahontan and Owens tui chubs.

Just to the north of the Owens River Basin lies the Mono Lake Basin, originally fishless. Mono Lake is still too saline to support fish, but a variety of fishes have been planted in its tributary streams as well as in a number of high-altitude lakes in the drainage system. The fishes present are an interesting mixture of species native to a wide variety of places: brown trout (Europe), brook trout (eastern United States), rainbow trout (coastal California), cutthroat trout (Lahontan system), golden trout (upper Kern River), tui chubs (Lahontan system), Owens sucker (Owens system), and threespine stickleback (coastal California).

COLORADO RIVER

The short section of the Colorado River that borders California bears little resemblance to the great river of a hundred years ago. The flows have been reduced and confined behind dams, forming large reservoirs like Lake Havasu. The formerly heavy silt load has been reduced, the reservoirs acting as settling basins, but in its place are salts, fertilizers, and other products of irrigation agriculture. Not surprisingly, the fish fauna has changed drastically, more so than in any other river system in California.

The original fauna was simple, since the California portion of the river was an ecologically uniform deep, muddy, sluggish channel with fluctuating flows and no large tributary streams. In the main channel were bottom-feeding humpback sucker and omnivorous bonytail, both species with bizarre body shapes adapted for moving about in strong currents. Preying on these two species, as well as on their own young, were giant Colorado squawfish. Desert pupfish may have been found in the shallow marshes on the river's edge. The only other fishes present were rare stragglers from upstream, such as speckled dace and flannelmouth sucker, and euryhaline wanderers from the Gulf of California, such as machete and spotted sleeper. Mullet, although abundant in the saline lower river now, were apparently originally uncommon migrants from the gulf.

Today, with the exception of mullet, the native fishes are extinct or rare in the California portion of the river. The river and reservoirs contain instead a conglomeration of introduced species: carp, red shiner, threadfin shad, several species of catfish, largemouth bass, striped bass, bluegill, green sunfish, mosquitofish, Mozambique mouthbrooder, etc. Obviously this is an unstable, artificial assemblage of fishes that will keep changing as long as man keeps changing the nature of the river and introducing new species into it.

SALTON SEA

The Salton Sea is the largest inland body of water within California, with a surface area of about 548 km^2. It fills the bottom of the Salton sink in the Imperial Valley, at an elevation of 71 m below sea level. The sea is shallow (maximum depth, 12 m), warm (summer tempeatures, 26 to 33°C; winter temperatures, 10 to 17°C), and saline (1971 salinity, 37 ppt). Although overflows from the Colorado River have filled the sink many times in the past, the bodies of water so created have usually dried up in a few years. The present sea was created in the summer of 1905 when, during a flood, the entire Colorado River started flowing through and enlarging the Alamo Channel, a canal dug to bring irrigation water to the Imperial Valley. The river continued to empty into the sink until February, 1907, when its flow was finally diverted back into its former channel through a massive earth-moving effort. The level of the sea is presently maintained through the inflow of irrigation water from the Imperial Valley. Unfortunately, the high salt content of the irrigation water combined with rapid evaporation from the sea itself means that the salinity of the sea is steadily increasing. This is reflected in the changes in its fish fauna. In 1915, the fishes were the same as those found in the Colorado River. At the present time they are mainly saltwater forms introduced from the Gulf of California (Table 3).

Numerous freshwater fishes, mostly tropical exotics, do exist, however, in the freshwater canals that flow into the sea. The three dominant fishes in the Salton Sea, bairdella (*Bairdella icistia*) orangemouth corvina (*Cynoscion xanthulus*) and sargo (*Anistremus davidsoni*), will not be treated beyond the brief discussion below, for the following reasons: their biology is discussed in detail in Walker (1961); they are saltwater forms with no tolerance of low salinities; and the salinity of the sea is steadily increasing, so that by 1975 it will be high enough (40 ppt) to severely stress all three species (Brocksen and Cole, 1972). If present trends continue, the species will probably disappear from the sea during the 1980s.

The bairdella, orangemouth corvina, and sargo were introduced into the Salton Sea between 1949 and 1956 by the California Department of Fish and Game to establish a sport fishery. The introductions were extraordinarily successful and the three species quickly became the dominant fishes in the open waters. Other species present in the sea are either restricted in their distribution to the shallow edges (longjaw mudsucker, desert pupfish, sailfin molly), confined to the inflowing irrigation canals (Mozambique

Table 3

Changes in the fish fauna of the Salton Sea, based on information in Evermann (1916), Coleman (1929), Dill (1944), and Walker (1961). A = abundant; C = common; R = rare; N = not recorded but probably present; – = absent. The species list does not include those found only in the freshwater canals tributary to the sea

Species	1916	1929	1942	1955-57	1971-73
Bonytail	C	–	–	–	–
Humpback sucker	C	C	–	–	–
Rainbow trout	R	R	–	–	–
Striped mullet	A	C	A	R	R
Desert pupfish	R	A	A	C	C
Carp	A	N	C	–	–
Mosquitofish	–	A	A	C	R
Longjaw mudsucker	–	–	N	C	C
Machete	–	–	C	–	–
Threadfin shad	–	–	–	A	R
Sargo	–	–	–	C	A
Bairdella	–	–	–	A	A
Orangemouth corvina	–	–	–	A	A
Sailfin molly	–	–	–	–	C

mouthbrooder, red shiner, desert pupfish, sailfin molly, other freshwater species), or enter the sea on a seasonal basis, through canals from the Colorado River (threadfin shad).

Because the number of fish species in the sea is small, the feeding relationships are relatively simple (Walker, 1961). Primary production is by the abundant planktonic algae, mainly diatoms, dinoflagellates, and green algae. These are fed upon by zooplankton, mostly rotifiers, copepods, and larval stages of the bottom invertebrates. Nothing seems to feed directly on the zooplankton, but the dead zooplankters, along with their fecal pellets and dead phytoplankton, sink to the bottom. There they decay and form a fine detrital ooze, the main food of the pile worm, *Neanthes succinea*. The pileworm is the main item in the diet of bairdella and sargo, which are fed on in turn by orangemouth corvina. The latter species, achieving weights of 14.5 kg in the sea, is the main object of the sport fishery.

Change

Ever since Western Civilization started dominating the California landscape, California's fish fauna has been changing. Thirty-seven percent of the fish species now present were introduced by man within the last one hundred years, and these fishes are now among the most abundant species in California's inland waters. The native fishes are quietly disappearing, especially from low-elevation regions where man's impact has been the greatest. In Clear Lake, Lake County, and in the San Joaquin River at Friant, two California localities from which reliable collecting records exist over the years, the fish faunas have changed from being dominated by native fishes to being dominated by introduced or planted species (Tables 4, 5). Many of the native fish species now endangered or extinct were among the most abundant fishes in aboriginal California and served as major sources of food for the Indians and early white settlers. Among these species are the Lost River and shortnose suckers of the Klamath River, the thicktail chub, Sacramento perch, and Clear Lake splittail of the Sacramento-San Joaquin River system, and the Colorado squawfish, bonytail, and humpback sucker of the Colorado River. The causes of the decline of native fish fauna are many but they fall into three basic areas: habitat changes, introductions, and fishing.

HABITAT CHANGES

Most of California's major inland waterways today bear little resemblance to the streams and lakes encountered by the first white explorers and settlers. The once turbulent and muddy lower Colorado River is now a giant dammed irrigation ditch and drain, carrying salts and other agricultural wastes to Mexico and occasionally to the Gulf of California. The giant lakes of the San Joaquin Valley are today vast grain farms. The Sacramento-San Joaquin Delta, once an enormous tule marsh dissected by meandering river channels, has been transformed into islands of farmland protected by high levees from the water that flows by in straight, dredged channels. Almost every stream of any size has been dammed at least once to control its flow. Thus, it is not surprising that habitat modification is the major cause of the changes in California's fish fauna. Different fish species are affected by different types of habitat change, however, so it is worthwhile to consider separately the effects of (1) stream-channel alterations, (2) dams and reservoirs, (3) dewatering of streams and lakes, (4) pollution, and (5) watershed changes.

Man has probably been altering the channels of California's streams ever since the first Spaniard stepped off a boat, shovel in hand. The first really drastic alterations, however, were those of the gold miners, who in their frantic search for tiny pieces of

Table 4

Changes in the fish fauna of Clear Lake, Lake County, based on information from Jordan and Gilbert (1894), Coleman (1930), Lindquist, Deonier, and Hancey (1943), Murphy (1951), Cook, Conners, and Moore (1964), and Moyle and Li (unpublished data). A = abundant; C = common; R = rare; P = present but status uncertain; N = not recorded but probably present; R* = rare in lake but common in tributary streams

	1894	1929	1939-41	1946-50	1961-63	1973
Native Species						
Pacific lamprey	P	—	—	—	—	—
Rainbow trout	C	C	—	—	—	—
Clear Lake splittail	A	A	A	R	R	—
Sacramento blackfish	A	A	A	A	A	A
Hitch	A	A	A	C	A	A
Sacramento squawfish	A	A	P	R	R*	R*
Thicktail chub	C	C	P	—	—	—
Sacramento sucker	A	A	P	C	R*	R*
Threespine stickleback	P	—	—	—	—	—
Tule perch	A	N	P	N	C	C
Sacramento perch	C	A	C	C	R	R
Prickly sculpin	C	N	P	N	C	C
Introduced Species						
Golden shiner	—	—	—	—	C	C
Carp	A	A	A	A	A	A
Mosquitofish	—	—	C	P	A	A
Mississippi silversides	—	—	—	—	—	A
Brown bullhead	A	A	A	A	A	A
Channel catfish	—	C	N	N	C	C
White catfish	A	N	A	A	A	A
Largemouth bass	—	C	C	C	C	C
Bluegill	—	A	A	A	A	A
Redear sunfish	—	—	—	—	—	R
Green sunfish	—	—	P	C	C	C
Black crappie	—	A	P	A	A	A
White crappie	—	—	—	—	A	A
Total species	15	17	18	17	20	21
Percent native	80	59	50	47	40	33

Table 5

Changes in the fish fauna of the San Joaquin River at Friant,
Fresno County, based on information from Rutter (1903),
Needham and Hanson (1935), Dill (1946), and Moyle and
Nichols (1974). N = the species was not recorded but
probably present; X = the species was present;
— = the species was absent

	1898	1934	1940-41	1970-71
Native Species				
Pacific lamprey	N	N	N	X
Pacific brook lamprey	N	N	N	X
Rainbow trout	X	X	X	X
Chinook salmon	X	X	X	—
Sacramento blackfish	N	X	X	—
Hitch	X	X	X	—
Hardhead	X	X	X	—
Splittail	X	—	—	—
California roach	X	X	X	—
Sacramento squawfish	X	X	X	—
Sacramento sucker	X	X	X	X
Tule perch	X	X	X	—
Prickly sculpin	N	X	X	X
Threespine stickleback	X	X	X	X
Introduced Species				
Brown trout	—	X	X	X
Carp	—	X	X	X
Brown bullhead	—	—	X	X
Mosquitofish	—	—	X	X
Green sunfish	—	—	X	X
Bluegill	—	X	X	X
Smallmouth bass	—	X	X	—
Largemouth bass	—	—	X	X
Total species	14	17	21	13
Percent native	100	77	62	40

metal, despoiled hundreds of miles of stream bed by placer mining. In the process of digging up the stream beds, they destroyed large salmon runs in Sierra Nevada foothill streams and turned shady pool-and-riffle trout streams into long, shallow, exposed runs. Many of these streams are still nearly barren of fish. Today the straightening and dredging of stream channels is being carried out in the name of flood control by agencies like the Soil Conservation Service. Channelized sections of Rush Creek, Modoc County, when compared to nonchannelized sections, contain fewer fish overall, much smaller trout, and fewer of the rare Modoc sucker. Only Pit sculpin and speckled dace manage to maintain large populations in the channelized sections (Moyle, in press). The decrease in size and numbers of fish were caused by the reduction of habitat diversity, especially the elimination of pools. Such effects are typical of other streams as well.

The dredged channels of the Sacramento-San Joaquin Delta are an example of stream-channel alterations on a mammoth scale. While fish are often surprisingly numerous in the channels, habitat variety, and thus the number of species, is limited. In particular, the elimination of most of the tule marshes through which the old channels meandered is probably the main reason for the extinction of the thicktail chub and for other native fishes having become only minor components of the fish fauna. Similar effects were observed when sloughs along the lower Colorado River were drained as part of a large channelization project (Beland, 1953a).

The most dramatic type of channel alteration in recent decades has been the construction of dams and reservoirs, an activity that bloomed with the advent of the Central Valley Project in the 1930s and has only slightly slowed down at the present time. One of the most severe effects of dams and reservoirs is that they block the upstream and downstream movements of fishes. Friant Dam, finished in 1946, completely prevented a large run of chinook salmon from reaching their spawning grounds. To make matters worse, while the reservoir was filling, flow down the San Joaquin River was almost completely cut off, preventing any salmon that might have spawned in the lower reaches of the river from doing so. Today the capture of a salmon in the upper San Joaquin River is a rare event (Moyle, 1970). A similar blockage of the migrations of Colorado squawfish may have been in part responsible for their extinction in California waters. A more subtle effect of dams is their isolation of the upstream areas. If a stream system located above a dam should lose its native fish fauna through natural or man-created disasters, there is no way this system could be recolonized by fishes from other nearby stream systems. For example, California roach are now absent from the small streams of the upper San Joaquin River above Friant Dam, with no hope of natural recolonization (Moyle and Nichols, 1974).

Reservoirs are also hard on the native fish fauna because they favor lake-adapted introduced species over native stream-adapted forms. Thus, in the Sacramento-San Joaquin system, squawfish and hardhead tend to disappear from reservoirs after an initial five to ten years of abundance. Reservoirs have, however, benefited some native fishes. Prickly sculpin and Sacramento sucker are permanently established in a number of Central Valley reservoirs, as are hitch and tui chub. Sacramento perch, virtually extinct in their native habitat, are extremely abundant in a number of alkaline reservoirs into which they have been introduced.

One of the main reasons for the construction of dams, reservoirs, and irrigation diversions is to catch runoff and send it, via canals, to where it can be used for irrigation, or for industrial and municipal consumption. This naturally leaves less water available for fish downstream from the dam. One of the most dramatic examples of the results of dewatering a stream is the continuous fall in the level of Pyramid Lake, Nevada, following diversion of most of the flow of the Truckee River for irrigation. The sandy delta that was exposed at the mouth of the river due to the declining lake level prevented both Lahontan cutthroat trout and cui-ui suckers from spawning in the river. The trout are now gone from the lake and the suckers are endangered. Similar reduction in flows of inlet streams during periods when they are used for spawning has apparently been at least partially responsible for the decline of the Clear Lake splittail in Clear Lake, Lake County (Cook, Moore, and Connors, 1966). Reduced stream flows have also altered the nature of the Sacramento-San Joaquin Delta and its fish fauna. Present flows are about half the natural level and by 1990 they will probably be reduced to about a third the natural level (Skinner, 1972). Besides reducing the aquatic habitat, such diminished flows are likely to increase the upstream penetration of salt water, decrease nutrient flow into the estuary, decrease the flushing action of the inflow and hence increase the effects of pollution, increase water temperatures, and decrease oxygen levels during the summer months. Such changes, unless controlled or mitigated in some way, are bound to have a deleterious effect on fishes of the Delta, particularly striped bass, chinook salmon, white sturgeon, and American shad (Skinner, 1972).

The ultimate reduction in fish habitat in California through dewatering has been the draining of lakes Tulare and Buena Vista on the floor of the San Joaquin Valley. They supported a small commercial fishery for turtles and native minnows in the nineteenth century. Unfortunately, the lakes were drained for farmland before anyone was able to take a look at the fish fauna but they probably were a major habitat for Sacramento perch, the now presumably extinct thicktail chub, and other depleted native fishes.

One of the sad realities of California is that water which is not used directly for one purpose or another is likely to be polluted to a greater or lesser degree. Pollution is especially hard on the native fishes. In the foothills of the San Joaquin Valley, most native fishes are able to live only in clear, undisturbed sections of stream. The exception is the California roach, which can be found in large numbers living in streams badly polluted with the effluent from small-town sewage-disposal systems. Fish kills from various types of pollution are common. In 1971, the fishes inhabiting the lower Pajaro River, including a run of steelhead, were virtually wiped out by the failure of the sewage treatment plant at Watsonville, which released large amounts of raw sewage into the river. Three years earlier, a similar kill took place in the Pajaro when a farmer washed out his crop-spraying gear in the river, releasing highly toxic pesticides (Lollock, 1968). Bury (1972) recorded a kill of over 2,500 Pacific lampreys, rainbow trout, Klamath smallscale suckers, and speckled dace in a small stream in Trinity County, due to a spill of 2,000 gallons of diesel oil. A kill of several hundred rainbow trout in Mill Creek, Mendocino County, occurred in August 1973, when an airplane carrying a load of fire-retardent chemicals and clay accidentally dumped the load into the stream rather than on a small wildfire burning nearby (H. W. Li, pers. comm.). Fish kills such as these, from a variety of causes, are not isolated incidents but are common occurrences that can, if repeated in one stream system, permanently alter the nature of its fish fauna.

Although direct fish kills by pollution are common, equally significant to fish populations are nonlethal forms of pollution that decrease growth, inhibit reproduction, or prevent migration. Laboratory studies of persistent pesticides, such as DDT, have shown that low levels can have such effects on salmon and trout, but the subtle nature of the effects usually renders it difficult to pin the decline of a fish population on pesticide levels. Equally subtle in their effects on fish populations are the rises in water temperatures caused by pumping river water through power plants as a coolant, and then returning it to the river. Small increases in stream temperatures can have severe long-term effects on the fishes. For example, striped bass spawning and migration is greatly inhibited if power plant effluent causes water temperatures to exceed 21°C (Talbot, 1966). So far, the effects of inland thermal pollution have been minimal in California, but as more power plants are built on streams with reduced flows, even lethal temperatures may be reached for many species of fish, especially trout and salmon.

Another environmental change that is likely to raise water temperatures is the deforesting and overgrazing of watersheds, particularly if the practices eliminate streambank vegetation shading the water. Such changes are likely to be most significant to marginal trout streams, where summer water temperatures normally approach the upper limits for trout. The removal of watershed vegetation, especially by logging operations, is likely also to affect stream flows, increase erosion and turbidity, compact streambeds, decrease dissolved oxygen levels, and create logjam barriers to fish migration (Burns, 1972). Streams in heavily logged or grazed areas tend to have greater flows in the summer because there is less vegetation to take up the water and lose it to the atmosphere through transpiration. The depletion of the vegetation also tends to increase winter and spring runoff, resulting in more damaging floods. In some situations, vegetation removal may actually create year-round flows in normally intermittent streams, improving the streams for some fish species. The large spring floods, however, may offset any gains by increasing streambank erosion, by silting in pools and riffles (or, alternately, by scouring and compacting them), by increasing water turbidity, and by piling up barriers of fallen trees and logs. Sloppy logging practices, such as using streambeds for roadways or as dumping grounds for slash, may exaggerate these effects, just as careful logging practices, such as leaving a belt of trees along the streams, can minimize them. Thus Burns (1972) found that sloppy logging along the Noyo River, Mendocino County, caused a decrease of 42 percent in young steelhead biomass and a decrease of 65 percent in young coho salmon biomass, yet careful logging along other similar streams actually increased production of these two species.

INTRODUCTIONS

The introduction of exotic fishes into California was both inevitable and necessary: inevitable because Western Man has seldom been satisfied with what he finds naturally in newly settled areas, necessary because his manipulation of the waterways has made many of them unsuitable for the native fishes. The introduced freshwater fishes of California have a worldwide origin, although most of them (thirty-three species) are from eastern North America. There are two species from other parts of western North America, six species from Central and South America, two species from Africa, three species from Europe, and five species from eastern Asia.

The reasons for introducing fishes are many, but there seem to be eight main ones: to improve sport and commercial fishing, to provide forage for game fishes, to provide bait for fishermen, for insect control, for weed control, for pets, for aquaculture, and by accident. Most of the deliberate introductions into California were meant to improve fishing. One of the most successful introductions of this type was carp, now considered to be a major pest. The introduced catfishes, basses, and sunfishes, however, form the backbone of California's warmwater fisheries. This is not surprising considering that the only widely accepted warmwater gamefish native to California is the Sacramento perch. Forage fishes for the gamefishes were introduced as reservoirs became one of the main aquatic habitats. These fishes have generally been small zooplankton feeders such as threadfin shad, Delta smelt (Japanese subspecies), and Mississippi silversides, although native fishes like tui chubs, hitch, and threespine stickleback have been tried. Golden shiner, red shiner, and fathead minnow have also been introduced as forage fish on occasion, but their spread has been mainly the result of releases from bait buckets or baitfish rearing ponds.

Mosquitofish and, more recently, Mississippi silversides were introduced to help control mosquitoes and gnats by feeding on the larvae. Mosquito control is likewise one reason given for introducing the Mozambique mouthbrooder, although it has also been justified as a sportfish, weed-control agent, aquarium fish, and aquaculture species. The weakest of these reasons is probably weed control and, as a result, other fishes (mainly other *Tilapia* species and grass carp, *Ctenopharyngodon idella*) are constantly being proposed as agents to check aquatic weeds in ponds and canals. *Tilapia zillii* was recently introduced for weed control into the Imperial Valley.

The introduction of these same species is sometimes argued by their proponents because they are potentially useful for aquaculture, converting vegetable matter into useful protein. It is unfortunate, however, that the appeal of these exotics has resulted in the native fish fauna being ignored as subjects for aquaculture, when some species, such as Sacramento blackfish, are eminently suited for it. The main fishes raised for food in artificial systems in California today are various catfishes and trouts.

The pet trade is another source of introductions. Fish dealers have released tropical fish into desert springs to have a ready source of supply, to the detriment of the pupfishes and their relatives. In the canals of the Imperial Valley, sailfin mollies, Trinidad rivulus, and other fishes have become established after escaping from ponds in tropical-fish farms. Pet-fish owners who have tired of their charges and released them in the nearest lake or stream are probably responsible for most wild goldfish populations and for the guppies that frequent sewage treatment plants.

A final source of exotic fishes has been accidental introductions. Logperch came in with a shipment of largemouth bass; rainwater killifish first probably arrived as eggs on oyster shells; and yellowfin gobies apparently were flushed into the Delta from the bilge of a cargo ship.

The introduced fishes have obviously radically changed the nature of California's fish fauna since they are now the most abundant fishes in much of the state's waterways. Nevertheless, the introductions themselves have been only partially responsible for the reduction of the native fish fauna. By and large, introduced species are most abundant in aquatic habitats modified by man while native fishes persist mostly in undisturbed areas. In the San Joaquin River system, for example, the aggressive, predaceous green sunfish is widely distributed in foothill streams. In undisturbed regions they occur only as scattered large adults, while native minnows remain abundant. If a stream section is dammed, bulldozed, or otherwise changed the sunfish quickly take over and the native fishes become uncommon (Moyle and Nichols, 1974). It is interesting to note, however, that in trout streams native and introduced trout species may coexist, apparently subdividing the resources available through behavioral interactions and specializations. Nevertheless, it is possible in some situations for introduced species to eliminate native ones through direct interactions: competition, predation, habitat interference, and hybridization.

Direct competition between two species for a resource (usually food or space) in limited supply, that results in one species being eliminated, is frequently invoked as a cause for faunal changes, but it is in fact very difficult to demonstrate. If a new species can survive in an undisturbed environment into which it has been introduced, it is likely that it will reach some sort of population equilibrium with the species already present, reducing the populations of the native fishes but not eliminating them (Johannes and Larkin, 1961). Thus, the introduction of golden shiners into a California trout lake usually results in decreased growth and reproduction of the trout population but the trout seldom disappear altogether. However, one native California fish species that seems to have been eliminated from its natural range due to competition from introduced species is the Sacramento perch. Its disappearance from the Sacramento-San Joaquin system was gradual (not obviously correlated with environmental changes), yet it is very successful in a wide variety of ponds, reservoirs, and lakes into which it has been introduced. The common denominator of these waters is the absence of ecologically similar but more aggressive species, particularly bluegill (Moyle, Mathews, and Bonderson, 1974).

Predation by an introduced species on a native one is another mechanism commonly invoked to explain the disappearance of species. The classic example of this is the projected elimination, by sea lamprey (*Pteromyzon marinus*) predation, of lake trout and other large fishes from the upper Great Lakes. Such situations, although spectacular, are also exceptional. Most predators will cease hunting a particular prey species long before it becomes extinct. It should be pointed out, however, that predation by green sunfish does seem to have been responsible for local extinctions of California roach, although habitat change may also have played a role. The sunfish invade the intermittent roach streams, which are ecologically similar to their native midwestern streams, and become trapped with the roach in the summer pools. Under these circumstances they can easily eliminate the roach from the streams (Moyle and Nichols, 1974).

Habitat interference occurs when an introduced species changes the habitat by its activities and the change forces the native forms to leave or die out. Carp are the main villains in this category since they root up the bottom, digging up aquatic plants and greatly increasing the amount of suspended matter in the water. Fishes (including many gamefishes) that require clear water for feeding or breeding may have their populations reduced or eliminated. In California the effect of carp is difficult to assess because they live mostly in disturbed habitats. It is possible, however, that they may be partially responsible for the supposed reduction in the clarity of Clear Lake, Lake County and for the gradual disappearance of its native fish fauna. Habitat alteration is one of the main objections to the introduction of herbivorous fishes (e.g., grass carp, Zill's cichlid) into natural waters, since they may eliminate or change the composition of aquatic plant communities important in the life cycles of fishes already present.

Hybridization between two closely related species or subspecies has been a problem primarily when fish are transferred from one drainage system in California to another. The Mojave tui chub is now an endangered subspecies because it has hybridized in most of its natural range with the introduced arroyo chub and the hybrids are almost identical with pure arroyo chubs (Hubbs and Miller, 1942). Results are similar when Lahontan cutthroat trout hybridize with introduced rainbow trout. Hybridization with rainbow trout has almost eliminated redband trout as a distinct form. The loss through hybridization of a distinctive population represents an irreplacable aesthetic and scientific loss, as well as the loss of a genetic reservoir of potential future use by man.

FISHING

Sport fishing and, to a lesser extent, commercial fishing are today major factors shaping the freshwater fish communities of California. Fishing is highly selective for both species and size of fish. Sport fishing is aimed primarily at large carnivorous species while freshwater commercial fishing is aimed at large fishes not reserved for sport fishing, such as carp and Sacramento blackfish. If sport fishing removes a large percentage of the fishes at the top of a food chain, the population structure of the species making up the lower links is bound to change. In simple systems, such as farm ponds containing only largemouth bass and bluegill, excessive harvest of the top carnivores (the bass) may irreversibly change the system, unless fishing imbalances are continuously corrected. Thus, harvest of large-sized largemouth bass from a pond may cause a population explosion among their prey, the bluegill. The bluegill in turn may greatly reduce the insect and zooplankton populations needed to support young bass, resulting in fewer bass than before and large numbers of stunted bluegill.

Similarily, removal of trout by fishing from streams that also contain squawfish may be partially responsible for the apparent dominance of squawfish in rivers, such as the American and Pit, which once provided excellent trout fishing. In an undisturbed stream, the faster growing rainbow trout can apparently dominate squawfish and keep them out of trout feeding areas (H. Li, pers. comm.). Removal of trout allows squawfish to exploit the food normally utilized by trout, presumably resulting in bigger and more squawfish. The larger population of big squawfish then presents more of a predatory threat to small trout, making recolonization more difficult. Assuming the foregoing hypothesis is true, questions that need to be answered are: (1) how much fishing pressure can such a trout population take before the situation becomes unbalanced, and (2) how can the balance be restored once it has been upset?

In other aquatic systems in California, such as reservoirs and warmwater streams, the effects of fishing on the fish communities is even less well understood than in trout streams, although overfishing of naturally reproducing populations of gamefishes seldom seems to be a problem. If fish populations decline, it is usually the result of environmental change rather than overfishing. One major exception to this rule, however, was the turn-of-the-century commercial fishery for white sturgeon in the Sacramento-San Joaquin Estuary, which so reduced the populations that only a complete prohibition of fishing for nearly fifty years allowed them to recover.

The imbalances created by heavy fishing are not always undesirable. Commercial fishing in lakes and reservoirs for carp, tui chubs, and other nongame fishes may create more favorable situations for gamefishes by making more food available to their young. The effects of the few such fisheries that now exist in the state are not known but it might actually pay to subsidize them to the extent that they would be willing to overfish the commercial species (especially carp) in order to provide better sport fishing.

THE FUTURE

It is possible to be both pessimistic and optimistic about the future of California's fish fauna, native and introduced. Pessimism comes easily in the face of the all too frequent fish kills, major and minor, that result when one of the products of our industrialized society enters a watercourse. Even more depressing are the rapes of watersheds by careless developers, loggers, dam builders and other groups who have a greater concern for quick profits and growth than they do for proper watershed management which can, in fact, be compatible with their aims. The massive transfer of water from one part of the state to another, mostly via th California Water Project, is another cause for concern, especially as flows through the Sacramento-San Joaquin Delta decrease and as dams are built on the few large, free-flowing streams still remaining. It is difficult for stream-adapted fish to live in the absence of flowing water and impossible for them to exist in the absence of any water at all. In addition to these stresses, the native fauna will have to cope with an inevitable increase in exotic species. In the Sacramento-San Joaquin system alone, three recently introduced species (Mississippi silverside, logperch, and yellowfin goby) are undergoing population explosions. It seems unlikely that any of the three will be particularly beneficial in the long run.

Despite the above trends there are reasons to be optimistic as well. Both public and official attitudes towards water utilitization have changed dramatically in the past few years as part of a general awareness of how rapidly the natural features of California have been disappearing. Hopefully, the changes in attitude mean that the destructive trends of the past are slowing down or even reversing themselves. Some of the more prominent signs of this are listed below.

1. A number of dam projects, specifically those on the Eel and Mad rivers, have been scuttled, or at least delayed, in recent years, due not only to public opposition but also to changes in the method of evaluating the worth of such projects. The possible destruction of natural areas and native faunas now has to be taken into account.

2. The National Environmental Policy Act, requiring reports on the environmental impact of a proposed project, has forced watershed users to at least consider the effects of their projects on water quality and fish populations. Short-term economic benefits still seem to take precedence over long-term environmental degradation but the environmental impact documents are a step in the right direction.

3. State legislation, such as the Wild Rivers Bill (1972) and the Coastal Intiative (1972) have done much to slow down the development of particularly fragile watersheds, giving conservationists a chance to acquire desirable natural areas now in private hands, and giving local, state, and federal agencies more time to develop comprehensive management plans.

4. The California Department of Fish and Game has established an endangered species program which has been effective in identifying rare and endangered fishes, promoting studies of their biology, and establishing management programs for them. Considering that the program was only officially established in 1972, the progress already made has been remarkable.

5. Management techniques used by fisheries biologists of the California Department of Fish and Game are becoming increasingly sophisticated, especially for trout and salmon streams. Native nongame fishes are no longer universally regarded simply as competitors of gamefishes that must be eliminated at all costs. As a result, large-scale stream poisoning programs, such as took place on the Russian River in 1957 (Pintler and Johnson, 1958), are much less common.

6. The continuing construction of artificial spawning channels and hatcheries may eventually reverse the downward trend in Pacific salmon and steelhead populations.

7. State and federal agencies that manage large chunks of public land in California are showing increasing interest in the management of the fisheries resources of these areas. The U. S. Forest Service and the Bureau of Land Management in particular have been conducting inventories of their fisheries resources in recent years and have been actively cooperating with the Department of Fish and Game in setting up management programs for rare or endangered fishes.

8. The deliberate introduction of new species on a "let's see what will happen" basis is no longer possible under regulations by the California Department of Fish and Game. A species has to be carefully evaluated by the department before even an experimental introduction is made into a closed system (e.g., the introduction of white bass into Nacimiento Reservoir). A number of potentially harmful species, such as piranha and golden orfe, have already been banned, even to aquarists, and many more species are likely to join the list.

9. A refuge for native fishes, complete with a barrier to prevent the immigration of introduced species, has been established in the Owens Valley (Miller and Pister, 1971). Hopefully, this is the first of many such refuges.

10. Attempts are now being made to propagate Colorado squawfish and humpback sucker in an Arizona hatchery, in order to reintroduce them into the lower Colorado River.

11. In recent years there has been a marked resurgence of studies of the freshwater nongame fishes of California. Research is underway at most of the state universities and colleges, as well as at the University of California, by independent investigators. Around the turn of the century such research was largely confined to what has been called the Stanford School of Ichthyology, under the aegis of David Starr Jordan and his disciples, especially Charles H. Gilbert and John O. Snyder. There was a resurgence of studies from the late 1940s to the early 1960s. Most of this research was done by Paul R. Needham and his students at U.C. Berkeley but, unfortunately, much of the

work was never published. Although pioneering work was done at these two schools, too many problems (e.g., gamefish/nongame fish interactions; natural history and distribution of native fishes) were left unsolved and both native fishes and fisheries management in California suffered.

12. Private organizations have become increasingly effective in helping to set aside natural areas, either by obtaining desirable lands and then transfering them to public agencies (e.g., The Nature Conservancy) or by pressuring the agencies themselves to purchase them.

13. Between 1961 and 1971 close to 6 million dollars was spent by the Department of Water Resources and the Department of Fish and Game to study the Sacramento-San Joaquin Estuary, including the Delta, in an effort to find ways to minimize the impact of the California Water Project on the fish and wildlife resources (Skinner, 1972). The studies, which are continuing, have made the estuary one of the best understood in the world and they will assure the survival of its important sport fisheries, if at a reduced level.

14. Carp, sucker, squawfish, and other nongame fishes, long despised by most fishermen, are gaining limited public acceptance as being both sporty and edible. Once an active fishery, such as exists in Europe, develops for native minnows and suckers, their long-term survival will be assured.

15. The survival of California's native fishes ultimately depends on a stabilized human population and stabilized or decreasing per capita energy consumption. Population growth rates have been decreasing in recent years and the growth in per capita energy utilization will necessarily decrease as energy sources dwindle. All this will mean less increase in the pressure on California's fish resources.

CONCLUSIONS

The composition of California's fish fauna is still changing, but the rate of change seems to have slowed somewhat. Given proper and imaginative management, trout and salmon populations should at least be able to hold their own in future years, although the catch per angler is bound to decrease as more people take up fishing. Warmwater gamefish populations should increase as better techniques for managing reservoir fisheries are developed and as more farm ponds are constructed. Fishing pressure on warmwater fishes should consequently increase, especially as more of California's freshwater anglers realize that there are species of fish worth catching besides trout. Some of this pressure will be absorbed by the increased willingness of anglers to accept species now generally considered to be undesirable, such as carp and Sacramento sucker.

Nevertheless, the future of California's native nongame fishes does not appear to be as hopeful as does the future of the state's largely introduced sport fishes. Refuges have been set up, or are proposed, for a number of rare or endangered forms but more are needed. If a species is not rare or endangered, it is largely ignored, even in Environmental Impact Reports. This is a tragedy because complex and fascinating natural associations of fishes and other organisms, as described in the ecology section of this book, are rapidly disappearing, even though the individual species may survive in various artificial or disturbed situations. Many of these species may in fact become endangered as their normal biotic (and abiotic) associates gradually become disassociated from each other as the environment is modified by man's activities. Only when a species achieves rare or endangered status are refuges set up, and they are likely to be either too little, too late, or extremely expensive. It seems obvious that if the native fish fauna is going to be preserved for future generations, aquatic habitats in each major drainage basin will have to be managed at least in part for native fishes. Given the heightened public awareness of ecology and the interest in natural history, perhaps a series of fish refuges could be set up that embody many of the principles of state and federal waterfowl refuges. Their primary purpose would be to provide habitat for the maintenance of native fish populations and their vertebrate and invertebrate associates but limited fishing and various noncomsumptive outdoor activities (e.g., fish watching) would be encouraged.

Fish Structure

Understanding the external and internal features of fish is not only necessary for identifying species but it also can provide useful insights into how fishes function in their environment (Fig. 6). This chapter will briefly discuss the portions of the internal and external anatomy of California fishes that reflect most conspicuously the way each species makes its living and those aspects which are useful for identification.

BODY SHAPE

The basic body shape often can give a general idea of how a fish makes its living. However, generalizations based on body shape alone must be made cautiously since the fish do not realize that they are supposed to be following man's rules. Although a number of systems have been devised for categorizing fish body shapes (see, for example, Keast and Webb, 1966), one of the most generally useful is that of Greenway (1965), who recognized five basic plans: rover predator, lie-in-wait predator, surface fish, bottom fish, and deep-bodied fish. A sixth basic shape, eellike, should be added to the list (Fig. 7).

The *rover predator* has the classical fish body shape, epitomized by trout or striped bass, with the center of gravity close to the center of the body. In lakes, these fishes continuously cruise around looking for and then pursuing active prey, especially other fishes. In streams, the streamlined rover-predator shape is ideal for swimming against swift currents.

The *lie-in-wait predator* is adapted for capturing prey from ambush. The body is elongate with the dorsal and anal fins set far back on the body, to assist the tail in producing the sudden powerful thrust needed for a quick dash after a prey organism. The head is often flattened dorsoventrally, with an elongate snout and large mouth. The best examples of fishes with this type of body shape, the northern pike (*Esox lucius*) and the gars (*Lepisosteus* spp.), do not occur in California. The Sacramento squawfish, however, is a rover predator with strong lie-in-wait predator affinities.

Surface fish are built for feeding on insects and zooplankton that live at or near the surface of lakes or other quiet water. They are usually small in size, with the dorsal fin placed on the posterior half of the body. The top of the head is frequently flattened and the mouth angles upwards. Examples in California are mosquitofish and California killifish.

Bottom fish are adapted for living on the bottom of lakes and streams, feeding on bottom organisms and, in many species, detritus. The head is often flattened dorsoventrally, so the back may rise at an angle to a short, upright dorsal fin. The

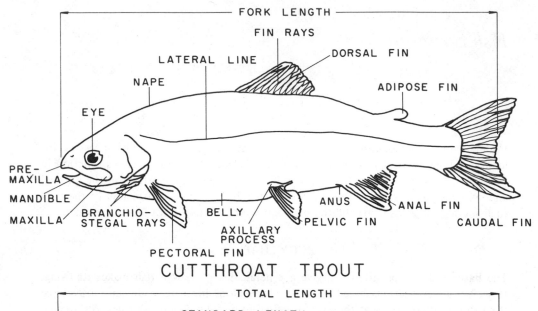

CUTTHROAT TROUT

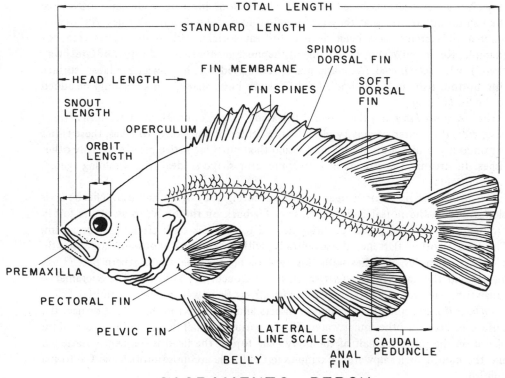

SACRAMENTO PERCH

Figure 6. External features and measurements of soft-rayed (upper) and spiny-rayed (lower) fish.

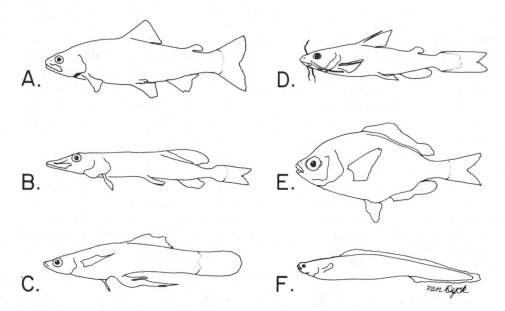

Figure 7. Major body types of fishes: (a) rover predator; (b) lie-in-wait predator; (c) surface fish; (d) bottom fish; (e) deep-bodied fish; (f) eellike fish.

mouth often faces downward and not infrequently has barbels associated with it. The pectoral fins are usually large and flattened. Adaptations for bottom living are often combined with a body shape approaching that of the rover predator, as in carp or Sacramento sucker. The catfishes and sculpins are the best examples in California of bottom fish.

Deep-bodied fish are basically adapted for maneuverability rather than speed or roving. They are typically found in quiet water and are very adapt at searching out and picking up invertebrates from the bottom or from aquatic plants. In deep-bodied fish, such as the sunfishes, the body depth is one-third to one-half the body length. The pectoral fins are usually high up on the body with the pelvic fins immediately below them. The body is laterally compressed, with long dorsal and anal fins. These characteristics may be combined with those of a rover predator in fishes that live in streams or feed on large prey (e.g., green sunfish). Rover and deep-bodied characteristics may also be combined in open-water, plankton-feeding fishes, which tend to be extremely compressed laterally and often possess a keel on the belly (e.g., threadfin shad).

The *eellike fish* are extremely elongate, with wedge-shaped or blunt heads and small, paired fins. They are adapted for squeezing into small crevices in rocks, logs, or beds of aquatic plants. California fishes with eellike bodies include gunnels and Japanese weatherfish.

SCALES

Except for sturgeon, which have primitive scales modified into bony plates, all California freshwater fishes that possess scales have either cycloid or ctenoid types. Cycloid scales are the typical round, thin, flat scales found on shad, minnows, trout, and other "primitive" fishes. Ctenoid scales are similar except that they have tiny, comblike projections on the exposed (posterior) edge of the scales. Ctenoid scales are characteristic of the most evolutionarily advanced fishes, such as perch and sunfish, but the advantage they may confer on these fishes is not clear.

The number and size of scales, regardless of type, tends to reflect the habitat of the fish species. Fishes that live in lakes or slow streams usually have large scales, since they seem to offer some measure of protection against predators, especially lampreys. Stream fishes, on the other hand, have many small scales, for streamlining (e.g., trout). Some groups of fast stream fishes, such as the sculpins, may be entirely without scales, although it should be noted that the catfishes, which primarily inhabit quiet water, also are scaleless.

FINS

Fins are composed of rays and spines. Rays make up the soft, flexible portions of the fins. They are segmented, often branched, and dumbell shaped in cross-section. Spines, in contrast, are normally stiff, unsegmented, unbranched, and round in cross-section. True spines are present mainly in the same advanced fishes that possess ctenoid scales, such as sunfish and perch. The "spines" present on catfish, carp, and goldfish are in fact stiff, thickened rays. Fin spines undoubtedly evolved to help protect their bearers, especially small fish, against predators. Once spines are held stiffly erect, they make the fish an uncomfortably sharp mouthful and they expand the perimeter of the fish, making it more difficult to swallow.

As noted in the section on body shape, the shape, size, and location of the various fins reflects how a fish makes its living. Although all the fins evolved together as a system that simulateously propels, stabilizes, and maneuvers the fish, it is easier to discuss them separately.

Pelvic fins. The farther forward the pelvic (ventral) fins, the more maneuverable the fish. Anteriorly positioned pelvic fins are a general characteristic of the more evolutionarily advanced fishes, including most deep-bodied forms (e.g., sunfish). For the purposes of identifying fishes, three basic positions of the pelvics are recognized: jugular, where the pelvics are well in front of the pectoral fins; thoracic, where the pelvics are immediately below the pectorals; and abdominal, where the pelvics are well behind the pectorals.

Pectoral fins. The higher up the pectorals are on the sides (with the pelvics immediately below), the more maneuverable the fish will be. There is a tendency for the pectoral fins of more roving fish to be more rounded than those of less active, related forms. Compare, for example, the fins of largemouth bass with those of bluegill. The pectorals of fish that rest on the bottom (suckers, sculpins) tend to be large and spread out laterally.

Dorsal and anal fins. These fins are usually long on roving or deep-bodied fishes, for stability while swimming. They are usually short on surface or bottom feeding fishes.

Caudal fin. The more active or faster swimming the fish, the more deeply the tail is likely to be forked. However, fish with less deeply forked tails tend to have more precise control over their movements. Fish adapted for living in flowing water usually have more deeply forked tails than those living in quiet water. Thus the channel catfish has a forked tail, while the brown bullhead has a rounded tail.

MOUTH

The shape of the mouth and the number, type, and placement of teeth reflects the feeding habits of each fish. Usually, the larger the mouth in relation to the size of the head, the larger the prey. Dorsally or ventrally placed mouths are indicators or surface and bottom feeding, respectively. Fish that chase down or ambush large prey, swallowing them whole, tend to have a "hard" mouth, with little capability of protruding the bones around the mouth, especially the premaxilla (squawfish). On the other hand, fish that pick or suck food from the water, bottom, or plants tend to have highly protrusible "lips" (bluegill, carp). Extreme protrusibility is characteristic of plankton feeders like threadfin shad, since they frequently swim around with their mouths open, straining out plankton with their gill rakers.

TEETH

Most California fishes, with the exception of the minnows and suckers, have teeth in their mouths. These teeth, however, are usually quite small, occurring in patches along the inside edge of the mouth, on the roof of the mouth, and on the tongue. Most of them face inwards since their main function is to keep live prey from wriggling back out again.

The location of the patches of teeth is important in the identification and systematics of some fish groups, such as sculpins and trout. *Vomerine teeth* are located on the center of the roof of the mouth, attached to the vomer, a bone which has a rounded head anteriorly and a long, narrow shaft that extends backwards. *Palatine teeth* are two oval patches of teeth located on each side of the vomerine teeth, usually where the roof of the mouth starts to slope downwards. *Basibranchial teeth* are found on the floor of the gill chamber, attached to the anterior portion of the bone to which the branchiostegal rays are connected.

In the minnows, suckers, and sunfishes the most well-developed teeth are the *pharyngeal teeth*, located on the fifth gill arch. This gill arch is not used for respiration and the teeth are apparently modified gill rakers. They are embedded in the tissues behind the gill-bearing arches, and so have to be carefully dissected out to be examined. They show remarkable modifications for feeding. Those of the redear sunfish are stout and peglike, for crushing food such as snails. Squawfish have knifelike pharyngeal teeth, for cutting up the fishes they swallow whole, while suckers have comblike teeth, for breaking up the masses of algae and detritus they swallow. The pharyngeal teeth of hardheads are knifelike when they are small and feed on aquatic insects but they gradually become molariform as they increase in size, reflecting a change to a broader diet that includes plants as well as insects.

The pharyngeal teeth of minnows are frequently used in taxonomy and identification. Most North American minnows have two rows of these teeth on the crescent-shaped pharyngeal arch. These rows are used to derive the pharyngeal tooth formula. A minnow with a pharyngeal tooth formula of 1,4-5,1 has one tooth on the lower row of each arch, four teeth on the upper row of the left arch, and five on the upper row of the right arch. Some minnows have but one row of teeth (formula = 0,4-4,0) and the introduced carp has three rows.

SENSE ORGANS

Vision. The fishes with large eyes in proportion to the size of the head tend to be active predaceous forms that feed most frequently at dawn or dusk, such as the Sacramento squawfish. Small eyes are found in fishes that feed largely by browsing on algae and detritus, such as suckers or California roach, or in fishes that have other well-developed, external sensory receptors, such as the barbels of catfish.

Touch. The long, whiskerlike barbels found around the mouths of bottom fishes such as catfish and sturgeon are primarily tactile organs, although they may have some function as taste organs in catfish. The papillose lips of suckers are also sensitive organs of touch. Fishes that can use tactile organs for locating food tend to feed at night and can exploit food resources available in deep or turbid water, below the limits of light penetration.

Hearing. Most fishes have a fairly well-developed sense of hearing. External ears are unnecessary because sound waves pass easily from water through the fleshy body of a fish, which is almost of equal density. To intercept sound waves, a fish must have its nervous system hooked up either to something considerably denser than water (e.g., earstones) or something considerably less dense than water (e.g., swim bladder). Most fishes rely on earstones (otoliths) for hearing, which permit them mainly to pick up low-frequency vibrations. The minnows, suckers, and catfishes, however, are also capable of picking up high-frequency sounds. They have a chain of four small bones, the Weberian ossicles, that connect the swim bladder to the inner ear. The vibrations of the swim bladder are conducted to the inner ear in much the same way that vibrations of the tympanic membrane in the ear of mammals are conducted down a chain of three small bones, to their inner ears. Fishes with Weberian ossicles have a range of hearing approximately equivalent to that of man.

Lateral line. The lateral line system consists (usually) of a single long canal located just underneath the skin on the sides of the fish, plus a complex pattern of canals on the head. The canals contain sensory endings, and are open to the outside through a series of pores. The lateral line system is sensitive to changes in turbulence and pressure in the water. Thus, it helps stream-dwelling fishes to locate the areas of least turbulence, where they can expend less energy keeping themselves in place. There are many other uses for this sensory system which are just beginning to be appreciated. In the identification of fishes it is frequently important to note whether or not the lateral line is clearly visible externally, and whether it extends all the way to the tail (complete) or not (incomplete). The functional significance of these different conditions is poorly understood.

INTESTINES

The intestines of predaceous fishes are usually short, with a well-developed stomach (largemouth bass, squawfish), while the intestines of detritus- and plant-feeding fishes are long and coiled, often without a recognizable stomach (suckers, Sacramento blackfish). Many fishes have pyloric ceca, blind pouches connected at the junction of the stomach and the small intestine. In some groups (smelt, salmon) the number of ceca can be used as an aid in identifying separate species and populations. Threadfin and American shads have well-developed gizzards, muscular chambers in the foregut that help to grind up the silica-coated diatoms they eat.

COLOR

The color and color patterns of fish species, or even of individual fish, can be highly variable and may depend on environmental conditions. Trout and salmon in lakes or oceans tend to become uniformly silver in color, and assume the "typical" species color patterns only when they are in streams or when they are spawning. Most species have typical color patterns that blend in well with their usual habitat background. However, striking color patterns, such as the dark lateral stripe of largemouth bass, may almost disappear in fish living in turbid water. Pelagic fishes, such as the threadfin shad and Clear Lake splittail, are silvery or white, since such coloration scatters light and makes them less visible to predatory fishes. Bottom fishes, in contrast, tend to be dark on the back and light on the belly, or are colored to match the substrate (suckers, sculpins). Fishes that regularly associate with aquatic vegetation, such as bluegill, tend to have irregular vertical bars on the sides, or other disruptive color patterns. Color also reflects breeding behavior. Fish that defend territories are generally brighter colored, at least during the breeding season, than are fishes that do not.

Identification

Most of the characters used to identify California fishes are discussed in the chapter on fish structure, are explained in the keys, or are shown in Figure 6. However, the measurements and counts listed below need more precise definitions to avoid confusion. Hubbs and Lagler (1958) should be consulted for even more detailed definitions, as well as for definitions of other counts and measurements used in fish taxonomy.

Standard length (SL) is the distance from the tip of the snout or lower jaw, whichever sticks out farther, to the end of the vertebral column. The end of the vertebral column can be found by flexing the tail. The slight projecting ridge that becomes visible is the end of the column.

Total length (TL) is the greatest length that can be measured, from the tip of the snout to the end of longest ray of the caudal fin, when the upper and lower lobes are squeezed together. Total length has to be used carefully since the tips of the caudal fin are frequently frayed or broken.

Fork length (FL) is the distance from the tip of the snout (or lower jaw) to the anterior-most location in the fork of the caudal fin. This measurement is commonly used by fisheries workers since it is more easily taken than standard length and less subject to variation than total length. However, many fishes lack forked tails.

Body depth is the greatest depth that can be measured, excluding the dorsal and anal fins.

Head length is the distance from the tip of the snout to the most distant point on the edge of the operculum.

Dorsal and anal fin rays are counted at the base of each ray to avoid counting branches. In soft-rayed fins which have an angular shape and a straight anterior edge, as in minnows and suckers, only principal rays are counted. The one or two small rudimentary rays in front of the first principal ray are ignored. In fins with a rounded anterior edge, where the fin rays gradually become longer towards the center of the fin, groups of fin rays are counted as one if their bases are much closer together than are the bases of the other fin rays.

Lateral line scales are the scales bisected by the lateral line, extending from the end of vertebral column (see standard length) to the edge of the opercular opening. The count represents the number of body scale rows, and so may be taken even if the lateral line is not externally visible. The count in such cases is called *scales in lateral series*. In fishes that lack scales but possess a visible lateral line, as in sculpins, *lateral line pores* may be counted.

Scales above lateral line are counted from the origin of the dorsal fin (first dorsal fin if there is more than one) down to the lateral line, not including the lateral line scale.

Scales below lateral line are counted from the origin of the anal fin up to the lateral line, preferably by following one scale row. The lateral line scale is not included in the count.

Scales before dorsal fin are the total number of scale rows that cross the back of the fish before the dorsal fin and behind the posterior dorsal end of the head. The end of the head is often marked with a line that separates the scaled from the unscaled portion.

Keys

FAMILY KEY

1a. Mouth with true jaws; gill cover (operculum) present 2

1b. Mouth jawless, a round sucking disc; no operculum present . . Petromyzontidae (lampreys).

2a. Sides with five rows of bony plates; upper lobe of tail much longer than lower (heterocercal, Fig. 8) . . Acipenseridae (sturgeons).

2b. Sides without 5 rows of bony plates; tail lobes about equal (homocercal) . . 3

3a. Heavy bone plate (gular plate) present on underside of lower jaw (Fig. 9) . . Elopidae (tarpons); machete, *Elops affinis.* [1]

3b. No gular plate present 4

4a. Scales on belly form a sharp, saw-toothed ridge . . Clupeidae (herrings).

4b. Belly smooth and usually rounded 5

5a. Adipose fin present 6

5b. Adipose fin absent 8

6a. Scales absent, barbels present on chin . . Ictaluridae (catfishes).

6b. Scales present, chin barbels absent 7

7a. Small fleshy or scaly appendage (axillary process) present at base of each pelvic fin . . Salmonidae (trout, salmon, whitefish).

7b. Axillary processes absent . . Osmeridae (smelts).

8a. Body flattened, asymmetrical; both eyes on one side . . Pleuronectidae (flounders); starry flounder, *Platichthys stellatus.*

8b. Body symmetrical, eyes on opposite sides of head 9

9a. Body encased in bony plates; snout long and tubular . . Syngnathidae (pipefishes).

9b. Body not encased in bony plates; snout blunt 10

10a. Body smooth, long and slender (eellike) 11

10b. Body not eellike 13

11a. 5-6 barbels present on each side of jaw; freshwater . . Cobitidae (loaches); Chinese weatherfish, *Misgurnus anguillicaudatus* [2] (Fig. 10).

11b. Barbels absent; estuarine 12

12a. Dorsal fin extends from caudal region to head . . Pholidae (gunnels).

12b. Dorsal fin extends from caudal region to middle of body . . Anguillidae (eels). [3]

[1]Machete are marine fish that occasionally enter the lower Colorado River. They were once common in the Salton Sea (Walker et al., 1961).

[2]Chinese weatherfish have been reported as established in the Westminster Flood Control Channel, Orange County (St. Amant and Hoover, 1969).

[3]A single European eel (*Anguilla anguilla*) and a single American eel (*A. rostrata*) have been taken from the Delta but it is highly unlikely that they are or will be established in California (Skinner, 1971).

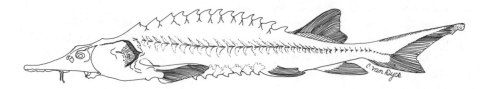

Figure 8. White sturgeon, showing bony plates (scutes) and heterocercal tail.

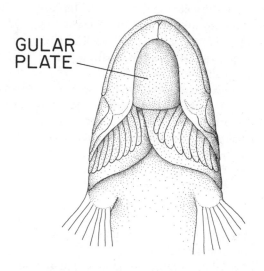

GULAR
PLATE

Figure 9. Gular plate (Elopidae) after Eddy (1957).

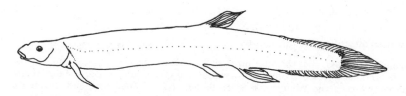

Figure 10. Chinese weatherfish (Cobitidae), 95 mm SL, China. CAS 24192.

13a. Pelvic fins united to form a sucking disc . . Gobiidae (gobies).

13b. Pelvic fins separated, not forming a disc 14

14a. Dorsal fin consists of 3 unconnected spines followed by a soft-rayed fin; usually a row of bony plates on side . . Gasterosteidae (sticklebacks); threespine stickleback, *Gasterosteus aculeatus.*

14b. All spines and rays of dorsal fin connected to others by membrane; no bony plates on side 15

15a. Scales absent, pectoral fins large and rounded . . Cottidae (sculpins).

15b. Scales present; pectoral fins not as above 16

16a. Spines present in dorsal fin (may be small and weak); dorsal fin either with spiny and soft-rayed portions or consisting of two separate fins 20

16b. No spines in dorsal fin (except carp and goldfish); dorsal fin single 17

17a. Scales present on head; caudal fin rounded 18

17b. Scales absent from head; caudal fin forked, often only slightly 19

18a. Anterior rays of anal fin of males elongated, modified into intromittent organ (Fig. 11); livebearing . . Poeciliidae (livebearers).

18b. Anal fin of male normal; egg layers . . Cyprinodontidae (killifishes and pupfishes).

19a. Mouth usually subterminal with fleshy papillose lips; no barbels; pharyngeal teeth comblike, 15 or more on each side . . Catostomidae (suckers).[4]

19b. Mouth usually terminal, with smooth lips; barbels present on a few forms; pharyngeal teeth never comblike, 10 or less per side . . Cyprinidae (minnows).

20a. Distinct scaled ridge present along base of dorsal fin . . Embiotocidae (surfperches).

20b. No such ridge present 21

21a. Anal fin spines 3 or more 25

21b. Anal fin spines 1-2 22

22a. Dorsal fin single; 1 stout spine precedes soft rays on dorsal fin . . Cyprinidae (carp and goldfish).

22b. Dorsal fin double; 4 or more spines on first dorsal fin 23

23a. Anal fin spines 2 . . Percidae (freshwater perches).

23b. Anal fin spines 1 24

24a. Caudal fin rounded; pelvic fins in front of pectorals . . Eleotridae (sleepers); spotted sleeper, *Eleotris picta*[5] (Fig. 12).

24b. Caudal fin forked, pelvic fin well behind pectorals . . Atherinidae (silversides).

25a. Spiny and soft-rayed portions of dorsal fin united, even if only slightly so . 26

25b. Spiny and soft-rayed portions of dorsal fin widely separated . . Mugilidae (mullets); striped mullet, *Mugil cephalus.*

26a. Well-developed pseudobranch (gill-like structure) present on inside surface of operculum (Fig. 13) . . Percichthyidae (temperate basses).

26b. Pseudobranch absent or inconspicuous 27

[4]Both the bigmouth buffalo and the shortnose sucker have terminal mouths but can be distinguished from cyprinids by their comblike pharyngeal teeth, lack of spines in the dorsal and anal fins (possessed by carp and goldfish), lack of barbels (carp), large size, and distinctive appearances.

[5]A single spotted sleeper, normally found in streams and estuaries of Mexico and Central America, was taken from a canal in Imperial County (Hubbs, 1953).

INTROMITTENT ORGAN

Figure 11. Mosquitofish, showing intromittent organ (gonopodium).

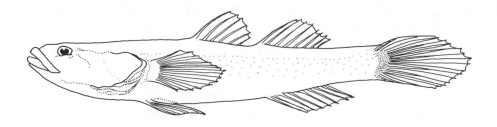

Figure 12. Spotted sleeper (Eleotridae), 57 mm SL, Mexico. CAS 51006.

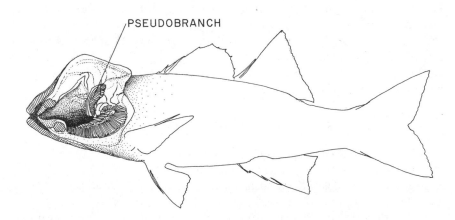

PSEUDOBRANCH

Figure 13. Pseudobranch on the inner surface of a striped bass operculum.

27a. One nostril present on each side of head; lateral line interrupted .. Cichlidae (mouthbrooders).

27b. Two nostrils on each side of head; lateral line continuous .. Centrarchidae (sunfishes and basses).

LAMPREY FAMILY, PETROMYZONTIDAE

1a. Eyes and sucking disc well-developed 2

1b. Eyes and sucking disc absent or poorly developed .. Ammocoetes of all species.

2a. Inner lateral plates 4, supraoral lamina with 3 distinct cusps (Fig. 14) 3

2b. Inner lateral plates 3, supraoral lamina with 2 cusps, often indistinct 4

3a. Total length greater than 21 cm .. Pacific lamprey, *Lampetra tridentata.*

3b. Total length less than 21 cm .. Pit-Klamath brook lamprey, *Lampetra lethophaga.*

4a. Horny plates in disc well-developed, with distinct points .. river lamprey, *Lampetra ayresi.*

4b. Horny plates in disc blunt, many barely visible .. Pacific brook lamprey, *Lampetra pacifica.*

STURGEON FAMILY, ACIPENSERIDAE

1a. 38-48 bony plates in row on each side of body; 44-53 dorsal rays; 28-32 anal rays .. white sturgeon, *Acipenser transmontanus.*

1b. 23-31 bony plates in row on each side of body; 33-40 dorsal rays; 21-31 anal rays .. green sturgeon, *Acipenser medirostris.*

HERRING FAMILY, CLUPEIDAE

1a. Last ray of dorsal fin long and threadlike; single black spot near operculum .. threadfin shad, *Dorosoma petenense.*

1b. Last ray of dorsal fin not elongated; either more than one or no black spots present near operculum 2

2a. Row of black spots on side; scales in lateral series more than 55 .. American shad, *Alosa sapidissima.*

2b. No black spots on side; scales in lateral series less than 55; marine .. Pacific herring, *Clupea harengeus pallasii.*

SMELT FAMILY, OSMERIDAE

1a. Mouth small, maxilla does not reach past middle of eye 2

1b. Mouth large, maxilla usually reaches beyond posterior margin of eye 3

2a. Head length more than 4X eye diameter and more than 2.5X longest anal ray; scales in lateral series 66-73; marine .. surf smelt, *Hypomesus pretiosus.*[6]

2b. Head length less than 4X pupil diameter and less than 2.5X longest anal ray; scales in lateral series 53-60; euryhaline .. delta smelt, *Hypomesus transpacificus.*

[6]Surf smelt are infrequent marine visitors to fresh and brackish waters from Monterey Bay north.

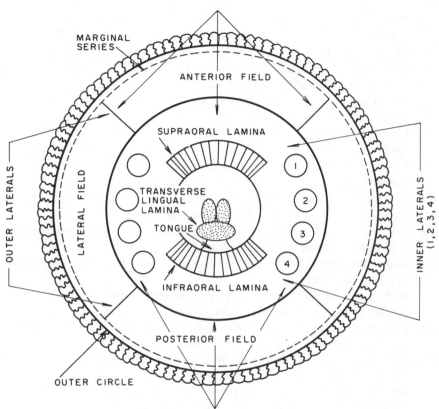

Figure 14. Diagrammatic disc of a lamprey, showing the position of the tooth plates, after Vladykov and Follett (1967).

3a. Lateral line reaches caudal fin, with 70-78 scales; strong concentric striations present on gill covers . . eulachon, *Thaleichthys pacificus*.

3b. Lateral line does not reach past dorsal fin base, 54-63 scales in lateral series; striations on gill covers weak or absent . . longfin smelt, *Spirinchus thaleichthys*.

SALMON AND TROUT FAMILY, SALMONIDAE

1a. Mouth small, maxilla does not reach center of eye; teeth weak or absent . .   2

1b. Mouth large, maxilla reaches to center of eye or beyond; teeth well-developed 3

2a. Dorsal fin saillike, base longer than head length . . arctic grayling, *Thymallus arcticus*.

2b. Dorsal fin short, base shorter than head length . . mountain whitefish, *Prosopium williamsoni*.

3a. Standard length less than 15 cm (juvenile fish)[7]   4

3b. Standard length greater than 15 cm (adult fish) 16

[7]For a more detailed key to the juveniles of anadromous salmonids, see McConnell and Snyder (1972).

4a. Parr marks absent, maximum size 5 cm SL .. pink salmon, *Oncorhynchus gorbuscha*.

4b. Parr marks present 5

5a. Anal rays 8-12, anal fin higher than long 6

5b. Anal rays 13-19, anal fin longer than high 13

6a. Dorsal fin with conspicuous dark spots 7

6b. Dorsal fin without dark spots 12

7a. Combined width of parr marks greater than or equal to combined width of spaces between parr marks; red or yellow spots present on live wild fish .. 8

7b. Combined width of parr marks less than combined width of spaces between parr marks; no red or yellow spots present on live wild fish 9

8a. Parr marks 8-9, adipose fin of live fish plain; no row of pale round spots along lateral line .. brook trout, *Salvelinus fontinalis*.

8b. Parr marks 10-12, adipose fin of live fish orange; row of pale round spots along lateral line .. brown trout, *Salmo trutta*.

9a. Body color pale to bright gold yellow; dorsal, anal, and pelvic fins with orange, yellow, or white tips 10

9b. Body color usually silver (may be gold in some cutthroat trout); dorsal, anal, and pelvic fins usually without colored tips 11

10a. Tips of anal and pelvic fins white; common in isolated Sierra Nevada lakes and streams .. golden trout, *Salmo aguabonita*.

10b. Tips of anal and pelvic fins yellow or orange; rare in a few tributaries to the McCloud and Pit rivers .. redband trout, *Salmo* sp.

11a. Red slash marks present along inner edge of lower jaw; black spots usually present on tail .. cutthroat trout, *Salmo clarki*.

11b. No red slash marks on lower jaw, few or no spots on tail .. rainbow trout, *Salmo gairdneri*.

12a. Distance from tip of snout to base of dorsal fin about one-half standard length; parr marks narrow vertical bars; Lake Tahoe region .. Lake trout, *Salvelinus namaycush*.

12b. Distance from tip of snout to base of dorsal fin less than one-half standard length; parr marks irregular blotches; McCloud River (rare) .. Dolly Varden, *Salvelinus* spp.

13a. Parr marks short, only a few reaching below lateral line, if at all 14

13b. Parr marks large, most reaching below lateral line 15

14a. Parr marks small and faint, usually entirely above lateral line; sides of living fish below lateral line iridescent green; uncommon .. Chum salmon, *Oncorhynchus keta*.

14b. Parr marks sharply defined, usually a few extending slightly below lateral line; sides of living fish below lateral line silvery .. sockeye salmon and kokanee, *Oncorhynchus nerka*.

15a. Parr marks wider than interspaces; adipose fin with clear area at base .. chinook salmon, *Oncorhynchus tshawytscha*.

15b. Parr marks narrower than interspaces; adipose fin completely speckled .. coho salmon, *Oncorhynchus kisutch*.

16a. Anal rays 13-19, anal fin longer than higher 17

16b. Anal rays 8-12, anal fin higher than long 21

17a. Conspicuous black spots on back and tail 18

17b. No such spots on back and tail (but fine speckling may be present) 20

18a. More than 160 scales in lateral line; spots on back large and oval shaped; exaggerated hump on back of adult males .. pink salmon, *Oncorhynchus gorbuscha.*

18b. Less than 150 scales in lateral line, spots on back small and round; hump of spawning males low 19

19a. Gums of lower jaw black; spots present on both lobes of tail; anal rays 15-17 .. chinook salmon, *Oncorhynchus tshawytscha.*

19b. Gums of lower jaw white to grey; spots present on upper lobe of tail only, or absent; anal rays 12-15 .. coho salmon, *Oncorhynchus kisutch.*

20a. Gill rakers short and stout; 19-26 on first gill arch; uncommon .. chum salmon, *Oncorhynchus keta.*

20b. Gill rakers long and slender; 30-40 on first gill arch .. sockeye salmon and kokanee, *Oncorhynchus nerka.*

21a. Body with dark spots on light background; teeth present on shaft of vomer (detectable as line of teeth running down the middle of the roof of the mouth) 22

21b. Body with light spots (red, orange, green, etc.) on dark background; teeth absent from shaft of vomer 26

22a. Small red or orange spots present on upper half of body, each surrounded by pale halo; adipose fin large .. brown trout, *Salmo trutta.*

22b. No small red or orange spots on body; adipose fin small 23

23a. Body color pale to bright gold yellow, with parr marks; dorsal, anal, and pelvic fins with white, orange, or yellow tips 24

23b. Body color usually silvery without parr marks (except Piute cutthroat trout); dorsal, anal, and pelvic fins usually without parr marks 25

24a. Tips of anal and pelvic fins white; isolated Sierra Nevada lakes and streams .. golden trout, *Salmo aguabonita.*

24b. Tips of anal and pelvic fins yellow or orange; small tributaries to the McCloud and Pit rivers .. redband trout, *Salmo* sp.

25a. Basibranchial teeth present;[8] red slash marks present along inner edges of lower jaw; scale rows between lateral line and base of dorsal fin 32-48 .. cutthroat trout, *Salmo clarki.*

25b. Basibranchial teeth absent; red slash marks on lower jaw absent; scale rows between lateral line and base of dorsal fin 25-32 .. rainbow trout, *Salmo gairdneri.*

26a. Tail deeply forked; leading edges of pelvic and anal fins plain; Lake Tahoe region .. lake trout, *Salvelinus namaycush.*

26b. Tail not deeply forked; leading edges of pelvic and anal fins white or creamed colored 27

---

[8]If basibranchial teeth are present, they can be detected by gently feeling the base of the trout's "throat" with one finger.

27a. Back dark and unspotted but mottled with wormlike markings; dorsal and caudal fins marbled . . brook trout, *Salvelinus fontinalis.*

27b. Back with pale spots, not mottled; dorsal and caudal fins plain 28

28a. Standard length 3.5-4.1X head length; branchiostegal rays 13-14 per side . . interior Dolly Varden, *Salvelinus sp.*

28b. Standard height 4.1-4.5X head length; branchiostegal rays 11-2 per side . . coast Dolly Varden, *Salvelinus malma.*

CATFISH FAMILY, ICTALURIDAE

1a. Tail forked 2

1b. Tail square or rounded 4

2a. Anal fin rays 30-36; anal fin nearly straight . . blue catfish, *Ictalurus furcatus.*

2b. Anal fin rays less than 30; anal fin rounded 3

3a. Anal fin rays 24-29; small dark spots usually present on sides . . channel catfish *Ictalurus punctatus.*

3b. Anal fin rays 19-23; no dark spots on sides . . white catfish, *Ictalurus catus.*

4a. Anal rays 24-27; chin barbels whitish . . yellow bullhead, *Ictalurus natalis.*

4b. Anal rays less than 24; chin barbels dark 5

5a. Anal rays 12-15; lower jaw projects beyond upper . . flathead catfish, *Pylodictis olivaris.*

5b. Anal rays 17-24; jaws even 6

6a. Membranes between anal fin rays blackened; body not mottled; whitish bar present at base of tail . . black bullhead, *Ictalurus melas.*

6b. Membranes between anal fin rays same color as or lighter than fin rays; body mottled; no whitish bar present at base of tail . . brown bullhead, *Ictalurus nebulosus.*

MINNOW FAMILY, CYPRINIDAE

1a. Dorsal fin with one or two spines 2

1b. Dorsal fin without spines 3

2a. Barbels present on each side of upper jaw . . carp, *Cyprinus carpio.*

2b. Barbels absent . . goldfish, *Carassius auratus.*

3a. Fleshy scaleless keel present between pelvic and anal fins . . golden shiner, *Notemigonus crysoleucas.*

3b. No such keel present 4

4a. Barbels present (may be tiny at end of maxilla) 5

4b. Barbels absent 7

5a. More than 90 scales along lateral line; deep bodied . . tench, *Tinca tinca.*

5b. Less than 90 scales along lateral line; slender bodied 6

6a. Upper lobe of caudal fin longer than lower; anal rays 7-9 . . splittail, *Pogonichthys macrolepidotus.*

6b. Caudal fin symmetrical; anal rays 6-7 . . speckled dace, *Rhinichthys osculus.*

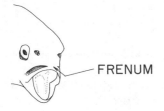

Figure 15. Frontal view of
the head of a hardhead,
showing the frenum.

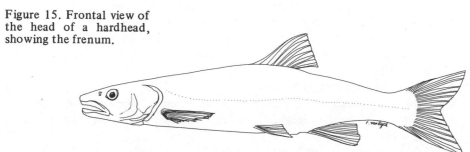

Figure 16. Sacramento squawfish body shape.

7a. Small ridge of skin (frenum) connects upper lip to head (Fig. 15) .. hardhead,
      Mylopharodon conocephalus.[9]
7b. Frenum absent   8
8a. Body slender, pikelike; snout long and pointed (Fig. 16)   9
8b. Body not pikelike; snout shorter 10
9a. Anal rays 9; Colorado River drainage .. Colorado squawfish, *Ptychocheilus
      lucius.*
9b. Anal rays 7-8; Sacramento-San Joaquin drainage .. Sacramento squawfish,
      Ptychocheilus grandis.
10a. Caudal peduncle extremely slender; Colorado River drainage .. bonytail, *Gila
      elegans.*
10b. Caudal peduncle thick or moderately thick 11
11a. More than 90 scales along lateral line .. Sacramento blackfish, *Orthodon
      microlepidotus.*
11b. Less than 75 scales along lateral line 12
12a. Lateral line does not extend beyond base of dorsal fin; adults with horizontal
      dark bar across dorsal fin .. fathead minnow, *Pimpehales promelas.*
12b. Lateral line extends well beyond base of dorsal fin; no dark bar on dorsal fin 13
13a. Scales along lateral line less than 40 .. red shiner, *Notropis lutrensis.*
13b. Scales along lateral line more than 43 14
14a. Anal fin rays 10-14 .. hitch, *Lavinia exilicauda.*
14b. Anal fin rays 7-9 15
15a. Origin of dorsal fin behind (usually only slightly) origin of pelvic fins 16
15b. Origin of dorsal fin above or before origin of pelvic fins 19

[9]A few speckled dace without barbels may key out here, but note thick caudal peduncle and
overhanging snout.

16a. Eyes large, distance between eye and tip of snout less than 1.5X width of eye 17
16b. Eyes small to moderate, distance between eye and tip of snout more than 1.5X width of eye . . speckled dace, *Rhinichthys osculus.*
17a. Anal fin rays 9; mouth terminal; sides with wide, dark band between two pale ones; Lahontan system . . Lahontan redside, *Richardsonius egregius.*
17b. Anal fin rays 7-8; snout slightly overhangs mouth; sides without bands as above 18
18a. Caudal fin moderately forked, depth of fork goes more than 3X into head length; pharyngeal teeth in 2 rows . . arroyo chub, *Gila orcutti.*
18b. Caudal fin deeply forked, depth of fork goes 2-3X into head length; pharyngeal teeth in 1 row . . California roach, *Hesperoleucis symmetricus.*
19a. Caudal peduncle thick, almost as broad as caudal fin . . thicktail chub, *Gila crassicauda.*
19b. Caudal peduncle moderately thick 20
20a. Upper lobe of caudal fin slightly longer than lower lobe; length of upper lobe about 1/3 of standard length; Clear Lake, Lake County . . Clear Lake splittail, *Pogonichthys ciscoides.*
20b. Caudal fin symmetrical; length of upper lobe 1/4 or less of standard length 21
21a. Lateral line scales more than 65; body depth usually 1/5 or less of total length; Klamath River system . . blue chub, *Gila coerulea.*
21b. Lateral line scales less than 65; body depth usually 1/5 or more of total length . . tui chub, *Gila bicolor.*[10]

SUCKER FAMILY, CATOSTOMIDAE[11]

1a. Mouth terminal; lips thin with few or no papillae 2
1b. Mouth subterminal, lips usually thick, with distinct papillae 3
2a. Dorsal fin long, 23-30 rays; lateral line scales 36-39; southern California . . bigmouth buffalo, *Ictiobus cyprinellus.*
2b. Dorsal fin short, 11-12 rays; lateral line scales 73-88; Klamath system . . shortnose sucker, *Chasmistes brevirostris.*[12]
3a. Upper and lower lips separated by deep indentations at corners of mouth; median notch of lower lip shallow (Fig. 17B) 4
3b. Upper and lower lips not separated by deep indentations; margin of lip continuous; median notch of lower lip moderate to deep (Fig. 17A) 5
4a. Pigmentation present on membranes between rays of caudal fin; axillary process at a base of pelvic fins a simple fold; southern California . . Santa Ana sucker, *Catostomus santaanae.*
4b. Pigmentation absent or very sparse on membranes between rays of caudal fin;

[10]Lateral line scales in Klamath tui chubs are less than 54.

[11]Some sucker species may be found outside their designated drainage systems. Tahoe and mountain suckers have been found in the Sacramento River system while Sacramento suckers may have been introduced into the Lost River, Modoc County.

[12]Great care should be taken identifying suckers from the upper Klamath system due to extensive hybridization between the three species. One of the best ways to separate them seems to be gill raker counts: *luxatus*, 24-28; *snyderi*, 30-35; and *brevirostris*, 34-39 (J. K. Andreason, pers. comm.).

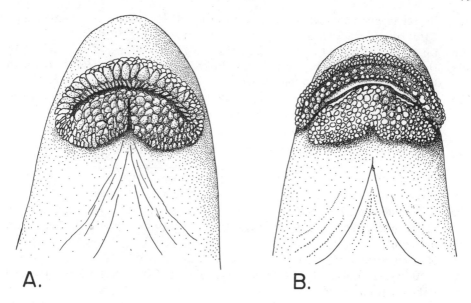

A.   B.

Figure 17. (a) Mouth of typical sucker (Sacramento sucker); (b) mouth of *Pantosteus*-type sucker (mountain sucker).

axillary process at base of pelvic fins well developed; Lahontan system .. mountain sucker, *Catostomus platyrhynchus*.

5a.   Well-developed, sharp-edged ridge before dorsal fin; Colorado River system .. humpback sucker, *Xyrauchen texanus*.

5b.   No such ridge present 6

6a.   Distinct hump on snout; lips thin, papillae only moderately developed, mouth subterminal; Klamath River . . Lost River sucker, *Catostomus luxatus*.[12]

6b.   Snout without hump; lips thick and papillose, mouth strongly ventral 7

7a.   Lateral line scales more than 80 8

7b.   Lateral line scales less than 80 10

8a.   Median indentation of lower lip moderate, 2 or more rows of papillae crossing midline; 5-6 rows of papillae on upper lip; lower Klamath River system .. Klamath smallscale sucker, *Catostomus rimiculus*.

8b.   Median indentation on lower lip deep, usually only one row of papillae crossing midline; 2-4 rows of papillae on upper lip 9

9a.   Skin-covered opening on top of head (frontoparietal fontanelle) small or absent (Fig. 18); adults usually less than 20 cm TL; middle Pit River . . Modoc sucker, *Catostomus microps*.[13]

9b.   Frontoparietal fontanelle well developed (Fig. 18); adults usually greater than 18 cm TL; Lahontan system . . Tahoe sucker, *Catostomus tahoensis*.

[13]Modoc suckers are sympatric only with Sacramento suckers, from which they can be readily told by their short dorsal fin (10-11 rays) and generally small size at maturity.

10a. Dorsal rays usually 10 or less; belly dusky; Owens River .. Owens sucker, *Catostomus fumeiventris*.

10b. Dorsal rays usually 11 or more; belly white to yellow 11

11a. Dorsal rays usually 11, occasionally 12; Klamath River system .. Klamath largescale sucker, *Catostomus snyderi.*[12]

11b. Dorsal rays usually 12 or more, rarely 11 .. Sacramento-San Joaquin River system .. Sacramento sucker, *Catostomus occidentalis*.

KILLIFISH FAMILY, CYPRINODONTIDAE

1a. Body depth more than 1/3 standard length; teeth flat, tricuspid 4

1b. Body depth less than 1/3 standard length; teeth conical, pointed 2

2a. Conspicuous small brown, grey, or white spots present on sides and dorsal fin; males bright blue green, females plain .. Argentine pearlfish, *Cynolebias bellottii.*[14]

2b. No conscpicuous spots on sides 3

3a. 8-10 rays in dorsal fin; oviducal pouch absent; Salton Sea area .. Trinidad rivulus, *Rivulus harti.*[15]

3b. 12-15 rays in dorsal fin; oviducal pouch covers anterior portion of anal fin in females; euryhaline; coastal areas California .. California killifish, *Fundulus parvipinnis*.

4a. Dorsal fin equidistant between base of caudal fin and snout; pelvic fins small, usually with 7 rays 5

4b. Dorsal fin closer to base of caudal fin than to snout; pelvic fins reduced or absent, usually with 6 or fewer rays 6

5a. Scales with spinelike projections on circuli, interspaces between circuli not reticulated (Fig. 19a), southern California .. desert pupfish, *Cyprinodon macularius*.

5b. Scales without spinelike projections on circuli; interspaces between circuli reticulated (Fig. 19b); Owens Valley .. Owens pupfish, *Cyprinodon radiosus*.

6a. Scales in lateral series 27-34; scales before dorsal fin 22-33, usually 25-30 . 7

6b. Scales in lateral series 25-26; scales before dorsal fin 15-24, usually 17-19 .. Amargosa pupfish, *Cyprinodon nevadensis*.

7a. Prominent ridge present on outer face of central cusps of teeth (Fig. 19d); pelvic rays usually 6-7 .. Salt Creek pupfish, *Cyprinodon salinus*.

7b. Prominent ridge not present on outer face of central cusps of teeth (Fig. 19c); pelvic rays usually 5 or less .. Cottonball marsh pupfish, *Cyprinodon milleri*.

LIVERBEARER FAMILY, POECILIIDAE

1a. Scales in lateral series 29-32; anal fin rays 6-7; intestine short and without coils; dorsal fin behind origin of anal fin .. mosquitofish, *Gambusia affinis*.

[14]Argentine pearlfish are established in several ponds in Los Angeles County (F. Legner, pers. comm.).

[15]Trinidad rivulus is reported to be established in canals near the Salton Sea (St. Amant, 1970).

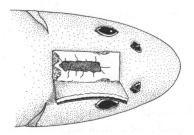

Figure 18. Cutaway view of dorsal surface of Tahoe sucker head, showing well-developed frontoparietal fontanelle.

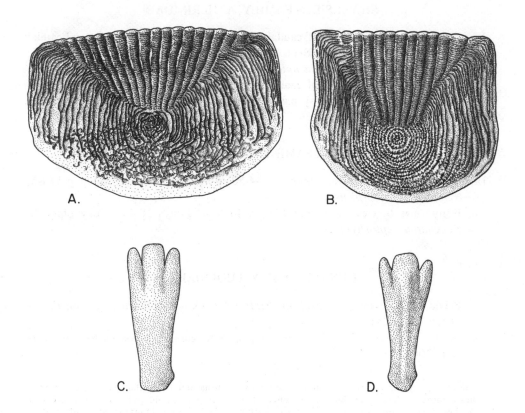

Figure 19. Scales and teeth of pupfish after Miller (1948): (a) scale of desert pupfish; (b) scale of Owens pupfish; (c) tooth of desert pupfish; (d) tooth of Salt Creek pupfish.

1b. Scales in lateral series 28 or less, anal fin rays 8-10; intestine long and coiled; dorsal fin origin in front of anal fin origin 2

2a. Dorsal fin with 12 or more rays .. sailfin molly, *Poecilia latipinna.*

2b. Dorsal fin with less than 12 rays 3

3a. Dorsal fin rays usually 10-12; scales in lateral series usually less than 26 .. variable platyfish, *Xiphophorus variatus.*[16]

3b. Dorsal fin rays usually 7-9; scales in lateral series 26-28 4

4a. Mature fish usually greater than 40 mm TL; males nearly equal in size to females; no red or green on body or fins .. shortfin molly, *Poecilia mexicana.*[16]

4b. Mature fish usually less than 40 mm TL; males much smaller than females; males usually with red or green on caudal fin .. guppy, *Poecilia reticulatus.*[17]

SILVERSIDES FAMILY, ATHERINIDAE

1a. Pigment spots on bottom of caudal peduncle between anal fin base and caudal fin base in 2 rows; less than 3 dorsal scale rows outlined by pigment .. Mississippi silverside, *Menidia audens.*

1b. Pigment spots on bottom of caudal peduncle not in distinct rows; more than 3 dorsal scale rows outlined by pigment; coastal streams .. topsmelt, *Atherinops affinis.*

PIPEFISH FAMILY, SYNGNATHIDAE

1a. Bony rings between vent and tail 44-50; dorsal rays 36-47 .. kelp pipefish, *Syngnathus californiensis.*[18]

1b. Bony rings between vent and tail 36-46; dorsal rays 28-44 .. bay pipefish, *Syngnathus leptorhynchus.*

GUNNEL FAMILY, PHOLIDAE[19]

1a. Pelvic fins present; V-shaped markings on back .. saddleback gunnel, *Pholis ornata* (Fig. 20a).

1b. Pelvic fins absent; back plain .. penpoint gunnel, *Apodichthys flavidus* (Fig. 20b).

---

[16]Variable platyfish and shortfin mollies are popular aquarium fishes that have been found in ditches feeding the Salton Sea but the presence of breeding populations has not been confirmed. Since they have become established in warm springs in Nevada and Montana, it would not be surprising to find them in warm springs in California.

[17]Guppies can be expected almost anywhere in the state where there is warm water. The presence of breeding populations in natural or seminatural waters has not been confirmed, but substantial populations exist in some sewage treatment ponds, such as that on the campus of the University of California, Davis.

[18]Kelp pipefish have been recorded from the mouths of streams flowing into Monterey Bay (Kukowski, 1972), but these records are probably misidentifications (C. L. Hubbs, pers. comm.).

[19]Both species of gunnels were collected in August 1973, in the Navarro River, Mendocino County, about 1 km from its mouth, at salinities of 19-23 ppt.

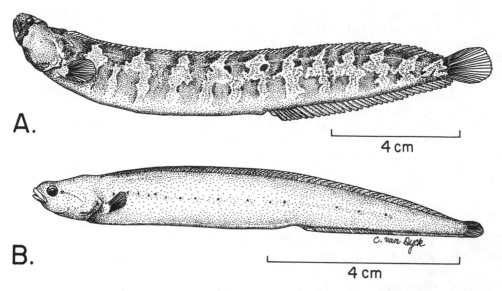

A.

4 cm

B.

C. van Dyck

4 cm

Figure 20. (a) saddleback gunnel, 14 cm SL; (b) pen point gunnel, 9 cm SL; Navarro River, Mendocino County.

SUNFISH FAMILY, CENTRARCHIDAE[20]

1a. Anal spines 5 or more 2
1b. Anal spines 3 4
2a. Dorsal fin spines 11-13; dorsal fin much longer than anal fin .. Sacramento perch, *Archoplites interruptus.*
2b. Dorsal fin spines 5-10, dorsal and anal fin bases about equal in length 3
3a. Dorsal fin spines 7-8; length of dorsal fin base equal to or greater than distance from origin of dorsal fin to eye .. black crappie, *Pomoxis nigromaculatus.*
3b. Dorsal fin spines 5-6; length of dorsal fin base less than distance from origin of dorsal fin to eye .. white crappie, *Pomoxis annularis.*
4a. Scales large, 53 or less in lateral series; sunfishes.[20] 5
4b. Scales small, 58 or more in lateral series, basses 9
5a. Teeth present on tongue; upper jaw (maxilla) extends beyond middle of eye .. warmouth, *Lepomis gulosus.*
5b. No teeth on tongue; upper jaw does not extend beyond middle of eye ... 6
6a. Pectoral fins short and rounded, contained about 4X in standard length; mouth large, upper jaw extends to middle of eye .. green sunfish, *Lepomis cyanellus.*
6b. Pectoral fins long and pointed, contained less than 3X in standard length; mouth small, upper jaw does not reach middle of eye 7

[20]Sunfishes that seem to be intermediate in their characteristics between two species may be hybrids. Hybrids most likely to be encountered are warmouth-bluegill, green sunfish-bluegill, green sunfish-redear sunfish, and green sunfish-pumpkinseed. The hybrids are usually dark but highly colored sterile males.

7a. Gill rakers long and slender (more than 2X longer than wide); posterior edge of opercular bone flexible . . bluegill, *Lepomis macrochirus.*

7b. Gill rakers short and stubby (about 2X longer than wide); posterior edge of opercular bone stiff 8

8a. Rear portion of dorsal fin usually speckled; living adults with scarlet spot on opercular lobe and blue and orange stripes on operculum . . pumpkinseed, *Lepomis gibbosus.*

8b. Rear portion of dorsal fin usually without speckles; living adults with orange or red margin on opercular lobe, and without conspicuous stripes on operculum . . redear sunfish, *Lepomis microlophus.*

9a. Soft and spiny portions of dorsal fin barely connected; dark, unbroken stripe on each side; upper jaw of adults extends behind eye . . largemouth bass, *Micropterus salmoides.*

9b. Soft and spiny portions of dorsal fin obviously connected; lateral stripe absent or broken; upper jaw of adults does not extend behind eye 10

10a. Lateral band of connected, uneven blotches on each side; lateral line scales usually less than 67 . . spotted bass, *Micropterus punctulatus.*

10b. Lateral band absent; lateral line scales usually 67 or more 11

11a. Rays in rear portion of dorsal fin usually 13-15; 12-13 scale rows above lateral line . . smallmouth bass, *Micropterus dolomieui.*

11b. Rays in rear portion of dorsal fin usually 11-12; 7-10 scale rows above lateral line . . redeye bass, *Micropterus coosae.*

TEMPERATE BASS FAMILY, PERCICHTHYIDAE

1a. Body depth less than 1/3 standard length; head 5X longer than second anal spine . . striped bass, *Morone saxatilis.*

1b. Body depth more than 1/3 standard length; head 3X longer than second anal spine . . white bass, *Morone chrysops.*

SURFPERCH FAMILY, EMBIOTOCIDAE

1a. Dorsal spines 10 or less; euryhaline . . shiner perch, *Cymatogaster aggregata.*

1b. Dorsal spines 15 or more; freshwater . . tule perch, *Hysterocarpus traskii.*

PERCH FAMILY, PERCIDAE

1a. Mouth small, upper jaw (maxilla) does not reach to below eye; snout overhangs upper lip . . bigscale logperch, *Percina macrolepida.*

1b. Mouth large, upper jaw extends to or past eye; snout does not overhang upper lip 2

2a. Body with strong vertical bands; caninelike teeth absent; anal rays 7-8 . . yellow perch, *Perca flavescens.*

2b. Body mottled, without strong vertical bands; caninelike teeth present; anal rays 12-13 . . walleye, *Stizostedion vitreum.*[21]

[21]Walleye probably do not exist in California any longer since all attempts to establish reproducing populations seem to have failed.

CICHLID FAMILY, CICHLIDAE

1a. Transverse bands present on sides; dorsal fin with yellow spots; substrate spawner . . Zill's cichlid, *Tilapia zillii*.

1b. Sides with 3-4 dark blotches, or with no markings, no yellow on dorsal fin; mouthbrooder . . Mozambique mouthbrooder, *Tilapia mossambica*.

GOBY FAMILY, GOBIIDAE

1a. Maxillary bone extends past the posterior margin of eye, nearly reaching opercular opening 4

1b. Maxillary bone usually does not extend past the posterior margin of eye . . 2

2a. Series of small dark bands on anterior edge of both dorsal fins; teeth tricuspid . . chameleon goby, *Tridentiger trigoncephalus*. [22]

2b. Dorsal fin bands absent; teeth not tricuspid 3

3a. Spines in first dorsal fin 8, less than 50 scales in lateral line . . yellowfin goby, *Acanthogobius flavimanus*.

3b. Spines in first dorsal fin 6-7, more than 60 scales in lateral line . . tidewater goby, *Eucyclogobius newberryi*.

4a. Anal fin elements 9-14, second dorsal fin elements 9-14 . . longjaw mudsucker, *Gillichthys mirabilis*.

4b. Anal fin elements 15-18, second dorsal fin elements 14-18 . . arrow goby, *Clevelandia ios*. [23]

SCULPIN FAMILY, COTTIDAE[24]

1a. Preopercular spine large and antlerlike . . Pacific staghorn sculpin, *Leptocottus armatus*.

1b. Preopercular spine(s) small and simple 2

2a. Pelvic elements 3[25] 3

2b. Pelvic elements 4 5

3a. Anal rays 10-13; tufts of cirri present on head and maxillae; euryhaline . . sharpnose sculpin, *Clinocottus acuticeps*. [26]

3b. Anal rays 13-17; no cirri on head; freshwater 4

4a. Preopercular spines 1+; chin speckled; middle Pit River . . rough sculpin, *Cottus asperrimus*.

[22]Chameleon gobies are introduced estuarine forms that can be expected from the lower reaches of California streams.

[23]The arrow goby is an occasional marine visitor to the lower reaches of coastal streams along the entire coast.

[24]Sculpins are highly variable. Carefully check your keying result with the accompanying table, species descriptions, and distributions.

[25]The spine of the pelvic fin is fused to the first ray, so the two are best counted as one "element."

[26]Sharpnose sculpins are rare marine visitors to California coastal streams from the Big Sur River north.

Table 6

Characteristics of eight easily confused species of California sculpins; parentheses indicate that the condition is the usual one but may vary

	Rough	Coastrange	Marbled	Piute	Prickly	Riffle	Pit	Reticulate
Anal rays	13-17	12-14	13-15	11-13	16-18	12-15	13-15	13-16
Dorsal rays	5-7	17-20	18-20	15-18	19-21	18-20	17-18	18-20
Dorsal spines	17-19	8-9	5-7	6-8	8-9	7-9	8-9	7-8
Dorsal fins	(separate)	(joined)	(joined)	(separate)	(joined)	variable	(separate)	(joined)
Pectoral rays	14-16	14-16	14-16	14-16	15-18	(15-16)	(13-15)	14-16
Preopercular spines	2	1+	1-2	1+	2-3	2-3	2-3	2-3
Lateral line pores	19-29	34-44	14-22	23+	28-43	22-36	31-39	20-32
Lateral line	(incomplete)	complete	(incomplete)	(complete)	complete	(incomplete)	(complete)	variable
Palatine teeth	absent	absent	absent	(absent)	present	(present)	absent	absent
Axillary prickles	present	present	variable*	absent	present	present	present	present
Drainage	Pit	coastal	Klamath, Pit	Lahontan	coastal Sacto.-San Joaquin	coastal Sacto.-San Joaquin	Pit	Rogue

*Usually absent in adults.

4b. Preopercular spines usually 3; chin without speckles; upper Klamath River .. slender sculpin, *Cottus tenuis*.[27]

5a. Anal rays usually 17-18 (rarely 15-16); palatine teeth (Fig. 21) well developed .. prickly sculpin, *Cottus asper*.

5b. Anal rays 12-15; palatine teeth (Fig. 21) variable 6

6a. Front and rear tubular nostriles of equal size, conspicuous; pelvic fins when depressed reach anus .. coastrange sculpin, *Cottus aleuticus*.

6b. Rear nostril smaller than front nostril, inconspicuous; pelvic fins when depressed usually do not reach anus 7

7a. Dorsal spines 8-9; palatine teeth absent; lateral line pores 31-36, Pit River system .. Pit sculpin, *Cottus pitensis*.

7b. Dorsal spines 5-8; palatine teeth variable; lateral line pores usually less than 32 8

8a. Lateral line pores 14-22; preopercular spine single; Klamath and Pit rivers .. marbled sculpin, *Cottus klamathensis*.

8b. Lateral line pores usually more than 22; preopercular spines usually more than one 9

9a. Axillary patch of prickles beneath pectoral fins absent; Lahontan system .. Piute sculpin, *Cottus beldingi*.

9b. Axillary patch of prickles present (Fig. 21) 10

10a. Palatine teeth usually present; coastal and Sacramento-San Joaquin systems .. riffle sculpin, *Cottus gulosus*.

10b. Palatine teeth absent; Rogue River drainage .. reticulate sculpin, *Cottus perplexus*.

[27]Slender sculpins have apparently not been collected in California but since they are abundant in Upper Klamath Lake, Oregon, they can be expected in the Klamath River.

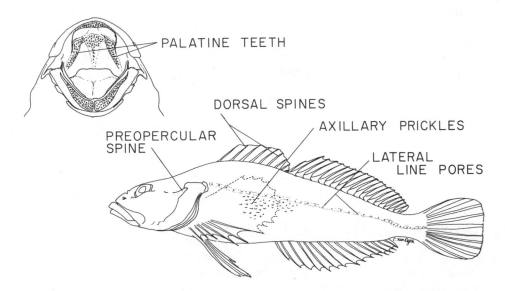

Figure 21. Characters used for identifying sculpins.

Lamprey Family, Petromyzontidae

The lampreys are primitive yet specialized aquatic vertebrates, eellike in form but lacking the jaws and paired fins of true fishes. Their internal organization allies them most closely to the long-extinct ostracoderms, the first-known vertebrates, which were heavily armored creatures that sucked organic ooze from ocean, lake, and river bottoms. Thus, lampreys have a persistent notochord, a cartilaginous skeleton, a single nostril, a small primitive brain, and two semicircular canals in each side of the head, rather than the usual three.

The survival of lampreys into modern times has depended on their ability to prey on the jawed fishes that replaced their ancestors. An adult lamprey will latch onto the side of a large fish with its suckerlike mouth and rasp a hole with its powerful tongue, which is covered with sharp, horny plates ("teeth"). The lamprey extracts blood and body fluids from the fish and drops off when satiated. Although the gaping wound left by the lamprey may be fatal, many fish do survive lamprey attacks. It is not unusual to find fish with two or more scars from lamprey attacks. Under normal conditions lamprey and their prey coexist successfully, the lampreys maintaining their populations without destroying those of their prey. In the Great Lakes, sea lampreys (*Petromyzon marinus*) invaded through the Welland Canal and nearly succeeded in wiping out the large fishes, presumably because the fish populations were not adapted to their style of predation. It is likely that, had not man intervened with lamprey-control measures, the sea lampreys would have become scarce in the Great Lakes once they had reduced the prey populations to a low level. Presumably a more or less balanced system would have evolved given a few thousand years. Such a system currently exists in the Finger Lakes of New York, where sea lamprey populations became established in the late Pleistocene.

The predatory portion of the lamprey life cycle is usually short (6 to 18 months) compared to the time spent as larvae (ammocoetes) in streams (usually 4 to 7 years). The adults migrate from a large body of water upstream into a small tributary to spawn. They build a nest in a gravel-bottomed area, spawn, and die. The eggs hatch and the ammocoetes are carried downstream to muddy-bottomed backwaters. They burrow into the mud and spend the next few years growing on a diet of detritus and algae.

One of the most fascinating aspects of lamprey biology is the frequent evolution of nonpredatory species from predatory ones. The nonpredatory species are generally small as adults and their rasping plates are reduced in size and number. The larval portion of their life cycle is like that of the predatory forms except that it tends to last longer and the ammocoetes thus tend to grow larger (Hardisty and Potter, 1971). The adults, however, do not migrate after metamorphosis but remain in their home streams where they spawn and die without feeding. The nonpredatory adult stage allows lampreys to live in small streams where few large fishes are present for food or where distances to large bodies of water are great.

The classification and identification of lampreys depends largely on the number, structure, and position of the horny plates (usually labelled teeth or laminae) in the sucking disc. The plates are named according to their position (anterior, posterior, or lateral) in the three concentric circles that can be visualized on the disc (Fig. 14). They are described in detail by Vladykov and Follet (1962) and Hubbs and Potter (1971). Lamprey identification, particularly of small forms, should be done with care using the original descriptions if possible, especially since there may be one or more undescribed forms in California. Ammocoetes are hard to identify because they lack the bony plates.

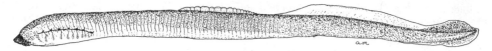

Figure 22. Ammocoetes of Pacific lamprey, 12 cm TL, San Joaquin River, Fresno County.

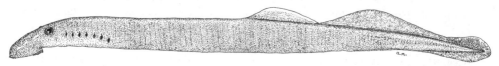

Figure 23. Dwarf form of Pacific lamprey, 24 cm TL, Clear Lake Reservoir, Modoc County.

Figure 24. Sucking disc of Pacific lamprey, after Vladykov and Follett (1958, 1967).

Pacific Lamprey
Lampetra tridentata (Gairdner)

Identification. Any large (over 40 cm TL) adult lamprey in California belongs to this species. However, dwarf (19 to 27 cm TL) populations do exist. Sharp, horny plates (teeth) are present in all areas of the sucking disc, more than in any other California lamprey. The most distinctive plate is the crescent-shaped supraoral lamina with three sharp cusps, the middle cusp smaller than the two lateral cusps. There are also four large, inner, lateral plates on each side. The middle two are tricuspid, the outer two bicuspid. The tongue ends in 15 to 25 small points (transverse lingual lamina), the middle one slightly larger than the others. The two dorsal fins are slightly separated. The second dorsal is continuous with the caudal fin. The dorsal fins are higher in males than in females and males lack an anal fin, which is conspicuous in females. Males also possess a small genital papilla. Ammocoetes have 64 to 70 segments between the anus and the last gill opening. The lower half of the oral hood is usually well pigmented.

Names. *Lampetra*, and probably the word lamprey, is derived from the Latin words *lambere*, to suck, and *petra*, stone. The words refer to their habit of clinging to stones in streams with their suckerlike mouth. *Tridentatus* (three-toothed) is a reference to the structure of the supraoral laminae. The Pacific lamprey was formerly placed in a separate genus *Entosphenus* and the arguments for putting it back there are compelling (McPhail and Lindsey, 1970). Lampreys are frequently called eels by fishermen.

Distribution. Pacific lampreys have been found in most Pacific coast streams from Unalaska down to the Santa Ana River, although large spawning runs are unusual south of Monterey Bay. In the ocean, they have been captured off Japan as well as off Baja California (Hubbs, 1967; McPhail and Lindsey, 1970). Dwarf landlocked forms are known from the upper Klamath River, Klamath Lake, and Goose Lake, and they may occur elsewhere as well (Hubbs, 1971).

Life History. Pacific lampreys, with the exception of landlocked populations, spend the predatory phase of their life in the ocean. Little is known about their oceanic life except that they attack a wide variety of large fishes, occasionally even taking on whales. Despite far-flung ocean distribution records, it is unlikely that Pacific lampreys normally wander far from the mouths of their home spawning streams, since their prey is most abundant in estuaries and other coastal areas. The oceanic phase presumably lasts one to two years, like that of the eastern sea lamprey (*Petromyzon marinus*). The landlocked forms spend the predatory phase in a lake or reservoir, feeding on suckers and other large fishes (Coots, 1955).

Adults, ranging in length from 30 to 69 cm, usually move up into the spawning streams between April and late July. In the Trinity River, Moffett and Smith (1950) observed some migration also occurring in August and September. Often lampreys will migrate several months before they spawn, hiding under stones and logs until fully mature. Most upstream movement takes place at night and tends to occur in surges rather than continuously. The lampreys can move considerable distances up rivers, stopped only by major barriers such as Friant Dam on the San Joaquin River. The remarkable ability of Pacific lampreys to surmount less formidable barriers is described by Kimsey and Fisk (1964, p. 6): "Great wriggling masses of lampreys are often seen ascending barriers and fish ladders on coastal streams in the early spring. . . . In many cases the flow is too great for the fish to move across the barrier in one attempt. They solve the problem by swimming until tired, then attaching themselves to the bottom and sides and resting for a while. When recovered, they make another attempt and move upstream several more feet. In this manner, by successive spurts and resting period, they move over various obstructions until they reach their spawning grounds."

Both sexes help construct a crude nest, 40 to 60 cm in diameter, by removing the larger stones from a gravel area where the current is not too swift. To remove a stone, the lamprey latches on to the downstream side and swimgs vigorously in reverse.

Usually the combination of lamprey pulling and current pushing is enough to move the rock to the downstream edge of the nest. The final result is a shallow depression with a pile of stones at the downstream end. For the spawning act, the female attaches to a rock on the upstream edge of the nest, while the male attaches himself to the head of the female, wrapping his body around hers. Both lampreys then vibrate rapidly and a small white cloud of eggs and milt is released. The fertilized eggs are washed into the gravel, especially at the downstream end of the nest, where they adhere to the rocks. After spawning the lampreys loosen rocks above the nest, causing silt, sand, and gravel to cover the eggs. Spawning is repeated on the same nest a number of times until both sexes are spent. They die shortly thereafter. If the fecundity of Pacific lampreys is similar to that of eastern sea lampreys, each female, depending on her size, lays 20,000 to 200,000 eggs.

After the eggs hatch the ammocoetes spend a short time in the nest gravel. Eventually they swim up into the current and are washed downstream to a suitable area of soft sand or mud. The ammocoetes burrow tail first into the sand or mud and begin lives as filter feeders, sucking organic matter and algae off the substrate surface. The ammocoetes do not stay in one area for their entire growth period. Thus, Long (1968) and Moffett and Smith (1950) were able to trap "migrating" ammocoetes at almost any time of the year. In the Trinity River, ammocoetes of all sizes down to 16 mm colonized areas from which they had been eradicated during the winter high-water period (Moffett and Smith, 1950). Most movement of the ammocoetes takes place at night. In three to seven years, they reach lengths of 14 to 16 cm and start to metamorphose into adults, developing large eyes, a sucking disc, silver sides, and dark blue backs (McPhail and Lindsey, 1970).

Status. Pacific lampreys are still abundant in most of their native areas, although dams across many streams have prevented access to former spawning grounds. Despite their predaceous habits, they seem to have little effect on fish populations. Lampreys were highly esteemed as food by a number of tribes of California Indians (Kroeber and Barrett, 1960), and are still considered a delicacy in some European countries.

References. Coots, 1955; Ganssle, 1966; Hubbs, 1967, 1971; Kimsey and Fisk, 1964; Kroeber and Barrett, 1960; Long, 1968; McPhail and Lindsey, 1970; Moffett and Smith, 1950; Scott and Crossman, 1974.

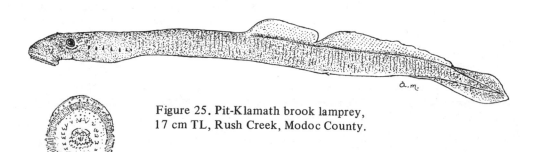

Figure 25. Pit-Klamath brook lamprey, 17 cm TL, Rush Creek, Modoc County.

Pit-Klamath Brook Lamprey
Lampetra lethophaga Hubbs

Identification. This is a small (less than 21 cm TL), nonpredaceous derivative of the Pacific lamprey. The disc resembles that of the Pacific lamprey but the plates are smaller and fewer. The three circumoral plates have two or three cusps each but frequently cusps are missing. The supraoral plate has three cusps, although the middle one may be degenerate or missing. The posterior circumoral plates number only 9 to 15. The cusps on the transverse lingual lamina are filelike and difficult to see. The mouth is small and puckered, the disc length less than 5 percent of the total length. The gut is atrophied in mature specimens.

Name. "The name *lethophaga*, figuratively referring to the elimination of feeding as adults, is formed by combining the Latinized expression *leth* . . . a forgetting or forgetfulness . . . (and) . . . *phag-*, to eat" (Hubbs, 1971, p. 151). Other names are as for the Pacific lamprey.

Distribution. The Pit-Klamath brook lamprey is apparently limited to the Pit River system in northeastern California (including Goose Lake) and the close-by upper Klamath River of south-central Oregon.

Life History. Virtually all of the available information on the biology of this nonpredaceous lamprey is found in Carl L. Hubbs' 1971 paper describing the species. The following is a summary of the limited life-history information presented there. The principal habitat of this species seems to be cool, clear streams or springs with sandy-muddy bottoms or edges. Trout are frequently found in the same waters, as are sculpins, speckled dace, suckers, and tui chubs.

The ammocoetes burrow into soft mud bottoms among aquatic plants. The time spent as ammocoetes seems to be at least four years, based on an analysis of ammocoete size classes. The maximum size is about 21 cm, which is also the minimum size for the dwarf predaceous race of the Pacific lamprey that lives in some of the same areas.

Metamorphosis probably takes place in the fall. Spawning does not begin until early spring, but may occur at anytime during the summer. Some populations of this lamprey, although they transform into the adult form, do not develop the nuptial features characteristic of "normal" spawners: the dark, contrasting coloration of back and belly, the united, thick, and frilled dorsal fins, and the enlarged anal fin. Some interbreeding may occur with the dwarf form of the Pacific lamprey in the Klamath River.

Status. The Pit-Klamath brook lamprey is widely distributed in both river systems and seems to be in no danger. Some man-made changes in the streams may actually benefit them; in Rush Creek, Modoc County, large numbers of ammocoetes were found in a silty-bottomed pool immediately below a channelized section of the stream. They were also common in muddy-bottomed irrigation diversions from the creek (Moyle, unpublished data).

References. Hubbs, 1971; Hubbs and Potter, 1971.

Figure 26. Sucking disc of river lamprey, after Vladykov and Follett (1967).

River Lamprey
Lampetra ayresi (Günther)

Identification. The river lamprey is small (average length about 17 cm) and predaceous, with well-developed horny plates in the sucking disc. The plates, however, become progressively blunter in spawning individuals. The middle cusp of the transverse lingual lamina is well developed. There are three inner lateral plates on each side, the outer two bicuspid. The supraoral plate has only two cusps. The eye is large compared to other California lampreys, the diameter being one-half to one times the distance from the posterior edge of the eye to the anterior edge of the first branchial opening. The number of myomeres is high, averaging 68 in adults, 67 in ammocoetes. Adult river lampreys are dark on the back and sides, silvery to yellow on the belly. The tail is darkly pigmented. As the lamprey becomes sexually mature, the gut degenerates and the dorsal fins grow closer together, eventually joining.

Names. In 1855, William O. Ayres described the river lamprey from a single specimen collected in San Francisco Bay and named it *Petromyzon plumbeus.* Unfortunately, that name had already been given to a European species of lamprey. So, in 1870, A. Günther renamed it *P. ayresi.* In 1911, C. T. Regan decided that this species and the European river lamprey, *Lampetra fluviatilis,* were identical. This diagnosis was accepted until 1958, when the careful redescription of the river lamprey by V. D. Vladykov and W. I. Follett showed that it is indeed a distinct species, *L. ayresi.* Other names are as given for the Pacific lamprey.

Distribution. River lampreys have been collected from coastal streams from fifteen miles north of Juneau, Alaska (McPhail and Lindsey, 1970) down to San Francisco Bay. In California, they appear to be most abundant in the lower Sacramento-San Joaquin River system.

Life History. Most of the rather limited life-history information on river lampreys is given in Vladykov and Follett (1958). River lampreys are anadromous but they will attack fish in both salt and fresh water. They have been found attached to salmonids in streams but other fishes are undoubtedly preyed on as well. In salt water, they have been recorded attaching to the dorsal surface of Pacific herring and Pacific salmon. The salmon most subject to predation by river lampreys are those of intermediate sizes (11 to 28 mm FL) but the incidence of predation is low, usually less than 2 percent even in good lamprey years (Roos et al., 1973). While in fresh water, adults spend most of their time in the lower reaches of the larger streams. Spawning, however, seems to take place in the small tributary streams, usually during April and May. Nest building and spawning behavior have not been recorded but they are probably similar to those of other species of *Lampretra.* Fecundity estimates of two females were 37,288 eggs for one 175 mm SL and 11,398 eggs for one 230 mm SL.

How long the ammocoetes spend in the mud is not known. Transformation does not take place until they are at least 117 mm SL. The largest river lamprey on record was 311 mm SL.

Status. River lampreys are apparently as common as they ever have been, but they have never been collected in large numbers in California.

References. Vladykov and Follett, 1958; McPhail and Lindsey, 1970; Roos et al., 1973.

Figure 27. Pacific brook lamprey, 17 cm TL, after Vladykov (1973).

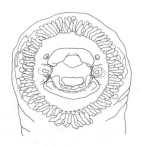

Pacific Brook Lamprey
Lampetra pacifica Vladykov

Identification. Pacific brook lampreys are small (to 18 cm TL), nonpredaceous, and rather similar to *L. richardsoni*, the brook lamprey of Oregon and Washington. The tooth plates on the oral disc are poorly developed and the plates on the anterior field may be missing from spawning adults. The supraoral plate is broad with a cusp at each end but none in the middle. There are 6 to 9 infraoral cusps and 2 to 4 posterior circumoral plates. The cusps on the transverse lingual lamina are too small and irregular to count. The disc length is less than 6 percent of the total length. There are 52 to 58 myomeres in the trunk of mature lampreys as well as of the ammocoetes. The coloration is dark on the back and sides and yellow to white on the belly.

Names. Pacifica refers to their distribution in Pacific coast streams. Other names are as for the Pacific lamprey. Records before 1973 usually refer to this species as either *L. planeri* or *L. richardsoni.*

Distribution. Pacific brook lampreys are known from low-altitude portions of the Sacramento and San Joaquin rivers and their tributaries, streams tributary to San Francisco Bay, coastal streams in northern California, and tributaries to the lower Columbia River in Oregon (Vladykov, 1973). Ammocoetes occurring in streams in the Los Angeles Plain may also belong to this species (C. L. Hubbs, pers. comm.).

Life History. Since Pacific brook lampreys are difficult to collect and were only recently described (Vladykov, 1973), little is known about their biology. Presumably the life history is similar to that of other nonparasitic lampreys, especially *L. richardsoni* (Schultz, 1930).

Status. Pacific brook lampreys are probably more common than collection records indicate, since special effort has to be made to collect them. However, it is unlikely that they can withstand severe pollution or habitat changes so they are probably now restricted to the less disturbed sections of streams. A certain amount of adaptability is reflected in the fact that they will use disposable beverage cans for shelter on occasion (Kottcamp and Moyle, 1972).

References. Kottcamp and Moyle, 1972; Schultz, 1930; Vladykov, 1973.

Sturgeon Family, Acipenseridae

Sturgeon are among the largest and most primitive of bony fishes. They are placed, along with paddlefishes, African bichirs, and numerous fossil fishes, in the infraclass Chrondrostei, from which the higher bony fishes evolved. The sturgeons themselves are not ancestral to modern bony fishes but are a highly specialized and successful offshoot of the ancestral chondrosteans. They have retained primitive features such as the heterocercal tail, fin structure, jaw structure, and spiracle. They have replaced the bony skeleton with one of cartilage and have a few large, bony plates instead of scales. They are highly adapted for preying on bottom animals which they detect with the row of extremely sensitive barbels on the underside of their snouts. They then protrude their extraordinary long lips and suck up the food. Some species will stir up the bottom with their shovellike snouts and then suck up the suspended organisms.

Sturgeons are confined to the temperate waters of the northern hemisphere. Only seven of the twenty-four species are found in North America, two in California. Although most species live primarily in salt water, moving up rivers only to spawn, a few species live exclusively in fresh water. The anadromous forms are the largest fish found in fresh water. The giant beluga sturgeon (*Huso huso*) which spawns in the Volga River of the USSR gets as long as 8.5 m (26 ft) and as heavy as 1,297 kg (2,860 lbs). White sturgeon are the largest freshwater fish in North America, supposedly growing as large as 820 kg (1,800 lbs) although the largest verified record seems to be 590 kg (1,300 lbs).

The history of the sturgeon fisheries over most of the world has been one of overexploitation followed by severe population reduction. The large size and sluggish nature of sturgeon make them vulnerable to netting and snagging and their valuable caviar, isinglass, and flesh has made such fisheries, while they last, very lucrative. However, as has been demonstrated in California and the USSR, proper management can restore overfished sturgeon populations, provided their spawning areas are not reduced by pollution and other competing uses of the water.

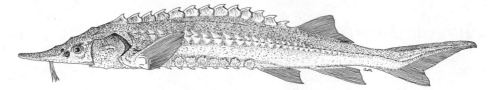

Figure 28. White sturgeon, 52 cm TL, Sacramento-San Joaquin Delta.

White Sturgeon, *Acipenser transmontanus* Richardson

Identification. White sturgeon have blunt, rounded snouts, with four barbels in a transverse row on the underside. The barbels are closer to the tip of the snout than to the mouth. Their mouths have highly protrusible lips but lack teeth. Each fish has five widely separated rows of bony plates on the body, each plate with a sharp spine. The dorsal row has 11 to 14 plates, the two lateral rows have 38 to 48 plates each, and the two bottom rows have 9 to 12 plates each. The dorsal fin has one spine and 44 to 48 rays, while the anal fin has 28 to 31 rays. The ventral surface is white, shading to grey brown on the back above the lateral row of scutes.

Names. Just where the "white" comes from in white sturgeon is a bit of a mystery since they are grey in color, but it probably refers to the pale color of their flesh compared to that of green sturgeon. *Acipenser* is Latin for sturgeon, while *transmontanus* means across the mountains, perhaps a reference to their wide distribution in the Columbia River system.

Distribution. White sturgeon are found in salt water from Ensenada, Mexico, north to the Gulf of Alaska but spawning sturgeon have been found only in large rivers from the Sacramento-San Joaquin system north. In California large runs occur only in the Sacramento and Feather rivers, but there may be small runs up the Russian, San Joaquin, Klamath, and Trinity rivers. The occasional capture of small sturgeon by anglers indicates that Lake Shasta may have a landlocked population that became established when Shasta Dam was built, trapping young sturgeon behind it. White sturgeon were planted in Lake Havasu on the Colorado River in 1967 and 1968, but the success of this introduction is not known (Minckley, 1973).

Life History. White sturgeon are one of California's important fish resources. Hence their life history has been investigated in some detail by the California Department of Fish and Game (Pycha, 1956; Skinner, 1962; Ganssle, 1966; Radtke, 1966; Stevens and Miller, 1970; McKechnie and Fenner, 1971; L. Miller, 1972a,b,c; Fry, 1973). The results of these studies form the basis for this summary.

White sturgeon spend most of their lives in the estuaries of large rivers, such as the Sacramento-San Joaquin, moving up into fresh water to spawn. In the estuaries they prefer mud bottoms and water with salinities less than that of seawater. A few do make extensive saltwater migrations, however, since they are occasionally captured far from any major stream system. They are also capable of completing their entire life cycle in fresh water. Populations are known to exist as far up the Columbia River as Montana, above barriers (dams) impassable to fish (Brown, 1971). Such a population may now be established in Lake Shasta on the upper Sacramento River.

The food of white sturgeon is taken on or close to the bottom. In the Delta, young sturgeon (around 20 cm FL) feed mostly on crustaceans, especially amphipods (*Corophium*) and oppossum shrimp, (*Neomysis*). As they get larger, their diet becomes more varied, although it still consists mostly of bottom-dwelling estuarine invertebrates: various species of clams, crabs, and shrimp. Fish also assume some importance in the diet of larger sturgeon, especially herring, anchovy, striped bass, starry flounder, and smelt. When herring move into the estuaries to spawn, white sturgeon feed heavily on the eggs. Other items recorded from stomachs of large sturgeon include onions, wheat, Pacific lampreys, crayfish, frogs, salmon, trout, striped bass, carp, squawfish, suckers and, in one case, a domestic cat (Carlander, 1969).

Young white sturgeon grow rapidly in the Delta, reaching 18 to 30 cm FL by the end of their first year. Growth gradually slows as they get older but they can reach 102 cm FL (40 inches), the smallest size anglers can legally keep, by their sixth or seventh year. In subsequent years they add 2 to 6 cm per year to their length. Just how large they can grow is a matter of some dispute since the largest fish were taken prior to 1900 and were subject to inaccurate measurements and exaggerated reporting. Nevertheless, they probably achieved at least 4 m FL and 590 kg (1,300 lbs.). Such large fish were probably over 100 years old and were the largest fish to occur in the fresh waters of North America. The largest white sturgeon taken in recent years, a 3.2 m FL fish from Oregon, was 82 years old (Carlander, 1969). The largest recent record from California is a 2.8 m FL, 21 kg female, aged 47, that was accidentally caught in a fish trap. Age of sturgeon is determined by taking cross-sections of fin rays or spines and counting the number of rings visible, on the assumption that a new ring is laid down every year.

Female white sturgeon are at least eleven or twelve years old and 1.1 to 1.5 m FL before they are sexually mature. The males generally mature at smaller sizes than the females. When they are ready to spawn they migrate upstream, although some upstream movement to the lower reaches of the rivers may take place in the winter months prior to spawning. Spawning seems to take place between mid-March and early June, when water temperatures range from 10 to 24°C. Exactly where and how white sturgeon spawn is not known but they can migrate several hundred miles upstream to find suitable spawning sites. They probably spawn either over deep gravel riffles or in deep holes with swift currents and rock bottoms. In the Sacramento-San Joaquin system, most spawning takes place in the upper Sacramento and Feather rivers. The San Joaquin River may have been an important spawning stream before its flows were reduced, since large sturgeon are still caught moving up it on occasion. When spawning is completed the sturgeons move back down to the estuaries. White sturgeon do not spawn every year and the interval between spawnings is not precisely known. It seems to be about five years in the Sacramento-San Joaquin system (L. Miller, pers. comm.).

Female sturgeon are very fecund: 1.1 to 1.5 m FL fish contain around 100,000 eggs. The number of eggs increases with size, so the 2.8 m FL female from the Sacramento River contained 4.7 million eggs. The eggs are adhesive after fertilization and stick to the substrate. The larvae hatch from the eggs in one to two weeks. The larvae stay close to the bottom and are washed downstream into the estuary. Juvenile sturgeon apparently have a greater tendency to live in the upper reaches of the estuaries than do the adults.

Status. White sturgeon in the Sacramento-San Joaquin Estuary are an almost classic case of a valuable fish resource being nearly wiped out by overfishing but restored through proper management. The large size and late age of maturity of sturgeons makes them extremely vulnerable to overfishing, so it is not surprising that they were decimated by the commercial fishery that started in the 1860s and lasted until 1901. The peak catch was 1.66 million pounds taken in 1887. By 1895 the catch was down to 300,000 pounds and declining annually. The fishery was closed in 1901 after less than 200,000 pounds were caught. Low catches in 1909, 1916, and 1917, when the fishery was reopened, indicated that the population had not recovered so the commercial fishery was closed for good in 1917.

In 1954, a year-round sport fishery was legalized, with a 102 cm size limit and one fish per day per fisherman bag limit. The fishery was an immediate success and large numbers of sturgeon were caught, mostly by snagging from party boats. Apparently because snagging was considered unsportsmanlike, this method was outlawed in 1956. Since no other effective method had been found to catch sturgeon on hook and line, the catch by anglers declined. Most of the sturgeon caught were taken by fishermen angling for other species, especially striped bass. In 1964, it was discovered that shrimp worked well as sturgeon bait and the sport fishery intensified. The catch now appears to have stabilized at 8,500 sturgeon per year or about 270,000 pounds. This represents an acceptable exploitation rate of catchable size sturgeon of 2 to 10 percent of the population per year. An independent estimate of the catchable-size sturgeon populations in the Sacramento-San Joaquin Estuary is 115,000 fish, with 95 percent confidence limits of 72,000 and 212,000 fish (Miller, 1972a).

The value of proper management of this fishery is clearly indicated by the fact that the present-day sturgeon catchs are, on a sustained yield basis, nearly 70 percent of the *average* commercial catch from 1875 to 1899 of 374,000 pounds. The unregulated commercial fishery nearly wiped out the populations in a short period of time, while the present managed sport fishery promises to yield continuous returns for years to come. Even large sturgeon occasionally appear in the catch again. In April, 1973, a 190 kg, 2.8 m FL sturgeon was caught in the Sacramento River, a hook and line record.

References. Brown, 1971; Carlander, 1969; Ganssle, 1966; L. Miller, 1972a,b,c; McKechnie and Fenner, 1971; Pycha, 1956; Skinner, 1962; Stevens and Miller, 1970.

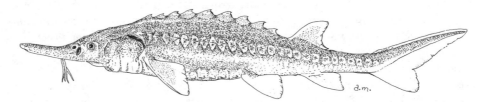

Figure 29. Green sturgeon, 22 cm TL, Klamath River Estuary. CAS 36968.

Green Sturgeon, *Acipenser medirostris* Ayres

Identification. Green sturgeon are similar in appearance to white sturgeon except that the barbels are closer to the mouth than to the tip of the long, narrow snout; the dorsal row of bony plates numbers 8 to 11, the lateral rows, 23 to 30, and the bottom rows, 7 to 10; the dorsal fin has 33 to 36 rays, the anal, 22 to 28; and the body color is olive green, with an olivaceous stripe on each side.

Names. Medirostris means moderate snout. The snout is more elongate than that of the white sturgeon but less so than that of many other species. Other names are as for the white sturgeon.

Distribution. Green sturgeon have been taken in salt water from Ensenada, Mexico, to the Bering Sea and Japan (Miller and Lea, 1972). They are found in the lower reaches of large rivers from the Sacramento-San Joaquin on north, including the Eel, Mad, Klamath and Smith rivers. They seem to be the most common sturgeon in the Klamath and Trinity rivers at the present time, and will migrate considerable distances upstream (Fry, 1973).

Life History. Much less is known about green sturgeon than white sturgeon because they are less abundant, they spend less time in estuaries and fresh water and seldom penetrate far up the rivers (except the Klamath and Trinity rivers), and they are held in low esteem by fishermen. The relative abundance of green sturgeon, at least in the Sacramento-San Joaquin system, is reflected in the numbers of the two species of sturgeon tagged in San Pablo Bay by the California Department of Fish and Game during their 1967 and 1968 sturgeon studies: 2,692 white sturgeon and 54 green sturgeon (Miller, 1972b). While tagged white sturgeon were mostly recaptured in fresh water or in the estuary, the five tagged green sturgeon were taken in salt water off Washington (2), Oregon (1), Santa Cruz, California (1), and San Pablo Bay (1). Although spawning of green sturgeon has not been confirmed for the Delta, juveniles are common in freshwater areas, especially in the summer. A particularly heavy concentration was found in shallow water of the lower San Joaquin River in the summer of 1964 (Radtke, 1966). In the Klamath River, the famous "sturgeon hole" about 1.5 km upstream from Orleans, Humboldt County, may be a major spawning grounds. Leaping and other frantic behavior indicative of spawning or courtship is frequently observed there in the spring and early summer.

The diet of adult green sturgeon appears to be similar to that of white sturgeon: bottom invertebrates and small fish (Ganssle, 1966). Juveniles in the Delta feed on opposum shrimp, *Neomysis*, and amphipods, *Corophium* (Radtke, 1966).

Nothing is known about age and growth in green sturgeon except that they can reach 2.3 m FL and 159 kg. However, they seldom exceed 1.3 m FL and 45 kg, at least in the Delta (Skinner, 1962).

Status. Because of its low numbers and bad reputation as food fish, the green sturgeon has not been subjected to as heavy fishing pressure as has the white sturgeon. Jordan and Evermann (1923, p. 7) express what is perhaps the most common attitude towards it: "As a food-fish, it is of very inferior rank; indeed, it is commonly believed to be poisonous, but this belief is without any warrant. Its flesh, however, is dark, has a strong, disagreeable taste, and an unpleasant odor, and is regarded as inferior to that of the white sturgeon." Even the roe has been rejected as unfit for caviar! In fact, the bad culinary reputation of green sturgeon probably stems mostly from the dark color of the flesh since, properly prepared, they can be quite tasty (L. Miller, pers. comm.). Recently a commercial fishery has developed for green sturgeon in Washington and Oregon.

References. Fry, 1973; Ganssle, 1966; Jordan and Evermann, 1923; L. Miller, 1972a,b; Miller and Lea, 1972; Radtke, 1966; Skinner, 1962.

Herring Family, Clupeidae

The herrings are one of the most successful families of fishes in the world, if sheer number of individuals is the primary criterion for success. They are also among the more structurally primitive of advanced bony fishes (Teleostei). Early in the history of teleost evolution, they achieved the plankton-feeding specializations that allow them to remain abundant despite the development of more advanced types of fishes. Herrings have highly protractile jaws and long, fine gill rakers for picking or filtering out zooplankters from the water. The intestine is long and convoluted. Herrings have silvery cycloid, deciduous scales and thin, deep bodies with a sharp keel on the belly. Since they live mostly in well-lighted surface waters, these features make it difficult for predatory fishes coming from below to pick out individual fish.

Although usually thought of as marine fishes, herrings are also very successful as anadromous and freshwater fishes. Thanks to man, the range of these forms has been greatly extended, especially in North America, with effects ranging from highly beneficial to disastrous. Small freshwater shads of the genus *Dorosoma* have long been considered as ideal forage fish for reservoirs and large lakes and have been distributed throughout the United States. Alewives (*Alosa pseudoharengeus*) made their way through canals to the Great Lakes where they have become extremely abundant. They are now considered to be nearly as great a pest as sea lampreys. Alewives have greatly reduced, through competition, the populations of many valuable sport and commercial fishes in the Great Lakes and become a public nuisance when they die by the millions at certain times of the year, clogging beaches and water intakes. Both threadfin shad and American shad were introduced into California with greater success than was perhaps ever imagined, with unknown effects on native fish and zooplankton populations. The one herring native to California's fresh waters is only an occasional visitor; Pacific herring (*Clupea harengeus pallasii*) occasionally wander into fresh water when they move into estuaries to spawn.

Herring and their close relatives, the anchovies (Engraulidae), are the most important commercial fishes in the world in terms of tons landed. Many of the marine stocks have been severely overfished, such as Pacific sardine off California, menhaden off the Atlantic coast, and more recently, the Peruvian anchoveta. Most herrings and herringlike fishes are reduced to fish meal, an important supplement in livestock, chicken, and people feeds. Thus, as marine stocks of clupeoids decline, it might become economical to harvest freshwater stocks, including those in California, to fulfill the demand for fish meal.

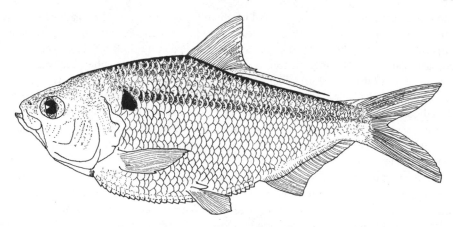

Figure 30. Threadfin shad, 10 cm SL, Sacramento-San Joaquin Delta.

Threadfin Shad, *Dorosoma petenense* (Günther)

Identification. Threadfin shad are small (rarely longer than 10 cm TL in California) with the typical deciduous scales, thin bodies, and sawtooth bellies of the herrings. They are distinguished by the long, threadlike final ray of the dorsal fin and by the single dark spot behind the operculum. The mouth is oblique, small, and toothless. The upper jaw is longer than the lower. The dorsal fin (14 to 15 rays) is falcate. Anal rays are 20 to 23; scales in the lateral series, 40 to 43; belly scutes (scales), 15 to 18 before the base of pelvic fins, 8 to 12 behind the pelvic bases. The intestine is long and convoluted, with a gizzardlike stomach. The gill covers are smooth or with a few faint striations. The overall color is silvery, although the back frequently has a black or bluish hue.

Names. Doro-soma means lance-body, referring to the eellike larvae. *Petenense* is after Lake Petén, Guatemala, from which the first specimens were described. The subspecies introduced into California is *D. p. atchafalayae* (after the Atchafalaya River, Louisiana). A synonymy of the scientific nomenclature can be found in La Rivers (1962).

Distribution. Threadfin shad are native to streams flowing into the Gulf of Mexico, south to Belize. In the Mississippi River and its tributaries they are found as far north as Oklahoma, Tennessee, and southern Arkansas. Shad from Watts Bar, Tennessee, were introduced into Lake Havasu on the Colorado River and San Vincente Reservoir, San Diego County, in 1953 by the California Department of Fish and Game. They have since been spread to warmwater reservoirs throughout the state (Burns, 1966). From these transplants, they have become established in the Sacramento-San Joaquin River system and its delta, as well as in most of the lower Colorado River and the Salton Sea. They are occasionally taken in salt water from Long Beach to Humboldt Bay (Miller and Lea, 1972). Besides California, threadfin shad have been planted successfully in Arizona, Nevada, Kentucky, Ohio, Virginia, West Virginia, Hawaii, and probably other states as well.

Life History. Threadfin shad inhabit the open surface waters of reservoirs, lakes, and large ponds, as well as the sluggish backwaters of rivers. In reservoirs they will congregate near the inlets of small streams or along the steep surfaces of dams. They are seldom found below depths of 18 m (Burns, 1966). Best growth and survival is found in waters that do not get colder than 7 to 9°C, but the shad can survive temperatures close to freezing for short periods of time. A sudden drop to a low temperature causes high mortalities, as do prolonged periods of cold water. The population in the Delta experiences heavy die-offs every winter when the water cools to 6 to 8°C (Turner, 1966). Threadfin shad are typically freshwater dwellers and become progressively less abundant in the Delta as salinity increases (Ganssle, 1966). Nevertheless they are established elsewhere in brackish water and they can survive and grow in sea water. Salt water apparently inhibits reproduction, however, since shad in the Salton Sea failed to reproduce despite continuous recruitment from the Colorado River and irrigation canals (Hendricks, 1961).

Threadfin shad form schools segregated by size, and hence by age. Although shad concentrate in surface waters, the young of the year tend to be found in deeper water than adults, especially at night (Johnson, 1970). When attacked by predatory fish such as striped bass, shad in a school will close together and hug the water surface, individuals leaping from the water at each attack.

Like all clupeids, threadfin shad are plankton feeders, straining zooplankton, phytoplankton, and detritus out of the water with their gill rakers and then grinding them in their "gizzards." Their feeding appears to be nonselective; planktonic organisms occur in their digestive tracts in roughly the same proportion as they occur in the water (Turner, 1966; Miller, 1967). In the Delta, threadfin shad are most abundant where there are the highest concentrations of crustacean zooplankters: warm, quiet, turbid sloughs (Turner, 1966).

Threadfin shad are fast growing but short lived. Under optimal conditions, during the first summer of life they can increase in length 1 to 3 cm per month, reaching 10 to 13 cm TL at the end of the summer. Normally they only reach 4 to 6 cm TL by the end of the first year and 6 to 10 cm TL by the end of the second. Few live longer than two years or achieve lengths longer than 10 cm TL, although some live as long as four years (Johnson, 1970) and achieve lengths up to 33 cm (Carlander, 1969). The largest threadfin shad recorded from California seems to be one 22 cm TL from the Salton Sea (Hendricks, 1961). Fish from the nonreproducing saltwater populations frequently achieve larger sizes than are normal for fresh water (Johnson, 1970). In fresh water, one of the main factors limiting growth is interspecific competition for food and space (Johnson, 1970). Thus, shad newly established in reservoirs tend to grow larger during their first year than do their counterparts from longer established populations.

Threadfin shad may spawn at the end of their first summer but they usually wait until their second (Johnson, 1971). Spawning can take place throughout the summer but it tends to peak in June. It is unlikely that each shad spawns more than once in a summer (Johnson, 1971). Most spawning takes place at temperatures above 21°C but some spawning has been observed in California reservoirs at 14 to 18°C (Rawstron, 1964). Spawning occurs most often at dawn and centers around floating or partially submerged objects such as logs, brush, aquatic plants, and gill nets. Small compact groups of shad swimming close to the surface approach such objects rapidly, turning away just prior to collision. As they turn away, the eggs and sperm are released (Lambou, 1965). The fertilized eggs stick to the surfaces of the objects. Spawning is usually accompanied by much splashing and by shad leaping out of the water. Each female produces 900 to 21,000 eggs, the number of eggs increasing sharply with the size of the fish (Johnson, 1971).

The eggs hatch in three to six days and the larvae immediately assume a planktonic existence. The larvae are long and slender and metamorphose into the adult form at about 1 to 1.5 cm TL.

Status. Threadfin shad were introduced to California in 1953 on the optimistic assumption that they were the ideal forage fish for California reservoirs and should greatly improve growth rates of game fishes. Their apparent desirability stemmed from their characteristic small size, high reproductive rate, and ability to occupy the open waters of reservoirs, which were presumed to be unexploited fish habitat. In many reservoirs managed for trout, especially those that receive large plants of catchable size fish, the growth of trout larger than 28 cm FL can be extremely rapid because they feed on shad. The success of striped bass in Millerton Lake, Fresno-Madera counties, is probably due largely to their diet of shad. In other reservoirs, large-sized largemouth bass, black and white crappie, and white catfish may utilize threadfin shad (Burns, 1966). Unfortunately, threadfin shad are largely unavailable to smaller warmwater game-fishes. Since the young of many centrarchids live in the open waters of reservoirs for extended periods of time, feeding on plankton, the shad may actually compete with them by reducing plankton populations. In particular, threadfin shad may eliminate large species of planktonic crustaceans from California reservoirs, as have other species of shad (*Alosa* spp.) in lakes in the eastern United States (Brooks and Dodson, 1965). These larger crustaceans are often important food for larval fishes, presumably since it takes less energy to capture and consume them. Thus, in some California reservoirs the growth and survival rates of young centrarchids, including largemouth bass, decreased after the introduction of shad (Burns, 1966).

The ability of shad populations to increase explosively has also created some problems. The 1,020 shad introduced into Lake Havasu on the Colorado River managed to provide enough offspring to colonize the entire lower Colorado River and the Salton Sea in less than eighteen months (Burns, 1966). In the Sacramento-San Joaquin system, they quickly established populations downstream from the reservoirs in which they were planted. In both systems it is not known what the overall effect of the shad has been, especially on native minnows and suckers with planktonic larvae, and on young centrarchids. In the Delta, shad serve as forage for striped bass and other piscivorous fishes but their importance does not appear to be proportional to their numbers, probably because they concentrate in deadend sloughs.

Their abundance and underutilization in some reservoirs had been a major reason for the experimental introduction of white bass (*Morone chrysops*), a species once considered unsuitable for California (Chadwick et al., 1966).

References. Brooks and Dodson, 1965; Burns, 1966; Carlander, 1966; Chadwick et al., 1966; Ganssle, 1966; Hendricks, 1961; Johnson, 1970, 1971; Lambou, 1965; La Rivers, 1962; R. V. Miller, 1967; Miller and Lea, 1972; Rawstron, 1964; Turner, 1966.

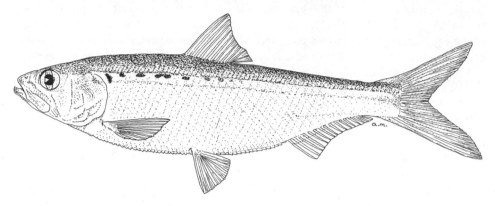

Figure 31. American shad, juvenile, 11 cm SL, Sacramento-San Joaquin Delta.

American Shad, *Alosa sapidissima* (Wilson)

Identification. American shad are large (to 76 cm FL) herring with thin, deciduous scales, thin bodies, and a sawtooth keel on their bellies. The mouth is terminal and the upper and lower jaws are about equal in size, the lower jaw fitting into the central notch of the upper. The dorsal fin (15 to 19 rays) is short and straight edged, without the greatly elongated last ray of the threadfin shad. Anal rays are 19 to 23, scales in the lateral series are about 60, belly scutes (scales) are 21 to 22 before the base of the pelvic fins and 16 to 17 behind the pelvic base. The gill rakers are long and slender, usually 60 or more below the sharp bend on the first arch. The gill covers have coarse, fanlike striations on their surfaces. Live fish tend to be steely blue on the back and silvery on the sides. They are distinguished by a row of spots that starts on the back just behind the operculum.

Names. Alosa is derived from the old Saxon name for the European shad (*Alosa alosa*), while *sapidissima* means most delicious, a fitting name for the most edible of the North American shads. American shad are often referred to as common or white shad.

Distribution. American shad are native to the Atlantic coast from Newfoundland to the St. Johns River, Florida. Between 1871 and 1881, over 800,000 fry were caught in New York and planted in the Sacramento River (Skinner, 1962). By 1879 they were well established. As a result of the California plants and later plants elsewhere on the Pacific coast, most notably the Columbia River, they are now found from San Pedro, California, to southeastern Alaska, where they spawn in the major rivers.

The main shad runs in California are in the Sacramento River up to Red Bluff and in the lower reaches of its major tributaries (particularly the American, Feather, and Yuba rivers), as well as the Mokelumne and Stanislaus rivers. Small runs are found in sloughs of the south Delta, the San Joaquin River, the Klamath River, the Russian River, and the Eel River. Apparently, the only landlocked population of American shad in existence is in Millerton Lake, Fresno-Madera counties, where the shad were accidentally introduced with striped bass between 1955 and 1957 (von Geldern, 1965; and more recent records).

Life History. Adult American shad, with the exception of the Millerton Lake populations, are found in fresh water only when they move up into rivers to spawn. Most young shad move out to sea shortly after hatching but a few spend a year or more in the freshwater portions of estuaries. What happens during the three to five years between hatching and spawning on the Pacific coast is largely unknown. In their native Atlantic they make extensive migrations up and down the entire coast from Florida to New Brunswick (Talbot and Sykes, 1958). The wide distribution of shad along the Pacific coast indicates that similar migrations take place here as well. Although little is known about the life of California's American shad in salt water, their life cycle in fresh water has been investigated by the California Department of Fish and Game as part of the Delta Fish and Wildlife Protection Study. Unless otherwise noted, the information presented here is derived from Skinner (1962) and Stevens (1966, 1972), who summarized the results of these investigations.

The first mature shad of each year's run appear in the fall in the lower portions of the estuaries where they gradually adjust to the lower salinities. They do not move into fresh water until water temperatures exceed 10 to 11°C. Peak runs, and spawning, usually occur at higher temperatures, 15 to 20°C. This means that the first shad appear in late March or early April but large runs are not seen until late May and early June. The runs become smaller again when water temperatures start exceeding 20°C, so few adults are seen after the first week of July. It is not known if American shad home to the exact freshwater area where they spawned but it would not be surprising considering their remarkable abilities to navigate and to detect minor changes in their environment (Leggett, 1973). The first runs consist largely of males, many of them unripe, while the later runs tend to be predominately females. The males are mostly three years old, while the females are mostly four. They range in size from 30 to 76 cm FL.

Adult shad in the Delta are unlike their counterparts on the Atlantic coast in that they feed while in fresh water. This is more than likely the result of the abundance of large zooplankters in the Delta as opposed to their scarcity and small size in most Atlantic spawning streams. Even in the Delta, however, the percentage of shad with empty stomachs is high and feeding virtually ceases once the main rivers are entered. The most abundant organism in their stomachs while in the Delta is the oppossum shrimp, *Neomysis mercedis*, followed by copepods, cladocerans, and amphipods. Occasional clams and fish larvae are also taken.

Spawning is a mass affair that takes place mostly in the main channels of the rivers. Each act is initiated when a male presses alongside a female. The two then swim rapidly side by side, releasing eggs and sperm. Other pairs of shad usually spawn at the same time, so that spawning is seen as a school of wildly swimming, thrashing fish. Spawning can occur at any time of the day but seems to be most frequent at night. Each fish spawns repeatedly, until the females have each released 30,000 to 300,000 eggs, the number depending on the size of the female. Most shad die after spawning but a few do return to the ocean and spawn again the next year. The warmer the water, the greater the postspawning mortality. Large numbers of dead shad are particularly noticeable when spawning occurs above 20°C.

Shad eggs are only slightly heavier than water so they stay suspended in the current, gradually drifting downstream. They can be found at almost any depth during the peak spawning season but are most numerous near the bottom. Hatching takes three to six days, depending on temperature; it is fastest at high temperatures but survival seems to be lower then.

Most newly hatched shad gradually move out to sea, lingering in the Delta for several weeks to several months. As the season progresses, the center of juvenile shad abundance moves closer to salt water. The entry into salt water takes place in September, October, and November but may start as early as late June. At hatching they are about 1 cm TL and they triple in length during the first month. By the time they have moved into salt water they have reached 8 to 18 cm TL.

While in the Delta, young shad feed in surface waters on zooplankton, especially *Neomysis*, copepods, and amphipods. Although young shad feed primarily in the water column, they are rather opportunistic and so will also take abundant bottom organisms, such as chironomid midge larvae, and surface insects (Levesque and Reed, 1972). Most feeding takes place during the day, reflecting their reliance on vision for prey capture. Summer concentrations of young shad in deadend sloughs where zooplankton is abundant indicates that they will seek out concentrations of food off the migration pathways. A few of the shad stay in these areas, and elsewhere in the Delta, for a year or more. Sooner or later even these shad must move out to sea because immature shad over 20 cm FL are rarely caught in the Delta.

Status. The introduction of American shad into California was extraordinarily successful. By 1879, eight years after the first introduction, a commercial shad fishery had developed. The fishery reached its peak in 1917 when 5,675,509 pounds were landed. Between 1918 and 1945, the catch ranged annually from 0.8 to 4.1 million pounds. Between 1955 and 1957, the catch exceeded a million pounds only once. Despite their reputation on the Atlantic coast as an excellent food fish, American shad have never been particularly popular on the west coast. Thus the commercial fishery was never very valuable despite its size. Female shad, from which roe was removed for shipment to the Orient, fetched 6 to 8 cents a pound in 1957, while male shad brought less than a penny a pound.

In 1957, the commercial fishery was banned in favor of the rapidly developing sport fishery. As a result, when shad migrate upstream, especially in the Yuba, Feather, and American rivers, sportsmen range the stream banks, often standing shoulder to shoulder when fishing is good. Spawning shad readily take a fly, jig, or small spinner and can put up spectacular fights on light tackle. Ripe males are also caught at night by "bumping," where a long-handled dipnet is held vertically in the water from the stern or side of a slowly moving boat. When a shad hits the net, the net is twisted and lifted and the shad is flipped into the boat. Some shad are also caught by dipping from the banks. The present shad fishery seems to be mostly for sport and a good many of the fish caught are either discarded or returned to the water. Fortunately, more and more fishermen are learning to appreciate the culinary qualities of shad, both fresh and smoked.

Since the current shad runs in the Sacramento River and tributaries have been estimated to contain somewhere between 750,000 and 4,000,000 three-to six-pound fish, the shad fishery should become increasingly popular as other sport fisheries decline or stabilize. A heavy fishery may create pressure to increase runs up the San Joaquin River, which appear to be limited now by a combination of turbidity, reduced flow, irrigation diversions, and other factors. The establishment of a small landlocked population in Millerton Lake is an interesting development but it seems to have limited potential as a sport fishery.

The future of American shad in the Delta seems fairly secure, yet competing uses of the water may affect their populations as the development of California's water resources proceeds. The sensitivity of shad to temperature changes indicates that careful investigations should be carried out before any nuclear power plants, with their heavy use of water for cooling, are built along waterways used by shad. The increasing diversion of the fresh water now flowing through the Delta, by the California Water Project, may also reduce shad populations by changing spawning and nursery areas. If the proposed Peripheral Canal is constructed, anywhere from 50 to 90 percent of the Sacramento River flow will be diverted during that time of the year when young shad are moving downstream. This poses a serious threat to shad (as well as to salmon, striped bass, and sturgeon) unless effective methods of screening are employed at the canal intake. Thus, while the Peripheral Canal may mitigate many of the problems connected with the present system of water transport across the Delta as well as future reduced flows (Skinner, 1972), it is also likely to cause a continued decline in Delta-dependent fisheries. Perhaps what is really needed is a complete change of priorities for the use of Delta water.

References. Ganssle, 1966; Leggett, 1973; Levesque and Reed, 1972; Stevens, 1962, 1966; Skinner, 1962; Talbot and Sykes, 1958; von Geldern, 1965.

Salmon and Trout Family, Salmonidae

The Salmonidae consists not only of salmon, trout, and char (subfamily Salmoninae), but also of whitefish (subfamily Coregoninae) and grayling (subfamily Thymallinae). All members of the family are native to the cooler waters of the northern hemisphere. They all possess an adipose fin and an axillary scale (usually visible as a distinct process) at the base of each pelvic fin. Salmon and trout have strong teeth in the jaws, small scales, and short dorsal fins. Grayling also have strong teeth but they have large scales and long dorsal fins, while whitefish lack strong teeth and have large scales but short dorsal fins. Trout (genus *Salmo*) can be distinguished from char (genus *Salvelinus*) by the presence of teeth·on the shaft of the vomer (a bone on the roof of the mouth) and by their spotting patterns. Trout have black spots on a light background while char have light spots, red, pink, orange, or gray in color, on a dark background.

The Salmonidae seems to be a family that evolved for living in the cold, nutrient-poor waters of recently glaciated areas. The advances and retreats of continental glaciers have meant that these waters are often transient or likely to be isolated at one time or another. Thus, an evolutionary premium has presumably been placed on salmonid fishes that are opportunistic in their feeding, adaptable in their behavior and life-history patterns, and capable of moving through salt water. The behavioral flexibility of salmonids has resulted in their colonization of most of the accessible coastal and headwater streams of the northern hemisphere, and of many coldwater lakes as well. Since anadromous salmonids tend to have strong homing behavior and since many headwater streams become isolated through geological events, local salmonid strains, both resident and anadromous, tend to develop in response to local conditions. Often these populations are morphologically quite distinct from other related populations but will hybridize readily if brought in contact by man. For example, in isolated mountain streams golden colored trout have evolved independently in many areas. They are normally recognized as distinct species or subspecies (e.g., golden trout, Piute cutthroat trout, redband trout) yet they will all hybridize readily with rainbow trout (and other *Salmo*) if given the opportunity. Such situations are characteristic of recently evolved forms and lead to innumerable taxonomic problems.

Because salmonids have a long history as major sport and commercial fishes, a delightful vocabulary has developed for the various stages of the typical salmonid life history. The spawning adults construct a redd (nest depression) in which *alevins* (sac-fry) hatch from the eggs. When the *fry* develop vertical bars on their sides, they are called *parr*. In anadromous forms, parr lose the parr marks and turn silvery as they start moving out to sea. They are then termed *smolts*. Fish that have spent only one year at sea but have returned to spawn are called *grilse*, although such males are more often called *jacks*. *Kelt* is a rarely used term for spawned-out fish.

At the present time, fifteen species of salmonids can be found in California, eleven native, four introduced. Despite the natural richness of California's salmonid fauna, numerous attempts have been made to establish other species as well. Attempts that have failed have been those to establish Japanese ayu, *Plecoglossus altivelus* (Anonymous, 1967), Bonneville cisco, *Prosopium gemmiferum* (Frantz and Cordone, 1965), lake whitefish, *Coregonus clupeaformis*, and Atlantic salmon, *Salmo salar* (Shapovalov, Dill, and Cordone, 1959).

Figure 32. Mountain whitefish, 28 cm SL, Sagehen Creek, Placer County.

Mountain Whitefish, *Prosopium williamsoni* (Girard)

Identification. Mountain whitefish can be distinguished from all other California fishes that possess an adipose fin by the combination of large scales (74 to 90 in the lateral line); a small, weak, toothless, ventral mouth; a short dorsal fin (11 to 15 rays); and a slender body that approaches being nearly cyclindrical in cross-section. The head is short (about 20 percent of total length) with a laterally compressed snout which overhangs the mouth. The gill rakers are short, 19 to 26 on each gill arch, and armed with small teeth. The branchiostegal rays are 7 to 10 per side; anal fin rays, 10 to 13; pelvic fin rays, 10 to 12; and pectoral rays, 14 to 18. The pelvic axillary process is well developed. The body color is silvery, sometimes dusky on the back. The scales on the back may be outlined in dark pigment. Breeding males develop nuptial tubercles on their head and sides. The young are silvery with two or more rows of dark spots on the sides, the lowermost covering the lateral line with 8 to 10 troutlike parr marks.

Names. *Prosopium* means mask, referring to the large preorbital bones in the skull, while *williamsoni* is after Lt. R. S. Williamson who commanded the Railroad Survey of California and Oregon in which this species was first collected. Mountain whitefish are frequently placed in the genus *Coregonus*, to which most other whitefishes belong (La Rivers, 1962).

Distribution. Mountain whitefish are found throughout the Columbia River system (including Wyoming, Montana, and Idaho), the upper reaches of the Missouri and Colorado river systems, the Lahontan system, the Bonneville system, and in most river systems in Alberta and British Columbia. In California they are found in Lahontan system streams and lakes (including Tahoe) on the east slope of the Sierra Nevada.

Life History. Mountain whitefish are most commonly found in streams with large pools that exceed one meter in depth and in cold mountain lakes. In the Lahontan system, most of their populations are located between 1,400 and 2,300 m in elevation. Often they are abundant in streams immediately above a lake or reservoir. In Lake Tahoe, they are generally found close to the bottom in fairly deep water, although they move into the shallows during the spawning season. They typically swim about in schools of five to twenty fish.

As the subterminal mouth and body shape suggest, they are bottom-oriented predators on a wide variety of aquatic insects (Sigler and Miller, 1963; Pontius and Parker, 1973). In Lake Tahoe, whitefish feed on bottom-dwelling forms: snails, dragonfly larvae, chironomid midge larvae, mayfly larvae, caddisfly larvae, crayfish, and amphipods. Small numbers (about 10 percent by volume) of zooplankters and surface insects are also taken (Miller, 1951). In both streams and lakes, mountain whitefish have shown a proclivity for fish eggs, especially those of their own species. The food found in whitefish stomachs seems to depend mostly on availability of the food organisms, although fish over 10 cm SL feed on a larger and greater variety of organisms than do smaller fish. Most feeding takes place at dusk or after dark.

Growth is highly variable, depending on habitat, food availability, and temperature regimes. At the end of their first year they can average 6 to 14 cm TL; second year, 10 to 22 cm TL; third year, 16 to 30 cm TL; fourth year, 20 to 33 cm TL; fifth year, 22 to 33 cm TL; sixth year, 28 to 36 cm TL; seventh year, 33 to 39 cm TL; eighth year, 35 to 42 cm TL, and ninth year, 37 to 44 cm TL (Scott and Crossman, 1973). The growth of the one California population investigated, from a small lake in Mono County, was in the lower half of the yearly range for the species (McAfee, 1966). The oldest fish on record is seventeen years (from Canada) while the largest seems to be one 51 cm FL and 2.9 kg, from Lake Tahoe (Cordone and Frantz, 1966).

Mountain whitefish spawn from October through early December, over bottoms of loose gravel. Most lake populations migrate into tributaries to spawn but some spawning may take place in the lake itself. Little is known about their spawning behavior but they are presumably mass spawners, since there is no evidence that they build redds or defend territories. They become mature in their third or fourth year. Each female lays an average of 5,000 eggs, but the fecundity varies with size, from 1,400 to over 24,000 (Scott and Crossman, 1973). The eggs hatch in the early spring and the newly hatched fish spend the first few weeks in the shallows of the stream. Fry from lake populations usually move into the lake fairly soon after hatching and seek out deep water.

Status. Mountain whitefish are a common but little appreciated gamefish in streams of the east slope of the Sierra Nevada. They are as tasty and sporting as trout, but their large scales and small mouths cause many fishermen to discard them as "trash fish." There is little evidence that they seriously compete with trout, especially native species. A thorough investigation of their life history and ecology in California lakes and streams is needed, emphasizing the effects of new reservoirs.

References. Cordone and Frantz, 1966; McAfee, 1966; Miller, 1951; Pontius and Parker, 1973; Scott and Crossman, 1973; Sigler and Miller, 1963.

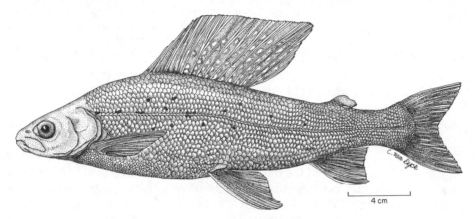

Figure 33. Arctic grayling, 25 cm SL, Alaska.

Arctic Grayling, *Thymallus arcticus* (Pallas)

Identification. Greatly enlarged, saillike dorsal fins, small, toothed mouths, and small adipose fins make arctic grayling unmistakable. Their bodies are long and compressed, heads small (about 25 percent of standard length), and eyes large. Their scales are large and cycloid (77 to 98 in lateral line). The fin counts are: dorsal rays, 19 to 24; anal rays, 11 to 14; pectoral rays, 14 to 16; and pelvic rays, 10 to 11. Adults are blue gray to iridescent purple on their backs and gray with scattered black speckles on their sides. An irregular dusky stripe lies immediately anterior to the pelvic fins. Their dorsal fins have rows of orange and iridescent green spots and are often bordered with orange. Mature males have dorsal fins that will reach their adipose fins when depressed and pelvic fins that nearly reach the anus, while the fins of females are shorter (McPhail and Lindsey, 1970). Juveniles have 10 to 20 narrow parr marks, plus numerous small spots above them.

Names. Grayling were supposed to smell like wild thyme, hence *Thymallus.* However, Sir D'Arcy Wentworth Thompson (quoted in McPhail and Lindsey, 1970) has stated: "For my part I think the odour was imagined by the grammarians to account for the name." *Arcticus* refers to their northern distribution. Although a number of different species of graylings were described from North America, only one is now recognized. A history of the scientific nomenclature is given in McPhail and Lindsey (1970).

Distribution. The native range of arctic grayling includes eastern Siberia, Alaska, and most of northwestern Canada (to Hudson Bay). In addition, there were isolated populations in the upper peninsula of Michigan (now extinct) and in the headwaters of the Missouri River system in Montana (now depleted). They have been planted in a number of northern and western states, with limited success. A number of attempts have been made to introduce arctic grayling into California. From 1903 to 1906 large numbers of eggs were imported from Montana and the progeny of these imports were raised in California hatcheries until 1921. No wild populations became established despite widespread planting (Emig, 1969). Equally unsuccessful attempts to establish them took place in 1924, 1929, and 1930, although the fact that grayling were present for nearly nine years after planting in Grayling Lake, Yosemite Park, indicates that they may have reproduced successfully at least once (Emig, 1969). A new grayling program was started in 1969 when eggs from Arizona were brought to the Hot Creek Hatchery. Plants were made in at least twenty-six mountain lakes, ponds, and creeks in Inyo, Nevada, Sierra, Plumas, Amador, Alpine, El Dorado, Placer, Lassen, Shasta, and Siskiyou counties (Gerstung, 1972). Most of the populations died out after a year or two, although a few have persisted, but without natural reproduction. All grayling populations in the state are now maintained entirely by planting hatchery-reared fish.

Life History. This summary is derived from the extensive literature on arctic grayling reviewed by Carlander (1969), Emig (1969), and McPhail and Lindsey (1970). Arctic grayling inhabit clear, cold lakes and streams. They have been reported surviving in water as warm as 23 to 26°C but they seem to be stressed if temperatures exceed 16 to 18°C for extended periods of time. They are one of the most tolerant salmonids to low oxygen levels, supposedly overwintering in lakes where oxygen levels drop to less than 1 ppm. However, many of the grayling planted in mountain lakes in California are winterkilled, indicating that they may not be as tolerant of low oxygen levels as once thought (Gerstung, 1972). One of the most critical factors for the maintenance of lake populations is the presence of tributary streams with accessible gravel-bottomed riffles for spawning.

Grayling, like most salmonids, are highly opportunistic in their feeding but during the summer months they feed heavily on flying insects. A characteristic of waters where grayling are abundant is the constant dappling of the surface by schools of feeding grayling. When terrestrial insects are not readily available, they will forage for aquatic insect larvae, crustaceans, snails, small fish, and salmon eggs. Their stomach contents have even included an occasional small rodent.

Growth in California populations of grayling can be excellent if the lakes are fertile with plenty of cover for small fish. Thus, in Bullpen Lake, Nevada County, and Devils Lake, Amador County, grayling planted as fingerlings reached 23 cm FL in their first year, 28 cm FL in their second year, and 34 cm FL in their third (Gerstung, 1972). More typically, they reach 8 to 18 cm FL in their third year. Males generally grow slightly faster than females. In their native range, the maximum size recorded is 53 cm SL (2.5 kg) and the maximum age, ten years.

Grayling become mature at the beginning of their third or fourth year and usually migrate up a spawning stream in May or June. Lake spawning may occur, but only rarely. The trigger for the spawning migration seems to be rising temperatures, although spawning will occur anywhere within the range of 4 to 11°C. If suitable inlet streams for spawning are lacking, mature grayling planted in lakes will often migrate down outlets and are then lost to the lakes (Gerstung, 1972). Males congregate in gravel-bottomed riffles, defending territories but not building redds. The spawning act is similar to that of trout except that the male folds his dorsal fin over the back of the female. The eggs are slightly adhesive and may be at least partially buried by the spawning activities of the adults. Each female lays 400 to 12,500 eggs, typically 2,000 to 4,000.

Status. Since arctic grayling have so far failed to establish any self-reproducing populations in California, they can be maintained only by a continued program of stocking. They seem to have only minor value in the management of mountain-lake fisheries. They have not proven to be much better at surviving in shallow, winterkill lakes than brook trout but in a few California lakes they have shown slightly better growth rates than trout. They can also provide surface angling in midsummer when trout may be difficult to catch. Most good grayling lakes, however, are also likely to be good trout lakes. Thus the main justification for continuing to maintain grayling populations in California is to provide a novelty fishery for a rather attractive fish (Gerstung, 1972). Even so, anglers fishing for trout will occasionally discard grayling thinking they are "chubs" (D. Ahrenholz, pers. comm.).

References. Brown, 1971; Carlander, 1969; Emig, 1969; Gerstung, 1972; McPhail and Lindsey, 1970; Minckley, 1973.

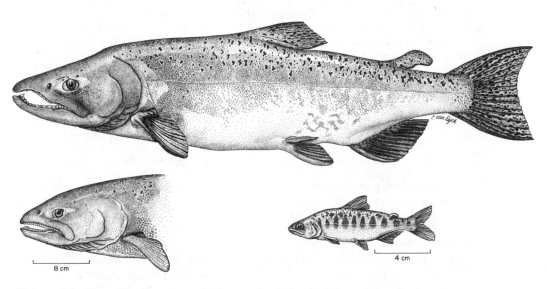

Figure 34. Chinook salmon, spawning male (64 cm SL) and female (60 cm SL); American River, Sacramento County; parr (9 cm SL), Mill Creek, Fresno County.

Chinook Salmon, *Oncorhynchus tshawytscha* (Walbaum)

Identification. Spawning adults are olive brown to dark maroon in color, without conspicuous streaking or blotches on the sides. Spawning males are darker than females, and have a hooked jaw and slightly humped back. There are numerous small black spots in both sexes on the back, dorsal fin, and both lobes of the tail. They can be distinguished from other spawning salmon by the color pattern, particularly the spotting on the back and tail, and by the dark, solid black gums of the lower jaw. They have 10 to 14 major dorsal fin rays, 14 to 19 anal fin rays, 14 to 19 pectoral fin rays, 10 to 11 pelvic fin rays, 130 to 165 pored lateral line scales, and 13 to 19 branchiostegal rays on each side of the jaw. The gill rakers are rough and widely spaced, with 6 to 10 on the lower half of the first gill arch. Spawning adults are the largest Pacific salmon, typically 75 to 80 cm SL (9 to 10 kg). The largest on record for California weighed 38.6 kg (Fry, 1973). Parr have 6 to 12 parr marks, each equal to or wider than the spaces in between them and most centered on the lateral line (or at least passing through it). The adipose fin of parr is pigmented on the upper edge, but clear at its base. The dorsal fin occasionally has one or more spots on it but the other fins are clear.

Names. King salmon is the most widely used name in California but chinook salmon, the most widely used name in Canada, has been adopted as the official common name by the American Fisheries Society. Other names often applied are spring salmon, quinnat salmon (especially in New Zealand), and tyee (for large adults). Chinook is the name of a large tribe of Indians that lived along the Columbia River. *Oncorhynchus* means hooked snout, while *tshawytscha* is an approximation of the word for these fish used by the natives of the Kamchatka Peninsula (USSR) as interpreted by Johann Julius Walbaum, a German naturalist employed by Catherine the Great of Russia.

Distribution. Spawning runs of chinook salmon once occurred as far south as the Ventura River but the southernmost runs at the present time occur in the Sacramento-San Joaquin system. In North America they occur in streams north to Point Hope, Alaska, and in Asia they are found from northern Japan to the Anadyr River, USSR. Since 1872 many attempts have been made to establish chinook salmon elsewhere in the world, but the only successful transplants seem to have been made to New Zealand and, possibly in recent years, the Great Lakes (Scott and Crossman, 1973). In northern California, runs occur in the Klamath, Trinity, Smith, and Eel rivers, as well as in a few smaller streams such as Redwood Creek, Mad River, and Mattole River (Fry, 1973). At the present time attempts are being made to establish a run up the Russian River. Prior to the construction of Shasta Dam, chinook salmon ran up into the upper reaches of the Sacramento River, the McCloud River, and the lower Pit River. Today they spawn only in the Sacramento River below the dam and in its tributary streams, especially the American and Feather rivers. Prior to the construction of Friant Dam, they also spawned in the upper San Joaquin River, and occasionally, the Kings River. Today only occasional salmon manage to spawn in either river, in years of high runoff (Moyle, 1970). In the San Joaquin system, large runs still exist only in the lowermost portions of the Stanislaus, Tuolumne, Mokelumne, and Consumnes rivers, largely as a result of artificial propagation.

Life History. The life history of chinook salmon is characterized by variability. In one spawning run, mature fish can be found at ages ranging from two to seven years. In one stream there are likely to be several distinct spawning populations, each spawning at a different time of the year. For example, fall, winter, and spring chinook runs exist in the Sacramento River. Even juvenile fish can adopt a variety of life-history strategies. Reimers (1973) recognized five major life-history types among the juveniles of fall-spawning chinook salmon of the Sixes River, Oregon. The types are defined according to the amount of time spent in the river, the estuary, and the ocean.

Most chinook salmon in California are fall spawners; they start to move upstream in the early fall, as the water begins to cool. Such fish spawn between October and February. In the past, a high percentage of the chinook salmon in the Sacramento-San Joaquin system ran up the rivers in May and June, and spent the summer in deep holes of upstream areas where water temperatures seldom exceeded 21 to 25°C. They would then spawn in late fall. Such runs are now gone because dams block access to the upstream areas. In the Sacramento River, however, Shasta Dam has actually caused an increase in water-run salmon. These fish move up in December through February but do not spawn until May or June. Cool water flowing from the base of the dam lowers water temperatures of the main river enough so that the eggs and young can survive the summer (Frey, 1971).

Spawning chinook salmon can migrate considerable distances upstream: over 2,000 km in the Yukon River, Alaska, and over 350 km in the Sacramento River. They home to the stream they were spawned in, using olfactory and visual cues to find their way back (Groves et al., 1968). Enough fish miss these cues so that in years of high water they can be found spawning in unexpected places. Most spawning runs are up fairly large streams; chinook salmon leave most of the smaller coastal streams entirely to coho salmon. However, spawning may occur in surprisingly small tributaries to the larger streams, although most spawning takes place in coarse gravel riffles in the main streams. For maximum egg survival, water temperatures have to be less than 14°C. Spawning behavior is similar to that of other Pacific salmon. Because the spawning fish are so large, redds over 3.6 m long and 30 cm deep may be constructed (Scott and Crossman, 1973).

Each female, depending on her size, lays 2,000 to 14,000 eggs. Eggs laid in the fall hatch in the spring (March to April) while those laid in the spring, by winter-run fish, may hatch in late August. The alevins remain in the gravel for two to three weeks, until the yolk sac is absorbed. Once they emerge, most California fry start moving downstream at once, seldom spending more than three to four weeks in fresh water. A majority of these fish also move through the estuaries fairly rapidly and enter the ocean when they are only two to four months old (4 to 8 cm SL). The peak of movement through the Sacramento-San Joaquin Estuary occurs in May and June (Sasaki, 1966). Small numbers of juvenile chinook salmon spend up to a year in the rivers or in the estuaries, a pattern that is much more common in northern populations than it is among California populations. However, the extent to which juvenile chinook salmon use estuaries along the north coast of California is poorly known.

While in fresh water, juvenile chinook salmon are opportunistic drift feeders and take a wide variety of terrestrial and aquatic insects. In the Sacramento-San Joaquin Delta, terrestrial insects are by far the most important food, but crustaceans are also taken in some numbers. Adult salmon feed mostly on fish.

Parr that are resident in streams defend feeding territories. The preferred locations for these territories are, at first, shallow, silty-bottomed areas along the stream edge, but as the fish grow larger they gradually move out into deeper and swifter water. Their precise habitat in any given stream depends on their interactions with resident juveniles of coho salmon and steelhead rainbow trout, as well as on food and cover availability (Chapman and Bjornn, 1969; Everest and Chapman, 1972; Stein et al., 1972).

Status. Although chinook salmon are the least abundant of the species of Pacific salmon, they are the most important species in California. Because fish spawned in California streams spend most of the marine portion of their life cycle off the California coast, the valuable sport and commercial fishery of the state depends on the maintenance of its own spawning streams. Since the commercial salmon fishery started in the 1860s, the total California salmon catch (up to 90 percent chinook) has varied from 2 to 14 million pounds (0.7 to 6.4 million kg) per year and the price per pound has increased steadily. Each year 40,000 to 130,000 salmon are also caught by anglers, so the worth of the salmon in recreational dollars is considerable as well.

There is little doubt that California chinook salmon populations have declined in the last one hundred years. Fortunately, the remarkable ability of the salmon to adapt to changing conditions has minimized the decline. Thus the loss of the large spring runs of salmon in the Sacramento River, caused by the construction of dams that blocked access to upstream spawning grounds, was at least partially compensated for by the development of winter runs, which take advantage of cool summer outflows from the dams. Chinook salmon still manage to spawn in many streams that have been radically altered by man's activities ranging from gold mining to water diversion for irrigation. For example, a few fish still spawn in Putah Creek, which flows through the University of California, Davis campus despite the fact that it has been dammed, the stream bed has been bulldozed, and the water has been polluted with agricultural and domestic runoff. They accomplish this feat by spawning when there is winter runoff and by having young that leave before the stream dries up in the summer. During years of high runoff, small numbers of chinook salmon wander into streams normally too small for spawning, including streams they had been forced to abandon as a result of man's activities. During such years, a few appear at the base of Friant Dam, Fresno-Madera counties, the construction of which eliminated the large runs that once spawned in the upper San Joaquin River. In 1969, a few salmon even managed to spawn in the Kings River, Fresno County, from which they had not been recorded for over twenty-five years (Moyle, 1970). Such incidents indicate that with the will and a commitment to release of minimal flows during critical times of the year, some salmon runs now gone could be reestablished, and most present runs can be maintained.

Despite the adaptability of the salmon and the value of the fishery, there are constant threats to the continued existence of many chinook salmon runs. Foremost among these are the proposed construction of more dams for hydroelectric power production, for flood control, and for water supply. One critical factor that needs investigation is the amount of flow needed in the spring to permit maximum survival of fry migrating out to sea (Jensen, 1972). The reduction in natural spawning created by dams and other projects can be at least partially compensated for by hatcheries, such as the Nimbus Hatchery on the American River, and by the construction and maintenance of artificial spawning channels. Such methods, however, can seldom completely make up the losses and, indeed, can never compensate for the aesthetic loss of being able to watch salmon spawn in a free-flowing stream.

For further information on California's salmon populations consult Skinner (1962), Hallock and Fry (1967), Hallock et al. (1970), Frey (1971), Jensen (1972), and Fry (1973).

References. Chapman and Bjornn, 1969; Everest and Chapman, 1972; Frey, 1971; Fry, 1973; Groves et al., 1968; Hallock and Fry, 1967; Hallock et al., 1970; Jensen, 1972; McAfee, 1966; McPhail and Lindsey, 1970; Moffett and Smith, 1950; Moyle, 1970; Reimers, 1973; Sasaki, 1966; Scott and Crossman, 1973; Skinner, 1962; Stein et al., 1972.

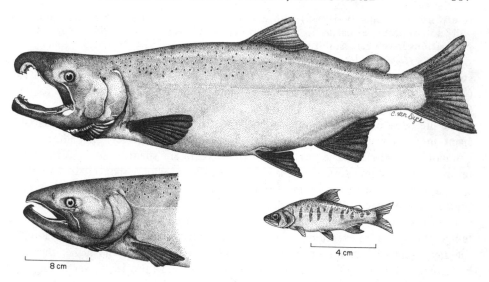

Figure 35. Coho salmon, spawning male (51 cm SL) and female (50 cm SL), British Columbia; parr (7 cm SL), Scott Creek, Santa Cruz County.

Coho Salmon, *Oncorhynchus kisutch* (Walbaum)

Identification. Spawning adults are dark, drab, and greenish on the head and back, dull maroon to brown with a bright red lateral stripe on the sides, and grey to black on the belly. Females are paler than males and usually lack the red stripe on the sides. Males have a hooked jaw and slightly humped back. Both sexes have small black spots on the back, dorsal fin, and upper lobe (only) of the tail. The gums of the lower jaw are grey (often dark grey) but the crowns of the gums, at the base of the teeth, are generally whitish (Fry, 1973). They also have 9 to 12 major dorsal fin rays, 12 to 17 anal rays, 13 to 16 pectoral fin rays, 9 to 11 pelvic fin rays, 121 to 148 pored lateral line scales, and 11 to 15 branchiostegal rays on each side of the jaw. The gill rakers are rough and widely spaced, with 12 to 16 on the lower half of the first arch. Spawning fish are typically 45 to 61 cm SL (3.5 to 5.5 kg) but fish weighing as much as 10 kg have been caught in California (Fry, 1973). Parr have 8 to 12 narrow parr marks that center on the lateral line and are slightly narrower than the spaces in between them. The adipose fin is finely speckled, giving it a grey color, but the other fins are without spots and are often tinged with orange.

Names. Silver salmon is the "official" common name in California but coho salmon has gained wide usage elsewhere and is the common name adopted by the American Fisheries Society. Coho is derived from an Indian dialect name for this species (Hart, 1973). *Oncorhynchus* means hooked snout, while *kisutch* is J. J. Walbaum's interpretation of the vernacular name used in the Kamchatka Peninsula (USSR). A synonymy of the scientific nomenclature can be found in Scott and Crossman (1973).

Distribution. In Asia, coho salmon spawn in coastal streams from northern Japan, north to the Anadyr River in the USSR. In North America they use streams from Point Hope, Alaska, south to the northern edge of Monterey Bay. They are rare in the Sacramento River despite attempts in 1956, 1957, and 1958 to establish runs by planting large numbers of fry in the system (Hallock and Fry, 1967). In recent years, the California Department of Fish and Game has been planting coho salmon in reservoirs (e.g., Lake Berryessa) with considerable success, although such populations will not reproduce naturally (Wigglesworth and Rawstron, 1974). Reproducing populations have been established in the Great Lakes.

Life History. Unless otherwise indicated this summary is based on the classic study of coho salmon in Waddell Creek, Santa Cruz County, by Shapovalov and Taft (1954), and on the summaries by McPhail and Lindsey (1970), Scott and Crossman (1973), and Fry (1973).

The life cycle of coho salmon is from two to five years. The first year is invariably spent in fresh water and the second year may be as well (rarely in California but commonly in Alaska). The next one to three years are spent at sea and the adults return to their home stream to spawn in the fall and winter months. In California, spawning can occur at any time from early September through March, but most spawning takes place in November through January. The typical coho spawning stream is a moderate-sized coastal stream, or the tributary to a larger river, that has summer temperatures seldom exceeding 21°C. The salmon move upstream from the sea during the day, usually in response to increased flows. They seldom ascend higher than 200 km upstream but much longer migrations are known from a few large river systems.

The redd site is chosen by the female. The preferred location is at the head of a riffle, in small- to medium-sized gravel. Spawning behavior is similar to that of other Pacific salmon. Frequently, more than one male will spawn simultaneously with a female. The extra males are often small jack coho that have ascended the streams after only a year at sea. Each female lays 1,000 to 5,000 eggs, depending on her size. The adults die after spawning.

The eggs hatch in eight to twelve weeks and the fry emerge from the gravel four to ten weeks later, depending on water temperatures. The fry school in the shallow stream edges, feeding on a wide variety of small invertebrates. As the fry become parr, the schools break up and individual fish establish territories. Most territories are located in the quiet water of the stream edge or in pools. As the parr grow larger, they expand their territories and move into deeper water. Small parr tend to occupy the shallow glides at the tail of pools, while larger parr tend to be found at the head of pools (Chapman and Bjornn, 1969). Young coho are voracious feeders, ingesting any organism that moves or drifts over their territories. A major part of their diet is aquatic insect larvae and terrestrial insects. Small fishes are taken when available.

One aspect of the biology of coho parr that has received considerable attention in recent years is their interaction with the parr of other salmonids. They will segregate from similar-sized juvenile steelhead trout, occupying pools while the steelhead occupy riffles (Hartman, 1965). Temperature plays an important role in segregating chinook salmon parr from coho parr; the coho stay in the cool tributaries (they prefer temperatures of 12 to 19°C) while the chinook live in the warmer main rivers. However, in some streams the two species may occupy the same habitat and then the more aggressive coho tend to dominate, causing the chinook salmon to have a reduced growth rate (Stein et al., 1972). Juvenile coho will also prey on other salmonids and this may be a major cause of early mortality for other species (Parker, 1971).

By the end of their first year, juvenile coho typically reach 10 to 12 cm SL. Since larger fish occupy larger territories, many coho are displaced by slightly larger neighbors and are forced to migrate downstream to seek a new location. At the end of the first year, there is usually not enough suitable habitat for coho territories and so the parr start transforming into smolts and migrate out to sea. This movement in turn stimulates most of the territorial coho parr to abandon their stations, turn to smolts, and migrate out to sea (Chapman, 1962).

At sea, coho salmon are pelagic and prey mostly on other fishes. They may wander widely but most stay fairly close to the coast within a few hundred km of the home spawning stream. In Lake Berryessa, planted coho feed almost exclusively on threadfin shad.

Status. Coho salmon are the most sought after of the Pacific salmon by sportsmen because their voracious feeding habits make them vulnerable to a wide variety of baits and lures and because they put up spectacular fights when hooked. In California, however, they are outnumbered in both the sport and commercial catch by chinook salmon, although the coho take does approach 50 percent of the California salmon landings in some years (Fry, 1973). The saltwater catch of coho salmon has actually increased in California in recent years, despite the deterioration of many of their coastal spawning streams, due especially to poor logging practices (Burns, 1972). Most of the increase in coho numbers can be attributed to hatchery operations in Oregon and Washington (Fry, 1973). Coho are perhaps the best suited of the Pacific salmon to hatchery production because they normally spend such a long time in fresh water. They can be raised in hatcheries to the size at which they will migrate to sea. The survival rate at this stage is high and the adults will return to the home hatchery area for spawning. The success of coho hatchery operations in California has resulted in the species being planted in reservoirs as a sport fish that will feed on threadfin shad. The planting programs have been quite successful (e.g., Lake Berryessa). The coho are economical to raise in hatcheries, are quite popular with anglers, and achieve high growth rates in reservoirs (Wigglesworth and Rawstron, 1974).

Despite the success of hatchery-raised coho salmon, special efforts should be made to preserve their natural spawning areas in coastal streams. Such areas are integral parts of some of the most aesthetically pleasing streams in California. They also produce large numbers of salmon at little cost to the fisherman. Most of the logging practices that degrade the streams are unnecessary and avoidable. A well-managed logging operation can actually enhance coho salmon production (Burns, 1972).

References. Burns, 1972; Chapman, 1962; Chapman and Bjornn, 1969; Fry, 1973; Hallock and Fry, 1967; Hartman, 1965; McPhail and Lindsey, 1970; Parker, 1971; Scott and Crossman, 1973; Shapovalov and Taft, 1954; Stein et al., 1972; Wigglesworth and Rawstron, 1974.

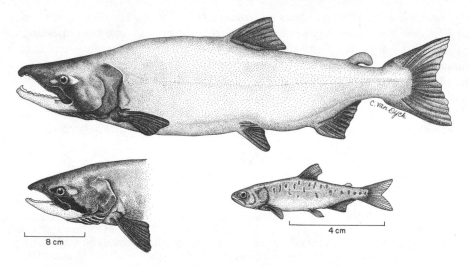

Figure 36. Sockeye salmon, spawning male (49 cm SL) and female (46 cm SL), British Columbia; parr (8.5 cm SL), Alaska. CAS 48486.

Sockeye Salmon (Kokanee)
Oncorhynchus nerka (Walbaum)

Systematic note. Kokanee are the nonanadromous form of sockeye salmon that are frequently referred to as a subspecies (O. *nerka kennerlyi*) of sockeye salmon. However, landlocked populations of sockeye salmon have evolved independently in many different places and these populations differ from each other in their characteristics, so there seems little reason to maintain the subspecific name (McPhail and Lindsey, 1970). Kokanee populations in California, established through introductions, have many different origins and so are not particularly homogeneous in their characteristics.

Identification. Spawning sockeye and kokanee with their solid bright red bodies and green heads are unmistakable. The males develop a distinct hump on the back and the snout becomes long and hooked, with large teeth. Both sexes lack black spots on the back or caudal fin and have 19 to 27 long, slender, and rough gill rakers on the lower half of the first gill arch. Nonspawning kokanee can be distinguished from trout by the lack of spotting (except occasional vague spots on the dorsal fin), long anal fin (13 to 18 rays), slender gill rakers, and slightly oblique mouth. They also have 11 to 26 complete dorsal rays, 11 to 21 pectoral rays, 9 to 11 pelvic rays, 120 to 150 lateral line scales and 11 to 16 branchiostegal rays on each side. Parr have 8 to 12 oval parr marks that are centered on the lateral line and are narrower than the white interspaces. The back has a blue green sheen, the sides are silvery, and the fins are without spotting.

Names. Sockeye salmon are often called red or blueback salmon and kokanee are sometimes called redfish. Sockeye is an approximation of the name given it by the Amerinds who lived along the Fraser River in Canada, as is kokanee. *Oncorhynchus* means hooked snout, while *nerka* is a Russian name for the sockeye. A synonomy of the scientific nomenclature is given in Scott and Crossman (1973).

Distribution. Sockeye salmon have been found in rivers of North America from the Sacramento north to the Yukon in Alaska (Hallock and Fry, 1967; Foerster, 1968). Those found in streams south of the Columbia system are probably nonspawning strays although, prior to the construction of Copco Dam in 1917, there may have been a small run up into Klamath Lake, Oregon, and its tributaries. In Asia, sockeye occur from northern Japan to the Anadyr River in the USSR. Kokanee occur naturally throughout the range of the species, including the upper reaches of the Columbia River system in Washington, Oregon, and Idaho (Scott and Crossman, 1973). They have been successfully introduced into coldwater lakes throughout Canada and the northern and western United States. Kokanee were brought into California in 1941 from Idaho and successfully established in Salt Springs Reservoir on the Mokelumne River. Progeny from this population were planted in a number of lakes in the Tahoe region, including Lake Tahoe. In 1951, kokanee from British Columbia were planted in Shasta Reservoir. Subsequently, plants were made in many of California's lakes and reservoirs, with varying degrees of success (Seeley and McCammon, 1966).

Life History. In California, anadromous sockeye salmon occur only as rare strays mixed in with runs of chinook salmon, so their life cycle will not be dealt with here. It is covered in great detail by Foerster (1968). In any case, the life cycle of kokanee is similar to that of sockeye salmon except that kokanee mature in lakes rather than the ocean. Unless otherwise indicated, this life-history summary is derived from Seeley and McCammon (1966) and Scott and Crossman (1973).

Kokanee are pelagic zooplankton grazers that prefer well-oxygenated water of 10 to 15°C. They will inhabit surface waters of a lake as long as temperatures remain in the preferred range or colder. As the surface waters warm up in late summer the fish gradually move deeper. In Lake Tahoe, they are found most of the year less than 4 m below the surface but in July through September they concentrate at depths of 17 to 40 m (Cordone et al., 1971). In large midelevation reservoirs (e.g., Shasta Reservoir) they stay in the hypolimnion during the summer. Occasionally, heavy kokanee mortality will occur when the hypolimnion becomes depleted of oxygen.

As the fine gill rakers of kokanee attest, their main food is zooplankton. In Lake Tahoe, they take mostly waterfleas (*Daphnia pulex*) and copepods, but emerging aquatic insects are eaten on occasion (Cordone et al., 1971). In some lakes emerging insects, especially chironmid midges, may be important food items and larval fish will be eaten when they are abundant. The food of kokanee changes little as the fish grow larger, although newly emerged fry in streams will subsist on aquatic insects for short periods of time. Feeding ceases in the winter and just prior to spawning.

Growth in kokanee is fairly rapid for a freshwater salmonid. They typically reach 10 to 25 cm TL in their first year, 18 to 31 cm TL in their second, 22 to 44 cm TL in their third year, and 23 to 47 cm TL in their fourth (Carlander, 1969). Lake Tahoe kokanee collected from 1960 to 1966 tended to be at the upper end of each length group, and fish over 53 cm TL (1.4 kg) were present (Cordone et al., 1971). However, growth rates seem to have decreased in recent years (S. Nicola, pers. comm.). In contrast, sea-run sockeye usually reach 65 to 80 cm TL (4 to 7 kg).

The size and age of spawning kokanee depends in part on growing conditions (e.g., food availability, light, and temperature regimes) and in part on the origin of the stock. Some populations will complete their life cycle in two years, while others will take as long as seven years (Lake Pend Oreille, Idaho). Most populations mature in four years, including those initially introduced into California and now present in Lake

Tahoe. In some instances fish from populations with four-year life cycles in their native lakes mature in three years in California, presumably as a result of better growing conditions. Most of the recent kokanee transplants into California, however, have been from populations with two-year life cycles because these populations also seem to have superior growth rates. Some plants of these fish have been made into lakes that already contained three-to-four-year life cycle fish but it is not known if the two groups of fish coexist, as they do naturally in some British Columbia lakes, or if they interbreed. Most kokanee are at least 20 cm TL before they spawn but mature fish as small as 16 cm TL have been recorded.

Kokanee normally spawn between early August and early February but spawning has been recorded in California as late as early April. The time of spawning is determined in part by the genetic background of the fish and in part by lake and stream temperatures. Spawning requires temperatures of 6 to 13°C. Most spawning takes place in streams, in gravel riffles a short distance from the lake. However, lake spawning in beds of gravel close to shore, usually at depths less than 8 m, is sometimes important. Lake spawning may be especially important in Lake Tahoe (Cordone et al., 1971).

The first sign that spawning is about to begin is the congregation of kokanee near the mouths of spawning streams or near lake spawning sites. Like other salmon, kokanee home to the stream in which they were hatched (or planted as fry) and locate the stream in part by its "odor" (Lorz and Northcote, 1965). The female builds the redd and defends the area from other females, while her male partner defends the area from other males. Spawning behavior is similar to that of pink salmon. Each female contains 200 to 1,800 eggs, larger fish containing more eggs. Many females die before releasing all of their eggs. Particularly low spawning success is found in Lake Tahoe kokanee where only 11 percent and 28 percent of the dead females examined by Cordone et al. (1971) in 1967 and 1968, respectively, were spawned out and 30 percent and 46 percent, respectively, had died without spawning at all. This low success is compensated in part by high survival rates of the eggs that are laid.

The fry emerge in April through June and move downstream immediately. Most movement takes place at night. Some may begin feeding while in the stream but most do not start until they enter the lake.

Status. Kokanee were originally introduced into California as a forage fish for trout in large reservoirs which would also provide a limited amount of angling. Enthusiasm for kokanee led to their becoming established, during the 1950s and 1960s, in a substantial proportion of the large lakes and reservoirs with temperature regimes suitable for them. They have largely failed as forage for trout although they are eaten in small numbers by lake trout in Lake Tahoe. In small lakes they may actually depress trout growth and population size by competing with them for zooplankton. Angling for kokanee has become popular only in recent years. Even so, most populations are probably underexploited because it takes specialized techniques to catch them during much of the season (e.g., trolling with small lures in the hypolimnion). The only time they seem particularly vulnerable to more conventional salmonid fishing techniques is when they congregate off stream mouths prior to spawning. This low fishing mortality when combined with the small plankton populations present in some California oligotrophic lakes and reservoirs, such as

Trinity Reservoir and Donner Lake, has lead to stunted kokanee populations (S. Nicola, pers. comm.).

References. Carlander, 1969; Cordone, Nicola, Baker, and Frantz, 1971; Foerster, 1968; Fry, 1973; Hallock and Fry, 1967; Lorz and Northcote, 1965; McPhail and Lindsey, 1970; Seeley and McCammon, 1966; Scott and Crossman, 1973.

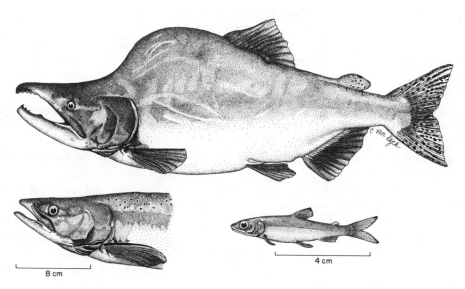

Figure 37. Pink salmon, spawning male (46 cm SL), female (44 cm SL), and parr (6 cm SL), Olsen Creek, Alaska.

Pink Salmon, *Oncorhynchus gorbuscha* (Walbaum)

Identification. Spawning male pink salmon have a pronounced purple hump behind the head, a greatly enlarged and hooked snout, and jagged teeth. Spawning females are trout like in form and olive green on the sides, with long, dusky, vertical spots. Pink salmon can be distinguished from other salmon by the combination of large black spots on the back, oval blotches on both tail lobs, and 16 to 21 gill rakers on the lower half of the first gill arch (McPhail and Lindsey, 1970). They have 10 to 16 complete rays in the dorsal fin, 13 to 19 in the anal fin, 14 to 18 in each pectoral fin, and 9 to 11 in each pelvic fin. The scales (147 to 198 in the lateral line) are deeply imbedded in spawning fish. Branchiostegal rays are 10 to 15 on each side of the jaw. The maximum size recorded for pink salmon is 76 cm SL (6.3 kg) but fish over 60 cm (2.5 kg) are unusual. The young in fresh water are always small (less than 5 cm TL), silvery, and without parr marks or spots on the dorsal fin.

Names. Humpback salmon is a widely used common name. *Oncorhynchus* means hooked snout, while *gorbuscha* is the Russian word for humpback.

Distribution. Spawning takes place in coastal streams of northeastern Asia, including Korea, Japan, and Siberia west to the Lena River, and in streams of northwestern North America from the MacKenzie River, Canada, around Alaska and the Aleutian Islands south to California. In California, pink salmon have been taken in the San Lorenzo, Sacramento, Russian, Garcia, Mad, and Klamath rivers, as well as in a number of smaller north-coastal streams (Hallock and Fry, 1967). The only established spawning run seems to be in the lower Russian River (Fry, 1967), although the run is extremely small. There may also be a small run up the Sacramento River (Fry, 1973) but spawning activity has not been observed there. In the ocean, pink salmon have been collected as far south as La Jolla (Hubbs, 1946). They have been transplanted successfully only to Lake Superior (Scott and Crossman, 1973).

Life History. Most pink salmon live only two years and much of that time is spent at sea. The adults can move into fresh water to spawn anytime from mid-June to early October. The only spawning actually observed in California took place in early October (Fry, 1967). They seldom move very far upstream and frequently spawn in intertidal areas, but they have been found nearly 320 km up the Sacramento River, in Battle Creek (Fry, 1973). The typical spawning ground is a gravel riffle in a moderate-sized stream, with a depth of 20 to 40 cm.

Spawning males are rather aggressive and defend territories in the riffles. They often inflict severe wounds on each other with their large jaw teeth during conflicts. While the males fight, the females dig the redds. Each redd is constructed by a female turning on her side and repeatedly "cutting" at the gravel with her tail, displacing gravel downstream. When the depression is deep enough the female signals the male of her readiness to spawn by sinking to the bottom of the redd until her anal fin touches the gravel. The male swims alongside the female and the two quiver and gape, while simultaneously releasing eggs and sperm. Not all the eggs are released in one spawning so the female digs a new redd above the old one and buries the eggs from the preceding spawning while doing so. She may thus dig several redds in succession, and spawn with more than one male. Within a few days after the female has laid her 1,000 to 2,000 eggs she dies, as do spent males.

The eggs hatch in four to six months, depending on water temperatures, but the alevins continue to remain in the gravel until the yolk sac is absorbed. They emerge in April and May and move downstream immediately, without feeding. The fry school in estuaries for several months before they finally move out to sea.

Status. Pink salmon are uncommon in California and probably have always been so. However, they are the single most abundant species of Pacific salmon (*Oncorhynchus* spp.) over the entire range of the genus, a fact accentuated by the overexploitation of the other, more valuable species. The overexploitation of pink salmon has been proceding apace in recent years, especially on the high seas, so their numbers too are dwindling. Despite the small size of the pink salmon run up the Russian River, it is of interest because it seems to be the southernmost for the species. It should thus be taken into account as further modifications are made of the river's flow (e.g., the proposed Dry Creek Dam) and as changes are made in the estuary by the Army Corps of Engineers.

References. Fry, 1967, 1973; Hallock and Fry, 1967; Hubbs, 1946; McPhail and Lindsey, 1970; Scott and Crossman, 1973.

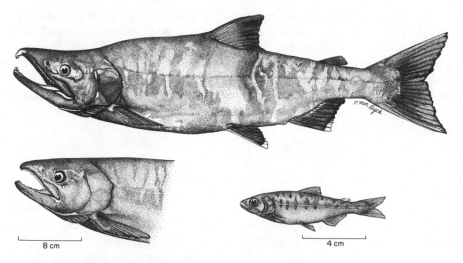

Figure 38. Chum salmon, spawning male (60 cm SL) and female (48 cm SL), British Columbia; parr (7 cm SL) Klamath River, Del Norte County.

Chum Salmon, *Oncorhynchus keta* (Walbaum)

Identification. Spawning male chum salmon are heavy-bodied, slightly humped, and have a long, hooked snout with conspicuous caninelike teeth at the end of the jaws. They are dark olive on the back and dirty maroon on the sides, with irregular greenish vertical bars on the sides. Females are similar in color, although the maroon color on the sides is less well developed; they lack a hump and the jaw is less hooked. Chum salmon can be distinguished from other salmon by the absence of black spots on the back and fins, and by the 11 to 17 short, smooth gill rakers on the lower half of the first gill arch (McPhail and Lindsey, 1970). They have 10 to 14 major rays in the dorsal fin, 13 to 17 in the anal fin, 14 to 16 in each pectoral fin, and 10 to 11 in each pelvic fin. The scales (124 to 153 in the lateral line) are deeply imbedded in spawning fish. Branchiostegal rays are 12 to 16 on each side of the jaw. Their maximum size is about 1 m SL (15 kg) but they typically are less than 80 cm SL (6 to 7 kg). The parr have 6 to 14 pale parr marks that seldom extend below the lateral line, and the width of the light areas in between the marks is greater than the width of the marks themselves. There is no spotting on the fins and the back is mottled green, the sides silvery green.

Names. Chum salmon are often called dog salmon, apparently in reference to the jaw teeth. *Oncorhynchus* means hooked snout, while *keta* is the Russian name for this salmon. A synonymy of the scientific nomenclature is given in Scott and Crossman (1973).

Distribution. The distribution of spawning chum salmon in streams flowing into the northern Pacific and Arctic oceans is virtually identical to that of pink salmon, although chum salmon will migrate much further upstream than will pink salmon. In California, chum salmon will occasionally stray up coastal streams as far south as the San Lorenzo River (Scofield, 1916; Rogers, 1974) and apparently about 30 to 210 ascend the Sacramento River annually as far as Mill Creek, Tehama County (Hallock and Fry, 1967). In the ocean, they have been taken as far south as off Del Mar, California (Messersmith, 1965).

Life History. Chum salmon normally complete their life cycle in three to five years, although a few may complete it in two. They spend little time in fresh water, the adults usually ascending only a short distance upstream to spawn and die, and the young descending downstream into the ocean soon after hatching. The main exceptions to this pattern are the populations that migrate as much as 2,000 km up rivers (e.g., Yukon River) that lack major barriers. Chum salmon appear to be unable to hurdle waterfalls and other barriers that present few difficulties of passage to other salmon species.

They prefer streams with temperatures of 12 to 14°C (Brett, 1952) for spawning, which generally takes place in gravel riffles. Spawning behavior is similar to that of pink salmon. A single female, in the process of digging a series of depressions for egg deposition, may displace gravel over an area 2.25 m^2 down to a depth of 40 cm. Each female lays 2,400 to 4,000 eggs depending on her size. Chum salmon are mostly summer and fall spawners. In the Sacramento River they have been captured from early August to early February (Hallock and Fry, 1967).

Depending on time of spawning and water temperature, hatching takes place in January or February but the alevins remain in the gravel for two to three months longer, until the yolk sac is absorbed. They leave the gravel at 30 to 35 mm TL. Most fry, because they were hatched from eggs laid close to the mouths of streams, enter the estuaries without feeding in fresh water. When they have long distances to travel downstream they will feed on aquatic insect larvae and crustaceans. They move downstream at night, in schools. Parr that live in fresh water while migrating downstream may grow to 6 to 8 cm TL. This would presumably be the case with parr spawned in the upstream areas of the Sacramento River, although collections of chum salmon parr are lacking from the river. Some populations of parr spend several months in the estuaries, moving in and out of fresh water and feeding on both marine and freshwater organisms (Mason, 1974).

Status. Although important commercially in Alaska and Canada, chum salmon contribute little to the commercial catch in California. The few that are caught off the California coast presumably originated in streams north of the state. Most of the chum salmon found in California streams are strays that had probably become mixed with schools of chinook or coho salmon out in the ocean. Such fish generally die without spawning. However, the fact that spawned-out carcasses are regularly found in tributaries to the Sacramento River indicates that some reproduction does occur and the yearly capture of small numbers of chum salmon in nets set in the river probably means that this reproduction is at least occasionally successful, since adult chum salmon home to the areas in which they were hatched. In addition, the California Academy of Sciences has a small collection of parr taken from the Klamath River in 1944 (uncatalogued).

References. Brett, 1952; Fry, 1973; Hallock and Fry, 1967; McPhail and Lindsey, 1970; Mason, 1974; Messersmith, 1965; Rogers, 1974; Scofield, 1916; Scott and Crossman, 1973.

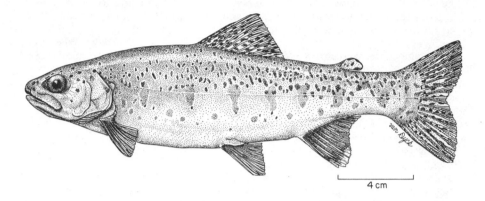

Figure 39. Rainbow trout, 21 cm SL, California.

Rainbow Trout, *Salmo gairdneri* Richardson

Systematic Note. Rainbow trout are the most abundant and widespread species of western *Salmo*. They are successful because they have been able to adapt to a wide variety of aquatic habitats (including fish hatcheries) and are flexible in their life-history patterns. As a result, many local populations of rainbow trout have distinctive characteristics, and have been given separate common and scientific names. Within these populations, however, variation is often considerable. Distinctive characteristics, especially color patterns, are often at least in part phenotypic responses to local conditions and may be lost is the fish are transferred to a hatchery or to another stream (Needham and Gard, 1959). The widespread mixing of rainbow trout from different populations by man, in hatcheries and through indiscriminate planting, has further blurred the distinctions between populations, especially in California. Thus, the six subspecies of rainbow trout in California that have been officially recognized by the California Department of Fish and Game (McAfee, 1966) are all of questionable validity.

The steelhead rainbow trout, *S. g. gairdneri*, is the anadromous form. Aside from their sea-going habits and large size at spawning there is little to distinguish them from rainbow trout that are resident in the same streams that steelhead use for spawning.

The Kamloops rainbow, *S. g. kamloops*, is a hatchery strain derived from trout native to Kamloops Lake, British Columbia, and planted mostly in large California reservoirs (e.g., Shasta Lake). The lack of truly distinctive characteristics in the original Kamloops rainbow trout (McPhail and Lindsey, 1970), together with changes in their genotype in California created by selection in hatcheries and interbreeding in the wild with other varieties, leaves little reason to continue to recognize the Kamloops trout as a subspecies. However, there may be some utility in continuing to recognize it as a lake-adapted hatchery strain (but without the formal trinomial nomenclature).

The Shasta rainbow trout, *S. g. stonei*, from the McCloud River, was the original California rainbow selected for hatchery culture (Wales, 1939). Widespread planting of derivatives of this form over California (and over the world) combined with hatchery selection pressures and hybridization with other forms have largely eliminated whatever distinctive traits they may once have had. Also, the original description may have been based on steelhead rainbow trout. It should be noted, however, that brilliantly colored populations of rainbow trout still live in the McCloud River. Their systematic position is worth investigating.

The Kern River rainbow trout, *S. g. gilberti*, is (or was) a distinctive, heavily spotted form from the upper Kern River. Schreck and Behnke (1971), however, consider it to be a subspecies of golden trout, an opinion that is disputed (C. L. Hubbs, pers. comm.). The systematic status of this form awaits resolution through further studies.

Eagle Lake rainbow trout, *S. g. aquilarum*, is a brightly colored form adapted for living in the highly alkaline waters of Eagle Lake, Lassen County. They have been variously classified as a cutthroat trout subspecies (Snyder, 1933), as a rainbow trout subspecies, and as a hybrid between native cutthroat and introduced rainbow trouts (Hubbs and Miller, 1948). If they are in fact a native rainbow trout population they are a zoogeographic enigma, since all other fishes present in the lake are native to the Lahontan system from which rainbow trout are otherwise absent. The present-day form does seem to be like rainbow trout in most of its characteristics and, regardless of its origin, is uniquely suited for Eagle Lake.

Royal silver rainbow trout, *S. g. regalis*, supposedly native to Lake Tahoe and now extinct, presents a zoogeographic puzzle similar to that of Eagle Lake rainbow trout. However, there is little reason to doubt that J. O. Snyder's 1912 description of "*Salmo regalis*" was based on large-sized rainbow trout derived from fish introduced in the 1860s and 1870s. His royal silver rainbow trout differs little from rainbow trout of known origin that have grown to large sizes in other large lakes.

Identification. Rainbow trout are highly variable in color, body shape, and meristic characters. Nevertheless, they can usually be recognized as silvery trout with numerous black spots on the tail, adipose fin, dorsal fin, and back (best developed anteriorly) and an iridescent pink to red lateral band. The cheeks (opercula) are also pinkish, the back iridescent blue to nearly brown, the sides and belly silver, white, or yellowish. Resident stream forms are generally darker than lake or sea-run forms. The mouth is large, the maxillary usually extending behind the eye. The teeth are well developed on the upper and lower jaws, on the head and shaft of the vomer, on the palatines, and on the tongue. Basibranchial teeth are absent. The dorsal fin has 10 to 12 principal rays; the anal fin, 8 to 12 principal rays; the pelvic fins, 9 to 10 rays each; and the pectoral fins, 11 to 17 each. The tail is slightly forked. There are 16 to 22 gill rakers on each arch and 9 to 13 branchiostegal rays. The scales are small, with 110 to 160 pored scales along the lateral line, 18 to 35 scale rows above the lateral line, and 14 to 29 below it.

The coloration of the young is similar to that of the adults except that the young also have 8 to 13 widely spaced parr marks centered on the lateral line (the interspaces are wider than the parr marks), 5 to 10 dark marks on the back between the head and dorsal fin, white to orange tips on the dorsal and anal fins, and few or no black spots on the tail (McPhail and Lindsey, 1970). Adults from small streams may retain much of the color pattern of parr.

Names. *Salmo* is the ancient Latin name for the Atlantic salmon (*S. salar*) and is probably derived from the Latin verb meaning "to leap." *Gairdneri* is after Dr. Meredith Gairdner, a Hudson Bay Company naturalist who assisted Sir John Richardson in his collections of Columbia River fishes. The scientific name is frequently listed in the older literature as *Salmo irideus*, the name given to nonsteelhead by Gibbons in 1855. Synonymies of the scientific nomenclature can be found in La Rivers (1961) and Scott and Crossman (1973).

Distribution. Rainbow trout are native to Pacific coast streams from the Kuskokwim River in Alaska down to northwestern Mexico, plus a few interior basins. In California, they are native to coastal streams from the Los Angeles River system and the Ventura River north to the Klamath River. They are also native to most of the Sacramento-San Joaquin system. They have been introduced into most of the suitable waters to which they were not native over most of the world. They are now present in South America, Africa, India and southern Asia, Japan, Europe, New Zealand, Australia, Tasmania, and Hawaii, as well as in most suitable waters of North America (MacCrimmon, 1971).

Life History*. The life-history patterns of rainbow trout range from the highly migratory, sea-going pattern of steelhead populations, to the pattern of many isolated populations in small streams, where an individual trout may complete its entire life cycle in a few hundred meters of stream. When in fresh water, most rainbow trout are found in cool, clear, fast-flowing permanent streams and rivers, where riffles tend to predominate over pools. In the Sacramento-San Joaquin system they also inhabit the Squawfish-sucker-hardhead Zone in the larger streams, even though temperatures may often approach the maximum they can withstand. Mountain lakes and the cold, deep waters of reservoirs also provide suitable habitat for rainbow trout, but such populations have to be artificially maintained if suitable spawning streams are lacking. Rainbow trout will survive temperatures of 0 to 28°C. They can withstand temperatures at the upper end of this range, however, only if they have been gradually acclimated to them and if the water is saturated with oxygen. Optimum temperatures for growth and for completion of most stages of their life history seem to be 13 to 21°C. At low temperatures, they can withstand oxygen concentrations as low as 1.5 to 2.0 ppm but normally concentrations close to saturation are required for growth. Their tolerance of the varying chemical conditions of water is also broad. They can live in water ranging in pH from 5.8 to 9.6. All other factors being equal, best growth seems to be achieved in slightly alkaline waters (pH of 7 to 8), although Eagle Lake trout have adapted to the highly alkaline waters of Eagle Lake (ph of 8.4 to 9.6).

While rainbow trout are the only fish species found in many California streams, more often than not they occur with other salmonids (especially brown trout and juvenile coho and chinook salmon), sculpins (*Cottus* spp.), speckled dace, suckers (*Catostomus* spp.), and Sacramento squawfish. It is unusual, however, to find more than three to four other species in abundance where rainbow trout are common. Rainbow trout are fairly flexible in their behavior and habitat requirements. They can interact successfully with other species of fish, avoiding as much as possible direct competition for food and space. In coastal streams, juvenile steelhead interact with juvenile coho and chinook salmon and, as a result, the species select different microhabitats (Hartman, 1965; Everest and Chapman, 1972). When brown trout and rainbow trout are found in the same stream, brown trout tend to select slow, deep pools with lots of cover, while rainbow trout select the faster water (Lewis, 1969). Rainbow trout also tend to feed more on drift organisms, while brown trout feed on the bottom. The interactions between rainbow trout and various nongame species are discussed in the ecology chapter of this book.

One of the main reasons rainbow trout are so successful at interacting with other fish species is that they are highly aggressive and defend feeding territories in streams. Other salmonids recognize the aggressive displays of rainbow trout (e.g., rigid swimming, flared operculae, nipping at the caudal peduncle of invading fish) and usually react either by fleeing or by challenging the trout with similar displays, perhaps driving it off its territory. The winners of such interspecific contests are determined by

---

*The literature on rainbow trout life history is so large, even just for California populations, that a literature review is far beyond the scope of this book. This summary is based largely on personal experience (e.g., Moyle and Nichols, 1973), the compilations of McAfee (1966), Carlander (1969), and Scott and Crossman (1973), the monograph of Shapovalov and Taft (1954), and the papers in Northcote (1969).

a number of factors, but relative size and habitat preferences play leading roles. Rainbow trout can generally drive nongame fishes such as suckers and squawfish, which do not respond to the displays themselves, from feeding territories by repeatedly rushing at the invaders and nipping at their sides and caudal peduncles (H. Li, pers. comm.).

Territorial displays are also extremely important in the intraspecific interactions of rainbow trout. In streams, rainbow trout set up feeding territories which they defend from each other. The number of territories depends on many factors, but probably the most important are size of the fish, speed of current, water temperature, and availability of cover. Superimposed on this territorial mosaic, however, is a dominance hierarchy in which larger fish are dominant over small fish and hold much larger territories. The smaller fish may actually hold small territories within the territory of the large fish. They interact with each other and a stable hierarchy develops to the point where they will actually help the dominant trout defend the entire territory against invading trout (Jenkins, 1969). These territorial interactions may be the most important factor limiting the number of trout in many streams, outweighing food availability.

The competitive interactions of rainbow trout with each other and with other fish species in lakes is less well understood than it is in streams. The trout tend to school and wander about within lakes, so aggressive behavior probably plays a minor role. The numerous observations of decrease in trout growth rates and population size following the introduction of another species (usually a cyprinid) into a pure trout lake, indicates, however, that direct competition for limited food resources takes place initially. Eventually, the trout and the new species will segregate by habitat and feeding strategies and the trout may subsist in part by preying on the other species. A classic, well-documented case of this sort is Paul Lake, British Columbia (Johannes and Larkin, 1961).

In the summer months, stream-dwelling rainbow trout feed mostly on drift organisms, but they will also take active bottom invertebrates. Thus, the stomachs from a sample of trout taken from one stream at the same time are likely to contain a hodgepodge of terrestrial insects, adult and emergent aquatic insects, aquatic insect larvae, amphipods, snails, and occasional small fish. Individual trout, however, tend to specialize in the type of organisms they feed on, even over a long period of time, and do not take the whole range of foods available (Bryan and Larkin, 1972). In the winter, feeding is considerably reduced over summer levels and the trout feed mostly on bottom-dwelling invertebrates. The most commonly taken bottom invertebrates at all seasons are either those that drift on a regular basis (e.g., baetid mayfly larvae, amphipods), those that are active bottom crawlers or live in exposed positions, or those that are large in size. The size of the organism taken tends to increase with the size of the feeding fish. Rainbow trout can feed at virtually any hour of the day or night but feeding activity is usually most intense around dusk.

In lakes, feeding varies with invertebrate availability. Although benthic invertebrates and zooplankton seem to be preferred, terrestrial insects will be taken in numbers when other foods are scarce. Rainbow trout in lakes also have a greater proclivity for feeding on fish than do stream-dwelling rainbows, although fish normally do not become an important item in the diet until the trout are 30 to 35 cm TL. Thus, large Eagle Lake trout subsist mostly on tui chubs, while trout in California reservoirs subsist on threadfin shad or delta smelt. Other fishes commonly eaten in California are sculpins and suckers. As in streams, feeding is most intense during the summer but can continue throughout the winter, at temperatures as low as 1°C (Elliott and Jenkins, 1972). Steelhead feed on estuarine invertebrates after they leave their home streams but fish gradually become more important in their diet as they increase in size. The large size and rapid growth achieved by steelhead, and to a lesser extent by lake-dwelling rainbow trout, can be attributed in a large part to their diet of fish.

Growth rates in rainbow trout are variable. In mountain lakes, they reach 11 to 17 cm TL in their first year, 14 to 21 cm TL in their second, and 20 to 23 cm TL in their third. In such lakes they seldom live longer than six years or grow over 40 cm TL. Growth rates are similar in small California streams. The most rapid growth in California is achieved in large lakes and reservoirs. In Eagle Lake, trout 20 to 23 cm TL are one year old, 43 to 46 cm TL are two years old, and 46 to 56 cm TL are three years old. Similar growth is achieved by fish planted as fingerlings in some reservoirs (e.g., Crowley Lake, Mono County) but generally it is somewhat slower, especially after the first year. Juvenile steelhead migrate out to sea at one to three years of age, at 13 to 25 cm TL. After one to two years at sea they return at 38 to 69 cm TL (1.4 to 5.4 kg). The largest known nonsteelhead rainbow trout, from Jewel Lake, British Columbia, weighed 23.9 kg (Hart, 1973), although the largest caught by angling (from Lake Pend Oreille, Idaho) weighed 16.8 kg. The largest such fish from California (Feather River) weighed 9.6 kg, while the largest California steelhead known (Smith River) weighed 9.7 kg (Anonymous, 1964). The largest steelhead on record, from Alaska, weighed 19.1 kg (Hart, 1973). The oldest rainbow trout known are those from Eagle Lake, at eleven years. Steelhead occasionally reach nine years old, but the maximum age for most nonsteelhead rainbow trout is seven years.

Most nonandromous rainbow trout mature in their second or third year, but the time of first maturity can vary from the first to the fifth year of life. Mature fish can be of any size from 13 cm on up. Most steelhead spawn for the first time after spending two to three years in fresh water and then one to two years in salt water. However, spawning fish, usually small males, that have spent only one year in each habitat do occur on a regular basis in some streams.

Most wild rainbow trout are spring spawners, from February to June, but low temperatures in high mountain areas may delay spawning until July or August. California steelhead trout also spawn in the spring, but they frequently migrate upstream in the fall several months before they actually spawn. In some north-coast streams, small numbers migrate upstream in the late spring, spend the summer in deep pools, and spawn in the spring of the following year. Steelhead and other rainbow trout have well-developed homing abilities, and usually spawn in the same stream and area in which they had lived as fry. This means that local races of trout tend to develop that are adapted to local conditions.

Successful reproduction of rainbow trout generally requires a gravel riffle, in which a redd can be dug by the female and the eggs successfully incubated. Spawning behavior is similar to that of brown trout. The number of eggs laid per female depends on the size and origin of the fish but ranges from 200 to 12,000 eggs. Rainbow trout under 30 cm TL typically contain less than 1,000 eggs, while steelhead contain about 2,000 eggs per kg of body weight. Both rainbow and steelhead usually spawn once a year, but it is not unusual for fish to skip a year between spawnings.

The eggs hatch in three to four weeks (at 10 to 15°C) and the fry emerge from the gravel two to three weeks later. The fry initially live in quiet waters close to shore and exhibit little aggressive behavior for several weeks.

Status. Rainbow trout are the most popular and widely distributed gamefish in California. The demand for them is far beyond the natural reproductive capacities of wild populations, so a considerable portion of the fishing-license revenues of the California Department of Fish and Game goes towards supporting hatcheries that rear domestic strains of rainbow trout for planting on a put-and-take basis. Most trout planted are 18 to 20 cm TL and are caught within two weeks of planting (Butler and Borgeson, 1965). This is fortunate because hatchery-raised fish are ill-adapted for surviving in streams and are likely to die of starvation or stress within a few weeks anyway. Mortality is highest when they are planted in relatively small numbers in a stream that also sustains a wild trout population, because the planted fish will be unable to break into the established dominance hierarchies of the wild trout. If large numbers are planted over a wild trout population, the effect of the sheer numbers is likely to disrupt the established hierarchies, making the wild fish more vulnerable to angling. Such streams generally have to be continually planted if any sort of trout fishery is to be sustained, since neither the wild nor domestic trout can maintain themselves very easily.

In lakes, the survival rates of planted fish are much higher than they are in streams because of the absence of dominance hierarchies in wild fish, the low expenditure of energy required to stay alive (and become adjusted to the environment) in the absence of current, and the lower vulnerability of the fish to angling. In lakes, it is often economical to plant fingerling trout in place of catchable size fish, which it seldom is in streams.

Despite the generally low survival rates of planted trout, especially in streams, a few often will survive and interbreed with wild trout. Thus, indiscriminate planting of rainbow trout has led to loss through hybridization of many distinctive local populations, not only of rainbow trout but of other closely related species such as golden trout, cutthroat trout, and redband trout. Only in recent years has the aesthetic value of distinctive local populations been recognized and efforts made to preserve the few that are still left.

Another problem of some concern to fisheries managers in California is the long-term decline of steelhead populations. The decline is largely attributable to degradation of the spawning streams through sloppy logging, dewatering, dam construction, and pollution. Hatchery production of young steelhead can compensate in part for the loss of naturally spawned fish but it cannot compensate for the loss of the streams.

References. Anonymous, 1965; Bryan and Larkin, 1972; Butler and Borgeson, 1965; Carlander, 1969; Elliott and Jenkins, 1972; Everest and Chapman, 1972; Fry, 1973; Hart, 1973; Hartman, 1965; Hubbs and Miller, 1948; Jenkins, 1969; Johannes and Larkin, 1961; La Rivers, 1962; Lewis, 1969; McAfee, 1966; MacCrimmon, 1971; Moyle and Nichols, 1973; Needham and Gard, 1959; Northcote, 1966; Schreck and Behnke, 1971; Scott and Crossman, 1973; Shapovalov and Taft, 1954; Snyder, 1933; Wales, 1939.

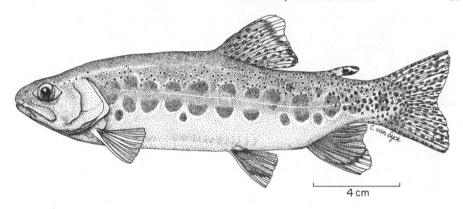

Figure 40. Golden trout, 18 cm SL, Clarence Lake, Fresno County.

Golden Trout, *Salmo aguabonita* Jordan

Systematic note. The systematics, origin, and zoogeography of golden trout are controversial. The latter two topics are covered in the introductory chapter on zoogeography and will not be repeated here. The golden trout was originally described as three separate species: *S. aguabonita*, from the south fork of the Kern River; *S. roosevelti*, from Golden Trout Creek; and *S. whitei*, from the Little Kern River. *S. gairdneri gilberti*, a heavily spotted "golden" trout from the main Kern River was also described (Evermann, 1905), as was *S. rosei*, from Culver Lake.

This naturally complex taxonomic picture was made even more complicated by early (prior to the original descriptions) intrabasin transfers of golden trout from the different streams of the Kern River Basin, and by the introduction of rainbow trout into the basin. Rainbow trout hybridize freely with golden trout. Thus, *S. rosei* is apparently a hybrid between at least two strains of golden trout and not a valid species (Schreck and Behnke, 1971). *S. roosevelti* and *S. aguabonita* have long been recognized as belonging to one taxonomic unit, usually referred to as *S. a. aguabonita*. Schreck and Behnke (1971) and Legendre et al. (1972) present evidence that *S. g. gilberti* and *S. whitei* also should be considered as one subspecies, *S. a. gilberti*. Their findings, however, have not been completely accepted. C. L. Hubbs (pers. comm.) and others consider this complex to be two subspecies, one of rainbow trout (*S. g. gilberti*) and one of golden trout (*S. a. whitei*). Recent studies by Kornblatt (1974) and Gold and Gall (in press) tend to support this view.

Identification. The coloration of golden trout is spectacularly bright. The belly and cheeks are bright red to red orange, the lower sides are bright gold, the central lateral band is red orange, and the back is deep olive green. Usually about 10 parr marks are present, even in adults, centered on the lateral line. Spots are large and concentrated on the dorsal and caudal fins. Body spotting is highly variable but spots are usually scattered across the back with a few below the lateral line. The pectoral, pelvic, and anal fins are orange, the latter fins having white to yellow tips preceded by a black band. The dorsal fin also has a white to orange tip. The following meristic information is derived from Schreck and Behnke (1971): scales in lateral series, 175 to 210; scales above lateral line, 34 to 45; pelvic rays, 8 to 10; gill rakers, 17 to 21; pyloric ceca, 25 to 40; vertebrae, 58 to 61. Basibranchial teeth are absent in pure golden trout (but present in some *gilberti* trout).

Names. Salmo is the Latin word for salmon while *aguabonita* means beautiful water and "is the name of a cascade on Volcano Creek, near which this trout abounds" (Jordan and Evermann, 1896).

Distribution. Golden trout are native only to the upper Kern River Basin, Tulare and Kern counties. Early records indicate that they were present in the basin in the upper main Kern River, the lower Little Kern River, Golden Trout Creek, and the South Fork of the Kern River (Schreck and Behnke, 1971). Even before they were formally described, they were being moved by enthusiastic fishermen to other drainages in the Sierra Nevada. Today they are found in over three hundred high mountain lakes and streams in California, mostly in Fresno and Tulare counties (Anonymous, 1968). They have also been established in mountain waters in a number of other western states and provinces, especially the Rocky Mountain states.

Life History. Golden trout are confined to clear, cold (less than 22°C) mountain lakes and streams above 2,100 m elevation. They seem to have coexisted with Sacramento suckers in parts of their native Kern Basin but they generally do not do well when other salmonids are present. They hybridize with rainbow trout, the rainbow phenotype becoming dominant, and tend to die out when brook trout are introduced into their waters. In a few streams in the Kern Basin, however, they have been able to hold their own against brook trout (J. P. Bartholomew, pers. comm.).

The high mountain habitat of golden trout seems to be related to the development of their brilliant colors. Although the colors may fade dramatically in golden trout kept in hatcheries or planted in lakes, they without doubt have a genetic basis (Needham and Gard, 1959). It is of interest, therefore, to speculate on the adaptive significance of the color patterns, particularly since similar brilliant coloration has evolved independently in other western *Salmo* from high mountain areas: redband trout, Piute cutthroat trout, Gila trout (*S. gilae*), Apache trout (*S. apache*), and Mexican golden trout (*S. chrysogaster*). The usual explanation given is that bright colors make the fish less visible to predators in clear streams with bottoms of bright, rust-colored volcanic rocks. While this may be a partial explanation of the phenomenon, especially in the smaller streams of the upper Kern Basin (W. Evans, pers. comm.), the bottoms of streams to which golden-colored trout are native are not consistently brightly colored. In any case, birds and mammals likely to prey on trout are infrequent in high mountain areas. An alternate explanation is behavioral. Most stream-dwelling trout species assume bright colors during the breeding season. It may be evolutionarily advantageous for the trout (especially males) to temporarily sacrifice some of their cryptic coloration to increase their chances of reproductive success. The brightest colored males tend to be the most attractive to females and have the greatest success defending their breeding territories. Stream-dwelling trout usually defend feeding territories when they are not spawning, but the advantages of being brightly colored are outweighed by the disadvantages of being more visible to predators. Since golden trout evolved in an area where predators were presumably scarce, it would be advantageous for them to retain brilliant colors even when not spawning. The most brightly colored fish would have the greatest success defending feeding territories, and be able to grow faster, increasing their reproductive success by achieving larger sizes and, perhaps, maturity at younger ages.

The food of golden trout is essentially every invertebrate that lives in or falls into their waters. In streams, these are primarily larval and adult aquatic insects, plus a few terrestrial forms. In lakes, their main foods are caddisfly larvae, chironomid midge larvae, and planktonic crustaceans (Curtis, 1934). The stomachs of golden trout, caught by the author from a high mountain lake in July, 1970, contained large caddisfly larvae, with cases, and hundreds of tiny seed shrimp (Ostracoda). The latter organisms were swarming among the beds of rushes that grew close to shore. The ability of golden trout to feed on such microcrustaceans has undoubtedly contributed to their success in mountain lakes.

Growth in golden trout is generally slow, as might be expected considering the low productivity and short growing season of their native waters. There is little published data on their growth in streams, but fish over 25 cm FL or five years of age are rare. In alpine lakes, they live six to seven years, generally reaching 4 to 5 cm FL in their first year, 10 to 15 cm FL in their second, 13 to 23 cm FL in their third, and 21 to 28 cm FL in their fourth (Curtis, 1934; Carlander, 1969). In lightly fished lakes, they will achieve lengths of 35 to 43 cm FL by their seventh year. Occasionally, golden trout will achieve large sizes in lakes. The largest from California (Virginia Lake, Madera County) weighed nearly 4.5 kg, while the largest on record, from Wyoming, weighed nearly 5 kg and was 71 cm TL (McAfee, 1966).

Golden trout become mature in their third or fourth year and spawn when water tempeatures reach 7 to 10°C, usually late June or July. They require gravel riffles in streams for successful spawning. Although spawning has apparently been observed in lakes, it is rarely, if ever, successful and attempts to establish golden trout in lakes without inlets or outlets suitable for spawning have failed (McAfee, 1966). Each female lays 300 to 2,300 eggs, the number depending on the size of the fish ($10.44X$ $FL_{cm}-1290$, according to Curtis, 1934).

The eggs hatch in about twenty days at 14°C. The fry emerge from the gravel at about 25 mm TL, two to three weeks after hatching. Fry from lake populations move into the lake at 46 mm TL (Curtis, 1934).

Status. Golden trout have been declared the official state fish of California and have been accorded high priority for preservation and management. Most populations receive only light angling pressure and can thus maintain themselves with minimal manipulation. A number of lake populations, however, are sustained entirely by annual plants of hatchery fish. In the upper Kern River Basin, special efforts are being made by the California Department of Fish and Game, in cooperation with the U. S. Forest Service and the National Park Service, to preserve the distinct populations of golden trout present in the South Fork of the Kern River and in the Little Kern River. Hopefully, studies underway by a number of scientists will clear up the taxonomic picture.

Despite the considerable publicity golden trout have received in California since their discovery, little work, outside of that of Curtis (1934) and Needham and Vestal (1938), has been done on their life history. In particular there is a need for studies of stream populations, especially those in the upper Kern Basin.

References. Carlander, 1969; Curtis, 1934; McAfee, 1966; R. R. Miller, 1972; Needham and Gard, 1959; Needham and Vestal, 1938; Schreck and Behnke, 1971.

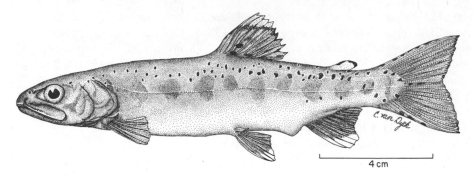

4 cm

Figure 41. Redband trout, 19 cm SL, Sheepheaven Creek, Shasta County.

Redband Trout, *Salmo* sp.

Systematic note. The name redband trout is used to cover a confusing complex of distinctive (or formerly distinctive) trouts that reportedly occur in isolated headwater streams of the McCloud, Pit, Klamath, and Columbia river systems of California, Nevada, and Oregon. R. J. Behnke, who has closely examined this complex, believes that each drainage system has (or had) its own form of redband trout, but that these forms have hybridized with each other in the past and with both native and introduced rainbow trout more recently (pers. comm., 1974). As a result, the forms have not yet been described in formal taxonomic terms although a study of the McCloud population (in Sheepheaven Creek) may lead eventually to such a description.

Redband trout, along with golden trout, presumably are derived from an ancestor that once occupied most of the Sacramento-San Joaquin system but was displaced, through competition and hybridization, by rainbow trout, leaving relict populations in areas isolated by the continuing rise of the Sierra Nevada. Thus, taxonomic arguments can be raised for lumping redband trout with rainbow trout or with golden trout or for describing them as one or more separate species. Whatever classification decision is ultimately accepted by fish taxonomists, it will have to be arbitrary since the taxonomic confusion stems from the evolutionary dynamism of the entire genus *Salmo* in the western United States. In any case, the remaining populations of redband trout are distinct and interesting fishes that deserve to be managed as a unique part of California's native fish fauna.

Identification. The following description, based on unpublished data of R. J. Behnke, refers to the Sheepheaven Creek population. Other populations are similar but have even greater variability due to hybridization with rainbow trout. Redband trout have pale yellow to golden sides crossed by a brick red lateral band. They retain parr marks throughout their lives and are variously spotted. The dorsal, anal, and pelvic fins' are tipped with orange or yellow. They have 153 to 191 scales along the lateral line and 33 to 40 scale rows above it. Gill rakers are 15 to 18; pyloric ceca, 35 to 45; branchiostegal rays, 9 to 10; and pelvic fin rays, 9 to 10 (mostly 9). About half possess basibranchial teeth.

Distribution. Redband trout were originally found in a number of small tributaries to the McCloud River, the Pit River, Goose Lake, and the Upper Klamath River, all in California. Populations also exist in the Owyhee Drainage Basin in Oregon and Nevada (R. J. Behnke, pers. comm.). The only pure population still known to exist in California is in Sheepheaven Creek, Siskiyou County, although attempts are being made by the California Department of Fish and Game to establish Sheepheaven redband trout in a nearby stream previously barren of trout.

Life History. What little is known about redband trout is summarized in Hoopaugh (1974). Sheepheaven Creek (elevation 1,433 m) is a small (flow about 28 1/sec), cold stream that flows in the summer for only about 2 km before sinking into its streambed. The drainage basin was recently logged over, with little effect on the trout populations. The total population of redband trout in Sheepheaven Creek is small; population estimates indicate that there are less than 250 fish greater than 80 mm FL. The largest fish taken was 21 mm FL and was probably four years old. Spawning takes place in late spring.

Status. Most populations of redband trout have lost whatever distinctive characters they once possessed through hybridization with rainbow trout introduced into their isolated streams. The apparent exception is the population, inhabiting the one-mile-long Sheepheaven Creek, which is now being managed as a threatened trout by the California Department of Fish and Game. Because of the small size of the population and because Sheepheaven Creek is entirely on private land, attempts are now being made to establish populations in other creeks. Eventually it is hoped that enough of these populations will be established to assure the continued existence of the species.

References. Behnke, 1972; Hoopaugh, 1974; R. R. Miller, 1972.

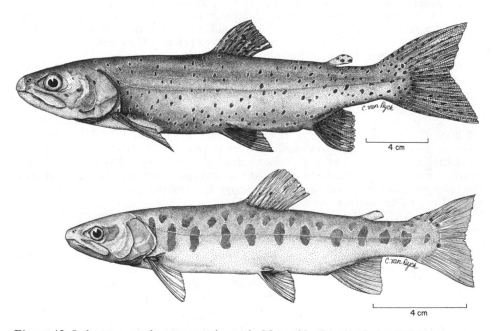

Figure 42. Lahontan cutthroat trout (upper), 25 cm SL, Granite Lake, Trinity County; Piute cutthroat trout (lower), 16 cm SL, Silver King Creek, Alpine County.

Cutthroat Trout, *Salmo clarki* Richardson

Systematic Note. Like the rainbow trout, the cutthroat trout is a highly variable species with numerous populations that have been described in the past as distinct species or subspecies (La Rivers, 1962; Scott and Crossman, 1973). On the opposite extreme, Needham and Gard (1959) have suggested that cutthroat trout and rainbow trout are so similar that they should be lumped together as one species. Three cutthroat trout subspecies are now generally recognized in California: the coast cutthroat, *S. c. clarki*; the Lahontan cutthroat, *S. c. henshawi*; and the Piute cutthroat, *S. c. seleniris*. While the three subspecies are not exactly free of taxonomic controversy, there seems little reason to dispute their validity at the present time.

Identification. Cutthroat trout are heavily marked with black spots and have two yellow to red slashes of pigment on the under side of the lower jaw and basibranchial teeth. The basibranchial teeth can usually be detected by feeling the floor of the "throat" with one finger. It should be noted, however, that the cutthroat slash marks may be faint or absent in young or sea-run cutthroat trout. Coast cutthroat are similar to rainbow trout in overall body color but the spotting is heavier, particularly below the lateral line and on the posterior half of the body. Spots are also frequently present on the anal and paired fins, which otherwise are uniform in color. Lahontan cutthroat are similar to coast cutthroat except that the body tends to be dark olive to reddish yellow and the spots larger and fewer. Piute cutthroat resemble golden trout, with vivid orange, yellow, and white body colors and parr marks retained by the adults. The body and caudal fin are largely without black spots, although there are generally a few on the dorsal and adipose fins. Cutthroat trout tend to have larger mouths (longer maxillary bones) and more slender bodies than rainbow trout. The teeth are well developed in the upper and lower jaws, head and shaft of the vomer, palatines, tongue, and basibranchial bones. The dorsal fin has 9 to 11 major rays; the anal fin, 8 to 12 major rays; pelvic fins, 9 to 10 rays each; and pectoral fins, 12 to 15 rays each. The tail is moderately forked. There are 15 to 28 gill rakers on each arch and 9 to 12 branchiostegal rays. The scales are usually smaller (116 to 230, usually 140 to 200, in the lateral line) than those of rainbow trout.

The parr have 9 to 10 oval parr marks centering on the lateral line that are covered with black speckles dorsally. The interspaces are wider than the parr marks. The fins are generally plain except for a dark leading edge on the dorsal and a few spots on the adipose. The cutthroat marks seldom are visible until the fish exceed 8 cm TL.

Names. Salmo is the ancient Latin name for salmon, while *clarki* is for Captain William Clark, coleader of the Lewis and Clark expedition to the Pacific coast. Synonymies of the scientific nomenclature can be found in La Rivers (1962) and Scott and Crossman (1973). The San Gorgiono trout (described as *Salmo evermanni*) is an extinct population of Lahontan cutthroat that was apparently temporarily established in the upper reaches of the Santa Ana River system following a very early transplant from Lake Tahoe (Benson and Behnke, 1961).

Distribution. Coast cutthroat live in coastal drainage systems from the Eel River, Humboldt County, north to Seward, Alaska. Various interior forms occupy headwater streams of the Missouri, Platte, Colorado, Rio Grande, and Saskatchewan river systems, as well as the Bonneville and Lahontan systems of the Great Basin. In California, Lahontan cutthroat are native to streams and lakes of the Lahontan system, on the east side of the Sierra Nevada. Piute cutthroat are native only to Silver King Creek, Alpine County, but they have been established elsewhere in the Sierra Nevada and the White Mountains.

Life History. Cutthroat trout are ecologically similar to rainbow trout. They are (or were) established in a wide variety of cool waters from large alkaline lakes (e.g., Pyramid Lake, Nevada) to small mountain lakes, from major rivers to small tributaries. Populations in coastal streams are usually anadromous, spending the summers in salt water but winters in fresh water. Coast cutthroat seem to prefer small streams (drainage basins of less than 13 km^2) or streams that have extensive, low-gradient reaches before they enter the sea (Hartman and Gill, 1968). When they are found in stream systems naturally with rainbow trout, coast cutthroat are usually most abundant in the small tributaries and headwaters, while rainbow trout are most abundant in the main streams. The literature on cutthroat trout life history is large (Cope, 1964), so this account is based largely on La Rivers (1962), Carlander (1969), Giger (1972), Scott and Crossman (1973), and McAfee (1966).

Stream-dwelling cutthroat trout are often rather sedentary, and may spend their entire life in less than 20 m of stream (R. B. Miller, 1957). On the other hand, Hanzel (in Armstrong and Morton, 1969) reported movements of wild cutthroat in Montana of over 150 km. Lake and sea-going cutthroat typically make extensive spawning migrations, although coast cutthroat, when in salt water, seldom move far from the estuary of their natal stream.

Like other trout, cutthroat trout defend feeding territories in streams. They feed mostly on drift, and their stomachs typically contain a mixture of terrestrial and aquatic insects. They are opportunistic so, generally, whatever is most abundant in the drift will be most abundant in their stomachs. In lakes, cutthroat trout tend to feed on insects taken at the water's surface or on zooplankton, although if neither is abundant they will feed on bottom-dwelling insect larvae, crustaceans, and snails (Calhoun, 1944; Andrusak and Northcote, 1971). Large trout (over 40 cm FL) will also feed on other fish, especially in large lakes like Tahoe and Pyramid. Coast cutthroat commonly feed on the young of other salmonids. In estuaries, coast cutthroat feed on shrimp and other larger crustaceans as well as on fish. Coast cutthroat feed actively when migrating downstream on their way out to sea but usually do not feed when migrating upstream to spawn (Giger, 1972).

Growth in cutthroat trout varies with the water temperature and the abundance of food organisms. Slowest growth is seen in small mountain streams and lakes, where Lahontan cutthroat will take four years to reach 38 cm FL (450 gm). The same size can be reached in less than two years in Pyramid Lake, Nevada, where temperatures are fairly warm and forage fish are abundant. Present-day Lahontan cutthroat seldom live longer than nine years or reach more than 61 cm TL (2.2 kg), but larger fish were once common in Tahoe and Pyramid lakes. The largest cutthroat trout known, from Pyramid Lake, was over 99 cm TL (18.6 kg). In contrast, Piute cutthroat trout seldom exceed 25 cm TL, as might be expected of trout inhabiting a cold mountain stream. In Oregon, coast cutthroat typically reach 20 to 25 cm FL in two to three years of stream life, feeding mostly on insects. Once they have migrated to salt water, where their main food is fish, their growth rate increases and they reach 35 to 40 cm FL in the next year or so (Giger, 1972). They will live up to eight years, reaching nearly 50 cm FL. Fastest growth in fresh water, for all subspecies, takes place in the spring and early summer.

Maturity is first achieved in their second to fourth year. In Lahontan and Piute cutthroat, spawning takes place between April and early July, while coast cutthroat spawn in the winter months, usually January or February. Both lake-dwelling Lahontan cutthroat and coast cutthroat migrate up streams to spawn, seeking out gravel riffles. Spawners generally home to the same stream and probably the same riffle in which they were hatched. The distances migrated are usually short, but migrations of over 100 km are not unusual. There is some evidence that Lahontan cutthroat trout from Pyramid Lake once moved up the Truckee River into Lake Tahoe (McAfee, 1966), a distance of about 160 km. The immediate stimulus for upstream migration in coast cutthroat is poorly understood, but lake-dwelling Lahontan cutthroat seem to respond to a combination of increasing daylight and increasing stream temperatures, probably moving when temperatures exceed 8 to 10°C. Spawning behavior is similar to that of brown and brook trout. Each female, depending on her size, lays 400 to 4,000 eggs (about 47 eggs per cm of FL). Each fish may spawn up to five times in its lifetime.

The eggs hatch in six to eight weeks, and the fry begin feeding about two weeks after hatching. Coast cutthroat usually spend the first two to three years in the stream, while Lahontan cutthroat tend to move into lakes in the first year. Individuals and populations of both subspecies, however, may spend their entire life cycle in streams.

Status. Coast cutthroat are abundant in the more northern parts of their range but are uncommon (compared to rainbow trout) in northern California streams (DeWitt, 1954), and probably always have been. In any case, the similarity of sea-run cutthroat to the more abundant steelhead rainbow trout means that most of those that are caught go unrecognized by fishermen. Piute cutthroat trout are considered to be a threatened trout by the California Department of Fish and Game because they have hybridized in part with rainbow and cutthroat trout introduced into Silver King Creek. Pure populations still exist in the upper reaches of the creek and efforts are presently underway to eliminate the hybrids. Populations have been established through transplants into Delaney Creek, Madera County, and Cottonwood Creek, Mono County. The former population is in decline, apparently due to competition from brook trout (D. Christensen, pers. comm.). The Cottonwood Creek population seems well established and is currently being studied by D. Wong, a graduate student at California State University, Long Beach. Once the future of this unique form is assured, limited angling will be permitted for it (S. Nicola, pers. comm.).

Lahontan cutthroat are also considered to be a threatened trout by the California Department of Fish and Game. Once widespread in the streams and lakes of the Lahontan system, they have been largely replaced by rainbow trout, brown trout, and brook trout in streams, as well as by lake trout in Lake Tahoe. In streams, they have hybridized extensively with rainbow trout and the rainbow trout phenotype has become dominant, for reasons which are not clear. Possibly, pure rainbow trout are more aggressive than either cutthroat trout or the hybrids and displace them from feeding territories. Not only would this make cutthroat trout and the hybrids more vulnerable to predation, but it would increase the growth rates, and hence the reproductive potential, of rainbow trout.

Competition and predation from introduced lake trout were presumably important factors in the complete elimination of cutthroat trout from Lake Tahoe. However, the cutthroat probably would not have disappeared nearly so quickly (or possibly not at all) had not a commercial fishery at the turn of the century killed a large part of the population. The cutthroat trout of Pyramid Lake, Nevada, were also reduced by commercial fishing but the main cause of their decline was the reduction in flow of the Truckee River, which made it inaccessible for spawning (La Rivers, 1962). They are presently maintained only by the planting of hatchery fish that are not of pure Pyramid Lake stock.

The California Department of Fish and Game, along with other state and federal agencies is presently attempting to locate pure wild populations of Lahontan cutthroat, and to preserve those that are known to exist in tributaries to the Carson, Truckee, and Walker rivers. Transplant sites for the establishment of new populations are also being sought. Thus it appears that at least some stream-adapted genotypes of

Lahontan cutthroat will be saved. However, the genotypes that produced such large fish in lakes Pyramid and Tahoe are gone forever, unless the pure Lahontan cutthroat population that still exists in Independence Lake (Alpine-Sierra counties) is an offshoot of these populations.

References. Andrusak and Northcote, 1971; Benson and Behnke, 1961; Calhoun, 1944; Carlander, 1969; Cope, 1964; DeWitt, 1954; Giger, 1972; Hartman and Gill, 1968; La Rivers, 1962; Lowrey, 1965, 1966; McAfee, 1966; R. B. Miller, 1957; Needham and Gard, 1959; Scott and Crossman, 1973; Sigler and Miller, 1963.

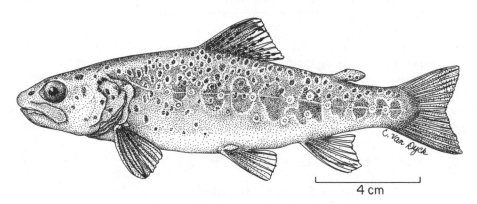

4 cm

Figure 43. Brown trout, 15 cm SL, California.

Brown Trout, *Salmo trutta* Linnaeus

Identification. Brown trout are the only trout in California with both red and black spots on the body. The black spots, which are large and variable in size, are present on the tail (few and often indistinct), adipose fin, dorsal fin, and sides. The red spots are present only on the lower sides. The trout are usually dark to olive brown on the back, shading to yellow brown on the sides, and white to yellow on the belly. Brown trout are slightly heavier bodied than other California trouts, with thicker caudal peduncles. The mouth is large, the maxillary extending beyond the rear margin of the eye. The jaw of spawning males is usually hooked. Well-developed teeth are present in both jaws, as well as on the head and shaft of the vomer, on the palatines, and on the tongue. Basibranchial teeth are absent. The dorsal fin has 12 to 14 major rays; the anal fin, 10 to 12 major rays; the pelvic fins, 9 to 10 rays each; and the pectoral fins, 13 to 14 rays each. The tail is straight-edged in adults but may be slightly forked in young fish. The anal fin is rounded on males but falcate (the rear edge slightly indented) in females. There are 14 to 17 gill rakers on each arch and 9 to 11 branchiostegal rays. The scales are small, 120 to 130 in the lateral line.

Names. *Salmo* is the Latin name for salmon, while *trutta* is the name for trout. Brown trout are often called German brown trout or Loch Leven trout, in reference to the places of origin of the American stocks. The original stocks have been so mixed that it is pointless to call these fish anything but just brown trout.

Distribution. Brown trout are native to Europe and western Asia. Since they are partially anadromous there, they are also found in the British Isles and Iceland. Brown trout were first introduced into North America in 1883. In 1894, eggs of the Loch Leven (Scotland) strain were brought to California and successfully reared, followed by those of the German strain in 1895 (Staley, 1966). They are now present in trout waters throughout the state. They have also become established in much of the United States and Canada, as well as parts of South America, Africa, India, Australia, and New Zealand (MacCrimmon et al., 1970).

Life History. Brown trout, because they are *the* trout of Europe and a favorite sport fish of serious anglers the world over, are perhaps the most studied of the trouts and chars, as is indicated by the accounts of Staley (1966), Frost and Brown (1967), Carlander (1969), and Scott and Crossman (1973). Adult brown trout are largely bottom-oriented pool dwellers but younger, smaller trout are as likely to be found in riffles as in pools. The optimum habitat for brown trout seems to be medium to large sized, slightly alkaline, clear streams with both swift riffles and large, deep pools. They are found, however, in the complete range of trout waters from spring-fed trickles to large lakes. Anadromous brown trout are rare in California (Fry 1973). Temperature is an important factor limiting their distribution. They can survive for short periods of time at temperatures in excess of 27°C but the most rapid growth occurs between 7 and 19°C. They seem to prefer, however, temperatures in the upper half of this range. Vincent and Miller (1969) found that they would not move into the upper reaches of Colorado streams unless water temperatures exceeded 13°C for extended periods of time.

In streams, nonreproducing brown trout are rather sedentary, seldom moving more than a few meters from one spot. Trout less than 25 cm TL set up feeding territories and a dominance hierarchy is usually established among the fish in one area. The largest, most aggressive fish defends the largest territory, which is usually located in one of the best positions in the stream for cover and food availability. Trout larger than 25 cm TL are more mobile and tend to remain under cover (undercut banks, logs, etc.) during the day, coming out to actively pursue prey during the evening. Even these large fish, however, generally patrol rather restricted areas (Jenkins, 1969).

The food of brown trout in streams changes with their size and the season. In general, the smaller the trout, the greater percentage of its diet will be made up of drift organisms, especially terrestrial insects. As the trout grow larger, they tend to spend more time selectively picking aquatic invertebrates from the bottom. Trout over 25 cm TL are active pursuers of large prey, especially other fish (including their own young) and active invertebrates such as crayfish and dragonfly larvae. There are, of course, many exceptions to this general description. In particular, trout of all sizes are prone to feeding on drift during the late summer when the populations of large aquatic insect larvae are reduced. They also feed on emerging aquatic insects when a large hatch is taking place. Most terrestrial insects are taken during the day, although feeding activity (mostly on aquatic organisms) is most intense at dawn and dusk. Active feeding, however, can be observed at nearly any time (Chaston, 1969). In lakes, small brown trout feed heavily on zooplankton, gradually switching first to bottom-dwelling insect larvae (especially chironomid midge larvae) and amphipods, and then (at sizes greater than 25 to 35 cm TL) to fish.

Growth in brown trout is as variable as the waters they inhabit. In California, they reach anywhere from 3 to 8 cm TL (usually 5 to 7 cm TL) in the first year; 7 to 22 cm TL (usually 13 to 16 cm TL) in their second; 13 to 36 cm TL (usually 19 to 28 cm

TL) in their third, and 23 to 45 cm TL (usually 35 to 41 cm TL) in their fourth (Carlander, 1969). Brown trout can reach large sizes: the largest known is a 103 cm TL (18 kg) sea-run individual from Scotland, while the largest recorded from California was a 10.9 kg fish from Regulator Lake (Anonymous, 1964). They can live as long as eighteen years, but the oldest known from California was only nine years old, from Castle Lake. Growth is usually faster in lakes than streams but this does not seem to apply to high alpine situations, where growth is poor in both habitats. Growth is affected by temperature, alkalinity, total dissolved solids, turbidity, population density, and food availability.

Brown trout usually become mature in their second or third year, although a few may wait as long as seven or eight years. Spawning takes place in the fall or winter, commonly in November and December in California. Most brown trout populations require streams with gravel riffles that have pea- to walnut-sized gravel for spawning. The most suitable locations are at the tails of pools, where the water is deeper, the current less turbulent, and cover close by. In some large lakes, successful spawning will occasionally take place on gravel bars close to shore.

The reproductive cycle and spawning behavior of brown trout is described and pictured in detail by Frost and Brown (1967). The initial stimulus for upstream movement to the spawning grounds is often a rise in water level, although selection of the spawning site does not occur until water temperatures have dropped to 6 to 10°C. The redd site is selected by the female and she soon starts a depression by turning on her side and digging with her tail (termed "cutting"). The gravel is moved downstream by the suction created by the upward movement of the tail and by the stream current. The initial cutting attracts a male, who defends the female and redd from other males. The male does not help with the construction of the redd but continually courts the female as she works. Courtship consists of swimming alongside the female and quivering. As the redd becomes deeper, courting becomes more intense. Finally the female sinks into the depression, with her anal fin resting on the bottom, and opens her mouth. The male immediately swims alongside her, quivering violently, mouth open, and releases his sperm as the female releases her eggs. The sperm is frequently visible to the observer for a few seconds as a white cloud on the bottom of the nest.

Following the spawning act, the female begins cutting again above the redd, simultaneously burying the newly fertilized eggs and digging a new redd. The spawning act must be repeated several times since each female normally lays only 100 to 250 eggs in each cut. Each female lays a total of 200 to 21,000 eggs, the number depending in part on her size (about 30 to 40 eggs per cm of FL).

The eggs hatch in four to twenty-one weeks, typically seven to eight weeks, depending on water temperature. The alevins emerge from the gravel and begin feeding three to six weeks later. The fry tend to live in the quiet waters close to shore, among large rocks or under overhanging plants.

Brown trout occasionally hybridize with brook trout, and the sterile offspring are known as tiger trout, after the distinctive banding on their sides.

Status. Brown trout are abundant in over 5,000 km of California streams and in numerous lakes (Staley, 1966). Their presence in the state is a mixed blessing. On the positive side, they provide some of the finest wild-trout angling in California. Their bottom feeding and piscivorous tendencies, coupled with their natural wariness, make them extremely difficult for the inexperienced angler to catch. Thus they can maintain substantial populations of large fish even in heavily fished streams that receive regular plants of rainbow trout. For the experienced angler they can provide much pleasure, if he can just keep the hatchery rainbows off his hook! A number of streams in California (e.g., Hat Creek, Owens River) are now being managed as wild brown trout streams.

On the other hand, brown trout often have a decidedly negative effect on the populations of other fishes, including other trout. In lakes and stream pools, the production of wild, catchable size trout of all species can sometimes be increased considerably by removing large brown trout that subsist mostly on the other fish. Competition and predation from brown trout may be one factor that has contributed to the decline of the Dolly Varden in the McCloud River. They may also have reduced populations of the rare Modoc sucker in Rush Creek, Modoc County, since there is a strong negative correlation between brown trout abundance and Modoc sucker abundance in the stream (Moyle and Marciochi, in press).

References. Anonymous, 1964; Carlander, 1969; Chaston, 1969; Frost and Brown, 1967; Fry, 1973; Jenkins, 1969; MacCrimmon et al., 1970; Moyle and Marciochi, in press; Staley, 1966; Scott and Crossman, 1973; Vincent and Miller, 1969.

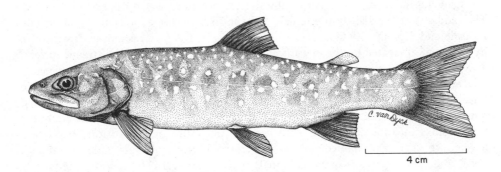

4 cm

Figure 44. Interior Dolly Varden, 16 cm SL, McCloud River, Shasta County. CAS 19889.

Interior Dolly Varden, *Salvelinus sp.*

Systematic Note. This species is in the process of being redescribed by T. Cavender of Ohio State University who provided the following information. It was originally described under a number of names: *Salmo (Salvelinus) spectabilis, bairdi, parkei, campbelli,* and others. It was then lumped with the coast Dolly Varden, but often treated as a subspecies, *Salvelinus malma parkei* or *S. malma spectabilis.* Furthermore, *S. malma* has been lumped in the past with the arctic char, *S. alpinus,* although the evidence now available seems to favor keeping the two species complexes separate (Scott and Crossman, 1973). In recent years, there has been a trend to once again recognize distinctive interior populations of Dolly Varden from Asia and North America, and a number of forms have been described or redescribed. However, the systematics of the Dolly Varden group is complex and is far from being settled (Behnke, 1972).

Identification. The interior Dolly Varden is similar to the coast Dolly Varden exept: the head is broader and longer, the head length going into the standard length 3.5 to 4.1X; the branchiostegal rays are 13 to 14 per side; the gill rakers average 17 per arch with visible teeth on the anterior margin of each raker; there is a fleshy nob at the tip of the lower jaw that fits into a notch on the top of the upper jaw; and the basibranchial teeth are in one row (T. Cavender, pers. comm.). The jaws are well developed, with strong teeth. The fish are olive green with small yellowish spots on the back and small, but conspicuous red spots on the sides. There are no black spots on the body and the fins are free of any spotting except for a few yellow spots on the base of the tail. The leading edges of the paired and anal fins are white or cream colored.

Names. Salvelinus is an ancient Scandinavian word for char. The name Dolly Varden has an interesting origin which was recounted to the author in a letter (March 24, 1974) from Mrs. Valerie Masson-Gomez:

"My grandmother's family operated a summer resort at Upper Soda Springs on the Sacramento River just north of the present town of Dunsmuir. She lived there all her life and related to us in her later years her story about the naming of the Dolly Varden trout. She said that some fishermen were standing on the lawn at Upper Soda Springs looking at a catch of the large trout from the McCloud River that were called "calico trout" because of their spotted, colorful markings. They were saying that the trout should have a better name. My grandmother, then a young girl of 15 or 16, had been reading Charles Dickens' *Barnaby Rudge* in which there appears a character named Dolly Varden; also the vogue in fashion for women at that time (middle 1870s) was called "Dolly Varden," a dress of sheer figured muslin worn over a bright-colored petticoat. My grandmother had just gotten a new dress in that style and the red-spotted trout reminded her of her printed dress. She suggested to the men looking down at the trout, "Why not call them 'Dolly Varden'?" They thought it a very appropriate name and the guests that summer returned to their homes (many in the San Francisco Bay area) calling the trout by this new name. David Starr Jordan, while at Stanford University, included an account of this naming of the Dolly Varden Trout in one of his books."

In Montana and Idaho, interior Dolly Varden are commonly called bull trout.

Distribution. Interior Dolly Varden are found in California only in the McCloud River, Shasta County. Since similar disjunct populations are also found in some tributaries to the Klamath River in Oregon and in the upper reaches of the Snake River in Idaho and Nevada (Behnke, 1972; T. Cavender, pers. comm.), they have apparently enjoyed a wider distribution in this region in the past. They are still widely distributed in the upper Columbia and Saskatchewan river systems in Idaho, Montana, and Alberta.

Life History. Little information is available on the biology of the McCloud River population of Dolly Varden (Wales, 1939), so most of the information summarized here is from Montana and Idaho populations (Armstrong and Morton, 1969; Carlander, 1969; C. J. Brown, 1971). Ecologically, Dolly Varden are similar to brown trout. They prefer to live on the bottom in deep pools of rivers and their larger tributary streams. They can also do well in large coldwater lakes and reservoirs (e.g., Flathead Lake and Hungry Horse Reservoir in Montana), although in California they do not seem to have been able to maintain populations in either McCloud or Shasta reservoirs, the two to which they have had access.

Young interior Dolly Varden, which occur more in riffles and smaller streams than the adults, feed heavily on aquatic insects. Much of their food may be taken as drift, but much is probably also captured on the bottom. Interior Dolly Varden over 25 cm

TL feed primarily on fish, including other salmonid species and their own young. Frogs, snakes, mice, and ducklings have also been found in their stomachs. Typically, Dolly Varden lie in wait underneath a log or ledge and then dash out to grab passing fish. Feeding is probably most intense in the evening and early morning, but I have watched Dolly Varden in a Montana stream capture small cutthroat trout at midday. Coast Dolly Varden will feed extensively on salmon fry, loose salmon eggs, and dead salmon carcasses, so it is likely that the interior form does so as well. The chinook salmon that spawned in the McCloud River prior to the construction of Shasta Dam may once have been a major, though seasonal, source of food.

Interior Dolly Varden grow slowly in most situations. In Montana, they typically reach 8 cm SL in their first year, 14 cm SL in their second, 20 cm SL in their third, 28 cm SL in their fourth, 36 cm SL in their fifth, and 43 cm SL in their sixth (C. J. Brown, 1971). The largest on record was 103 cm TL (14.5 kg), from Lake Pend Oreille, Idaho. The largest confirmed Dolly Varden from the McCloud River was 66 cm TL (3.4 kg), although one from McCloud Reservoir weighed 4.1 kg (Fry, 1973). A fish that lived for nineteen years in the Montana Shasta hatchery weighed 6.1 kg at the time of death (McAfee, 1966).

Dolly Varden spawn in their fourth or fifth year. They usually migrate upstream to spawn in gravel riffles of small, clear tributary streams. Migrations of over 150 km are not unusual. Spawning takes place in late summer or fall, apparently in September and October in the McCloud River. Spawning behavior is similar to that of brook trout (Needham and Vaughn, 1952). Each female, depending on her size, lays 1,000 to 9,000 eggs (Brunson, 1952). Young Dolly Varden generally spend the first two to four years of their lives in the small spawning streams.

Status. Interior Dolly Varden are now a common and prized gamefish in Montana and Idaho, but for a long time they were held in low regard by fishermen and fisheries managers because of their tendency to prey on other salmonids. The isolated populations in the southernmost parts of their range, in Oregon, Nevada, and California, are doing poorly. The McCloud River population, unique because of its extreme southern location, is either extinct or close to it. There have been no reliable records of the capture of a Dolly Varden from the McCloud River since 1968. An intensive survey of the McCloud River and its tributaries in the summer of 1974 by the author and three graduate students (J. Sturgess, W. Tippetts, and D. Alley) failed to produce any Dolly Varden. Efforts to collect them from McCloud and Shasta reservoirs have also been unsuccessful (D. Hoopaugh, pers. comm.).*

It is indeed a pity that the only population of Dolly Varden in California has been allowed to disappear for they were once abundant and much sought after. Their existence was probably one of the reasons much of the land along the McCloud was bought up in the late 1800s by private fishing clubs. The clubs maintained the river and its immediate watershed in pristine condition, assuring that the Dolly Varden would maintain its populations. Unfortunately, the construction of Shasta Dam in 1944 caused the lower reaches to be flooded by the reservoir and the construction of McCloud Diversion Dam created a block in the upper reaches. The decline of the Dolly Varden is probably due to a number of factors working in concert: inundation of habitat; upstream extension of the range of potential competitors, such as squawfish,

*In late July, 1975, we confirmed the identity of a large (48 cm SL) angler-caught interior Dolly Varden from the McCloud River. A second fish (52 cm SL) was caught and released by J. Sturgess two weeks later. The California Department of Fish and Game is now surveying potential spawning streams to get more of an idea of population size and to see if fish can be captured for artificial propagation.

caused by the flooding of barriers and the stabilization of flows; elimination of the runs of chinook salmon, which may have deprived the piscivorous Dolly Varden of a yearly influx of enough protein to maintain the population; and the blocking of upstream spawning migrations. In addition, the introduction of the ecologically similar brown trout may have contributed to the decline. Brown trout can reproduce at younger ages and hence have greater reproductive potential. The stabilization of stream flows by McCloud Dam may have created conditions that favored brown trout over Dolly Varden.

References. Armstrong and Morton, 1969; Behnke, 1972; C. J. Brown, 1971; Brunson, 1952; Carlander, 1969; McAfee, 1966; Needham and Vaughn, 1952; Wales, 1939.

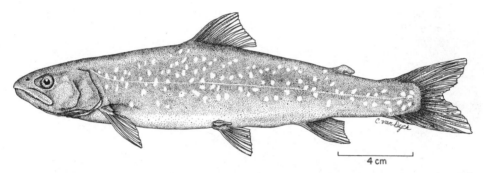

4 cm

Figure 45. Coastal Dolly Varden, 21 cm SL, Alaska.

Coast Dolly Varden
Salvelinus malma (Walbaum)

Identification. Dolly Varden tend to be less deep bodied than other California trouts. The head length goes into the standard length, 4.1 to 4.5X (T. Cavender, pers. comm.). The mouth is large, usually reaching past the posterior margin of the eye, with well-developed teeth in the jaws, on the tongue, and roof of the mouth. The basibranchial teeth (located on the floor of the gill chamber) are usually in more than one row. There are 11 to 12 branchiostegal rays on each side and fewer than 17 gill rakers on each gill arch. Visible teeth are present on the dorsal and ventral surfaces of the gill rakers, but absent from the inner (middle) surface (T. Cavender, pers. comm.). The dorsal fin has 10 to 12 major rays; the anal fin, 9 to 11 major rays; the pelvics, 9 to 11 rays; and the pectorals, 14 to 16 rays. There are 105 to 142 scales along the lateral line. The color patterns of coast Dolly Varden are variable, but usually they are dark olive green on the back, paler on the sides, and white on the belly. There are yellow to orange spots on the back, red spots on the sides, and few or no spots of any color on the fins. The leading edge of the paired fins is creamy or white, often followed by a thin, black line.

The parr have 8 to 12 irregular parr marks, the width of the marks being greater than the width of the light areas between them. In fish less than 8 cm SL the parr marks may appear as irregular blotches (Scott and Crossman, 1973). The sides are finely speckled below the lateral line. The fins lack distinctive spotting.

Names. Malma is the vernacular name for Dolly Varden in the Kamchatka Peninsula. For other names see interior Dolly Varden.

Distribution. Coast Dolly Varden are known from California only from a few specimens collected in the late 1800s from the McCloud River (T. Cavender, pers. comm.). An occasional fish may stray into the Klamath River or other northcoast streams, but there are no known records of this. They are common in coastal streams from northern Oregon north along the Pacific coast to the Seward Peninsula, Alaska, and in Asia, from the Anadyr River, USSR, to the Yalu River, Korea.

Life History. Coast Dolly Varden usually move out from their stream system into the estuary in the spring, spend the summer there or in nearby coastal regions, and then move back up into the stream to spend the winter. Other aspects of their life history in fresh water are similar to those of the interior Dolly Varden (see Armstrong and Morton, 1969; Scott and Crossman, 1973).

Status. There are no recent records of coast Dolly Varden from California, but they were probably never very common in the state. They are presented in this summary mostly to contrast them with the interior form.

References. Armstrong and Morton, 1969; McPhail and Lindsey, 1970; Scott and Crossman, 1973.

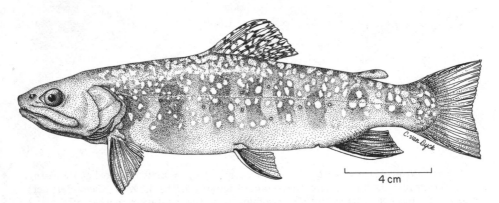

4 cm

Figure 46. Brook trout, 19 cm SL, First Lake, Inyo County.

Brook Trout, *Salvelinus fontinalis* (Mitchill)

Identification. Brook trout are distinguished from other trout by the combination of dark olive green back with lighter colored wavy lines (vermiculations), red spots on the sides surrounded by blue halos, and white edges on the pectoral, pelvic, and anal fins. The mouth is large and slightly oblique with the maxillary extending past the posterior margin of the eye. Teeth are present in both jaws, on the head of the vomer, and on the tongue and palatine bones, but absent from the shaft of the vomer and basibranchial bones. There are 110 to 132 scales in the lateral line, 10 to 14 rays in the dorsal fin, 9 to 12 in the anal fin, 11 to 14 in the pectoral fins, and 8 to 10 in the pelvic fins. Spawning males are deep bodied with hooked lower jaws (kype), while the females develop a protruding genital papilla. Both sexes may become brightly colored when spawning, with dusky to black bellies, red sides, and red lower fins. Young fish have 8 to 12 wide parr marks, some as wide as the eye, and usually a few red, yellow, or blue spots.

Names. Brook trout are frequently called eastern brook trout in California and speckled trout in Canada. Brook char would actually be a better name, since most members of the genus *Salvelinus* are called chars while most members of the genus *Salmo* are called trout. When Mitchell described the species in 1815, however, from a stream in New York, he placed it in the genus *Salmo*, from which it was removed in 1878 by D. S. Jordan. *Salvelinus* is the Latinized version of an ancient Scandinavian word for char while *fontinalis* means living in springs.

Distribution. Brook trout are native to the northern half of the eastern United States and to eastern Canada. A few populations are native as far south as Georgia, in Appalachian mountain streams. The first introductions to California were 6,000 trout brought in by the California Fish Commission in 1872. Between 1872 and 1879 thousands of eggs were imported from New Hampshire and Wisconsin, to be raised in the hatchery at Berkeley. By 1890 they were being raised in large numbers and had been distributed throughout the state (McAfee, 1966). They are now established in mountain (mostly Sierra Nevada) streams and lakes from the San Bernardino Mountains north to the Oregon border. Only a few populations exist in coastal streams. They are also widely distributed in mountainous regions of the western United States, as well as South America, Asia, New Zealand, and Europe (MacCrimmon and Campbell, 1969).

Life History. Brook trout are fish of clear, cold lakes and streams. Despite their continuous and widespread planting throughout California, populations have become established mostly in small, spring-fed headwater streams and in isolated mountain lakes. These are the coldest of California's trout waters, so it is not surprising to find that brook trout are among the most cold tolerant of salmonids, feeding at temperatures as low as 1°C (Elliott and Jenkins, 1972). They seem to prefer temperatures of 14 to 19°C but can survive temperatures up to 26°C, if acclimated to them (Carlander, 1969). However, growth is poor or nonexistent at temperatures much above 19°C.

In streams, brook trout often hold territories (or the partial territories described by Jenkins, 1969) which they defend against all other trout, including individuals of other species. Such territories are generally located behind rocks that break the current, permitting the trout to stay in back eddies without expending much energy. A trout holding a territory has exclusive rights to the invertebrates that drift over it or live in it. In lakes, brook trout tend to swim about as individuals, schooling only when alarmed. However, faceplate observations in Chiquito Lake, Madera County (elevation 1,700 m) during August, 1973, showed that they will congregate in large numbers over springs, presumably attracted to the lower water temperatures (J. P. Bartholomew, pers. comm.).

Brook trout in streams feed mainly on terrestrial insects and aquatic insect larvae. Both types of food are taken primarily as drift, on or close to the surface of the water. Brook trout are not particularly selective in their feeding, but concentrate on whatever organisms are most abundant. They also do some bottom feeding, indicated by the fact that 20 percent of their summer diet in Sagehen Creek is sculpins (Dietsch, 1959). The diet of brook trout in lakes is similar to the stream diet, except that young trout feed heavily on zooplankton and large trout feed more on fish. Feeding in both lakes and streams has definite daily and seasonal rhythms. Brook trout will feed any time there is sufficient light to see their prey but most intensive feeding occurs in the evening, when insects are most active, and in early morning. In mountain lakes, some feeding takes place under the ice in winter, mostly on aquatic insect larvae, zooplankton, and molluscs, but the amount consumed is small compared to summer feeding (Elliott and Jenkins, 1972). There is also frequently a period in midsummer when the pace of feeding slackens due to high water temperatures. This is particularly noticeable in shallow "meadow" lakes and in small streams.

Growth in brook trout is highly dependent on length of the growing season, water temperature, population density, and availability of food, although other factors, such as water chemistry, the presence of other trout species, heredity, and fishing pressure also frequently affect growth. In California the fastest growth occurs in lakes and streams of moderate elevation that do not contain large populations either of brook trout or of other fishes. In such situations brook trout will reach 15 cm TL by the end of their first year, 18 to 20 cm TL by the end of their second year, and 23 to 25 cm TL by the end of their third year. Somewhat slower growth, however, is typical of most California populations, so the trout seldom exceed 30 cm TL (340 gm). The largest brook trout from California, caught in 1932 from Silver Lake, Mono County, was over 60 cm TL and weighed 4.4 kg. On the opposite end of the size spectrum are brook trout from Bunny Lake, Mono County. Here, poor growing conditions have produced fish that are only 24 to 28 cm TL even though they are over twenty years old (N. Reimers, pers. comm., 1974). The Bunny Lake trout are the oldest brook trout on record from anywhere. Brook trout that live longer than four or five years are rare.

Accompanying this short life span is a generally early age of maturity. Male brook trout may spawn at the end of their first summer of life, at less than 10 cm TL, while females may mature at the end of their second summer, at 11 to 12 cm TL. It is more common however, for the males to mature in their second or third year, at 12 to 15 cm TL, and females to mature in their third or fourth year, at 15 to 20 cm TL.

Brook trout are fall spawners, but the specific time depends on water temperatures. Usually they spawn in California from mid-September to early January, at water temperatures of 4 to 11°C. However, some reproductive activity was observed in Frying Pan Lake, a high-altitude lake in Madera County, in mid-August, when water temperatures were considerably higher (J. P. Bartholomew, pers. comm.).

Spawning sites are chosen by females, who seek out areas with the following characteristics, in approximate order of importance: upwelling through the bottom; water temperatures colder than the surrounding water; pea- to walnut-sized gravel; and nearby cover. Thus the preferred site for a redd construction is a gravel-bottomed spring in a stream, close to an undercut bank or log. Such a site presumably assures maximum egg survival. Since the upwelling and the coarse gravel provide constant flow around the eggs, the cold, constant temperatures slow development so the eggs will not hatch before spring, and the cover offers protection from predators for the brilliantly colored spawners. Frequently one or more of the ideal site characteristics may be missing from water where brook trout are established. They will then spawn in suboptimal areas and enough eggs usually will survive to assure continuance of the population. Thus brook trout have been observed spawning in gravel riffles, sandy-bottomed springs, and gravel-bottomed shallows of lakes. Their adaptability to lake conditions in particular has permitted brook trout to main populations in mountain lakes that lack the accessible inlets or outlets most other salmonids require.

Once a female has chosen a spawning site, she begins to dig the redd by turning on her side and shoving up gravel with rapid movements of her tail. Usually this behavior does not begin unless there are males in the vicinity. The males are attracted to the digging female and one quickly becomes dominant and defends the redd site against all other males. Often redds are located in territories already defended by males. The female chases away other females although the male will also perform this task on occasion. As the female digs, the male courts constantly by swimming alongside her, nudging and quivering. When the redd is complete (the size depends on the size of the female), the female swims slowly to the bottom of the redd and the male quickly swims alongside her, quivering. Together they swim over the bottom of the redd, releasing eggs and sperm simultaneously, the milt visible as a white cloud. The female almost immediately begins to sweep gravel over the eggs with her tail. This new digging activity covers the newly spawned eggs and serves to start a new redd just upstream from the old one. Since only 15 to 60 eggs are laid at one time and since wild brook trout females contain anywhere from 50 to 2,700 eggs, each female has to repeatedly dig new redds. In California, the average fecundity seems to be between 200 and 600 (McAfee, 1966). Males also spawn repeatedly, usually with more than one female, and females frequently switch mates between spawnings. Spawning activity can occur at any time of the day or night but tends to peak in the early morning or at dusk.

Because the eggs have to overwinter at low water temperatures, development time is long, usually 100 to 144 days at water temperatures of 2 to 5°C. At 13°C, however, development only takes about 35 days (McAfee, 1966). For the first three to four weeks after hatching, the alevins remain in the gravel in late April and May, gradually becoming more active as the yolk sac is absorbed and the water warms up. The fry in streams move into the shallow edges, among emergent plants, or into the back waters of pools where they feed on small crustaceans. In lakes, they move into shallow water as well, concentrating in areas somewhat protected from wave action.

Brook trout occasionally hybridize in the wild with brown trout, producing offspring known as tiger trout, a name which seems to fit both the hybrid's striped color pattern and its voracious feeding habits. Such hybrids are usually sterile. In hatcheries, brook trout have been crossed with both rainbow trout and lake trout. The brook trout-lake trout cross has produced the splake trout, a fertile hybrid which has been stocked in a number of lakes in the eastern United States and Canada.

Status. Brook trout are the principal species of gamefish in over 1,000 lakes and 2,200 km of stream in California (McAfee, 1966). In most of these waters their populations are self-sustaining. Only small numbers are still raised in California hatcheries, compared to the number of rainbow trout raised. This has not always been the case. In the 1890s and early 1900s large numbers were raised and planted, many in the fishless waters of the high Sierras. The planting was done by fisheries workers, foresters, and laymen enthusiastic about the beautiful colors, edibility, and angling qualities of brook trout but unfortunately ignorant of their biology. Although they are the only trout species that will perpetuate itself in many mountain lakes without tributaries for spawning, they also tend to overpopulate these lakes, resulting in large numbers of small trout barely worth fishing for. Part of the problem may be caused by the inability of larger fish to survive the long winters after using their reserves for spawning. Thus, a common management practice for brook trout lakes that do have tributaries suitable for spawning is to poison out the brook trout and then plant rainbow or golden trout.

In streams brook trout are sometimes a problem because they can compete with native trouts, even displacing some of the rarer forms. In Long Canyon Creek, Tulare County, brook trout have almost completely replaced golden trout. However, in nearby creeks golden trout have managed to hold their own, outnumbering brook trout by ten to one (J. P. Bartholomew, pers. comm.).

Detailed suggestions for managing brook trout in California can be found in McAfee (1966).

References. Carlander, 1969; Dietsch, 1959; Elliott and Jenkins, 1972; Evermann and Bryant, 1919; Hale and Hilden, 1969; MacCrimmon and Campbell, 1969; McAfee, 1966; Moyle, 1969; Reimers, 1958.

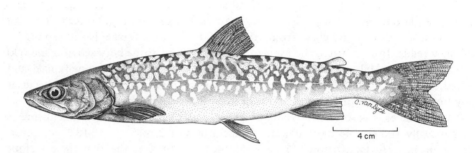

Figure 47. Lake trout, 23 cm SL, Lake Tahoe, Placer County.

Lake Trout, *Salvelinus namaycush* (Walbaum)

Identification. Lake trout can be readily recognized by their deeply forked tail with pointed lobes, and by their color pattern of irregular white spots on a background of light green to grey that covers the entire body, including the head and fins. The spots may be obscured if the trout has assumed a silvery color overall. There may be a pale white border on the leading edges of the paired and anal fins. Lake trout are heavy bodied. The head is broad and about 25 percent of the standard length. The mouth is large, the maxillae extending past the posterior margin of the eye. Well-developed teeth are present on the jaws, head of the vomer, palatines, tongue, and basibranchial bones. There are 16 to 26 gill rakers per arch and 10 to 14 branchiostegal rays on each side. The dorsal fin has 8 to 10 major rays; the anal fin, 8 to 10 major rays; the pelvic fins, 8 to 11 rays; and the pectoral fins, 12 to 17 rays. The scales are small, 116 to 138 in the lateral line.

Parr have 7 to 12 irregular parr marks which are equal to or narrower than the interspaces in width. The fins are without color and the back has small, irregular white spots.

Names. Lake trout are often called mackinaw trout by California fishermen. Taxonomists sometimes place lake trout in a distinct genus, *Cristivomer*, to separate them from the rest of the chars, *Salvelinus* (Scott and Crossman, 1973). A synonomy of the scientific nomenclature is given in La Rivers (1962). *Namaycush* is an Indian name for this species. For other names, see brook trout.

Distribution. Lake trout are native to most of the interior of Canada, coastal drainages of Alaska (except the Yukon River), and the Great Lakes and St. Lawrence drainages of the United States (Scott and Crossman, 1973). Relict populations are present in some Montana lakes (C. J. Brown, 1971). They have been widely introduced into deep, cold lakes in the United States, New Zealand, Sweden, South America, and probably elsewhere. They were first introduced into California (Lake Tahoe) in 1885 or 1886, and a number of subsequent plants assured that they became established. They are present in California only in Tahoe, Donner, Fallen Leaf, and Stony Ridge lakes, all in the Tahoe Basin (McAfee, 1966).

Life History. Because lake trout are the most important gamefish in Lake Tahoe (Cordone and Frantz, 1966), their life history has been extensively investigated in the lake (R. G. Miller, 1951; Hanson and Wickwire, 1967; Hanson and Cordone, 1967; Frantz and Cordone, 1970). Numerous investigations carried out elsewhere are summarized in McAfee (1966) and Scott and Crossman (1973).

Lake trout ordinarily inhabit the deep, cold waters of lakes, although in the more northern parts of their range they may also live in shallow water and in rivers. In Lake Tahoe, they are usually found deeper than 30 m and have been collected as deep as 430 m. In spring and fall, however, they may move into shallow water to feed. They are one of the least tolerant salmonids to high temperatures, preferring water less than 13°C and dying if it becomes much warmer than 23°C. Their salinity tolerance is also low for a salmonid: 11 to 13 ppt is the maximum they can withstand. Lake trout dwell on or close to the bottom. A number of them may concentrate around a deep reef or other topographic feature but they exhibit little social behavior outside the breeding season.

The diet of Lake Tahoe lake trout changes with the size of the fish as well as with the season of the year (Frantz and Cordone, 1970). Trout less than 13 cm FL feed mostly (91 percent by weight) on zooplankton (primarily *Daphnia pulex*) but also take chironomid midge larvae and pupae. Zooplankton continues to be important (33 percent by weight) to trout between 13 and 25 cm FL but Piute sculpins are the main item in the diet (56 percent). As the trout increase in size, zooplankton cease to be of much importance in the diet and they start preying on virtually every available fish species in the lake and, to a lesser extent, on crayfish (9 to 12 percent of the diet of trout over 38 cm FL). Piute sculpin are the most common species preyed on by trout 25 to 50 cm FL, although they also consume Tahoe suckers, tui chubs, and mountain whitefish. For trout over 50 cm FL, the favorite prey is Tahoe sucker (45 percent), followed by other trout species (17 percent) and mountain whitefish (11 percent). Very few Lahontan redside, speckled dace, or kokanee salmon are taken by lake trout of any size, reflecting the usual restriction of the trout to bottom habitats in deep water. They also take surprisingly small numbers of their own young. Feeding activity is most intense during the spring and fall months.

Growth in Lake Tahoe is slow even for lake trout, which is a slow-growing species in general (Hanson and Cordone, 1967). The trout, however, are long lived (up to seventeen years in Tahoe, up to forty-one years elsewhere) so they can achieve large sizes (over 1 m FL and 9.1 kg in Tahoe, and 1.26 m and 28.6 kg in Lake Athabasca, Saskatchawan). In Lake Tahoe, the average fork lengths for ages one through ten are, respectively, 12, 18, 25, 32, 38, 43, 48, 53, 58, and 62 cm. This pattern of growth has remained relatively constant during the forty years records have been kept. Most growth takes place in June through September. It does not cease in the winter but only slows down.

Lake trout in Lake Tahoe become mature for the first time in their fifth through eleventh year, but spawn every year thereafter (Hanson and Wickwire, 1967). They spawn from mid-September to mid-November in deep water (but less than 37 m), over bottoms covered with rubble and boulders. Lake trout are unique among North American chars, trout, and salmon in that they do not build redds or defend breeding territories. Instead, the males arrive first in the breeding area and sweep the rocks clean of silt and debris by fanning with their fins or rubbing with their bodies. Most spawning takes place at night. Each female spawns with one or more males simultaneously, after a brief courtship ceremony. The fertilized eggs fall between the crevices of the rocks and are left unattended by the adults. In Lake Tahoe, each female lays an average of 3,400 eggs, with a range of 900 to 11,500. The number of eggs laid depends in part on the size of the female.

The eggs hatch in four to six months, and the fry remain among the rocks for the first month or so. There is little information available on their ecology for the next one to two years, although it is generally assumed they continue to live on the bottom in deep water.

Status. Lake trout are a well-established and popular game-fish with self-sustaining populations in the Tahoe Basin. Most are taken by trolling with bait and lures close to the bottom in deep water. The specialized nature of the fishery makes it a stable one and there is no evidence yet of overharvest. Their slow growth rate, late age of maturity, and vulnerability to trolling, however, does make lake trout susceptible to overfishing so the populations must be monitored.

It is doubtful that lake trout will ever be planted in California outside the Tahoe Basin. The few additional lakes to which they might be suited already have fisheries for other salmonids over which lake trout would have few, if any, advantages. Indeed, lake trout may have been one of the main reasons Lahontan cutthroat, which they replaced ecologically, are now extinct in Lake Tahoe. Presumably, the combination of competition and predation from lake trout made it impossible for the cutthroat trout to recover from the ravages of the turn-of-the-century commercial fishery.

References. Cordone and Frantz, 1966; Frantz and Cordone, 1970; Hanson and Cordone, 1967; Hanson and Wickwire, 1967; La Rivers, 1962; McAfee, 1966; Scott and Crossman, 1973.

Smelt Family, Osmeridae

Smelts are small, silvery fishes, with adipose fins that both show their close relationship to salmonid fishes and distinguish them from similar but distantly related fishes, such as silversides (family Atherinidae). McAllister (1963) characterized smelt as elegant and tasty, many of them having a "curious cucumber odor." McPhail and Lindsey (1970), however, noted that at least one writer has labeled this odor as being that of putrid cucumbers. Smelt are also characterized by having teeth in the jaws, no axillary processes, 8 rays in the pelvic fins, and adhesive, demersal eggs. Because each smelt species is rather variable, but at the same time similar to other species, considerable confusion exists in the literature as to the identity of many populations. McAllister's 1963 revision of the family has cleared up much of the confusion and should be consulted by anyone seriously working with smelt.

The origin of the word smelt is not known but it is tempting to relate it either to smell, for obvious reasons, or to smolt, the silvery immature stage of salmon. Both relationships are doubtful since a Latin version of the word has been around since at least the eighth century and similar words are present in a number of Germanic languages.

The tastiness of smelt has made them much sought after for food while their tendency to congregate in large numbers to spawn in streams or along beaches has made the seeking easy. They are today probably more important economically as sport fish than as commercial fish, at least in North America. They give much pleasure to masochistic fishermen, who plunge into freezing surf and cold rivers to scoop them up with dip nets. Although best when eaten fresh, they were formerly dried in large numbers. Dried eulachon, which have high oil content, were burned as candles by Indians.

Smelt are almost always associated with coastal regions, in both fresh and salt water, in subarctic to temperate zones of the northern hemisphere. Species may be marine, freshwater, anadromous, or estuarine in habit. Some anadromous species have landlocked populations. One such population of rainbow smelt (*Osmerus eperlanus*) has become established recently in the Great Lakes, where it forms the basis of a popular sport and commercial fishery. The Sacramento-San Joaquin Delta is particularly rich in smelt, with large resident populations of two species, longfin smelt and Delta smelt. Both species are still abundant, despite changes in water quality and flow.

Because of their small size and pelagic habits, various species of smelt have been introduced as forage fish into large lakes and reservoirs. In California, the Japanese subspecies of the Delta smelt has been introduced successfully into a number of reservoirs. Where the introductions were successful, gamefishes have been found to prey on the smelt. However, considering the fact that smelt are highly predaceous despite their small size, surprisingly few studies have been made evaluating the effects of introduced populations on zooplankton, larval fishes, and the growth of adult gamefishes.

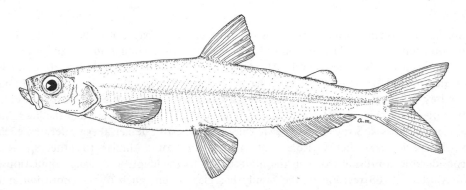

Figure 48. Delta smelt, 8.3 cm SL, Sacramento-San Joaquin Delta.

Delta Smelt, *Hypomesus transpacificus* McAllister

Systematic note. H. transpacificus was originally considered to be the same species as *H. olidus*, the pond smelt. Hamada (1961) realized that the two species were distinct but ran into some nomenclatural difficulties: he considered the present *H. transpacificus* to be *H. olidus* and the present *H. olidus* to be a new species, *H. sakhalinus.* McAllister (1963) clarified matters by redescribing *H. olidus* and describing and naming *H. transpacificus*, with Japanese (*nipponensis*) and California (*transpacificus*) subspecies. Thus, in the Japanese literature, most references to *H. olidus* are in fact to *H.t. nipponensis* while, in the American literature, references to *H. olidus* in the Delta are to *H.t. transpacificus. H. olidus* does not occur in California waters. To further confuse the literature on *Hypomesus*: (1) some Russian systematists now regard the two *H. transpacificus* subspecies as full species (D. E. McAllister, pers. comm.) and (2) the only other species in the genus, *H. pretiosus* (surf smelt), is also occasionally confused with *H. olidus*. (Surf smelt occasionally occur in California estuaries.)

Identification. Delta smelt are slender bodied, characterized by a small, flexible mouth with a maxilla that does not extend past the middle of the eye. They lack strong concentric striations on the gill covers. The pectoral fins, when pressed against the body, reach less than two-thirds of the way to the pelvic fin bases. The lateral line is incomplete but there are 53 to 60 scales in the lateral series. The number of dorsal rays is 9 to 10; pelvic rays, 8; pectoral rays, 10 to 12; anal rays, 15 to 17; gill rakers on the first arch, 27 to 33, pyloric ceca, 4 to 5; and branchiostegal rays, 7. The orbit width goes into the head length 3.5 to 4.0X, while the longest anal ray goes 2.2 to 2.3X into the head length. There are small, pointed teeth on the upper and lower jaws. The lining of the gut cavity is pale with a few speckles. In life, Delta smelt have a steely blue sheen on the sides and seem almost translucent. There are usually no, or only one, chromatophores between the mandibles.

The above description applies mostly to the native *H.t. transpacificus*. The introduced *H. t. nipponensis* has more pectoral rays (12 to 14), fewer dorsal rays (7 to 9), and fewer anal rays (13 to 15). There are 10 or more chromatophores between the mandibles (McAllister, 1963).

Names. Delta smelt were formerly identified with pond smelt (*H. olidus*), and so the name pond smelt is consequently still in common usage among California fisheries workers. When McAllister (1963) described Delta smelt as a distinct species he proposed that the Japanese common name, wakasagi, also be used in North America. Delta smelt was adopted instead by the American Fisheries Society (1970). *Hypo-mesus* means below-middle, referring to the position of the pelvic fins, while *transpacificus* "refers to (their) occurrence on both sides of the Pacific and to the friendship of Japanese and Canadian ichthyologists" (McAllister, 1963, p. 36).

Distribution. The native subspecies is found mainly in the waters of the Sacramento-San Joaquin Delta below Mossdale on the San Joaquin River and Isleton on the Sacramento River. They also occur seasonally in Suisan Bay, Carquinez Strait, and San Pablo Bay. They are most abundant in Montezuma Slough and the main channels and the Delta from Martinez to Antioch (L. Miller, pers. comm.). The Japanese subspecies was introduced in 1959 into six reservoirs as a forage fish, apparently because the native smelt were difficult to collect (Wales, 1962). The original reservoirs receiving them were Dodge Reservoir (Lassen County), Dwinnel Reservoir (Siskiyou County), Freshwater Lagoon (Humboldt County), Spalding Reservoir (Nevada County), Sly Park Reservoir (El Dorado County), and Big Bear Lake (San Bernadino County). They have since been introduced into other reservoirs, including Shastina Reservoir (Siskiyou County). Although the status of some of the introduced populations is in doubt, the Japanese subspecies can be expected anywhere in the lower Klamath River system, in the Sacramento River system, and possibly in other systems as well.

Life History. Little is known about the biology of the introduced populations of Delta smelt in California, so only the population native to the Sacramento-San Joaquin Delta will be discussed here. These smelt are seldom found at salinities greater than 10 ppt and the bulk of the population lives at salinities of less than 2 ppt for most of the year (Ganssle, 1966). They school in large numbers in the open surface waters of the Delta and have definite seasonal movements. In the fall (September to November), most of the population is concentrated in the lower reaches of the Delta and upper Suisun Bay. They then disperse into the channels and deadend sloughs of the Delta, apparently for spawning (Radtke, 1966). The adults and young-of-the-year stay here until late summer, when they gradually begin moving downstream.

For most of the year, the main food of Delta smelt is planktonic copepods, although cladocerans, amphipods, and insect larvae are also taken on occasion. In the fall, however, when they are in Suisun Bay, oppossum shrimp (*Neomysis*) also become an important food source (Moyle, unpublished data).

Delta smelt are fast growing and short lived. Most growth occurs in the first six to nine months of life, when they reach 55 to 70 mm SL. Most of the food taken after that apparently contributes to the development of sex products, since in the next three months only 3 to 9 mm is typically added on to the length (Erkkila et al., 1950; Radtke, 1966). The smelt that survive spawning continue to grow, reaching lengths up to 120 mm SL.

The spawning period is long. Ripe smelt can be collected from December to April, although they are most common in February and March. Females 64 to 80 mm SL lay anywhere from 1,400 to 2,800 eggs. The size of the female seems to have little correlation with the number of eggs spawned (Moyle, unpublished data). Apparently, most Delta smelt die after spawning because the number of large smelt that can be collected by trawling gradually declines as the spawning season progresses. The presence of a few very large smelt, however, indicates that either some survive spawning or else do not mature until the second year. The site of spawning is not known but the eggs are probably attached to aquatic plants close to shore.

There is some evidence that reproduction can fail completely some years. Erkkila et al. (1950) collected no young-of-the-year smelt in their second year of sampling, although their previous year's work, as well as that of Ganssle (1966) and Radtke (1966) would lead one to expect large numbers of them.

Status. Delta smelt are still one of the most abundant fishes in the Sacramento-San Joaquin Delta and the Japanese subspecies is doing well in a number of reservoirs. However, considering the limited range of the native subspecies (which may deserve species status) and its short life cycle, its populations should be watched closely. Two successive years of low spawning success could decimate the Delta populations and, unfortunately, little is known about environmental conditions necessary for spawning success. It is possible that the reduced flows projected for the Delta or the change in flow patterns created by the proposed Peripheral Canal (especially in deadend sloughs where most spawning may occur), could have a negative effect on Delta smelt populations.

References. Erkkila et al., 1950; Ganssle, 1966; Hamada, 1961; McAllister, 1963; Radtke, 1966; Wales, 1962.

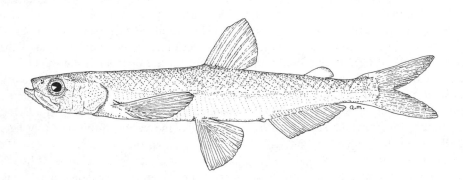

Figure 49. Longfin smelt, 9.4 cm SL, Sacramento-San Joaquin Delta.

Longfin Smelt, *Spirinchus thaleichthys* (Ayres)

Identification. Longfin smelt can be distinguished from other California smelts by their long pectoral fins (which reach or nearly reach the base of the pelvic fins), incomplete lateral line, weak or absent striations on the opercular bones, low number of scales in the lateral series (55 to 62), and long maxillary bones (extend just short of the posterior margin of the eye). The number of dorsal rays is 8 to 10; anal rays, 18 to 21; pelvic rays, 10 to 12; gill rakers, 38 to 47; and pyloric ceca, 4 to 6. The orbit width goes into the head length 3.6 to 4.5X and the longest anal rays go 1.4 to 2.2X into the head length (McAllister, 1963). The lining of the gut cavity is silvery with a few scattered speckles. The sides of living fish appear translucent silver while the back has an olive to iridescent pinkish green hue. Mature males are usually darker than females, with enlarged and stiffened dorsal and anal fins, a dilated lateral line region, and breeding tubercles on the paired fins and scales (McAllister, 1963).

Names. The longfin smelt was considered to be two species at one time: *S. thaleichthys*, known as the Sacramento smelt, and *S. dilatus*, known as the longfin smelt. McAllister (1963) found that there was little reason to separate the two "species" and chose longfin smelt as being the most appropriate common name. *Spir-inchus* means breath-beginning, referring to the conspicuous duct that connects the air bladder (= lung) to the gut. *Thaleichthys* means rich fish but is probably a reference to the related eulachon, *Thaleichthys pacificus.*

Distribution. Populations have been found in estuaries along the Pacific coast of North America from Prince William Sound, Alaska down to the Sacramento-San Joaquin Estuary. The latter population is the main one in California, but a smaller one lives in Humboldt Bay and the Eel River.

Life History. Longfin smelt are euryhaline. In the Sacramento-San Joaquin Estuary they can be found in water ranging from nearly pure sea water to completely fresh water. However, they are most abundant in San Pablo and Suisun bays, where salinities normally are greater than 10 ppt. They seem to occupy mostly the middle or bottom of the water column. They also have definite seasonal migrations, spending early summer in San Pablo and San Francisco bays, and then moving into Suisun Bay in August. In the winter they congregate for spawning at the upper end of Suisun Bay and in the lower reaches of the Delta. There is a mass movement of young smelt downstream into the bays in April and May (Ganssle, 1966). The pattern of movement between Humboldt Bay and the Eel River seems to be similar.

The main food of longfin smelt is the opposum shrimp, *Neomysis mercedis*, although copepods and other crustaceans are important at times, especially to small fish (Moyle, unpublished data). This is similar to their feeding habits in Lake Washington, Washington (Dryfoos, 1965).

Growth in California populations seems to be similar to that of more intensively studied Washington populations (Dryfoos, 1965). Most growth in length takes place in the first nine to ten months of life, when they typically reach 6 to 7 cm SL. During the first winter, growth levels off but there is another period of growth, during the second summer and fall, when the smelt reach 9 to 11 cm SL. Weight gains may be considerable during this latter period as the gonads develop. A few smelt, mostly females, will live yet another year, reaching lengths of 12 to 14 cm SL.

Spawning apparently takes place from December through February, since large smelt become rare after this time. The eggs are adhesive (Dryfoos, 1965) so they probably are deposited either on rocks or on aquatic plants in the freshwater sections of the lower Delta. A majority of the Delta spawning occurs in the lower Sacramento River. Each female lays between 5,000 and 24,000 eggs (Dryfoos, 1965, Moyle, unpublished data). However, the mean number for ten females from Lake Washington was 18,104 (Dryfoos, 1965) which seems to be higher than in California populations. The eggs hatch in forty days at $7°C$ (Dryfoos, 1965). Most of the smelt die after spawning but a few females may survive to spawn a second time.

Status. Longfin smelt are abundant in the Sacramento-San Joaquin Estuary, common in Humboldt Bay, and abundant in other estuarine food chains. Although edible, they have little commercial value.

References. Dryfoos, 1965; Ganssle, 1966; Jensen, 1957; McAllister, 1963; Radtke, 1966.

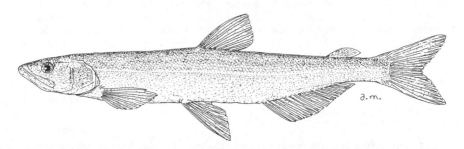

Figure 50. Eulachon, 13.6 cm SL, Klamath River, Del Norte County.

Eulachon, *Thaleichthys pacificus* (Richardson)

Identification. Eulachon have compressed, elongate bodies and large mouths, the maxilla usually extending just past the middle of the eye. The gill covers possess strong concentric striations and the pectoral fins, when pressed against the body, reach about two-thirds of the way to the bases of the pelvic fins. The lateral line is complete, with 7 to 78 scales. There are 8 to 11 pyloric ceca, 18 to 23 dorsal rays, 8 pelvic rays, 10 to 12 pectoral rays, 18 to 23 anal rays, 17 to 23 slender gill rakers on the first arch, and 7 to 8 branchiostegal rays. The jaws have small, pointed teeth which may be missing from spawning fish, especially males. The lining of the gut cavity (peritoneum) is pale with dark speckles. In life eulachon are brown to dark blue on the back and head with a silvery white belly and unmarked fins. Spawning males develop a distinct midlateral ridge and numerous distinct tubercles on the head, body, and fins. Females may also have tubercles but they are poorly developed.

Names. Eulachon (pronounced oolak-on) is the Chinook Indian name for this fish. They are also known as candlefish. The flesh is so oily that dried eulachon were burned by the Indians as candles, after the insertion of a wick. *Thaleichthys* means rich fish, a reference to their oily flesh, while *pacificus* refers to their exclusively Pacific distribution.

Distribution. In California, spawning eulachon run up the Klamath River in large numbers. Small runs are found in Redwood Creek and the Mad River, Humboldt County (Odemar, 1964). They are common north along the Pacific coast to the eastern Bering Sea (McPhail and Lindsey, 1970), and a few have been collected as far south as off Bodega Head, Sonoma County (Odemar, 1964).

Life History. Eulachon spend most of their life in salt water, moving up rivers to spawn in large number in the spring. In the Klamath River, most eulachon migration takes place in March and April and the fish seldom penetrate more than 10 to 12 km upstream. Spawning takes place en masse over bottoms of pea gravel and sand. Each of the 25,000 or so eggs laid by each female is surrounded by two membranes. The outer membrane ruptures when the egg hits the bottom. This membrane is attached by a short stalk to the inner membrane which still surrounds the egg, so that the egg is anchored to the bottom until it hatches in two to three weeks (Carl and Clemens, 1953). The feeble, transparent larvae (4 to 5 mm TL) are quickly washed to sea by river currents.

At sea the larvae are widely distributed by ocean currents. For the next two to three years the immature fish form part of some of the deep echo-scattering layers of the open waters of the ocean, where they feed on copepods and other crustaceans (Barraclough, 1964). They can grow to 30 cm TL during this time but fish over 20 cm TL are unusual.

Most eulachon mature during their third year, move upstream to spawn, and then die, although a few live to spawn once again the following year (Barraclough, 1964). They do not feed while in fresh water.

Status. Eulachon spawning runs are still large in the Klamath River and they provide the basis for a sport dipnet fishery, concentrated in the estuary. At one time eulachon were important to the local Indians for food, fuel, and oil but they have never been particularly important as commercial fish in California. Farther north, especially in British Columbia, they support a small but valuable commercial fishery because they are considered to be one of the tastiest of the smelts despite their oily flesh. Perhaps the greatest value of eulachon, however, lies in their importance as food for marine and anadromous sport fishes. When eulachon move into the estuaries, the salmon and sturgeon present often glut themselves on them, much like the fishermen on shore.

References. Barraclough, 1964; Carl and Clemens, 1953; Clemens and Wilby, 1961; McPhail and Lindsey, 1970; Odemar, 1964.

Minnow Family, Cyprinidae

The true minnows, together with their relatives the catfishes and the tropical characins, are the most abundant and widely distributed group of freshwater fishes in the world. There are over two hundred fifty species of minnows in North America alone, including the introduced carp and goldfish. They range in length as adults from a few centimeters to 1.8 meters (Colorado River squawfish).

The typical native North American minnow is a small, scaled, unspecialized fish. The body is elongate, silvery in color, and often has a dark band running down the side. The caudal fin is forked and the dorsal fin is short, located just above the pelvic fins. True spines are absent from the fins, although carp, goldfish, and spine daces have rays which are hardened and resemble spines. There are never any teeth in the mouth, but pharyngeal teeth are well developed. Scales are cycloid and typically are evenly distributed over the body but are absent from the head. Socially, most minnows are schooling fish. During the breeding season, however, males of many species stake out territories and defend them from other minnows. Breeding males usually develop small, hard tubercles on their bodies and fins, particularly around the snout. The more conspicuous the tubercles, the more likely that the species builds nests and defends territories. The tubercles are inconspicuous on most native California minnows.

Many factors contribute to the success of the Cyprinidae. Perhaps the most important are a well-developed sense of hearing, the fear scent they release when injured, pharyngeal teeth, and high fecundity.

The hearing of minnows is acute because they possess a series of small bones, the Weberian ossicles, which connect the swim bladder to the inner ear. The swim bladder, being filled with air, intercepts sound waves that are passing through the water (and the body of the fish), causing the swim bladder walls to vibrate. The vibrations of the swim bladder wall are then carried to the inner ear by the Weberian ossicles, much as the bones in the middle ear of mammals carry sound from the eardrum to the inner ear. Their auditory system allows the minnows to hear a much wider range of sound frequencies than most other fishes can (Lowenstein, 1957). Although the primary functions of such acute hearing are presumably protection and food-finding, it is also used in breeding. The males of a number of minnow species make sounds during courtship.

The sense of smell is also well developed in minnows, and it is important in helping them avoid predators. If a minnow is injured by the attack of a predator so that the skin is broken, a special chemical present in the skin is released into the water. The olfactory organs of the minnows are highly sensitive to this fear substance. When they detect it in the water, the minnows immediately go into a protective behavior pattern, usually fleeing or hiding. This mechanism is particularly valuable in weedy or turbid waters where predators are difficult to see.

Pharyngeal teeth have contributed to the success of the minnows in much the same way that specialized jaw teeth have contributed to the success of mammals on land. They allow the minnows to specialize in their feeding habits and to break up ingested food. These teeth, located in the "throat" on the last gill arch on each side, grind the food against the hard plate on the roof of the mouth. Minnows with different feeding habits tend to have different shapes, sizes, and numbers of pharyngeal teeth. Sacramento squawfish have pointed, knifelike pharyngeal teeth, well-suited for cutting up the fish and large invertebrates they feed on. Adult hardheads, which live in the same waters as squawfish, have pharyngeal teeth that are flattened on the end, for crushing algae and small invertebrates. Young hardheads that feed primarily on aquatic invertebrates have more knifelike teeth, which are gradually replaced by the more flattened teeth as the fish grow older (Reeves, 1964).

Since the teeth for each species are distinctive, they can be used in taxonomic identification. The number of teeth is particularly useful and pharyngeal teeth formulas frequently accompany descriptions of minnow species. Most native minnows have two rows of teeth on each side, so a typical formula reads 1,4-4,1, indicating one tooth on the inside row and four teeth on the outside row on each side. It is not unusual for the number of teeth on each side to differ slightly.

Minnows also have a rapid rate of reproduction. When a minnow species enters a new area, such as a recently impounded reservoir, it can rapidly build up its numbers and become permanently established. A 23 cm SL hitch may lay 26,000 eggs; a 50 cm SL Sacramento squawfish, 18,000 eggs; and a 50 cm SL carp, 500,000 eggs.

Despite all these advantages, many native minnow species are declining in numbers as the environment deteriorates beyond their ability to cope with the changes or as they are displaced by more aggressive introduced fishes such as carp. Thicktail chub, Colorado squawfish, and bonytail have all become extinct in California within the past fifty years. Another presumably extinct species, the Clear Lake minnow (*Endemichthys grandipinnis*) of Hopkirk (1973) may in fact by a hitch-blackfish hybrid and so will not be treated further in this book. Other minnows (Clear Lake splittail, Mojave tui chub, Owens tui chub) have become rare and will probably survive only if suitable habitat for them is preserved.

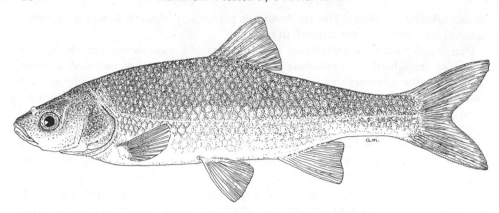

Figure 51. Tui chub, 15 cm SL, Tule Lake, Siskiyou County.

Tui Chub, *Gila bicolor* (Girard)

Systematic note. The tui chub is a highly successful species that presents some fascinating problems in systematics. Almost every isolated or partially isolated drainage system in California, Nevada, and Oregon supports at least one distinctive form. One of California's early ichthyologists, J. O. Snyder, was so impressed by the differences among the various forms that he described most of them as separate species. Today, Snyder's species have been reduced to subspecies. The taxonomic confusion created by Snyder's work and by the variable nature of the tui chubs themselves still has not been satisfactorily resolved. It probably never will be because the evolutionary plasticity of the species resists taxonomic pigeon-holing. Tui chubs are successful because they have been able to adapt to the severe long- and short-term climatic fluctuations characteristic of the interior basins where they are most common.

Despite the variability of tui chubs, a number of forms, usually labelled as subspecies, are widely recognized in California. Unfortunately, only three of them are relatively noncontroversial: *G. b. snyderi* of the Owens River (Miller, 1973); *G. b. mohavensis* of the Mojave River (often recognized as a species); and *G. b. bicolor*, of the Klamath system. The tui chubs of Goose Lake and of the upper Pit River, although probably deserving subspecies status, are in need of study because they were assigned to *G. b. bicolor* by Evermann and Clark (1931), to *G. b. formosa* by Snyder (1918) and Bond (1961), and to a distinct subspecies, *G. b. thallassina*, by Snyder (1908a) and by Hubbs and Miller (1948). The name *G. b. formosa* was originally applied to tui chubs that were supposed to have lived in the Sacramento-San Joaquin Valley. Since only a few poorly preserved specimens of the form are known, the subspecies may be based on a mislabelled collection (C. L. Hubbs, pers. comm.). An undescribed subspecies apparently exists in the slough that drains the now dry Cowhead Lake, in extreme northeastern Modoc County (C. L. Hubbs, pers. comm.).

Perhaps the most intriguing systematic problem among tui chubs is the relationship between the two forms in the Lahontan system, usually listed as the subspecies *G. b. obesa* and *G. b. pectinifer* (Hubbs, 1961; Hubbs, Miller, and Hubbs, 1974). The two forms are different enough in their morphology so that Snyder (1918) placed them in separate genera. The differences in the gill rakers, which are finer and more numerous in *pectinifer* than they are in *obesa*, are particularly striking. Miller (1951) found that the differences in gill rakers, as well as some slight morphological differences, reflected differences in ecological niche: *G. b. obesa* is the form found in streams and in lakes and is a shallow-water bottom feeder. Some overlap in diet and habitat does exist, however, and the young of both forms tend to school together in shallow water. The taxonomic picture is further clouded because the two forms commonly interbreed. In Eagle Lake, interbreeding has made it difficult to distinguish them morphologically or ecologically (Kimsey, 1954). In Lake Tahoe and Pyramid Lake, however, they maintain their identities despite some interbreeding (Hubbs, 1961). Presumably the two forms have interbred in Eagle Lake and other lakes that lack the huge areas of deep open water characteristic of Lake Tahoe and Pyramid Lake, which would give an efficient plankton-feeding form a strong selective advantage. Despite the energetic advantages of having two semi-specialized forms in a large lake rather than one generalized one, it is not clear how the two forms manage to maintain their identities in Lake Tahoe and Pyramid Lake in the face of actual and potential interbreeding. Distinctive breeding habits and differential predation on the two forms and their hybrids by various types of trout may contribute to maintenance of the distinct forms (see life-history section for details).

What, then, is the relationship between the two forms? It would be tempting to call them separate species, as Hopkirk (1973) does, but the Eagle Lake and other similar populations demonstrate that the two forms do not always maintain reproductive isolation. They do not even make very good subspecies since, according to Mayr (1966), subspecies are taxonomically distinct populations that are found in separate geographical subdivisions of the species range. There is also some question as to the reliability of using differences in gill rakers as the primary morphological means of separating the two forms into taxonomic entities. As Uyeno (1966, p. 59) pointed out, gill rakers in the genus *Gila* and its relatives ". . . reflect ecological adaptations more than they do phylogeny."

Whatever the forms are labelled (species, subspecies, semi-species, incipient species, ecotypes, or polymorphic variants), the arguments for each label will remain largely academic until thorough systematic and ecological studies are made throughout the Lahontan system. "Whenever reproductive isolation and morphological differentiation do not coincide, the decision as to species status must be based on a broad evaluation of the particular case. The solution is generally a rather unsatisfactory compromise" (Mayr, 1966, p. 26).

Identification. Tui chubs are typically chunky, large-scaled (44 to 60 along the lateral line) fishes with small, terminal, and slightly oblique mouths, stubby gill rakers, and a decurved lateral line. The gill rakers range in number from 8 to 24, the left gill arch usually bearing a few more than the right arch. The gap between the gill rakers is wider than the base of the gill rakers themselves. Both the dorsal and anal fin rays are 7 to 9 (usually 8). All fins are rounded and short. The head becomes larger relative to the rest of the body in older fish and is usually somewhat convex in profile. A distinct hump may develop behind the head. The single-rowed pharyngeal teeth (5-5, 5-4, or 4-4) are slightly hooked, with narrow grinding surfaces. Live fish tend to be dusky olive, brown, or brassy on the back and white to silver on the belly. The younger the fish, the more silvery the overall body color.

The *pectinifer* forms differ from the above description in that the gill rakers are more numerous (29 to 40) as well as being long and slender. The distances between gill rakers are usually less than the width of the gill rakers themselves. The mouth is more oblique than that of the typical chubs and the profile of the head is slightly concave. The overall color is more silvery, so that the contrast between the belly and back is not as striking (Miller, 1951).

Names. The origins of the words *Gila* and chub are explained under thicktail chub. *Bicolor* means two-colored. The scientific name for this species has a complex history, detailed in La Rivers (1962). In most of the literature the name used is *Siphateles bicolor* or else *Siphateles* in combination with one of the names now used to designate subspecies. When Bailey and Uyeno (1964) merged *Siphateles* into the genus *Gila*, the name became *Gila bicolor*. Unfortunately, the blue chub of the Klamath River system also had the name *Gila bicolor*, so Bailey and Uyeno (1964) adopted for it the early synonym, *coerulea*. Thus, *G. bicolor* in the literature prior to 1964 is in fact *G. coerulea*. The name tui chub is derived from the Paiute Indian name for the species "tui-pagwi," where "pagwi" seems to be the Paiute word for minnow (Loud, 1929).

  Distribution. Tui chubs are widely distributed in the Klamath and Lahontan systems and are present in the Owens and Mojave rivers as well as in the upper Pit River and Goose Lake of the Sacramento-San Joaquin system. They have been introduced into several reservoirs in the Sacramento River system (e.g., Lake Alamanor). Outside of California, they are found in a number of interior basins of Oregon and Nevada. They were widespread in the Columbia River system in Washington and Oregon, into which they may have been introduced.

  Life History. Tui chubs occur in a wide variety of habitats but most commonly they are found in the weedy shallows of lakes or the quiet waters of sluggish rivers. *G. b. "pectinifer"* appears to be more restricted in its habitat than the other chubs, since it is found primarily in the open waters of large lakes. Tui chubs do well under a wide variety of limnological conditions, from the cold, clear, oligotrophic waters of Lake Tahoe to the warm, turbid, eutrophic waters of Pyramid Lake, Nevada, where the total dissolved solids are more than 4,700 ppm, mostly (75 percent) sodium chloride.

  In large, deep lakes, tui chubs tend to form large schools in shallow water, frequently associated with submerged objects or beds of aquatic vegetation. In Lake Tahoe, both *"obesa"* and *"pectinifer"* forms over 16 cm TL tend to move into deep water (down to 50 m) during the day and return to the shallows at night. The *"pectinifer"* schools apparently stay well off the bottom while the *"obesa"* schools stay close to it. Thus, the *"obesa"* chubs more commonly fall prey to the lake trout, a deep-water benthic predator, than do the *"pectinifer"* chubs (Miller, 1951). Small chubs of both types remain in shallow water most of the time, although strong wave action will drive chubs of all sizes into deep water.

  In shallow lakes with heavy growths of aquatic vegetation, such as Tule Lake, Modoc County, schooling is much less noticeable. The chubs tend to be dispersed among the vegetation in small groups, presumably as protection against predatory birds that are attracted to large schools. In the fall, in all types of lakes, the chubs tend to seek out deep water where they spend the winter, presumably on the bottom in a semi-dormant state. The spring reappearance of the chubs, at least in Eagle Lake, Pyramid Lake, and Lake Tahoe, is both sudden and spectacular, usually coming in mid-May (Snyder, 1918; Miller, 1951; Kimsey, 1954). Snyder (1918, p. 66-67) described the spring return in Pyramid Lake vividly: "On May 20 the weather suddenly settled and became warm . . . About 2 o'clock the following morning there was heard a vigorous lapping of the water, which in the quiet air appeared entirely without cause until it was found to accompany the leaping of vast numbers of fishes. Far out and up and down the shores the surface of the water fairly boiled. Spring had come, and with it, in the dim light of early morning, myriads of fishes from the depths of the lake. Daylight revealed them everywhere, along the shore, among the boulders, and in the algae, hovering in enormous schools over the bars and moving about in the clear water of the sheltered bays."

  Tui chubs are opportunistic omnivores but they concentrate on invertebrates associated with the bottom or with aquatic plants. Thus *G. b. bicolor* from ponds in Lassen County were observed feeding on aquatic insect larvae and crustaceans usually found with aquatic plants (Kimsey and Bell, 1956), but chubs from Big Sage Reservoir, Modoc County, were observed feeding on a mixture of plant material, plankton, insect larvae, and small tui chubs (Kimsey and Bell, 1955). Miller (1951) found the food of *G. b. obesa* in Lake Tahoe to be 89 percent benthic invertebrates, 5 percent fish and fish eggs, 3 percent plankton, and 3 percent plants. The bottom food consisted mostly of snails, small clams, caddisfly larvae, midge larvae, and crayfish. Snyder (1918) observed that *G. b. obesa* in Pyramid Lake would move into recently flooded shallow areas at night to feed on insects, algae, and plant material. An exception to the benthic feeding rule is *G. b. pectinifer* which, with its long gill rakers, feeds almost exclusively (92 percent) on plankton, mostly crustaceans (Miller, 1951). The "hybrid" population in Eagle Lake apparently also feeds largely on plankton, although plant material, insect larvae, water mites, and surface insects can make up significant portions of the diet (Kimsey, 1954). One of the main items in the present diet of the rare Mojave tui chub, now largely confined to a pond at Warm Springs Resort, is bread crumbs cast by guests of the resort (Vicker, 1973). Young-of-the-year tui chubs feed on planktonic crustaceans and rotifers, gradually switching to larger organisms as they increase in size (Kimsey and Bell, 1955; Miller, 1951).

Growth during their first summer of life is fairly rapid, the chubs reaching 22 to 42 mm SL. Subsequent growth is slow compared to that of other large cyprinids. By the end of their second summer they are typically 37 to 98 mm SL and in subsequent summers they add 20 to 50 mm to their length depending on the body of water. Thus, age VI fish from Big Sage Reservoir were only 21 cm FL, compared to similar aged fish from Eagle Lake which averaged 33 cm FL (Kimsey and Bell, 1955). The oldest fish whose age could be determined by Kimsey (1954) were age VII, ranging in length from 31 to 35 cm FL. Larger fish, up to 41 cm, have been collected but not aged. Tui chubs are usually mature at age II.

Most spawning takes place between late April and late June, although in Lake Tahoe spawning apparently continues until the end of July (Miller, 1951). Multiple spawning by a single female is probably common, since all eggs do not ripen at the same time. Thus, Kimsey (1954) found that a single 28 cm FL female contained 11,200 ripe eggs, while Bond (1948) found that the total number of eggs in fish 15 to 28 cm TL ranged from 4,140 to 25,000. Ripe fish have been found at temperatures between 8 and 16°C. They usually spawn over beds of vegetation in shallow water but the spawning act has never been described in detail. Miller (1951) indicated that Lake Tahoe chubs spawn over sandy bottoms in shallow water or in the mouth of streams. It is not known if the *obesa* and *pectinifer* forms spawn in different localities in the lake, since they seem to have the same requirements for spawning sites. However, if the two forms maintain their separate schools during the breeding season they could maintain their genetic identities, even if they spawned in the same area. The presence of intermediate forms, which usually school with the *obesa* chubs, indicates that the two forms breed at the same localities at least some of the time and may hybridize.

Newly laid eggs are 1.5 to 1.9 mm in diameter and adhere to aquatic plants or to the bottom substrate. The eggs hatch in less than nine days and the larvae start feeding soon after hatching. In Eagle Lake, they remain among the aquatic plants until they are 1 to 2 cm TL; then they move into the shallow water along shore (Kimsey, 1954). In Lake Tahoe, the newly hatched fry concentrate in shallow nursery areas that contain cover and much organic matter, as well as the fry of other cyprinids. As they grow, they spread out along the shore and can be found in both rocky and sandy areas (Miller, 1951). Scale formation starts at 20 to 25 mm SL.

Status. Tui chubs in the Klamath and Lahontan systems are still abundant, especially in large lakes and reservoirs, as are the chubs in Goose Lake and the upper Pit River. They can overpopulate a new reservoir to the detriment of the gamefishes, but usually their value as forage fish far outweighs their effect as gamefish competitors. They make excellent forage fish because they have a high reproductive rate, a comparatively slow growth rate, and a preference for the littoral areas where most sport fish feed. They are a major source of food for trout in Eagle Lake, Lake Tahoe, and Pyramid Lake, and for largemouth bass and Sacramento perch in some warmer waters. In Eagle Lake, tui chubs are a minor sport and food fish in their own right. Large lake and reservoir populations may have some value in the future for commercial fish meal.

Elsewhere in California, tui chubs are not faring so well. The Owens tui chubs have been depleted by the diversion of the Owens River to Los Angeles and by the introduction of predatory fishes into the system. In Crowley Lake, Mono County, they have hybridized with *G. b. obesa*, introduced as bait by fishermen (Miller, 1973). Mojave tui chubs have been almost exterminated because of the introduction of arroyo chubs (*G. orcutti*) in the Mojave River. The two species have hybridized so extensively that typical Mojave tui chubs have virtually disappeared from the main river (Hubbs and Miller, 1942; Miller, 1961a). A pure population exists in the Mojave system only in an artificial, spring-fed pond at Zzyzx Springs near Baker, San Bernardino County. A few successful transplants have been made to other isolated Southern California localities (Leach and Fis, 1972). Mojave tui chubs are now fully protected by California state law.

References. Bailey and Uyeno, 1964; Bond, 1948, 1961; Harry, 1951; Hopkirk and Behnke, 1966; Hubbs, 1961; Hubbs and Miller, 1942, 1948; Hubbs, Miller, and Hubbs, 1974; Kimsey, 1954; Kimsey and Bell, 1955, 1956; La Rivers, 1962; Leach and Fisk, 1972; R. G. Miller, 1951; R. R. Miller, 1961a, 1973; St. Amant and Sasaki, 1971; Snyder, 1908a,c, 1918, 1919; Uyeno, 1961; Vicker, 1973.

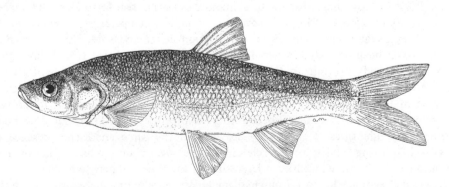

Figure 52. Blue chub, 15 cm SL, Tule Lake, Siskiyou County.

Blue Chub, *Gila coerulea* (Girard)

Identification. Blue chubs resemble Klamath tui chubs, with which they are usually associated, except that they have finer scales (58 to 71 in the lateral line), are not as deep bodied, have longer tails, and have longer heads with larger mouths, the maxillary reaching the eye. There are 9 dorsal rays, 8 to 9 anal rays, and 14 to 17 rays in each pectoral fin. The two-rowed pharyngeal teeth (2,5-5,2) are sharp and slightly hooked. The lateral line is decurved. They seldom exceed 34 cm SL and, in life, tend to be silvery blue on the sides and dusky on the back. Spawning males become brightly tinged with orange on the sides and fins.

Names. The origins of *Gila* and chub are explained under thicktail chub. Blue (*coerulea*) chub is somewhat of misnomer since they are no more or less blue than most California minnows. For reasons explained under tui chub, blue chubs were listed as *Gila bicolor* before the 1964 paper of Bailey and Uyeno.

Distribution. Blue chubs are widely distributed in the Klamath and Lost river systems of Oregon and California.

Life History. Little is known about the habits of blue chubs, despite the fact that they school conspicuously in a variety of habitats, from small streams and rivers, to shallow reservoirs and deep lakes. In upper Klamath Lake, Oregon, Vincent (1968), found them most numerous along rocky shores or out in the open water. They seemed to avoid marshy shore areas. Apparently, only the complete lack of oxygen in the lower layers of Klamath Lake prevents them from occupying the deep areas of the lake in summer, since they have been gill netted in waters with a dissolved oxygen concentration of less than 0.1 mg/1 (Vincent, 1968). As winter sets in and oxygen levels rise in the deep areas, the chubs generally move down into them.

Blue chubs are omnivorous as indicated by the generalized body shape and tooth structure. Twenty chubs collected from Willow Creek, Modoc County, in August 1972 (all age I, 29 to 59 mm SL) had fed mostly (66 percent by volume) on chironomid midge larvae and pupae, with small numbers of water boatmen, water fleas, other aquatic insect larvae, and various flying insects. Sixteen age II chubs from the same place (61 to 109 mm SL) were feeding heavily on filamentous algae (68 percent), with aquatic and terrestrial insects making up most of the rest of the diet.

Spawning occurs in May and June, over shallow rocky areas, at temperatures from 15 to 18°C. Spawning behavior was witnessed by C. R. Hazel (pers. comm.) in Upper Klamath Lake, Oregon: "On the afternoon of May 4, 1966, I observed an estimated 200-300 blue chubs spawning at the shoreline on the northern end of Eagle Ridge. Spawning was taking place from near the surface to a depth of 0.3 to 0.5 m. The bottom was composed of large gravel and rubble of volcanic origin. The water was clear with a low concentration of blue-green algae (*Aphanizomenon*) ... (and) ... the water temperature was 17°C. Two to several males would approach a female and exhibit rapid and violent agitations of the water, making it impossible to see exactly what was taking place. In some instances, the female was pushed from the water onto dry land and in a few situations, eggs were spawned outside the water. After these activities, egg masses were found attached to (submerged) rocks either on the sides or near the bottom edge. Many of these depositions were found along rocky edges at depths to 0.5 m."

Nothing has been published on age and growth of blue chubs or on early life history.

Status. Blue chubs are one of the most abundant fishes in the Klamath and Lost river systems. They are doing well in reservoirs (e.g., Clear Lake and Tule Lake, Modoc County), in the face of introduced predatory fishes such as yellow perch, largemouth bass, and Sacramento perch.

References. Bailey and Uyeno, 1964; Vincent, 1968.

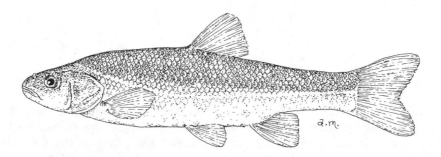

Figure 53. Arroyo chub, 8.9 cm SL, Santa Clara River, Los Angeles County.

Arroyo Chub, *Gila orcutti* (Eigenmann and Eigenmann)

Identification. Arroyo chubs are small (usually less than 12 cm TL but occasionally as large as 30 cm), chunky minnows with small mouths and moderately large eyes. They have 7 anal fin rays, 8 dorsal rays, 5 to 9 gill rakers, and 48 to 62 lateral line scales. The dorsal fin origin is placed well behind the origin of the pelvic fins. The pharyngeal teeth (2,5-4,2, but variable) are closely spaced and strongly hooked, with black tips. The lateral line reaches the caudal peduncle and is not decurved. In life, they are silvery or grey to olive green on the back and white on the belly, usually with a dull grey lateral band in between.

Names. Arroyo chubs are named for the gullies and small canyons (arroyos) of their native southern California. *Gila* and chub are explained under thicktail chub. *Orcutti* is for the botanist C. R. Orcutt who, in 1889, collected the first specimens, using a blanket as a seine (Eigenmann and Eigenmann, 1893).

Distribution. Originally native to the streams of the Los Angeles Plain (including Malibu Creek), the upper Santa Clara River system and, reportedly, the San Luis Rey and Santa Margarita river systems of San Diego County, California, arroyo chubs apparently have been introduced successfully into the Santa Ynez, Santa Maria, Cuyama, and Mojave river systems.

Life History. Arroyo chubs are adapted for surviving in the warm fluctuating streams of the Los Angeles Plain. Prior to the arrival of civilization and concrete, these streams were muddy torrents in the winter and clear intermittent brooks in the summer. Generally the slowest moving sections of stream, where the bottoms are of sand or mud, are preferred by the chubs. The chubs were then associated with Santa Ana suckers, speckled dace, and threespine sticklebacks. The only extensive studies on the biology of arroyo chubs are those of Greenfield and Deckert (1973) and Greenfield and Greenfield (1972) who worked in the Cuyama River, Santa Barbara County.

Arroyo chubs are omnivorous grazers, feeding heavily on algae and other plants as well as on small crustaceans and aquatic insect larvae. Although their stomachs contain mostly plant material (60 to 80 percent), they probably derive most of their nutrition from the invertebrates associated with the plants. Thus, they will feed extensively on the roots of floating water fern (*Azolla*) when the roots are infested with nematode worms. Invertebrates increase in number and variety in the diet during the spring and are least abundant during the winter months.

Nothing appears to be known about age and growth in arroyo chubs but they seldom exceed 75 mm SL.

Breeding takes place, usually in pools, in March and April. Behavior is presumably similar to that of tui chubs. Introduced arroyo chubs have hybridized in the wild with both Mojave tui chubs and with California roach. As a result of the hybridization, Mojave tui chubs have been completely eliminated from their native Mojave River, and the population that exists there now phenotypically resembles arroyo chubs.

California roach-arroyo chub hybrids and backcrosses are abundant in the Cuyama River. When stream flows are high the two species segregate, the chubs in the large pools and reservoirs, the roach in the riffles and smaller pools. During low water flows the two species are forced together and hybridization takes place. In this situation the chubs tend to disappear, their populations reduced by competition from the roach and the roach-chub hybrids (Greenfield and Deckert, 1973).

Status. Although still common in many of its native streams, populations of arroyo chubs should be watched closely because most are found in areas with large human populations. Serious consideration should be given to setting aside and managing sections of stream specifically for arroyo chubs and other fishes native to the area. Since they seem rather susceptible to predation, a management scheme probably would have to include eliminating introduced predatory fishes such as green sunfish and largemouth bass.

References. Eigenmann and Eigenmann, 1893; Greenfield and Deckert, 1973; Greenfield and Greenfield, 1972; Hubbs and Miller, 1942.

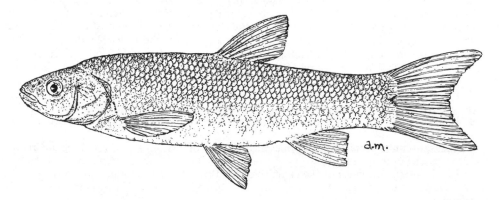

Figure 54. Thicktail chub, 11 cm SL, collection locality unknown. CAS 11060.

Thicktail Chub, *Gila crassicauda* (Baird and Girard)

Identification. Thicktail chubs are heavy-bodied fish with short, deep, and thick caudal peduncles, small, cone-shaped heads, 8 rays in both the dorsal and anal fins, and 9 rays in each pelvic fin. The scales are large, 49 to 60 along the lateral line. The pharyngeal teeth (2,5-4,2) are sturdy and hooked. The 8 to 14 gill rakers (usually 10 to 12) are stubby and toothlike in appearance. The backs of living fish range in color from greenish brown to purplish black, while the sides and belly are generally yellowish (Miller, 1963).

Names. Chub is an old English name, of unknown origin, originally given to a heavy-bodied European minnow, *Leuciscus cephalus*, but now also applied to a number of North American minnows. Thicktail is a reference to the wide caudal peduncle. Other common names include Sacramento chub and thicktail. *Gila* is after the Gila River, New Mexico, from which it was thought the first fish referred to this genus had been obtained. They actually came from the Zuni River in New Mexico (R. R. Miller, pers. comm.). *Crassicauda* means thicktail.

Range. Thicktail chubs were probably once found throughout the Central Valley in lowland areas, as well as in Clear Lake and in streams tributary to San Francisco Bay. There are unconfirmed records from the Pajaro and Salinas rivers. If thicktail chubs still survive today, they are in isolated sloughs of the Valley floor.

Life History. Little is known about the habits of these interesting minnows, since no one took an interest in them until they had become extremely rare. What little is known is summarized in Miller (1963) who examined 101 fish, ranging in length from 49 to 268 mm SL. He estimated that these fish comprised 98 percent of the fish in scientific collections. Thicktail chubs were originally abundant in lowland lakes, sloughs, slow-moving stretches of river and, during years of heavy run-off, the surface waters of San Francisco Bay. The stubby gill rakers, short intestine, and stout, hooked, pharyngeal teeth indicate that thicktail chubs were carnivorous, probably feeding on small fish and large aquatic invertebrates. Thicktail chubs have occasionally hybridized with hitch and the hybrids were originally described, in 1908, as a separate species.

Status. At one time thicktail chubs were abundant enough to be sold in the San Francisco fish market (Miller, 1963). Their bones are among the most abundant in Indian middens along the Sacramento River (Schulz and Simons, 1973). However, the last known thicktail chub was collected from the Cache Slough, near Rio Vista, in 1958. The species is now either very rare or extinct since neither the extensive fish sampling of the Delta in recent years by the California Department of Fish and Game nor the continuous examination of fishes retrieved from the Delta-Mendota Canal by the Bureau of Reclamation and from the California Aqueduct by the California Department of Water Resources at their facilities near Tracy have turned up any thicktail chubs (Fisk, 1972). A recent search of likely sloughs of the Sacramento and San Joaquin rivers has also been unsuccessful (M. Caywood, pers. comm.). At the present time, thicktail chubs certainly deserve to be placed on the fully protected list of California fishes, so that appropriate measures can be taken to preserve them in case a population should be discovered.

Thicktail chubs seem to have achieved their rare or extinct status by being unable to adapt to the extreme modification of their valley-floor habits, particularly the removal of tule beds, the drainage of the large, shallow lakes, the reduction in stream flows, the modification of stream channels, and the introduction of exotic predators and competitors.

References. Fisk, 1972; Miller, 1963; Rutter, 1908; Schulz and Simons, 1973.

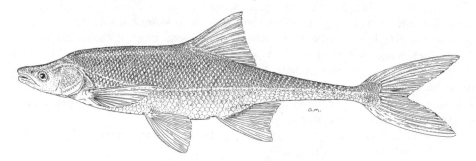

Figure 55. Bonytail, 30 cm SL, Green River, Wyoming.

Bonytail, *Gila elegans* Baird and Girard

Systematic note. The bonytail is one member of a complex of closely related *Gila* species and subspecies that inhabit the Colorado River system. Miller (1946) thought that the forms could best be placed in two species: *G. cypha*, the bizarre humpback chub of the Grand Canyon, and *G. robusta*, the Colorado chub, with four subspecies: *G. r. robusta*, *G. r. elegans*, *G. r. seminuda*, and *G. r. intermedia*. The different forms presumably evolved, in isolation, to meet special ecological conditions in the Colorado system's varied waterways: *G. cypha* for the swift and turbulent water of the Grand Canyon; *G. robusta*, with the exception of *G. r. elegans*, for the quiet pools and slower moving waters of the main tributaries; and *G. r. elegans* for the fast waters of the main river. A careful systematic review of these forms by Holden and Stalnaker (1970), however, revealed that *G. cypha* has hybridized with *G. robusta* in recent years and questioned its validity as a species. On the other hand, their analysis confirmed the previous conclusion of Minckley and Deacon (1968), that *G. r. elegans* deserved full species status as *G. elegans*. The work of Vanicek and Kramer (1969), which indicated that *G. elegans* and *G. robusta* are ecologically and reproductively segregated, tends to support this conclusion.

Identification. Bonytails are readily recognized by their extremely narrow caudal peduncles with deeply forked tails, their fine, embedded scales (75 to 88 along the lateral line), and their small, flattened heads with small, elliptical eyes. There is usually a conspicuous hump behind the head. Scales may be lacking on the dorsal and ventral surfaces, as well as on the caudal peduncle. Dorsal and anal rays number 10 to 11; pelvic rays, 9 to 10. The pharyngeal teeth (2,5-4,2) are closely spaced, compressed, and hooked. The color of the back and sides ranges from dusky green to metallic blue, with fine speckling, while the belly is silvery to white. Breeding males become reddish orange on the head and sides below the lateral line. Young fish lack the exaggerated morphology of the adults and bear a fairly close resemblance to young Colorado squawfish.

Names. Elegans means elegant. Members of the Colorado *Gila* complex are commonly referred to by nonichthyologists as Colorado chubs. Other common names for bonytail include Gila trout and swiftwater Colorado *Gila*.

Distribution. Bonytails are found throughout the Colorado River and its larger tributaries, mostly in the main channels. In California they are (were) found only in the Colorado River where it borders the state.

Life History. Bonytails are usually considered to be primarily inhabitants of the swifter waters of the large rivers of the Colorado system. This conclusion is based on their streamlined morphology. The fine, deeply embedded scales, narrow caudal peduncle, and nuchal hump are all considered to be swiftwater adaptations (La Rivers,

1962). However, their habitat requirements need to be carefully reevaluated, since Vanicek and Kramer (1969) did not capture any in swift water but found them only in pools and eddies. It is possible that, although they spend most of their time in quiet water, they forage for food in swift water. There they presumably would have a competitive advantage over roundtail chubs, with which they often occur. The streamlined shape would also be advantageous during times of flood (Minckley, 1973). The water in which they are generally found is muddy and the bottom is of clay, mud, silt, and/or boulders, with few aquatic plants.

The feeding habits of bonytails have been studied extensively only by Vanicek and Kramer (1969). They found large bonytails (over 20 cm TL) to be omnivorous surface feeders, taking terrestrial insects, filamentous algae, and plant debris such as leaves, stems, seeds, and horsetail stems. They do not seem to be selective in their feeding, taking every variety of food that falls on the water. Small fish (less than 3 cm TL) feed mostly on aquatic insect larvae and become more dependent on surface food as they grow larger.

Growth in small bonytails is similar to that of small roundtail chubs, from which they are difficult to distinguish: 55 mm TL and 1 gm at age I, 100 mm TL and 8 gm at age II, and 158 mm TL and 31 gm at age III (Vanicek and Kramer, 1969). However, as they grow larger, they increase in length faster than roundtail chubs, but the weight increase is smaller in proportion to length, a consequence of their more elongate, streamlined form. The largest and oldest fish encountered by Vanicek and Kramer (1969) was seven years old, measured 39 cm TL, and weighed 422 gm.

Spawning apparently takes place in May and June, once the water temperatures exceed 18°C, over gravel riffles or rubble-bottomed eddies (Vanicek and Kramer, 1969, Sigler and Miller, 1963). Breeding behavior was observed in Lake Mojave, Nevada, in May by Jonez and Sumner (1954). About 500 bonytails had congregated over a gravel-covered shelf, 9 m deep. As is typical of such cyprinid spawning groups, the males outnumbered the females by two to one, and each spawning female was attended by three to five males. The eggs were broadcast over the gravel, to which they adhered. The spawning areas were not defended by any of the fish. The spawners were 28 to 36 cm TL. A 31 cm TL female contained 10,000 eggs.

Young fish are apparently planktonic for a short time after they hatch but they are soon found in the quiet, shallow waters of the river's edge.

Status. At one time, bonytails were one of the commonest fish on the lower Colorado River but, by 1942, they were quite rare (Dill, 1944). They now seem to be extinct in the California portion of the Colorado River because the swift muddy water they require has been impounded and changed in character. They still seem to be fairly common in the upper reaches of the Colorado River but even there the populations are declining (Miller, 1961a; Vanicek and Kramer, 1969). The take, possession, and sale of bonytails is currently forbidden by California state law but their preservation is really in the hands of the states upstream from California. Bonytails are likely to be around for future generations to study and enjoy only if large stretches of the Colorado River are left with substantial natural flows.

References. Dill, 1944; Holden and Stalnaker, 1970; Jonez and Sumner, 1954; La Rivers, 1962; Leach and Fisk, 1972; R. R. Miller, 1946, 1961a; Minckley, 1973; Minckley and Deacon, 1968; Sigler and Miller, 1963; Vanicek and Kramer, 1969.

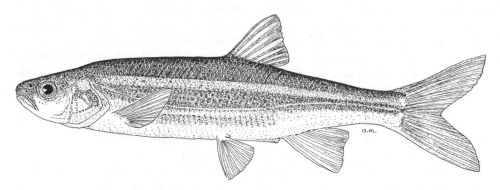

Figure 56. Lahontan redside, 11 cm SL, Sagehen Creek, Placer County.

Lahontan Redside, *Richardsonius egregius* (Girard)

Identification. Lahontan redsides are rather small and slender minnows (body depth goes 4X into the standard length) with large eyes. They are best identified by their spectacular breeding colors: a scarlet stripe on each side, a shiny olivaceous back, and a silvery belly. In nonbreeding fish the red color is greatly reduced, but the stripe is still visible as a dark lateral band. The mouth is slightly oblique, the maxillary barely reaching the front edge of the eye. There are 7 to 8 (usually 8) dorsal rays, 8 to 10 (usually 9) anal rays, and 52 to 63 scales along the lateral line. The scales on the back behind the head tend to be crowded before the dorsal fin. The pharyngeal teeth (2,5-4,2) are strongly hooked, while the gill rakers are stubby, tending to expand towards the tip. The intestine is S-shaped, shorter in length than the body.

During the breeding season both sexes develop breeding tubercles on the body and head, but those on the males are larger and more numerous and also occur on the pectoral fins. Males tend to be darker in color with a more intensely red stripe. When pressed down, the pectoral fins of the males usually reach the base of the pelvic fins, while those of the female do not (Evans, 1969).

Names. A variety of unofficial common names have been applied to the Lahontan redside, all referring to its breeding colors: Lahontan redshiner, Lahontan redside shiner, redside minnow, redside bream, red-striped shiner. *Richardsonius* is after Sir John Richardson (1787-1865), an English naturalist who described the only other species assigned to this genus, *R. balteatus. Egregius* means surprising. Just what Charles Girard was surprised at when he described this species in 1858 from a single specimen is not known. The somewhat confusing history of its scientific nomenclature is given in La Rivers (1962).

Distribution. Lahontan redsides are native to the streams and lakes of the Lahontan system in western Nevada and southeastern California. There are also a number of records from the Sacramento River system. Kimsey (1950) reported a population in Mill Creek, at the headqaters of the Rubicon River, in the Sacramento system. This population, with those of other Lahontan fishes, may have been the result of a bait-bucket introduction, although the creek drains a low divide separating the two systems. A more likely bait-bucket introduction is the population existing in Bucks Lake, which drains into the north fork of the Feather River (R. A. Flint, pers. comm.). Rutter (1908) found redsides, and other Lahontan fishes, in Warner Creek, a tributary to the north fork of the Feather River.

Life History. The habitat of Lahontan redsides was well described by Snyder (1918, p. 54): "This beautiful little fish is almost universally distributed throughout the brooks, rivers, and lakes of the region. It is found not only in the lower courses of the rivers where the water is deep and quiet, but it also stems the swift currents of the high mountain tributaries, following closely in the wake of the smallest trout. . . . It delights in the slow riffles and the quiet, shallow pools, where large numbers may be seen swimming lazily about over the submerged bars, occasionally turning their silvery sides to the bright sun. In the lakes it congregates in large schools, swimming about submerged logs, tops of fallen trees, wharves and other sheltered places."

Since Snyder's description, only two life-history studies on the Lahontan redsides, both from Lake Tahoe, have appeared (Miller, 1951; Evans, 1969). In Lake Tahoe, redsides are a littoral zone species, second in abundance only to the speckled dace. Most swim at depths of less than 10 m, although they have been collected at depths down to 30 m (Evans, 1969). Typically, they swim about in large schools close to the surface, generally staying over areas that have rocky bottoms. During the winter months, after water temperatures drop below 10°C, redsides disappear from the shallow areas. Presumably they spend the cold months relatively inactive, on rocky bottoms 3 to 18 m deep (Evans, 1969).

As the hooked pharyngeal teeth, short gill rakers, short intestine, and oblique mouth suggest, redsides are opportunistic feeders on invertebrates. In Lake Tahoe, Miller (1951) found that 38 percent of their diet, by volume, was surface insects, 28 percent bottom-living insect larvae, and 25 percent planktonic crustaceans. Another 8 percent consisted of Tahoe sucker eggs, ingested while the suckers were spawning. Schools of redsides preying on sucker eggs were also noted by Snyder (1918). The surface insects were primarily flying terrestrial forms: butterflies and moths, beetles, wasps, and ants, while the bottom forms were larvae of chironomid midges, blackflies (Simulidae), aquatic beetles, and stoneflies (Plecoptera). Redsides are opportunistic feeders and the predominant items in their stomachs varied with the area from which they were collected as well as with the time of day. Thus, the percentage of bottom organisms in different samples ranged between 9 to 99 percent, the percentage of surface organisms, 8 to 87 percent, and the percentage of planktonic forms, 0 to 92 percent (Miller, 1951). Redsides feed at any time of the day or night but flying insects seem to be favored in the evening and night, while bottom and planktonic forms are favored during the day.

Lake Tahoe redsides averaged 34 mm SL (1 gm) at age I, 51 mm (2.5 gm) at age II, 67 mm SL (7 gm) at age III, and 77 mm SL (9.5 gm) at age IV (Evans, 1969). The largest Lahontan redside on record is 14 cm SL (Snyder, 1918) but fish over 8 cm are uncommon.

Most redsides become mature in their third or fourth summer. A few may attain maturity in their second. The average number of eggs in sixteen females examined by Evans (1969) was 1,125. The right ovary of each fish contained the majority of eggs. Spawning can take place at any time from late May through August, but most such activity seems to occur in the last two weeks of June, at water temperatures between 13 and 24°C. In order to spawn, Lake Tahoe redsides either migrate up tributaries to sand and gravel areas at the downstream end of pools or they move into shallow (less than 1 m) areas along the shore, with bottoms of gravel or small rocks.

Spawning, according to Miller (1951), "provides a scene of excitement, urgency, and confusion from which the observer despairs of any constructive outcome." Groups of twenty to one hundred spawning fish swim about in a tight swirling school close to the bottom. The release of the sex products occurs when a small cluster of fish seems to press itself against the rocks on the bottom. The eggs sink into the crevices between the rocks and adhere to the undersurfaces.

After hatching, young fish leave the spawning grounds for shallow areas of quiet water, in covers or near the mouths of the spawning streams. Frequently they will occur in schools mixed with the young of other cyprinid species. These areas usually have a protective cover of floating debris.

Lahontan redsides hybridize with tui chubs and speckled dace in Lake Tahoe (Hopkirk and Behnke, 1966; Calhoun, 1940).

Status. Lahontan redsides are still abundant in most of their native range. La Rivers (1962) found that they were gone from many of the upstream areas of Nevada streams where they had been found by Snyder (1918).

References. Calhoun, 1940; Evans, 1969; Hopkirk and Behnke, 1966; La Rivers, 1962; R. G. Miller, 1951; Murphy, 1963; Snyder, 1918.

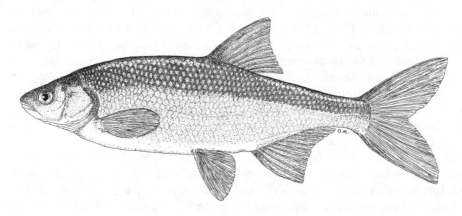

Figure 57. Hitch, 24 cm SL, Sacramento-San Joaquin Delta.

Hitch, *Lavinia exilicauda* Baird and Girard

Identification. Hitch superficially resemble golden shiners in their laterally compressed bodies, small heads with upward pointing mouths, moderately large scales, and decurved lateral lines. However, hitch lack a sharp keel on the belly, are thicker bodied, grow larger (over 35 cm TL), have a narrower caudal peduncle, and have 10 to 13 rays in the dorsal fin. Anal fin rays are usually 10 to 14, lateral line scales 54 to 62, and gill rakers 17 to 26. The pharyngeal teeth (5-4 or 5-5) are long and narrow, slightly hooked yet with fairly broad grinding surfaces. When small, hitch are silvery in color with a black spot at the base of the tail. Older fish lose the spot and become darker in color, approaching brownish yellow on the back.

Names. "Hitch" is a Pomo Indian name for this fish, as is the related name "chi" (Murphy, 1948b). *Lavinia* is a Latin feminine name whose application to the hitch is somewhat of a mystery. The narrow caudal peduncle inspired *exilicauda* (slender tail).

Distribution. Hitch are found throughout the Sacramento-San Joaquin drainage system, in streams tributary to Monterey and San Francisco bays, in Clear Lake, and in the Russian River. Three subspecies of the hitch have been recognized although they need to be reevaluated: *L. e. exilicauda* from the main river systems; *L. e. harengus*, from the Pajaro and Salinas rivers (probably invalid); and *L. e. chi* from Clear Lake (Miller, 1945; Hopkirk, 1973).

Life History. Hitch are characteristic of warm, low-elevation lakes, sloughs, slow-moving stretches of river, and ponds. When they are found in foothill streams, they are associated with large, sandy-bottomed pools with moderate growths of aquatic vegetation (Moyle and Nichols, 1973). Their quiet water habitat is reflected in their rather deep and laterally compressed body shape. Before modern-day alterations of their habitat, hitch were associated with such fishes as Sacramento perch, Sacramento blackfish, thicktail chub, and splittail. Today their most common fish associates are introduced species, especially catfishes, centrarchids, and carp (Moyle and Nichols, 1973; Turner and Kelley, 1966). Although their occurrence in the main Sacramento-San Joaquin system is somewhat spotty today, they have become permanently established in a number of reservoirs, such as Bass Lake, Madera County, and Beardsley Reservoir, Tuolumne County. Some of these reservoirs are cold and deep enough to support good trout populations.

The feeding habits of hitch have not been given the extensive study they deserve. Studies by Lindquist et al., (1943), Murphy (1948b), and S. F. Cook (unpublished data) indicate that, in Clear Lake, Lake County, hitch less than 5 cm TL feed in schools in shallow water on all stages of the Clear Lake gnat (*Chaoborus asticopus*) and on planktonic crustaceans. Large fish school out in open water, feeding on phytoplankton, planktonic crustaceans, and, to a lesser extent, flying and emerging insects. The deep compressed body, small upturned mouth, long slender gill rakers, and high but flat-topped pharyngeal teeth tend to confirm hitch as omnivorous open-water and surface feeders.

The growth rate of hitch in Clear Lake, studied by Murphy (1948), is fairly rapid: about three months after hatching their average length was 4.4 cm, and by the end of their first year they ranged in length from 8 to 12 cm. Subsequently, they increased 2 to 5 cm per year, the increase becoming less as the fish got older. In large fish, weight increased faster than length: 20 cm fish weighed 90 to 100 gm, 25 cm fish about 200 gm, and 30 cm fish about 350 gm. Growth of hitch in Beardsley Reservoir, Tuolumne County, is slower than that of Clear Lake hitch. S. J. Nicola (in press) found that Beardsley hitch were only 4 to 5 cm SL at the end of their first year and 9 to 11 cm SL by the end of their second, with subsequent yearly increments of 2 to 4 cm. Both Murphy and Nicola showed that females grew faster and larger than males. The largest fish Murphy examined was a 34 cm female in its fifth year. Older fish were taken from Beardsley Reservoir by Nicola, but none were as large.

Female hitch usually become mature in their second or third year, while males may mature in their first, second, or third year (Kimsey, 1960; Nicola, in press). They are rather prolific: 44 females examined by Nicola contained 3,000 to 26,000 eggs, with a mean of 9,000. An estimate of 112,000 eggs in one female examined by Murphy (1948b) is apparently an error. Spawning takes place in March through July when large schools of fish either migrate up into small streams or into the shallow waters of a lake or pond. Stream spawning generally occurs earlier than lake spawning. In both situations, fine- to medium-gravel bottoms, swept clean by wave action or current, and water tempeatures of 14 to 18°C seem to be necessary for spawning (Murphy, 1948; Kimsey, 1960). In the tributaries to Clear Lake, late heavy rains generally precede the spectacular spawning runs (Murphy, 1948). Spawning is a mass affair accompanied by vigorous splashing. A ripe female is closely followed by one to five males, who apparently fertilize the eggs immediately after their release. There is no territoriality or fighting. The fertilized eggs are not adhesive but sink into the interstices of the gravel. They then absorb water, swelling to about four times their initial size (Murphy, 1948). The swelling may help lodge the eggs in the gravel, to keep them from being washed away, although large numbers of viable eggs were observed slowly being washed downstream in Middle Creek (March, 1974). The rate of drift may have been slow enough so that the eggs could hatch before reaching the lake.

Hatching takes place in about ten days and the larvae take another ten days to become free-swimming (Murphy, 1948; Swift, 1965). Once they start swimming, the fry of stream-spawned Clear Lake hitch quickly move down into the lake, at about 2.5 cm TL (Murphy, 1948). This behavior has undoubtedly contributed to the success of hitch, since it permits reproduction in streams that dry up in the summer (Cook et al., 1966). The small hitch spend the next two months schooling in the lake's littoral region.

Hitch have hybridized with California roach and thicktail chubs under unusual circumstances (Miller, 1945, 1963). Hitch-roach hybrids are common in the pools of the intermittent middle reaches of the Pajaro River (J. Smith, pers. comm.).

Status. The hitch is one native fish species that seems to have held its own in the face of changes in its habitat and introduction of exotic predators and competitors. However, they are much less abundant in the Delta than they once were. Although hitch have had some value as bait fish (their sale is now prohibited) and they still have small value as a commercial fish, they are largely regarded as a nuisance by fisheries managers. They seem to grow too fast to be of much value as forage fish. In reservoirs, large populations may inhibit the growth of game fishes, including trout. However, in Clear Lake, hitch and game fishes coexist, for reasons unknown. This indicates that more needs to be known about their biology, especially outside of Clear Lake, before they are condemned as being completely worthless.

References. Burns, 1966; Cook et al., 1966; Evermann and Clark, 1931; Hopkirk, 1973; Kimsey, 1960; Lindquist et al., 1943; Miller, 1945, 1963; Moyle and Nichols, 1973; Murphy, 1948b; Swift, 1965; Turner, 1966c.

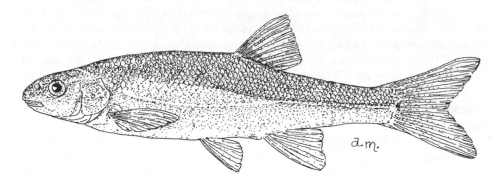

Figure 58. California roach, 5.5 cm SL, Rush Creek, Modoc County.

California Roach, *Hesperoleucus symmetricus* (Baird and Girard)

Identification. Adult California roach are small (usually less than 100 mm TL) and chunky bodied. The eyes and head are relatively large; the mouth is small and slanted at a downward angle. The dorsal fin is short (7 to 10 rays) and set behind the insertion of the pelvic fins. There are 6 to 9 anal rays. The scales are small, 47 to 63 along the lateral line and 32 to 38 before the dorsal fin. The pharyngeal teeth are 5-4 and, although narrow and slightly hooked, appear to be adapted for grinding. The upper half of the roach is usually dark, ranging from dusky gray to steel blue. The lower half is usually a dull silvery. During the breeding season, patches of red orange appear on the chin, on the operculum, and at the bases of the paired and anal fins. The males may develop numerous tiny breeding tubercles on the head at this time.

Names. The common name of California roach is derived from their superficial resemblance to one of the common minnows of Europe, the roach (*Rutilus rutilus*). Other frequently used names are western roach and Venus roach. *Hesperoleucus* is derived from the Greek words for western and white; *symmetricus* means symmetrical.

Distribution. California roach are found throughout the Sacramento-San Joaquin drainage system. The only population known outside the system is in the Cuyama River, San Luis Obispo and Santa Barbara counties, and is presumably the result of a bait-bucket introduction. The population present in the Eel River may also have been introduced (Fite, 1973). In 1913, J. F. Snyder described five forms as distinct species from streams now isolated from the main system: (1) the Monterey roach, *Hesperoleucus subditus*, from streams flowing into Monterey Bay; (2) the Venus roach, *H. venustus*, from the Russian River and streams flowing into San Francisco Bay; (3) the short-finned roach, *H. parvipinnis*, from the Gualala River, Sonoma County; (4) the Navarro roach, *H. navarroensis*, from the Navarro River; Mendocino County; and (5) the northern roach, *H. mitrulus*, from streams flowing into the Pit River and Goose Lake, Modoc County. These species are currently recognized as being, at best, subspecies of the California roach, *H. symmetricus* (Murphy, 1948). The nominate subspecies *H. s. symmetricus* is described in Hubbs and Wallis (1948).

Life History. In the main Sacramento-San Joaquin system, California roach are typically found in the small, usually intermittent, tributaries to the larger streams. In the San Joaquin River system, they are found most abundantly in the small streams of the Sierra Nevada foothills at moderate elevations (average 460 m). Populations are also present in a few warm, alkaline streams on the west side of the San Joaquin

Valley. In coastal streams, including the Russian River, roach are one of the most abundant fishes in the main channels and are dominant in the warm tributaries.

The key to the success of California roach seems to be their ability to survive where larger native fishes cannot. Large numbers of them can be found crowded together in the pools left behind when foothill streams stop flowing in the summer. These pools, although often well shaded, may have water temperatures approaching that of the air (30 to 35°C), and low dissolved oxygen concentrations (1 to 2 ppm). Most other native foothill fishes appear to have lower temperature and higher dissolved oxygen requirements than roach. In Fresno County, roach have been found in isolated, shady, rock-bottomed pools as small as 30 cm in diameter and 10 cm deep. Elsewhere they have been found in large numbers in streams heavily polluted by sewage.

The ability of roach to survive in small tributaries has presumably also lead to their colonization, through stream captures, of coastal streams where other cyprinids are absent, such as the Navarro and Gualala rivers. Such colonization could not have taken place through salt water because they are unable to tolerate even slight increases of salinity. In August, 1973, healthy roach were collected in the Navarro River at salinities of 3 ppt but those trapped downstream by the incoming tide died by the time salinities reached 9 to 10 ppt.

The main food of roach is filamentous algae (Barnes, 1957; Fite, 1973; Greenfield and Deckert, 1973). Despite the predominance of algae in the stomachs during the summer, aquatic insects and small crustaceans often make up 25 to 30 percent of the stomach contents by volume. Crustaceans are especially important in the diet of small roach. The type of insect larvae taken depends on which forms are most available in the quiet water the roach inhabit. Thus, in the Eel River, small midge, mayfly, caddisfly and stonefly larvae, along with elmid beetles, aquatic bugs, and amphipods, were taken roughly in proportion to their abundance on the bottom (Fite, 1973). One roach examined from the Navarro River contained three larval lampreys. In the winter, animal food virtually disappears from the diet and diatoms and desmids usually become the important food items, especially for small roach. Since roach pick most of their food off silty bottoms, their stomachs usually contain considerable amounts of detritus and debris. Despite this preference for bottom feeding, they will also take terrestrial insects and water striders from the surface on occasion.

Growth in roach is highly seasonal. Fry (1936) found they grew most rapidly in the early summer, presumably because food was most abundant then. These roach were mature at about two years of age, when they were 45 mm SL. Similar results were obtained by Barnes (1957) for roach in Bear Creek, Colusa County. Growth is much faster in the Russian and Navarro rivers, where roach frequently exceed 45 mm SL in their first summer, reaching 60 to 70 mm in their second summer and 80 to 90 mm in their third summer (K. Harshberger and C. Staley, unpublished data). The oldest roach on record is a five-year-old specimen from San Anselmo Creek, Marin County, but few roach live longer than three years.

Spawning takes place from March through June although spawning activity has been observed in late July in the Russian River. The fish move up from the pools into shallow, flowing areas where the bottom is covered with small rocks 3 to 5 cm in diameter. The fish spawn in schools, each female laying 250 to 900 eggs, a few at a time, in crevices between the rocks. They are immediately fertilized by one or more males following close behind the female. The eggs are adhesive and stick to the rocks as they are deposited. They hatch in two to three days and the newly hatched fish remain in the crevices until they grow large enough to swim actively around. The population of roach studied by Barnes (1957) apparently spawned in emergent vegetation and the newly hatched fry remained among the plants for some time.

Roach hybridize extensively with hitch in the Pajaro and Salinas rivers (Miller, 1945), especially in pools in the intermittent middle sections of the rivers, and with arroyo chubs in the Cuyama River (Greenfield and Greenfield, 1972).

Status. Because roach occur mostly in small, intermittent streams that contain few other fishes, especially game fishes, little is known about the state of their populations. A survey of the streams of the Sierra Nevada foothills above the San Joaquin Valley by Moyle and Nichols (1974) indicated they were still fairly common in many areas but were absent from the upper San Joaquin River and its tributaries, Fresno County, and from the Fresno River, Madera County. They were present in both systems in the late 1800s (Evermann and Clark, 1931). The disappearance of roach from these regions is probably the result of a combination of modification of their streams by man, isolation of populations by barriers on the main streams, and introduction of green sunfish. Although roach can withstand extreme environmental conditions, excessive siltation of their pools, combined with the removal of shade plants, has created conditions too severe even for them, particularly during years of drought. Once a population has been eliminated, recolonization from other populations is difficult because the presence of dams and reservoirs on the main streams, combined with large populations of introduced predatory fishes, prevents migration. Green sunfish are an additional threat to roach because they can also survive and reproduce in the harsh environment of intermittent streams. The sunfish are more aggressive and predaceous than roach and so may be gradually replacing them throughout much of their range, in part by preying on them.

Fortunately, the roach populations in coastal streams are not threatened, partially because many of the streams are managed for steelhead and salmon spawning. Although roach have been accused of competing for food and space with juvenile steelhead in such streams, Fite (1973) has effectively demonstrated that niche overlap is minimal.

References. Barnes, 1957; Evermann and Clark, 1931; Fite, 1973; Fry, 1936; Greenfield and Deckert, 1973; Greenfield and Greenfield, 1972; Kimsey and Fisk, 1964; Miller, 1945; Moyle and Nichols, 1973; Murphy, 1948; Snyder, 1912.

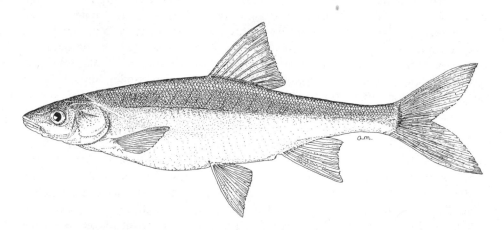

Figure 59. Sacramento blackfish juvenile, 14 cm SL, Putah Creek, Yolo County.

Sacramento Blackfish, *Orthodon microlepidotus* (Ayres)

Identification. Sacramento blackfish can be readily recognized by their tiny scales (up to 105 in lateral line), cone-shaped head with a flat, sloping forehead, round elongated body, small eye, and wide, slightly upturned mouth. There are 9 to 11 rays in the dorsal fin, 8 to 9 in the anal. The pharyngeal teeth (6-6, 6-5) are long, straight, and knifelike with a narrow grinding surface on the dorsal side of each tooth. The gill rakers are large and expand towards their tips into a broomlike fringe (Murphy, 1950). The color of small fish tends towards silvery grey. Larger fish become progressively darker, especially on the back. The combination of fine scales and dark color gives large fish a dull, olivaceous sheen.

Names. The common names usually refer to the shiny dark coloration of the adults, hence "Sacramento blackfish," "greaser blackfish," "greaser," and "blackfish." In the older literature, they are sometimes referred to as "hardheads," a name now reserved for *Mylopharodon conocephalus. Orthodon* means straight teeth; *microlepidotus*, small scales.

Distribution. Sacramento blackfish are native to the main Sacramento-San Joaquin river system, Clear Lake, and the Pajaro and Salinas rivers. They were apparently introduced into the Russian River. Introductions have also been made into reservoirs on the Carmel River, in southern California, and in the Truckee Meadows area of west-central Nevada (Burns, 1966), although the status of these populations is questionable.

Life History. Sacramento blackfish are most abundant in the warm, shallow, and usually turbid waters of the Central Valley floor, especially where current is slow or absent. Thus, they are one of the most abundant fish in Clear Lake, Lake County, and once apparently dominated the large lakes, now drained, of the San Joaquin Valley. In the Sacramento-San Joaquin Delta, Turner (1966) found they were most abundant in the San Joaquin River portion near Mossdale, where the concentration of dissolved solids was higher than in most of the rest of the Delta. They are common to very abundant in oxbows and other nutrient rich waters of the Delta (M. Caywood, pers. comm.). Other fishes common here are hitch, goldfish, carp, and white catfish.

The feeding habits of blackfish are unusual for a North American cyprinid; they are primarily filter feeders on planktonic algae and zooplankton, including rotifiers, cladocerans, copepods, and suspended detritus (Cook, et al., 1964; Murphy, 1950). They do not appear to be particularly selective in their feeding. Plankton occurs in their stomachs in roughly the same proportions as they occur in the water, so phytoplankton predominate (Murphy, 1950). The presence of sand in some stomachs indicates that they may also feed on the bottom at times. Their digestive system reflects a general reliance on filter feeding for small, hard-to-digest organisms. The broomlike gill rakers filter out tiny organisms while the knifelike pharyngeal teeth probably break up larger masses of ingested material. The intestine is long (six to seven times the body length) and convoluted, providing the surface area necessary for the slow breakdown of plant material. Cook et al. (1966) suggested that the nonselective feeding habits may cause the annual summer kills of blackfish that occur in Clear Lake. The fish ingest large amounts of bluegreen algae which may be toxic under certain conditions. However, the die-offs may also be the result of the fish being unable to withstand other midsummer conditions, such as low oxygen and high temperatures, after being weakened from spawning.

Limited observations by Murphy (1950) indicated that young-of-the-year fish (less than 8 cm FL) are more selective in their diet than are larger fish, feeding more on the bottom and more on invertebrates, such as midge (*Chaoborus*) larvae and small cladocerans. The differences in feeding habits also reflect differences in habitat. Young-of-the-year fish occur in small schools close to shore while older fish school in open water away from shore.

Growth of Sacramento blackfish is fairly rapid. Murphy (1950) found that in Clear Lake they were about 10 cm FL and weighed 30 gm at the end of their first year, growing rapidly to 25 to 26 cm FL and 230 gm during their second year. During the third year growth differences between males and females became evident, the males reaching 34 to 35 cm FL (625 gm), the females, 36 to 37 cm FL (710 gm). Growth was slower in the following years, although the male-female differences became more pronounced. The longest fish recorded by Murphy was 50 cm FL, the heaviest was 1.5 kg., and the oldest was five years.

Sacramento blackfish are mature by their second or third year. Mature males grow tiny breeding tubercles and seem to be darker than the females during the breeding season. Spawning occurs between April and July, at water temperatures ranging from 12 to 24°C in warm, shallow areas with heavy growths of aquatic plants. Because of turbid water, observations of blackfish spawning are few and incomplete. Murphy (1950) observed spawning activity by a small school over a bed of aquatic vegetation in 90 cm of water. The males followed the females closely, apparently fertilizing the eggs as they were extruded onto the plants. Similar behavior was observed by Cook et al. (1966) over rocks in water less than 18 cm deep. Spawning seems to be physiologically hard on blackfish. They develop spawning checks on the scales (Murphy, 1950) indicating that the scales are partially resorbed to provide a last-minute supply of nutrients for the developing gonads. In Clear Lake few fish manage to survive their second spawning and this may account for the annual summer die-offs noted there.

In the Truckee Meadows area of Nevada, introduced blackfish have hybridized with tui chubs, *Gila bicolor* (La Rivers, 1962).

Status. The herbivorous filter-feeding habits of blackfish, coupled with their ability to survive in warm, turbid waters, allows them to continue to be successful despite changes in their environment. Nevertheless, they are probably less abundant than formerly. They have done well when introduced as forage fish in reservoirs. Such introductions have largely ceased, however, since there is some evidence (Burns, 1966) that blackfish are not particularly useful as a forage fish. They grow too fast and, when young, may consume small invertebrates also eaten by young gamefish. Despite this, in Clear Lake they are at times important in the diet of the largemouth bass.

At the present time, their chief value seems to be as commercial fish, sold live in the oriental fish markets of San Francisco. Fifty to one hundred thousand pounds per year are now being taken from Clear Lake. Regardless of their commercial value, Sacramento blackfish merit further study for their role in aquatic food chains because they are one of the few North American fishes that seem to be largely herbivorous.

References. Burns, 1966; Casteel and Hutchinson, 1973; Cook et al., 1964, 1966; Kimsey and Fish, 1964; La Rivers, 1962; Murphy, 1950; Turner, 1966.

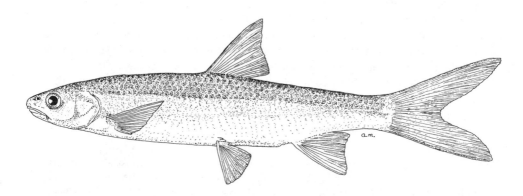

Figure 60. Sacramento splittail, 19 cm SL, Sacramento-San Joaquin Delta.

Sacramento Splittail, *Pogonichthys macrolepidotus* (Ayres)

Identification. These large (up to 40 cm FL) cyprinids are readily recognized by the enlarged upper lobe of the tail, barbels (sometimes weak or absent) at the corners of the slightly subterminal mouth, and small head (head length goes into body length less than 4.5 times). The dorsal rays are 9 to 10; pectoral rays, 16 to 19; pelvic rays, 8 to 9; anal rays, 7 to 9; the lateral line scales, 57 to 64 (usually 60 to 62); and the gill rakers, 14 to 18 (usually 15 to 17). The pharyngeal teeth, usually 2,5-5,2 but variable, are hooked and have narrow grinding surfaces. The inner tooth rows are very small. Live fish are a dull silvery gold on the sides; the older the fish, the duller the color. The back is usually a dusky olive grey. Adults develop a distinct nuchal hump on the back. During the breeding season, the paired and caudal fins are tinged with red orange (retained by some fish all year) and the males become darker colored, developing tiny white tubercles on the head.

Names. *Pogon-ichthys* means bearded fish, referring to the typically well-developed barbels, while *macro-lepidotus* means large-scaled.

Distribution. Formerly widely distributed in the lakes and rivers on the floor of the Central Valley, Sacramento splittail now seem to be confined to the Delta region and the lower reaches of the Sacramento River, up to the Red Bluff Diversion Dam (M. Caywood, pers. comm.). There is also a single highly questionable record from the Russian River (Pintler and Johnson, 1958).

Life History. Surprisingly little is known about the life history of this fish. They live mostly in the slow-moving stretches of the main rivers and the Delta. For a cyprinid, they are extremely tolerant of brackish water. Following the high flows of winter, it is common to find splittail in the diluted waters of Suisun Bay, San Pablo Bay, and the Carquinez Straits. Messersmith (1966) found that they were most common in the Carquinez Straits from February through April, when salinities were less than 5 ppt. A few, however, were captured in May and June when salinities had risen to 10 to 12 ppt. There also seems to be a resident population of splittail in Napa Marsh, where the water is brackish much of the year (M. Caywood, pers. comm.).

Their small subterminal mouth, maxillary barbels, large upper tail lobe, and generalized pharyngeal teeth suggest that splittail are adapted for feeding in areas of moderate current on bottom invertebrates, such as amphipods, aquatic insect larvae, and oppossum shrimp. Two splittail collected from the Delta in September, 1972, were feeding on small clams. When water levels rise in February and March, splittail may move into flooded areas to feed on earthworms (M. Caywood, pers. comm.). Rutter (1908) reported large numbers of splittail feeding on loose eggs in upstream areas where salmon were spawning. Splittail no longer occur in these areas.

Spawning takes place from early March to mid-May, when splittail congregate in deadend sloughs. They apparently spawn over flooded streambank vegetation or over beds of aquatic plants, mostly in the evening (M. Caywood, pers. comm.). No studies have yet been published on age, growth, or other aspects of their life history.

Status. The range of Sacramento splittail has been drastically reduced since the arrival of civilization in the Central Valley. They are today the most abundant native minnow in the Delta (M. Caywood, pers. comm.) but they are not particularly abundant compared to introduced fishes such as striped bass. They do not appear to be in any immediate danger of extinction but their ecological requirements are just beginning to be understood (a detailed life-history study is being conducted by M. Caywood, California State University, Sacramento). Their reproductive cycle may be especially vulnerable to interference by man. They seem to require deadend sloughs with beds of submerged vegetation for spawning, and a number of the sloughs that are important for spawning are proposed as outlets for the Peripheral Canal. Whether or not the movement of water through these sloughs from the canal will disrupt splittail spawning needs to be taken into consideration for the following reasons: splittail are thought to be one of the most primitive North American cyprinids (Hopkirk, 1973) and an irreplaceable member of the Sacramento-San Joaquin fish fauna; they are the object of a small sport fishery that is particularly important to the Chinese-Americans who catch them in flooded areas in the spring; and they are of some importance as forage for striped bass (Thomas, 1967). They may also have some potential for aquaculture.

References. Ganssle, 1966; Hopkirk, 1973; Kimsey and Fisk, 1964; Messersmith, 1966; Rutter, 1908; Thomas, 1967; Turner and Kelley, 1966.

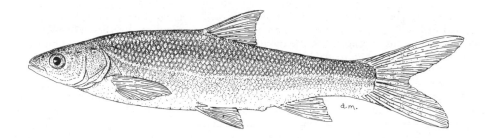

Figure 61. Clear Lake splittail, 21 cm SL, Clear Lake, Lake County.

Clear Lake Splittail, *Pogonichthys ciscoides* Hopkirk*

Identification. Similar in most respects to the Sacramento splittail, Clear Lake splittail differ in the following ways: more gill rakers (18 to 23, usually 21 to 23), more lateral line scales (60 to 69, usually 62 to 65), smaller fins, terminal mouth with absent or poorly developed barbels, reduced nuchal hump in adults, tail fin more symmetrical, and well-developed nuptial tubercles on the head and sides of breeding males (Hopkirk, 1973).

Names. Ciscoides means ciscolike, referring to the superficial resemblance of splittails to ciscoes (family Salmonidae) of the Great Lakes and elsewhere. Other names are as for Sacramento splittail.

Distribution. They are confined to Clear Lake, Lake County, and tributary streams. Occasional individuals are found in the outlet, Cache Creek.

Life History. Not much is known about Clear Lake splittail, since little interest was taken in them until recently, long after their populations had suffered a decline. They were not recognized as distinct from the Sacramento splittail until 1967 (Hopkirk, 1973). Most of the distinctive features of the Clear Lake splittail seem to be adaptations for lake living. They once apparently schooled in large numbers over most of the lake, concentrating in the littoral areas. Summer die-offs of large splittail, and other Clear Lake minnows, seems to be an annual event, although its exact cause is not known. Clear Lake splittail seem to depend less on bottom food than Sacramento splittail. They have been recorded feeding on ovipositing gnats and gnat egg rafts on the surface, as well as on bottom-living gnat larvae and on emerging pupae (Lindquist et al., 1943; Cook et al., 1964). Seventy-six percent of the diet of twenty-two splittail examined by S. F. Cook (unpublished data) was zooplankton; the rest, insects or detritus.

Clear Lake splittail spawn in the inlet streams in April and May, frequently migrating several miles upstream to suitable gravel riffles. It is not known how long the newly hatched splittail remain in the streams before returning to the lake, but it is probably at least three weeks. Once in the lake, they apparently spend the first few months in the littoral zone.

Status. Clear Lake splittail are now rare in the lake and have been so since a precipitous decline in their numbers took place in the early 1940s (Cook et al., 1966).

*The validity of this species is questioned by Clark Hubbs (*Copeia* 1974(3):808-809).

Hitch and squawfish in the lake also suffered population declines at the same time. The two most likely causes of the declines are the reduction in flow of the spawning streams and the increase in the number of bluegill in the lake. Water flows in the spawning streams have been reduced by irrigation demand. This may be particularly critical in dry years, when sudden reduction in water flows may either trap spawning adults or prevent young fish from moving into the lakes (Murphy, 1951). The three minnow species that have declined in the lake are all stream spawners in April and May. Hitch, however, are in less trouble than splittail or squawfish because they are also capable of spawning in the lake and their young apparently do not spend as long in the streams as those of the other two species (Murphy, 1951). Competition from Mississippi silversides and bluegill, now the dominant fish in the littoral areas that once supported large numbers of small cyprinids, may help keep splittail numbers low (Cook et al., 1966). Clear Lake splittail should be placed on the list of threatened fishes of California. Efforts should be made to assure that future spawning runs are successful and to learn more about their biology.

References. Cook et al., 1964, 1966; Hopkirk, 1973; Lindquist et al., 1943; Murphy, 1951.

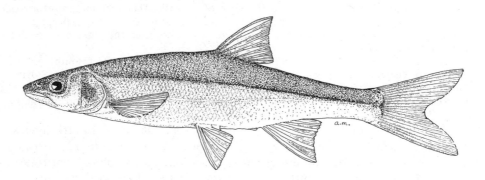

Figure 62. Hardhead, 11 cm SL, Ash Creek, Modoc County.

Hardhead, *Mylopharodon conocephalus* (Baird and Girard)

Identification. Hardheads are large, occasionally exceeding 60 cm SL, and look much like Sacramento squawfish except that the head is not as pointed, the body is slightly deeper and heavier, the maxilla does not reach past the front margin of the eye, and a small bridge of skin (frenum) connects the middle of the premaxilla to the head. They have 8 dorsal rays, 8 to 9 anal rays, and 69 to 81 scales along the lateral line. The pharyngeal teeth (2,5-4,2) are large and molariform in adults, slender and hooklike in young fish. Young fish are silvery in color, gradually turning brown to dusky bronze on the back as they mature. Small tubercles occur on the snouts of spawning males.

Names. The origin of the name hardhead is obscure, particularly since it was frequently applied to Sacramento blackfish, Sacramento squawfish, and other large minnows in the early literature. *Mylopharodon* means grinding pharyngeal teeth, referring to their molariform shape, while *concephalus* means coneshaped head.

Distribution. Hardheads are found throughout the main Sacramento-San Joaquin system and in the Russian River system. They are absent from all other coastal drainage systems.

Life History. Typically, hardheads are found in the more undisturbed sections of larger streams at low and middle elevations, although they have been captured as high as 1,338 m (Reeves, 1964). In the Sierra Nevada foothills, they are most abundant in warm, clear streams with large and deep, rock- or sand-bottomed pools. Sacramento squawfish and Sacramento suckers are common where hardhead occur, and introduced fishes, particularly centrarchids, are few (Moyle and Nichols, 1973). Hardheads are almost never found where squawfish are absent. Populations of hardheads have become permanently established in Redinger and Kerckhoff reservoirs on the San Joaquin River, Fresno County, but this seems to be an exceptional situation. More commonly they are abundant in reservoirs only for the first few years after they are built, disappearing as introduced fishes become abundant. This has happened in Shasta Lake, Shasta County; Folsom Lake, El Dorado County; Lake Berryessa, Napa County; Don Pedro Reservoir, Tuolumne County; and Millerton Lake, Fresno County (Reeves, 1964).

Hardhead are largely bottom browsers, feeding on small invertebrates and aquatic plants in quiet water. Both plankton and surface insects may be taken on occasion. Fish under 20 cm SL feed primarily on aquatic insect larvae, especially those of baetid mayflies and caddisflies, and on small snails (Reeves, 1964; R. Nichols, unpublished data). In Shasta Lake, young hardheads fed mainly on planktonic cladocerans (Wales, 1946). As the fish get older and larger, aquatic plants, particularly filamentous algae, seem to become more and more important in their diet. Follett (1928) noted large hardheads feeding on sedge (*Carex*) leaves. This dietary change is reflected in changes in the morphology of the pharyngeal teeth (Reeves, 1964). The adult fish may not get much of their nutrition from the plants themselves but rather from the small animals that are attached to the plants.

Reeves (1964) studied the growth rate of two hardhead populations from the American River drainage and found that they reached about 70 mm (48 to 119 mm) FL by the end of their first year. In subsequent growing seasons, they grew 60 to 70 mm per year, although growth tended to slow down as the fish got older. The oldest fish encountered were in their sixth year, measured 457 to 460 mm FL, and weighed about 900 gm. If the older records are accurate (e.g., Jordan and Evermann, 1896), much larger hardheads, up to 1 m in length, occur occasionally, although there are no recent records of fish this size.

Hardheads become mature after their second year and spawn in the spring. Extensive upstream spawning migrations, into smaller tributary streams, are common. Populations established in Pine Flat Reservoir, Fresno County, move up into the permanent tributary streams in April and May. Spawning behavior has never been described but hardheads most likely are mass spawners in gravel riffles. Fecundity is fairly high; a 394 mm FL female contained 21,800 eggs (Burns, 1966).

Status. Hardheads, although still widely distributed in the Sacramento-San Joaquin system, are much less abundant than they once were, especially in the San Joaquin portion. In the foothills above the Valley, Moyle and Nichols (1974) found hardheads in only 12 of 130 stream localities. Where they occurred, they were abundant. Reeves (1964) presents evidence that their distribution always has been spotty and characterized by "local abundance." It is important to note, however, that hardheads are abundant mostly in the larger, more undisturbed streams, such as the

Chowchilla River (Madera County), the Napa River (Napa County), and the Pit River (Shasta and Modoc counties), that are largely free of introduced predators (largemouth bass and smallmouth bass) and competitors (carp). Even though they may become abundant in reservoirs, occasionally even achieving "pest" status, this seems to be mainly a temporary phenomenon, associated with low populations of nonnative lake-adapted fishes. Thus, populations of hardheads should be monitored in the future. If their apparent decline continues, measures should be taken to preserve them, preferably by setting aside suitable sections of stream.

References. Burns, 1966; Evermann and Clark, 1931; Hubbs and Wallis, 1946; Jordan and Evermann, 1896; Moyle and Nichols, 1973, 1974; Reeves, 1964; Rutter, 1908; Wales, 1946.

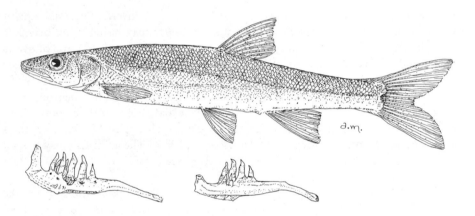

Figure 63. Sacramento squawfish juvenile, 10 cm SL, Putah Creek, Modoc County. Pharyngeal teeth are from a 46 cm SL adult, Russian River, Mendocino County.

Sacramento Squawfish, *Ptychocheilus grandis* (Ayres)

Identification. The Sacramento squawfish has an elongate body with a flattened, tapered head (pikelike). The mouth is large, the maxilla extending behind the front margin of the eye, and without teeth. The pharyngeal teeth (2,5-4,2) are long and knifelike. There are 8 rays in the anal fin, 8 in the dorsal, and 73 to 86 scales along the lateral line. Large fish (up to 114 cm SL) are generally a dark brownish olive on the back and a dingy yellow on the belly. Small fish tend to be more silvery on the sides and belly and have a dark spot at the base of the tail. The fins of breeding adults are tinged with reddish orange.

Names. The name squawfish seems to have been given to this fish (and three similar species) by the early white settlers of the Pacific states because it was a common food fish of the Indians. Many other names have also been applied to it: Sacramento pike, chub, whitefish, hardhead, chappaul, bigmouth, boxhead, and yellowbelly. *Ptychocheilus* means folded lip, "the skin of the mouth behind the jaws being folded" (Jordan and Evermann, 1896); *grandis* means large.

Distribution. Sacramento squawfish are found throughout the main Sacramento-San Joaquin River system, the Pajaro and Salinas rivers, the Russian River, and the upper Pit River. The Salinas River population seems to be recently established since J. O. Snyder failed to collect any there in 1913.

Life History. Today Sacramento squawfish are most abundant in the larger intermittent and permanent streams of the Sierra Nevada foothills between 100 and 650 m elevation (Moyle and Nichols, 1973; Taft and Murphy, 1950). These streams are generally clear, showing few signs of modification by man. Squawfish spend most of their time in the deep, well-shaded, sand- or rock-bottomed pools that are characteristic of these streams. They are usually associated with other species of native fishes, especially hardhead and Sacramento sucker. In higher elevation (500 to 650 m), permanent foothill streams, they frequently occur with rainbow trout although they apparently do not thrive in waters where temperatures seldom rise above 15°C. In the Merced River, for example, squawfish are rarely found much above the lower boundaries of Yosemite National Park (650 m) although Sacramento suckers are common in the park, indicating that these waters are accessible to squawfish (Hubbs and Wallis, 1948). Squawfish are generally rare or absent in disturbed habitats where introduced fishes, especially carp and the various centrarchid species, are present in large numbers (Moyle and Nichols, 1973). However, large numbers of small squawfish can be found in sloughs of the Delta where introduced fishes are common. These squawfish probably are all washed down from the rivers and do not reproduce in the Delta (M. Caywood, pers. comm.).

As their pikelike appearance and sharp pharyngeal teeth suggest, squawfish are predatory. Before the introduction of other predatory fishes, such as the largemouth bass, large Sacramento squawfish were undoubtedly at the top of the aquatic food chain in the Central Valley and the surrounding hills. They may take their prey on the bottom, at the surface, or in between, depending on food availability and other fish species present. Thus, Taft and Murphy (1950) found that squawfish under 18 cm SL fed largely on bottom-dwelling aquatic insect larvae, a diet similar to that of closely related northern squawfish (*P. oregonensis*). However, R. Nichols (unpublished data) has found that small squawfish, collected from foothill streams in association with hardheads, were feeding mostly (64 percent) on surface insects, while the hardheads were concentrating on the bottom-dwelling insect larvae. As the fish grow larger, large aquatic organisms become more important in their diet, especially crayfish and fish. Squawfish over 18 cm SL feed mostly on fish, including small squawfish, other minnow species, suckers, sculpins, trout, and salmon (Taft and Murphy, 1950; Thompson, 1959; Burns, 1966).

In streams, Sacramento squawfish, like northern squawfish, are often rather sedentary in habit. Taft and Murphy (1950) observed a single tagged squawfish in the same pool for three years. On the other hand, regular migrations also occur: upstream for spawning and feeding when stream flows are high, downstream when stream flows become reduced in the summer. Young squawfish typically swim about in schools in the shallow water of large stream pools or reservoirs. Large fish are generally more solitary and spend most of their time underneath submerged rocks and logs, from which they ambush prey organisms. In the evening large fish will come out and actively forage for food.

The growth rate of the squawfish varies with the season. Taft and Murphy (1950) found that growth in an intermittent stream population was very rapid between the time the young squawfish hatched from their eggs in May until the time when the stream stopped flowing in early July. During this time they increased in size from 10 to 15 mm SL to 30 to 40 SL, with scale formation taking place at about 20 mm. Between July and November, growth was very slow (5 to 7 mm increase in length) because the fish were crowded into warm pools. The growth rate then increased during the winter months when the water was again flowing, although the lower water temperatures presumably kept the fish from growing as rapidly as they did in the early summer. By the end of the first year, the fish were 44 to 74 mm SL. A similar pattern of growth is probably found in older fish as well as in other intermittent stream populations. Fish from larger and more permanent streams grow faster and larger than those from intermittent streams (Burns, 1966), although growth in the Russian River seems to be exceptionally slow (D. Dettman, unpublished data). Thus, two-year-old fish may range in size from 72 to 142 mm SL, three-year-old fish from 100 to 210 mm SL, four-year-old fish from 145 to 260 mm SL, and five-year-old fish from 205 to 320 mm SL. The largest Sacramento squawfish known, 115 cm SL and weighing 14.5 kg, was caught in Avocado Lake, Fresno County, which occupies an abandoned gravel pit just off the Kings River. The oldest on record was nine years old (Taft and Murphy, 1950) although older fish undoubtedly exist. Despite their apparent longevity and ability to reach large sizes, squawfish grow slowly compared to other large minnows, such as carp or hardhead.

Sacramento squawfish are sexually mature by the beginning of their third or fourth summer, at 20 to 25 cm SL. Ripe fish move upstream during April and May to spawn in gravel riffles when water temperatures exceed 14°C. In reservoirs they may spawn on gravel areas near shore.

Spawning behavior of the Sacramento squawfish has not been recorded in detail but it is undoubtedly similar to that of the northern squawfish, observed by Patten and Rodman (1969) in a Washington reservoir. They estimated that a maximum of 5,000 to 8,000 adult northern squawfish congregated over a rocky-bottomed area near shore, at depths between 12 m (the upper limits of the thermocline) and 3 m. Most of the congregating fish were males, outnumbering the females 50-200:1. Any female swimming past the swarm of males would immediately be pursued by one to six males. Spawning occurred when a female dipped close to the bottom and released a small number of eggs, which were simultaneously fertilized by one or more males swimming close behind her. The fertilized eggs sank to the bottom and adhered to the rocks and gravel.

High fecundity is indicated by a 50 cm SL female Sacramento squawfish that contained 17,730 eggs (Burns, 1966). In northern squawfish, the eggs hatch in four to seven days at 18°C, and the fry begin schooling in another seven days (La Rivers, 1962; Burns, 1966). These events are probably similar in the Sacramento squawfish since soon after spawning occurs, schools of fry can be observed in the shallow pool edges.

Status. Sacramento squawfish, although still common, are less abundant than they used to be. They were once found in large numbers in the lakes and rivers of the Valley floor but are now much less common there, as well as in Clear Lake, Lake

County (Cook et al., 1966) and in the Delta (Turner, 1966c). Three factors working in combination seem to be mostly responsible for their reduction: the creation of reservoirs, the siltation of the lowland streams, and the introduction of other predatory fish species. When the warm-water streams are still clear and free flowing, squawfish are abundant. Where the streams are laden with silt or pollutants and introduced fishes are abundant, squawfish tend to be absent. Populations often become established in new reservoirs, where they may persist for long periods of time. However, like hardhead, squawfish tend to disappear after initially establishing large populations. Persistance seems to depend largely on the presence of suitable spawning streams.

Sacramento squawfish are generally overrated as predators or competitors of trout and salmon. Although northern squawfish have been shown to prey heavily on young sockeye salmon in some areas (Foerster and Ricker, 1942), there is little evidence that Sacramento squawfish are serious predators on young chinook salmon, the principal salmon species that occurs where they are common. In some streams squawfish may prey on trout or compete with them for food and space. Most of these streams are marginal for trout in any case, since water temperatures in the summer approach or exceed the maximum trout can withstand. In cold trout streams squawfish seem to be rare or absent, even if the water is accessible to them (Moyle and Nichols, 1973). In the Sacramento River below Shasta Dam, squawfish were replaced by trout because the water discharged from the dam was substantially colder than it had been in its natural state (Taft and Murphy, 1950). However, there are a number of formerly productive trout waters, especially some of the larger tributaries to the Sacramento River, that now support mostly squawfish and hardheads. The reasons for the apparent change in fish fauna are unclear but changes in water quality and flows combined with the presence of impoundments that large squawfish can use for refuge during times of stress (winter, dry summers) may be mainly responsible.

If the predatory nature of Sacramento squawfish gives them a bad reputation, it also gives them sporting qualities, recognized by Jordan and Evermann (1931), Taft and Murphy (1950), Burns (1966), and every angler who hooks one (until he discovers the fish he has been fighting is not a trout or bass). Although modern anglers generally disdain such large cyprinids as food fish, the California Indians ate them regularly. Perhaps more efforts should be made to educate California angles to the good points of squawfish, rather than trying to eradicate them from streams where the standard sport fishes do poorly. In any case, squawfish merit preservation as an interesting part of California's native fauna.

References. Burns, 1966; Cook et al., 1966; Foerster and Ricker, 1942; Hubbs and Wallis, 1948; Jordan and Evermann, 1896, 1931; La Rivers, 1962; Moyle and Nichols, 1973; Patten and Rodman, 1969; Taft and Murphy, 1950; Thompson, 1959.

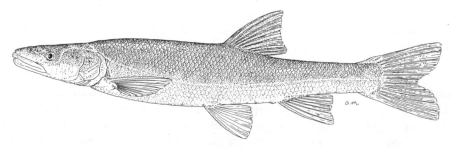

Figure 64. Colorado squawfish, 35 cm SL, Green River, Wyoming.

Colorado Squawfish, *Ptychocheilus lucius* Giard

Identification. Colorado squawfish are similar in shape and color to Sacramento squawfish, except that the head and eye are smaller in relation to the rest of the body, the body is more slender, and the head is more elongate. There are 9 rays in the dorsal fin, 9 rays in the anal fin, 80 to 95 scales in the lateral line, and the pharyngeal teeth are 2,5-4,2.

Names. The trivial name *lucius* means pike, referring to the superficial resemblance of squawfish to true freshwater pikes (Esocidae). Jordan and Evermann (1923) listed its common name as "white salmon of the Colorado" or "whitefish." Other names are as for Sacramento squawfish.

Distribution. Formerly found throughout the Colorado River and its major tributaries, it appears to be absent today from the lower Colorado River and rare elsewhere, although it is in the process of being cultured and reintroduced.

Life History. The Colorado squawfish is a big-river species. The large adults are typically found in deep, fast-flowing waters of the Colorado River and in large pools of its tributaries. Smaller fish frequent quiet water of the river's edge or shallow pools with sand or silt bottoms (Vanicek and Kramer, 1969). Unlike Sacramento squawfish, Colorado squawfish seem to do well in turbid, silty water which occurs naturally in the Colorado River system.

Like Sacramento squawfish, they are predatory. Fish less than 50 mm TL feed mostly on cladocerans, copepods, and chironomid midge larvae. Aquatic insect larvae are the most important food for fish between 50 and 100 mm TL, while fish, especially other minnows, are the dominant food for those greater than 100 mm TL (Vanicek and Kramer, 1969). Colorado squawfish over 200 mm TL feed almost exclusively on other fish, but do so sporadically; Vanicek and Kramer found that 39 percent of the stomachs of large squawfish they examined were empty.

Presumably because they occupied the position of chief piscivore in a major river system, Colorado squawfish achieved large sizes. Jordan and Evermann (1896) indicate that they occasionally exceeded 1.8 m TL and 45 kg, making this species the largest native North American cyprinid. However, few weighing more than 18 kg have been captured since 1930 (Sigler and Miller, 1963). Vanicek and Kramer (1969) collected none larger than 61 cm TL and 2.3 kg. Like the Sacramento squawfish, Colorado squawfish are slow growing. The Green River, Colorado-Utah, population studied by Vanicek and Kramer was 44 mm TL at year I, 95 mm TL at year II, 162 mm TL at year III, 238 mm TL at year IV, and 320 mm TL at year V. After the fifth year, the growth rate decreased, so that a 61 cm TL squawfish was age XI. Vanicek and Kramer also found that the growth rate of squawfish in a stretch of river below a new dam slowed down considerably following impoundment, apparently because the temperature regime of the river had changed, being either colder or warmer on the average than it had been prior to the construction of the dam.

Colorado squawfish mature between ages V and VII. Spawning takes place in July and August in the Green River, Wyoming, and seems to depend on water temperatures rising above 18°C coupled with dropping water levels (Vanicek and Kramer, 1969). In other areas, spawning may take place in the late spring (Sigler and Miller, 1963). Details of spawning habits have not been recorded but they are undoubtedly similar to those of the Sacramento and northern squawfishes. There is some evidence that

Colorado squawfish may once have made extensive spawning migrations (Sigler and Miller, 1963; Dill, 1944), which have now been blocked by dams.

Status. Colorado squawfish were once very abundant in the lower Colorado River (Minckley, 1973) but by the early 1960s they were probably extinct there. They are rare enough elsewhere to be regarded as an endangered species (Leach et al., 1974). Their disappearance is most likely the result of the drastic changes in the nature of the Colorado River, caused by large dams built in recent years. Neither the extensive reservoirs behind the dams nor the cold, clear water that flows from them provides the habitat necessary for squawfish survival. In addition, the dams block spawning and migration, curtailing reproduction. In the waters flowing from Flaming George Dam on the Green River, Vanicek (1970) found that Colorado squawfish, along with other native fishes, have been replaced by rainbow trout. In areas where squawfish still survive their growth rate is reduced and large fish are rare. Vanicek and Kramer (1969) listed several factors besides habitat change which might have caused this: competition from introduced channel catfish; death from having channel catfish, with erect fin spines, lodged in their throats; overexploitation by fishermen; and an excessively heavy load of exotic parasites acquired from introduced fish species. It is unlikely that breeding populations of Colorado squawfish will ever become reestablished in the California portion of the Colorado River as long as the present water conditions persist, although attempts are now being made to breed them in the Willow Beach Hatchery, Arizona, in order to reintroduce them to the river (S. Nicola, pers. comm.). It can only be hoped that other states that still possess stretches of river suitable for this fish will preserve these areas in their natural state. The best such remaining stream for this purpose is the lower Yampa River, Colorado (Holden and Stalnaker, 1975).

References. Dill, 1944; Jordan and Evermann, 1896, 1923; Holden and Stalnaker, 1975; Leach et al., 1974; Sigler and Miller, 1963; Vanicek, 1970; Vanicek and Kramer, 1969.

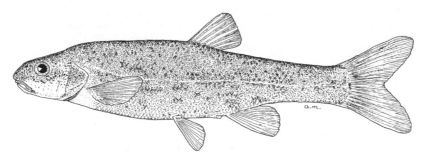

Figure 65. Speckled dace, 7.4 cm SL, Sagehen Creek, Placer County.

Speckled Dace, *Rhinichthys osculus* (Girard)

Systematic Note. No freshwater fish in the western United States is as widely distributed or occupies such a wide variety of habitats as does the speckled dace. Its adaptability is reflected in its variability and many distinct forms of it exist. Jordan and Everman (1896), for example, divided the complex into twelve species. Although systematists now seem to have little trouble placing the many forms into *Rhinichthys osculus* (Hubbs, Miller, and Hubbs, 1974), the status of the many described (and undescribed) subspecies can only be called chaotic. Of the California subspecies, only the Lahontan speckled dace, *R. o. robustus* (from the Lahontan system including Lake Tahoe), and the Klamath speckled dace, *R. o. klamathensis* (from the Klamath River system), seem to create few taxonomic problems. The Nevada speckled dace, *R. o. nevadensis*, seems to cover at least four distinct forms from isolated portions of the Death Valley system, including one from the Owens River. The name *R. o. carringtoni*, which has been applied mostly to the forms in the Sacramento-San Joaquin system and southern California, in fact seems to belong to a form from the Snake River in Utah (C. L. Hubbs, pers. comm.). It is obvious that the systematics and nomenclature of the entire complex throughout the western United States need to be examined in detail. The task, however, is likely to be extremely difficult, tedious, and time consuming. Such a study could be rewarding if undertaken with the idea of documenting evolutionary trends within one species. It will be extremely frustrating, however, if the main idea is to "straighten out" the confusing nomenclature since the species is too variable to fit in nicely with the type concepts of species.

Identification. Speckled dace are a small (less than 9 cm TL), highly variable species, distinguished by their small, subterminal mouths, pointed snout, small scales (47 to 89 in lateral line), thick caudal peduncle, and slender body. The origin of the dorsal fin (6 to 9 rays, usually 8) is set well behind the origin of the pelvic fins. The anal fin normally has 7 rays (rarely 8, frequently 6). The pharyngeal teeth (1,4-4,1 or 2,4-4,2) are strongly hooked with a slight grinding surface. Usually there is a tiny barbel at the end of each maxilla and a small frenum may or may not be attached to the premaxillae. Color is highly variable but usually consists of dark blotches on the rear half of the fish that often coalesce to resemble a dark lateral band. The bases of the fins of both sexes turn orange to red during the breeding system. Males may or may not develop tubercles on the pectoral fins.

Names. Speckled dace have a variety of unofficial common names, all of which include the word "dace:" western dace, Pacific dace, spring dace, dusky dace, etc. The word "dace" is derived from the same Middle English word that gave rise to "dart" and was originally applied only to *Leuciscus leuciscus*, a lively European cyprinid. *Rhinichthys* means snout-fish; *osculus*, kissing, refers to the small mouth. The history of the scientific nomenclature for *R. osculus* is complicated. However, the generic name used in the older literature was most often *Agosia* or *Apocope*, while the species name is usually a variant of one of the names now used to designate subspecies. Fairly complete synonymies are given in La Rivers (1962) and Cornelius (1969).

Distribution. Speckled dace are the only fish native to all of the major Western drainage systems from the Colorado River south to Sonora, Mexico. They are found throughout California, although they are absent from most coastal streams. The population in San Luis Obispo Creek seems to have originated from an early bait-bucket introduction (C. L. Hubbs, pers. comm.).

Life History. Speckled dace are primarily inhabitants of cool, flowing, rocky-bottomed permanent streams and rivers. They are also successful in a variety of other situations: warm permanent streams, such as the Owens River; large lakes, such as Lake Tahoe and Eagle Lake; small mountain lakes; the outflows of desert springs; and warm intermittent streams. In streams, their usual habitat is among the rocks in riffles, as might be expected from their streamlined body shape and subterminal mouth. In lakes, they are found on rocky or sandy bottoms, mostly in the zone stirred up by wave action (less than 1 m deep), although they are common down to 8 m in Lake Tahoe and have been taken there as deep as 61 m (Baker, 1967). Dace adapted to warm water are surprisingly tolerant of high temperatures. John (1964) found that dace from intermittent streams in Arizona survived temperatures as high as 33°C, and daily fluctuations of 10 to 15°C. In Nevada, populations live in springs with temperatures of 28 to 29°C.

Speckled dace are seldom found singly, yet they avoid forming conspicuous schools except during the breeding season. Typically, small groups appear to forage among the rocks as loose units. In Lake Tahoe and the Trinity River they are most active at night, spending the day quietly among the rocks or in slightly deeper water (Miller, 1951; Moffett and Smith, 1950). Their nocturnal habits and ability to hide among the rocks make them relatively invulnerable to predation by other fishes. Lake Tahoe dace become inactive during the winter, although they do remain in the shallow rocky areas (Baker, 1967). In streams, however, they may be active all year.

In general, speckled dace can be characterized as bottom browsers on small invertebrates. This feeding pattern is reflected in their subterminal mouth, pharyngeal tooth structure, and short intestine. However, they will feed on large flying insects at the water's surface and on zooplankton. Thus, Miller (1951) found that 81 percent of the food of Lake Tahoe dace was benthic invertebrates (snails and larvae of blackflies, caddisflies, mayflies, and beetles), while 12 percent consisted of planktonic crustaceans and water mites. In the upper Trinity River, Jhingran (1948) showed that their diet changed with the season. In the winter, the dominant food was chironomid larvae with occasional mayfly and stonefly nymphs. The nymphs became dominant in the spring, yielding to flying insects in the summer. In the fall, filamentous algae were important. Speckled dace may also consume the eggs and larvae of suckers and of other minnows.

Age and growth in speckled dace are difficult to study, since the scales have been thought to be unreliable as indicators of age (Jhingran, 1948). This may be due partially to the fact that some growth in stream populations can occur during the winter. However, length-frequency analyses from the Trinity River and Lake Tahoe indicate that dace reach 20 to 30 mm FL by the end of their first summer (Baker, 1967; Jhingran, 1948). In subsequent years, they add, on the average, 10 to 15 mm to their length, the females growing slightly faster than the males. In the Trinity River, apparently few fish survive their third winter and the largest captured by Jhingran (1948) was 85 mm FL. In Lake Tahoe, the largest fish recorded by Baker (1969) was also about 85 mm FL, but there seemed to be five or six year classes in his samples. The fish studied by John (1964) lived three to four years at most.

Dace usually become mature in their second summer. Speckled dace are capable of spawning throughout the summer but most such activity occurs in June and July, probably induced by rising water temperatures (Jhingran, 1948). In intermittent streams, spawning may be induced by flooding (John, 1963). In lakes, schools of dace seek out shallow areas of gravel for spawning or else they migrate a short distance up inlet streams where spawning occurs primarily on the gravel edge of riffles. The males congregate in a small spawning area from which they remove the algae and detritus, leaving a bare patch of rocks and gravel. When a female enters this area she is immediately surrounded by a knot of males. The female wriggles the rear portion of her body underneath a rock or close to the gravel surface and releases a few eggs while the males simultaneously release sperm (John, 1963). The eggs sink into the interstics of the rocks and adhere to them. The eggs hatch in six days (at 18 to 19°C) and the larval fish remain in the gravel for seven to eight days (John, 1963). Speckled dace are known to hybridize with Lahontan redside (Calhoun, 1940), presumably because both minnows occasionally spawn at the same time and place.

After emerging from the gravel, the fry tend to concentrate in the warm shallows of streams, especially in the channels between large rocks. In Lake Tahoe, the fry, along with those of other cyprinids, move into shallow nursery areas, usually quiet swampy coves with an accumulation of floating debris. Scales first appear at 13 mm FL (Jhingran, 1948).

Status. The Death Valley forms should all be considered endangered for the same reasons as the various pupfish species. The speckled dace of the Sacramento-San Joaquin system seems to be uncommon over the southern portions of its range, but may always have been so. None were collected by Moyle and Nichols (1973) in the Sierra Nevada foothills above the San Joaquin Valley and J. Smith (pers. comm.) has found them to be rare in the Pajaro River. They are common in the Pit River system. The Klamath and Lahontan speckled dace are widely distributed and in no trouble, in part because they often frequent streams preserved for salmon and trout. As a consequence, there is some concern by fisheries managers that they may compete for food and space with young salmonids. Large populations in small lakes, where food is limited in amount and variety, may in fact limit trout production. However, in large streams and lakes, their habitat preferences and feeding behavior result in the utilization of food largely unavailable to salmonids. Studies of interactions for food and space between dace and salmonids are currently underway (Li and Moyle, unpublished data). The habitat preferences of speckled dace, especially in lakes, also makes them largely unavailable as forage fish (Miller, 1951).

References. Baker, 1967; Calhoun, 1940; Cornelius, 1969; Jhingran, 1948; John, 1963, 1964; La Rivers, 1962; R. G. Miller, 1951; R. R. Miller, 1968; Moffett and Smith, 1950; Moyle and Nichols, 1973; Pister, 1972; Sigler and Miller, 1963.

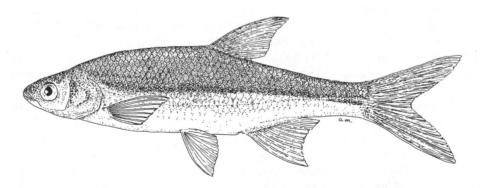

Figure 66. Golden shiner, 8.2 cm SL, Clear Lake, Lake County.

Golden Shiner, *Notemigonus crysoleucas* (Mitchill)

Identification. Golden shiners, although closely resembling hitch, can be readily recognized by their deeply compressed body, small head with an upward pointing mouth, large deciduous scales, and sharp keel on the belly between the pelvic fins and anus. The lateral line curves downward from the head, with 47 to 54 scales. There are 8 rays in the dorsal fin, 11 to 15 in the anal fin, 9 in the pelvic fins, and 15 in the pectoral fins. The pharyngeal tooth formula is 0,5-5,0. Golden shiners are usually under 25 cm SL. They often have a golden sheen to their scales, although a silvery color is also common, especially in smaller fish. The fins are colorless and lack dark basal spots.

Names. Notemigonus means angled back, referring to the fish's angular body shape, while *crysoleucas* is a combination of the Greek words for gold and white.

Distribution. Golden shiners are native to most of eastern North America, including the Mississippi River system. They occur as far north as Quebec and as far south as Texas and Florida. They were introduced into southern California in 1891 and their wide use as a bait fish has resulted in their spread to most suitable waters in California, including the Sacramento-San Joaquin system, and the Colorado River (McKechnie, 1966). They are one of the most abundant fishes in the swampy sections of the upper Pit River in Big Valley.

Life History. Golden shiners live primarily in warm ponds, lakes, and sloughs where they are associated with dense mats of aquatic vegetation. They can tolerate both the low summer oxygen levels in these waters and temperatures as high as 35°C. In the San Joaquin Valley they are most abundant in low-elevation reservoirs and sloughs where they are found with other introduced fishes such as largemouth bass, various species of sunfish, and mosquitofish (Moyle and Nichols, 1973). Occasionally they become established in cold trout lakes, to the detriment of the trout populations.

As the compressed body shape, deeply forked tail, and upturned mouth indicate, golden shiners are active fish that feed mostly on the surface or in midwater (Keast and Webb, 1966). Their triangular pelvic and pectoral fins give them considerable maneuverability, enabling them to capture small swimming organisms with some precision. Zooplankton, particularly cladocerans like *Daphnia*, seem to be the most important food for golden shiners of all sizes, followed closely by small flying insects taken at the water's surface. S. F. Cook (unpublished data) found that 95 percent of the diet of golden shiners in Clear Lake, Lake County, was zooplankton. Larger individuals will occasionally take small fish, molluscs, and aquatic insect larvae. When animal food is in short supply, filamentous algae can be found abundantly in their stomachs.

The golden shiner is a schooling fish. The schools stay mostly in littoral areas but may roam widely in a body of water.

Not surprisingly, golden shiners grow faster in warm waters than in cold. In lowland California ponds they can reach 76 mm TL in one year, while in higher, colder waters they will only reach 36 to 46 mm TL. By the end of their second year they can reach 140 mm TL, after which growth slows down somewhat. Females generally grow faster and achieve larger sizes than males. The maximum age recorded for golden shiners is nine years and the maximum length is about 260 mm SL (Carlander, 1969).

The spawning season for golden shiners lasts from March through August in California, the exact time depending on water temperature. Spawning usually begins when the water temperature reaches about 20°C, although it has occurred at temperatures as low as 15°C. The shiners spawn in schools early in the morning. Each female deposits her adhesive eggs on submerged vegetation and bottom debris, where they are fertilized immediately by one or more males. Occasionally, active nests of largemouth bass are selected as spawning sites. The survival of eggs and larvae may actually be higher in this situation, presumably because the adult bass protects the nest (Kramer and Smith, 1960).

The eggs hatch in four to five days. The newly emerged fry school in large numbers close to shore, feeding on small planktonic organisms.

Status. Golden shiners are the most extensively propagated bait fish in California and thus support a rather valuable small industry. The very fact they are widely used as bait fish has resulted in their introduction throughout the state, with unknown effects on the native minnow fauna. They are considered to be valuable forage for game fishes, particularly in warm-water reservoirs, although they may compete for food with young sunfish and bass. Similarly, when they become established in trout lakes, they apparently compete with the young trout for food and space since trout production becomes much lower.

References. Dobie et al., 1956; Kramer and Smith, 1960; McKechnie, 1966; Keast, 1966, 1967; Keast and Webb, 1966; Carlander, 1969; Moyle and Nichols, 1973.

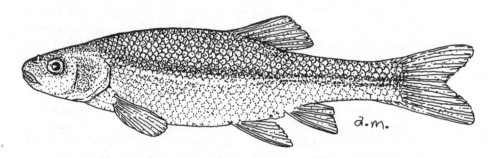

Figure 67. Fathead minnow, 6 cm SL, Suisun Creek, Solano County.

Fathead Minnow, *Pimephales promelas* Rafinesque

Identification. Chunky, bluntheaded fish seldom exceeding 85 mm TL, fathead minnows can be distinguished by their thickened first dorsal ray, small, slightly oblique mouth, and the crowding of scales behind the head. The lateral line seldom extends beyond the anterior half of the body. There are 44 to 48 scales in the lateral series. Dorsal rays are 8, pelvic rays 8, anal rays 7, and pharyngeal teeth 4-4 with oblique grinding surfaces. The intestine is two to three times the body length and the peritoneum is black. Breeding males have conspicuous tubercles on the snout, chin, and pectoral fins and a spongy pad on the back of the head. The back is usually dark, tending towards brown or olive, the sides dull and dusky. Breeding males turn nearly black, particularly on the head, with two wide pale vertical bands on their sides.

Names. The word minnow is an Old English word of possible Latin origin. In Great Britain it is applied primarily to the cyprinid *Phoxinus phoxinus* but in America the use of the term has been broadened to include all small cyprinids. *Pime-phales* means fat helmet ornament; *pro-melas*, before black. Both terms refer to the head of spawning males which is dark colored, with a conspicuous fatty pad on top.

Distribution. Fathead minnows are native to most of the eastern and midwestern United States and Canada, as well as to parts of northern Mexico, except for the Atlantic slope and the Gulf states east of the Mississippi River. Their use as bait fish has resulted in introductions throughout the West. They probably first came into California as bait used in the Colorado River fishery in the early 1950s (Shapovalov et al., 1959). As the bait industry grew, they were spread throughout the state, although established populations are fortunately few. They are found in large numbers, however, in some small streams of the San Joaquin Valley, such as Los Banos and Ulatis creeks (M. Caywood, pers. comm.).

Life History. Fathead minnows can survive in a wide variety of habitats, but they seem to do best in the pools of small, muddy streams and in ponds. Cross (1967) characterized them as pioneers, the first to invade and the last to disappear from intermittent streams and other fluctuating aquatic environments. They are capable of tolerating alkalinities of over 2,100 mg/l (McCarraher, 1972) as well as low dissolved oxygen, high organic pollution, high turbidities, and temperatures up to 33°C. However, they seem to be poor competitors with other fish species, especially other cyprinids, in more stable environments (Cross, 1967). When they do occur with other species, they are generally found in association with beds of aquatic vegetation.

Despite their terminal mouths, fathead minnows are largely bottom browsers on filamentous algae, diatoms, small invertebrates, and organic matter (Keast, 1966). This diet is indicated by their grinding pharyngeal teeth and long intestine. It is likely that in the absence of other fishes, they feed on whatever small organisms are most abundant on the bottom, in midwater, or among aquatic plants.

Growth rates of fathead minnows are highly variable, influenced by factors such as temperature, food availability, and population size. Growth normally ceases at low temperatures but this may be the result of low food availability. Prather (1957) found experimentally that growth was possible at temperatures of 2 to 7°C if the fish were well fed and not overcrowded. At the end of their first growing season they range in length from 25 to 64 mm TL reaching up to 84 mm in their second season (age I fish). Comparatively few fish reach ages II or III or approach the maximum recorded length of 109 mm TL (Carlander, 1969). Size also depends on sex since males grow larger than females.

The age of sexual maturity is variable: first spawnings have been recorded at ages 0, I, and II (Carlander, 1969). This variability in age of maturity has undoubtedly contributed to their success in fluctuating environments. Another factor contributing to their success is their ability to spawn repeatedly, throughout the summer, once water temperatures exceed 15 to 16°C (Dobie, et al., 1956). Thus, although a female can contain anywhere from 600 to 2,300 eggs, usually less than a third of the eggs will be ripe at any one time. Total egg production per female, especially in a newly established population with a low density of fish, may greatly exceed the number of eggs each is capable of containing at one time. Dobie et al. (1956) recorded a single female spawning twelve times in eleven weeks, producing 4,144 eggs.

Breeding males are highly territorial, which accounts for their larger size, dark coloration, and well-developed breeding tubercles. The center of each territory is usually a flat stone, board, or branch, at a depth of 30 to 90 cm, which serves as an egg-laying site. Root masses, water lilies, and vertical stakes may also be used (Cross,

1967). The males defend their nests from other males with such vigor that occasional injuries result, especially eye damage, presumably from contacts with the breeding tubercles. The males improve each nest site by enlarging a hollow underneath the rock or stick and by removing small pieces of debris. Since the eggs are usually laid on the undersurface, the male may clean it off by rubbing with the pad on the back of his head. The pad may also be used for tending the eggs (Wynne-Edwards, 1932).

While the males are defending their territories, the females are swimming nearby in loose schools. When one is ready to spawn, she approaches a male who then goes through a courtship display which culminates in her being led into the nest and the eggs laid. The males may spawn with several females over an extended period of time, since nests have been found that contained over 12,000 eggs in various stages of development (Carlander, 1969).

The eggs, about 1.3 mm in diameter, hatch in four to six days at temperatures around 25°C (Dobie et al., 1959). The newly hatched larvae are about 4.8 mm TL and remain in the nest for the first few days after hatching.

Status. Fathead minnows, along with golden shiners and red shiners, are legal bait minnows in California, which means that they have been widely distributed in the state. They have also been planted in reservoirs as forage fish (Shapovalov et al., 1959). However, few populations seem to have become established. This is not too surprising since most fishing with live bait takes place in reservoirs and large rivers where suitable fathead minnow habitat is lacking. They also seem to be of major importance as bait minnows compared to golden shiners. Nevertheless, their use as bait minnows in California should probably be banned in the future to safeguard native fishes, especially California roach, that live in the intermittent stream habitat favored by fathead minnows.

References. Bell, 1960; Carlander, 1969; Cross, 1967; Dobie et al., 1956; Keast, 1966; McCarraher, 1972; Prather, 1957; Sigler and Miller, 1963; Shapovalov et al., 1959; Wynne-Edwards, 1932.

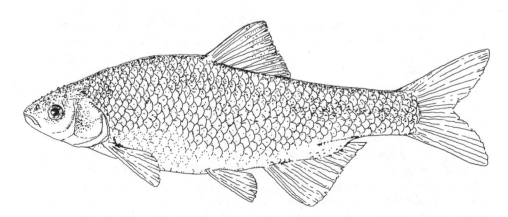

Figure 68. Redshiner, 5 cm SL, ditches along Salton Sea, Imperial County.

Red Shiner, *Notropis lutrensis* (Baird and Girard)

Identification. Red shiners are small (less than 8 cm TL) minnows with deep, compressed bodies and a terminal, oblique mouth. The lateral line is decurved, with 33 to 36 scales. There are 8 rays in the dorsal fin, 8 to 10 in the anal, and 8 in each pelvic. The pharyngeal teeth are 0,4-4,0, or 1,4-4,1, with narrow grinding surfaces. Breeding males have numerous tubercles on the head, sides, and fins. Nonbreeding fish are buff to olivaceous on the back, silver on the sides (with a faint dark lateral band), and white on the belly. Breeding males have red to orange caudal, anal, pelvic and pectoral fins and steely blue sides. Their heads are red on top, pinkish on the sides, with conspicuous purplish crescents immediately behind them.

Names. The generic name *Notropis*, applied to over one hundred species of North American minnows, is a misnomer, since it means keeled back. Rafinesque, when he described the genus in 1818, used fish that were partially dried out, the shrinkage producing a "keel" on the back (Jordan and Evermann, 1896). *Lutrensis* means otter, referring to Otter Creek, Arkansas, from which the first specimens were collected.

Distribution. Red shiners are native to streams of those western and central states that drain into the Mississippi River and the Rio Grande. Their use as a bait minnow led to their establishment in the Colorado River between 1950 and 1953 (Hubbs, 1954) and in freshwater ditches around the Salton Sea. It is likely that most of these fish are descendants of red shiners that escaped from an Arizona bait farm, which had brought them in from Texas. Attempts to introduce them elsewhere in the state have so far been unsuccessful, although they are a legal bait minnow and so can be expected almost anywhere.

Life History. Like fathead minnows and California roach, red shiners thrive in unstable environments such as intermittent streams. In Kansas they are most abundant in warm, muddy streams where few other fish species occur (Cross, 1967). They are extremely tolerant of high temperatures, having been collected from water as warm as 39.5°C (Carlander, 1969). According to Cross (1967) they become most abundant during years of drought when extreme conditions eliminate more specialized fishes. In the Colorado River, they seem to be most common in backwaters and sloughs, avoiding areas of strong current.

Red shiners characteristically swim about in large schools, feeding on whatever organisms are most abundant, especially small crustaceans, aquatic insect larvae, surface insects, and, when necessary, algae. Morphologically, they seem best adapted for taking small invertebrates in midwater or from aquatic plants in quiet water. Most feeding is done during daylight hours, although there may be a peak of feeding activity at dawn (Harwood, 1972).

Growth is most rapid during the first summer, when they may reach 25 to 30 mm SL. In subsequent years they can grow 5 to 15 mm per year, achieving a maximum of 80 mm SL. The oldest red shiner recorded by Carlander (1969) was age III. They become mature as yearlings.

Spawning occurs at water temperatures between 15 and 30°C, which permits a long breeding season. Cross (1967) recorded spawning in Kansas from May to October, most of it occurring in June and July. Red shiners spawn in quiet water on a variety of substrates, including aquatic plants, gravel and sand bottoms, tree roots, logs, and other submerged debris. Active sunfish nests may also be used. Apparently, red shiners can either spawn in groups or on territories held by individual males. In nonterritorial spawning observed by Minckley (1959), males courted females by swimming closely beside them with erect fins. A chase for a meter or so usually followed, often resulting in one or more fish leaping from the water. Spawning occurred when male and female swam side by side, fins erect, over suitable substrate. The numerous breeding tubercles of males are used for contacting the females during courtship and holding them during spawning (Koehn, 1965).

Status. Despite the fact that the red shiner is one of the three legal bait minnow species in California, it has only become established in one major river system, the Colorado. Even its establishment there was unexpected since it was once felt that the river lacked suitable habitat for it (Miller, 1952). The red shiner has spread rapidly in the Colorado River as well as tributary streams. In the Moapa River, Nevada, establishment of the red shiner, and other exotic species, has been associated with the decline of native fishes (Deacon and Bradley, 1972). Attempts to get populations going in northern California for bait and forage have so far failed (Kimsey and Fisk, 1964). Because red shiners have potential for becoming established in the warm intermittent streams of California where they would compete with endemic fishes, their use as bait fish outside the Colorado River system should be discouraged.

References. Bell, 1960; Cross, 1967; Deacon and Bradley, 1972; Harwood, 1972; Hubbs, 1954; Kimsey and Fisk, 1964; Koehn, 1965; Miller, 1952; Minckley, 1959.

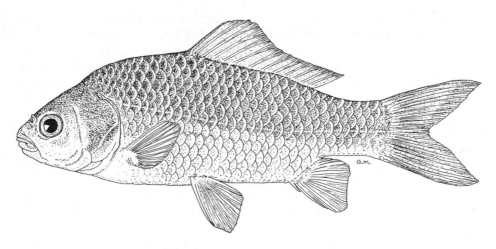

Figure 69. Goldfish, 16 cm SL, Putah Creek, Yolo County.

Goldfish, *Carassius auratus* (Linnaeus)

Identification. Wild goldfish can be as variable in color and body shape as those sold in pet stores. However, in wild populations, there is strong selection (presumably by predatory birds) for the more protectively colored wild phenotype: usually olive on the back, silvery to bronze on the sides, white on the belly. Like carp, goldfish are heavy bodied and possess stout, serrated spines at the beginning of the dorsal and anal fins. Unlike the carp they lack barbels at the corners of their thin-lipped terminal mouths. Counting the spine (actually a hardened ray), they have 18 to 19 rays in the dorsal fin, 6 to 7 in the anal fin. There are 28 to 31 large scales along the lateral line, while the pharyngeal teeth are 0,4-4,0, blunt, and comblike. Breeding males develop small tubercles on the sides of the head and on the pectoral fins.

Names. Carassius is the Latinized common name (French, *carassin*; German, *Karausche*) of the closely related Crucian carp (*Carassius carassius*), a native of western Europe. *Auratus* means gilded or golden.

Distribution. Originally, wild goldfish ranged from eastern Europe to China. They are now established in suitable waters the world over. In California large established populations are present in some southern California reservoirs and in the canals and sloughs of the Central Valley. Individuals from recent releases and from natural spawnings are likely to be found almost anywhere in the state where the water is sufficiently warm.

Life History. Although goldfish are known to survive water temperatures from 0 to 41°C, populations generally become established only in warm, often oxygen-deficient water in areas where winters are mild. They seem especially well-suited to fertile ponds and sloughs with heavy growths of aquatic vegetation. Goldfish can become established in cold, more oligotrophic lakes provided there is a littoral area large and warm enough for breeding.

Goldfish are by and large grazers on phytoplankton, as their long intestine and closely spaced gill rakers suggest. They also consume zooplankton, large amounts of organic detritus, and aquatic macrophytes, indicating that they feed on the bottom as well as in midwater. Adult goldfish collected in November from the sloughs of the San Joaquin River in Fresno County were feeding mostly (58 percent) on algae, primarily planktonic diatoms together with a few strands of filamentous algae. The rest of their diet was organic detritus with a few fragments of higher plants. The diet of seventy-one goldfish collected from sloughs of the Sacramento River in November and April was similar, except that the April fish also had eaten chironomid larvae and cladocerans (4 percent by volume). Dobie et al. (1956) indicated that goldfish will also occasionally take insects and small fish. Young-of-the-year goldfish feed more on zooplankton and small aquatic insect larvae.

Growth rates in goldfish are highly variable, depending on environmental conditions. Overcrowding particularly stunts their growth. Thus, at the end of the first growing season they may range in length from 15 to 105 mm SL (Trautman, 1957). In Sacramento River sloughs, normal growth in subsequent years is 15 to 25 mm per year, the amount decreasing with age (R. Greenlee, unpublished data). Thus, goldfish in their fourth year from the Sacramento River were 117 to 161 mm SL, although similar-aged fish from the San Joaquin River were 165 to 215 mm SL. Goldfish may reach 41 cm TL and 1.5 kg. Trautman (1957) suggested that "goldfish" much larger than this are actually goldfish-carp hybrids. Females generally grow larger and live longer than males. As a result, the male:female sex ratio in goldfish populations changes from 1:1 in small fish to 13-16:100 in fish over 15 cm TL (Breder and Rosen, 1966). Maximum ages of twenty-five to thirty years have been recorded for aquarium goldfish (Carlander, 1969).

Goldfish are mature by their second or third year, males almost always maturing during the second year. The number of eggs per mature female varies with the size and health of the fish but 14,000 seems to be about average. Nine fish (average length, 135 mm SL) from the Sacramento River contained an average of 19,900 eggs, the numbers ranging from 8,000 in a 121 mm SL fish to 29,600 in a 168 mm SL fish (R. Greenlee, unpublished data).

Spawning requires temperatures of 15 to 23°C. At higher or lower temperatures the gonads do not develop completely and any eggs laid do not develop successfully. Overcrowding will also inhibit spawning. Under normal conditions goldfish spawn several times per season, laying 2,000 to 4,000 eggs each time (Dobie et al., 1956). In California, the first spawning takes place in April or May. Spawning usually occurs at sunrise on sunny days, over aquatic vegetation, flooded grass, roots, leaves, and other submerged objects. The spawning act is similar to that of carp, the male following close behind the female and fertilizing the eggs immediately after their release. The eggs are highly adhesive and hatch in five to seven days.

Goldfish are known to hybridize with carp and the hybrids may be fertile, resulting in extensive back-crossing. In Lake Erie the hybrids are more abundant than either parent species (Trautman, 1957). Such hybrid swarms, although unreported so far from California, seem likely in areas where the two species occur together.

Status. Although goldfish are widely distributed in California, their ecological role is not well understood. They probably compete with native fishes for food and space and yet grow too fast to be of much value as forage fish. Dobie et al. (1956) indicated that, like the carp, large populations of goldfish can severely disturb gamefish habitats. Thus, their prohibition as a bait minnow should remain in effect. The control of pet releases, although highly desirable, seems to be impossible.

References. Breeder and Rosen, 1966; Carlander, 1969; Cross, 1967; Dobie et al., 1956; Trautman, 1957; Wheeler, 1969.

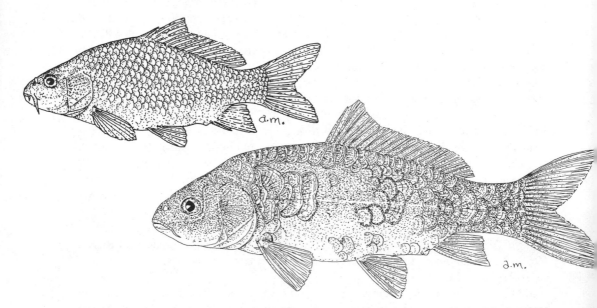

Figure 70. Carp, normal, 15 cm SL (upper); large-scaled variety, 18 cm SL (lower); both from sloughs along Sacramento River.

Carp, *Cyprinus carpio* Linnaeus

Identification. Carp are large-scaled, heavy-bodied minnows with two barbels hanging from the upper lip on each side of their subterminal mouths. The dorsal fin is elongate, consisting of 17 to 21 rays preceded by a stout, serrated spine (actually a hard ray). The anal fin also has a spine, followed by 5 to 6 rays. The pelvic fins contain 5 to 7 rays while the caudal fin usually as 19, 17 of which are branched. There are 32 to 38 scales along the lateral line in most wild carp although there are varieties that lack scales completely (leather carp) or have only a few patches of large, irregular scales (mirror carp). The pharyngeal teeth (3,1,1-1,1,3) are large and molariform. Adult carp are gold green in color with red tinged pectoral, pelvic, and anal fins. Juveniles tend to be whitish grey in color.

Names. The word carp, and its relative *carpio*, is an ancient one. Forms of it were used by the Roman and Celtic peoples of Europe. The generic name *Cyprinus*, first used by Linnaeus in 1758, seems to be an indirect reference to its fecundity, since the name is probably derived from Cyprus, the island home of Venus.

Distribution. The carp were originally native to Asia but became established early in Europe by planting. Because of the high esteem they held (and hold) in Europe as food and sport fish, they were brought to California in 1872 by Julius A. Poppe, who stocked a pond in the Sonoma Valley with five carp from Germany. In 1877 the California Fish Commission started culturing carp with 88 it imported from Japan. Also in 1877 the United States Fish Commission in Washington, D. C., started raising carp with 345 imported from Germany. From these sources carp were planted all over the United States and Canada. By 1897 carp were so widely distributed and their disadvantages were starting to become so apparent that official stocking was halted. The damage was already done, however, so that today carp are found in most rivers and reservoirs throughout the United States. In California, they seem to be absent only from the Klamath River system.

Life History. Carp are most abundant in warm, turbid water at low altitudes but they also manage to live in some trout streams and in a few cold-water reservoirs at high altitudes such as Shaver Lake, Fresno County (1,320 m). They are generally associated with eutrophic waters with silty bottoms and good growths of submerged and emergent aquatic vegetation. Carp are active at water temperatures of 4 to 34°C, although the optimum temperature for growth seems to be around 24°C (McCrimmon, 1968). One of the main reasons carp have succeeded so well in the West is their ability to survive under adverse conditions. They can withstand exceptionally high turbidity, sudden temperature changes, and low oxygen concentrations (0.5-3.0 ppm).

Carp prefer shallow water and have seldom been recorded occurring deeper than 30 m. They usually overwinter, however, in the deeper waters of lakes and streams, moving into shallow water to feed and breed as the water warms up in the spring. If the preferred feeding areas are exceptionally shallow, the carp will move in to feed only during the early morning and evening.

In general carp are omnivorous bottom feeders, although animal food, particularly aquatic insect larvae, seems to be more important in their diet than plant food. The diet changes with age. Newly hatched carp feed on both zooplankton (rotifers, copepods, etc.) and phytoplankton (algae). As they increase in size, they begin to feed more and more on the bottom, on insect larvae. By the end of their first summer they are feeding on most of the available bottom invertebrates. Adult carp have been recorded feeding heavily on aquatic plants and on algae, although it seems likely that the small animals that grow attached to the plants are more important nutritionally to the fish than the plants themselves. The preferred animal foods of carp are aquatic insect larvae, especially midge larvae (Chironomidae), followed by aquatic crustaceans, molluscs, and annelid worms. Fish, probably dead before eaten, and fish eggs, including carp eggs, have been found in carp stomachs.

Undoubtedly one of the carp's most undesirable traits is its feeding behavior. Typically, they root around on silty bottoms, stirring up aquatic insects which they then pick out of the water. They will frequently take the silt up into their mouths and then spit it out. This allows the fish to pick out the organisms thus suspended in the water. The effect of this behavior is to uproot aquatic plants, which provide cover and food for other fishes and food for waterfowl, and to greatly increase the turbidity of the water, cutting down on the sunlight available for plant growth.

Although the turbidity created by carp feeding frequently is responsible for the disappearance of gamefish from an area, more often than not the carp were not the creators of the adverse conditions but rather they moved into an area already disturbed by man's activities. The ability of carp to move into new areas, favorable and unfavorable to other fish, has been well documented by Sigler (1958). A tagged carp in the Missouri River moved 1100 km upstream in just over two years.

Growth of carp varies considerably with the summer water temperatures, length of the growing season, quality of the water, and food availability. During their first summer of life they may reach 7 to 36 cm SL with an average of 10 to 15 cm SL. During their second year they can double in length, and add 10 to 12 cm during each following year, although growth tends to slow down after the fourth or fifth year. Increase in weight follows a similar pattern, although it too can be highly variable. Sigler (1958) found that 30 cm SL carp from Bear Lake, Utah, weighed anywhere from 117 to 1,729 gm, with an average of 683 gm. In the wild, carp seldom live longer than twelve to fifteen years or exceed 80 cm SL and 9,000 gm in weight. However, they have been recorded as living as long as forty-seven years in captivity. The largest carp ever caught, from South Africa, weighed 39.9 kg, while the largest caught in North America from Iowa weighed 26.9 kg. One of the largest carp recorded for California was caught in Lake Nacimiento, San Luis Obispo County, California, and weighed 26.3 kg (files, California Department of Fish and Game, Region 4).

Spawning takes place in the spring and early summer when water temperatures start to exceed 15°C. The first indication of spawning is large schools of carp swimming slowly about in open water, usually close to shore, their dorsal fins and backs frequently breaking the surface. Soon they separate into smaller schools, each containing one or two females and three or four males. These schools move into shallow, weedy areas, preferably recently flooded, and quickly begin to spawn, accompanied by much splashing. Spawning can occur at any time of the day and night, but seems to peak in the late evening and early morning.

A female lays about 500 eggs at a time and, depending on her size, will deposit 50,000 to 2,000,000 eggs during the season. The eggs are adhesive and stick to the plants and bottom debris in the spawning area. They hatch in three to six days. The newly hatched larvae are 5.0 to 5.5 mm TL. They quickly drop to the bottom or attach to the vegetation where they live on the contents of their yolk sac for the next few days. Soon they start feeding on zooplankton and, as their fins develop, become more and more active swimmers. By the end of their first week, most carp fry have moved into beds of emergent or submerged vegetation. They seldom leave this protective cover until they are 7 to 10 cm TL when they are fairly secure from predation.

Status. The introduction of carp to North America was a serious mistake. They have displaced or greatly reduced the populations of many native fishes and have been responsible for the destruction of much gamefish and waterfowl habitat. They have low value as forage fish since the most vulnerable stages of their life history are spent hidden in the aquatic weeds. However, they do have virtues as a food and gamefish that are slowly being recognized in California. They grow rapidly and achieve large sizes in polluted water that will support few other fish. They can provide good sport as they are wary, often surprisingly difficult to catch, and put up a good fight when hooked. They can be a real culinary treat when properly prepared. Already a substantial commercial fishery exists for them in Clear Lake, Lake County, and in some reservoirs.

Control of carp is both difficult and expensive. Probably the most effective means are intensive commercial fishing in large bodies of water and the use of selective fish poisons in small bodies of water. Certainly, efforts should be made to exclude carp from waters that do not now contain them.

References. Burns, 1966; Carlander, 1969; McCrimmon, 1968; Moyle and Kuehn, 1964; Sigler, 1958.

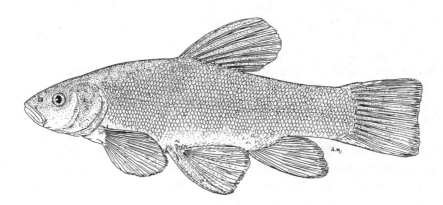

Figure 71. Tench, 23 cm SL, reservoir near Lobitas Creek, San Mateo County.

Tench, *Tinca tinca* (Linnaeus)

Identification. Tench are deep-bodied, thick, covered with tiny, deeply imbedded scales (90 to 115 in the lateral line), and very slimy. The mouth is small and terminal with a single barbel at the end of each maxilla. The caudal fin is not forked and the dorsal and anal fins are well rounded, each with 8 to 9 rays. The pharyngeal teeth are in a single row, usually 5-4. In California tench may reach sizes of 60 to 80 cm TL and 2 to 3 kg. Mature males possess a thick ray on the edge of each pelvic fin. The color of the back varies from dark green to black, becoming bronze on the sides and belly. Some individuals may be a gold bronze color overall. The fins are dark.

Names. Tinca is the Latin word for tench and the Old English name tench is derived from it.

Distribution. Tench are native to most of Europe, except northern Scandanavia. Twelve to twenty-four 10 to 15 cm TL fish were brought to California from Italy in 1922 and introduced as sport and food fish into a private reservoir near Lobitas Creek, San Mateo County, by an Italian-American rancher (Shapovalov, 1944; Skinner, 1972). They are still present in this reservoir (as of 1973). They were subsequently spread to other ponds and reservoirs in Santa Cruz and San Mateo counties, but only a few still have them. Supposedly, they were introduced successfully into the lower Trinity and Klamath rivers (Kimsey and Fisk, 1964), but there seem to be no recent records of them from these rivers (M. Coots, pers. comm.).

Life History. Little work has been done on tench biology in California. This summary is based on studies done in Europe (Wheeler, 1969; Varley, 1967) and in Tasmania (Weatherley, 1959), where they have also been introduced.

Tench are fish of warm, quiet waters doing best in farm ponds, oxbow lakes, sloughs, deep, slow-moving stretches of rivers, and castle moats. They are generally associated with muddy bottoms and heavy growths of aquatic macrophytes. Tench can survive water temperatures as high as 30 to 35°C, oxygen concentrations less than 1 ppm, and salinities up to 12 mg/1. Although tench from northern Europe can apparently withstand temperatures close to freezing, California tench, being descended from south European populations, may not be able to withstand such low temperatures. The optimum temperatures for growth seem to be between 12 and 30°C.

Tench are rather sluggish in their movements and are not very aggressive towards other tench or towards other fishes (Sterba, 1959), earning them the reputation of "Physician of Fishes" (Walton, 1653). Usually tench are solitary in habit and strongly nonmigratory. During the hot summer months, however, they tend to congregate in deep holes and shady areas, seeking cooler water.

Invertebrates that live on the bottom or on aquatic plants are their main food. Tench 6 to 12 cm TL feed primarily on aquatic insect larvae, especially those of mayflies, damselflies, chironomid midges, and caddisflies. Larger fish seem to depend on whatever large invertebrates are most abundant. Thus, Weatherley (1959) found that large tench from one pond fed mostly on pulmonate snails; from another, on oligochaete worms, and from another, on insect larvae, especially chironomids. Most of the guts he examined also contained mud, indicating that the food was taken on the bottom. Algae and aquatic plants become important in their diet only when overcrowding in a pond reduces the amount of invertebrate food available. Like bluegill, tench are probably not able to survive on a purely vegetarian diet. Tench less than 6 cm TL feed on small crustaceans among the aquatic plants, especially cladocerans, copepods, and amphipods. Small chironomid larvae and water mites may also be taken. Newly hatched fry take mostly small crustaceans, especially nauplii, along with rotifers and diatoms.

Growth of tench is generally slow for a large cyprinid, averaging about 3 cm per year for the first four years and becoming progressively slower thereafter. A 30 cm TL fish will probably be at least nine years old. In Tasmania, Weatherley (1959) found that tench grew fastest in farm ponds, slowest in a large lake, and moderately well in a sluggish river. In Europe, tench commonly reach 64 cm TL and weights of 2 kg, although fish weighing nearly 4 kg have been caught. Shapovalov (1944) indicated that tench in California may reach 2 to 3 kg.

Tench mature during their third or fourth year, the males usually achieving maturity one year before the females of the same age. Spawning takes place in the summer (May through August in Europe), after the water has reached a temperature of 18°C. Tench school for spawning in areas of heavy plant growth, each female laying around 500,000 eggs per kg of body weight (Varley, 1967). The adhesive green eggs, each about 1.2 mm in diameter, stick to the aquatic plants. They hatch in six to eight days, and the 2 to 3 mm long fry begin feeding a day or so later.

Status. Tench were illegally introduced into California. Fortunately, their slow growth, confinement to isolated ponds in small coastal drainages, and generally low desirability seem to have kept them from spreading. However, their hardiness in and out of the water and their high fecundity does make their spread into other river systems rather easy. Although they seem to be innocuous compared to carp, their potential for offering competition for food, especially to gamefishes and native cyprinids, is high enough so that their introduction into other waters should be prevented if at all possible. Since they are presently found only in a few small ponds without public access, their further spread seems unlikely, especially since the local ranchers seem to have lost interest in them. A thorough survey of their populations, however, is needed.

References. Kimsey and Fisk, 1964; Shapovalov, 1944; Sterba, 1959; Varley, 1967; Walton, 1653; Weatherley, 1959; Wheeler, 1969.

Sucker Family, Catostomidae

The suckers are a highly successful group of fishes, even though they lack the diversity of species and ways of making a living of their close relatives, the minnows. With the exception of a few plankton-feeding forms, they are bottom browsers, sucking up or scraping off small invertebrates, algae, and organic matter with their fleshy, protrusible lips. Their comblike pharyngeal teeth serve to keep large, undigestible items from entering the long, coiled intestine. The ability of suckers to thrive on an abundant food source little exploited by other fishes, combined with the mobility given them by their solid, muscular bodies, has permitted a comparatively small number of species to become abundant in a wide variety of habitats, from mountain and foothill streams, to reservoirs and lakes, to lowland sloughs and large rivers. In addition, they possess many of the characteristics that have made the cyprinids so successful, including a well-developed sense of hearing, fear scents, and high fecundity.

The sucker success story is primarily a North American one. They originally evolved from cyprinid ancestors in northeastern Asia, spreading eventually across the Bering Straits land bridge into North America. They then died out in Asia, with the exception of one species in China, *Myxocyprinus asiaticus*, presumably because they were unable to compete with the advanced carplike cyprinids that have taken over most of Asia's fresh waters in geologically recent times. These advanced cyprinids never were able to get into North America until given an assist by modern man. In North America's comparative isolation, the suckers perfected their bottom-browsing way of life through natural selection, to the point where one species, the longnose sucker (*Catostomus catostomus*), has managed to reinvade northeastern Asia with a considerable degree of success.

In western North America, sucker evolution has resulted in three basic types of suckers: (1) deep-bodied plankton feeders with terminal mouths that inhabit open waters of large lakes and sluggish rivers, (2) small mountain suckers with horny plates underneath their lips for scraping algae and invertebrates from rocks in fast-moving streams, and (3) typical suckers, which occupy a wide range of habitats. The specialization of the lake suckers and mountain suckers allows two or more sucker species to exist in waters which presumably would otherwise support only one species.

The success of suckers has given them a bad reputation among fishermen and fisheries managers, who frequently accuse them of competing with gamefish for food and space. In some instances, the accusation is justified. Occasionally, large sucker populations depress those of gamefishes apparently by consuming invertebrates needed as forage by the young gamefishes. These situations, however, most often occur in disturbed or overfished streams, particularly those near reservoirs. Too often, in natural streams the presence of suckers and the absence of gamefishes is considered to be a cause and effect relationship, when in fact the lack of gamefishes may be due to poor habitat, low water quality, or overfishing. Suckers may even be beneficial to gamefish populations, as forage fish that utilize food (algae and detritus) largely unavailable to gamefishes. They also have some importance as commercial fish and have potential as gamefish: they reach large sizes, put up a good fight on light tackle, and are quite edible, if a bit bland and bony. Hubbs and Wallis (1948) pointed out that the Indians of the Yosemite Valley actually preferred suckers to trout for food.

Eleven species of suckers occur in California but only one of them, the bigmouth buffalo, is introduced. An additional species, the flannelmouth sucker (*Catostomus latipinnis*), is usually listed as a member of California's fish fauna but is omitted here. Primarily an inhabitant of the upper Colorado River, it rarely, if ever, was found in the California portion of the river, even prior to man's drastic changes of the lower river. An undescribed sucker (*Catostomus* sp.) lives in Wall Canyon Creek on the Nevada side of Surprise Valley. These suckers may wash into Surprise Lake, the sump on the valley floor in Modoc County, California, during times of high runoff (C. L. Hubbs, pers. comm.).

It is a sad comment on the state of California's native fish fauna that six of the ten native sucker species are rare, endangered, or potentially endangered. The life histories of these species are, by and large, poorly known. Even the four common species have not been studied to any great extent.

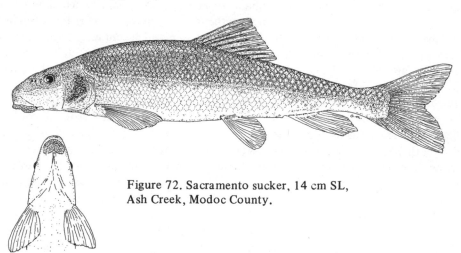

Figure 72. Sacramento sucker, 14 cm SL, Ash Creek, Modoc County.

Sacramento Sucker, *Catostomus occidentalis* Ayres

Identification. Sacramento suckers are "typical" suckers, with subterminal mouths and large fleshy lips covered with papillae (5 to 6 rows on the upper lip). The lower lip is evenly joined to the upper on both sides and usually has a deep median indentation. The dorsal fin (11 to 15 rays, usually 12 or more) is slightly longer than high, the origin usually closer to the caudal base than to the tip of the snout. The pectoral fins are rounded or pointed, and the anal fin has 7 rays, occasionally 6 or 8. There are 57 to 75 scales along the lateral line, with 10 to 17 scale rows above it and 8 to 12 below it. Adult suckers tend to be greenish on the back and dirty yellow gold on the belly, with a faint, dark red stripe in between. The stripe is most prominent on spawning males. Spawning males also have numerous tubercles on the pelvic, anal, and caudal fins. Young suckers are grey all over, slightly darker on top, with 3 to 4 dark spots on the sides.

Names. Western sucker and Sacramento western sucker are frequently-used, unofficial common names. *Cato-stomus* means inferior (down) mouth, while *occidentalis* means western.

Distribution and systematics. The Sacramento sucker is widely distributed in the Sacramento-San Joaquin system, with four subspecies. *C. o. occidentalis*, the typical form with slightly pointed pectorals, is found in the Sacramento and San Joaquin rivers and tributaries, as well as in the Russian River, Clear Lake, and streams tributary to San Francisco Bay. *C. o. mniotiltus* is a slightly heavier-bodied, coarser-scaled form found in the Pajaro and Salinas rivers. *C. o. humboldtianus*, with rounded pectorals and a large mouth, is confined to the Eel, Bear, and Mad rivers of Humboldt County. *C. o. lacusanserinus*, from Goose Lake and probably the upper Pit River, is similar to *C. o. occidentalis*. It was described by Fowler in 1913 on the basis of one specimen and quite possibly does not deserve subspecies status. A thorough systematic review of these subspecies is needed.

Life History. Sacramento suckers are found in a wide variety of waters, from cold, rapidly flowing streams to warm, nearly stagnant sloughs. They seem to be most abundant in clear, cool streams, especially in the pools, and in lakes and reservoirs at moderate elevations (200 to 600 m). Adults tend to be most numerous in large bodies of water, while juveniles are most abundant in tributary streams where adults have spawned. They are usually associated with native minnows, especially squawfish, hardhead, and California roach. In the Russian River, which contains all age classes of suckers, the different sizes are found in different microhabitats (J. Norton and J. White, unpublished data). Postlarval suckers (less than 14 mm SL) concentrate over detritus bottoms in the warm, quiet, protected stream margins. Juvenile suckers (19 to 100 mm SL) prefer the shallow, slow-flowing water along the edge, at depths of 8 to 10 cm, with sandy bottoms. Adult suckers are found in the deep water of pools or beneath undercut banks during the day.

In both lakes and streams, adult suckers are often found in small groups which seem to be aggregations of individuals attracted to optimal habitats, such as the head of a large pool or the edge of a bed of vegetation in a lake, rather than true schools. Schooling behavior is exhibited by young-of-the-year suckers. Feeding can be an almost continuous activity, but usually suckers are most active at night. In streams, most suckers spend the day browsing on the bottom of deep pools, moving up into the riffles to forage in the evening. In lakes, they spend daylight hours in fairly deep water, moving into shallows to feed at night. Feeding activity is greatly reduced during the colder months of the year. Then, dense aggregations of large suckers are sometimes found underneath ledges and logs in the deep pools of large rivers.

The food of Sacramento suckers is much like that of other sucker species: algae, detritus, and invertebrates associated with the bottom. In a study of the feeding habits of Sacramento suckers from Hat Creek, Shasta County, Brauer (1971) found that, in suckers over 40 cm long, 40 percent of the volume of the digestive tract contents consisted of algae, mostly diatoms. The bulk of the remaining portion consisted of invertebrates, especially chironomid larvae and caddisfly larvae. In smaller suckers (11 to 22 cm), hydracarinid mites and blackfly larvae were also important. In suckers less than 9 cm long, cladocerans were an important part of the diet. The sample upon which Brauer's study is based, however, is somewhat biased since it consisted of suckers collected on one September day, following a poisoning operation. A more realistic picture is perhaps given by an analysis of sucker feeding habits in the Russian River, August, 1973, by J. Norton and J. White (unpublished data). They found that postlarval suckers with their terminal mouths and short digestive tract, are initially surface and midwater feeders on early instars of aquatic insects. As they transform into juveniles, with subterminal mouths and long intestines, their food consists mostly of diatoms, filamentous algae, and protozoans. Small juveniles (24 to 38 mm) eat a wide variety of small organisms, as well as undigestible items such as sand grains, suggesting the development of the rather indiscriminate feeding of adults. The bulk of their diet, and that of large adults, is filamentous algae, diatoms, and detritus. Invertebrates made up less than 20 percent of their diet.

Growth in Sacramento suckers is as variable as their habitats. In the upper Merced River (Yosemite Park), where the water is cold the year around and the bottom is comparatively free of potential sucker food, yearling fish averaged only 47 mm SL (Hubbs and Wallis, 1948). Suckers of comparable age in the lower Merced River and Hat Creek averaged 80 mm SL (Brauer, 1961; Burns, 1966). Growth in following years in the latter two localities was highly variable. The annual increments in length ranged from 12 to 87 mm, averaging 43 mm. The largest fish encountered by Brauer (1971) was 48 cm long, aged ten years. Much larger (60 cm) and older fish undoubtedly exist. Large numbers of adult suckers may depress the growth and survival of juveniles. Thus, Brauer found that 81 percent of the large sucker population in Hat Creek was adults age VI and older. Less than 10 percent of the population was less than four years old. The young suckers apparently were forced by the adults into more exposed habitats, where food was harder to obtain and where they were more vulnerable to predation.

Spawning usually occurs for the first time in a Sacramento sucker's fourth or fifth year of life. Most spawning takes place in streams, over gravel riffles, between late February and early June. However, the presence of larval suckers in mid-August in the Russian River indicates that spawning can take place in late July and early August. Ripe suckers in lakes and reservoirs often congregate at the mouths of streams prior to migration. B. Cates (unpublished manuscript) found that the immediate trigger for spawning runs up Big Creek, from Pine Flat Reservoir, Fresno County, was sudden warming of the creek water after a series of warm days. Over a period of five years, spawning runs began at temperatures ranging from 5.6 to 10.6°C. A sudden cooling spell may halt migration until the water warms up again. Once the migration has started, the suckers may move considerable distances upstream. It is not unusual to find young-of-the-year suckers 10 to 20 km from the nearest source of adults. Spawning also takes place in lakes and reservoirs. Shoreline spawning has been observed in Pine Flat Reservoir where spring freshets were flowing into the lake.

Sacramento sucker spawning behavior seems to be like that of other catostomids. Large numbers congregate in the spawning area, with each spawning female accompanied by two to five males. The eggs are broadcast over the gravel, to which they adhere after sinking into the interstices. In largescale suckers (*C. macrocheilus*), whose spawning behavior closely resembles that of Sacramento suckers, vigorous splashing during spawning by the female and closely attending males creates a slight depression in the gravel. The eggs sink into this depression and may be buried by the shifting gravel (McCart and Aspinwall, 1970). Fecundity increases with the size of the female. Females 28 to 38 cm FL contained 4,700 to 11,000 eggs (Burns, 1966).

The eggs hatch in three to four weeks and the young are soon washed into warm shallows, where they sometimes occur in large schools. Typically, they will spend the next two to three years in the spawning stream before finally moving down to a reservoir or large river during fall high water.

Status. Sacramento suckers usually are unable to maintain their populations in waters dominated by introduced fishes, especially carp and goldfish. However, their wide distribution and ability to live in a variety of habitats assure their continued survival. Population declines have been experienced in the sloughs of the Sacramento and San Joaquin rivers, in Clear Lake, Lake County, and in some reservoirs.

References. Brauer, 1971; Burns, 1966; Fowler, 1913; Hopkirk, 1973; Hubbs and Wallis, 1948; MacPhee, 1960; McCart and Aspinwall, 1970; Moyle and Nichols, 1973; Snyder, 1908.

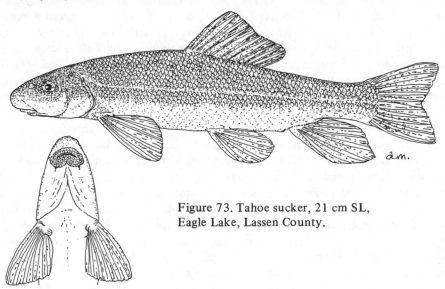

Figure 73. Tahoe sucker, 21 cm SL, Eagle Lake, Lassen County.

Tahoe Sucker, *Catostomus tahoensis* Gill and Jordan

Identification. Tahoe suckers have large heads (4 times into standard length), long snouts (1/2 of head length), and fine scales (82 to 95 in lateral line, 16 to 19 rows above it, 12 to 15 below). The caudal peduncle is thick, the least depth going 12 times into the standard length. Their subterminal mouths are large, with the papillose lower lips so deeply incised that only one row of papillae crosses completely. The fontanelle on the top of the head (beneath the skin) is usually well developed. The dorsal fin has 10 to 11 rays; the anal, 7; and the pectorals, 14 to 16. Live fish tend to be dark olive on the back and upper half of the sides, the dark contrasting sharply with the yellow or white of the belly and lower half of the sides. There is usually a well-defined lateral band on the sides. In breeding males this band becomes a bright red stripe running across brassy colored sides. Breeding tubercles are well developed on the anal and caudal fins.

   Names. Named for Lake Tahoe, this species has also been called Nevada sucker and red sucker. The sandbar sucker, *C. arenarius* of Snyder (1918), has proven to be the same species as *C. tahoensis* (Hubbs and Miller, 1951). A complete synonymy is given in La Rivers (1962). Other names are as for the Sacramento sucker.

   Distribution. Tahoe suckers are native to the Lahontan drainage system of California and west central Nevada, including the Truckee River, Susan River, Lake Tahoe, and Eagle Lake. Either through tributary capture or introduction by fishermen, Tahoe suckers have apparently become established in the upper reaches of the Feather and Rubicon rivers, in the Sacramento system (Kimsey, 1950), although recent records are lacking.

   Life History. Tahoe suckers are the "typical" suckers of the Lahontan system of California and their life history is similar to that of Sacramento suckers. They occur in a wide variety of habitats but achieve their greatest sizes and numbers in large lakes such as Lake Tahoe and Pyramid Lake, Nevada. In Lake Tahoe, adults tend to be found at moderate depths, while young are either in shallow water or in tributary streams. Miller (1951, p. 155) reported "herds" of Tahoe suckers in Lake Tahoe, at depths of 10 to 13 m, "moving over the bottom and feeding in a manner suggesting the grazing of sheep." Occasional suckers are found as deep as 300 m (Willsrud, 1971). The most usual fish associates of Tahoe suckers are rainbow and cutthroat trout, tui chubs, Lahontan redsides, and speckled dace. In streams they are frequently found also with mountain suckers. In such situations Tahoe suckers usually inhabit the pools and are most abundant in the lower reaches of the stream, while mountain suckers concentrate in the riffles and are most abundant in the upper reaches.

   Like most suckers, Tahoe suckers feed most actively at night. A wide variety of organisms, as well as inorganic and detrital material, is ingested but most of the food is algae and small benthic invertebrates. In Pyramid Lake, algae, midge larvae (Chironomidae), and small crustaceans usually found in algal mats are the dominant foods of adults (La Rivers, 1962). In Lake Tahoe, midge larvae, amphipods, and annelid worms "in a bulky matrix of sand" are dominant (Miller, 1951). A variety of other invertebrates and algae are eaten in lesser amounts. Postlarval suckers (less than 4 cm FL) feed mostly on zooplankton, chironomid larvae, and small terrestrial insects. As they grow larger, they become increasingly bottom oriented but less selective in their feeding. As a result the variety of organisms taken increases, as does the amount of sand and detritus, until the diet is the same as that of adult suckers, at about 13 cm FL (Willsrud, 1971).

   Growth in Tahoe suckers from Lake Tahoe is remarkably constant, averaging 25 to 33 mm for fish two to eleven years old (Willsrud, 1971). Growth is faster during the first year of life, the suckers averaging about 58 mm FL at the end of it. The annual increment is less in suckers over eleven years old, usually between 5 and 10 mm. It should be pointed out, however, that there is considerable variation in the lengths of fish of each age class. A ten-year-old fish can be anywhere from 21 to 41 cm FL. Males and females have similar rates of growth. Suckers over 40 cm FL are uncommon in Lake Tahoe, although suckers up to 61 cm TL have been found in Pyramid Lake,

Nevada. The oldest fish collected by Willsrud (1971) was fifteen years. The suckers mature at four to five years of age, 20 to 30 cm FL.

Spawning takes place in either lakes or streams from April to early June, the time of year depending on altitude and water temperature. In Lake Tahoe, suckers spawning in the tributary streams are mostly less than 25 cm FL, although larger fish are common in the lake. The large fish are presumed to spawn in the lake itself (Willsrud, 1971). Lake spawning takes place over rock and gravel bottoms, at depths of 5 to 18 m. In streams, the preferred spawning grounds are gravel riffles with few large rocks. Stream spawning is generally preceded by nighttime upstream migrations, when water temperatures reach 11 to 14°C. La Rivers (1962) indicated that Tahoe suckers will migrate over 50 miles up the Truckee River, from Pyramid Lake, in about one week.

Spawning was described by Snyder (1918): "The males appear first on the spawning beds and are always represented there in large numbers, each female being attended by from two to eight or more. Twenty-five males were seen attending one female in a pool. Occasionally another female would enter the pool from below, when she would be met and inspected by a school of males and then allowed to pass without further notice. Several of these passing females proved on examination not to be ripe. On account of the presence of so many males nothing definite can be observed of the spawning act, more than the eggs are extruded and shaken down in the gravel by the female while the males struggle over and under her, churning the water to foam by their activities . . ."

During the spawning season, males space themselves evenly on the spawning riffles, but do not seem to be territorial or even aggressive. When a female approaches they will leave their stations, spawn, and then resume them again (Willsrud, 1971). Intense spawning activity may result in the creation of a nestlike depression in the sand or gravel (Snyder, 1918) although none were observed in runs of suckers from Lake Tahoe (Willsrud, 1971). The violent spawning act, however, does seem to assure that most of the adhesive yellow eggs get buried in the gravel.

Fecundity varies with the size of the female. Willsrud (1971) found that the number of eggs ranged from 2,415 in a 15 cm FL female to 35,556 in a 43 cm FL female. Although fecundity is highly variable, an approximate length-fecundity relationship for fish between 15 and 38 cm FL can be derived from the data of Willsrud (1971): fecundity = 2500 + 1000X, where X is the cm of fork length in excess of 15 cm.

Tahoe suckers commonly hybridize with mountain suckers (Hubbs et al., 1943). In Sagehen Creek, Nevada and Sierra counties, 6.6 percent of the suckers are such hybrids (Flittner, 1953).

Status. Tahoe suckers are abundant throughout their range and are important forage fish for trout in large lakes. In Lake Tahoe, suckers make up 34 percent of the diet of lake trout and 28 percent of the diet of rainbow trout (Miller, 1951). Although no fishery exists for them at the present time, both Snyder (1918) and La Rivers (1962) reported them to be excellent eating.

References. Flittner, 1953; Hubbs et al., 1943; Hubbs and Miller, 1951; La Rivers, 1962; R. G. Miller, 1951; Snyder, 1918; Willsrud, 1971.

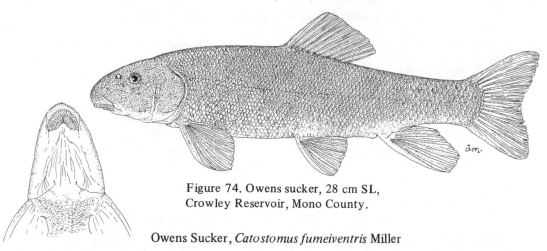

Figure 74. Owens sucker, 28 cm SL,
Crowley Reservoir, Mono County.

Owens Sucker, *Catostomus fumeiventris* Miller

Identification. Owens suckers are similar to Tahoe suckers except that they are coarser scaled (lateral line scales 66 to 85, usually less than 80, 13 to 16 rows above, 9 to 11 below), have more pectoral rays (16 to 19), and are duller in color, especially during the breeding season. Live fish are slate colored, occasionally becoming very dark, and usually have dusky bellies. The dusky bellies are especially noticeable in spawning males, which, however, do not develop the lateral red stripe characteristic of Tahoe suckers. The larval and juvenile stages are described by Miller (1973).

Names. Owens suckers were first described by Snyder (1919a) as a population of *C. arenarius*, a species now merged with *C. tahoensis*. Although they were subsequently recognized as being distinctive by C. L. Hubbs in 1938 and were so noted by Shapovalov (1941), they were not formally described as such until 1973, by R. R. Miller. *Fumei-ventris* means smoky belly, referring to the characteristic color pattern.

Distribution. Owens suckers are native to the Owens River and tributaries but they have been introduced into June Lake in the Mono Lake Basin, and possibly into the Santa Clara River Basin (by escape from the Los Angeles Aqueduct).

Life History. Little work has been done on the biology of the Owens sucker but it is probably similar in most respects to that of Tahoe suckers (E. P. Pister, pers. comm.). They apparently spawn from late May through early July, at least in the tributary streams of the Owens River and Crowley Lake, Mono County. The larval suckers may be found in abundance in the weedy edges and backwaters of the streams (Miller, 1973).

Status. Owens suckers seem to be the one fish species native to the Owens River that has thrived despite the disruption of the system by the city of Los Angeles. They are abundant in Crowley Reservoir, Mono County, and elsewhere in the system where there is still enough water for fish to live. As a precautionary measure they have also been introduced into a native fish sanctuary in the Owens Valley, along with Owens tui chubs and Owens pupfish. The status of the introduced Santa Clara River population is uncertain, although Hubbs, et al., (1943) reported extensive hybridization with Santa Ana suckers.

References. Hubbs, Hubbs, and Johnson, 1943; R. R. Miller, 1973; Shapovalov, 1941; Snyder, 1919a.

Klamath Largescale Sucker*, *Catostomus snyderi* Gilbert

Identification. Klamath largescale suckers are best distinguished from Sacramento suckers by their shorter dorsal fins (11 to 12 rays, usually 11), the base being shorter than or equal to the length of the longest ray, and their greater number of gill rakers (more than 25, usually 30 to 35). The origin of the dorsal fin is slightly nearer to the snout than to the base of the caudal fin. Anal rays are 7. Scales are large (69 to 77 in the lateral line, 13 to 14 scale rows above, 10 to 11 below) and the mouth is small, with papillose lips. The lower lip in deeply incised in the middle so that only one row of papillae goes all the way across. The upper lip is narrow with 4 to 6 rows of papillae. The lateral line canals on the head seem to be particularly well developed. Coloration is presumably similar to Sacramento suckers, although breeding fish have not been described.

Names. *C. snyderi* is named for J. O. Snyder, the California ichthyologist who first recognized that Klamath largescale suckers were undescribed and called this fact to the attention of C. H. Gilbert, his teacher at Stanford University (Gilbert, 1897).

Distribution. Most Klamath largescale suckers are found in the Klamath River system above Klamath Falls and in the Lost River. Occasional specimens are also taken in the lower Klamath River.

Life History. Perhaps less is known about Klamath largescale suckers than about any other suckers that occur in California. Adults frequently live in lakes or reservoirs, migrating upstream to spawn in March and April. In upper Klamath Lake, Oregon, juvenile suckers are found in shallow water (Evermann and Meek, 1897). Presumably, most aspects of their life history are like those of Sacramento suckers. Apparently, they commonly hybridize with shortnose suckers and Lost River suckers (J. K. Andreasen, pers. comm.).

Status. The general lack of records of Klamath largescale suckers indicates that they never have been particularly common, even in the upper Klamath River. The life history, distribution, and status of this species need careful investigation.

References. Evermann and Meek, 1897; Gilbert, 1897; Koch and Contreras, 1973; Vincent, 1968.

*Not illustrated but similar to Sacramento sucker.

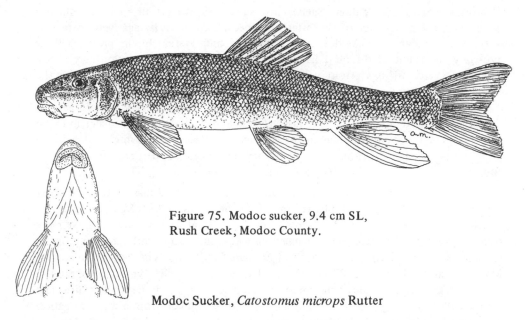

Figure 75. Modoc sucker, 9.4 cm SL,
Rush Creek, Modoc County.

Modoc Sucker, *Catostomus microps* Rutter

Identification. Modoc suckers are small (up to 19 cm SL), with short heads (head length goes into body length 4.5 times), small eyes (orbit width less than 5.5 percent SL), and small scales (80 to 89 in lateral line, usually around 81, scales below lateral line 9 to 12, above lateral line 15 to 17). There are 10 to 11 rays in the dorsal fin, 7 in the anal. The axillary process is absent from the pelvics. The lower lip has a deep medial notch, with only one of the 5 to 6 rows of papillae connecting the two halves. The upper lip usually has only 2 rows of papillae. The fontanelle on the top of the head is usually closed, or nearly so. In life, they are deep grey to greenish brown above, changing to yellow or white on the belly. Breeding fish develop a red lateral stripe, orange fins, and breeding tubercles on the fins and body.

Names. Modoc suckers occur primarily in Modoc County which was named for the Modoc Indians. *Microps* means small eye. Other names are for the Sacramento sucker.

Distribution. Modoc suckers are most abundant in Rush Creek and its main tributary, Johnson Creek, Modoc County. Small populations are also found in upper Ash Creek, Lassen County, and the interconnected Washington, Turner, and Hulbert creeks, Modoc County (Moyle, 1974). All these streams are tributary to the upper Pit River but there are no records from the river, except an unconfirmed individual from Dorris Reservoir, near Alturas, Modoc County.

Life History. The sections of stream in which Modoc suckers are found are characterized by low summer flows (mean: 113 1/sec in 1973). Some may actually be intermittent. The suckers are most abundant in areas dominated by large, shallow, muddy-bottomed pools, partially shaded by overhanging trees and shrubs, and containing cool (less than 25°C), moderately clear water. They are largely absent from stream sections dominated by riffles, including channelized sections (Moyle and Marciochi, in press). Even in areas where they are most abundant, Modoc suckers seldom dominate the fish fauna; usually, they make up less than 20 percent of the fishes present. They are commonly associated with speckled dace, rainbow trout,

California roach, Pit sculpin, Sacramento sucker, brown trout, and Sacramento squawfish. The abundance of the latter four species, however, is negatively correlated with the abundance of Modoc suckers (Moyle and Marciochi, in press). This is probably the result of different habitat preferences, although predation may play a role in the cases of brown trout and squawfish. Modoc suckers have been found in the stomachs of brown trout.

Modoc sucker feeding habits are like those of other sucker species: over 75 percent detritus and algae, the rest aquatic insect larvae and crustaceans that occur in or on muddy substrates or among clumps of filamentous algae. Chironomid midge larvae seem to be particularly important since they made up 18 percent of the diet of fourteen suckers examined by Moyle and Marciochi (in press).

Modoc sucker growth rates for the first four years of life are similar to those of other sucker species that occur in similar streams. Thus they average 7 cm SL at one year, 11 cm SL at two years, 14 cm SL at three, and 18 cm SL at four. However, unlike most other sucker species, including Sacramento sucker, they apparently seldom grow to sizes larger than 15 cm SL nor live longer than four years. The largest and oldest Modoc sucker known was 28 cm SL and five years old. The typical small size of Modoc suckers may be an adaptation to the small cool streams in which they live. The largest collection of Modoc suckers over 15 cm SL was taken from a warm irrigation ditch which had deep (2 to 3 m), permanent pools.

Modoc suckers partially compensate for their small size and short lives maturing at an early age. Most males and females mature in their third year, at about 12 cm SL. A few males, however, do mature during their second year. Spawning seems to take place in riffles between mid-April and late May, although actual spawning has not been observed. The females have a high fecundity for their size: two females, 162 and 165 mm SL, contained 6,395 and 12,590 eggs respectively.

Status. Modoc suckers are known from only two widely separated tributary systems of the Pit River, the Rush-Ash Creek system, and the Washington-Turner-Hulbert system. Since they appear to require small isolated streams for their existence, it is unlikely that they will be found in the Pit River itself, although it has not been properly surveyed. Moyle (1974) estimated that the total number of Modoc suckers in the streams they are known to inhabit is under 5,000 fish, with a majority of them living in Johnson Creek just above its confluence with Rush Creek, Most of the Modoc sucker habitat is privately owned, in areas that are heavily used for grazing sheep and cattle. Lower Rush Creek, which may once have supported much larger Modoc sucker populations, has been extensively channelized and the suckers are absent from channelized sections. Fortunately, the important sections of Johnson Creek are controlled by the U. S. Forest Service, which has shown in interest in maintaining the Modoc sucker populations. Nevertheless, with its restricted distribution and small numbers, the Modoc sucker clearly deserves the rare and fully protected species status given it by the California Department of Fish and Game (Leach et al., 1974) and the threatened species status given it by the Office of Endangered Species, U. S. Fish and Wildlife Service (1973).

References. Leach, Brode, and Nicola, 1974; Martin, 1967, 1972; Moyle, 1974; Moyle and Marciochi, in press; Rutter, 1908.

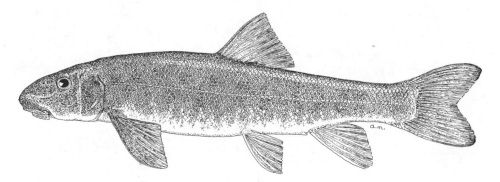

Figure 76. Klamath smallscale sucker, 18 cm SL, Scott River, Siskiyou County.

Klamath Smallscale Sucker, *Catostomus rimiculus* Gilbert and Snyder

Identification. "Typical" suckers with subterminal mouths, Klamath smallscale suckers have fine scales (81 to 93 in lateral line, 15 to 18 above, 11 to 13 below), 10 to 12 dorsal rays, 6 to 7 anal rays and 16 to 18 pectoral rays. The eyes are small and the fontanelle on the top of the skull is either narrow or closed. The lips are large with large papillae. The upper lip has 5 rows of papillae and the lower lip has 4 rows, 2 of which go completely across the lip since the median cleft is shallow. In life, Klamath smallscale suckers are dusky on the back and sides and yellow to white on the belly. Breeding colors have not been recorded.

Names. Rimi-culus means split-small, referring to the shallow cleft of the lower lip. Other names are as for the Sacramento sucker.

Distribution. Klamath smallscale suckers are confined to the Trinity River system, the Klamath River below Klamath Falls, and the Rogue River in Oregon.

Life History. Despite their wide distribution in three river systems, little is known about the life history of Klamath smallscale suckers, although it is unlikely that it differs in any major respect from the life histories of other typical suckers. Klamath smallscale suckers seem to be most abundant in the deep, quiet pools of the main rivers and in the slower moving stretches of tributaries. They are also common in reservoirs of the lower Klamath River, such as Copco Lake. Moffett and Smith (1950, p. 19) reported that "it is common to see large schools feeding along the bottom of pool areas any time of the year." Presumably Klamath smallscale suckers migrate up tributary streams to spawn in the spring, since juvenile suckers are most abundant in such streams. Klamath smallscale suckers seldom achieve large sizes, the largest on record being 41 cm SL (Gilbert, 1898). Growth is slow. Suckers taken in April and May, 1973, from the main river by D. Ahrenholz averaged only 11 cm SL at age II, 15 cm at age III, 16 cm at age IV, 23 cm at age V, 26 cm at age VI, 31 cm at age VII, 33 cm at age VII and 34 cm at age IX (Moyle, unpublished data).

Status. Klamath smallscale suckers are abundant throughout their range. They may have some value as forage fish for salmonids, although the smallest fish are found in tributaries where large resident trout are uncommon (Moffett and Smith, 1950).

References. Gilbert, 1898; Moffett and Smith, 1950; Snyder, 1908.

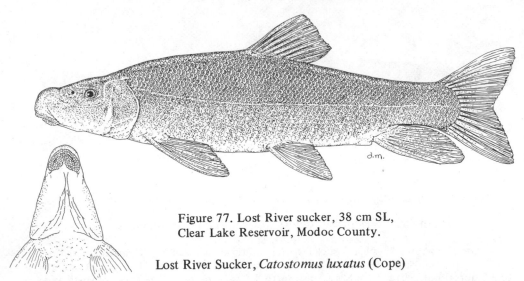

Figure 77. Lost River sucker, 38 cm SL,
Clear Lake Reservoir, Modoc County.

Lost River Sucker, *Catostomus luxatus* (Cope)

Identification. Lost River suckers are distinguished by subterminal, almost terminal, mouths, long, slender heads with a small hump on the snout, short, triangular gill rakers (24 to 33 on the first arch), thin lips with only a moderate number of papillae, and large size (up to 1 m TL and 4.5 kg). They have 11 to 12 dorsal rays, 7 to 8 anal rays, 10 pelvic rays, and 82 to 88 scales along the lateral line, with 14 above it and 8 below. Like most suckers, they are dark on the back and sides, fading to white or yellow on the belly.

Names. These suckers are frequently placed in their own genus, *Deltistes*, but they were originally described as members of the genus *Chamistes*, to which they bear a superficial resemblance. *Luxatus* means dislocated or put out of joint, referring to the crumpled appearance of the snout. In the Klamath Lake area, Lost River suckers are known as mullets. The Klamath Indians called them "tswam" (Cope, 1879).

Distribution. Lost River suckers are native to the Lost River system including Tule Lake, Upper Klamath Lake, Lower Klamath Lake, and Sheepy Lake, in Oregon and California. In recent years they have been collected from Copco Reservoir on the Klamath River and Clear Lake Reservoir on the Lost River.

Life History. Few studies have been made of the biology of Lost River suckers, despite their importance in the past as food, commercial, and sport fish. Apparently, they are primarily a lake species and spend most of their time in fairly deep water. Their feeding habits have not been recorded but the morphology of their mouth and gill rakers suggest that they either feed on hard-shelled bottom invertebrates or on large planktonic organisms. Attempts by Coots (1965) to do an age and growth analysis were unsuccessful because the scales seemed to lack distinct annual bands.

Spawning takes place in March, April, and May. The suckers run up the tributary streams, formerly in "incredible numbers" (Gilbert, 1898). Spawning runs have been reported in the tributaries to Upper Klamath Lake, Sheepy Creek from Sheepy Lake, Lost River from Tule Lake and Willow, and Boles Creek from Clear Lake Reservoir. They also spawn in springs in Upper Klamath Lake. Juveniles have not been collected from the spawning streams, so it is likely that they wash down into the lakes soon after hatching.

Status. In 1879, Cope reported that Lost River suckers, fresh and dried, were one of the staple foods of the Modoc and Klamath Indians. They were still abundant in 1894, when Gilbert (1897, p. 6) found them to be "the most important food fish in the Klamath Lake region." Gilbert also mentioned that attempts had been made to can the suckers commercially, as well as to render them for oil. Prior to 1924, large numbers were taken annually from Sheepy Creek for consumption by people and hogs (Coots, 1965). After 1924, most of Sheepy Lake, Lower Klamath Lake, and Tule Lake were drained for farming. Although the lakes were reflooded after the farming attempts failed, the sucker populations never recovered. Consequently, Lost River suckers have been declared an endangered species by the California Department of Fish and Game. An interagency, interstate recovery team is currently investigating the small populations that exist in Copco Lake and Clear Lake Reservoir. The suckers in Upper Klamath Lake, Oregon, seem to have fared better than in California, although their populations are also depleted. Coots (1965) reported that they still provide a significant sport fishery (by snagging) in Oregon during the spawning season. Fairly large numbers still made spawning runs up the Williamson River, Oregon, as of 1972 (C. E. Bond, pers. comm.). Unfortunately, they appear to have hybridized extensively with the equally rare shortnose sucker and the Klamath largescale sucker (J. K. Andreasen, pers. comm.; Koch and Contreras, 1973b), making their preservation as a species difficult. The only pure population in California seems to exist in Clear Lake, a reservoir subject to uncontrolled fluctuations (Leach et al., 1974).

References. Coots, 1964; Cope, 1879; Gilbert, 1897; Contreras, 1973; Koch and Contreras, 1973b; Leach and Fisk, 1972; Leach, Brode, and Nicola, 1974.

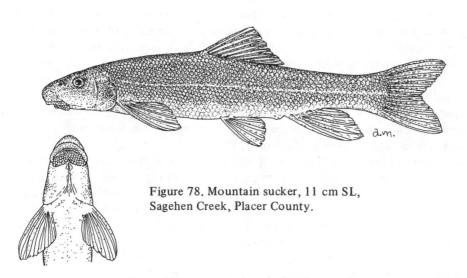

Figure 78. Mountain sucker, 11 cm SL, Sagehen Creek, Placer County.

Mountain sucker, *Catostomus platyrhynchus* (Cope)

Identification. Mountain suckers are small (usually less than 25 cm SL), with deep notches at the junctions of the upper and lower lips and a shallow median incision on the lower lip. Papillae are large on the lower lip but usually absent from the outer edge of the upper lip. The jaws have cartilaginous scraping edges. The fontanelle beneath the skin on the top of the skull is a narrow slit or closed. There are 23 to 37 gill rakers on the external row of the first arch and 31 to 51 on the internal row. There are 60 to 108 lateral line scales, usually 75 to 92; 8 to 13 dorsal rays, usually 10; and 9 pelvic rays. The axillary processes at the base of the pelvic fins are well developed. The intestine is 4.5 times longer than the standard length of the fish and the peritoneum is black. Pigmentation is absent from the membranes connecting the rays of the tail. Live fish are white to light gold yellow on the belly and dusky brown to greenish on the back and sides, usually with a dark lateral band or series of blotches. In breeding fish the lateral band becomes dark red orange, and the fins become tinged with red orange. Breeding males have well-developed tubercles on the anal and caudal fins, as well as minute tubercles over the entire body. Breeding females have small tubercles on the dorsal and lateral part of the head, body, and caudal peduncle.

Names. Other common names include Lahontan Mountain Sucker, mudsucker, and flatnose sucker. *Platy-rhynchus* means flat-snout, although the snout is, if anything, rounder than in most other sucker species. Until the excellent monograph by G. R. Smith (1966), mountain suckers found in California were classified as *Pantosteus lahontan*. *P. lahontan* was lumped by Smith with *P. platyrhynchus*, and *Pantosteus* was reduced to a subgenus of *Catostomus*, hence *C. platyrhynchus*. A complete synonymy is given in Smith (1966).

Distribution. In California, mountain suckers are found in the Lahontan system and probably in the headwaters of the North Fork of the Feather River, in the Sacramento system. The California Academy of Sciences has at least one specimen taken in the lower Sacramento River. Mountain suckers are widely distributed throughout the West, in the headwaters of the Columbia, Missouri, and Colorado river systems and in the Lahontan and Bonneville basins. A complete distributional map can be found in Smith (1966).

Life History. The characteristic habitat of mountain suckers is small, clear mountain streams, 3 to 15 m wide and less than 1 m deep, with rubble, sand, or boulder bottoms. They are usually found in the pools, especially those containing aquatic macrophytes, or behind submerged rocks or logs in swift water. However, they have also been collected from a variety of other situations such as large rivers, turbid streams, and, occasionally, lakes and reservoirs. They have been recorded from altitudes ranging from 0 to 2,800 m and at temperatures of 1 to 28°C (Smith, 1966). Fingerling mountain suckers (less than 13 cm) are most often found among aquatic plants in quiet backwaters or pools (Hauser, 1969).

Mountain suckers feed largely by scraping algae, mostly diatoms, small invertebrates, and detritus, from rocks and other surfaces with the hard edges of their jaws. They are capable of feeding in fairly swift water but will also feed on soft bottoms in quiet water. Plant material seems to be more important in their diet than it is for most other sucker species. This is reflected in their long intestine and black peritoneum. Hauser (1969) found that, in Montana, invertebrates were more important for small (less than 3 cm) suckers than they were for larger fish, but that filamentous algae seemed to become more important in the diet as the fish grew larger.

During their first year of life, mountain suckers grow to 6 to 7 cm TL, reaching 9 to 10 cm during their second year. In subsequent years, they usually add 1 to 2 cm to their lengths (Hauser, 1969). Females grow larger and live longer than males. Thus, the oldest males encountered by Hauser were age VII, while the oldest females were age IX. Females can achieve sizes up to 25 cm TL, although fish over 18 cm are unusual.

Mountain suckers become mature sometime between their second and fifth year.

Mature males have been recorded as small as 6 cm TL, but usually they are 8 to 11 cm before they spawn. Ripe females are at least 9 cm (Smith, 1966). The number of eggs per female, in twenty-one fish examined by Hauser, ranged from 990 to 3,710, larger females usually having more eggs than smaller females.

The exact spawning time has not been recorded in California, although Snyder (1918) found ripe females in Nevada between July 13 and 30. Elsewhere they spawn from May through mid-August at water temperatures ranging from 11 to 19°C (Hauser, 1969; Smith, 1966). For any single population it is unlikely that the spawning season lasts more than three weeks. Spawning presumably takes place over gravel riffles, but breeding behavior has not been described. Limited spawning migrations may also occur. Mountain suckers inhabiting Stampede Reservoir, Sierra County, apparently migrate up Sagehen Creek to spawn and the creek then serves as a nursery area for the young (D. Erman, pers. comm.). Mountain suckers will hybridize with Tahoe suckers, *C. tahoensis* (Hubbs et al., 1943).

Status. Mountain suckers are abundant and widely distributed. Their small size and vegetarian habits make it unlikely that they compete with trout that share streams with them. They may even serve as forage for larger salmonids.

References. Hauser, 1969; Hubbs, Hubbs, and Johnson, 1943; Sigler and Miller, 1963; Smith, 1966; Snyder, 1918.

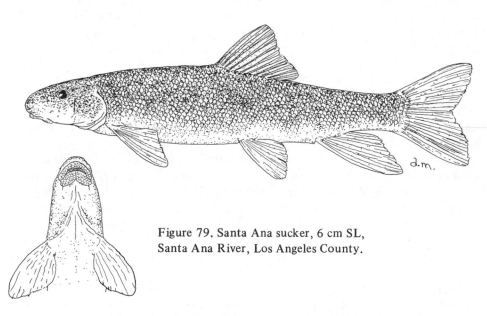

Figure 79. Santa Ana sucker, 6 cm SL, Santa Ana River, Los Angeles County.

Santa Ana Sucker, *Catostomus santaanae* (Snyder)

Identification. Santa Ana suckers resemble mountain suckers, to which they are closely related. They also are small (less than 16 cm SL) and have deep notches at the junctions of the upper and lower lips, with a shallow median notch in the lower lip. Papillae are large on the lower lip but poorly developed on the upper lip. The jaws have cartilaginous scraping edges inside the lips. The fontanelle beneath the skin on the top of the head is closed in fish larger than 7 cm SL. There are 21 to 28 gill rakers on the external row of the first arch and 27 to 36 on the internal row. There are 67 to 86 lateral line scales; 9 to 11 dorsal rays, usually 10; and 8 to 10 pelvic rays. The axillary process at the base of the pelvic fins is represented only as a simple fold. Pigmentation is present on the membranes connecting the rays of the tail. In life the color is "silvery below, darker above, with irregular dorsal blotches; (the) melanophore pattern on scales often gives the impression of longitudinal lateral stripes" (Smith, 1966, p. 54). Breeding males can have tubercles on most parts of the body, although they are heaviest on the anal fin, caudal fin, and caudal peduncle. Females grow tubercles on the caudal peduncle and fin.

Names. Both common and trivial names are after the Santa Ana River, from which the first specimens were collected. Santa Ana suckers were formerly placed in the genus *Pantosteus.* A complete synonymy is given in Smith (1966).

Distribution. They are found only in the Santa Clara, Los Angeles, San Gabriel, and Santa Ana river systems of southern California (Smith, 1966). The Santa Clara River population is probably derived from an early introduction (C. L. Hubbs, pers. comm.).

Life History. The streams in which Santa Ana suckers live are generally small, less than 7 m across, and shallow, with currents ranging from swift in the canyons to sluggish in the bottomlands. All the streams are subject to periodic severe flooding. Santa Ana suckers seem to be most abundant where the water is cool (less than 22°C) and unpolluted, although they can survive in fairly turbid water. Boulders, rubble, and sand are the main bottom materials they are associated with, together with growths of filamentous algae and *Chara* (Smith, 1966). The only substantial study of the life history of this species is that of Greenfield et al. (1970), and the following account is based on their work.

Like mountain suckers, Santa Ana suckers feed mostly on algae, especially diatoms, and detritus, which they presumably scrape from rocks and other surfaces. In the Santa Clara River, 98 percent of their diet consists of algae and detritus, although small numbers of aquatic insect larvae are also taken. Larger fish generally feed more on insects than do smaller fish.

Age and growth studies are difficult because Santa Ana suckers lack strong annuli on the scales. Nevertheless, by examining otoliths and length-frequency distributions, Greenfield et al., (1970) were able to come to the following conclusions about a Santa Clara River population: at the end of their first six months of life, Santa Ana suckers averaged 44 mm SL; they matured during their second summer and usually died at the end of their third summer, at 75 to 110 mm SL; a few suckers lived through a fourth summer (age III+), reaching 14 to 16 cm SL; and males and females grew at the same rate.

Spawning takes place from early April to early July, with the peak of activity in late May and June. Fecundity is exceptionally high for a small sucker species, ranging from 4,423 eggs in a 78 mm SL female to 16,151 eggs in a 158 mm SL female. The combination of early maturity, protracted spawning period, and high fecundity allows Santa Ana suckers to quickly repopulate streams following periodic severe floods which can decimate the populations.

Development of the eggs and larvae is described by Greenfield et al. (1970). The mouth becomes subterminal in position when the larvae reach 16 mm SL.

Status. Santa Ana suckers still seem to be common in their four small river systems. The rivers, unfortunately, flow through the ever-spreading urban sprawl of the Los Angeles area. As a result, they are subject to dams, draining, pollution, and channelization, together with excessive floods due to poor watershed management. The lower Los Angeles River is now little more than a concrete storm drain. It would seem wise, therefore, to set aside several refuges for this endemic species which, along with the arroyo chub and the unarmored threespine stickleback, faces extinction if present trends continue.

References. Greenfield et al., 1970; Smith, 1966.

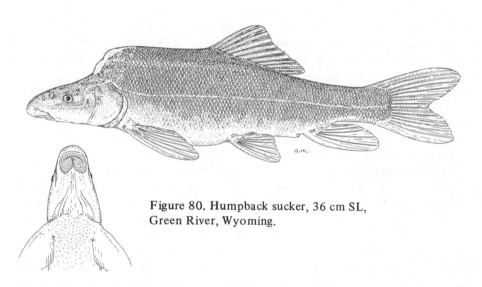

Figure 80. Humpback sucker, 36 cm SL, Green River, Wyoming.

Humpback Sucker, *Xyrauchen texanus* (Abbott)

Identification. Humpback suckers, over 2 cm TL, are distinguished by the sharp-edged keel on the back before the dorsal fin. In other respects they resemble members of the genus *Catostomus*: subterminal mouth with weakly papillose lips, 68 to 87 lateral line scales, 13 to 16 dorsal rays, 7 anal rays, 36 to 50 gill rakers, and a well-developed fontanelle. The lower lip has a deep median cleft which completely separates the two halves. Live fish are dusky to olivaceous on the back and yellow orange on the belly. Spawning males become nearly black on the back and sides and brilliant orange on the belly and anal fin. They develop conspicuous breeding tubercles on the caudal fin and peduncle, anal fin, pelvic fins, and head. Larvae are described by Winn and Miller (1954).

Names. Xyrauchen translates as "razor nape," hence the frequently used (but unofficial) common name, razorback sucker. Just why C. C. Abbott used the trivial name *Texanus* when he described the species is not known, for it does not occur in Texas. Possibly he mistook the Colorado River for a smaller stream of the same name in Texas (R. R. Miller, pers. comm.). Complete synonymy is given in La Rivers (1962).

Distribution. Widely distributed in the Colorado River system, humpback suckers occur in California only in the parts of the main river that border the state.

Life History. The conspicuous, knife-edged hump of these fish seems to be an adaptation for living in the swift muddy waters of large rivers. The hump, together "with the long, flat, sloping head, undoubtedly steadies the fish against the bottom in currents where the water has a tendency to push down on the anterior portion of the body while the dorsal keel provides increased stability when faced into the current" (La Rivers, 1962, p. 360). However, humpback suckers also are found in the quiet waters and reservoirs on the river. Usually they are associated with bottoms of sand, mud, and rock in areas where aquatic vegetation is sparse (Sigler and Miller, 1963).

Humpback suckers generally swim about in small schools, often in water less than 1 m deep, feeding on the bottom. Their usual food seems to be algae and detritus, although aquatic insect larvae may also be consumed (Jonez and Sumner, 1954; Dill, 1944). The food of larval, postlarval, and juvenile suckers has not been studied. However, since they school in large numbers in warm, shallow water at river or reservoir edge, presumably they feed like the young of other sucker species, on diatoms and small invertebrates at first, gradually becoming indiscriminate bottom browsers as they get older.

Little is known about their age and growth. They can reach large sizes so presumably they are fairly long lived. Although Sigler and Miller (1963) recorded total lengths up to about 1 m and weights over 7 kg, humpback suckers over 60 cm TL and 4.5 kg are unusual. Females generally grow larger than males.

Spawning takes place during March, April, or May in tributary streams or shallow waters of reservoirs, over bottoms of silty sand, gravel, or rocks. Water temperatures are usually between 12 and 18°C. Spawning behavior, as described by Douglas (1952) and Sigler and Miller (1963), is similar to that of other suckers. "One female is attended by 2 to 12 males, the group moving slowly in circles of three to five feet in diameter. Upon reaching a suitable spawning site, the female, closely pressed by the male on either side, settles on the bottom and starts to vibrate her body. When this act reaches a convulsive stage, the eggs and milt are simultaneously expelled. As this occurs, the three fish move forward and upward, leaving a cloud of silt and sand as spawning is consummated" (Sigler and Miller, 1963, p. 107). Frequently, at the end of the spawning act, one or more of the suckers will leap out of the water. The eggs adhere to the bottom substrate in the spawning area. Humpback suckers hybridize with *Catostomus* species in the Colorado River system (Hubbs and Miller, 1952).

Status. Humpback suckers were once one of the most abundant fishes in the Colorado River, and served as a major food source for the Mojave Indians and other tribes that lived along the river. Commercial fisheries have existed for them at various times and places. By 1942, however, they were uncommon in the California portion of the river (Dill, 1944), although Miller (1961a) thought that they were at least holding their own, the only native fish to do so. Today, they are considered to be a rare species by the California Department of Fish and Game (Leach and Fisk, 1972). Despite their ability to live and reproduce in reservoirs, their populations have continued to decline, presumably because they have been unable to adapt to the drastic changes in the nature of the lower Colorado River, or to competition and predation from introduced fishes. They are now fully protected by California state law, but their preservation really is in the hands of the states up river, where they seem to be more common (but still depleted). Ideally, a section of river should be set aside and managed for native fishes, including Colorado squawfish and bonytail, as well as humpback sucker. If setting aside suitable habitat is not feasible, attempts should be made to determine the exact causes of the decline of humpback sucker populations. If reproductive failure, due to lack of suitable spawning grounds or egg predation, is the main cause then serious consideration should be given to large-scale artificial propagation. Such efforts might even be further justified as a means of building up an unusual sport and commercial fishery. The first attempts to culture this sucker are now being made at the Willow Beach Hatchery on the Colorado River, Arizona.

References. Dill, 1944; Douglas, 1952; Hubbs and Miller, 1952; Jonez and Sumner, 1954; La Rivers, 1962; Leach and Fisk, 1972; Miller, 1961a; Sigler and Miller, 1963; Winn and Miller, 1954.

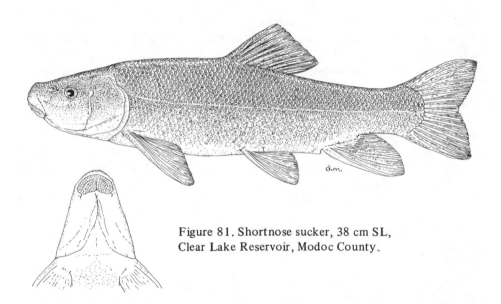

Figure 81. Shortnose sucker, 38 cm SL, Clear Lake Reservoir, Modoc County.

Shortnose Sucker, *Chasmistes brevirostris* Cope

Identification. Shortnose suckers are distinguished by their large heads with oblique, terminal mouths and thin, striated lips. Lip papillae are minute or absent. The snout is blunt, frequently with a small hump, while the body is nearly cylindrical. The gill rakers, 34 to 49, are slender, triangular, and densely tufted at the ends. Lateral line scales are 73 to 82 with 11 scale rows above and 12 to 13 below. There are 7 to 8 anal rays, 11 to 12 dorsal rays, and 17 pectoral rays. Live fish are dark on the back, ranging from silvery to white on the belly. Spawning fish have a reddish cast to the scales.

Names. Chasmistes means "one who yawns," referring to the large, flexible mouth, while *brevi-rostris* translates as short-snouted. Gilbert (1897) described an additional species of *Chamistes, C. stomias,* from Upper Klamath Lake, and Evermann and Meek (1898) described *C. copei.* The former "species" seems to represent large, spawned-out specimens of *C. brevirostris,* each with a well-developed hump on the snout (or perhaps hybrids with the Lost River sucker), while the latter "species" seems to represent large specimens without the snout hump. The Klamath Indians called shortnose suckers *Xoöptu* (Cope, 1879).

Distribution. Shortnose suckers are (were) native mainly to Upper Klamath Lake and Lake of the Woods, Oregon, as well as their tributary streams during the spawning season. However, in recent years, a few fish have been taken from Copco Reservoir, Siskiyou County, below Upper Klamath Lake, and also from Boles Creek, Modoc County, apparently on a spawning run from Clear Lake Reservoir on the Lost River (Leach and Fisk, 1972). Their presence in Clear Lake indicates that they may be native to the Lost River and Tule Lake, although canals have connected the Lost River to the Klamath River, immediately below Upper Klamath Lake, for a long time.

Life History. Although the biology of shortnose suckers has been little studied, inferences can be drawn by comparing what information does exist to the life history of the cui-ui (*Chasmistes cujus*), a similar and slightly better-known species from Pyramid Lake, Nevada. Shortnose suckers and cui-ui spend most of the year in the open waters of large lakes. The morphology of the mouth and gill rakers of both species suggests that they feed primarily on zooplankton and to a lesser extent on phytoplankton, which they strain from the water. Stomach analyses of cui-ui confirm this (La Rivers, 1962).

Age and growth studies on shortnose suckers are difficult because the scales seem to lack distinctive annual marks (Coots, 1965). Fish over 50 cm SL are unusual.

Spawning takes place in April and May, when they migrate up streams tributary to the lakes. Runs have been observed in the Williamson River, Oregon, and Willow and Boles creeks, Modoc County (Coots, 1965). Spawning behavior is probably similar to that of cui-ui, described by Koch (1973), which is similar to that of other sucker species. Two 49 cm FL females examined by Coots (1965) contained 36,763 and 56,217 eggs, respectively. Spawning seems to be hard on adult populations since Gilbert (1897) observed large numbers of dead and dying fish immediately following the spawning season.

Fry of shortnose suckers apparently move into the lakes to assume a planktonic existence soon after hatching, for there are no records of young fish being captured in streams.

Status. Shortnose suckers have been officially declared an endangered species and are fully protected by California state law (Leach, Brode, and Nicola, 1974). In California, they may never have been common, except possibly in Tule Lake, but early records are lacking. Suitable habitat in the state today seems to exist only in two man-made reservoirs, Copco Lake and Clear Lake. Shortnose suckers were once extremely abundant in Upper Klamath Lake, Oregon (Gilbert, 1897) and were considered to be a valuable food fish by the Indians. Yet three years of extensive sampling in the lake in the mid-1960s by C. E. Bond and students (e.g., Vincent, 1968) failed to produce a single specimen. However, Bond (pers. comm., 1972) has observed that in recent years a few have been caught, apparently in increasing numbers, by snag fishermen in the Williamson River, Oregon. Causes of the decline of shortnose suckers in Upper Klamath Lake are not known. In Lake of the Woods, Oregon, however, they were eliminated by "rough fish" control measures (Bond, 1966).

Unfortunately, the suckers that are left seem to be hybridizing extensively with Lost River suckers and Klamath largescale suckers (J. Andreasen, pers. comm., 1973; Koch and Contreras, 1973b). The hybridization is presumably the result of habitat disruption in the region associated with agriculture. Clear Lake Reservoir may contain the only pure populations left (California Department of Fish and Game, 1974).

A cooperative study of shortnose suckers, with the intent to find the best ways of saving them, is now underway by several federal and state agencies in both Oregon and California. If necessary, artificial propagation should be tried, since techniques have been developed by Koch and Contreras (1973a) for the closely related cui-ui.

References. Bond, 1966; Contreras, 1973; Coots, 1965; Cope, 1879; Evermann and Meek, 1898; Gilbert, 1897; Koch and Contreras, 1973a,b; La Rivers, 1962; Leach and Fisk, 1972; Snyder, 1918; Vincent, 1968.

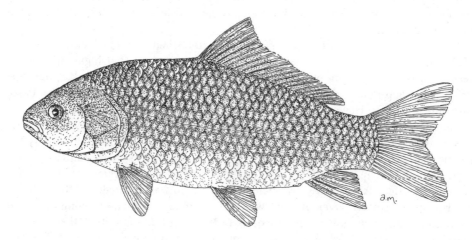

Figure 82. Bigmouth Buffalo, 40 cm SL, Iowa.

Bigmouth Buffalo, *Ictiobus cyprinellus* (Valenciennes)

Identification. Bigmouth buffalo are readily recognized by their large, thin-lipped, oblique mouths, deep robust bodies, and long, falcate dorsal fins (23 to 30 rays). The heads are large, with blunt and rounded snouts, small eyes, and head fontanelles closed in adults. Lateral line scales are 36 to 39; anal fin rays, 8 to 10; and pelvic rays, 10 to 11. Pharyngeal teeth are weak, intestines long, and gill rakers fine (more than 60 on the first arch). Overall color tends to be dull grey or bronze, darkest on the back, turning to white or yellowish on the belly, with darkly pigmented lower fins.

Names. Both the generic name (*Ictio-bus*, meaning fish-bull) and the common name reflect the buffalolike appearance of these fish, produced by the large heads and high arched backs. The resemblence is particularly striking when an imaginative observer sees a school of dark-backed fish "grazing" in shallow water. *Cyprinellus* means small carp, a misnomer considering that bigmouth buffalo grow to large sizes.

Distribution. Bigmouth buffalo are native to the Mississippi River system from Minnesota to its mouth, west up the Missouri River into Montana, and east into Lake Erie. They also are found in the Red River, up into Saskatchewan and Manitoba. They have been introduced into reservoirs of the Gila River in Arizona and into the Los Angeles Aqueduct system in southern California, where they are (or were) found in at least eleven reservoirs. It is not known how they were introduced into California but Evans (1950) speculated that commercial fishermen in the 1940s may have transplanted some from Arizona, to provide a source close to the Los Angeles fresh-fish market.

Life History. Although bigmouth buffalo are largely unstudied in California, their abundance and importance as commercial fish elsewhere has led to numerous studies. This summary, therefore, is based largely on data found in Carlander (1969) and in the excellent life-history study of Johnson (1963).

The principal habitat of bigmouth buffalo is quiet, shallow (less than 5 m deep) water of large, sluggish rivers, lakes, and reservoirs. They seem to be quite tolerant of turbid water and so may coexist with carp. They are normally found in schools swimming close to the bottom but on warm summer days individuals can occasionally be observed "loafing," barely moving, close to the surface of the water, often with the dorsal fin exposed.

The oblique mouth, fine gill rakers, and intestinal contents dominated by cladocerans and copepods have led many workers to conclude that bigmouth buffalo feed primarily by straining plankton from the water column. In some lakes, this type of feeding apparently does predominate (e.g., Starostka and Applegate, 1970; McComita, 1967). However, a careful examination of the crustaceans fed on by bigmouth buffalo by Johnson (1963) indicated that most of them belonged to species living on the bottom or among aquatic plants. Bottom feeding is also indicated by the frequent presence in bigmouth buffalo intestines of detritus, algae, aquatic insect larvae, molluscs, and other bottom-dwelling organisms (Minckley et al., 1970). Apparently, they feed mostly by swimming in schools at an angle to the bottom, stirring up the surface layer of mud with their snouts and then straining out small organisms with their gill rakers. Johnson (1963, p. 1416) described their feeding behavior: " . . . several fish were observed swimming at an angle of about 55° to the bottom, bouncing with short up-and-down movements as they proceeded along the bottom, both forward and backward, in a manner best described as 'skipping.' As the fish contacted the bottom, swirls of muddy water were raised in a search for food through the mud and debris. In the hatchery, captive buffaloes have often been observed feeding on fish-food pellets. They swim forward, at an angle of about 55°, along the bottom of the holding tank littered with food particles. A clear pathway appears behind the fish, as the food is sucked up with much the same effect as a vacuum cleaner."

Even in populations that feed mostly on the bottom, some time is spent feeding on plankton, since planktonic crustaceans and diatoms are typically found in their intestines in small amounts. Regardless of where in the environment they are taken, crustaceans make up the major part of the diet of bigmouth buffalo of all sizes, but aquatic insect larvae may be important in the diet of fry and of very large fish. Algae, especially diatoms, may become important to fish of all sizes during the colder months, when animal food is scarce. Feeding does occur during all months of the year but less is consumed at lower temperatures.

Like feeding, growth varies with temperature. Fish in warm southern waters grow faster than fish in colder northern waters. In southern waters, which presumably have temperature regimes similar to reservoirs in southern California, bigmouth buffalo may reach 10 to 29 cm TL at the end of their first growing season and 28 to 39 cm TL by the end of their second, with weights ranging from 640 to 1,530 gm. In subsequent years, they add 2 to 9 cm annually to their length, the increment decreasing with age.

Females grow slightly faster, live longer, and get larger than males. Bigmouth buffalo with total lengths of 1 to 1.2 m and weights of 30 to 36 kg are occasionally taken from the Mississippi River but fish over 70 cm TL and 6.5 kg are unusual. Typical bigmouth buffalo in the California commercial catches weighed 2.7 to 3.6 kg (Evans, 1950). Bigmouth buffalo seldom live beyond age VI or VII, although fish as old as age XX are on record from Saskatchewan.

Maturity sets in at age III or IV, at 30 to 48 cm TL. Spawning occurs in the spring, probably April and May in California, when the fish move into shallow water, especially recently flooded weedy areas. Optimum temperatures seem to be between 15 and 18°C, but spawning has been observed from 14 to 27°C. Spawning is accompanied by much splashing and seems to be the typical mass affair of suckers. Eggs are spread over the spawning area, adhering to vegetation, sticks, and rocks. The high fecundity of females (400,000 to 750,000 eggs), combined with their longevity allows bigmouth buffalo populations to survive years of repeated reproductive failure. Young-of-the-year fish are found in large schools in shallow water.

Status. Bigmouth buffalo are presumably still present in reservoirs of the Los Angeles Aqueduct system, although their populations may have declined. They once supported a small commercial fishery there, rating just above carp as food fish (Davis, 1963), but the fishery apparently no longer exists (Bell, 1971). They have considerable potential for aquaculture, since they grow rapidly under pond conditions and take artificial food readily. However, great care should be taken to avoid having them released elsewhere in the state because they are likely to compete for food and space with native minnows and suckers, and with the young of game species. They grow too rapidly to be of much value as forage fish and have little potential as gamefish, since they do not take bait readily.

References. Bell, 1971; Carlander, 1969; Cross, 1967; Davis, 1963; Evans, 1950; Johnson, 1963; McComita, 1967; Minckley et al., 1970; Starostka and Applegate, 1970.

Catfish Family, Ictaluridae

The North American catfishes (Ictaluridae), with about forty-three recognized species, are but a small part of the large catfish order (Siluriformes) that contains over two thousand species, most of which live in the fresh waters of the tropics. They are closely related to the minnows and characins (Cypriniformes) since they possess Weberian ossicles, the small chain of bones used to transmit sound from the air bladder to the inner ear.

Within the Ictaluridae there are three distinct groups: the large, "typical" catfishes and bullheads (*Ictalurus* and *Pylodictis*), the small madtoms (*Noturus*), and the blind cave catfishes (*Satan*, *Trogloglanis*, and *Prietella*). All of these fishes have much in common: (1) nocturnal, bottom feeding habits; (2) no scales; (3) 8 barbels: 2 on the snout, 2 on the end of the maxillae, and 4 on the chin; (4) a well-developed adipose fin; (5) hundreds of tiny teeth arranged in bands on the roof of the mouth; and (6) rays that have been modified into moderate to heavy spines on the pectoral and dorsal fins. The spines are apparently the main reason why catfishes are not taken as often by predatory fishes as one would expect from their large numbers. The spines can be locked into an erect position, making the fish a larger mouthful, and the sheath of skin over the spine contains a poison which can be injected into an unlucky predator or fisherman. The spines are used by fishery workers to determine catfish ages, since annual rings are visible in thin cross-sections.

The ictalurid catfishes are native only to waters east of the Rocky Mountains except in Mexico (Miller, 1958). The seven species found in California have all been introduced.

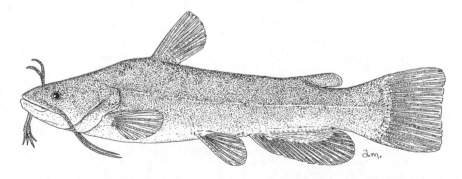

Figure 83. Black bullhead, 16 cm SL, Sacramento-San Joaquin Delta.

Black Bullhead, *Ictalurus melas* (Rafinesque)

Identification. Black bullheads can be distinguished from other catfishes by the combination of square-tipped, slightly notched tail; darkly pigmented membranes between 17 to 24 light-colored rays of the rounded anal fin; pigmented chin barbels, always darker than the chin; pectoral fin spines smooth to rough but never toothed posteriorly; jaws equal in length, although the upper sometimes protrudes slightly; and base of caudal fin usually with a pale vertical bar. They are stout bodied and vary in color from brownish yellow to black, with yellow to white bellies. The young are black.

Names. Icta-lurus means fish-cat, while *melas* means black. The black bullhead, along with other bullhead species, was originally placed in the genus *Ameiurus*. A complete synonymy of the scientific nomenclature is given by La Rivers (1962). The name bullhead was originally applied in England to freshwater sculpins. It was presumably transferred to various catfishes in North America because of similarities in head shape.

Distribution. Black bullheads are native to much of eastern North America, as well as to most of the Mississippi drainage system (Hubbs and Lagler, 1958). They seem to have been introduced successfully into most of the rest of the continental United States. They were one of the earliest (1874) introductions to California (Curtis, 1949) and are found in every major drainage system. They are rather uncommon compared to the ubiquitous brown bullhead although the two species seem to be equally abundant in the Delta (Turner, 1966).

Life History. Little work has been done on the black bullhead in California and this summary is based on work done in other states (Sigler and Miller, 1963; E. Miller, 1966; Cross, 1967; Carlander, 1969; Minckley, 1973). The preferred habitats of black bullheads are ponds, small lakes, river backwaters, and small stream pools with warm and turbid water, muddy bottoms, slow currents, and few other fish species. They are capable of surviving water tempeatures up to 35°C. Considering that they are quick to invade new areas and are abundant in intermittent streams in the Midwest, it is surprising that they are not more common in streams of the Central Valley foothills. Although numerous in some ponds in the San Joaquin Valley, they were not found in intermittent foothill streams by Moyle and Nichols (1974).

Black bullheads are highly social and are usually found in loose schools. Adults tend to be in physical contact with each other during the day, when they remain quietly buried in beds of aquatic plants or under some other cover. They come out to forage actively at night. Young-of-the-year black bullheads, in contrast, swim about during the day in tight schools. Despite their diurnal habits, young black bullheads feed mostly at dawn and dusk although the adults presumably feed continuously throughout the night (Darnell and Meierotto, 1965). Black bullheads of all sizes are omnivorous bottom feeders. They feed extensively on aquatic insects, crustaceans, and molluscs, occasionally taking live fish and scavenging on dead ones. In reservoirs they will feed heavily on earthworms and terrestrial insects as water levels rise over previously dry areas and will move out into open water to feed when planktonic midge larvae are abundant (Applegate and Mullan, 1967). Their stomachs almost invariably contain substantial amounts of detritus, algae, and pieces of aquatic plants, although the nutritional value of this material to the bullheads has not been determined.

The growth of black bullheads is highly variable and depends on conditions in their environment, especially food availability and the degree of overcrowding. Under optimal conditions, with artificial feeding, they can reach 30 cm TL (500 gm) in a year. However, in the wild they need anywhere from three to nine years to reach a similar size. The maximum size is apparently around 46 cm TL (950 gm). For the most part, it is unusual to find black bullheads over 20 cm TL although what they lack in size they will make up for in numbers. Cross (1967) reported wild pond populations as dense as 227 kg/ha.

Two of the main reasons black bullheads often form stunted populations are their small size at maturity (17 to 23 cm TL) and their high fecundity, which varies from 1,000 to 7,000 eggs per female (Dennison and Bulkley, 1972). They spawn in June and July, usually after water temperatures exceed 20°C. A sudden rise in water temperature may trigger spawning (Dennison and Bulkley, 1972). Before spawning, the female of each pair constructs a shallow nest depression by fanning away fine materials with her pectoral fins and pushing out larger objects with her snout. As the nest nears completion the male frequently touches the female with his barbels or rubs up against her. When they are ready to spawn, they line up head to tail and the male wraps his tail fin over the head of the female. The female quivers and releases a number of eggs, which the male fertilizes (Wallace, 1967). The eggs stick to each other, forming a yellow mass on the bottom of the nest, which one mate (or possibly both) fan with continuous circling.

Once they hatch, the young stay together for two to three weeks in a tight ball which seems to be in continuous motion. The ball of young is guarded by one or both parents until the young disperse somewhat to form normal schools.

Status. It is fortunate that black bullheads are not especially common in California since they all too frequently form populations consisting of individuals too small for harvest. In other states they are generally considered to be a nuisance that crowds out more desirable species, especially in ponds, yet seldom provides satisfactory fishing. They are important forage fish in some lakes, however.

References. Applegate and Mullan, 1967; Carlander, 1969; Cross, 1967; Curtis, 1949; Darnell and Meierotto, 1965; Dennison and Bulkley, 1972; E. Miller, 1966; Minckley, 1973; Seaburg and Moyle, 1964; Sigler and Miller, 1963; Turner, 1966; Wallace, 1967.

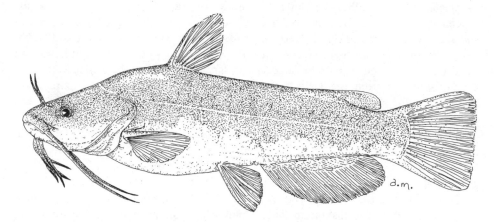

Figure 84. Brown bullhead, 18 cm SL, Clear Lake, Lake County.

Brown Bullhead, *Ictalurus nebulosus* (Lesueur)

Identification. Brown bullheads are similar to black bullheads except that the membranes of the anal fin are the same color as the 21 to 24 rays; the pectoral and dorsal fin spines are toothed on their posterior edges and so feel very rough; the base of the caudal fin does not have a pale vertical bar; and adults are a bright yellow brown with faint mottling on the sides and white to yellow bellies. The young are black.

Names. Brown bullheads are also called horned pout, common bullhead, and mud cats. *Nebulosus* means clouded, referring to the mottled coloration. A synonymy of the scientific nomenclature is given in La Rivers (1962). Other names are as for black bullhead.

Distribution. Brown bullheads are native to most of the United States east of the Mississippi River, as well as southeastern Canada, the Dakotas, and Oklahoma. They were introduced into central California in 1874 (Curtis, 1949) and are present in most warm waters of the state.

Life History. Brown bullheads are *the* bullhead for most of California, apparently because they can adapt to a wide variety of water habitats from warm, turbid sloughs to clear mountain lakes. They are most successful, however, in larger bodies of water, like the Sacramento-San Joaquin Delta, Clear Lake (Lake County), and foothill reservoirs, where they are usually associated with the deep end of the littoral zone (2 to 5 m), beds of aquatic plants, and muddy or sandy bottoms. They can live in water ranging from nearly 0° to 37°C, although optimum temperatures for growth seem to be in the range of 20 to 35°C.

Their social behavior is similar to that of the better studied black bullhead. Adults school and are most active at night. In large lakes in California they have proven to be quite mobile; tagged fish have been recaptured as much as 26 km away from the point of release (Emig, 1966). However, they do tend to concentrate in favorable habitats, such as weedy bays or sloughs. Loeb (1964) reported that they will bury themselves in muddy bottoms and become dormant at low temperatures, although Keast (1967) showed that they will feed at temperatures as low as 4°C.

Foraging brown bullheads swim along the bottom at an angle, their barbels just touching the substrate. When they detect a food organism, they quickly turn around and snap it up, often taking in detritus or algae at the same time (Keast and Webb, 1966). When small (less than 60 mm TL), they feed mostly on chironomid larvae and small crustaceans, but they take larger insect larvae and fish as they increase in size. Brown bullheads from the Delta were found to be feeding largely on amphipods, isopods, crayfish, dragonfly larvae, and snails (Turner, 1966). In Clear Lake they feed extensively on the recently introduced Mississippi silversides. However, like the black bullhead, they are omnivorous scavengers so that almost anything of suitable size can be expected in their diet.

The growth of brown bullheads is fairly rapid. They normally reach 7 to 10 cm TL in their first year, 10 to 14 cm TL their second, 14 to 20 cm TL in their third, and 19 to 28 cm TL in their fourth. Much faster and slower rates have been recorded (Carlander, 1966). The maximum length known is about 53 cm TL, the maximum weight about 2.2 kg, but fish over 30 cm TL and 450 gm are usually uncommon. The oldest fish on record was captured from Clear Lake eight years after it had been tagged. Since it was already 25 cm TL when tagged, it was probably at least ten years old (McCammon and Seeley, 1961).

Brown bullheads normally breed for the first time in their third year. The spawning season in California is not precisely known but it most probably occurs in May and June. Females lay between 2,000 and 14,000 eggs, depending on size (Carlander, 1966). The breeding behavior and care of young is similar to that of black bullheads (Breeder and Rosen, 1966).

Status. Brown bullheads are one of the most abundant warmwater gamefishes in California, yet their tastiness and ease of capture (by bait fishing at night, on the bottom) are not fully appreciated by California anglers. As a result, most populations are underexploited (Emig, 1966) and anglers who fish for them are rewarded by large catches of good-sized (e.g., 25 to 35 cm TL) fish. A particularly large and unexploited population exists in Clear Lake, Lake County.

References. Breeder and Rosen, 1966; Curtis, 1949; Emig, 1966; Keast, 1967; Keast and Webb, 1966; La Rivers, 1962; Loeb, 1964; McCammon and Seeley, 1961; Turner, 1966.

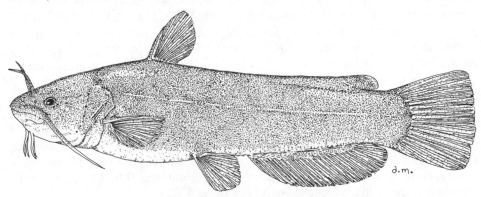

Figure 85. Yellow bullhead, 21 cm SL, Colorado River.

Yellow Bullhead, *Ictalurus natalis* (Lesueur)

Identification. Yellow bullheads resemble black bullheads except that the anal fin has 24 to 27 rays which are the same color as the membranes between the rays and are all nearly the same length, giving the fin a less rounded appearance; the chin barbels are white; the pectoral and dorsal fin "spines" are saw-toothed on their hindmost surfaces; and there is no pale vertical bar on the caudal fin base. They are the most heavy bodied of the bullheads and are yellow brown to black, without any mottling. The belly and chin are white.

Names. Natalis translates as "having large buttocks," a reference to the obese specimens originally described by Lesueur in 1819. Other names are as for black bullheads.

Distribution. Yellow bullheads are native to most of the United States east of the Rocky Mountains, south from the Great Lakes. Because of their scarcity and similarity to brown bullheads, their distribution in California is not well known but they seem to be common only in the Colorado River. They are present in small numbers in the Lost River, Modoc County (Contreras, 1973), and may be established in a few reservoirs in southern California. They were introduced into the Sacramento-San Joaquin Delta in 1874 (Curtis, 1949) and are apparently still present in some sloughs in small numbers (M. Caywood, pers. comm.).

Life History. Yellow bullheads are usually found in clear, warm streams with permanent flows and rocky bottoms or in the shallow, weedy bays of clear, warm lakes (E. Miller, 1966; Cross, 1967; Minckley, 1973). Thus, lack of suitable habitat may explain why they are so uncommon in California. Compared to the volume of information available on black and brown bullheads little is known about the biology of yellow bullheads. However, their life history does not seem to be strikingly different from the other two species, even though there are habitat differences.

Yellow bullheads are noctural and omnivorous, taking in plant material along with aquatic insects, molluscs, crustaceans (especially crayfish), and fish (E. Miller, 1966). They appear to be slightly more piscivorous than the other two species.

Growth is similar to that of brown bullheads and they can achieve lengths of over 47 cm TL and weights of over 1 kg (Carlander, 1969). Breeding age, behavior, and time are also similar to brown bullheads (Breder and Rosen, 1966), as are fecundities (Carlander, 1969).

Status. Yellow bullheads are uncommon in California and are likely to remain so. There is little reason to attempt to establish them where they are not already present since they do not seem to have any outstanding advantages over other species of catfish.

References. Breder and Rosen, 1966; Carlander, 1969; Contreras, 1973; Cross, 1967; Curtis, 1949; Dill, 1944; E. Miller, 1966; Minckley, 1973.

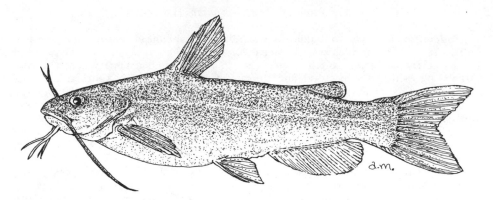

Figure 86. White catfish, 11 cm SL, Clear Lake, Lake County.

White Catfish, *Ictalurus catus* (Linnaeus)

Identification. White catfish have the most bullheadlike (stout) body shape of the fork-tailed catfishes present in California. The lobes of the tail are rounded, the upper often slightly longer than the lower, and the fork is shallow. There are 18 to 24 rays in the anal fin, 5 to 6 soft rays in the dorsal fin, and 8 to 9 soft eays in each pectoral fin. The head becomes disproportionately large in individuals over 40 cm TL. The maxillary barbels are long and dark colored, while the chin barbels are white. Their bodies are usually grey blue to blue black in color, with white bellies. Some may have a mottled appearance and those taken from extremely turbid water may be very pale.

Names. Icta-lurus means fish-cat, while *catus* is self-explanatory. White catfish are the "fork-tailed catfish" of much of the early California fish literature. A synonymy of the scientific nomenclature is presented in La Rivers (1962).

Distribution. White catfish were originally found in the lower reaches of coastal streams from Delaware and New Jersey down into Florida, including a few streams entering the Gulf of Mexico. California populations are apparently all derived from fifty-four to fifty-six fish imported in 1874 and planted in the San Joaquin River near Stockton (Skinner, 1962). They seem to be present now in every major drainage system except the Klamath and Colorado. They have subsequently been introduced into a number of other states, including Nevada.

Life History. White catfish evolved in the sluggish lower reaches of large, coastal streams, so it is not surprising to find them abundant in the upper reaches of the Sacramento-San Joaquin Estuary. They avoid the deep, swift channels favored by channel catfish and are most abundant in slow-current areas, such as Frank's Tract (a submerged island), and in deadend sloughs, which they share with bullheads (Turner, 1966). However, they tend to avoid heavy beds of aquatic plants and water less than 2 m deep. They are the only catfish common in Suisun Bay, and they can live in salinities as high as 11 to 12 ppt (Ganslle, 1966; Perry and Avault, 1969). Although seemingly best adapted to the above conditions, they are also very successful in large, warmwater lakes, reservoirs, and some farm ponds. They require water that exceeds 20°C in the summer and can survive temperatures of 29 to 31°C (Kendall and Schwartz, 1968). In reservoirs they concentrate at depths of 3 to 10 m during late spring and early summer. They tend to disperse in the summer, although the bulk of the population is located below 10 m. If the reservoir stratifies, depth distribution is modified and the catfish seek out temperatures greater than 21°C. In the winter, the catfish are found mostly at depths of 17 to 30 m (von Geldern, 1964). Tagging studies indicate that white catfish wander about the lakes and reservoirs they inhabit, but that there are no regular seasonal migrations (McCammon and Seeley, 1961; Rawstron, 1967).

White catfish are carnivorous bottom feeders, but they occasionally swim out into the surface waters of reservoirs to prey on plankton-feeding fishes. On the bottom, they eat whatever organisms are most available, smaller fish taking smaller organisms. Thus, young-of-the-year catfish (4 to 10 cm FL) in the Delta feed mostly on amphipods (*Corophium*), oppossum shrimp (*Neomysis*), and chironomid midge larvae. As they get older, their diet becomes more diversified and includes fish and large invertebrates, but amphipods and oppossum shrimp are still the most important items (Turner, 1966). This may explain why adult white catfish in the Delta are slower growing than other populations which feed more on fish. In reservoirs, threadfin shad are particularly important, although in Clear Lake, Lake County, a wide variety of fishes are taken (E. Miller, 1966). In recent years, Mississippi silversides have become perhaps the most important item in the diet of Clear Lake catfish. White catfish also commonly feed on carrion; parts of dead birds and mammals have been found in their stomachs as have parts of American shad that had died after spawning (E. Miller, 1966; Borgeson and McCammon, 1967).

The growth rates of white catfish in California seem to be slightly faster than those of brown bullhead but slower than those of channel catfish. They commonly reach larger sizes (30 to 40 cm FL) than bullheads but this is due mostly to greater longevity (eight to eleven years). The growth rates of California populations that have been investigated (Delta and Clear Lake) are comparable to those of white catfish in the eastern United States only for the first three years of life; thereafter they are slower (Carlander, 1969). One of the slowest growing populations known is that in the Delta, which for the first six years of life average 79, 132, 175, 213, 251, and 292 mm FL, respectively. In contrast, Clear Lake white catfish for the first six years average 107, 168, 226, 277, 320, and 348 mm FL, respectively (E. Miller, 1966). In their native habitat, white catfish can attain lengths of nearly 60 cm TL and weights of 3 kg.

White catfish mature at 20 to 21 cm FL, which means in California that they are usually three to four years old. Spawning takes place in June and July, when water temperatures exceed 21°C (E. Miller, 1966). Reproductive and parental behavior are similar to those of the bullheads (Breder and Rosen, 1966). Each female lays 2,000 to 4,000 eggs, which hatch in about a week at 24 to 29°C.

Status. White catfish are the most important catfish for sport fishing in the Sacramento-San Joaquin system, although they may eventually be replaced in this role by the larger, faster growing channel catfish. Their popularity is due mostly to their ubiquity and abundance. In most California waters they are underharvested, in part because they seem to be harder to catch than other catfishes in the state (E. Miller, 1966) and partly because fishing for catfish has only recently become a popular pastime when compared to fishing for trout, salmon, striped bass, and centrarchids. As a result, white catfish, as well as other catfishes, will be able to absorb a considerable amount of increased fishing pressure on them, caused by the decline of populations of other gamefish species. Nevertheless it seems unlikely that white catfish will ever be extensively propagated in California for stocking in reservoirs, since channel catfish seem to be better suited for this type of operation. They are, however, uniquely suited for the Delta, and are likely to remain a popular sport fish there despite their slow growth.

References. Borgeson and McCammon, 1967; Breder and Rosen, 1966; Carlander, 1969; Ganslle, 1966; Goodson, 1965; Kendall and Schwartz, 1968; La Rivers, 1962; McCammon and Seeley, 1961; E. Miller, 1966; Perry and Avault, 1969; Rawstron, 1967; Skinner, 1962; Turner, 1966; von Geldern, 1964.

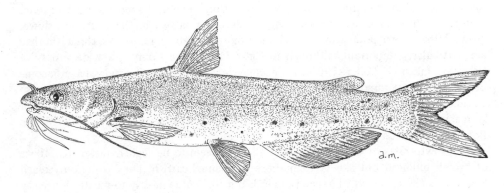

Figure 87. Channel catfish, 24 cm SL, Clear Lake, Lake County.

Channel Catfish, *Ictalurus punctatus* (Rafinesque)

Identification. Channel catfish are elongate, small-headed catfish distinguished by deeply forked tails, with pointed lobes; rounded anal fins with 24 to 29 rays; upper jaws that project beyond the lower jaws; and tiny, but conspicuous, black spots scattered lightly on the sides, which may be faint or absent on large fish. Their dorsal fins have 5 to 6 soft rays and each pectoral fin has 4 to 5 rays. The maxillary barbels are longer than the head and black in color. Their normal color is grey blue on the sides, often with an olive gold tinge, fading to white on the belly. Spawning males become dark colored, with enlarged heads, thickened lips, fatty pads behind and above eyes, and thickened fin membranes. Nonbreeding adults can be sexed using the characteristics given for flathead catfish.

Names. Icta-lurus means fish-cat, while *punctatus* means spotted. Spawning males are frequently called chuckle-headed catfish or mistaken for blue catfish. Channel catfish have also been called spotted catfish. A synonymy of the scientific nomenclature is given in La Rivers (1962) and in Cross (1967).

Distribution. Channel catfish were originally distributed throughout the Mississippi-Missouri river system southward into northeastern Mexico, but their range has been expanded through introductions to almost all parts of North America where there are suitable waters. They were first introduced into the Sacramento-San Joaquin system in 1874 but the introduction failed, as did several subsequent attempts until the early 1940s. They became established in the Colorado River in the 1920s (E. Miller, 1966). They can be expected in every drainage system of the state, including those for which no records as yet exist.

Life History. As their streamlined bodies and deeply forked tails indicate, channel catfish are adapted for living in the main channels of large streams. In rivers, adults typically spend the day in pools or beneath log jams or undercut banks, moving into riffles to feed at night. Young-of-the-year channel catfish, however, will live fulltime in riffles, taking advantage of rocks that break the current. Supposedly, the optimal habitat for channel catfish of all sizes is clear, rapidly flowing, warmwater streams, with sand, gravel, or rubble bottoms (E. Miller, 1966). However, they grow well in a wide variety of water bodies, from farm ponds to reservoirs to turbid, muddy-bottomed rivers like the lower Colorado. This tolerance of a wide range of conditions is one of the main reasons that they are the most commonly cultured North American catfish. Although they can live in waters with oxygen concentrations as low as 1 to 2 ppm, they grow best at levels above 3 ppm and at temperatures above 21°C. They can withstand temperatures of 36 to 38°C (Allen and Strawn, 1968). Despite their tolerance for moderate salinities, channel catfish in the Delta avoid brackish water (Turner, 1966).

Channel catfish are reputed to be omnivorous but the detritus and plant material that is frequently found in their stomachs may be the result of accidental ingestion with invertebrates and fish they catch on the bottom. They are not fussy eaters, however, since they adjust readily to living on commercial catfish food in captivity and consume a wide variety of organisms in the wild. For small channel catfish, less than 20 cm FL, the main food is crustaceans (amphipods in the Delta), and the larvae of aquatic insects. As they grow larger, fish and crayfish become increasingly important although catfish of all sizes will take aquatic insects that are abundant. Usually, fish over 30 to 38 cm TL are piscivorous but any organism large enough to be consumed, including small mammals, will be eaten (E. Miller, 1966; Turner, 1966; Busbee, 1968; Jearald and Brown, 1971).

Channel catfish are, on the average, one of the fastest growing species of catfish, but there is considerable variation in growth rates from population to population. In good habitat they typically will reach 7 to 10 cm TL in the first year, 12 to 20 cm TL in the second, 20 to 35 mm TL in the third, 30 to 40 cm TL in the fourth, and 35 to 45 in the fifth (Carlander, 1969). In California, channel catfish generally grow rather rapidly (E. Miller, 1966), although Kimsey et al. (1957) found that the channel catfish in Lake Havasu Reservoir on the Colorado River grew considerably more slowly than did the population in the main river. Fish from the river reached 53 cm FL in their seventh year, while those in the reservoir took twelve years to reach the same size. In their native range, channel catfish have been reported reaching over 1 m TL, weighing nearly 20 kg (South Carolina) and living for nearly forty years (Quebec). In California, fish over 53 cm TL (1.5 kg) or over ten years old are unusual.

The age and size of channel catfish at first spawning are highly variable; ages from two to eight years have been recorded, as have lengths of 18 to 56 cm TL (Carlander, 1969). Spawning takes place from April through June in California and a few channel catfish may spawn more than once in a season (Dill, 1944; Carlander, 1969). However, it is not unusual for planted populations not to reproduce at all, especially in reservoirs and ponds, so the populations have to be maintained by continuous stocking. Such programs are often especially worthwhile because catfish in nonreproducing populations may grow faster than those in self-reproducing populations.

Probably the main reason some populations of channel catfish fail to reproduce naturally is the lack of suitable spawning sites. They require cavelike sites for their nests, preferring old muskrat burrows, undercut banks, or log jams. In ponds, they will reproduce if provided with old barrels or similar containers for nest sites. Spawning also requires temperatures of 21 to 29°C, with 27 to 28° being optimum (Clemens and Sneed, 1957). Spawning and parental behavior are similar to those of bullheads, except that the females seem to have little to do with guarding the eggs and young (Breder and Rosen, 1966). Each female lays 2,000 to 70,000 eggs, depending on her size (Carlander, 1969). The eggs hatch in six to ten days and the young start actively swimming about one to two days after hatching.

Status. Channel catfish are fast becoming one of the more popular sport fish in California because they are easy to raise in hatcheries, are one of the easiest and most sporting catfish to catch, and are capable of reaching large sizes. As trout waters decrease in amount and quality, it is even possible that state hatchery production of channel catfish could someday rival that of trout in numbers, if not in weight. The California Department of Fish and Game now raises catchable-size (25 cm TL) channel catfish for stocking in reservoirs on a large scale (E. Miller, 1966). It is doubtful, however, that fishing for channel catfish will ever have the mystique that is associated with trout fishing, at least for the California angler. One reason, of course, is that the setting for the fishery is seldom as attractive (even at night!). It is also a much more passive type of fishing, with less of the prey stalking that is involved in trout fishing.

Channel catfish also have tremendous potential for fish farming. Their tolerance of brackish water means that catfish farming could become a profitable way to use farm land with soils that have become saline through the evaporation of irrigation waters, such as exist in the Imperial Valley. Eating commercially raised catfish may someday be as popular in California as it is in the southern United States (especially if it is relatively inexpensive).

References. Allen and Strawn, 1968; Breder and Rosen, 1966; Busbee, 1968; Carlander, 1969; Clemens and Sneed, 1957; Cross, 1967; Dill, 1944; Jearald and Brown, 1971, Kimsey et al. 1957; La Rivers, 1962; E. Miller, 1966; Perry, 1968; Perry and Avault, 1969; Turner, 1966.

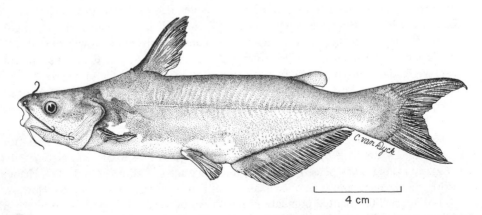

4 cm

Figure 88. Blue catfish juvenile, 17 cm SL, Fish Breeders Inc. fish farm, Imperial County.

Blue Catfish, *Ictalurus furcatus* (Lesueur)

Identification. Blue catfish, with their deeply forked tails and grey color, resemble channel catfish except that their anal fins are longer (30 to 35 rays) with straight edges; their bodies are stouter and steeply humped before the dorsal fins; their eyes are smaller; their maxillary barbels are pale in color and just barely longer than their head; and they are without spots. They tend to be a plain pale grey blue on their backs, turning paler on the sides, with white bellies. They can be sexed using the methods given for flathead catfish.

Names. In the midwestern United States, blue catfish are often called white catfish, fulton, or Mississippi catfish. *Icta-lurus* means fish-cat, while *furcatus* means forked. A partial synonymy of the scientific nomenclature is given in Cross (1967).

Distribution. Blue catfish are native to the main channels of the Mississippi River and its main tributaries from Minnesota and South Dakota southward into Mexico. They were introduced into Lake Jennings, Sutherland Reservoir, El Capitan Reservoir, San Vincente Reservoir, and the Santee lake chain, San Diego County, from 1969 to 1972, as well as into ponds of a commercial fish breeder in Imperial County. The California Department of Fish and Game has recently approved their importation into northern California, both to be released for sport fishing and to be raised in fish farms for meat production (Pelzman, 1971), although the decision is being reevaluated. Since they are likely to be spread by agency, accident, and fishermen they can be expected in suitable waters anywhere in the state.

Life History. The deep channels of big rivers are the original habitat for blue catfish, but they also do well in large reservoirs and in fish-farm ponds. In the rivers they remain on the bottom during the day in deep (8 to 10 m) areas with moderate currents. They seem to avoid muddy-bottomed pools and backwaters, except in the spring when they move in to spawn. At night they are often found feeding in rapids or other swift-flowing parts of the river. In reservoirs they prefer deep water, but may move into the littoral zone to feed at night. They can survive a wide range of temperatures (0 to 37°C) and salinities (up to 11 to 22 ppt), although they seem to grow best at temperatures around 27°C and at salinities of less than 7 to 8 ppt (Perry, 1968; Pelzman, 1971).

The feeding habits of blue catfish are similar to those of channel catfish, except that they are even more piscivorous and more nocturnal. They feed mostly on crustaceans and aquatic insects when young but will take fish when they are as small as 10 cm TL. Once they reach 20 to 30 cm, fish are their main source of food, although large invertebrates may also be eaten (Brown and Dendy, 1961). They also seem to take larger fish than will channel catfish. In southern California reservoirs (M. Lembeck, pers. comm.), they feed heavily on the Asiatic clam, *Corbicula*, although it is doubtful that the catfish will be able to control this pest.

The growth rates of blue catfish seem to be about the same as, or slightly less than, those of channel catfish living in the same waters (Carlander, 1969; Perry and Avault, 1969). Limited data from southern California reservoirs indicates that blue catfish growth there is decidedly slower than that of channel catfish (M. Lembeck, pers. comm.) but the two species have similar growth rates in warmwater reservoirs in other states (Pelzman, 1971). Exceptional growth of blue catfish in California has been observed only in El Capitan Reservoir, which is deep and turbid. Unlike channel catfish, blue catfish can reach lengths of over 1.6 m and weighs of over 45 kg, at least in their native big rivers. Just how large they actually can get is debatable since most of the "record" catfish were caught before reliable records were kept (Cross, 1967). However, it seems probable that blue catfish weighing 90 to 100 kg may once have been caught. None approaching such weights have been caught in the last one hundred years (Cross, 1967). Just how old such monster catfish would be is also a matter of conjecture, but 75 to 100 years or more would not seem unreasonable.

Spawning takes place in early summer, when water temperatures reach 21 to 25°C. Blue catfish use hole nests like channel catfish so it can be assumed that their spawning and parental behavior are similar. No natural reproduction has yet been observed in California reservoirs.

Status. There seem to be three main reasons why blue catfish were introduced into California: commercial catfish farmers wanted to try raising them, they could provide a trophy catfish sport fishery, and they might be useful in the control of nuisance clams (Pelzman, 1971). Their supposed potential as trophy fish will probably lead to their spread into most of California's catfish waters. However, as fishing pressure on catfish populations increases, it seems likely that few, if any, will get any bigger than channel catfish. Given their ecological similarity to channel catfish, blue catfish add little to California's sport fisheries except another species. If they are planted in reservoirs they will probably mostly replace channel catfish. Since blue catfish seem to grow more slowly and are harder to catch than channel catfish (M. Lembeck, pers. comm.) their planting may actually decrease the catfish catch.

References. Brown and Dendy, 1961; Carlander, 1969; Cross, 1967; Pelzman, 1971; Perry, 1968; Perry and Avault, 1969; Richardson et al., 1970.

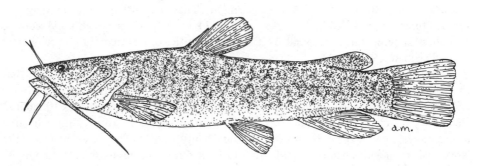

Figure 89. Flathead catfish, 14 cm SL, Rio Conchas, Mexico.

Flathead Catfish, *Pylodictis olivaris* (Rafinesque)

Identification. Flathead catfish have an extremely large, flat head with small eyes and mouth. The lower jaw projects beyond the upper. The caudal fin is slightly rounded and slightly indented in the middle while the anal fin is short (12 to 15 rays) and rounded, the adipose fin large and projecting. The spine in each pectoral fin is rough on both sides. Flathead catfish are black when young, with a yellow to white dorsal patch on the caudal fin. As they increase in size they first become a mottled olive on the sides and then a plain olivaceous yellow brown. Males can be told from females by their "distinct posteriorly directed genital papilla with a small, round urogenital opening at the tip. The genital papilla of females is more recessed and less distinct. The urogenital opening of the female is larger, appearing as a longitudinal slit" (Turner and Summerfelt, 1971, p. 109).

Names. According to Jordan and Evermann (1896), *Pylodictis* (*Pilodictis*) is a misspelling of *Pelodichthys*, meaning mud fish; *olivaris* refers to their greenish coloration. They are often called mud cats by fishermen.

Distribution. Flathead catfish were introduced by the Arizona Game and Fish Department into the lower Colorado River in 1962. They have since spread into the canals of the Imperial Valley (Botroff et al., 1969). They are native to most of the Mississippi drainage system, as well as to the Rio Grande and rivers in northeastern Mexico.

Life History. Flathead catfish inhabit the turbid waters of large rivers and reservoirs. The adults tend to live on the bottom of deep pools, or under rocks and logs in riffles or other fast-glowing areas (Minckley and Deacon, 1959). Adults are solitary for most of the year and seldom wander far from their home pools.

The feeding behavior of flathead catfish reflects their sedentary habits. They usually lie in wait in one place until a suitable prey organism comes near enough to be inhaled with a sudden opening of the enormous mouth. Adults (25+ cm TL) feed mostly at night when their main prey, fish and crayfish, are more vulnerable to visual deception. Small flatheads (less than 10 cm TL) feed largely on aquatic insect larvae, gradually becoming more piscivorous as they grow larger (Minckley and Deacon, 1959).

Growth is fastest in large muddy rivers with an abundance of smaller fishes for prey. Although flathead catfish may be present in other types of waters, ranging from clear streams to large reservoirs, they usually grow more slowly. Thus, one-year-old fish may be anywhere from 8 to 25 cm TL; two-year-olds, 15 to 16 cm TL; and three-year-olds, 20 to 74 cm TL (Carlander, 1969). They are long-lived, however, so that even under poor growth conditions they may reach respectable sizes. They can live as long as nineteen years and achieve lengths greater than 1.4 m and weights greater than 24 kg (Carlander, 1969). Their age and growth in the lower Colorado River have not been investigated but it is probable that their growth is quite rapid (Minckley, 1973). It is still not unusual to catch large (9 to 13 kg) flathead catfish from the lower Colorado.

Male flathead catfish usually do not become mature until they are three to five years old and exceed 38 cm TL, while females wait until they are four to six years old and in excess of 46 cm TL (Carlander, 1969). Spawning takes place in early summer (June th rough early July), after the fish have formed pairs and either constructed a nest depression or have occupied and enlarged submerged holes in the stream bank.

The male courts the female in the nest by rubbing repeatedly against her. When she is ready to spawn he wraps his tail around her head, and the female releases 30 to 50 eggs, which the male swims over and fertilizes (Breder and Rosen, 1966). Each female lays 4,000 to 59,000 eggs, depending on her size (Turner and Summerfelt, 1971). Once the female has laid all her eggs, the male chases her off the nest. He guards the eggs and keeps them stirred up with his mouth and fins to make sure that none smother. After hatching, the young form a tight school which stays in or around the nest for several days, guarded by the male. The school gradually disperses as the young assume their solitary existences (Breder and Rosen, 1966; Cross, 1967).

Status. Flathead catfish appear to be well established in the lower Colorado River, although not much is known about their populations. Their solitary nature and voracious feeding habits (including cannibalism) assures that they will usually be less abundant than the other catfishes in the river. However, they may be more abundant than angler catches indicate since catching them requires both a knowledge of their habits and the desire to sit for long night hours by a deep pool, fishing on the bottom with large baitfish. The patience of the fisherman is also tried by the fact that flathead catfish normally take their time in swallowing the bait and it is all to easy to jerk it out of the fish's mouth. Actually, the best way to catch them is with the traditional trot, jug, or set line which is left overnight in a favorable spot. Such rigs are illegal in California, however.

References. Botroff et al., 1969; Breder and Rosen, 1966; Carlander, 1969; Cross, 1967; Minckley and Deacon, 1969; Turner and Summerfelt 1971.

Killifish Family, Cyprinodontidae

Killifishes are found the world over (except Australia) in both fresh and salt water, but they are most successful in extreme habitats that exclude other fish species. Thus, species live in isolated desert springs at wide ranges of temperatures and salinities, in the fluctuating conditions of estuaries, and in highly saline inland seas and lakes. Some species (annual cyprinodonts) in Africa and South America have even adapted to temporary ponds, laying eggs that survive in bottom soil after the pond dries up. The eggs hatch quickly upon the return of seasonal rains.

Killifishes are small, aggressive fishes, usually with strong sexual dimorphism. The striking colors of the males of many tropical species have made them popular among aquarists. All have large eyes and small terminal mouths with highly protrusible lips. Unlike minnows, with which they are frequently confused, they possess small teeth in the jaws. All killifishes lay eggs, unlike their close relatives the poeciliids (e.g., mosquitofish), which give birth to free-swimming young. Most killifishes are elongate, flattened on top, and have oblique mouths, all adaptations for surface feeding. The native pupfishes depart from this form in being deep bodied with terminal mouths and omnivorous feeding habits.

In recent years much has been learned about fish evolution, ecology, behavior, and physiology through the study of the pupfishes living in desert waters in the western United States and Mexico. Scientific and public attention has focused particularly on the pupfishes of the Death Valley system of California and Nevada. In springs, streams, and swamps of this area, seven species and six subspecies of pupfish and killifish have evolved, each form in a different locality. Most remarkable of these fish is the Devil's Hole pupfish (*Cyprinodon diabolis*), a tiny species which occupies (or did occupy — its situation is precarious) the smallest known range of any vertebrate animal, the 20 square meters of a submerged limestone shelf in a deep spring in Nevada. For perhaps 100,000 years this species has maintained itself with a population that fluctuates between 200 and 700 individuals (R. R. Miller, 1961b).

Unfortunately, even the isolated and harmless pupfishes are being threatened by man's activities. At least three Death Valley forms have become extinct in recent years and most of the others are threatened. The situation in the lesser known desert waters of Mexico may be even worse. The U.S. Department of the Interior's Pupfish Task Force (1971) lists five causes of the decline of pupfish populations: introduction of predatory and competing fishes, such as largemouth bass, mosquitofish, goldfish, and various tropical fishes; destruction of habitats through the clearing and leveling of land around the springs; pumping of water from the springs and underground aquifers which feed them, resulting in dropping water levels and drying up of the springs; the presence of pesticides and other chemicals in the spring ecosystems; and over-collecting by scientists and aquarists. Concern for the Death Valley pupfishes resulted in the formation of the Desert Fishes Council in 1969, made up of individuals from numerous public and private agencies. The council has been successful in coordinating the efforts of the agencies to preserve and study the pupfishes and in publicizing plight of the pupfishes. Their task, however, is far from completed (Pister, 1974).

The cyprinodonts of California's inland waters include five species of pupfish, one introduced estuarine species, one marine species, and two introduced tropical species. The tropical species (Trinidad rivulus, *Rivulus harti*, and Argentine pearlfish, *Cynolebias bellottii*) will not be discussed extensively because both species are probably only temporarily established. The Trinidad rivulus, a rather attractive brown and green cyprindont from Colombia and Venezuela, was reported established only in a small ditch flowing into the Salton Sea (St. Amant, 1969). The ditch once drained a now defunct tropical-fish farm. Argentine pearlfish, a bright blue South American species adapted for living in temporary ponds, is established only in some experimental ponds on the University of California, Riverside, campus (E. F. Legner, pers. comm.). Attempts have been made to establish this species and other "annual" fishes for mosquito control in other southern California ponds and in rice fields of the Central Valley, but the attempts seemed to have failed so far. Before further plants of any "annual" fish species are made, much consideration should be given to their possible effects on the poorly known invertebrate fauna that exists in temporary ponds in California.

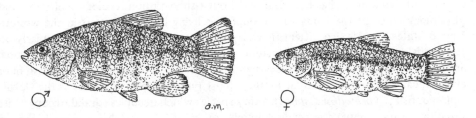

Figure 90. Desert pupfish male (left) 3 cm SL, and female (right), 2 cm SL, canal near Salton Sea, Imperial County.

Desert Pupfish, *Cyprinodon macularius* Baird and Girard

Identification. Desert pupfish are small (less than 75 mm TL), chunky fish with a single series of incisorlike tricuspid teeth in each jaw. The middle cusp of each tooth is spatulate. Scales are large and regular, usually 26 in the lateral series. The circuli on the scales have spinelike projections and the interspaces are regular, without reticulations. Fin rays are 9 to 12 in the dorsal, 9 to 12 in the anal, 14 to 18 in each pectoral, 14 to 20 in the caudal, and 2 to 8 in each pelvic (usually 7). The dorsal fin is equidistant between the base of the caudal fin and the snout. Males are larger and stouter than females and during the breeding season become bright blue with lemon yellow tails and caudal peduncles. The tail has a black terminal band. Females are tan to olive, with a lateral band of 5 to 8 disrupted vertical bars. Males also possess the bars but they are not as prominent.

Names. Cyprino-don means carp with teeth, while *macularius* translates as spotted. The name pupfish was coined by Carl L. Hubbs, once of the first people to take an interest in them, after he observed their "playful" aggressive behavior. Prior to Robert R. Miller's definitive work (1943b,c, 1948) most species of *Cyprinodon* in the southwest were lumped with *C. macularius.*

Distribution. Desert pupfish were found originally in California, Arizona, and Baja California, along the lower Colorado and Gila rivers, and in the Sonoyta River of northern Sonora, Mexico. Populations have become established in the Salton Sea and in its main tributary, San Felipe Creek. They have also been introduced into a special spring sanctuary in Anza-Borrego State Park, California. A sanctuary also exists in Organ Pipe Cactus National Monument, Arizona (Quitobaquito Spring).

Life History. Few fish can live in the extreme range of environmental conditions inhabited by desert pupfish: salinities ranging from nearly twice that of sea water (68 ppt) to that of fresh water (Barlow, 1968); temperatures from 45°C in the summer to 9°C in the winter; and oxygen levels from saturation down to 0.1 to 0.4 ppm (Lowe et al., 1967). They can also survive 10 to 15 ppt changes in salinity as well as daily temperature fluctuations of 22 to 26°C (Kinne, 1960; Lowe and Heath, 1969). One thing they cannot withstand is the presence of large numbers of predaceous or competing fishes. As a result, they are mostly found in habitats too extreme for other species, such as saline pools at the edge of the Salton Sea, isolated springs, and marshes at the river's edge. Most of our knowledge of their life history is based on the Salton Sea populations (Barlow, 1958a,b, 1961b; Walker et al., 1961).

Typically, desert pupfish swim in loose schools, from which small groups break off to forage. The schools tend to be made up of fish of similar size and age. During the breeding season, males become territorial and the schools then consist either entirely of adult females or entirely of juveniles. Smaller fish tend to be found in shallower water than larger fish. This may be a reflection of the slightly higher temperatures they require for optimal growth (Kinne, 1960) or a way they can avoid being eaten by adult pupfish (R. Haas, pers. comm.). In the Salton Sea, pupfish of all sizes move in and out of shallow water during the day, apparently to avoid temperatures higher than 36°C (Barlow, 1961b). Thus, they move into shallow water to forage in the early morning but, as the sun warms the shallows, they move back into deeper water (about 40 cm) and remain there, relatively less active until evening. As the water cools, they gradually move inshore to forage again. Foraging activity ceases at night but, as dawn approaches, the fish move back into the warmer deep water, remaining there until the shallows start to warm up. Some populations of desert pupfish bury themselves in loose debris on the bottom and become dormant when colder water temperatures set in during the winter (Cox, 1966). They may also avoid excessively high temperatures by burrowing.

What the pupfish forage for depends on what small invertebrates and algae are available to be picked off the substrate. In the Salton Sea this means ostracods, copepods, and occasionally insects and pile worms. Elsewhere, aquatic crustaceans, aquatic insect larvae, and molluscs are important. Since desert pupfish are rather unselective in their feeding behavior, their gut usually contains large amounts of algae and detritus as well as invertebrates; occasionally, they will eat their own eggs and young (Cox, 1972).

Growth is rapid and varies with temperature and salinity. For young fish the most rapid growth (in the laboratory) occurs at 30°C and 35 ppt salinity, while for older fish the optimum temperatures for growth are 22 to 26°C, at salinities of about 15 ppt (Kinne, 1960). In the Salton Sea desert pupfish are 4 to 5 mm TL at hatching and double in size in less than eight weeks. At twenty-four weeks, they are 15 to 28 mm TL. Maximum length at the end of the first growing season is 45 to 50 mm TL (Kinne, 1960). Since desert pupfish can become sexually mature at 15 mm TL, it is possible for them to complete their entire life cycle in one summer. Most, however, do not breed until their second summer, by which time they may have reached 75 mm TL.

Spawning takes place from April to October, whenever temperatures exceed 20°C. The first sign of reproductive activity is a few brightly colored males busily patrolling their territories. These territories are usually located in water less than 1 m deep and center on some small submerged object or bump on the bottom (Barlow, 1961b). The depth of the territory depends somewhat on water temperature. The territories are often located in deeper water in the summer than they are in the spring (Cox, 1966). The size of the territory depends on the size of the fish, the number of breeding males, and water temperature. Normally each male defends 1 to 2 square meters but the areas may be as large as 5 to 6 square meters.

The basic spawning behavior, as described by Barlow (1961b), is as follows: a female, when ready to spawn, is attracted to a territorial male and leaves her school. She approaches the male who moves towards her. The female then tilts head first towards the bottom and nips at it, usually taking a small piece of the substrate in her mouth. When she renews her horizontal position, she spits the piece out. This may occur several times in succession. She then halts close to the bottom. The male swims up to the female and lies parallel to her. The two fish then bend together into an "S" and the male cups his anal fin around the vent of the female. The female trembles and lays a single egg, which is fertilized by the male. Several eggs may be deposited on the bottom in this manner in quick succession, each spawning act taking less than a minute. Depending on her size, a female may lay 50 to 800 eggs or more during a season (Crear and Haydock, 1970).

The eggs hatch in ten days at 20°C and the larvae start feeding on small invertebrates within a day after hatching (Crear and Haydock, 1970). The larvae are frequently found in shallow water where environmental conditions may be severe, but they can survive higher salinities than adults (90 ppt) and sudden salinity changes up to 35 ppt (Crear and Haydock, 1970).

Status. Desert pupfish have disappeared from much of their native range due to changes in flows of the Colorado and Gila rivers. The Salton Sea populations are depleted and mostly confined to tributary streams, possibly due to the establishment of competing mosquitofish and sailfin mollies (Fisk, 1972). However they do not appear to be in any immediate danger. A desert pupfish sanctuary has been established in a large spring in Anza-Borrego State Park, and the fish are flourishing there. Desert pupfish are easily bred and maintained in aquaria and have some potential as laboratory animals (Crear and Haydock, 1970).

References. Barlow, 1958a,b, 1961b; Cowles, 1934; Cox, 1966, 1972; Crear and Haydock, 1970; Fisk, 1972; Kinne, 1960; Lowe and Heath, 1969; Lowe et al., 1967; R. R. Miller, 1943, 1948; Walker et al., 1961.

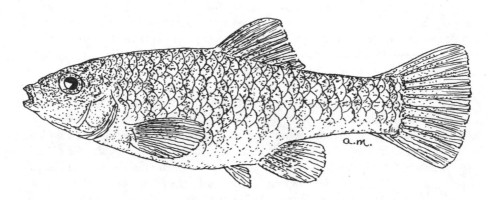

Figure 91. Amargosa pupfish female, 4.2 cm SL, Inyo County.

Amargosa Pupfish, *Cyprinodon nevadensis* Eigenmann and Eigenmann

Identification. Amargosa pupfish are one of the most variable species of pupfish but can be recognized by the following combination of characteristics: circuli of scales without spinelike projections but interspaces reticulated; scales large, 23 to 28, usually 25 to 26, in lateral series; scales before dorsal fin 15 to 24, usually 16 to 18; dorsal fin closer to base of caudal fin than to tip of snout; pelvic fins small, occasionally missing, but usually with 6 rays (range: 0 to 9); and central cusps of teeth truncate or pointed, without a conspicuous ridge (Miller, 1948). Anal rays are 8 to 11, usually 10; pectoral rays are 11 to 18, usually 15 to 17; caudal rays are 14 to 22, usually 16 to 19; gill rakers are 14 to 22, usually 15 to 17; and preopercular pores are 7 to 17, usually 12 to 14. Meristic counts, especially scales and pelvic fin rays, tend to decrease with an increase in average temperature of the water and to increase with an increase in salinity (Miller, 1948). The body is deep, especially in large males. Breeding males turn bright blue over the entire body, including the caudal peduncle, and have a black band at the end of the tail. Vertical bars on females are variable, ranging from 6 to 10 distinct vertical bands to a few very faint bars.

Names. "The name *nevadensis* indicates a desire on the part of the describers to honor the region each of California, but the reasons for such a desire apparently are lost in obscurity, for the Eigenmanns were well aware that the type locality was in California" (La Rivers, 1962, p. 503). Other names are as for desert pupfish.

Distribution. Amargosa pupfish are confined to the Amargosa River Basin in California and Nevada. The species is broken up into a number of isolated populations, six of which are currently recognized as subspecies: *C. n. nevadensis*, from Saratoga Springs in the southeastern corner of Death Valley, San Bernardino County; *C. n. calidae*, originally from north and south Tecopa Hot Springs, Inyo County; *C. n. amargosae*, in permanent waters of the Amargosa River, ditches from Tecopa Hot Springs, and Tecopa Bore (an outflow of an artesian well), San Bernardino County; *C. n. shoshone*, from Shoshone Springs, Inyo County; *C. n. mionectes*, from a number of springs in Ash Meadows, Nye County, Nevada; and *C. n. pectoralis*, from School Spring and Scruggs Spring, Nye County, Nevada. The subspecies can be further broken down into recognizable populations, each inhabiting a different spring.

Life History. Amargosa pupfish are the most widespread of the Death Valley pupfishes, with subspecies and populations adapted to a wide variety of aquatic environments. The populations in the Ash Meadows area, Nye County, Nevada, inhabit freshwater springs that range in temperature from 21 to 33°C, each spring varying only 2 to 7°C annually. In contrast, the highly saline Amargosa River varies from close to freezing in the winter to nearly 40°C in the summer, with daily fluctuations as great as 15 to 20°C. Most of the habitats support heavy growths of algae and associated invertebrates, with emergent cattails and rushes along the edges.

One of the more interesting habitats of Amargosa pupfish is Tecopa Bore, the outflow of a recently (1967) drilled artesian well that has been colonized by pupfish from a marsh connected to the Amargosa River. The temperature at the head is 47.5°C but it may be close to freezing, depending on air temperature, by the time the water reaches the marsh after flowing about 1 km. The maximum temperature the pupfish can withstand for any length of time is about 42°C. In the stream they tend to concentrate in the stretch of water that is 42°C, since the bluegreen algae they feed on is most abundant there (J. H. Brown, 1971). Frequently the wind will blow cooler water upstream and the pupfish quickly take advantage of the temporary availability of ungrazed pastures. When the wind dies, the fish move back downstream. Occasionally, pupfish are caught in water warmer than 42°C where they become moribund and die unless they are quickly washed into cooler water.

The main food of Amargosa pupfish seems to be algae, especially bluegreen algae. They have the long, convoluted intestines characteristic of aquatic herbivores and teeth adapted for nipping. However, small invertebrates are also important in the diet, and they are effective predators on mosquito larvae. In areas with heavy growths of emergent vegetation, they are even more effective than mosquitofish (Danielsen, 1968).

Growth in Amargosa pupfish is rapid, especially in warm, constant springs where they can reach 25 to 30 mm SL and sexual maturity in four to six weeks (Miller, 1948). Maximum length is about 60 mm SL. Growth rates, and generation time, are much less in fluctuating environments. Thus, pupfish in springs may have eight to ten generations per year, while stream populations have only two to three (Miller, 1961b). Short generation time has allowed some populations of Amargosa pupfish to maintain themselves with extremely small numbers of fish. The population of Mexican Spring, which contains about 80 gallons of water, is estimated to be twenty to forty fish, half of which are adults at any one time (J. H. Brown, 1971).

Spawning behavior is similar to that of desert pupfish, with minor differences (Liu, 1969).

Status. Amargosa pupfish, as a species, are widespread and easy to breed in captivity and so are in no great danger of extinction. However, it can only be regarded as a tragic blow to our national biological heritage that a number of the isolated subspecies (e.g., *C. n. calidae* and *C. n. shoshone*) and populations have become extinct in recent years, and others will soon be extinct if action is not taken to preserve their habitats. The study of the differences among the populations has given, and is continuing to give, profound insights into factors affecting the evolution of species and the rapidity with which speciation can take place. The presence of pupfish also focuses public attention on a unique cluster of habitats that contain endemic forms of invertebrates and plants as well as pupfish. Preservation of pupfish populations, which would be nearly meaningless without preservation of their habitats, thus preserves a series of miniature ecosystems for scientists and citizens to learn from for years to come (Pister, 1974). The task of preserving Amargosa pupfish habitats continues to be difficult, since most of them are on private land that is being developed for agriculture or other purposes. The Desert Fishes Council is currently working against time to save them.

References. J. H. Brown, 1971; Brown and Feldmeth, 1971; La Rivers, 1962; Liu, 1969; R. R. Miller, 1948, 1961b; Pister, 1974; U.S. Department of Interior, 1971.

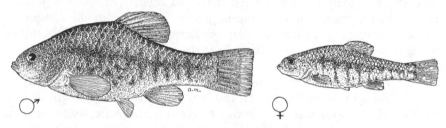

Figure 92. Owens pupfish male, 4.1 cm SL (left), and female, 3.5 cm SL (right), Inyo County.

Owens Pupfish, *Cyprinodon radiosus* Miller

Identification. Owens pupfish resemble desert pupfish but they lack the spinelike projections on the circuli of the scales and have reticulated spaces between the circuli. The scales are large, 26 to 27 in the lateral series. The middle cusps of the teeth are more truncate than spatulate. Dorsal rays are 10 to 12 (usually 11); anal rays, 9 to 12 (usually 10); pectoral rays, 13 to 17 (usually 14 to 15); pelvic rays, 6 to 8 (usually 7); and caudal rays, 16 to 19. The dorsal fin has a thickened first ray and is equidistant between the base of the caudal fin and the tip of the snout. Gill rakers are 15 to 20 (usually 16 to 19). The head is more slender and the caudal peduncle is longer than in other Death Valley pupfishes. Males are larger and deeper bodied than females but the differences are not as striking as in other California *Cyprinodon*. Breeding males are bright blue, with purplish lateral bars. Unlike those of other pupfishes, these bars do not narrow ventrally. Preserved fish lack the black border on the tail which is present in life in many breeding males. Females are similar to other pupfish females. A detailed description of the breeding colors can be found in Miller and Pister (1971).

Names. *Radiosus* "refers to the high number of dorsal, anal, and pelvic rays" (Miller, 1948, p. 98). Other names are as for the desert pupfish, with which the Owens pupfish was confused until Miller described it as a distinct species.

Distribution. Originally, Owens pupfish were found in the Owens River system from Lone Pine, Inyo County, to Fish Slough and its springs, Mono County. Now they are present only in Warm Springs, near Lone Pine (Miller and Pister, 1971) and in refuges constructed around springs at Fish Slough, designated as the Owens Valley Native Fish Sanctuary.

Life History. Owens pupfish once occupied a wide variety of shallow water habitats in Owens Valley: spring pools, sloughs, irrigation ditches, swamps, and flooded pastures along the Owens River. The water they lived in was clear and warm, often with heavy stands of emergent bulrushes in shallow water and dense mats of *Chara* on the bottoms of the pools. Water temperatures probably ranged annually from about 10 to 25°C. The sanctuaries to which Owens pupfish are now confined have large, clear pools with extensive shallow areas as well as holes up to 2 m deep. Like other pupfishes, they were most abundant where other species of fish, especially predaceous forms, were absent. They were originally associated with Owens tui chubs (*Gila bicolor snyderi*), Owens suckers (*Catostomus fumeiventris*), and speckled dace (*Rhinichthys osculus*), but these fishes were presumably found most often in deeper water than the pupfish.

Owens pupfish forage in small schools, feeding mostly on aquatic insects. Fish examined by Kennedy (1916) were feeding heavily on chironomid midge larvae and to a lesser extent on mayfly larvae and beetle larvae and adults. The presence of Owens pupfish in shallow water among emergent plants, coupled with the comparative absence of mosquitoes in the Owens Valley, led Kennedy (1916) to conclude that the pupfish kept the mosquitoes under control. As the pupfish became rare, mosquitoes became a problem (Miller, 1948).

Little has been recorded on the growth rates of Owens pupfish except that they can reach a maximum length of 60 mm TL (50 mm SL). The average length of those studied by Miller (1948) was 33 mm SL. Presumably, they are similar to other pupfishes in their ability to reach 30 to 45 mm SL during the first growing season and to breed before they are a year old. Spawning behavior is similar in most respects to that of desert pupfish (Liu, 1969).

Status. Owens pupfish are internationally recognized as an endangered species and are fully protected by California state law (Leach and Fisk, 1972). Once thought to be extinct, their rediscovery and preservation is a dramatic and heartening story (Miller and Pister, 1971) that hopefully signals a reversal of the general trend towards species elimination in North America. When Owens pupfish were originally described by Miller (1948), much of their habitat had disappeared due to the removal of Owens River water by the city of Los Angeles. The presence of largemouth bass, carp, and mosquitofish in what habitat remained made it appear unlikely that any pupfish survived. Thus, it came as a surprise when, in 1963, R. K. Liu, then a graduate student at the University of California, Los Angeles, discovered that two biologists from the California Department of Fish and Game had collected Owens pupfish in 1956, but had not told anyone because they had not realized the pupfish were thought to be extinct. After an unsuccessful search in 1963, a pool in the slough containing about 200 fish was located by C. L. Hubbs, R. R. Miller, and E. P. Pister. Realizing the position of the Owens pupfish was precarious, in 1967 they carefully examined the slough and laid plans for the construction of a refuge, complete with barriers to keep out exotic fish. The sanctuary pools were ready for stocking with pupfish in June, 1970, which was none too soon. In August, 1969, a series of natural events nearly dried up the marshy pool containing the last of the pupfish. Fortunately for the pupfish, R. E. Brown, also a UCLA graduate student, saw that the pool was nearly dry and took immediate action, rescuing about 800 fish. These fish were placed in live cages in deeper parts of the slough and temporary sanctuaries were hastily constructed. The rapid construction of both the temporary and permanent sanctuaries was a bit of a miracle, engineered by E. P. Pister of the California Department of Fish and Game, since it required the cooperation of innumerable public and private agencies, including the California Department of Fish and Game, the California Division of Foestry, the Los Angeles Department of Water and Power, the Bureau of Land Management, the Nature Conservancy, and the John Muir Institute (Miller and Pister, 1971).

References. Kennedy, 1916; Leach and Fisk, 1972; Liu, 1969; Miller, 1948; Miller and Pister, 1971; Snyder, 1917.

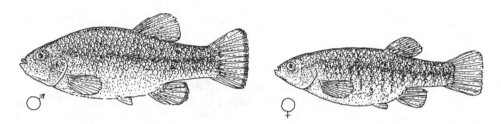

Figure 93. Salt Creek pupfish male, 2.8 cm SL (left), and female, 2.5 cm SL (right), Salt Creek, Inyo County.

Salt Creek Pupfish, *Cyprinodon salinus* Miller

Identification. Salt Creek pupfish are the most slender of the Death Valley pupfishes. They are distinguished by small scales (28 to 29 in the lateral series) that have reticulated interspaces between the circuli, and tricuspid teeth with prominent median ridges. The maximum length is about 65 mm TL. The dorsal fin (8 to 11 rays, usually 9 to 10) is closer to the base of the caudal fin than to the snout. Anal rays are 9 to 11 (usually 10); pectoral rays, 14 to 17 (usually 15 to 16); and caudal rays, 15 to 19 (usually 16 to 17). The pelvic fins are small and occasionally absent, but usually they have 6 rays. Gill rakers number 18 to 22, usually 19 to 21, and are shorter and more compressed than in other pupfishes. Scales are absent from most of the preorbital region of the head. Breeding males become deep blue on the sides and iridescent purple on the back. The caudal peduncle and fin is never yellow but the black terminal band is conspicuous. The sides of spawning males have 5 to 8 broad vertical bands, which may be either continuous or interrupted. Females are less deep bodied than the males and usually have 4 to 8 continuous vertical bars on the sides, which narrow ventrally. The vertical bars become less conspicuous in older fish.

Names. Salinus means salt. Other names are as for desert pupfish.

Distribution. Salt Creek pupfish are confined to a 2-1/2 km stretch of Salt Creek, which starts about 2 km below its origin in seepages on Mesquite Flat, in the northern part of Death Valley. Miller (1968) reported that additional populations have been established through transplants at Soda Lake, San Bernardino County, and at River Springs, Mono County.

Life History. Salt Creek is a unique habitat for fish, and Salt Creek pupfish are its sole piscine inhabitants. The creek starts flowing from seepages located about 60 m below sea level and ends, depending on the amount of flow, at 80 to 90 m below sea level. The upper end of the creek, which exists as surface water only in the winter and spring, meanders muddily across Mesquite Flat for 1 to 2 km before sinking into a narrow, shallow canyon. The flow through the canyon is permanent and thus supports pupfish the year around. The stream channel on the canyon floor is carved 3 to 7 m deep into alkaline mud and consists partially of a series of interconnected pools, some of which are as large as 10 by 25 m and 2 m deep. The pools are edged with heavy growths of saltgrass, pickleweed, and saltbush. The plants may completely roof over the interconnecting channels and hang over the edges of the pools, providing shelter for the fish. The pools contain heavy growths of aquatic plants which are favored by the pupfishes (Miller, 1943b). Below the pool area the stream becomes quite shallow and exposed. Pupfish will inhabit as much of this area as the fluctuating water flow permits.

Water temperatures range from close to freezing in the winter to nearly 40°C in the summer, although deep water in the pools seldom exceeds 28°C. Salinity is close to that of sea water but the boron levels (39 ppm) and total dissolved solids (23,600 ppm) are exceptionally high for any water containing fish (Miller, 1943b). In the laboratory, Salt Creek pupfish can tolerate temperatures up to 42°C (Brown and Feldmeth, 1971) and salinity about twice that of sea water (LaBounty and Deacon, 1972).

One of the most remarkable aspects of the biology of Salt Creek pupfish is their population fluctuations. When water flows are high the population grows rapidly, spreading beyond the normal limits of permanent water flow. Miller (1943b) has estimated that peak populations number in the millions. The rapid population buildup indicates a generation time of two to three months. As water temperatures rise and the stream shrinks in the summer, the fish die by the thousands. Predators, such as ravens and herons, take advantage of this accessible food supply, as did the Panamint Indians who caught them in baskets and baked them (Miller, 1943b).

Most other aspects of the behavior and life history of Salt Creek pupfish are similar to the desert pupfish (Liu, 1969).

Status. Salt Creek is located entirely within Death Valley National Monument, so the pupfish continue their dramatic population cycles interrupted only by tourists. Even the tourists rarely see the fish, since to do so normally requires a walk of several hundred yards from the Salt Creek parking lot.

References. Brown and Feldmeth, 1971; LaBounty and Deacon, 1972; Liu, 1969; Miller, 1943b.

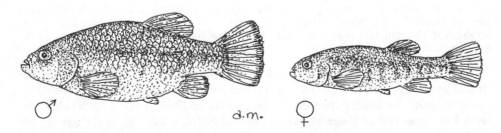

Figure 94. Cottonball Marsh pupfish male, 2.6 cm SL (left), and female, 1.5 cm SL (right), Cottonball Marsh, Inyo County.

Cottonball Marsh Pupfish, *Cyprinodon milleri* LaBounty and Deacon

Identification. Cottonball Marsh pupfish are similar to Salt Creek pupfish except that they have shorter, slenderer caudal peduncles; smaller pelvic fins, usually with less than 6 fin rays (or they may be absent altogether); dorsal and pelvic fins located in a more posterior position; shorter dorsal fins with 8 to 10 rays, usually 8 to 9; and larger jaw teeth, with the central cusps more spatulate, narrower at the base, more sharply separated from the lateral cusps, and lacking the ridge on the outer faces. Scales in the lateral series are 27 to 34; predorsal scales, 26 to 33; anal fin rays, 9 to 11; pectoral fin rays, 13 to 16; caudal fin rays, 15 to 18; gill rakers, 17 to 21; and preopercular pores are 7 to 16. Sexual differences and coloration are similar to Salt Creek pupfish.

Names. *Milleri* is for Robert Rush Miller, Curator of Fishes at the Museum of Zoology, University of Michigan, whose studies form the backbone of our knowledge of pupfishes. Prior to LaBounty and Deacon (1972), Cottonball Marsh pupfish were considered to be a population of Salt Creek pupfish. Other names are as for desert pupfish.

Distribution. Cottonball Marsh pupfish are confined to two joined marshy areas with a combined total of about 260 hectares of surface water. Collectively, the areas are known as Cottonball or Pupfish Marsh. The marsh is located in the northwest portion of Death Valley, near the sink of Salt Creek.

Life History. Most of what is known about these pupfish is found in LaBounty and Deacon (1972), since their habitat is so isolated and severe that they were overlooked until recently. Cottonball Marsh, located 80 m below sea level, is an extraordinary habitat, even for pupfish. The pupfish live in exposed shallow pools, the rims encrusted with gypsum and salt (mostly sodium sulfate). The pools become smaller and shallower as the summer progresses, exposing the fish to high extremes of temperature and salinity. The soil around the pools is too saline to support even the hardiest terrestrial plants such as pickleweed and saltgrass. In the water, however, there are good growths of algae and, in the less saline pools, stands of emergent rushes. The algae support large populations of amphipods, ostracods, and small snails upon which the pupfish presumably feed as well as on the algae itself. The salinities of the pools range from 14 ppt to 160 ppt (about 4.6 times that of sea water), depending on the time of year and closeness to the seepage water source. Pupfish can be found in all the pools, although they are less abundant in the highly saline ones. Temperatures vary from close to freezing in the winter to nearly 40°C in the summer, which approaches the maximum temperature they can withstand (Brown and Feldmeth, 1971). Daily fluctuations in temperature are also extreme, paralleling those of the air. In shallow water the daily fluctuations may reach 15°C, although in the deeper areas (33 cm maximum) the fluctuations may be only 2 to 3°C (Naiman et al., 1973).

In most aspects of their life history and behavior, Cottonball Marsh pupfish seem to be similar to Salt Creek pupfish, from which they were derived. It is estimated that Cottonball Marsh became separated from Salt Creek only a few thousand years ago, but the extreme habitat has promoted very rapid differentiation of the pupfish population.

Status. Cottonball Marsh is located in an isolated portion of Death Valley National Monument which is unlikely ever to be popular, even with tourists. Barring an unexpected cessation of the water seeping into the marsh, their future seems secure.

References. Brown and Feldmeth, 1971; LaBounty and Deacon, 1972; Naiman et al., 1973.

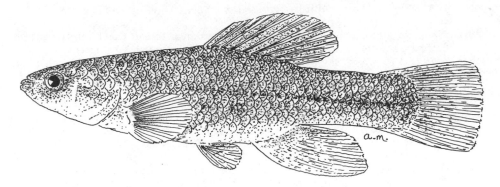

Figure 95. California killifish, 7.5 cm SL, Los Osos Creek, San Luis Obispo County.

California Killifish, *Fundulus parvipinnis* Girard

Identification. California killifish are little (to 115 mm SL), thick-bodied fish with small pelvic fins, rounded caudal and dorsal fins, and several rows of conical teeth in their small oblique mouths. They have 3 to 37 scales in the lateral series, 11 to 13 rays in the anal fin, 12 to 15 rays in the dorsal fin, and 7 to 11 gill rakers. Their overall color is olive green on the back and sides and yellowish brown on the belly. Males have about 20 short black bars on the side and turn dark brown on the back when breeding. Females lack the bars but have a faint lateral band. An oviducal pouch covers the first rays of the anal fin of females.

Names. Killifish is an American word for cyprinodont fishes dating back to colonial days but its origins are obscure. It is perhaps derived from kill-fish since some eastern members of the genus *Fundulus* are poisonous (White et al., 1965). A more likely explanation is that killifish is a contraction of "killing fish," since the word *killing* was used to describe exceptionally effective (deadly) fishing bait (Oxford English Dictionary, 1971). Killifish are also known as top minnows. *Fundulus* is derived from *fundus*, Latin for bottom, because the first species of the genus described has the habit of burrowing in bottom mud. *Parvi-pinnis* means small-finned, referring to the pelvics.

Distribution. California killifish are found in shallow coastal waters from the Salinas River, Monterey County (Kukowski, 1972) to southern Baja California (Miller and Lea, 1972). Occasionally populations are found in freshwater streams or brackish lagoons of southern California, most notably San Juan Creek, Orange County (Miller, 1939, 1943a).

Life History. Despite the fact that California killifish have been used as laboratory animals for physiological studies, little seems to be known about their life history. They are most abundant in saltwater lagoons and estuaries but can tolerate a wide range of salinities so populations have become established in a number of freshwater streams (Miller, 1939, 1943a). They can live in water ranging from completely fresh to that having salinities up to 128 ppt. Small fish are more resistant to sudden changes of salinity than are larger fish but the larger fish can withstand lower oxygen levels (Keys, 1931). The presence in fresh water of fish of all sizes, including ripe males and females, indicates that they can complete their entire life cycle in fresh water. Like other members of the genus *Fundulus* they are probably omnivorous, taking advantage of the most abundant invertebrates and algae in their environment.

Breeding takes place mostly from May to June but may continue through July and into August if water temperatures are low early in the year (Keys, 1931). There is some evidence that breeding may follow lunar cycles, with spring peaks about the time of the new moon and consequent high tides (Foster, 1967a).

Status. Although competing uses of fresh water in southern California may have eliminated much of the suitable freshwater habitat for California killifish, they are still abundant in salt water.

References. Feldmeth and Waggoner, 1972; Foster, 1967a,b; Keys, 1931; R. R. Miller, 1939, 1943a.

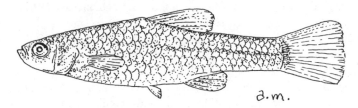

Figure 96. Rainwater killifish, 2.4 cm SL, tidal marsh, Solano County.

Rainwater Killifish, *Lucania parva* (Baird and Girard)

Identification. Rainwater killifish are small (usually less than 41 mm SL), guppylike fishes with large eyes, chunky bodies, oblique mouths with a single row of tiny conical teeth, rounded dorsal and caudal fins, and small pelvic fins. Scales in the lateral series are 23 to 29 (usually 27); anal rays, 8 to 13 (usually 9 to 10); dorsal rays, 9 to 14 (usually 11); caudal rays, 12 to 18 (usually 14 to 16); pectoral rays, 10 to 15 (usually 13 to 14); pelvic rays, 4 to 7 (usually 6); and gill rakers, 4 to 12 (usually 6 to 9). Basic color is olivaceous on the back, silvery blue grey on the sides, and yellowish on the belly. Males have black edges on the anal and pectoral fins and blackened anterior dorsal rays. Females have a membranous oviducal pouch covering the anterior portion of the anal fin.

Names. Lucania seems to be a nice-sounding name without meaning, coined by Charles Girard, while *parva* means small. For common names see California killifish.

Distribution. Rainwater killifish are native to coastal waters from Massachusetts and Florida, around the Gulf of Mexico to the lower Rio Panuco in Mexico. They are also present in the Rio Grande and the Pecos River, Texas and New Mexico. They have become established in recent years in springs in Utah, Irving Lake in southern California, sloughs and streams flowing into San Francisco Bay, Lake Merritt in Oakland, and Yaquina Bay, Oregon. How they were introduced into these areas is a bit of a mystery but Hubbs and Miller (1965) present circumstantial evidence that the populations in San Francisco and Yaquina bays started from eggs attached to live oysters imported from the east coast for culture. The Lake Irvine and Utah fish apparently fist came in with shipments of gamefishes from a federal hatchery along the Pecos River, New Mexico (Hubbs and Miller, 1965).

Life History. Little is known about the life history of rainwater killifish in California and only limited information is available on their biology elsewhere

(Renfro, 1960; Harrington and Harrington, 1961; Hubbs and Miller, 1965; Foster, 1967a,b). They are primarily inhabitants of brackish waters but they can live in water ranging from fresh to that nearly twice as saline as sea water. In California, populations are known from both the brackish stretches of coastal streams and from freshwater lakes. There is some evidence that they normally migrate into fresh water to breed and then move back into brackish water, in areas dominated by emergent and submerged vegetation. Such migrations may be spectacular; as many as 270,000 fish have been observed moving downstream in a Virginia river in a four-hour period (Beck and Massmann, 1951).

Rainwater killifish feed on whatever invertebrates are abundant in their habitat. In a Florida marsh they ate mostly mosquito larvae (51 percent) and copepods (32 percent). The remainder of the diet consisted of miscellaneous crustaceans and aquatic insects. The diversity of the diet increased with size; small fish (less than 15 mm TL) fed almost exclusively on mosquito larvae while larger fish (greater than 35 mm TL) fed mostly on a variety of crustaceans (Harrington and Harrington, 1961).

Growth is rapid, and sexual maturity can be reached in three to five months, at a minimum length of 25 mm TL. Females grow larger than males, reaching a maximum size of 62 mm TL (Foster, 1967). The time of breeding is not known for California populations but it is probably from May through July.

Breeding begins when males set up territories over or near beds of aquatic plants or algae (Foster, 1967). They assume a cross-hatched breeding pattern on the sides and display vigorously to the males holding nearby territories. When a female approaches, the male circles rapidly around her. If she is interested in spawning, she stops and he moves quickly beneath her, rubbing the top of his head against the underside of her head. In this position they swim to the surface of the water, to a point just above a suitable substrate for egg attachment. The male then wraps himself around the female, placing his vent close to hers, and fertilizes the eggs as they are released.

The eggs hatch in about six days at 75°F, and the larvae settle down to the bottom. They assume an active existence in about a week, when the yolk sac is absorbed (Foster, 1967).

Status. Rainwater killifish appear to be well established in California, at least in the San Francisco Bay area. Their spread southward down the coast seems likely, although special efforts will have to be made to document this since they superficially resemble the ubiquitous mosquitofish.

References. Beck and Massmann, 1965; Foster, 1967a,b; Harrington and Harrington, 1961; Hubbs and Miller, 1965; Renfro, 1960.

Livebearer Family, Poeciliidae

Livebearers are closely related to killifishes, differing from them mainly in their method of reproduction. Instead of laying eggs, female poeciliids incubate them internally, giving birth to free-swimming young. The males have elongated rays in their anal fins that permit them to be used as intromittent organs for placing packets of sperm in the vents of the females. Livebearers are small, active fishes, seldom exceeding 10 cm TL, and are extremely diverse in morphology and coloration. Since the family evolved in Central America and diversified in the absence of competing freshwater fishes, they have adapted to a wide variety of habitats, in water ranging from salt to fresh (Rosen and Bailey, 1963). Their colorfulness, hardiness, and readiness to breed in captivity have made them one of the most popular groups of aquarium fishes. Intensive breeding in aquaria of guppies, mollies, and platies has produced many bizarre body shapes and color patterns and has given scientists insights into fish evolution and genetics.

Central America is still the center of poeciliid abundance and diversity but the family has spread to both North and South America. At least twelve species are native to the United States, including the mosquitofish. Because of the high regard they hold as mosquito-control agents, mosquitofish have become, through introductions, the most widely distributed freshwater fish in the world. All livebearers found in California are introduced. Only two species, the sailfin molly and the mosquitofish, are common enough to warrant detailed treatment here. At least two other species, the shortfin molly, *Poecilia mexicana*, and the variable platyfish, *Xiphophorus variatus*, have been collected from freshwater ditches around the Salton Sea (St. Amant and Sharp, 1971) but it is uncertain if permanent breeding populations have been established. Green swordtails (*X. helleri*) have been collected from flood-control channels in Orange County (St. Amant, 1969). Populations of other platy and molly species, as well as the guppy (*P. reticulata*), can be expected since they have been found in warm springs in Nevada and Montana and in Alberta, Canada. Such populations are either the result of releases by aquarists tired of their charges or escapees from tropical fish farms. Guppies occasionally establish populations in sewage-treatment ponds but so far no populations have been recorded from natural waters in California.

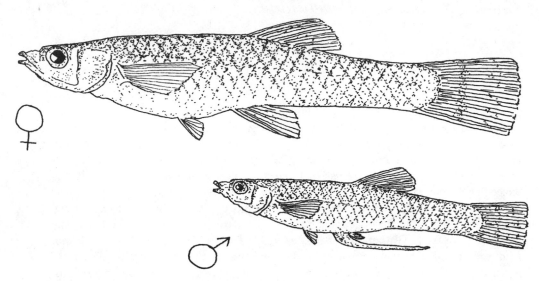

Figure 97. Mosquitofish female, 2.5 cm SL (upper), and male, 1.2 cm (lower), Putah Creek, Yolo County.

Mosquitofish, *Gambusia affinis* (Baird and Girard)

Identification. Mosquitofish are small (to 60 mm TL), stout-bodied fish with short, flattened heads and small oblique mouths. The dorsal fin (6 to 7 rays) is placed behind the origin of the anal fin (9 to 10 rays, although branching often gives the impression of more). The anal fin of males is rodlike since it is used as an intromittent organ (gonopodium). The caudal fin is rounded. Scales are large, 29 to 32 in the lateral series, frequently outlined with pigment on the back and sides. The intestine is short, with a single loop. Males are much smaller (to 35 mm TL) and less stout bodied than females. Overall color is generally grey or olivaceous, lighter on the belly, with few conspicuous markings.

Names. Gambusia was coined by F. Poey, a Cuban naturalist, who is quoted by Jordan and Evermann (1896, p. 679): "The name owes its etymology to the provincial Cuban word *Gambusino* which signifies nothing, with the idea of a joke or farce. Thus one says 'to fish for *Gambusinos*' when one catches nothing." *Affinis* means related, apparently to *G. holbrooki*, a species described first by Louis Agassiz in an unpublished manuscript. *G. holbrooki* was formally described by Girard in 1859 and is currently recognized as a subspecies of *G. affinis*. A complete synonymy is given in Rosen and Bailey (1963).

Distribution. Mosquitofish are broken up into two subspecies, *G. a. affinis*, native to central North America from southern Illinois to Alabama and Texas, and *G. a. holbrooki*, native to the Atlantic coast from New Jersey to Florida. The two subspecies may deserve species status (C. L. Hubbs, pers. comm.). Because of their reputation as mosquito-control agents they have been introduced into suitable areas over most of the world. They were introduced into California in 1922 and have since been spread over the state. The subspecies introduced seems to have been mostly *G. a. affinis*.

Life History. As might be expected of a fish that has become established in warm waters over most of the Earth, mosquitofish can survive in a wide range of environmental conditions. They are found in brackish sloughs as well as in warm ponds, lakes, and streams. They are particularly well adapted for life in shallow, often stagnant, ponds and the shallow edges of lakes and streams where predatory fishes are largely absent and temperatures are high. They can survive temperatures up to 37.3°C (Carlander, 1969) as well as extreme daily temperature fluctuations. They generally cannot withstand prolonged exposure to cold water (less than 4°C), although Krumholz (1948) has demonstrated that they can be acclimated to climates as severe as that of northern Illinois. Low oxygen levels in the water also pose few problems for mosquitofish. Their small size, flat head, and oblique mouth permit them to use the few millimeters of water close to the surface into which oxygen diffuses from the air. In the Sierra Nevada foothills, mosquitofish are most abundant in disturbed portions of intermittent streams, especially warm, turbid pools. Often, large schools can be observed swimming in the shallow pool edges where water temperatures can approach the thermal maximum for mosquitofish (Moyle and Nichols, 1973).

If submerged and emergent aquatic plants are present in the water, mosquitofish tend to be found among them, but only if the plant growth is not too heavy. When plant growths are heavy, mosquitofish remain close to the edges of the plant patches, seldom penetrating very far inward.

Mosquitofish are omnivorous and opportunistic feeders, usually taking their prey close to the water surface. Although mosquito larvae and pupae can form a substantial portion of their diet, they apparently do not feed selectively on them. Instead, they feed on whatever organisms are most abundant. Thus, Harrington and Harrington (1961) found that mosquitofish were the least specialized of the small fishes living in a Florida marsh, feeding voraciously on mosquito larvae and pupae when they were abundant, but otherwise subsisting on a mixed diet of algae, zooplankton, fishes, terrestrial insects, and miscellaneous aquatic invertebrates. A similar mixed diet was found in mosquitofish inhabiting a southern California stream (Greenfield and Deckert, 1973). Under crowded conditions or during periods when animal food is scarce, mosquitofish may feed extensively on filamentous algae and diatoms (Rees, 1958). The food of mosquitofish does not change with the size of the fish, except that larger fish can ingest larger organisms.

Growth in mosquitofish depends primarily on sex, productivity of the water, and temperature (Krumholz, 1948; Goodyear et al., 1972). Males almost stop growing once the formation of the gonopodium is complete. Thus males seldom exceed 31 mm TL and most reach their maximum size in one growing season. Females may reach 50 mm TL in one growing season, although smaller sizes are more common. Maximum growth is possible when the productivity of the water is high and warm temperatures prevail for extended periods of time. Most fish die in the same summer they reach maturity, so few fish live more than fifteen months (Krumholz, 1948). Overwintering fish are generally juveniles or adults that achieved maturity late in the growing season.

Males may become mature at 19 to 21 mm TL, while females usually reach at least 24 mm TL before becoming gravid. Under optimal conditions, females can become gravid at six weeks of age. Since the gestation period is only three to four weeks, 3 to

4 generations per year are possible in the warmer parts of California. In addition, large females can give birth to at least four broods of young in a season (usually April through September in California). Thus, the potential for rapid population growth in mosquitofish is very high. Each female contains 1 to 315 embryos, the number usually increasing with the size of the fish. However, the number may decrease with age, at the approach of the end of the reproductive season, and as conditions become more crowded (Krumholz, 1948). Cannibalism may help limit population size under crowded conditions.

Courtship and copulation are constant activities among mosquitofish, although individual acts are brief and variable in pattern (Itzkowitz, 1971). Two types of courtship displays can be observed. In the infrequent but conspicuous frontal display, the male swims in front of the female, orienting his body at a 90° angle to hers. He partially folds the dorsal and anal fins, bends his body into a "S," and quivers for a few seconds. Then he quickly swims around behind and below the female and attempts to shove his gonopodium into the female's genital opening. The lateral display is similar to the frontal display except that it is performed alongside the female, close to her head, and the male does not bend or quiver so much. Often no courtship display precedes an attempt at copulation (Peden, 1972). With or without courtship displays, most attempts at copulation are unsuccessful, usually because the female is not receptive. Receptive females tend to swim slowly or remain nearly stationary. In aquaria, they are quickly surrounded by males, although one male is usually dominant over the rest (Itzkowitz, 1971).

Status. Mosquitofish are just as popular for mosquito control in California as they are over most of the world, so they continue to be planted in warm waters throughout the state. As mosquitoes have developed resistance to pesticides, the use of mosquitofish has increased. In Central Valley rice fields it has been demonstrated that mosquitofish can both be more effective and less costly than pesticides in controlling mosquitoes (Hoy et al., 1972).

The success of mosquitofish as mosquito-control agents can be attributed to a number of factors: a high reproductive rate that permits rapid population buildups from small initial plants of fish; a method of reproduction (ovoviviparity) that frees them from the need for a special spawning substrate; an ability to live in the extreme environmental conditions which also favor mosquitoes; omnivorous feeding habits that allow them to live on other organisms, including algae, when mosquitoes are not abundant; a preference for habitats where predators are usually absent; an ability to develop resistance to pesticides, so that they can be used in areas where pesticides are also used (Rosato and Ferguson, 1968); and their ease of culture.

While the above characteristics have made mosquitofish extremely useful to man in disturbed or artificial bodies of water, they can also make mosquitofish a problem species in undisturbed situations. Mosquitofish have been accused of eliminating small fish species the world over through predation and competitive interactions (Myers, 1965), and a number of such cases in southwestern United States have been documented by Miller (1961a) and Minckley and Deacon (1968). In California, it is quite likely that mosquitofish have contributed to the decline of a number of pupfish populations, presumably by devouring substantial portions of their food supply and, possibly, young pupfish. However, in most cases the destruction of habitat and the introduction of predatory fishes have initiated the pupfish declines, while simultaneously creating conditions that favor mosquitofish.

Another problem created by the popularity of mosquitofish is that it has prevented serious consideration of native fishes and invertebrates for mosquito control, even through they might be more effective locally than mosquitofish. For example, Danielsen (1968) has demonstrated that pupfish are more effective mosquito predators in emergent vegetation than are mosquitofish. This may explain why mosquitoes became a problem in the Owens Valley after the Owens pupfish were eliminated, despite the introduction of mosquitofish.

The omnivorous nature of mosquitofish also can create problems because the fish can disrupt food chains in small bodies of water by reducing populations of invertebrate predators and grazers. In small experimental ponds, introduction of mosquitofish resulted in large blooms of phytoplankton after the zooplankton grazers had been eliminated by the fish (Hurlbert et al., 1972). It is even possible that an improper introduction of mosquitofish can result in an increase in mosquitoes. Mosquitofish can reduce populations of the invertebrate predators of mosquitoes before the fish can build up populations large enough to control the mosquitoes by themselves. Thus Hoy et al. (1972) found that mosquito populations in rice fields stocked with only a small number of mosquitofish were larger than populations in either control fields with substantial numbers of invertebrate predators (mostly Notonectidae) or in fields into which large numbers of mosquitofish had been stocked.

Despite the enormous amount of work that has been done on mosquitofish, much still needs to be done in California, particularly on their interactions with other fish species, including the young of native minnows and gamefishes, and on their effects on undisturbed ecosystems.

References. Carlander, 1969; Danielsen, 1968; Goodyear et al., 1972; Greenfield and Deckert, 1973; Harrington and Harrington, 1961; Hoy et al., 1972; Hurlbert et al., 1972; Itzkowitz, 1971; Krumholz, 1948; Lewis, 1970; Miller, 1961; Minckley and Deacon, 1968; Moyle and Nichols, 1973; Myers, 1965; Peden, 1972; Rees, 1958; Rosato and Ferguson, 1968; Rosen and Bailey, 1963.

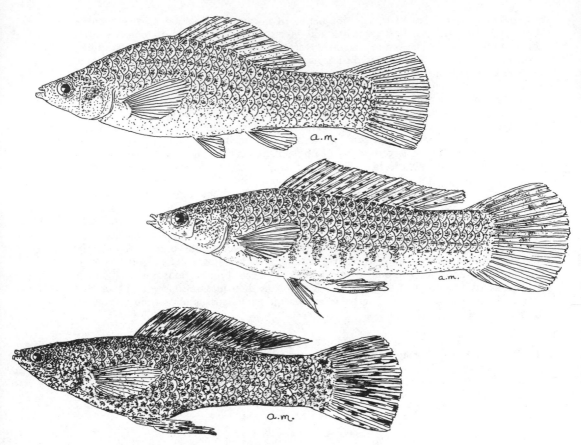

Figure 98. Sailfin molly female, 5 cm SL (upper), normal male, 6 cm SL (middle), and "checkered" male, 5 cm SL (lower), Salton Sea, Imperial County.

Sailfin Molly, *Poecilia latipinna* (Lesueur)

Identification. Sailfin mollies are chunky bodied with thick caudal peduncles, rounded tails, and oblique mouths. Males are brightly colored with long (12 to 15 rays), saillike dorsal fins and with gonopodia modified from the first rays of the anal fin (9 to 10 rays). The dorsal fin of females is shorter and the anal fin is unmodified. The pectoral fin has 13 rays, the pelvics have 6 rays, and the lateral line has 26 to 28 scales. Color patterns are highly variable but distinctive, especially for males. True wild-type sailfin molly males are brown on the back, which gradually changes to iridescent blue or pink on the sides, and white on the belly. There are 5 to 6 horizontal bands on the sides made up of red, blue, or green spots and 5 to 9 faint vertical bands starting beneath the pectoral fins. The dorsal fin is pale blue, with rows of black spots and a yellow border. The female coloration is similar to that of males, but paler. Most California populations, however, seem to be derived from black or checkered mollies of the aquarium trade, so many of the fish are likely to be solid iridescent black with an orange border on the dorsal fin, or heavily speckled on the sides with varying numbers of black "checkers" which merge into one another.

Names. Sailfin mollies are often listed under the generic name *Mollienesia*, although Rosen and Bailey (1963) synonomized it with *Poecilia. Poecilia* means many-colored while *latipinna* means broad fin. Black mollies of the aquarium trade are usually sailfin mollies, although the large fin usually does not develop under aquarium conditions.

Distribution. Sailfin mollies are native to coastal North America from South Carolina to northeastern Mexico (R. R. Miller, pers. comm.). The only large permanent populations in California live in the canals around the Salton Sea, as well as in the sea itself. Because of their commonness as aquarium fish it is not unusual to find them, at least temporarily, in ponds and canals in other parts of southern California. Populations have also been established in springs in Death Valley although most, if not all, of these populations are in Nevada.

Life History. Sailfin mollies are native to warm, brackish coastal swamps so it is not surprising that they have done so well in the salty irrigation water of the Imperial Valley. Because they can tolerate salinities up to 87 ppt, they can even move with ease through the Salton Sea (Barlow, 1958a). They can withstand a fairly wide range of temperatures but 24 to 28°C seems to be best for breeding and growth. Sailfin mollies feed primarily on algae and detritus. Mollies collected in ditches near the Salton Sea in July, 1973, were feeding on detritus (86 percent by volume) and algae (14 percent). Invertebrates are eaten only when they are superabundant and even then the main consumers are the smaller mollies (Harrington and Harrington, 1961). They grow rapidly on this diet, however, and can reach 8 to 10 cm TL in a year under optimal conditions of temperature and salinity. In the Salton Sea, individuals 12 to 15 cm TL are occasionally taken, although few exceed 8 cm TL. The largest fish are usually females.

Courtship and copulation are quick and simple, much like that of mosquitofish. Females can store sperm, so several batches of eggs can be fertilized internally from one copulation. For this reason, it is possible to start a population with one pregnant female. Females also generally outnumber males. In Salton Sea ditches (July, 1973) the male:female ratio was 1:13. Ripe eggs are shed by the ovaries into the ovarian cavity, where they are fertilized and incubated. The number of young produced by each female depends on her size, water temperatures, and salinities, but a large female under optimum environmental conditions can produce up to 120 young at a time (Sterba, 1959). In Salton Sea ditches, mollies normally produce 20 to 60 young but one large (59 mm SL) female contained 141 embryos. The young are large (9 to 12 mm TL) and self-sufficient at birth.

Status. Sailfin mollies are a pest in the Death Valley region because they compete with native pupfishes for the limited resources of desert springs. They are perhaps the most abundant fish in many of the canals flowing into the Salton Sea and, as the salinity of the sea itself increases, they may be the last fish species in the area to be able to use it to any extent.

References. Barlow, 1958; Harrington and Harrington, 1961; Rosen and Bailey, 1963; Sterba, 1959.

Silverside Family, Atherinidae

The silversides are a group of silvery, streamlined pelagic fishes abundant in tropical and temperate coastal environments. A number of species, including four in the eastern United States, live in fresh water. Silversides are often called smelt because of their superficial resemblance to the true smelts (Osmeridae). However, they lack adipose fins and lateral lines, and have two widely separated dorsal fins, the first composed of spines. The three silversides native to California, all marine, are California grunion (*Leuresthes tenuis*), jacksmelt (*Atherinopsis californiensis*), and topsmelt (*Atherinops affinis*). Topsmelt are occasionally found in the lower reaches of coastal streams but the only completely freshwater silverside in California is the introduced Mississippi silverside.

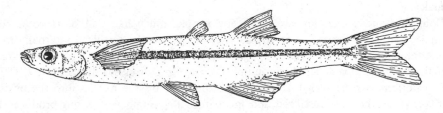

Figure 99. Mississippi silverside, 8.5 cm SL, Clear Lake, Lake County.

Mississippi Silverside, *Menidia audens* Hay

Identification. Mississippi silversides are long (SL is 6 to 7 times body depth) and slender, with large eyes, oblique mouths, and heads flattened on top. The two dorsal fins are widely separated, with 4 to 5 weak spines in the first fin and 1 spine and 8 to 9 rays in the second. The anal fin has 1 spine and 17 to 18 rays while the lateral line has 39 to 44 scales. In life the fish are translucent white with a wide silvery band on each side. The upper rows of scales are outlined with pigment spots and there are two rows of pigment spots on the bottom of the caudal peduncle, between the anal fin base and the caudal fin base.

Names. Menidia seems to be derived from an old Italian word for small silvery fish, since the genus was first described by Charles Lucien Jules Laurent Bonaparte, a nephew of Napoleon and the author of *Fauna Italica. Audens* means daring; the first Mississippi silversides was collected from the Mississippi River near Memphis, Tennessee, far from the brackish water inhabited by most members of the genus.

Distribution. Mississippi silversides are native to the lower reaches of large streams in the Mississippi River system, from Arkansas and Oklahoma southward. They were introduced into the Blue Lakes and Clear Lake, Lake County (the latter introduction unauthorized), in 1967 (Cook and Moore, 1970). Following their population explosion in Clear Lake, they have been found in its outlet, Cache Creek, and in Putah Creek, which is connected to the lake by irrigation ditches. In 1968 experimental introductions by the California Department of Fish and Game were made into small, isolated lakes in Alameda and Santa Clara counties and they have since been spread illegally into a number of reservoirs in these counties, including Anderson, Del Valle, and Lexington (Moyle et al., 1974). They are also present in some private ponds above Lake Berryessa, Napa County, but they have not yet (July, 1975) been collected from the reservoir itself. It is quite likely that they will soon be established in the Delta, as well as other suitable waters in the state.

Life History. Mississippi silversides are most abundant in the littoral zone of large, warmwater lakes and reservoirs where they may school in enormous numbers. Although they may also venture out into the open waters of the lakes, they seldom penetrate deeper than 2 m. In the littoral zone they tend to concentrate in protected areas with sand or gravel bottoms. Despite their delicate appearance and tendency to die when handled, Mississippi silversides survive in a wide range of conditions. Large numbers were taken in August, 1972, from a warm, stagnant, and extremely turbid pool in an intermittent section of Cache Creek, the outlet of Clear Lake. These fish must have arrived in the pool in the spring, after being washed down over 87 km of stream that includes a steep series of rapids. They can also survive salinities close to that of sea water, at least for short periods of time (Hubbs et al., 1971).

Schooling is the predominate social pattern of silversides. Fish of similar sizes school together, often in tens of thousands of fish. In Clear Lake, the segregation of size groups is especially striking when a school of large fish passes over that of smaller fish, without any mixing taking place. There also seems to be some diurnal movement of silversides in Clear Lake: the fish move some distance offshore in the early morning hours, at least on calm nights. The schools also seem to break apart at this time. Lights suddenly flashed on the surface of the water from a drifting boat at night reveal large numbers of silversides swimming close to the surface, with no sign of schooling. This is contrary to the observations of Mense (1967) in Lake Texoma, Oklahoma, who detected no diurnal movement patterns.

Mississippi silversides feed primarily on zooplankton, generally selecting the larger species, especially among the cladocerans. B. Bachen and R. Elston (unpublished manuscript) found that 68 to 80 percent of the diet at Clear Lake during August, 1973, was planktonic Cladocera. The fish also take the planktonic instars of chironomid midges and chaoborid gnats, but only when the instars are abundant (J. Prine, unpublished data). The silversides show a peak of feeding one to three hours after daybreak and another just before dusk; they will take food at night but the average size of organisms in their stomachs increases as light decreases (B. Bachen and R. Elston, unpublished manuscript). Thus, while cladocercans dominate the daytime diet in Clear Lake, amphipods and inseçt larvae dominate the nighttime diet.

The life cycle of silversides is characterized by fast growth and short lives. In their first year, despite a virtual cessation of growth in the winter, they will reach 8 to 10 cm TL (Mense, 1967). Most spawn and die in their second summer of life, although a few females may live through another year, reaching lengths of 15 to 16 cm TL. Females grow faster and larger than males (F. Fisher, pers. comm.). There are usually two peaks of spawning in Clear Lake, one in May and the other in August, with lesser amounts at other times from April through September. At least three size classes of silversides are evident by the end of the summer.

Spawning takes place over beds of aquatic plants or among emergent vegetation where schools of males apparently station themselves while waiting for passing schools of females. These males are presumably more vulnerable to local predatory fishes so the male:female ratio drops considerably as the spawning season progresses (Hubbs et al., 1971).

The spawning act has been described by Fisher (1973, p. 315):

"On May 11, 1973, during mid-morning, silversides were observed spawning in Lexington Reservoir, over a gentle slope in water 1 to 24 inches deep. Water temperature was 68°F. The slope was covered with rooted aquatic plants and some inundated terrestrial plants. The vegetation formed a mat 1 to 2 inches thick. A school of 25 to 150 individuals would approach parallel to the shoreline led by one or more females with visibly swollen abdomens. When sampled, one school contained 2 large females and 39 smaller males. When a school turned onto the slope, males began to swim vigorously around the female, nipping and prodding at her abdomen. Occasionally during this frenzied activity, a female would suddenly break free, closely accompanied by 3 to 5 males. She would dive, along with the males, into the rooted vegetation. There, both sexes began trembling violently. While lying on her side in close contact with the males, the female laid her eggs. Upon completion, she would rapidly swim away, still closely pursued by several males. The spawning group rejoined the larger school and left the shallow area. Examination of the vegetation showed each female deposited from 10 to 20 eggs. As each school passed, the females made a single spawning pass and were not observed to repeatedly broadcast eggs."

The success of spawning seems to depend on the water being between 17 and 34°C, the range of temperatures at which the eggs will develop. The optimum temperatures are 20 to 25°C (Hubbs et al., 1971). Each female carries about 1,000 eggs (range 384 to 1,699) but may spawn several times during the summer (Mense, 1967). Hubbs et al. (1971) estimated that a single female could lay over 15,000 eggs in a summer if spawning were continuous (which it does not seem to be in California).

The larvae hatch in four to thirty days, depending on the water temperature. The larvae presumably join the plankton for several weeks following hatching, before joining the larger fish in the littoral zone, although direct evidence for this is lacking.

Status. Mississippi silversides became the most abundant fish in the littoral zone of Clear Lake within two years after their introduction, a testimony to their powers of reproduction. They are now spreading (or are being spread by man) rapidly in the Sacramento-San Joaquin system and are likely to be another cause of ecological change in the system's waterways, natural and artificial, in the next few years. It therefore seems worthwhile to summarize their possible effects on the Clear Lake ecosystem, even though study of this problem has only just begun by Hiram W. Li and the author.

Virtually everything, good and bad, that has happened to Clear Lake since 1967 has been attributed by someone to the silverside's population explosion. Their potential effects fall into four basic areas: effects on other fishes, effects on invertebrates, effects on algae, and effects on pesticide cycling.

Introduced populations of silversides seem to have two main effects on the populations of fishes already present: the silversides become important prey for littoral zone gamefishes, especially largemouth bass and crappies, and they replace potentially competing species. In Clear Lake, Cook and Moore (1970) thought that the silversides would have a positive effect on gamefish populations by providing abundant year-round forage for them. Indeed, virtually every gamefish in the lake, including large bluegill (not normally piscivorous), feed heavily on them. However, there is no guarantee that the silversides have either increased gamefish population sizes or individual growth rates; they may have simply replaced forage species already present. The original forage fishes in Clear Lake were the young of native minnows, especially splittail, which early residents noted were enormously abundant in shallow water. The minnows were replaced gradually by young bluegill; Cook et al. (1964) reported taking as many as 10,000 small bluegill in one seine haul. In the 1940s the dominant fishes in the stomachs of largemouth bass were still native minnows but by the 1950s the dominant species were bluegill (McCammon et al., 1964). Today, silversides seem to be the preferred food, probably because they are now the most abundant littoral zone species, having largely replaced bluegill (although bluegill are still common).

The ability of Mississippi silversides to replace other littoral zone fishes has been demonstrated in Oklahoma where they have almost completely replaced the ecologically similar brook silversides (*Labidesthes sicculus*) in at least two reservoirs (Gomez and Lindsey, 1972). Just what replacement effects they have had in Clear Lake have not yet been thoroughly studied but they may have reduced populations not only of bluegill but of native minnows and juvenile bass as well. Despite the abundance of bluegill, Cook et al. (1964) reported that about 20 percent of the fish in their seine hauls were hitch or blackfish. Today these minnows make up less than 1 percent of such samples.

Competition from large populations of silversides could be the final blow to the Clear Lake splittail, an already rare species of minnow whose young once dominated the inshore environment. Such competition may also be limiting growth and survival of largemouth bass under 8 cm FL, since small bass feed primarily on zooplankton and aquatic insects (McCammon et al., 1964). However, it is quite possible that during the critical summer months such food is superabundant and therefore not an object of competition between species.

The main justification for introducing Mississippi silversides into Clear Lake was to help control the pestilent Clear Lake gnat (*Chaoborus astictopus*) and chironomid midges (Cook and Moore, 1970). Although the silversides do feed on the planktonic instars of these insects at times, their potential for control is limited, since they feed mostly on zooplankton and seem to be concentrated in the littoral zone, while the gnats and midges occupy the entire lake. Nevertheless, the enormous biomass of silversides that must exist in the lake by midsummer cannot help but have some effect on the insect populations, even if they are only a relatively small part of the diet. There is already some evidence that the silversides may be controlling at least minor potential nuisance hatches of the midges and gnats, permitting the Clear Lake Mosquito Abatement District to apply fewer pesticide treatments to the lake (J. Prine, pers. comm.). This level of control, however, may also have been achieved previously by other fishes, but went unrecognized.

Another reason given for introducing silversides was that they might act as a nutrient bank in the summer, thus limiting the large nuisance blooms of bluegreen algae that plague the lake at times. There is no sound evidence yet that they in fact will limit algae growth, especially that of bluegreens, and the possibility now seems rather remote since Horne and Goldman (1972) have shown that bluegreen algae become dominant *because* of a nutrient shortage (nitrogen). As dissolved nitrogen compounds in the water column become used up by other less bothersome types of algae, the bluegreens take over because they can fix atmospheric nitrogen. In addition, Hurlbert et al. (1972) have proposed that large populations of silversides may actually increase green algae blooms by reducing the zooplankton populations that might keep the algae under control by grazing.

A final effect of the silversides, proposed by Rudd and Herman (1972) is that they may have modified the cycling of chlorinated hydrocarbon pesticides in the lake, to the benefit of the populations of piscivorous birds, especially western grebes (*Aechmophorus occidentalis*). Between 1949 and 1957 large amounts of chlorinated hydrocarbons were applied to the lake for gnat control, as well as to pear orchids in the Clear Lake Basin for insect control. These persistant pesticides entered lake food chains, becoming increasingly concentrated in the organisms at each higher link, and continually being recycled. The concentrations were fatal to many of the western grebes at the top of the chain and were apparently the cause of reproductive failure in those that survived, even long after application of chlorinated hydrocarbons to the system had ceased. Following the population explosion of silversides, the grebes successfully nested again and have continued to do so. The reasons for this sequence of events are obscure, yet they may be related to the spreading of the pesticide load over a large biomass of silversides, which the grebes feed on either directly, or indirectly, by consuming silverside predators (Rudd and Herman, 1972). It is also possible that other factors, unrelated to the silversides explosion, are involved here (R. Garrett, pers. comm.).

References. Cook, 1968; Cook, Conner, and Moore, 1964; Cook and Moore, 1970; Fisher, 1973; Gomez and Lindsey, 1972; Horne and Goldman, 1972; Hubbs, Sharp, and Schneider, 1971; Hurlbert, Zedler, and Fairbanks, 1972; McCammon, LaFaunce and Seeley, 1964; Mense, 1967; Moyle, Fisher, and Li, 1974; Rudd and Herman, 1972; Saunders, 1959; Sisk and Stephens, 1964.

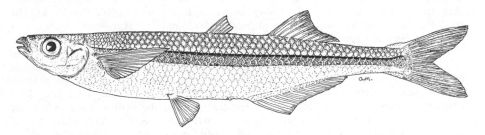

Figure 100. Topsmelt, 18 cm SL, Navarro River Estuary, Mendocino County.

Topsmelt, *Atherinops affinis* (Ayres)

Identification. Topsmelt are small and slender, with flattened backs and small oblique mouths. The first dorsal fin has 5 to 9 spines and is separated from the second dorsal (1 spine, 8 to 14 rays) by 5 to 8 scale rows. The anal fin has 1 weak spine and 19 to 25 rays; the pectoral fins have 13 rays. The lateral line is absent but there are 63 to 65 scales in the lateral series. The jaw teeth are tiny, forked, and arranged in one row on each jaw. Adults have bright green backs and silvery bellies, separated by a wide silver to pale stripe. Juveniles are almost uniformly translucent white, although the midline stripe is still conspicuous and more than 3 scale rows on the back are outlined with pigment spots. The pigment spots on the base of the caudal peduncle are in a scattered pattern, not in rows.

Names. The word smelt has always been associated with this fish, which is unfortunate since it is only superficially similar to the true smelts. *Atherin-ops* literally means *Atherina*-appearing, denoting the resemblance of topsmelt to European silversides, genus *Atherina. Atherina* is the Latinized version of the ancient Greek word for silversides, which was derived from their word for spike or arrow. *Affinis* means related, referring to jacksmelt (*Atherinopsis californiensis*) with which topsmelt are often found.

Distribution. Topsmelt can be expected in the lower reaches of any coastal stream in California, since they are found from Baja California to Vancouver Island, British Columbia (Miller and Lea, 1972).

Life History. Topsmelt are primarily saltwater fish, preferring shallow bays, sloughs, and estuaries. They are, however, one of the commonest marine fishes found in the lower reaches of coastal streams, although seldom are they found in completely fresh water. In the Navarro River, August, 1973, small schools were observed and collected in areas of slow current only at salinities greater than 9 to 10 ppt. They were often associated with schools of shiner perch. Although topsmelt can reach lengths of over 35 cm SL, those found in intertidal areas are generally less than 10 cm SL, presumably young of the year.

Given their large eyes and surface-feeding body shape, it is surprising to find that topsmelt are, in general, bottom-grazing or seaweed-browsing vegetarians. Topsmelt in the Navarro River, 49 to 56 mm SL, were feeding on diatoms and filamentous algae (50 percent by volume), detritus (29 percent), chironomic midge larvae (10 percent), and amphipods (10 percent). The type of organisms, coupled with the detritus and sand grains present in each stomach, indicates bottom feeding.

Status. Topsmelt are an abundant and tasty marine fish but are of only small significance in coastal streams.

References. Jordan and Evermann, 1896; Miller and Lea, 1972.

Stickleback Family, Gasterosteidae

The sticklebacks are a small, cohesive family of fishes, abundant in Europe, northern Asia, and North America. They are famous for their pugnacity and for their stereotyped breeding behavior which they perform readily in aquaria. As a result, their behavior has probably been studied in greater detail than that of any other group of freshwater fishes. Their bodies are spindle-shaped with pointed heads, narrow caudal peduncles, and are protected with sharp spines on the back and pelvic fins. Most species of sticklebacks have both resident freshwater and anadromous populations, although a few are exclusively marine or fresh water. Typically, they inhabit quiet water among heavy growths of aquatic plants and feed on small invertebrates. Only one of the five species currently recognized for North America occurs in California.

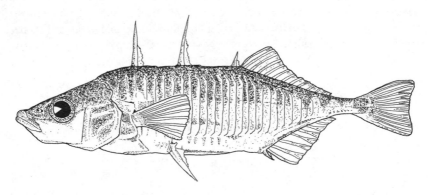

Figure 101. Threespine stickleback, 3 cm SL, San Joaquin River, Fresno County.

Threespine Stickleback, *Gasterosteus aculeatus* Linnaeus

Systematic note. The study of threespine sticklebacks gives headaches to those taxonomists who are mainly interested in pigeonholing distinct forms, each with a nice name. To a student of evolution, however, such study can provide fascinating insights into the processes of speciation. The confusing taxonomy of threespine sticklebacks is the result of their wide distribution, anadromous nature, and ability to repeatedly establish nonanadromous freshwater populations.

There are two major centers of threespine stickleback distribution, Eurasia and North America. In each area two basic forms exist: a robust anadromous form with a row of plates extending along each side to the caudal peduncle, which is keeled, and a smaller freshwater form with bony plates on the anterior portion of the body only.

The two forms of sticklebacks from all areas have generally been treated together as subspecies: *Gasterosteus aculeatus trachuras* for the anadromous form, *G. a. leiurus* for the freshwater form. This treatment, unfortunately, does not take into account the following factors: differences exist between North American and Eurasian stickle-backs; freshwater forms have evolved independently in many streams on both continents; freshwater populations in some areas have undergone further evolution into forms distinct from other freshwater populations, perhaps at the species level (e.g., Moodie, 1972); and the morphological and ecological separation between freshwater and anadromous forms varies from complete separation to complete interbreeding.

Thus, Hagen (1967), in a classic study of isolating mechanisms, found that the two forms in a British Columbia stream behave as "good" species. Yet, in California many populations appear to be interbreeding mixtures of the two forms. "Pure" populations of both types also exist in California (Miller and Hubbs, 1969) but there appears to be little correlation between plate number and habitat. Despite these difficulties it is still convenient in most situations in North America (but not in California) to treat the two forms as subspecies, using the names suggested by Miller and Hubbs (1969): *G. a. aculeatus* for the fully plated, usually anadromous form, and *G. a. microcephalus* for the partially plated, freshwater form. In addition, *G. a. williamsoni*, an unplated form, exists in some streams in southern California. Ultimately, the nomenclature may come full circle back to *leiurus* and *trachurus*, with the names either not italicized or used in quotes, in recognition of the fact that they stand for repeated phenomena of speciation, rather than for the geographically defined populations that normally constitute subspecies.

Identification. Threespine sticklebacks are small (maximum size of 8 cm TL), laterally compressed fish, with three sharp spines on the back in front of a soft dorsal fin. Their eyes are large, mouths terminal but slanting upwards, caudal peduncles narrow, and pelvic fins each reduced to a single stout spine and a small ray. Except for the rare *G. a. williamsoni*, they have 1 to 35 bony plates on the sides, but lack scales. "Pure" *G. a. aculeatus* have 28 to 35 plates, "pure" *G. a. microcephalus* have 1 to 8 plates. Gill rakers are 17 to 26; dorsal rays, 10 to 24; anal rays, 6 to 10; and pectoral rays, 9 to 11. *G. a. williamsoni*, in addition to lacking plates (occasionally tiny ones occur), has shorter, weaker spines and more rounded pectoral and caudal fins than do the other forms. Adults in fresh water are usually olive to dark green on the back and sides, with white to golden bellies. The fins are generally colorless. Breeding males usually have bright red bellies, blue sides, and iridescent blue or green eyes. Breeding females become lighter dorsally and silvery ventrally. The colors are often subdued in inland populations. Anadromous populations tend to be larger and brighter than nonanadromous populations.

Names. Gaster-osteus means belly-bone, while *aculeatus* means spined. The complex nomenclatural history of threespine sticklebacks is reviewed in Miller and Hubbs (1969).

Distribution. Threespine sticklebacks are found in coastal waters from Mediterranean Europe, north to Russia and across to Japan and Korea. In North America populations, are found on the East Coast down to Chesapeake Bay and on the West Coast down to Baja California. They are absent from arctic and interior North America. In California, they can be found in coastal streams along the entire coast, upstream to major fish barriers such as falls. They are widely distributed in the Central Valley. Populations can also be found in many reservoirs, such as Big Bear Lake, San Bernardino County, where they were introduced. *G. a. williamsoni* populations were once abundant in streams in the Los Angeles Basin, but now occur naturally only in the upper Santa Clara River and in the Cuyama River Basin. They have been introduced into the Mojave River (Miller and Hubbs, 1969).

Life History. Threespine sticklebacks are quiet-water fish, living in weedy pools and backwaters, or among emergent plants at stream edges, over bottoms of sand and mud. Marine populations are apparently pelagic, staying close to shore, although they have been collected up to 500 miles offshore (McPhail and Lindsey, 1970). By and large, they require cool water for long-term survival. It is unusual to find them in water much warmer than 23 to 24°C. It is also unusual to find them in turbid water since they are visual feeders, as the large eyes suggest.

Freshwater populations feed primarily on bottom organisms or organisms living on aquatic plants (Hagen, 1967; Hynes, 1950). Anadromous populations, perhaps as a reflection of their pelagic existence while in salt water, feed more on free-swimming crustaceans, although bottom organisms are also taken. While feeding, sticklebacks tend to move about in a jerky fashion, stopping frequently to investigate potential prey organisms. They hover at an angle to the prey, using the opposing forces of the pectoral fins and tail, and then quickly pick it off the substrate. Individual sticklebacks (and populations) tend to specialize in feeding on a rather limited number of organisms in their environment (e.g., chironomid midge larvae, ostracods) and are rather slow to learn to exploit new sources of food (Beukema, 1963).

Unless they are breeding, sticklebacks school, albeit loosely. Schooling seems to help the fish find concentrations of food. When one fish starts to feed, the others in the school come to investigate.

The small size, slow movements, and shallow-water habits of sticklebacks make them ideal prey for avian and piscine predators. The spines evolved to make them a less ideal prey, since a stickleback with rigidly erect dorsal and pelvic spines is very hard to swallow (Hoogland et al., 1956). Similarly, the bony plates appear to function as armor. Freshwater populations that occur where the number of potential predators is high tend to have more plates than populations where there are few potential predators (Hagen and Gilbertson, 1972). Nevertheless, sticklebacks are frequently important as prey of salmonids and of birds. Many populations are heavily infested with the intermediate stages of bird tapeworms. These larval tapeworms can grow to occupy most of the body cavity of the fish, causing them to swim sluggishly near the surface of the water. This in turn makes them more vulnerable to kingfishers and herons. Digestion releases the larval tapeworm into the gut of the bird where it grows to adulthood.

Most sticklebacks appear to complete their life cycle in one year. Usually a majority of the sticklebacks in one area will be of uniform size, although the presence of an occasional large individual indicates that a few live for two or possibly three years. Freshwater sticklebacks in California seldom exceed 60 mm TL, while anadromous sticklebacks commonly reach 80 mm TL. Females are usually larger than males.

As the amount of daylight increases in the spring and the water warms up (April through July), threespine sticklebacks move into breeding areas. For the anadromous forms, this means moving first into shallow regions of estuaries and then up into fresh water. They generally spawn earlier than freshwater populations. The males soon begin to assume their breeding colors and move away from their schools, to set up territories among the beds of aquatic plants. Once a territory is established, nest construction begins. The male excavates a shallow pit by taking up mouthfuls of sand and dropping them several cm away from the nest site. Next he gathers strands of algae and pieces of aquatic plants and deposits them in the pit. The next material is pasted together with a sticky kidney secretion. When the sticky pile is large enough, the male wriggles through it until a tunnel is created.

Meanwhile, schools of females, glistening and egg-swollen, cruise back and forth in the vicinity of the territories. Once the nest is finished, the male approaches passing females, performing the zig-zag courtship dance described by Tinbergen (1953). If a female is ready to spawn she will respond to the dance by following the male to the nest. She enters the nest and after a few nudges from the male begins laying eggs. When finished laying, she leaves the nest and the male goes in and fertilizes the eggs. He then chases the female away and repairs the nest. Usually several females are courted in this fashion for each nest. Each female lays 50 to 300 eggs, in several spawnings.

Once the nest has its complement of eggs, the male begins incubation behavior, which consists of maintaining a head stand, at an angle, in front of the nest, while using the pectoral fins to fan water over the developing eggs. The movement of the pectoral fins is counterbalanced by sweeps of the tail. When not fanning the eggs, the male defends the nest vigorously from other sticklebacks and other potential predators.

The eggs hatch in six to eight days at 18 to 20°C, but the fry remain in the nest for the first couple of days. Once they begin swimming about, the male guards the school of fry carefully, grabbing wanderers in his mouth and spitting them back into the main school. As the fry become more active and the male's task of guarding them becomes more difficult, he gradually loses interest. The male may then begin the spawning cycle again or go off and join a school of other fish that have finished reproducing. The young fish likewise join schools of similar-sized fish.

Status. Threespine sticklebacks are abundant and widespread, and have even managed to colonize irrigation canals and reservoirs. They can be important forage fish. *G. a. williamsoni*, the unarmored form, is currently endangered (Leach and Fisk, 1972), and is fully protected by California state law. Most populations in the Los Angeles Basin have become extinct due to the "development" of their streams in urban areas. The few remaining populations are threatened as civilization marches on.

References. Baggerman, 1957; Beukema, 1963; Hagen, 1967; Hagen and Gilbertson, 1972; Hynes, 1950; Leach and Fisk, 1972; McPhail and Lindsey, 1970; Miller and Hubbs, 1969; Moodie, 1972; Tinbergen, 1953; Vrat, 1949.

Pipefish Family, Syngnathidae

The Syngnathidae is a bizarre family of fishes that includes pipefishes and seahorses. They are distantly related to sticklebacks. The family is mostly marine; only the gulf pipefish (*Syngnathus scovelli*) of the Atlantic coast has been reported living in fresh water in the United States. Pipefish are readily recognized by their slender, elongate bodies which are completely enclosed in rings of bony plates. Their snouts are long and tubular, the dorsal fins single, and the pelvic fins absent in males. Pipefish swim in a more or less upright position, blending in with strands of seaweed, eelgrass, and filamentous algae. The males incubate the fertilized eggs in a large brood pouch, and the young remain there until they reach lengths of 1 to 2 cm.

Two species have been recorded from coastal streams in California, kelp pipefish (*S. californiensis*) and bay pipefish (*S. leptorhynchus*). The records for kelp pipefish are probably erroneous (C. L. Hubbs, pers. comm.), but bay pipefish will occasionally establish populations in low-salinity areas.

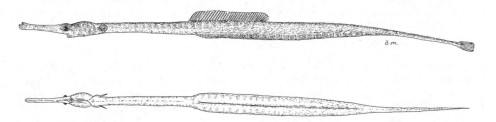

Figure 102. Male bay pipefish, 18 cm SL, dorsal and ventral views to show brood pouch, Navarro River, Mendocino County.

Bay Pipefish, *Syngnathus leptorhynchus* Girard

Identification. The elongate armored body together with the long snout make bay pipefish unmistakable. They have 17 to 20 body rings, 36 to 39 tail rings (tail rings start at the anus), 28 to 44 dorsal rays, 3 to 5 anal rays, and 11 to 13 pectoral rays. Bay pipefish collected in streams have ranged from pale green to dark brown in color. Males can be recognized by the long brood pouch, which consists of two large folds posterior to the anus, and by the absence of the anal fin.

Names. The systematics, and consequently the nomenclature, of pipefishes is confusing. We follow Miller and Lea (1972) in using *S. leptorhynchus* in preference to *S. griseolineatus*. Bay pipefish may in fact be a subspecies of *S. californiensis* (Herald, 1941). *Syn-gnathus* means "together-jaw," referring to the tubelike mouth; *lepto-rhynchus* means slender-snout.

Distribution. Bay pipefish are found in marine environments from Baja California to Sitka, Alaska. They are the only pipefish found north of San Francisco Bay. In coastal streams they have been reported only from the mouth of the San Lorenzo River, Santa Cruz County (Kukowski, 1972) and from the Navarro River, Mendocino County.

Life History. Bay pipefish are included as part of California's inland fish fauna because they were abundant in the lower Navarro River, from the mouth to about 5 km upstream, in August, 1973. The minimum salinity they were found at was 9 ppt, although it is quite likely that they experience lower salinities when more fresh water is flowing or during extreme low tides. Most of the pipefish observed were bright green juveniles, living in beds of filamentous algae, although a few larger individuals (20 to 25 cm TL) were also present.

In salt water, bay pipefish usually inhabit beds of eelgrass, feeding on small crustaceans they suck up with their tubelike mouths. Mating, and the subsequent transfer of eggs to the brood pouch of the males, takes place in May and June, although males have been found carrying young in mid-August in the more northern parts of their range (Clemens and Wilby, 1961). The total incubation time is usually between two and three weeks. Two adult males collected from the Navarro River had empty brood pouches. Adult bay pipefish can reach 33 cm TL.

Status. The lack of records of bay pipefish from coastal streams probably results from the difficulty in collecting them by seine. However, their abundance in the Navarro River is possibly caused by reduced (by man) stream flows that permit the tides to extend their influence further upstream, creating low salinity areas with favorable pipefish habitat.

References. Clemens and Wilby, 1961; Herald, 1941; Kukowski, 1972; Miller and Lea, 1972.

Temperate Basses Family, Percichthyidae

The fishes of the family Percichthyidae are among the most generalized members of the great order Perciformes, the group of advanced, spiny-rayed fishes that dominates the salt and fresh waters of the world. They therefore probably bear strong resemblence to the ancestral members of the order. Until recently, the temperate basses were considered to be members of the Serranidae, a family which had become a taxonomic garbage can for the more primitive perciform fishes (Gosline, 1966). The Percichthyidae, as defined by Gosline, contains the four North American freshwater basses of the genus *Morone* (*Roccus*) and a number of marine basses, including the giant sea bass (*Stereolepis gigas*) found off California. Two species of *Morone* have been introduced into California, the white bass and the striped bass. They can be distinguished from other spiny-rayed fishes in the state by the presence of a conspicuous small gill (pseudobranchia) on the underside of each gill cover, the separation of the spiny- and soft-rayed portions of the dorsal fin, and the narrow horizontal black stripes on the sides.

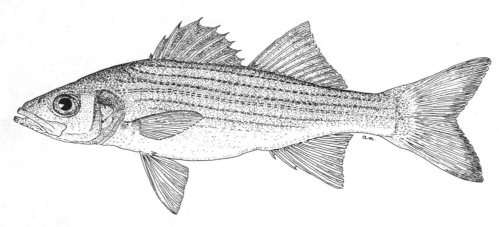

Figure 103. Striped bass juvenile, 18 cm SL, Sacramento-San Joaquin Delta.

Striped Bass, *Morone saxatilis* (Walbaum)

Identification. The streamlined, silvery white body, with its 6 to 9 black horizontal stripes and sharply separated spiny- and soft-rayed portions of the dorsal fin, make the striped bass instantly recognizable. There are 9 spines in the leading half of the dorsal fin, 1 to 2 spines and 12 rays in the following half. The anal fin has 3 spines and 9 to 11 rays; the pectorals, 16 to 17 rays; and the lateral line, 57 to 57 scales. There are two small but distinct spines on the operculum. The mouth is large, but the maxilla does not reach past the hind margin of the eye. The tongue has two distinct patches of teeth on its surface. The eye is small, less than one-fourth of head length.

Names. The generic name has changed back and forth over the years between *Morone* and *Roccus*. It is hoped that it will remain as *Morone* since the American Fisheries Society now recognizes that name. Unfortunately, Mitchill, who first used *Morone* in 1814, neglected to explain how he arrived at the word. *Saxatilus* means living among rocks, apparently a reference to the rather inappropriate, old common-name of rockfish. (Similarly, *Roccus* is a latinization of the word rock.)

Distribution. Striped bass are native to streams and bays of the Atlantic coast from the St. Lawrence River in the north down to the St. Johns River in Florida, as well as to streams flowing into the Gulf of Mexico from Florida to Louisiana. They were introduced to the Pacific coast in 1879 and 1882, when a total of 432 fish from two shipments were planted in the Sacramento-San Joaquin estuary. So successful was the introduction that by 1888 a commercial fishery had started up for them and the catch reached over 1.2 million pounds by 1899 (Skinner, 1962). They have since been found in salt water from 25 miles south of the Mexican border to southern British Columbia. The main population, however, is still that of the Sacramento-San Joaquin estuary and river system, although smaller populations are also present in the Coos, Umpqua, and Coquilla rivers and their estuaries in Oregon. Small runs may also exist in the Russian and Klamath rivers. A self-reproducing landlocked population now lives in Millerton Lake, Fresno-Madera counties, while a large population in San Luis Reservoir, Merced County, is continually replenished with small bass pumped in through canals from the Delta. Populations maintained by planting now exist in San Antonio Reservoir, Monterey County, and Lake Mendocino, Mendocino County. Reproducing populations are apparently also established in the lower Colorado River, although these populations are augmented by repeated stocking (Minckley, 1973). As hatchery techniques are refined, other reservoirs are likely to be planted with striped bass as well.

Life History. Striped bass are one of the most studied species of fish in the world, so any short account of their life history is bound to be a summary of more detailed reviews of the primary literature (Raney, 1952; Skinner, 1962; Turner and Kelley, 1966; Talbot, 1966; Goodson, 1966; Turner, 1972).

Striped bass move regularly between salt and fresh water, and they usually spend much of their life cycle in estuaries. It is not surprising, therefore, to find that they are remarkably tolerant of a wide range of environmental conditions. They can survive temperatures as high as 35°C, although they are under stress once temperatures exceed 25°C. Adults are capable of withstanding abrupt temperature changes (up to 27°C) that are simultaneous with changes from sea water to fresh water. Younger fish are less tolerant of such changes. Low oxygen (4 ppm) and high turbidity can also be withstood by striped bass, although extreme conditions will inhibit reproduction. Besides these rather broad water-quality requirements, striped bass have three basic habitat requirements for successful completion of their life cycle: a large river for spawning, with sufficient velocity to keep the eggs and larvae suspended off the bottom but not so fast that it washes them into quiet water before the larvae can actively swim (in some streams, tidal currents help keep the eggs and larvae suspended); a large body of water (e.g., San Francisco Bay, the Pacific Ocean) with large populations of forage fishes for the adults to feed on; and an estuary where juvenile striped bass can take advantage of large invertebrate populations. In California, only the Sacramento-San Joaquin system, with its large complex estuary, has satisfied all these conditions, although small landlocked populations maintain themselves in Millerton Lake, by using the upper San Joaquin River for spawning, and in reservoirs of the lower Colorado River.

The Atlantic populations of striped bass make extensive migrations along the coast, the adults spending much of their time out at sea. In contrast, the Sacramento-San Joaquin striped bass seem to spend most of their lives in San Pablo and San Francisco bays. However, the extent of their oceanic migrations is not precisely known so such movements may be more common than is now supposed (L. Miller, pers. comm.). There is a mass movement of the bass out of the bays into fresh water in the fall. They overwinter in the Delta, moving back into salt water in the spring, following the upstream spawning migration.

Striped bass are gregarious pelagic predators. This is reflected in their streamlined body shape, their silvery coloration, and their feeding habits. In the Delta, adults feed mostly on threadfin shad and smaller striped bass, while in San Pablo Bay they take a wide variety of pelagic fishes as well as bay shrimp (*Crago* spp.). Juvenile striped bass, in contrast, are primarily invertebrate feeders, the importance of fish in the diet increasing as the bass increase in size. Young of the year (5 to 23 cm SL) rely mostly on the oppossum shrimp, *Neomysis mercedis*, although amphipods, copepods, and small threadfin shad may be important foods on occasion. The diet of juvenile bass (13 to 35 cm FL) is similar to that of the young of the year, but fish are more important, especially late in the summer when young-of-the-year striped bass and shad become available. Subadult bass (age 2+, 26 to 47 cm FL) are primarily piscivorous, like the adults, although invertebrates are still important in the winter and spring when small fishes are hard to find. Despite the seemingly limited nature of the striped bass diet, they are in fact rather opportunistic feeders and almost any fish or invertebrate that is found with them will sooner or later appear in their stomachs.

Growth is most rapid during the first four years. In the Delta they typically reach 2 to 3 cm FL in the first year, 23 to 35 cm FL in the second, 38 to 39 cm FL in the third, and 48 to 50 cm FL in the fourth. In subsequent years they will add 1 to 3 cm to their length annually. Growth in Millerton Lake is somewhat faster. By the end of the fourth year Millerton bass are typically 55 to 56 cm FL, and after that they add 4 to 5 cm per year. Striped bass will reach about 125 cm FL (41 kg) in California, although bass 180 cm FL (56 kg) have been recorded from the Atlantic coast. Large striped bass are difficult to age using either scales or otoliths but the maximum age seems to be in excess of thirty years. The oldest and largest bass are invariably females.

The age of maturity for females is four to six years. A few males may mature at the end of their first year, but most of them wait until they are two to three years old. As a result, males are typically 25 cm FL when they spawn for the first time, while females are about 45 cm FL.

Spawning may begin in April, when the bass, usually males first, start to move into suitable areas. Spawning peaks in May and early June. The exact time and location of spawning depends on the interaction of three factors: temperature, flow, and salinity

(Turner, 1972). No spawning will occur until temperatures reach at least 14.4°C. Optimum temperatures appear to be from 15.6 to 20.0°C and spawning will cease above 21.1°C. When flows are high in the Sacramento River, the water takes longer to warm up so spawning takes place later in the year. It also takes place further upstream than is usual, since the bass migrate upstream while waiting for temperatures to rise. When flows are high in the San Joaquin portion of the Delta, spawning may actually occur further downstream than usual, since the salt water is pushed further downstream. Years of high flow when the large volume of runoff dilutes the salty, irrigation waste water that normally makes up much of the river's flow, are virtually the only time when successful spawning occurs in the San Joaquin River upstream from the Delta. Because of the interaction among these factors there are two main spawning areas in the Delta: the Sacramento River from Isleton to Butte City and the San Joaquin River and its sloughs from Venice Island down to Antioch.

Striped bass are mass spawners. In the Sacramento River, thousands of large bass aggregate close to the banks, just off the main current (Miller and McKechnie, 1968). Groups of five to thirty fish, predominately males, break off from the main group and swim out into the main river, close to the surface. During the spawning act the group mills about. Individuals frequently turn on their sides, accompany this action with vigorous splashing at the surface. Although spawning can occur at any time of the day, peak activity is usually during the late afternoon or early evening. Female bass are very prolific. Depending on her size, a female will release anywhere from 11 thousand to 1-2 million eggs in a season.

The eggs are slightly heavier than fresh water so they slowly sink to the bottom. If they remain on the bottom for any length of time they will not survive, but even a slight current will keep them suspended. They hatch in about forty-eight hours at 19°C. The larvae are virtually helpless, dependent on their yolk sacs for nourishment for the next seven to eight days. The larvae then begin feeding on small zooplankters. During this helpless period, the eggs and larvae in the Sacramento River are carried into the Delta and Suisin Bay. In the San Joaquin River, outflow is balanced by tidal currents so that eggs and larvae stay suspended in the same general area in which spawning took place. Essentially, the larval bass from both rivers are most abundant where salt and fresh water meet. Thus, when they begin to feed they are concentrated in the most productive portions of the entire estuary.

One of the most important tasks of the Delta Fish and Wildlife Protection Study (California Department of Fish and Game) has been to find out what factors affect the survival of larval striped bass, since a high survival rate of larval bass generally means larger adult populations. Although many factors, such as temperature, salinity, predation, food availability, and pollution, will affect larval survival rates, one of the most important factors appears to be the amount of summer outflow through the Delta. The higher the summer flows, up to 10,000 cfs, the larger the numbers of larval bass that survive to the juvenile stage (Turner, 1972). The correlation between young striped bass abundance and high flows is very strong, but what may be important is not the amount of outflow per se but the percent of the outflow that is diverted into various water projects. Striped bass abundance is negatively correlated with the percent of the total outflow that is diverted (L. Miller, pers. comm.).

Status. It has been estimated that the net economic worth of the striped bass fishery in the Delta is about 7.5 million dollars per year and that about two million days are spent annually fishing for the bass (Turner, 1972). The Millerton Lake fishery is very small but it does provide a significant trophy fishery for the residents of the southern San Joaquin Valley. Obviously, the striped bass fishery is worth protecting and enhancing, especially in the face of projected changes to the Sacramento-San Joaquin estuary. This has in fact been one of the main goals of the Delta Fish and Wildlife Protection Study, which officially started in 1961, although striped bass investigations had been underway for a good many years before 1961.

The investigations indicate that striped bass populations have declined since the early 1960s, as has angler success. The population of legal-sized adult bass (40+ cm FL) in 1972 was estimated to be about 1.4 million fish, down from earlier populations of around 3 million fish (Turner, 1972). This may be a temporary decline, however, since the present low populations seem to be due to the poor conditions, especially low outflows, that existed for young-of-the-year survival in the early 1960s. Nevertheless, the decreased flows projected for the future will have serious detrimental effects on Sacramento-San Joaquin striped bass populations unless protective action is taken. According to Turner (1972, p. 42): "Present knowledge indicates that the striped bass population can be protected or enhanced by:

1. Minimizing the losses of eggs, larvae, and young fish to water diversion.

2. Reducing water velocities in the river channels in the north and south Delta in late spring and early summer to increase production of food for young fish.

3. Providing a positive net downstream flow towards the ocean to guide adult fish in their migration.

4. Maintaining water quality suitable for striped bass spawning during the spring in the main San Joaquin River and adjacent sloughs from Antioch upstream to Venice Island at least.

5. Providing sufficient outflow during May through July for adequate survival of young striped bass.

6. Maintaining adequate temperature and dissolved oxygen conditions during the summer and fall, with requirements of *Neomysis* being most critical."

Some additional striped bass fishing may result from stocking hatchery-raised fish in reservoirs that contain large populations of threadfin shad but lack suitable spawning grounds for the bass.

References. Fry, 1973; Goodson, 1966; Miller and McKechnie, 1968; Raney, 1952; Skinner, 1962, 1972; Talbot, 1966; Turner, 1972; Turner and Kelley, 1966.

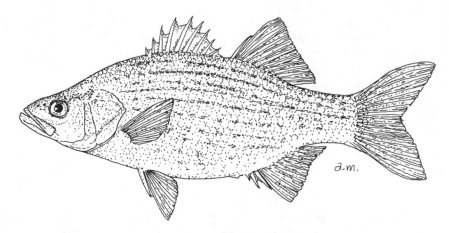

Figure 104. White bass, 25 cm SL, Lake Nacimiento, San Luis Obispo County.

White Bass, *Morone chrysops* (Rafinesque)

Identification. White bass look like striped bass, but they are deep-bodied with the body laterally compressed and the back rising up steeply behind the head. The dorsal fins are separate, with 9 spines in the first and 1 spine and 13 rays in the second. The anal fin has 3 spines, distinctly graduated in size, and 11 to 13 rays. The pelvic fins have 1 spine, 5 rays; the pectoral fins have 15 to 17 rays; and the lateral line has 50 to 55 scales. The head is small and the mouth relatively large, the maxillae extending to or slightly beyond the middle of the eye, and the lower jaw slightly projecting. There is a single patch of teeth on the tongue. White bass are silvery white on the sides with 6 to 9 brownish stripes, which are frequently interrupted.

Names. White bass have, in the past, been placed in the genera *Lepibema* and *Roccus*, as well as *Morone*. *Chrysops* means golden eye although the eye is not conspicuously golden. Other names are as for the striped bass.

Distribution. White bass are native to the Great Lakes region, the Mississippi River system, and the southern United States (including parts of Texas). They have been introduced into warmwater reservoirs throughout the United States and more introductions can be expected. Experimental introductions were made into Nacimiento Reservoir, San Luis Obispo County, starting in 1965 (von Geldern, 1966), although the first fish to reproduce were those planted in 1968 (C. von Geldern, pers. comm.). They have since been planted in the lower Colorado River but there is little evidence of natural reproduction there (C. von Geldern, pers. comm.).

Life History. White bass inhabit the open waters of large lakes and reservoirs and slow-moving rivers. Sigler and Miller (1963) suggested that white bass will not establish themselves in lakes of less than 300 to 500 acres. They can live in a wide variety of limnological conditions (Chadwick et al., 1966) but seem to do best in warm, slightly alkaline lakes and reservoirs. Their salinity tolerances are not known but they can probably survive in brackish waters since they are found in the lower reaches of coastal streams along the Gulf of Mexico.

Most of the time, white bass remain in surface waters, roaming in schools. They tend to be off shore during the day but move inshore at dusk, where they follow the shoreline while foraging for food (Sigler and Miller, 1963). Usually they are after fish, especially pelagic species, although some populations of white bass rely almost entirely on zooplankton (Priegel, 1970). Aquatic insects and crayfish may also be important on occasion. In Nacimiento Reservoir, adult bass feed mostly on threadfin shad (C. von Geldern, pers. comm.). Young-of-the-year white bass are primarily pelagic zooplankton feeders, usually changing to the adult diet in their second year (Priegel, 1970; Chadwick et al., 1966).

Growth is extremely rapid, especially in the southern part of their range, but varies considerably from lake to lake. Thus, at the end of their first year they can range in size from 9 to 31 cm TL; at the end of their second, 17 to 39 cm; at the end of their third, 26 to 43 cm TL; and at the end of their fourth, 28 to 46 cm TL (Chadwick et al., 1966; Priegel, 1971). The growth exhibited by Nacimiento Reservoir white bass, however, seems to typify that of most white bass populations: year I, 22 to 25 cm FL; year II, 30 to 33 cm FL; and year III, 33 to 36 cm FL (C. von Geldern, pers. comm.). White bass seldom weigh more than 1.5 kg (45 cm TL) but the largest on record weighed almost 2 kg. This fish was caught in 1972 from Ferguson Reservoir on the Colorado River, where it was probably a survivor from one of a series of plants made in the 1960s into Lahontan Reservoir in Nevada (none of which reproduced). White bass will live nine years in the northern parts of their range but seldom live more than six in western reservoirs.

Spawning normally takes place for the first time in the spring of the second year of life. As the water warms up, large schools of ripe fish congregate at the mouths of inlet streams or near suitable spawning areas in the lake (usually steep, rock- or gravel-covered bottoms). Large streams seem to be preferred, however, and they will migrate up to 150 miles upstream to a spawning ground (Chadwick et al., 1966). Normally they move just a short distance from the lake, to a gravel- or rock-bottomed area where the water is 1 to 3 m deep, and begin spawning when temperatures reach 13 to 17°C. The Nacimiento Reservoir population apparently spawns in the Nacimiento River, although the exact location is not known (C. von Geldern, pers. comm.). Spawning behavior is a mass affair, similar to that of striped bass. The eggs sink to the bottom, where they stick to the substrate. They hatch in forty-six hours at 16°C (Riggs, 1955).

Status. White bass have received very good press notices in recent years, as exemplified by the statement in Sigler and Miller (1963, p. 123): "The white bass is a short-lived, fast growing fish capable of producing an almost unbelievable amount of sport. In some areas in the South where a few years ago it was unknown, it is now the number one sport fish. It is a relatively easy fish to catch. It fights well when hooked and has good table qualities. In areas where there is an abundance of small fish, either game or forage, it is able to effectively reduce these to a large poundage of sport fish. It is popular with fishermen of all ages."

Their popularity in the West seems to stem from the spectacular fishery in Lake Texoma, Oklahoma, that developed following its impoundment in 1944. One of the main justifications for the subsequent spread of white bass was that they would be able to utilize and hopefully control the large threadfin shad populations that had developed in many western reservoirs (also the result of optimistic planting programs). Considering the rather uncritical reception white bass have received elsewhere as an ideal gamefish for reservoirs, the California Department of Fish and Game has moved with commendable caution in its own experimental introduction program for this fish. They have taken special care not to introduce it into the Sacramento-San Joaquin system, where it might become established in the Delta and compete with striped bass for food and space. Nacimiento Reservoir is on a coastal drainage system with no interior connections, and white bass were already established in reservoirs upstream from the California portion of the lower Colorado River.

Although white bass have shown excellent growth in the two California waters where planted, they otherwise have not completely lived up to their reputation. They have apparently failed to reproduce in the lower Colorado River and have done so only on an irregular basis in Nacimiento Reservoir. They have failed to have much effect on the superabundant threadfin shad populations and there is some evidence that, in Nacimiento Reservoir, threadfin shad may control the white bass populations rather than the expected reverse (C. von Geldern, pers. comm.). The official cautious attitude towards white bass introduction should be continued, especially considering the fact that uninformed fishermen have been known to make unauthorized transfers of fish from one body of water to another.

References. Chadwick et al., 1966; Cross, 1967; Priegel, 1979, 1971; Riggs, 1955; Sigler and Miller, 1963; von Geldern, 1966.

Sunfish Family, Centrarchidae

The Centrarchidae is a small family (thirty species) that contains some of the most important gamefishes in North America: the sunfishes (*Lepomis* spp.), the "black" basses (*Micropterus* spp.), and the crappies (*Pomoxis* spp.). It also contains a number of less well-known forms. The family evolved in North America, but now enjoys a world-wide distribution, thanks to enthusiastic planting by man. Although the fossil record indicates that they once occupied waters over much of the United States, mountain building and the increasing ardity of interior drainage basins seem to have eliminated them from most of North America west of the Rocky Mountains, probably during the Miocene period (Miller, 1958). One species that did manage to survive in the West is the Sacramento perch, of the Sacramento-San Joaquin system. As a result of its isolation and lack of competition from other related species, it has retained many primitive structural and behavioral features, making it a good representative of the ancient fishes that gave rise to the more advanced sunfishes. It is not surprising, therefore, that the Sacramento perch virtually disappeared from its native habitat following the introduction of eleven species of advanced centrarchids from the eastern United States.

The members of the family are, by and large, inhabitants of warm ponds, lakes, and slow-moving streams. They are all carnivorous and protect their eggs and young from predators. All but the Sacramento perch construct nests for protection. Structurally, centrarchids are characterized by united soft- and spiny-rayed portions of the dorsal fin; terminal mouths, with small teeth in bands and protractile premaxillary bones; small, membrane-covered pseudobranchs; strong pharyngeal teeth; ctenoid scales; and short intestines with pyloric ceca.

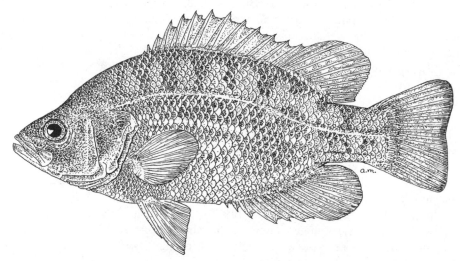

Figure 105. Sacramento perch, 12 cm SL, Yolo by-pass, Yolo County.

Sacramento Perch, *Archoplites interruptus* (Girard)

Identification. The Sacramento perch has more spines (12 to 13) in the dorsal fin than any other centrarchid. It is fairly deep bodied (depth goes 2-1/2 times into standard length) with a large oblique mouth, the maxillary reaching to about the middle of the eye. The spinous portion of the dorsal is continuous with the soft-rayed portion (10 rays). The anal fin has 6 to 7 spines and 10 rays. There are 38 to 48 scales along the lateral line, 25 to 30 long gill rakers, and numerous small teeth on the jaws, tongue, and roof of the mouth. The overall color tends towards brown, with 6 to 7 irregular, dark vertical bars on the sides, black spots on the operculae, and a white belly. Live fish tend to have a metallic green to purple sheen on the sides.

Names. Archoplites is derived from the Greek words for anus and armature, referring to the conspicuous, spiny anal fin; *interruptus* refers to the irregular bars on the sides.

Distribution. Although originally widely distributed in the Sacramento-San Joaquin rivers, the Pajaro and Salinas rivers, and Clear Lake, Lake County, today Sacramento perch are found only in scattered localities in California, principally farm ponds and reservoirs into which they have been introduced. The population in the Russian River is presumably also derived from introductions. Large populations have become established in San Luis Reservoir, Merced County, Clear Lake Reservoir, Modoc County, Crowley Lake, Inyo County, Lake Almanor, Plumas County, and Blue Lake, Lake County. They were introduced into Nevada, probably in 1877, and are now abundant in Pyramid and Walter lakes, as well as in other localities (La Rivers, 1962). Since then, they have been successfully planted in alkaline lakes in Utah, Colorado, Nebraska, North Dakota, and South Dakota (McCarraher and Gregory, 1970). Almost all recently established populations are derived from the population that still exists in Brickyard Pond (Greenhaven Lake), in Sacramento.

Life History. Sacramento perch are the only centrarchids native west of the Rocky Mountains. In isolation from the eastern centers of centrarchid evolution, they have retained the large number of fin spines and generalized centrarchid body shape that are more characteristic of fossil sunfishes than of other modern forms. In addition, neither their reproductive nor social behavior seems to be as complex as that of the eastern centrarchids. In the absence of competition from the more "advanced" forms, they, along with Sacramento squawfish, became the dominant piscivorous fishes in waters teeming with forage fishes. Thus, early observers, such as Lockington (1878), were impressed with their abundance and potential as food fish. They were also one of the most common fishes caught by California Indians (Schulz and Simons, 1973).

Originally, Sacramento perch were inhabitants of sloughs, sluggish rivers, and lakes of the Central Valley floor. Perhaps the most important characteristic of their habitat was the presence of beds of rooted and emergent aquatic vegetation, which served as spawning grounds and as nursery areas for young fish. Since the quality of the waters they lived in tended to fluctuate with floods and droughts, Sacramento perch evolved the ability to withstand high turbidities, high temperatures, and high salinities and alkalinities. McCarraher and Gregory (1970) found that they could survive and reproduce in chloride-sulfate waters with salinities up to 17,000 ppm and in sodium-potassium carbonate waters with total alkalinities of over 800 ppm. These waters exclude most other fish species.

Sacramento perch are rather sluggish in their movements. They seem to spend most of their time on or close to the bottom near submerged objects, moving little except their operculae and paired fins. When a prey organism is sighted, they stalk it slowly until they are close enough to seize it with a sudden rush. The prey is seized by "inhaling" it with a sudden expansion of the buccal cavity and then clamping down on it with the numerous small teeth in the mouth.

The prey organisms taken depend on the size of the fish, the body of water, and the time of year. Young of the year feed mostly on small crustaceans (amphipods, cladocerans, ostracods, and copepods) that are usually associated with the bottom or with aquatic plants. As the fish get larger, aquatic insect larvae and pupae, especially those of chironomid and chaoborid midges, become increasingly important. In large bodies of water, such as Pyramid Lake, Nevada, fish over 90 mm TL feed primarily on other fish, especially cyprinids and smaller Sacramento perch. In small lakes and ponds, aquatic insects continue to be important in the diet of large perch, small crustaceans and fish assuming minor dietary roles. In general, the diet of invertebrate-feeding Sacramento perch tends to be most varied in the summer months when planktonic and surface organisms are taken along with the usual bottom forms. In winter and fall, the perch concentrate on insect larvae, especially chironomid larvae, which they pick off the bottom or from vegetation. However, like most temperate zone fishes, Sacramento perch are highly opportunistic in their feeding and occasionally glut themselves on some organism that is temporarily superabundant, such as waterboatmen (Corixidae) or aquatic beetles. Feeding can take place at any time of the day or night (Moyle, Mathews, and Bonderson, 1974) but there seem to be peaks of activity at dusk and dawn.

Although the diets of sunfishes (*Lepomis* spp.) and Sacramento perch are often very similar in California, the perch generally grow faster and larger than the sunfishes. Age I fish are usually 7 to 15 cm TL, age II are 10 to 19 cm TL, age III are 13 to 24 cm TL, and age IV are 18 to 28 cm TL (McCarraher and Gregory, 1970). Nine-year-old fish from Pyramid Lake range in size from 35 to 42 cm TL (Mathews, 1962). These seem to be the largest and oldest fish recorded in recent years although Jordan and Evermann (1896) gave a maximum length of 61 cm and La Rivers (1962) mentioned a 3.6 kg perch from Walker Lake, Nevada. As in most fish, growth in older perch is mostly in weight rather than in length. Thus, a 10 cm TL perch from Pyramid Lake weighed about 15 gm, a 20 cm perch, 150 gm, a 30 cm perch, 550 gm, and a 40 cm perch, 1200 gm (Mathews, 1962). Overcrowding, diet, and the sex of the fish will affect the growth rate. Stunted populations can occur in underharvested farm ponds while populations of large, fast-growing fish occur in lakes where the adults are primarily piscivorous. Mathews found that females grow faster and have lower mortality rates than males, so that large perch tend to be predominately females.

Unlike the introduced sunfishes, Sacramento perch, except when breeding, show little intraspecific aggressive behavior when kept in aquaria or small ponds. They also do not school strongly, although they will congregate in favorable localities, especially for breeding.

Sacramento perch breed for the first time during their second or third summer of life. The fecundity of females is higher than that of most centrarchids but varies with the size of the fish. Mathews (1962) found the number of eggs in sixteen females 120 to 157 mm TL from Lake Anza, Contra Costa County, to range from 8,370 to 16,210 with a mean of 11,438; sixteen females 196 to 337 mm TL from Pyramid Lake contained from 9,666 to 124,720 eggs. Spawning occurs in California from the end of March to the beginning of August, although late May and early June are generally the peak times. Water temperatures usually have to be between 21° and 29°C for spawning (McCarraher and Gregory, 1970).

Reproductive behavior was described by Murphy (1948a) and Mathews (1965). The perch congregate in shallow areas (20 to 50 cm deep) with heavy growths of aquatic macrophytes or filamentous algae. Rock piles and submerged roots or sticks may also attract fish ready to spawn. Shortly before spawning begins, the males start defending small territories over the chosen substrate. No nests are built nor is the substrate usually altered in any way. The selected areas, however, are defended vigorously from other males by chasing, nipping, and by flaring the opercular flaps. Fish of other species are also chased away from the breeding areas. While patrolling their territories, the males frequently engage in a rapid quivering movement of their tails which Mathews (1965) considers to be a sexual recognition signal. When a female is ready to spawn, she becomes rather restless and approaches a territorial male who promptly chases her away. By persistently coming back to the territory, the female eventually gains acceptance by the male and spawning begins. During the spawning act both sexes either release their sex products simultaneously while inclined laterally at a 45° angle to the bottom, or the female releases the eggs first and they are then immediately fertilized by the close-following male.

After spawning the female leaves the territory. The male continues to defend it for several days against other perch and potential egg predators, including other centrarchids and catfish, for the two days it takes the eggs to hatch and for another two days or so until the larval fish are unable to swim well (Mathews, 1965). In contrast to this description, Murphy (1948a) found that both sexes left the territory shortly after spawning, although his observations were more limited than those of Mathews.

Young-of-the-year fish either remain among the aquatic plants or congregate in shallow water.

Status. Sacramento perch today are probably as abundant in other western states as they are in California, thanks to their ability to live in alkaline waters that will not support other sport fishes (McCarraher and Gregory, 1970). Their decline in California was rapid. Rutter (1908) found that they were rare in his 1898-1899 survey of Central Valley fishes, although he also noted that they were taken in "marketable quantities" in the Delta region. Between 1888 and 1899, 40,000 to 432,000 pounds were sold annually in San Francisco (Skinner, 1966). Today, Sacramento perch are rare even in the Delta (Turner, 1966b). In Clear Lake, Lake County, they have declined steadily since the 1930 fish survey which found them still abundant. By the late 1940s their numbers had been greatly reduced but they were still common enough for Murphy (1948a) to observe spawning in the lake. Between 1961 and 1961 an exhaustive fish-sampling program in the lake turned up only nine adult Sacramento perch and no juveniles (Cook et al., 1966). More recent surveys have turned up only occasional individuals.

Three hypotheses have been advanced to explain the decline of Sacramento perch: habitat destruction, egg predation, and interspecific competition. Habitat destruction, especially the draining of lakes and sloughs and the reduction of aquatic weedbeds needed for spawning, is the hypothesis favored by Rutter (1908) and Mathews (1962). However, the fact that the perch have declined in areas where suitable habitat still exists (e.g., Clear Lake, sloughs of the Delta) makes it unlikely that this is the only reason, although it has been a contributing factor.

Egg predation, especially by catfish and carp, as the cause of decline was first advanced by Jordan and Evermann (1896) and was supported by the observations of Murphy (1948a) that the perch did not defend their spawning sites. However, the observations of Mathews (1965) that they in fact do defend the sites against potential egg predators tends to make egg predation unlikely as a primary cause of the decline.

Interspecific competition for food and space may be the single most important cause of the decline since, almost invariably, local declines of Sacramento perch populations have been associated with increases in the numbers of introduced centrarchids, especially bluegill. In aquaria and small ponds, bluegill and green sunfish dominate Sacramento perch, chasing them away from favored places. Such behavior in the wild could force young perch out of shallow weedy areas and into more exposed waters where they would be more vulnerable to predation and have less food available to them. Bluegill could similarly keep Sacramento perch away from spawning areas even though bluegill build nests in the clearings rather than in the vegetation itself. The importance of interspecific competition is also reflected in the fact that Sacramento perch today are successful mostly in relatively simple fish communities where they can occupy the position of top littoral carnivore. However, in Brickyard Pond (now Greenhaven Lake), in Sacramento, Sacramento perch have long coexisted with other sunfishes, including bluegill, although Sacramento perch seem to be by far the most abundant gamefish.

The decline is probably due to all three factors working together, since habitat alteration and fish introductions have occurred simultaneously throughout the Central Valley. No Sacramento perch, no matter how aggressive, is likely to be able to defend its spawning area against a determined school of egg-eating bluegill or large carp. Thus, consistent defeats in interspecific encounters, especially of young fish, may just serve to accelerate a decline started by other factors.

To halt the general downward trend in California Sacramento perch populations, the

California Department of Fish and Game has tried in recent years to establish them in Central Valley farm ponds (Fisk, 1972). However, their tendencies to die out when other centrarchid species are introduced, to overpopulate and become stunted when left by themselves, and to be difficult to catch with standard centrarchid fishing techniques have not made this task easy. Such efforts should nevertheless be continued and experiments should be run to determine what other fish species can be stocked with perch to provide maximum growth and prevent stunting. Sacramento perch are worth developing as a gamefish not only because they are native Californians but also because they are scrappy fighters, grow rapidly in the Central Valley climate, and can achieve larger sizes than introduced sunfishes, their main farm-pond rivals.

References. Acetiuno, 1974; Cook et al., 1966; Fisk, 1972; Jordan and Evermann, 1896; La Rivers, 1962; Lindquist et al., 1943; Lockington, 1878; McCarraher, 1972; McCarraher and Gregory, 1970; Mathews, 1962, 1965; Miller, 1958; Moyle, Mathews, and Bonderson, 1974; Murphy, 1948a; Rutter, 1908; Schulz and Simons, 1973; Sigler and Miller, 1963; Skinner, 1966; Turner, 1966b.

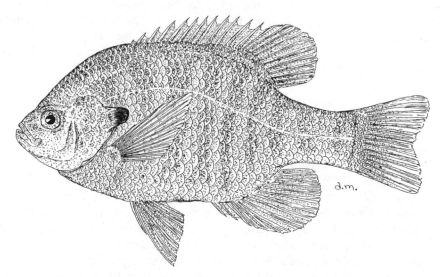

Figure 106. Bluegill, 13 cm SL, Clear Lake, Lake County.

Bluegill, *Lepomis macrochirus* Rafinesque

Identification. Bluegill are easily told from other California sunfishes by the combination of flexible blue or black flap on the rear of the operculum; long, slender gill rakers; long, pointed pectoral fins (13 rays) that are contained in the standard length about three times; and narrow, vertical black bars on the sides. The anal fin has 3 spines with 10 to 12 rays; the dorsal has 10 spines with 10 to 12 rays; and the pelvic fins have 1 spine with 5 rays each. There are less than 53 scales on the lateral line, typically 41 to 45. Living, nonbreeding fish usually have an iridescent purple sheen. Breeding males become very dark olive to bronze on the back and sides and have orange breasts. The pelvic and anal fins turn an iridescent black and a large dark spot develops on the soft-rayed portion of the dorsal fin. Most adult bluegill possess a posterior dorsal fin spot of some sort.

Names. The gills of bluegill are pink, as they are for most fish, so the common name is presumably derived from the sometimes blue flap on the operculum. California anglers often refer to bluegill (and other sunfishes) as "perch" or "bream." *Lepomis* means scaled cheek, since the scales present on the operculum were once considered to be a significant distinguishing feature. *Macrochirus* translates as large hand, referring to the long pectoral fins.

Distribution. Bluegill were originally distributed throughout much of eastern and southern North America, north to Ontario and the Great Lakes region, west through the Mississippi drainage system, and south into Florida and northeastern Mexico. They were introduced into California in 1908 and are now established in suitable waters throughout the state, as they are in all western states and provinces.

Life History. The ability of bluegill to survive and reproduce under a wide variety of environmental conditions has made them one of the most abundant freshwater fishes in California. Although they do best in warm, shallow lakes, reservoirs, ponds, and sloughs at low altitudes, occasional populations of stunted bluegills may become established in the shallow waters of higher, colder lakes such as Shaver Lake in Fresno County (1670 m). They can also survive in waters of high turbidity and surprisingly low oxygen content (less than 1 ppm), but maximum growth and reproduction occurs in fairly clear waters with moderate levels of dissolved oxygen (4 to 8 ppm). Bluegill are often associated with rooted aquatic plants, in which they hide and feed, and with bottoms of silt, sand, or gravel. They seldom go much deeper than 5 m.

Bluegill are highly opportunistic feeders, taking whatever animal food is most abundant in their shallow-water habitat. The mouth is relatively small but it is lined with small teeth and the upper lip is protrusible. The bluegill is thus capable of ingesting a wide variety of organisms. The larvae of aquatic insects, such as midges, mayflies, caddisflies, and dragonflies, seem to be preferred, followed by planktonic crustaceans, flying insects, and snails. Small fish, fish eggs, and crayfish may be eaten when available. Goodson (1965) found that bluegill, ranging from 10 to 26 cm FL in Pine Flat Reservoir, Fresno County, fed largely on fish eggs, midge larvae, and cladocerans in March through June, switching to flying insects in July through October, and going back to midge larvae and cladocerans in November through February. For larger fish, threadfin shad also formed an important part of the diet in winter months. In the Sacramento-San Joaquin Delta, Turner (1966b) found that an amphipod (*Corophium*), an isopod (*Exosphaeroma*), and chironomid larvae and pupae dominated the summer diet of bluegill. When animal food becomes scarce, the adult fish will feed extensively on algae and other aquatic plants although they are unable to support themselves nutritionally on such a diet (Kitchell and Windell, 1970). Feeding for the bluegill is a nearly continuous activity in the summer, reaching a peak in intensity in the midafternoon and again just after dark (Keast and Welsh, 1968).

Bluegill will feed almost anywhere: in shallow water, on the bottom, in midwater in the aquatic vegetation, and on the surface. Their deep body and flexible fins are adapted for hovering at all levels and then darting forward to pick up a food item (Keast and Webb, 1966). The body is kept from rolling sideways in the water by undulations of the large, nonspiny portions of the dorsal and anal fins, as well as by movements of the upper lobe of the tail. The long pectoral fins, assisted by the pelvic fins, also help stabilize the fish but their primary function is for maneuvering. For this purpose they can be moved independently of each other with a wristlike action.

Individual bluegill spend most of their lives in a rather restricted area, even in large bodies of water. This presumably gives each fish the familiarity with an area which it needs to find food and to avoid predators such as largemouth bass.

Yearly growth of bluegills in California lakes and reservoirs is slower than that of bluegills in the southern United States where the growing season is similar. California growth rates are similar to those of bluegills in midwestern lakes but California bluegill seldom reach the sizes commonly achieved by bluegill from the other two areas. At hatching California bluegill are 5 to 6 mm TL. By the end of their first year they have reached a length of 4 to 5 cm TL and they will grow 2 to 5 cm in each subsequent year. Thus, a typical 15 cm California bluegill will be four to five years old and weigh about 90 gm. A large (23 cm) bluegill from California is likely to be eight to nine years old and weigh over 300 gm. However, growth in the bluegill, as in most fish, will vary with the condition of the water in which it lives. Exceptionally cold or turbid water is likely to produce stunted fish. Growth is most rapid in water between 15° and 25°C.

Spawning begins in the spring when water temperatures reach 18 to 21°C and may continue throughout the summer. The spawning fish may be only one year old but usually they are two or three. The male constructs a nest in shallow water by excavating, with vigorous fanning movements of its fins, a depression 20 to 30 cm in diameter and 5 to 15 cm deep. Nests are constructed on bottoms of gravel, sand, or mud that contain pieces of debris, such as twigs or dead leaves. A number of males usually build their nests in close proximity to each other, but each male defends its nest and the area around it from all other males and from potential egg predators such as minnows and catfish. The females, meanwhile, swim about in schools in the general area of the nesting colony. When one is ready to spawn, she approaches the nesting area and is approached in turn and courted by a male, usually the largest one in the immediate vicinity. The male attracts the female to the nest and the two spawn side by side. Courtship movements are accompanied by distinctive grunting sounds (Gerald, 1971). Each male may court and spawn with several females in succession. The fertilized eggs adhere to the debris on the bottom of the nest. The male continues to defend the nest of eggs after he is through spawning and then guards the school of young for several days after they hatch.

Bluegill are very prolific. Single females lay 2,000 to 50,000 eggs, depending on the size of the fish. As many as 62,000 young bluegill have been reported hatching from one nest, although more typically 2,000 to 18,000 young are produced per nest (Emig, 1966).

At water temperatures around 20°C, the eggs hatch in two to three days and the fry soon start to swim about. Gradually they move away from the nests and into nearby aquatic plant beds. Mortality due to predation by various fishes and invertebrates is very high at this time. In the vegetation they grow 10 to 12 mm TL and then move out into the surface waters over the deep regions of the lake, where they remain for six to seven weeks feeding on planktonic crustaceans (Werner, 1967, 1969). By the time the bluegill fry return for good to the aquatic weedbeds near shore they have grown to 21 to 25 mm TL.

Status. Bluegill are one of the most widespread and abundant gamefish in California. Fishing usually has little effect on their populations because of their high reproductive rates. In some waters, they have become too abundant, and severe intraspecific competition has limited individual growth. The result is large populations of stunted fish, which may in turn limit populations of other gamefishes both by eating eggs and young and by eating food that the young fish need to survive.

It is possible that the characteristic small size of bluegills in California is the result of their limited genetic background. Apparently, most bluegill in the state are descended from fish collected in one or two midwestern localities that may have had small strains of bluegills. Attempts are now being made by the California Department of Fish and Game to introduce large, fast-growing bluegills from Florida, to see if they will continue to be fast growing once they become established in the state.

References. Applegate et al., 1967; Emig, 1966; Gerald, 1971; Goodson, 1965; Keast and Webb, 1966; Keast and Welsh, 1968; Kitchell and Windell, 1970; Moyle and Nichols, 1973; Seaburg and Moyle, 1964; Werner, 1967, 1969.

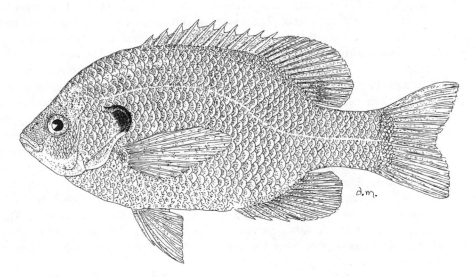

Figure 107. Redear sunfish, 15 cm SL, Lost Lake, Fresno County.

Redear Sunfish, *Lepomis microlophus* (Günther)

Identification. Redear sunfish are deep bodied, with small oblique mouths (barely reaching the front margin of the eye), long, pointed pectoral fins, short, stiff opercular flaps, and stubby gill rakers (only 2 to 3 times longer than wide). They differ from the similar pumpkinseed sunfish by the absence of any conspicuous patterns on either the sides or the fins, except an orange red edge around the dark blotch on the opercular flap. The dorsal fin has 10 spines, 11 to 12 rays; the anal fin has 3 spines, 10 to 11 rays; the pelvic fins have 1 spine, 5 days; and the pectoral fin has 13 rays. There are 35 to 37 lateral line scales. Adults are light olive on the back and a pale mottled brown to silvery on the sides. Young of the year may have 7 to 8 faint vertical bars on the sides. The dorsal fin is dusky, without a dark spot on the rear portion.

Names. Shellcracker is a widely used, unofficial common name for redear sunfish in much of their native southern United States. *Microlophus* means small crest, presumably after the short opercular flap. Other names are as for bluegill.

Distribution. Redear sunfish are native to the southeastern United States and to the Rio Grande and lower Mississippi drainage systems. They have been widely planted throughout the warmer regions of the United States, first appearing in the lower Colorado River in 1948 to 1949. They have since been introduced to a variety of waters in southern California and the Central Valley. Given the proclivity of sportsmen (and biologists) for moving fish around, they can be expected elsewhere in the state as well.

Life History. The preferred habitat of redear sunfish is the deeper waters of warm, quiet ponds, lakes, and river backwaters with substantial beds of aquatic vegetation. Reproduction and growth are inhibited in water that is too turbid, probably because the low light penetration limits aquatic plant growth and forces the sunfish into shallow water where they have to compete for food and space with other sunfish species, especially bluegill. They are usually most abundant in water deeper than 2 m.

Redear sunfish feed mostly by picking hardshelled invertebrates off the bottom and from aquatic plants with their protrusible lips. The prey is then crushed by their heavy set of molarlike pharyngeal teeth; the soft parts are swallowed and the hard parts are ejected. The short gill rakers make the ejection of hard parts, especially pieces of snail shell, easier although most of the material is literally spit out. The short gill rakers also permit the easy ejection of sand, mud, and bottom debris the sunfish may take up when grabbing snails or burrowing mayflies (*Hexagenia*). Redear sunfish seem particularly well adapted for feeding on snails, which form a major portion of the diet especially in the winter months (Wilbur, 1969). However, when given a choice they will select bottom-dwelling insect larvae (e.g., dragonfly, midge, and mayfly larvae) and amphipods over snails (Wilbur, 1969). Such organisms often form the bulk of their diet in the summer. It is possible that snails are important mostly where redear have to coexist with other species of sunfish that are slightly better adapted for feeding on insects, especially when food is in short supply (winter months).

The growth rates of redear sunfish in central California lakes and reservoirs are slightly faster than those of bluegill in the same bodies of water but slower than redear sunfish in their native south. An exceptionally slow-growing population occurs in Lost Lake, Fresno County, a small, turbid, former gravel pit with only small amounts of aquatic vegetation. Lost Lake redear sunfish average 48 mm TL at the end of their first year, reaching 92 mm TL in their second, 135 mm TL in their third, 163 mm TL in their fourth, 189 mm TL in their fifth, and 215 mm TL in their sixth (Moyle, unpublished data). In contrast, Lake Berryessa, Napa County, has a fairly fast-growing population for central California: 69 mm TL in the first year, 128 mm TL in the second, 140 mm TL in the third, and 170 mm TL in the fourth. Growth slows down considerably after the fourth year so redear sunfish in Lake Berryessa exceeding 200 mm TL are uncommon (Skillman, 1969). The maximum size attained by redear sunfish in California seems to be about 31 cm TL (540 gm) and the maximum age about seven years.

In their native range, redear sunfish usually become mature at lengths of 13 to 18 cm

TL, when they are one or two years old (Wilbur, 1969). If the length-maturity relationship holds true for California populations then they probably are unable to spawn until their third or fourth year. This might be the main reason why redear sunfish seldom have stunted populations in California, in contrast to bluegill.

Spawning takes place throughout the summer, starting as soon as water temperatures exceed 22 to 24°C (Emig, 1966). The males construct nests in colonies, although each nest is defended vigorously by its owner from the other males. The nests are depressions about 35 cm in diameter and 5 to 10 cm deep, constructed in bottoms of sand, gravel, or mud, usually at depths of 2 to 3 m. Nest building and spawning behavior are apparently similar to those of other sunfishes, especially pumpkinseed (Wilbur, 1969). Males, however, make species-specific popping sounds during courtship (Gerald, 1971).

Redear sunfish will hybridize with other species of sunfish, the crosses producing mostly fast-growing, sterile males.

Status. Redear sunfish are underexploited in California so large individuals are common. They are harder to catch than bluegill, their most common associates, because they live in deeper water and feed on or close to the bottom. In many waters where they maintain substantial populations of large fish, fishermen do not even realize that they exist and settle for catches of small bluegill. Nevertheless, redear sunfish are a worthwhile species to stock in farm ponds and reservoirs because they will not overpopulate and become stunted. Increasing the angler harvest of redear sunfish is mostly a matter of letting the anglers know where they are and how to fish for them. In the southern United States they are much sought after as a gamefish.

References. Cross, 1967; Emig, 1966; Gerald, 1971; Skillman, 1969; Wilbur, 1969.

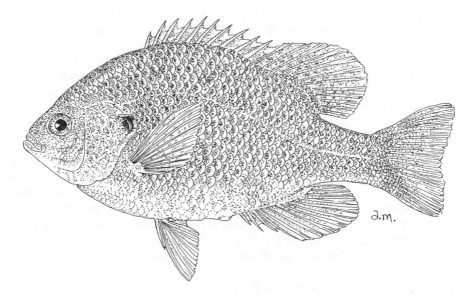

Figure 108. Pumpkinseed, 12 cm SL, Iron Gate Reservoir, Siskiyou County.

Pumpkinseed, *Lepomis gibbosus* (Linnaeus)

Identification. Like redear sunfish, pumpkinseed are deep bodied (only slightly more so), with small oblique mouths, long, pointed pectoral fins, short, stiff opercular flaps, stubby gill rakers, and heavy, molariform pharyngeal teeth. Unlike redear sunfish, they have small spots on the soft portion of the dorsal fin and adults have conspicuous orange and blue streaks on the dark operculum. The opercular flap is covered with a bright red spot. The dorsal fin has 10 spines, 10 to 12 rays; the anal fin has 3 spines, 10 to 11 rays; the pelvic fins have 1 spine, 5 rays; and the pectoral fins have 12 rays. There are 35 to 40 scales in the lateral line. The background color of the body is grey green to greenish brown with superimposed spots of orange, yellow, blue, and green and with 7 to 10 faint blue green vertical bands. The throat and belly are yellow to orange. Juveniles are a more uniform grey green color, with fairly conspicuous vertical bars.

Names. In their native East and Midwest, pumpkinseeds are frequently called common sunfish or simply *the* sunfish. Pumpkinseed aptly describes their body shape; *gibbosus*, means humped or rounded or, according to Jordan and Evermann (1896), "formed like the full moon." Other names are as for bluegill.

Distribution. Pumpkinseed are native to eastern North America from southern Canada down the Atlantic coast to South Carolina, west to the Great Lakes region, and to the northern half of the Mississippi River system. They have been widely introduced throughout North America, Europe, and probably other temperate regions of the world as well. The exact date of their introduction into California is not known but they are now established in ponds, reservoirs, and backwaters of the Klamath and Lost rivers and in Honey Lake and the sloughs of the Susan River, Lassen County. The only established population in southern California is in Big Bear Lake, San Bernadino County. It would not be surprising to find them elsewhere in the state, especially in southern regions where attempts have been made to establish populations (Hubbell, 1966).

Life History. Pumpkinseed are ecologically similar to redear sunfish, preferring lakes, sloughs, or sluggish streams with beds of aquatic plants that support large populations of snails. They do not show the redear's apparent preference for deep water, however, and they seem to be adapted for living in much cooler waters, especially those that have large seasonal fluctuations in temperature.

Like redear sunfish, pumpkinseed feed by picking hardshelled invertebrates from the bottom or from aquatic plants. Snails are usually the most important item in their diet, but aquatic insects are apparently preferred. In the summer, when aquatic insect larvae are most abundant, they will frequently be the most common prey taken despite large snail populations (Seaburg and Moyle, 1964). Aquatic insects also predominate in the diet when pumpkinseed occur in the absence of other species of sunfish (e.g., Keast, 1966; Kimsey and Bell, 1956). Pumpkinseed of all sizes feed on the same kinds of food, except that the larvae feed on zooplankton. They will feed at almost any time of the day or night but peak activity is generally at dawn or dusk. Feeding ceases when water temperatures drop below 6.5°C (Keast, 1968b).

Pumpkinseed grow rather slowly for a sunfish, although this may be mostly an effect of the cooler waters they inhabit. Their growth in Honey Lake, Lassen County, approximates the average growth they achieved in their native Midwest: one year, 25 mm FL; two years, 66 mm FL; three years, 112 mm FL; and four years, 132 mm FL (Kimsey and Bell, 1956). Although they can live as long as twelve years, they seldom exceed 30 cm FL (Hubbell, 1966).

Maturity sets in during the second or third year and does not seem to be strongly dependent on size, since populations of stunted pumpkinseed, all under 10 cm FL, are not unusual. Spawning takes place in the late spring and early summer as soon as water temperatures approach 20°C. The males construct nests in shallow water (less than 1 m deep) in bottoms of sand, gravel, or woody debris. The nests are built in colonies but defended individually. Each male may spawn with several females and guards the eggs until they hatch, usually in three to five days. The number of eggs laid by each female varies from 600 to 3,000, the fecundity increasing with the age and size of the female (Hubbell, 1966). As soon as the newly hatched young are able to swim, they leave the nest and venture into the open waters, where they drift among and feed on zooplankton for several weeks (Faber, 1967).

Pumpkinseed will hybridize in the wild with most other members of the genus *Lepomis*, but especially bluegill and green sunfish. The hybrids are almost always fast-growing but sterile males.

Status. Pumpkinseed are well established only in the Klamath and Lahontan systems. Although they are the most beautifully colored of all the sunfishes now in California, their spread to other systems should be discouraged. The ecologically similar redear sunfish probably grows faster in central and southern California and does not seem to produce stunted populations.

References. Dill, Coots, and Douglas, 1955; Faber, 1967; Hubbell, 1966; Keast, 1966, 1968b; Keast and Welsh, 1968; Kimsey and Bell, 1956; Moyle, 1969; Seaburg and Moyle, 1964.

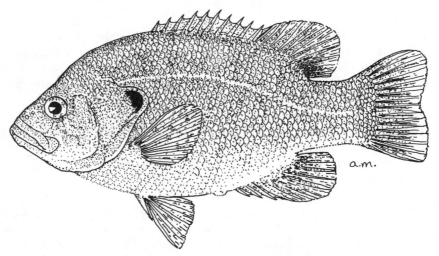

Figure 109. Green sunfish, 12 cm SL, Putah Creek, Yolo County.

Green Sunfish, *Lepomis cyanellus* Rafinesque

Identification. The bodies of green sunfish are stouter than but not as deep as those of other California sunfishes. Their pectoral fins are soft (13 to 15 rays) and rounded; their mouths are large, the maxillae extending past the front margin of the eyes; their opercular flaps are short and stiff; and their gill rakers are long and slender. Their dorsal fins have 9 to 10 spines, 10 to 12 rays; anal fins have 3 spines, 8 to 9 rays; pelvic fins have 1 spine, 5 rays; and the lateral line has 45 to 50 scales. There are no teeth on the tongue except in a few very large individuals. Large adults are dark olive on the back becoming lighter on the sides with iridescent green flecks. The breast and bellies are yellow orange and there are usually green iridescent streaks on the cheeks. Both dorsal and anal fins have a large dark blotch on the rear of the soft-rayed portion. Young show fine, closely spaced chains of iridescent green that give the impression of a very fine bluegreen grid on the sides. The backs, sides, and fins of breeding males turn very dark and the fins usually have bright yellow margins.

Names. Cyanellus means green. Few other names see bluegill.

Distribution. Green sunfish were originally native to most of the Mississippi drainage system, including the Great Lakes, but their original distribution pattern has been obscured by widespread introductions. They were introduced into California in 1891 and have since been spread throughout the state by well-intentioned fishermen and biologists, who often thought they were planting bluegill. They seem to be absent only from the Klamath River system.

Life History. Green sunfish are inhabitants of small, warm streams (especially those that become intermittent in the summer), ponds, and lake edges. They are generally rare in habitats that contain more than three or four other species of fish. Thus, in lakes and reservoirs they are usually only locally abundant in shallow weedy areas that exclude most other species. In the Sierra Nevada foothills above the San Joaquin Valley, they are the most widely distributed fish species, native or introduced, but they are abundant mostly in intermittent streams that have warm, turbid, muddy-bottomed pools containing beds of aquatic plants and populations of other introduced fishes, such as largemouth bass and mosquitofish (Moyle and Nichols, 1973). They will often be the sole inhabitants of such streams, especially those that have been heavily disrupted by man. It is not unusual to find a few large green sunfish in undisturbed sections of stream dominated by native fishes but they only seem to be able to take over physically disrupted areas where the native fishes have been depleted. A major exception to this is streams normally dominated by California roach. Like roach, green sunfish are a pioneer species, well adapted for moving into areas with low populations of other species and capable of surviving where other species cannot. They can survive high temperatures (over $36°C$), low oxygen levels (less than 3 ppm), and high alkalinities (up to 2,000 mg/l, McCarraher, 1972).

Green sunfish are very aggressive, although young of the year frequently school. Older fish tend to be territorial for feeding. In a small aquarium, one fish, usually the largest, quickly assumes dominance over the others and will keep them in a restricted area of the aquarium while it defends the rest as its territory. Green sunfish will also chase other species of fish from their territories. Such territoriality may not be as pronounced in the wild but, once a large green sunfish has been located in a stream, it can generally be found in the same area for long periods of time. This aggressiveness may be one reason why they are so quick to colonize new waters, since small fish are presumably always seeking feeding areas not dominated by large fish.

As their large mouths and aggressive natures indicate, green sunfish are opportunistic predators on the larger, more active invertebrates that occur with them, and on small fish. When small (less than 8 cm SL), they feed mostly on crustaceans and aquatic insect larvae, especially mayfly larvae, but as they increase in size they depend more on large aquatic insects, terrestrial insects, crayfish, and fish (Applegate et al., 1967; Moyle, 1969). In California, common prey species are mosquitofish, small sunfish (including their own young), and California roach.

Compared to other sunfishes, green sunfish grow slowly and seldom reach sizes greater than 15 cm SL. They usually reach 3 to 5 cm SL in their first year, 5 to 10 cm SL in their second, and 8 to 13 cm SL in their third. Such growth seems to be typical for populations in California reservoirs (E. Miller, 1970). They can grow to over 30 cm SL, achieve weights of nearly 1 kg, and live as long as ten years. Green sunfish that even approach such longevity and size are extremely unusual, especially in California, since in good habitats they are so prolific that large stunted populations quickly develop. Thus, it is not unusual to find four- to five-year-old fish that are only 10 to 12 cm SL.

One of the reasons green sunfish often form stunted populations is that they can reproduce at 5 to 7 cm SL, usually maturing at the beginning of their third year. Spawning activity is most intense in May and June but often continues into July and August. It usually does not begin until water temperatures exceed 19°C. The first noticeable activity is the congregation of male green sunfish in shallow water. One to two days later, the males start to dig nests, singly or in colonies, preferably on fine gravel bottoms near overhanging bushes or other cover. Each male defends his nest against other males and, to a lesser extent, females. Females that get past the males' defenses (using a special circling behavior) are quickly courted and spawned with, sometimes two at a time (Hunter, 1963). Courtship is accompanied by gruntlike sounds (Gerald, 1971). During spawning, females turn on their sides, vibrating and releasing eggs, while the males remain alongside in an upright position, simultaneously releasing sperm (Hunter, 1963). Each male may spawn several times with different females. The eggs adhere to the nest substrate and the male generally guards them for five to seven days, enough time for the young to hatch and become free swimming. Little is known about the ecology of larval green sunfish.

Green sunfish commonly hybridize with bluegill, pumpkinseed, warmouth, and any other sunfish species with which they occur. Much of this hybridization seems to be due to small male green sunfish dashing into the nests of the other species while a pair is spawning, the intruding male releasing some milt of its own.

Status. The introduction of green sunfish into California can only be regarded as unfortunate. They provide little in the way of sport or food and a great deal in the way of competition for (and predation on) native nongame fishes and other gamefishes. They have probably been responsible for the elimination of California roach in parts of the San Joaquin Valley (Moyle and Nichols, 1974). In ponds, and occasionally in trout lakes, they will form large stunted populations that seriously affect population size and growth of more desirable gamefishes (McKechnie and Tharratt, 1966). It is fortunate that green sunfish are seldom able to establish large populations in California's larger streams, lakes, and reservoirs.

References. Applegate et al., 1967; Carlander, 1950; Cross, 1967; Dill, 1944; Etnier, 1968; Gerald, 1971; Hunter, 1963; McCarraher, 1972; McKechnie and Tharratt, 1966; E. Miller, 1970; Moyle, 1969; Moyle and Nichols, 1973, 1974; Sigler and Miller, 1963.

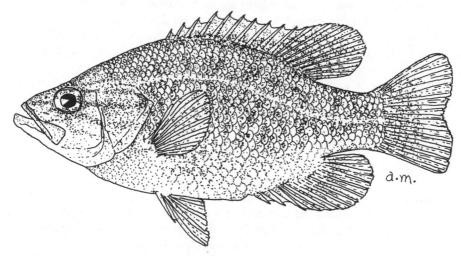

Figure 110. Warmouth, 12 cm SL, Sacramento River, Yolo County.

Warmouth, *Lepomis gulosus* (Cuvier)

Identification. Warmouth look like stout green sunfish, except that they are brown and have teeth on their tongues. Their pectoral fins are short and rounded (12 to 14 rays); their mouths are large, the maxillae extending past the front margin of their eyes; their opercular flaps are short and stiff; and their gill rakers are long and slender. Their dorsal fins have 10 to 11 spines, 9 to 11 rays; anal fins have 3 spines, 9 to 10 rays; pelvic fins have 1 spine, 5 rays; and the lateral line has 35 to 44 scales. Their overall color is brown, with an iridescent purple tinge to their scales, and yellow bellies. Faint vertical bars may sometimes be present on their sides. Four to six dark brown bars radiate across their cheeks from their eyes and mouths. Their eyes are red.

Names. The origin of the name warmouth is obscure, but it quite likely is based on a fancied resemblence of the markings on the head to the warpaint of American Indians. Warmouth are frequently called warmouth bass and, occasionally, goggle-eye. Prior to the publication of the third edition of the American Fisheries Society's list of fish names (1970), warmouth were placed by themselves in the genus *Chaenobryttus*, often as *C. coronarius.* They are now considered to be a part of *Lepomis* because of their close relationship to green sunfish. An alternative used by Minckley (1973) is to place green sunfish and warmouth together in *Chaenobryttus. Gulosus* means large mouth.

Distribution. Warmouth are native to most of the United States east of the Mississippi River, including the Atlantic seaboard. They were introduced into southern California in 1921 (Evermann and Clark, 1931) and were soon spread to the Central Valley. They are now widespread in the waters of the Valley floor and in a few reservoirs at higher elevations (e.g., Bass Lake, Madera County). They mysteriously appeared in the Colorado River in 1961 (Lanse, 1965) and are now abundant there.

Life History. Most warmouth in California are found where there is abundant vegetation and other cover in the warm, turbid, muddy-bottomed sloughs and backwaters of the Sacramento, San Joaquin, and Colorado rivers. They also do well in ponds. They are fairly adaptable, however, and are common in Bass Lake, Madera County, a cool, fluctuating reservoir that also supports substantial salmonid populations. Most of what is known about warmouth comes from the classic study of Larimore (1957) in Illinois, which is the main source for this summary.

Warmouth are opportunistic predators that tend to hide quietly in ambush. Fish less than 5 cm TL feed mostly on small crustaceans, but start taking small insect larvae and snails as they increase in size. By the time the warmouth reach 10 to 13 cm TL, they are feeding mostly on aquatic insects. Larger fish take larger organisms, and fish and crayfish are usually important in the diets of fish over 13 cm TL. In the Sacramento-San Joaquin Delta, warmouth of all sizes feed on oppossum shrimp (*Neomysis*), amphipods (*Corophium*), and aquatic insects, although larger fish also take crayfish and fish (Turner, 1966b). Peaks of feeding seem to be in the early morning and at dusk.

Warmouth are fairly long lived but they are so slow growing that an individual over 28 cm TL and 450 gm would be a giant of its species. Typically, they reach 3 to 9 cm TL in their first year, 6 to 14 cm TL in their second, 9 to 17 cm TL in their third, 11 to 20 cm TL in their fourth, and 13 to 21 cm TL in their fifth. They often live six to eight years. Since they often form stunted populations, 10 cm TL fish that are four to six years old can occur. Fish in newly established populations, on the other hand, may show rather fast growth for the first year or two, reaching 10 to 12 cm TL in their first year. Warmouth collected by Lanse (1965) from the Colorado River appear to belong in the latter category.

Warmouth mature in their second or third summer, at 7 to 10 cm TL. Spawning takes place in the late spring and early summer, when temperatures reach about 21°C. Warmouth are nongregarious nest builders and their breeding and parental behavior is very similar to that of green sunfish. They will hybridize with other members of the genus *Lepomis*. It is not unusual to find bluegill-warmouth hybrids in sloughs along the Sacramento River.

Status. Warmouth add little to the warmwater sport fishery of California. Although they put up a good fight on ultra-light tackle, they are too small, too slow growing, and too uncommon in California to be worth any special management considerations, except the elimination of stunted populations. Their role in the sloughs and reservoirs where populations are established is poorly known, especially their relationships with other fish species.

References. Cross, 1967; Lanse, 1965; Larimore, 1957; Minckley, 1973; Turner, 1966b.

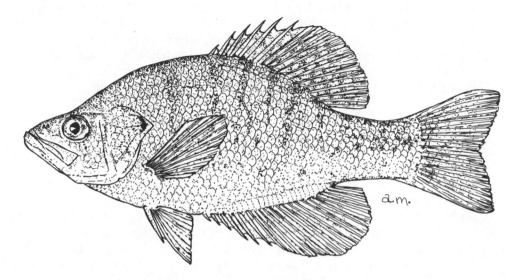

Figure 111. White crappie, 11 cm SL, Clear Lake, Lake County.

White Crappie, *Pomoxis annularis* Rafinesque

Identification. White crappie have deep, laterally compressed bodies and small heads with a sharp depression in the profile above the eyes. Their mouths are large and oblique, so the lower jaws appear to project. Their large, rounded, dorsal and anal fins are nearly equal in size, and the length of the dorsal fin base is much less than the distance from the origin of the dorsal fin to the eye. There are 5 to 6 spines, 13 to 15 rays in their dorsal fins; 5 to 6 spines, 17 to 18 rays in their anal fins; 1 spine, 5 rays in their pelvic fins; and 14 to 15 rays in their rounded pectoral fins. The lateral line is arched, with 38 to 45 scales. Living fish are iridescent olive green on their backs and silvery white on their sides, usually with 10 or fewer indistinct, dark vertical bars. Dorsal, anal, and caudal fins are checkered with dark spots. Breeding males become very dark, the head and breast turning nearly completely black.

Names. The name crappie is of unknown origin, but it is probably a modified Indian word for these fishes. White crappie are sometimes called calico bass or strawberry bass, names that are more frequently applied to black crappie. *Pom-oxis* means cover-sharp, referring to the fact that the operculum ends in a blunt point rather than in a distinct flap, as is characteristic of sunfish. *Annularis* means having rings.

Distribution. White crappie were originally distributed throughout the Mississippi River Basin from Minnesota southward, as well as in much of the Great Lakes Basin and in Gulf and Atlantic coast states north to North Carolina. They have been planted throughout the United States, the first successful plant in California apparently taking place in 1917 with sixteen fish in a pond in San Diego County. White crappie from this pond were spread throughout southern California but they were not planted north of the Tehachapi Mountains until 1951 (Goodson, 1966). They are now present in many reservoirs and sloughs of the Sacramento-San Joaquin system and can consequently be expected anywhere in the state where there is suitable habitat.

Life History. White crappie are most abundant in warm, turbid lakes, reservoirs, and river backwaters. They seem to have slightly greater tolerances than black crappie for high turbidities, alkaline water, current, high temperatures, and lack of aquatic vegetation and other cover (Hansen, 1951; Goodson, 1964). They are schooling fish and the schools are often rather localized in their distribution. Individuals, however, may move considerable distances within a body of water (Grinstead, 1969). During the day they tend to congregate around submerged logs or boulders, in quiet water 2 to 4 m deep. They may move out into open water to feed during evening and early morning. In the winter, they are apparently rather inactive, remaining close to the bottom in deep water (Grinstead, 1969).

The feeding mechanisms of white crappie are unusual in that they have long, fine gill rakers, suitable for straining small zooplankters from the water, combined with large, protrusible mouths that are suitable for ingesting large prey, especially fish. Thus, the stomachs of white crappie typically contain planktonic crustaceans, plankton-feeding fish, or both (Goodson, 1966; Mathur, 1972). However, they are also opportunistic in their feeding and will take other types of fish and aquatic insects when readily available. Zooplankton are the main food of crappie under 14 cm FL and fish tend to predominate in the diet of larger individuals. In California reservoirs, threadfin shad are especially important prey. In Clear Lake, Lake County, Mississippi silversides have recently become important in their diet. Young-of-the-year white crappie feed mostly during the day, with a peak of feeding in the midafternoon (Mathur and Robbins, 1971), although they seem to forage most actively about dusk.

Growth of white crappie in California reservoirs is generally somewhat slower than where they are native. They reach 5 to 10 cm FL in their first year, 11 to 18 cm FL in their second, 17 to 21 cm FL in their third, and 20 to 27 cm FL in their fourth (Goodson, 1966). The introduction of threadfin shad into Lake Isabella, Kern County, increased the growth rates of white crappie, especially those in their second and third years (Bartholomew, 1966). They seldom live longer than seven to eight years or grow larger than 35 cm FL (0.8 kg). Elsewhere they have reached nearly 2.4 kg.

White crappie become mature in their second or third spring, at sizes of 10 to 20 cm TL. Spawning usually begins in April or May, when temperatures reach 17 to 20°C. The males construct nests in colonies, underneath or close to overhanging bushes or banks, in water less than 1 m deep (Hansen, 1951, 1965). Nests are occasionally built in water as deep as 6 to 7 m. They usually consist of shallow depressions in hard clay bottoms (rarely in sand or gravel), near or in beds of aquatic plants, algae, or submerged plant debris (Hansen, 1965). The eggs adhere to the plant material which typically collects in the nest. Spawning and parental behavior have not been described in much detail, but they seem to be similar to the sunfishes. The fecundity of females is highly variable and the number of eggs (range: 970 to 213,000) is only partially related to her size.

Status. White crappie seem to do fairly well in warm, turbid reservoirs of California if provided with adequate forage. Despite the comparative recentness of their introduction into the Central Valley, they are now widespread and seem to be displacing black crappie in some areas. Turner (1966b) and M. Caywood (pers. comm., 1974) found that white crappie were very rare in sloughs of the Delta, while black crappie were common. In 1973, white crappie were one of the most abundant species in sloughs along the Sacramento River, in Yolo County, while black crappie were rare. White crappie were introduced to Clear Lake, Lake County, in 1957, where they now appear to be slightly more abundant than the long-established black crappie. Whether or not this is a good thing is debatable, since black crappie seem to grow larger in

California than white crappie. How these two species interact presents a fascinating problem in behavior and ecology that needs to be resolved.

References. Bartholomew, 1966; Cross, 1967; Goodson, 1966; Grinstead, 1969; Hansen, 1951, 1965; Mathur, 1972; Mathur and Robbins, 1971.

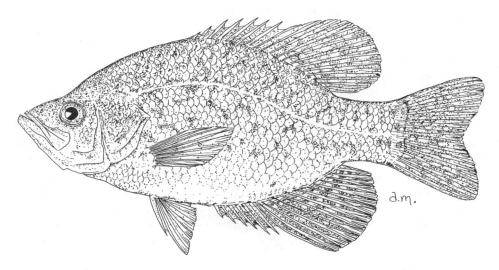

Figure 112. Black crappie, 10 cm SL, Clear Lake, Lake County.

Black Crappie, *Pomoxis nigromaculatus* (Lesueur)

Identification. The body shape of black crappie is similar to that of white crappie except that they are slightly deeper and heavier bodied. They can be told from white crappie by their longer dorsal fins (7 to 8 spines, 15 to 16 rays), the bases of which are about the same length as the distance from the fin origin to the middle of the eye. Their body coloring consists of heavy black spotting that is not arranged in vertical bands. The spots on the dorsal, anal, and caudal fins are not arranged in any sort of pattern. Breeding fish turn nearly solid black on the anterior halves of their bodies. Black crappie have 6 spines, 16 to 18 rays in their anal fins; 1 spine, 5 to 6 rays in their pelvic fins; 14 to 15 rays in their pectoral fins; and 38 to 44 scales in their arched lateral lines.

Names. *Nigro-maculatus* means black-spotted. A synonymy of the scientific nomenclature is given in La Rivers (1962). Other names are as for white crappie.

Distribution. The native distribution of black crappie was apparently similar to that of white crappie except that they occurred considerably farther north in the Great Lakes region of Canada (Scott and Crossman, 1973). They were first successfully introduced into California in 1908 (Goodson, 1966) and can now be expected almost anywhere in the state where there is warm, quiet water.

Life History. Black crappie are most successful in large, warm, clear lakes and reservoirs with large beds of aquatic plants, although they have also established populations in a number of clear, steep-sided California reservoirs that lack aquatic plant beds. Like white crappie, they tend to be found in highly localized schools that spend their days around large submerged objects but move offshore to forage in open water in the evenings and early mornings.

The feeding mechanisms of black crappie are almost identical to those of white crappie, so it is not surprising that their diets are similar. They are primarily midwater feeders; zooplankton and small Diptera larvae predominate in the diet of small fish (to 10 to 12 cm SL) while fish and aquatic insects predominate in larger fish (Keast and Webb, 1966; Keast, 1968a). However, it is not uncommon to find large amounts of planktonic crustaceans in the stomachs of fish up to 16 cm SL. In sloughs of the Sacramento-San Joaquin Delta, oppossum shrimp (*Neomysis*), amphipods (*Corophium*), and planktonic crustaceans are the main foods of black crappie under 10 cm FL, while fish, mostly threadfin shad and juvenile striped bass, are the main foods of adults. California populations are capable of feeding throughout the year, since Keast (1968a) found that black crappie will feed at temperatures as low as 6 to 7°C. Black crappie will feed at virtually anytime of the day or night but feeding tends to peak around noon, midnight, and early morning (Keast, 1968a).

Growth in California populations of black crappie is, on the average, somewhat slower than growth in populations in the eastern United States, although some populations (e.g., Clear Lake, Lake County) have excellent growth rates. In California, they can range in size from 4 to 8 cm FL at the end of their first year, 12 to 21 cm FL at the end of their second, 15 to 28 cm FL at the end of their third, and 17 to 33 cm FL at the end of their fourth (Goodson, 1966). The maximum age for black crappie seems to be about ten years, and the maximum size is about 2.27 kg, although a fish over 1 kg is unusual. The largest recorded for California weighed 1.8 kg (Goodson, 1966).

Black crappie mature in their second or third year at 10 to 20 cm TL. Spawning begins in March or April as temperatures exceed 14 to 17°C and may continue into July. Nests are shallow depressions fanned out by males in bottoms ranging from mud to gravel. They are usually built in water less than 1 m deep near or in beds of aquatic plants. A male generally constructs a nest 2 to 3 m from his nearest neighbor, so the spawning fish form a loose colony. Reproductive behavior is poorly known but it is presumably similar to that of white crappie and the sunfishes (Breder and Rosen, 1966). Each female lays between 10 and 200 thousand eggs, depending in part on her size.

The newly hatched fry are guarded for a short period of time by the males but they soon rise off the nests and spend the next few weeks drifting in open water, presumably feeding on plankton (Faber, 1967).

Status. Black crappie are abundant and popular gamefish in many California lakes and reservoirs. They seem to provide particularly good fishing in the spring and early summer. They apparently are being replaced by white crappie in some of the more turbid waters of the Central Valley, a phenomenon that presents an interesting problem in fish interactions.

References. Breder and Rosen, 1966; Cross, 1967; Faber, 1967; Goodson, 1966; Keast, 1965, 1968a,b; Keast and Webb, 1966; L. Miller, 1965; Scott and Crossman, 1973; Turner, 1966b.

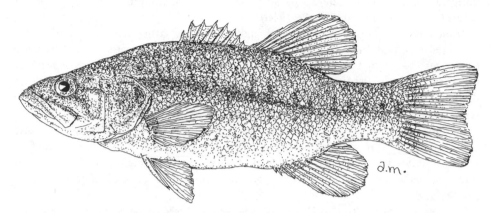

Figure 113. Largemouth bass, 12 cm SL, Sacramento-San Joaquin Delta.

Largemouth Bass, *Micropterus salmoides* (Lacépède)

Identification. Largemouth bass are distinguished by maxillae that extend well past the hind margin of their eyes; deeply notched dorsal fins, with 9 spines and 12 to 13 rays; and a single, continuous, heavy black lateral stripe on each side. They are the heaviest bodied of California "black" bass. Their anal fins have 3 spines and 10 to 12 rays; pectoral fins, 13 to 17 rays (usually 14 to 15); and lateral lines, 58 to 69 scales. The scales on their cheeks, in 9 to 12 rows, are about the same size as the scales on the operculum. Scales are absent from the bases of the dorsal and anal fins. In color, they tend to be plain olive gray on the back and white on the belly, with the stripe in between, and no other conspicuous markings. The young lack any orange in the caudal fin.

Names. All members of the genus *Micropterus* are commonly referred to as black bass, hence largemouth black bass. In much of the older literature, largemouth bass are placed in a separate genus *Huro*. Lacépède based his description of the genus *Micropterus* on a single specimen of smallmouth bass with a deformed dorsal fin in which the last few rays were separated from the fin, giving the appearance of a separate fin. Thus, *Micropterus* means short fin (Jordan and Evermann, 1896). *Salmoides* means troutlike. A synonymy for the scientific nomenclature is given in Hubbs and Bailey (1940).

Distribution. Largemouth bass were first introduced into California in 1874 (Skinner, 1962) and have since been spread to suitable waters throughout the state. They are native to most of the Mississippi River system as well to the Gulf and Atlantic coast states, north to North Carolina. Thanks to their popularity as gamefish, they now enjoy virtually a worldwide distribution. Most largemouth bass in California are presumably northern largemouth (*M. salmoides salmoides*), although in recent years a number of experimental introductions have been made of Florida largemouth (*M. salmoides floridanus*).

Life History. Warm, quiet waters with low turbidities and beds of aquatic plants are the usual habitat of largemouth bass. They are abundant in farm ponds, lakes, reservoirs, sloughs, and river backwaters. They are common in foothill streams above the San Joaquin Valley but occur mostly in disturbed areas where there are large, permanent pools with heavy growths of aquatic plants or, in some cases, near the outflows of farm ponds with similar growths (Moyle and Nichols, 1973). Optimum temperatures for growth are 20 to 30°C, while their minimum oxygen requirement seems to be 1.5 to 2.0 ppm (Emig, 1966).

Adult bass are solitary hunters. Each individual may either remain in a relatively restricted area that frequently centers around a submerged rock or branch (Lewis and Flickinger, 1967) or it may wander widely. Certain places in large lakes repeatedly yield large bass to fishermen, at intervals, indicating that each fish may establish a "home range" for a number of days at one spot and then move on to a new area. In reservoirs and lakes they remain close to shore and seem to be most abundant in water 1 to 3 m deep. Young-of-the-year bass also stay close to shore in schools that cruise about in the open. In crowded ponds, older and larger bass may also school. Bass of all sizes are active most of the day and they may also be active at night. Usually, however, they become quiescent after darkness sets in, following a peak of intense foraging activity at dusk.

Largemouth bass, with their large gape and roving body shape, are admirably suited for capturing the abundant fishes and large invertebrates that occur with them. For the first month or two following hatching, the fry feed mainly on rotifers and small crustaceans, but by the time they are 50 to 60 mm SL they are feeding largely on aquatic insects and fish fry, including those of their own species (Keast, 1966; Applegate et al., 1967). In ponds, if one keeps track of an individual school of nest mates for a month or more after hatching, it soon becomes obvious that as the schools become smaller, one or two members of each school become noticably larger than the rest, presumably by feeding on their fellow bass fry. Once largemouth bass exceed 100 to 125 mm SL they usually subsist primarily on fish. However, Lewis et al. (1961) have shown that both individuals and populations of bass can be highly selective in their feeding, occasionally preferring crayfish, tadpoles, or frogs to fish, as well as preferring one fish species to another. The preferred prey in one population can vary from year to year and the apparent preference cannot always be explained in terms of relative abundance of the prey organisms. Thus in Clear Lake, Lake County, small bluegill have been abundant in shallow water since the 1920s, yet in 1948 largemouth bass over 12 cm FL were feeding mostly on Sacramento blackfish (Murphy, 1949). In 1956 to 1958 they were feeding mostly on bluegill (blackfish were uncommon on the littoral area, however, according to McCammon et al., 1964). By 1973 they had switched to feeding mostly on the superabundant Mississippi silversides. In California reservoirs they feed largely on threadfin shad, golden shiners, and bluegill (Goodson, 1965).

Growth in largemouth bass is highly variable, depending on genetic background, food availability, inter- and intraspecific competition, temperature regimes, and other limnological factors. Thus, they can reach anywhere from 5 to 20 cm TL in their first year, 7 to 32 cm TL in their second, 15 to 37 cm TL in their third, and 20 to 41 cm TL in their fourth. The maximum size anywhere seems to be 76 cm TL or 10.2 kg, and the maximum age, sixteen years (Emig, 1966; Scott, 1967). Large bass in California reservoirs (35 to 45 cm TL, 0.6 to 2.2 kg) are usually four to five years old (Emig, 1966), indicating that their growth compares favorably with that of bass from midwestern states. Since Florida largemouth bass grow even faster (in Florida) than northern largemouth (the variety in California), attempts have been made to improve California bass growth rates by introducing the Florida subspecies (Emig, 1966). So far the attempts have not met with notable success, indicating that growth is more influenced by environment than heredity (L. Miller, 1965). However, Florida largemouth bass are much less vulnerable to angling to they often reach larger sizes in heavily fished reservoirs (von Geldern, 1974).

Food availability for bass may be affected by competition and by the amount of cover available to prey. Competition effects are likely to be most severe for young-of-the-year bass because they feed on zooplankton and other small invertebrates favored by many other fishes. In California reservoirs threadfin shad may depress the growth (and survival) of young bass, presumably by reducing invertebrate populations. This is at least partially compensated for by the increased growth of adult bass that prey on the shad (E. Miller, 1970; von Geldern, 1971). Heavy beds of aquatic plants or large amounts of submerged brush may also depress bass growth by providing hiding places for prey, especially small fish.

Largemouth bass spawn for the first time during their second or third spring, at about 18 to 21 cm TL. The first noticeable spawning activity is nest building by males, which starts when water temperatures reach 14 to 16°C, usually in April (Emig, 1966; K. Miller and Kramer, 1971). Spawning activity will often continue through June, at temperatures up to 24°C. Nests are generally shallow depressions fanned by the males in sand, gravel, or debris-littered bottoms at depths of 1 to 2 m. Rising waters in reservoirs may cause active nests to be located as deep as 4 to 5 m (K. Miller and Kramer, 1971). The nests are often build next to submerged objects and are rarely, if ever, in colonies such as are typical of sunfishes. Spawning and parental behavior is similar to that of smallmouth bass although defensive behavior by males seems to be less vigorous (Breder and Rosen, 1966). Each female lays, in one or more nests, a total of 2,000 to 94,000 or more eggs, the number depending on her size. The eggs adhere to the next substrate and hatch in two to five days. The sac fry then usually spend five to eight days in the nest or its vicinity (Emig, 1966).

Status. Largemouth bass are perhaps the most sought after warmwater gamefish in California. Many California reservoirs and farm ponds provide much excellent bass fishing, with sizable populations of large, fast-growing fish. Unfortunately, the overall quality of bass fishing in California has declined in recent years due to three main factors: overfishing, reservoir aging, and competition from threadfin shad and other plankton-feeding fishes (von Geldern, 1974).

Largemouth bass, being voracious predators, are extremely vulnerable to angling, which is one of the main reasons they are such popular gamefish. This means, however, that in many reservoirs at least half the population of legal-size fish are caught each year. If such fishing pressure is sustained for a number of years, the catch rate declines and the fish caught are, on the average, smaller. Proposed measures to remedy the situation are to establish Florida largemouth bass in heavily fished lakes, since they are less vulnerable to angling; set minimum size limits of 30 to 35 cm TL; and develop hatchery technology so that largemouth bass, which are near catchable sizes, can be planted (von Geldern, 1974).

In many reservoirs a decline in bass populations will occur regardless of fishing pressure. Such declines are often associated with aging of the reservoirs. For a variety of reasons, not fully understood, new reservoirs often develop outstanding populations of bass and other gamefishes which gradually decline as the reservoir matures. In some situations, the manipulation of reservoir water levels to increase food availability or spawning success may maintain relatively large populations of bass (Heman et al.,

1969). Such manipulation, however, is seldom possible because it is likely to conflict with the uses for which the reservoir water was originally intended, such as irrigation and power production.

It is somewhat ironic that plankton-feeding fishes, particularly threadfin shad, which were introduced in part to provide forage for largemouth bass, have also contributed to their decline in some reservoirs. Competition for zooplankton between shad and bass fry apparently greatly reduces the survival rate of the fry. Thus, when mild winters result in increased overwinter survival of shad, there tends to be poor spring survival of largemouth bass fry (von Geldern, 1974). Similar competition with the Mississippi silversides may be responsible for the apparent decline of largemouth bass populations in Clear Lake.

Despite the fact that largemouth bass occur mostly in habitats disturbed or created by man, in a few instances they have probably been at least partially responsible for the elimination of populations of native fishes through predation (Minckley, 1973). In California, their introduction into the Owens Valley seems to have been a major contributing factor to the decline and near extinction of the Owens pupfish (Miller and Pister, 1971).

References. Applegate et al., 1967; Breder and Rosen, 1966; Emig, 1966; Goodson, 1965; Heman et al., 1969; Hubbs and Bailey, 1940; Keast, 1966; Lewis, 1970; Lewis and Flickinger, 1967; Lewis et al., 1961; K. Miller and Kramer, 1971; R. Miller and Pister, 1971; Minckley, 1973; Moyle, 1969; Moyle and Nichols, 1973; Murphy, 1949; Scott, 1967; Seaburg and Moyle, 1964; Skinner, 1962; von Geldern, 1971, 1974.

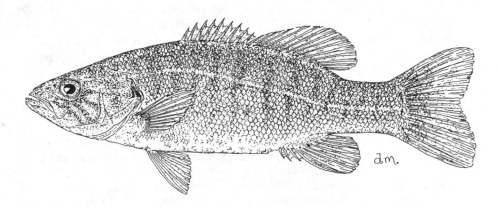

Figure 114. Smallmouth bass, 10 cm SL, Cache Creek, Yolo County.

Smallmouth Bass, *Micropterus dolomieui* Lacépède

Identification. Smallmouth bass are chunky bodied, with mouths (maxillae) that do not reach the hind margin of their eyes, broadly joined, spiny (9 to 10 spines) and soft (13 to 15 rays) portions of the dorsal fins, and no conspicuous horizontal stripes on the sides. Their anal fins have 3 spines and 10 to 12 rays; pectoral fins, 16 to 18 rays; and lateral lines, 66 to 78 scales. The scales on the cheeks (in 14 or more rows) are smaller than those on the opercula. Small scales are present near the bases of the soft portions of the dorsal and anal fins. Adults are greenish to dark brown olive on their sides, often with faint, vertical, dark mottled bars, and white on their bellies. There are three dark, faintly iridescent bands, radiating from the eyes and mouth, on the side of their heads. Young of the year are darker than the adults, with orange caudal fins tipped (submarginally) with single black bands.

Names. Dolomieui is after M. Dolomieu, a French minerologist who was apparently a colleague of Lacépède. A synonymy of the scientific nomenclature is given in Hubbs and Bailey (1940). Other names are as for largemouth bass.

Distribution. Smallmouth bass are native to most of the Mississippi River system, including the Great Lakes drainage, but they have been introduced into suitable waters throughout North America and other parts of the world. They were first introduced into central California in 1874 (Curtis 1949) and have since been spread to most of the larger streams in the Sacramento-San Joaquin system (including the Russian River) and into southern California.

Life History. The waters preferred by smallmouth bass are large, clear lakes and clear streams and rivers with many large pools, abundant cover, and cool (20 to 27°C) summer temperatures. In California, they are most abundant in the larger tributaries to the Sacramento and San Joaquin rivers, at elevations between 100 and 1,000 m. This is almost entirely in the squawfish-sucker-hardhead zone, so they are often associated with native minnows and suckers and, occasionally, rainbow trout. Their stream habitat has been considerably diminished by the flooding of many of the best areas by reservoirs. They have managed to become established in a number of reservoirs, however, where they are usually most abundant near the upstream ends. They also tend to concentrate in narrow bays or in areas along shore where rocky shelves project under water.

The social behavior of smallmouth bass is similar to that of largemouth bass, although smallmouth have less of a tendency to wander and are less solitary. In lakes, local populations of bass often develop that seldom exchange members with other populations (Forney, 1961). Feeding habits are also similar to largemouth bass. Smallmouth bass fry feed largely on crustaceans and aquatic insects until they are about 5 cm TL, when they start feeding heavily on fish. Smallmouth of all sizes are frequently cannibalistic. They are not, however, obligatory piscivores. Crayfish, amphibians, and insects often become dominant foods of local populations or seasonally (Webster, 1954; Emig, 1966; Applegate et al., 1967; Mullan and Applegate, 1968).

Growth in smallmouth bass seems to be somewhat less variable than it is for largemouth bass, presumably because smallmouth bass are more restricted in their habitat requirements. At the end of their first year, they range from 6 to 18 cm TL; at the end of their second, 14 to 27 cm TL; at the end of their third, 19 to 27 cm TL; and at the end of their fourth, 25 to 41 cm TL. Growth in Central Valley reservoirs is excellent, so four-year-old fish are typically 35 to 39 cm FL and older fish longer than 40 cm FL are not uncommon (Emig, 1966). Growth in California streams is presumably slower. The largest smallmouth bass known (from Kentucky) was 69 cm TL and weighed 5.4 kg.

Smallmouth bass usually become sexually mature for the first time during their third or fourth year. Their reproductive behavior is probably the best known of any member of the genus *Micropterus* (Webster, 1954; Latta, 1963; Emig, 1966; Breder and Rosen, 1966; Schneider, 1971). As the water warms up in the late spring, the bass move into shallow water in lakes or into quiet areas of streams. Some lake populations of bass will migrate short distances up a stream to spawn. The males start fanning out nest depressions, 30 to 60 cm in diameter, with their fins when water temperatures reach 13 to 16°C. They usually build the nests on gravel or sand bottoms at depths of 1 m, near submerged logs, boulders, or other cover, but nests have been recorded on substrates ranging from mud to roots to large rocks at depths down to 5 m.

Males defend their nest sites vigorously from other males and to a lesser extent from passing females. Ripe females eventually convince males of their identities by their persistence in returning to nests and other behavioral differences, and by changing color so the mottled markings on their sides become very distinct. Once a pair bond has formed, the pair of bass begins slowly circling above the nest, the male nipping the female on her sides. The female occasionally sinks into the nest and rubs her abdomen on the bottom. When they are ready to spawn, the pair settles into the nest, the male parallel with the bottom, the female at variable angles. Both fish stiffen, quiver, and release the sex products. The female releases 10 to 50 eggs at a time, in 4 to 45 second intervals. When spawning is finished the female leaves the nest or is chased away by the male. Females may spawn in more than one nest and males may spawn with more than one female. Females lay 2,000 to 21,000 eggs, depending on size.

The male guards the nest until the eggs hatch, usually in three to ten days. The newly hatched fry remain on the bottom of the nest for three to four days before they start to become active and rise off the bottom. The male then herds them together into a dense school, which he continues to guard for one to three weeks. By the time the fry reach 2 to 3 cm TL they are too active for the male to herd and they soon disperse into shallow water.

Status. Compared to largemouth bass, smallmouth bass are of minor importance as sport fish in California. Their populations are scattered, mostly small, and have probably declined as more dams have been built across foothill streams. However, the populations in the upper reaches of reservoirs like Pine Flat, Millerton, and Folsom provide excellent fishing for large, fast-growing fish. Rivers like the Merced, Stanislaus, and Russian also have substantial populations of smallmouth bass, although the bass tend to be smaller than those found in the reservoirs. All of these populations are probably underexploited.

In Arizona, smallmouth bass have apparently been responsible for reducing or eliminating populations of native fishes in some streams (Minckley, 1973). This may have happened in California as well, although it would be difficult to distinguish the effects of smallmouth bass predation from those of habitat destruction by man.

References. Applegate et al., 1967; Breder and Rosen, 1966; Cross, 1967; Emig, 1966; Forney, 1961; Hubbs and Bailey, 1940; Latta, 1963; Minckley, 1973; Moyle and Nichols, 1974; Mullan and Applegate, 1968; Schneider, 1971; Webster, 1954.

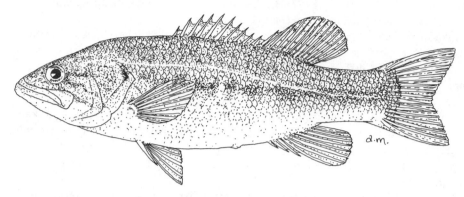

Figure 115. Spotted bass, 21 cm SL, Merle Collins Reservoir, Yuba County.

Spotted Bass, *Micropterus punctulatus* (Rafinesque)

Identification. Spotted bass look like smallmouth bass with single, irregular, black horizontal stripes on each side (made up of connecting blotches) and maxillae that extend past the middle of the eyes, occasionally even slightly beyond the hind margin of the eyes. The dorsal fins have 9 to 11 spines in the anterior half, which is not deeply notched where it attaches to the posterior half (9 to 11 rays). Their anal fins have 3 spines, 9 to 11 rays (usually 10); pectoral fins, 14 to 17 rays; lateral lines, 59 to 69 scales. The scales on their cheeks, in 12 to 17 rows (usually 13 to 16), are smaller than the scales on their opercula. Scales are usually present on or near the bases of the soft portions of their dorsal and anal fins. Their coloration is olivaceous on the back and white on the belly, with the blotched stripe in between. There are usually a series of smaller rows of spots below the midline stripe. The caudal fin of young of the year has a black spot at its base and is orangish with a black tip.

Names. Punctulatus means spotted. For other names see largemouth bass, with which spotted bass are commonly confused.

Distribution. Northern spotted bass (*M. punctulatus punctulatus*) were introduced into California from Ohio in 1933, propagated at the Central Valley Hatchery, and widely planted in foothill streams of the lower Sacramento and San Joaquin valleys (McKechnie, 1966). The only populations which are known to have become established are in the Consumnes River and the Feather River, especially in Oroville Reservoir. Alabama spotted bass (*M. punctulatus henshalli*) were planted in Perris Reservoir, San Bernadino County, in 1973 but it is not known yet if the population is maintaining itself (J. St. Amant, pers. comm.). Spotted bass are native to the Mississippi River system from Illinois southward, as well as to Georgia and the Gulf states.

Life History. Spotted bass seem to do well in three types of warm waters: small, clear creeks; moderate sized, clear, low-gradient (less than 0.5 m per km) sections of river; and reservoirs (McKechnie, 1966; Cross, 1967). In California they are found mostly in the latter two situations. In streams they are secretive pool dwellers, avoiding riffles and backwaters with heavy growths of aquatic plants. In reservoirs, adults tend to stay in fairly deep water, close to the bottom of the epilimnion, although the young generally remain near shore, in shallow water. Young-of-the-year are usually found in small schools (presumably of nest mates), but larger fish tend to be solitary. Each adult frequently remains in one limited area for most of the year, such as a single stream pool, but spawning migrations are common in the spring

(Gerking, 1953; Trautman, 1957). In reservoirs they may seek out deep water (30 to 40 m) following the fall overturn (McKechnie, 1966).

Like other basses, spotted bass are predators on the larger invertebrates and fish that occur with them. The diet changes with size, reflecting differences of both mouth size and habitat of the different life-history stages. In an Illinois stream, bass less than 75 mm TL fed mostly on aquatic insects and crustaceans while larger fish consumed, in order of importance, aquatic insects, fish, crayfish, and terrestrial insects. Crayfish and fish were increasingly important in larger fish (Smith and Page, 1969). In Arkansas reservoirs, bass under 50 mm TL fed mostly on terrestrial or aquatic insects, while larger fish fed heavily on fish and to a lesser extent on aquatic insects (Mullan and Applegate, 1968, 1970). Spotted bass commonly feed on their own young and those of other bass species.

Spotted bass are rather slow growing and short lived, so they seldom reach the sizes achieved by largemouth or smallmouth bass. They reach 66 to 155 mm TL in their first year, 152 to 323 mm TL in their second, and 207 to 406 mm TL in their third (Applegate et al., 1967). They seldom live longer than four to five years, so they seldom exceed 40 cm TL. The maximum size is about 51 cm TL and 2.9 kg (McKechnie, 1966). Growth rates of California populations have not been studied, but one of the main reasons for the recent experimental introduction of the Alabama subspecies by the California Department of Fish and Game is that it seems to grow faster and to achieve larger sizes than the northern subspecies already present (R. Rawstron, pers. comm.).

Maturity sets in during their second or third year and the bass spawn in late spring, when water temperatures rise above 18°C (Howland, 1931). Nests are constructed in low-current areas on bottoms ranging from mud to gravel. Breeding and parental behavior are similar to that of the smallmouth bass, except that males do not guard the young as long, probably because the young are rather active and soon leave the nest area. Spotted bass seem to be one of the least fecund of the black basses, with each nest producing only 2,000 to 2,500 young (Howland, 1931). This may be related to their comparatively small size at spawning.

Spotted bass have hybridized with smallmouth bass in California (R. Rawstron, pers. comm.). The extent and significance of this hybridization needs investigation, as does their entire life history.

Status. Spotted bass were originally introduced into California to occupy foothill river habitat that is intermediate between that preferred by largemouth and smallmouth bass. This type of habitat seems to be found only in the Feather and Consumnes rivers, where spotted bass have maintained populations now for nearly forty years. Their distribution in the state will probably be deliberately expanded only if the Alabama subspecies proves successful. Their main advantage over smallmouth and largemouth bass, which achieve larger sizes, is their reputation as a fish that puts up a superb fight on light tackle. They seem to have met with considerable approval from anglers who fish for them in Oroville Reservoir, although the fishery is a small one (R. Rawston, pers. comm.).

References. Cross, 1967; Gerking, 1953; Howland, 1931; Hubbs and Bailey, 1940; McKechnie, 1966; Minckley, 1973; Mullan and Applegate, 1968, 1970; Smith and Page, 1969; Trautman, 1957.

Redeye Bass*, *Micropterus coosae* Hubbs and Bailey

Identification. "A beautiful fish in every respect, the redeye bass has color characteristics not found in other basses. The eyes and fish are brick red, and the deep bronze back changes to a greenish or purplish cast, depending on the habitat. The transverse flexuous bands on the sides and the opercular and basal caudal spots are indistinct on fish of all sizes. The young of this species can be distinguished from the other basses by the absence of the subterminal black band across the caudal lobes and the red coloration of the fins" (Parsons, 1953, p. 202). There is no lateral band and the maxillae seldom extend beyond the middle of the eye. They have 9 to 11 dorsal spines and 11 to 13 (usually 12) dorsal soft rays, in shallowly notched dorsal fins. Their anal fins have 3 spines, 9 to 11 rays (usually 10); their pectoral fins, 14 to 17 rays (usually 15 to 16); their lateral lines, 67 to 72 scales. The scales on their cheeks, usually in 14 rows, are smaller than the opercular scales. Scales are usually present on the bases of the soft portions of the dorsal and anal fins.

Names. Prior to Hubbs and Bailey (1940), redeye bass were considered to be a small form of smallmouth bass. *Coosae* is after the Coosa River system in Georgia where the type specimens were collected. For other names see largemouth bass.

Distribution. Between 1962 and 1964, redeye bass were planted in Alder Creek (Sacramento County), Stanislaus River (Tuolumne County), Dry Creek (Nevada County), Santa Ana River (Riverside County), Sisquoc River (Santa Barbara County), and Santa Margarita River (San Diego County), but only the Sisquoc River population seems to be established (R. Rawstron, pers. comm.). Redeye bass are native to river systems that flow into the Gulf of Mexico, in Georgia, Alabama, Tennessee, and Florida.

Life History. Redeye bass are adapted for living in small, clear, upland streams of the Deep South and do poorly in most other situations, especially if other bass species are present. They were originally introduced into California because of the resemblance of many foothill streams to those of their native region. These streams usually do not support any gamefishes except squawfish. Most of what little is known about the biology of redeye bass is the result of the work of Parsons (1953) in Tennessee.

Redeye bass feed like trout. They are opportunistic predators that depend heavily on terrestrial insects. They also consume aquatic insects, fish, crayfish, fish eggs, and salamanders. They can be extremely slow growing, averaging as little as 2 to 3 cm per year and taking ten years to reach 25 cm TL, although in a Florida stream they reached 39 cm TL in five years (Parsons and Crittenden, 1959). Their maximum size seems to be close to 39 cm TL.

Redeye bass move up into small tributary streams or the heads of pools in larger streams to spawn in late spring, when temperatures rise to 17 to 21°C. They become mature at about 12 to 13 cm TL, presumably at two to four years of age. Fecundities are high, considering the size of the females: 2,084 and 2,334 eggs in 15 cm TL and 21 cm TL females, respectively. Spawning behavior is similar to that of smallmouth bass.

Status. The introduction of redeye bass in California has been, by and large, unsuccessful and interest in them has waned. Despite their bright colors and reputed tenacity as gamefish, their small size makes it unlikely that they would ever have

*Not illustrated.

achieved much popularity. Their inability to become established in streams of the Sierra Nevada foothills is particularly fortunate because this region is one of the few in California where native fish communities still exist in a relatively undisturbed state.

References. Goodson, 1966; Hubbs and Bailey, 1940; Kimsey, 1957; Parsons, 1953; Parsons and Crittenden, 1959.

Perch Family, Percidae

The perches are an exclusively freshwater group of fishes confined to temperate North America and Eurasia. None are native west of the Rocky Mountains in North America. They are readily distinguished from other freshwater spiny-rayed fishes with ctenoid scales and thoracic pelvic fins by their two well-separated dorsal fins (the first composed entirely of spines) and by the presence of only 1 to 2 spines in the anal fin.

There are three distinct subdivisions of the perch family: the darters, the walleye and pikeperches, and the yellow perches. The darters are an abundant (110+ species) and colorful group of small, slender, bottom fishes, native only to eastern North America. Like sculpins, they lack a functional air bladder. One darter species, the bigscale logperch (*Percina macrolepida*), has been introduced into California. Walleye (*Stizostedion vitreum*), like the European pikeperches of the same genus, are predaceous inhabitants of the deep water of lakes. They are a favorite sport and commercial fish in midwestern North America where they are native. Because of this popularity they have been introduced throughout the United States. Introductions into California reservoirs, most recently El Capitan Reservoir in San Diego County, have so far been unsuccessful due to lack of reproduction and catches by anglers have been low. The yellow perch (*Perca flavescens*), a favorite prey of the walleye where the two species occur together naturally, is the only member of the perch family besides the bigscale logperch which has been successfully introduced into California.

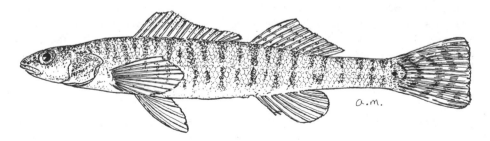

Figure 116. Bigscale logperch, 6.2 cm SL, Putah Creek, Yolo County.

Bigscale Logperch, *Percina macrolepida* Stevenson

Systematic note. Bigscale logperch were recently described from Texas by Stevenson (1971). They were formerly considered to be part of the logperch (*P. caprodes*) species complex. Bigscale logperch in California were thus originally identified as *P. caprodes*. Jamie Sturgess, a graduate student of the author, in the course of an investigation of the life history of the California population, recognized that they were in reality bigscale logperch, a fact confirmed by Dr. Stevenson.

Identification. Bigscale logperch are long and slender, readily recognized by their pointed, projecting snouts, yellowish bodies with 14 to 16 complete dark vertical stripes and a dark spot at the base of the tail, two well-separated dorsal fins, and small size (usually less than 12 cm SL). The scales are ctenoid and cover the breast, cheeks, opercles, and nape. A few scales are sometimes present on the top of the head (supra-occipital region) but they are usually lacking in California fish. There is a row of large spiny scales on the belly and 77 to 90 scales along the lateral line. The first dorsal fin has 13 to 15 spines; the second dorsal, 12 to 15 rays; the anal fin, 2 spines and 7 to 10 rays; and the pelvic fins, 1 spine and 5 rays each. The pectoral fins are enlarged and fan-shaped, with 13 to 15 rays. Breeding males may become dark on their heads and sides, and have an orange bar on their dorsal fins.

Names. *Percina* means little perch, while *macrolepida* means big scales. In clear streams they can frequently be observed resting on submerged logs, hence logperch.

Distribution. Bigscale logperch occur in a number of drainage systems in Texas, Oklahoma, and northeastern Mexico (Stevenson, 1971). They were accidentally imported into California from the Trinity River, Texas (M. M. Stevenson, pers. comm.) in 1953 by the U.S. Fish and Wildlife Service. They were apparently mixed in with a shipment of largemouth bass and bluegill planted in three small lakes on Beale Air Force Base, Yuba County (McKechnie, 1966). During wet years these lakes overflow into a small tributary of the Yuba River. As a result, bigscale logperch are now abundant in sloughs of the lower Sacramento River and Delta. At the present time they seem to be rapidly extending their range in the Sacramento-San Joaquin system. They are now common in the lower Sacramento River and Delta and have been collected as far south in the San Joaquin Valley as Mendota (Farley, 1972; Moyle, Fisher, and Li, 1974). Further extensions of their range can be expected in the near future.

Life History. Bigscale logperch are found in a wide variety of lake and stream habitats. They are most common in the slower moving stretches of warm, clear streams or in the shallow waters of lakes, on bottoms of mud, gravel, rock, sticks, or large pieces of debris. In California they are most abundant in the muddy bottomed, turbid sloughs of the Delta and lower Sacramento River. They have also been found in the warm summer pools of the intermittent sections of Cache Creek, Yolo County.

Bigscale logperch are incapable of sustained swimming so they spend most of their time motionless on the bottom, where their barred color pattern makes them very difficult to see, even in clear water. They move only for short distances at one time, usually propelling themselves with quick, short sweeps of the pectoral fins. Although they commonly occur in small groups, neither schooling nor territorial behavior seems to be well developed, at least outside the breeding season.

When feeding, bigscale logperch visually inspect the bottom around them for food organisms, occasionally flipping over twigs, leaves, and small rocks with their projecting snouts. They will also rise quickly from the bottom to snap up small, free-swimming organisms. They are highly opportunistic in their feeding. Usually whatever insect larvae are most abundant dominate the stomach contents, together with amphipods and planktonic crustaceans. Planktonic crustaceans tend to be most important in the diet of young logperch. Examination of the stomachs of 121 logperch from sloughs of the Delta in the winter and spring of 1973 revealed a wide variety of insect larvae (chironomid midge, mayfly, beetle, stonefly, damselfly, dragonfly) as well as crustaceans (copepods, cladocerans, amphipods, *Neomysis*). Fish eggs were found in a number of the fish (J. Sturgess and R. Hobbs, manuscript). Logperch collected from a recently flooded grassy area were feeding on earthworms, while those collected in small sloughs were feeding heavily (50 percent by volume) on copepods.

Little is known about age and growth in bigscale logperch. In the Delta, one-year-old fish ranged from 48 to 81 mm SL (mean, 63 mm) and two-year-olds from 75 to 102 mm SL (mean, 90 mm). A single three-year-old fish was 104 mm SL (J. Sturgess and R. Hobbs, manuscript).

Logperch usually mature in their second year. Spawning of recently captured fish has been observed in aquaria in late February (J. Sturgess, pers. comm.). Unlike most darters, logperch are not strongly territorial. Bigscale logperch collected from California sloughs have spawned in a vertical position in aquaria, depositing the eggs on the stems of aquatic plants (J. Sturgess, pers. comm.). This behavior is different from that of other *Percina* species, which spawn in gravel riffles (Winn, 1958a,b), and may explain why they have managed to become so abundant in sloughs. Only 10 to 20 eggs are laid at each spawning, so each female spawns many times, with different males, over an extended period.

Status. Bigscale logperch populations in California are apparently still expanding. What effect they have on native and game fishes is not known. Since they have been found so far primarily in disturbed lowland areas where there were no other small bottom fishes, they presumably do not compete much for food with the other fishes present. On the other hand, large populations (which are so characteristic of a newly introduced animal rapidly expanding its range) could locally deplete bottom invertebrates or have significant effects as fish-egg predators. Logperch (*P. caprodes*) have low value as forage fish; they are seldom found in the stomachs of gamefishes (Mullan and Applegate, 1968). McKechnie (1966) states: "(Bigscale) logperch add nothing to our fauna and do not benefit our fisheries." However, it must be admitted that they do make interesting and attractive aquarium fish. In addition, their populations seem to be depleted in at least part of their native range (R. R. Miller, pers. comm.), so the California populations may be able to serve as a source for their reintroduction into native streams at some future date.

References. Cross, 1967; Faber, 1967; Farley, 1972; Keast and Webb, 1966; McKechnie, 1966; Moyle, Fisher, and Li, 1974; Mullan and Applegate, 1968; Winn, 1958a,b.

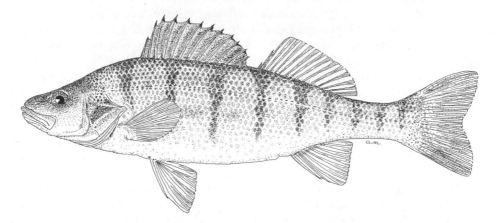

Figure 117. Yellow perch, 19 cm SL, Iron Gate Reservoir, Siskiyou County.

Yellow Perch, *Perca flavescens* (Mitchill)

Identification. Yellow perch can be readily recognized by their yellow bodies with 6 to 8 dark vertical bars on each side, their two well-separated dorsal fins, and the two spines (with 7 to 8 rays) in their anal fins. Their bodies are moderately deep (standard length 3 times depth) and their heads large (25 percent or more of total length). There is a single small spine on each operculum. The first dorsal fin has 13 to 15 spines; the second dorsal, 2 to 3 spines and 13 to 15 rays; and the pelvic fins, 1 spine and 5 rays each. The scales are large (54 to 70 in the lateral line) and ctenoid. The pectoral and pelvic fins, usually yellow, may become reddish orange in spawning males.

Names. Perch (and hence *Perca*) is derived from the ancient Greek word for dusky, perhaps a reference to the dusky back and bars of the European perch. *Flavescens* means yellow. Good arguments can be raised for regarding the American perch as a subspecies of the very similar European perch, *P. fluviatilis* (McPhail and Lindsey, 1970).

Distribution. Yellow perch are abundant in reservoirs (especially Copco Lake) and dredge ponds of the Klamath River, where they were first discovered in 1946 (Coots, 1956). They have since been found all the way down to the mouth of the river. These fish are presumably descendents of perch planted in the upper Klamath River in Oregon. The only official introductions of the yellow perch into California were those made into some southern California reservoirs and the Sacramento River between 1891 and 1918. The perch became established in the Sacramento River and the Delta but apparently were never particularly abundant. These populations declined, holding out in sloughs of the Delta into the 1950s. There seem to be no recent records from the Sacramento-San Joaquin system.

Yellow perch are native to the northern half of North America ease of the Rocky Mountains, north as far as the Mackenzie River in Canada, south through the Great Lakes region, and down the Atlantic coast to South Carolina. They have been introduced into most of the western states.

Life History. Yellow perch usually inhabit the weedy backwaters of rivers, the shallow waters of lakes, and large ponds. They do best in warmwater situations but occasionally large populations of stunted fish become established in lakes cold enough to support trout. In lakes they are almost always associated with heavy growths of aquatic plants and tend to occur in loose schools on or just above the plant beds, at depths of 1 to 10 meters. Schooling is the typical social behavior pattern of adult perch. Even in aquaria they swim together and seldom exhibit any aggressive interactions. The schools are larger and more compact for immature perch (less than 10 cm TL) than they are for adults, reflecting the fact that the young inhabit the open waters, usually at depths of 1 to 4 m, rather than the aquatic plant zone.

The feeding habits of perch change with size and thus with habitat. Larval and juvenile perch are primarily zooplankton feeders, but the variety of organisms consumed increases with size. As the schools of young perch move into shallow water, invertebrates associated with the bottom and with aquatic plants gradually become more important in their diet, especially aquatic insect larvae, snails, and various crustaceans. Adult perch browse methodically among the aquatic plants and along the bottom, selecting the larger invertebrates such as crayfish, dragonfly larvae, and snails. Small fish may also be important in the diet. The terminal scooplike mouth with its protrusible lips and small teeth is well suited for capturing such prey (Keast and Webb, 1966). In the Klamath River, the main foods are small crustaceans, snails, aquatic insect larvae, and fish, mostly minnows, suckers, and sunfish (Coots, 1956). Yellow perch are capable of capturing small salmonids but no evidence has been found so far that they do so. Most feeding takes place during the day, with peaks of activity in the morning and at dusk (Keast and Welsh, 1968).

Growth of perch in the Klamath River is slow but similar to growth observed in other waters. They average 9 cm TL by the end of their first year, 15 cm TL by the end of the second, 20 cm TL by the end of the third, 23 cm TL by the end of the fourth, and 27 cm TL by the end of the fifth (Coots, 1956). Elsewhere, yellow perch may reach (rarely) 53 cm TL, 1.9 kg, and thirteen years, although a perch exceeding 30 cm TL, 0.4 kg, and five years would be unusual in California. It is not unusual for large populations of stunted perch to develop in small bodies of water where overcrowding reduces growth through severe intraspecific competition.

Yellow perch are usually ready to spawn during their second year. Spawning takes place over submerged beds of aquatic plants in quiet water, at temperatures ranging from 7 to 14°C. The first sign of spawning, which takes place in April and May in the Klamath River, is the presence of large schools of ripe adult perch over the plant beds. Prior to spawning, the females become restless and swim slowly around the spawning area. Periodically, males in small groups swim up to a cruising female and follow her for a short distance, nudging her vent. When the female is ready to spawn, she makes a series of rapid turns or other quick movements. Two to three males quickly approach her and start jockeying for a position immediately below her vent. The female then starts swimming rapidly, releasing a long string of eggs enclosed in a gelatinous sheath. As the eggs are released, the males in turn release a cloud of sperm, enveloping the eggs (Hergenrader, 1969). The strands of eggs may be as long as 2 m, but are more typically 30 to 50 cm long. They are draped over the aquatic plants. Each female lays 5,000 to 76,000 eggs, the number being proportional to the length of the fish (Tsai and Gibson, 1971).

The eggs hatch in ten to twenty days. The larvae, about 6 mm TL, may start to feed on zooplankton soon after hatching but they possess some reserve food in the yolk sac until they reach about 7 mm TL (Houde, 1969). The larvae are attracted to light, so they swim up into the surface waters. Since they are weak swimmers, they are at the mercy of lake and stream currents for the first few weeks.

Status. Yellow perch are a favorite gamefish in many parts of their range, and are of considerable commercial importance in Canada. Their firm white flesh is quite tasty and they are readily caught on live bait (especially worms and minnows) and small spinners. However, they are not particularly desirable for California since they are smaller and slower growing than most other gamefishes. They can also survive and reproduce in some trout lakes, reducing the growth of trout by competing with them for food. In such cold waters they are usually too small themselves to be worth fishing for.

Although they are abundant in reservoirs and ponds along the Klamath River, the fishery for them is small. Most yellow perch caught there are taken incidentally by trout, salmon, and catfish anglers. Hopefully, they will never be reintroduced into the Sacramento-San Joaquin system or elsewhere in California.

References. C. J. Brown, 1971; Coots, 1956; Hergenrader, 1969; Houde, 1969; Hsai and Gibson, 1971; Keast and Webb, 1966; Keast and Welsh, 1968; McPhail and Lindsey, 1970; Moyle, 1969a.

Cichlid Family, Cichlidae

The cichlids are an abundant and diverse group of sunfishlike fishes, native to Africa, the Middle East, southern India, South America, and Central America north to the Rio Grande in Texas. They are favored as aquarium fishes because of their fascinating breeding habits (many incubate their eggs in the mouth), bright colors, and pugnacious behavior. Most cichlids are pond and lake dwellers and are very prolific. As a result, they have been promoted throughout the tropical and subtropical areas of the world as a source of low-cost protein. In the United States they are also promoted as gamefish and for aquatic-weed control. Consequently, cichlids have been released throughout the southern United States. As Hubbs (1968) points out, most of these releases have been ill advised, without enough consideration being given to the long-term effects of the introductions.

At the present time, the cichlids established in California are all members of the generalized genus *Tilapia*. These are large-headed, moderately deep-bodied fishes with two incomplete lateral lines, a long dorsal fin, and two or more rows of teeth in the jaws. In 1971, the California Department of Fish and Game authorized the introduction of three spieces of *Tilapia* (*mossambica, hornorum,* and *zillii*) for weed control in irrigation canals of southern California (Pelzman, 1973). The introductions of *T. mossambica* and *T. zillii* have been moderately successful and their effects on aquatic flora and fauna are now under study (W. J. Hauser, pers. comm.).

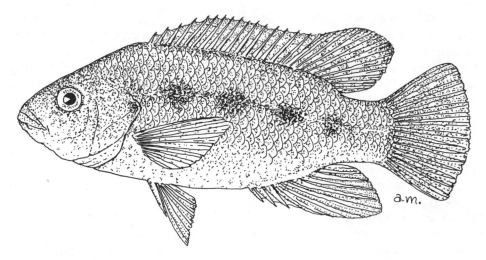

Figure 118. Mozambique mouthbrooder, 17 cm SL, Imperial County.

Mozambique Mouthbrooder, *Tilapia mossambica* (Peters)

Identification. The snout of Mozambique mouthbrooders is bluntly pointed with a large mouth that usually extends to or past the outer margin of the eye. The scales are cycloid, 29 to 33 in the lateral series, and are in 2 to 3 rows on the cheek below the eye. The dorsal fin has 15 to 16 spines, 10 to 12 rays; the anal fin has 3 to 4 spines, 9 to 10 rays; the pectoral fins have 14 to 15 rays each. The caudal fin is rounded. The gill rakers are short, 14 to 20 on the first arch. The color is highly variable due to the interbreeding of fish of different origins. However, females and nonbreeding males are normally a pale grey to washed-out yellow in color, with 3 to 4 dark spots generally visible on the sides. Spawning males have enlarged mouths and blue thickened upper lips; their bodies turn black, often with mottling or an iridescent blue tinge; the throat and lower part of the head become pale while the dorsal fin becomes black with a red border, the caudal fin gets a wide red band at the end, and the pectoral fins turn red. The fins are free of distinct spotting.

Names. *Tilapia* is derived from the native African (Bechuana) word *thlape* meaning fish, while *mossambica* describes the geographic area to which they are native (Jubb, 1967). In the older literature, *T. mossambica* is sometimes referred to as *T. natalensis*. The Mozambique mouthbrooder was, until recently, considered to have two distinct strains, the Javanese strain and the Zanzibar strain. The latter strain is now considered to be a distinct species, *T. hornorum.*

Distribution. Mozambique mouthbrooders are native to coastal streams of southeast Africa, especially the Zambesi River, Mozambique. They have been widely introduced into tropical and subtropical regions of the world including the southern United States, Arizona, and California. In California they are established in the irrigation systems of Imperial, Palo Verde, and Bard valleys, Imperial and Riverside counties (St. Amant, 1966a; Hoover and St. Amant, 1970) and in the lower Colorado River, near the Mexican border (E. McClendon, pers. comm.). The first fish to become established, in the early 1960s, were probably escapees from a tropical-fish farm but these were augmented by authorized introductions in the late 1960s and early 1970s. Attempts to establish them in the San Diego area have so far failed but their popularity with anglers will probably soon result in their being illegally established wherever California waters will support them.

Life History. Although Mozambique mouthbrooders are native to tropical Africa, they can survive temperatures as low as 5°C and as high as 43°C for short periods of time. The normal range for living, however, seems to be 11 to 38°C, with the optimum for growth around 30°C (St. Amant, 1966b). In California ponds they usually suffer heavy mortalities when water temperatures drop below 12°C for long periods of time (Hoover, 1971). They normally inhabit fresh water but they are capable of living and breeding in sea water (Brock and Takata, 1954; Jubb, 1967). The preferred habitat seems to be warm, weedy ponds, canals, and river backwaters. In the lower Colorado River they are abundant mostly in areas influenced by warm, salty irrigation water (E. McClendon, pers. comm.).

The long coiled intestines and studies of feeding habits of Mozambique mouthbrooders suggest that they are largely herbivorous, feeding on planktonic algae and aquatic plants (Kelly, 1957; Avault et al., 1966). However, since they lack the enzyme cellulase and since algae cells pass unbroken through the gut, their ability to digest much of the algae they ingest has been questioned (Fryer and Iles, 1972). Aquatic invertebrates always make up at least part of the diet and are especially important in the diet of young fish. Fish raised in an effluent pond near San Diego fed mostly on a variety of aquatic insect larvae, amphipods, and some adult insects (St. Amant, 1966b). In aquaria they will readily capture and eat small fishes, as well as taking various kinds of artificial foods. Thus, they appear to be rather omnivorous and nonselective in their feeding. This may explain in part why they have not been shown to be particularly effective in controlling either aquatic plants or mosquito larvae (Avault et al., 1966; St. Amant, 1966b), except in small experimental ponds (Legner and Medved, 1973). Their ability to act as biological control agents is further complicated by the territorial behavior of adult males. Because the males will drive all other *Tilapia* out of their territories, wild populations seldom reach densities needed for weed or insect control (Legner et al., 1973).

The ability of *Tilapia* to grow extremely rapidly in ponds is one of the main reasons they have been distributed over much of the tropical world after they were first promoted for pond culture in the late 1930s. In experimental ponds in Alabama, they grew in eighteen weeks from an average of 73 mm TL and 6.6 gm to 166 mm and 42.8 gm (Kelly, 1957). In California, all-male hybrids between *T. mossambica* and *T. hornorum* grew in experimental ponds at rates of 25 to 61 mm per month (St. Amant, 1966b) while in more natural situations they grew at maximum rates of 23 to 28 mm per month (Hoover, 1971). Males grow faster and get larger than females, achieving a maximum size of about 39 cm TL and a maximum age of eleven years (Fryer and Iles, 1972). The maximum size achieved so far in California seems to be about 38 cm TL (W. Hauser, pers. comm.).

Mozambique mouthbrooders usually become mature at lengths of 12 to 14 cm TL, a size they can reach in less than six months after hatching. They will breed continually as long as water temperatures are above 20°C. Breeding begins when the males leave the schools of nonbreeding fish and establish territories in shallow, weedy areas. They clear an area about 30 cm in diameter of weeds and then dig a shallow pit. From that time on the males are continually active, digging, courting, spawning, feeding, and fighting with neighboring fish (Baerends and Baerends-Van Roon, 1950). Courtship begins with the male approaching a school of females with special invitation displays. If a female is ready to spawn she follows the male back to his territory, which they circle around, the female occasionally biting at the bottom. During the circling the female suddenly releases a number of eggs. She then turns around and takes them into her mouth. The male ejects milt at the spot the eggs were dropped and the female takes the milt into her mouth as well, fertilizing the eggs with "mumbling movements" of the jaw (Baerends and Baerends-Van Roon, 1950). This act is repeated until the female has laid 100 to 400 eggs, the number depending on her size. Once spawning is completed, the male chases the female out of the territory and starts courting other females.

For the next eleven to twelve days the female goes into hiding while she incubates the eggs. By the end of the incubation period the young are capable of swimming by themselves and are ejected by the female. They then form a school that follows the female around. When a threatening fish approaches, the female attacks it. If unsuccessful in driving the intruder away, the female will call the young to her mouth with special movements. They then enter it or cluster around her head. This behavior ceases after four to eight days and the young are on their own (Baerends and Baerends-Van Roon, 1950).

Status. Mozambique mouthbrooders appear to be well established in irrigation systems of the lower Colorado River Basin. As Hoover and St. Amant (1970) pointed out, their range in California will undoubtedly be extended by misinformed anglers. For anglers, the main advantage of *T. mossambica* is their ability to grow and reproduce rapidly in warm waters which will not produce satisfactory fishing for sunfishes (Kelly, 1957; McConnell, 1966). In ponds, if the fish are not harvested at a high rate, their rapid rate of reproduction will soon produce a large population of stunted fish. Such stunting can be prevented by stocking all-male hybrids of *T. mossambica* and *T. hornorum* (St. Amant, 1966b) but this would require a major hatchery operation if done in any quantity. Although the present range of *T. mossambica* is limited by their intolerance of low temperatures, selective breeding in a hatchery for temperature tolerance or even natural selection in marginal areas where they have been planted might produce strains that could live in the cooler waters of California.

Introducing Mozambique mouthbrooders elsewhere into California is not particularly desirable. Their growth in most of the state's natural waters would probably be at best not much better than that of the sunfishes already present. They also could compete with established gamefishes for food and space. In addition, they seem to have only limited value for either mosquito or aquatic-weed control, even under an optimal temperature regime.

Perhaps the biggest disadvantage of any program using *T. mossambica* is that it may lead to other species of *Tilapia* that have lower temperature tolerances becoming established in the state. A mistake in identifying *Tilapia* imported from elsewhere would be easy to make. Thus, Pelzman (1972) strongly recommended against the importation of *T. sparrmani* since it could become established in central California and presumably compete with gamefishes. *T. aurea* (= *T. nilotica*) and *T. zillii* could probably likewise become established. Unfortunately, most workers with *Tilapia* recommend it as a sport fish or aquatic-weed control agent, even though most of the studies have been done in experimental ponds or aquaria. The effects of *Tilapia* on established aquatic systems and on other fish species, especially centrarchids, is seldom considered. It seems that the safest course for California would be to ban the importation of all *Tilapia* species north of the Tehachapi Mountains, except for experimentation under controlled conditions. This ban would have to include the home aquarium market for the entire state since aquarists frequently release unwanted charges into natural waters.

References. Avault et al., 1966; Baerends and Baerends-Van Roon, 1950; Brock and Takata, 1954; Fryer and Iles, 1972; Hoover, 1971; Hoover and St. Amant, 1970; Jubb, 1967; Kelly, 1957; Legner and Medved, 1973; Legner, Fisher, and Medved, 1973; McConnell, 1966; Pelzman, 1972; St. Amant, 1966a,b.

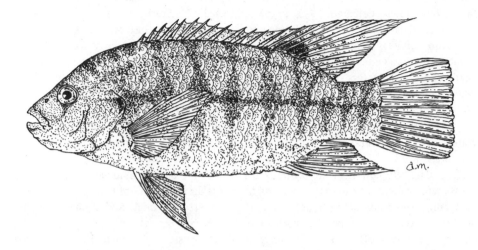

Figure 119. Zill's cichlid, 12 cm SL, Imperial County.

Zill's Cichlid, *Tilapia zillii* (Gervais)

Identification. This *Tilapia* has the typical cichlid body, elongate yet deep and laterally compressed, and the long dorsal fin. The dorsal fin has 14 to 16 spines and 10 to 13 rays, many of the latter considerably longer than the spines. The anal fin has 3 to 4 spines, 7 to 10 rays, and the pectorals have 14 to 15 rays each. There are 28 to 30 cycloid scales in the lateral series. The 8 to 12 gill rakers are shorter than those of Mozambique mouthbrooders. The typical nonbreeding coloration is dark olive on the back and light olive or yellow brown on the sides, the sides often with an iridescent sheen and 6 to 7 poorly defined vertical bars. The belly is yellow to white and the fins are brown to yellow. The dorsal fin has a dark "eye-spot" on the soft-rayed portion, often outlined in yellow, along with numerous small yellow spots on the entire fin. The operculum also has a distinct dark spot. Spawning fish become shiny dark green on the back and sides, with red and black on the throat and belly and distinct vertical bands on the sides. Their heads turn dark blue black, mottled with blue green spots.

Names. There is no widely used common name for this species since most fisheries workers simply use the easily pronounced scientific name. Zill's cichlid is, however, used by Sterba (1959). The fish is named for M. Zill, a naturalist who provided Paul Gervais with the specimen upon which the species description was based. *Tilapia* is discussed under *T. mossambica.*

Distribution. Zill's cichlid is native to north and west Africa and the Middle East, although its distribution in this region has been considerably expanded by man (Lowe, 1955). They are being widely introduced into the warmer parts of the world for aquaculture and aquatic-weed control. In the United States they are present today in Hawaii, Arizona, and California (Pelzman, 1973). In California they are well established in the irrigation systems of the Imperial Valley. They are probably also established in the Coachella and Palo Verde valleys, and have been reported from a few ponds in Kern and Santa Clara counties (Pelzman, 1973). The latter populations do not seem to have become established permanently. They have recently been planted in over twenty ponds, lakes, and creeks in Los Angeles, Orange, and Riverside counties (R. Pelzman, pers. comm.) but the status of these populations is not known.

Life History. Because of their potential for aquaculture and aquatic-weed control, as well as their readiness to breed in aquaria, the life history of Zill's cichlid is fairly well known (Pelzman, 1973; Fryer and Iles, 1972; Sterba, 1959).

Zill's cichlids normally inhabit large lakes and rivers but they adapt well to ponds, irrigation ditches, and other artificial habitats. They are particularly well suited to saline irrigation waters such as exist in the Imperial Valley, since populations have been reported in waters of 29 to 35 ppt salinity. They are also capable of living at a wide range of temperatures and are able to survive, for varying periods of time, temperatures as low as 8 to 10°C. In Napa County, Zill's cichlid survived two winters in ponds with temperatures that dropped down to 10°C but died during the third winter when temperatures dropped even lower for an extended period of time (Pelzman, 1973).

Regardless of where they are found, Zill's cichlids are usually associated with aquatic plants which form an important part of the adult diet. Their dentition is well-adapted to feeding on plants. The inner rows of jaw teeth are small and multicuspid, for holding onto leaves, while the teeth in the outer row are sharp and incisorlike, for cutting the leaves off. The leaves are ground up by stout pharyngeal teeth. Despite their specialized dentition and the publicity these cichlids have received as herbivores, they actually appear to be omnivorous, consuming invertebrates (especially those associated with aquatic plants) as well as algae and higher plants. Occasionally they will even take other fish, usually individuals that are already dead or dying (Pelzman, 1973). Young Zill's cichlids are more carnivorous than the adults and seem to depend on small crustaceans during the first few months of life.

Long-established populations of Zill's cichlids typically do not grow very fast, even in their native Africa where they reach 5 to 12 cm TL in the first year. They can double in size in the next one to two years, reaching 14 to 25 cm TL by the end of their third year; males grow faster than females. However, in irrigation systems of the Imperial Valley with low fish densities and abundant food, Zill's cichlids grow exceptionally fast, reaching an average of 17 cm TL in their first year and 25 cm TL in their second. The largest two-year-old fish known from these ditches was 315 mm TL and weighed 708 gm (W. J. Hauser, pers. comm.). In Africa, fish over 35 cm TL and 800 gm are rare, and are likely to be over six years old. Under crowded pond conditions, however, growth is often exceedingly slow and the fish may take two years to reach 7 cm TL, a size at which they will breed. Normally they reach 13 to 14 cm TL before breeding, although in Imperial Valley ditches, males and females may become mature at 7 to 8 cm TL and 11 to 12 cm TL, respectively (Legner and Hauser, unpublished data).

The breeding behavior of Zill's cichlid was described and illustrated by Sterba (1959) and Fryer and Iles (1972). It is unusual for a member of the genus *Tilapia* in that no mouthbrooding takes place. Instead, the fish lay their eggs in sand or mud buttoms, constructing a nest depression much like that of sunfishes (*Lepomis*). Courtship and pair formation begin once the water has warmed up to about 20°C. Once a pair bond has formed, the two fish build the nest, defend the territory around it, court, and spawn. The eggs are often laid in rows of 50 to 100 and then fertilized. Egg laying continues until 1,000 to 6,000 have been laid. The site of egg laying, although usually in the territory of the pair, is not necessarily the nest, which seems to be built more as part of courtship than as a necessity for incubation. One or both members of the pair tend the eggs by fanning a current of water across them or by picking out debris and dead eggs. The eggs hatch in two to three days. During incubation, the pair constructs one or more small depressions nearby. After hatching, the young are transferred by mouth or by fin fanning to the depressions where they remain for three to four days until the yolk sac is absorbed and they become free-swimming. The school of fry is abandoned by the parents in another one to two days and within a month the pair may spawn again. Under optimal temperature and food conditions, Zill's cichlid will apparently breed throughout the year, but in southern California water temperatures are probably suitable for breeding for less than six months. Even so, each pair would presumably be capable of producing four to six broods in this time.

Status. As a result of the authorized introductions in 1971, Zill's cichlid is well established in southern California. The decision to introduce them was ill-advised, since it seems to have been made with limited knowledge of their temperature tolerances and their ability to control aquatic weeds. Zill's cichlid may be capable of living in at least the San Joaquin Valley, although heavy die-offs occur even in the winter waters of the warm Imperial Valley (W. J. Hauser, pers. comm.). Their spread to the Central Valley is a distinct possibility, given the ease at which some uninformed fisherman, farmer, or biologist could transfer them. Should they become established, they will add little to the fishery due to their small size. If their ability to consume aquatic plants is as great as their proponents claim, they may actually destroy the aquatic weed beds in natural waters that are needed by other fishes for food production or cover.

Zill's cichlid is in fact quite effective in controlling weeds in the canals of the Imperial and Coachella valleys, although control is best achieved by making large annual plants of artificially reared fish (W. J. Hauser, pers. comm.). In low numbers, they seem to be rather selective in the plants they will eat. Thus, the main effect of wild populations may be to change the composition of the aquatic plant community, without affecting plant density. Because of doubts over their impact on established aquatic communities, Pelzman (1973) has recommended that the California Department of Fish and Game ban the species from central and northern California and attempt to control its distribution in the southern regions, at least until more is known about its biology.

References. Fryer and Iles, 1972; Lowe, 1955; Minckley, 1973; Pelzman, 1973; Sterba, 1959.

Surfperch Family, Embiotocidae

The surfperches are twenty species of live-bearing fishes found mostly in the shallow waters of the Pacific Ocean along the coast of North America. Only one species, the tule perch, occurs exclusively in fresh water, although the shiner perch often enters the mouths of Pacific coast streams. Five other species have been recorded from stream mouths also, but they do not occur on a regular basis. Surfperches are deep-bodied, spiny-rayed fishes, distinguished by a scaled ridge that runs along the base of the dorsal fin. However, the surfperch feature that has fascinated biologists since 1853, when Louis Agassiz described the family for the first time, is their viviparity; they give birth to young rather than laying eggs as most marine fish do. The embryos develop in the enlarged ovaries of the female and obtain nourishment for growth by absorbing the rich ovarian fluid which surrounds them. The dorsal and anal fins of the embryo are large and vascular and lie in close contact with the convoluted, vascularized ovarian wall, indicating that they are used to obtain oxygen from the blood of the mother fish. The young fish can become sexually mature soon after they are born.

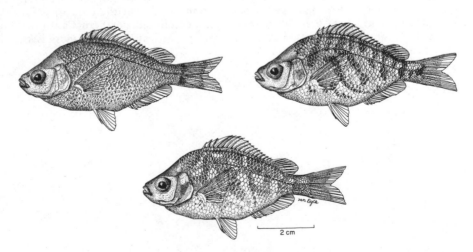

Figure 120. Tule perch, each 6 cm SL, showing color phases, unbarred (top left), narrow barred (top right), wide barred (bottom), Russian River, Mendocino County.

Tule Perch, *Hysterocarpus traski* Gibbons

Identification. Tule perch are small (to 15 cm TL), deep-bodied fish with small, terminal mouths. Adults often have a pronounced hump between the head and the dorsal fin. The dorsal fin has 15 to 19 spines and 9 to 15 rays. The rays make up 24 to 38 percent of the length of the dorsal fin. The anal fin has 3 spines and 20 to 26 rays, with a fleshy enlargement of the anterior portion in males. The pectoral fins have 17 to 19 rays and the lateral line has 34 to 43 scales. The color of living fish is variable but the back is generally dark, often a bluish or purplish, while the belly color ranges from white to yellow. There are three color phases (pictured above) related to the bars on the sides: wide barred, narrow barred, and unbarred.

Names. Hysterocarpus means womb-fruit, referring to their viviparity; *traski* is in honor of Dr. J. B. Trask who sent the first specimens to the describer, W. P. Gibbons, in 1854. Tule is the Aztec word, modified by the Spaniards, for bulrush (*Scirpus* spp.) with which the perch are commonly associated.

Distribution. Tule perch are native to low-elevation waters of the Sacramento-San Joaquin River system, as well as to Clear Lake, Coyote Creek, and the Russian, Napa, Pajaro, and Salinas rivers. In the Pit River (and its reservoirs) they occur as far up as the large falls in Shasta County. They are now apparently extinct in the Pajaro, Salinas, and San Joaquin rivers. Hopkirk (1962, 1973) recognized three subspecies, *H. traski lagunae* from Clear Lake, *H. traski pomo* from the Russian River, and *H. t. traski* from the rest of Sacramento-San Joaquin system. The validity of these subspecies has been questioned by Hubbs (1974). Populations of the latter have recently become established in O'Neill Forebay of San Luis Reservoir, Merced County, and in the nearby retention reservoir on Los Banos Creek.

Life History. Tule perch are basically inhabitants of large, low-elevation streams. In these streams they occupy a wide range of habitats, from sluggish, turbid channels in the Delta to clear, swift-flowing sections of river. Despite their deep bodies, they can live in fast water by taking advantage of eddies behind submerged boulders and logs, or by staying in the slower moving backwaters and edges. In most situations they are associated with beds of emergent aquatic plants or overhanging banks. These areas are important for feeding, breeding territories, and protection of young of the year. Tule perch seldom venture into brackish water, although they seem to be tolerant of it. In Clear Lake, Lake County, they are most abundant over sand and gravel bottoms (rather than mud), in areas where algae blooms are comparatively light.

Tule perch are adapted for feeding on small, hard-shelled invertebrates associated with the bottom or aquatic plants, although they will also feed in midwater on zooplankton. The deep body shape and maneuverable fins, combined with large eyes and protrusible premaxillary bones of the upper jaw, allow the fish to suck or pick up small invertebrates. Both the jaw teeth and the pharyngeal plates are large, for crushing the food. In the Sacramento-San Joaquin Delta, tule perch feed mostly on small amphipods, together with a few midge larvae (Chironomidae) and small clams (Turner, 1966d). Fish collected in brackish water near the mouth of the Napa River, Napa County, were feeding predominately on small brachyuran crabs, although midge larvae and pupae were also important, especially for immature fish (Hopkirk, 1962). In Clear Lake, Lake County, they seem to be primarily midwater feeders, concentrating on zooplankton in the cold season, and chironomid midge and mayfly larvae in the warm season (Cook, 1964). In the Russian River, Mendocino County, tule perch feed on a wide variety of bottom and plant-dwelling invertebrates but most important are the larvae of chironomid midges, baetid mayflies, and blackflies (D. Alley, D. Hilton, and C. van Dyck, unpublished data).

Tule perch are gregarious, especially when feeding. In rivers, small groups can be observed strung out in a line by the current, moving slowly upstream while periodically picking at the bottom. In Clear Lake, they school in large numbers, especially off tule beds and overhanging trees. However, breeding males in the Russian River were observed to hold small territories under overhanging branches or plants close to shore. Each male defends the territory against other males as well as against fish of other species. The apparent purpose of the territories is to attract females for mating, since courtship can be frequently observed within them. However, each male does not appear to hold one territory for more than a day or so and courtship and mating can also occur away from the territories.

One such instance of nonterritorial courtship and mating was observed by John Norton (pers. comm.) in August, 1973: "Two tule perch each about 75 mm SL were observed at a depth of 1 m behind a few boulders about 2.5 m from shore. The darker of the two fish (probably the male) pecked at the operculum of the other, who did not flee. This opercular nipping continued for nearly 5 minutes. The two fish then went into a short tail chase, head to tail, head to tail, for a single revolution. They separated and opercular nipping was resumed for another minute. This was followed by both fish opening and closing their mouths, with the lips coming in contact. Next the fish attempted to align themselves side by side, facing the same direction. After several attempts, they pressed their caudal fins and peduncles together, rotating until the anal fins were in contact. Together, the bodies of the two fish formed a V, with the anal region forming the vertex. Next the anal fins were pressed close together, followed by a thrust, a jerk, and separation. Activity from the time the caudal fins were first pressed together until the fish separated took approximately 15 seconds. This mating sequence was then repeated and followed by fighting."

Presumably, when the anal fins were pressed together, the male injected sperm into the female using his modified anal fin spines. Fertilization of the eggs does not take place immediately after intromission (Bundy, 1970). Instead, the female stores the sperm until about January, when fertilization occurs. Mating occurs in July through September and the young are born in May or June, when food is abundant. The number of young produced per female is 22 to 83, the number increasing with the size of the fish (Bundy, 1970). The young are born head first and begin to school soon after birth. Since they become sexually mature shortly after birth, many of the territorial males observed in the Russian River in August were young of the year.

Growth in tule perch is most rapid during the first eighteen months after birth, when they are 3 to 4 cm SL (Bundy, 1970). However, the growth rate varies from population to population. At the end of their first summer, Russian River fish reach 5 to 8 cm SL; Clear Lake fish, 6 to 9 cm SL; and Delta fish, 8 to 10 cm SL (Bundy, 1970; D. Alley, D. Hilton, and C. van Dyck, unpublished data). The growth differentials are maintained, so that by the end of the third year, they will be about 10 to 11 SL, 11 to 15 cm SL, and 14 to 16 cm SL, respectively. Tule perch apparently seldom exceed 16 cm SL or five years of age.

Status. Tule perch are abundant in the Russian River, Clear Lake, and locally in the Sacramento Valley. They are one of the most abundant fishes in Lake Britton, a reservoir on the Pit River, Shasta County (D. Hoopaugh, pers. comm.). Although they are still common in the Delta, their populations seem to be greatly reduced from their former abundance. They appear to be extinct in the San Joaquin, Pajaro, and Salinas rivers. It is likely that many of their populations are declining slowly, although their actual status is hard to determine since they are fairly difficult to collect. However, they are absent from many of the localities where they were collected around the turn of the century, as recorded by Evermann and Clark (1931).

Habitat change seems to be the major cause of their decline. They tend to disappear from streams with reduced flows, increased turbidity, heavy pollution, or reduced cover, especially reduced emergent vegetation. Their sensitivity to environmental conditions is reflected in the extreme difficulty of maintaining them in captivity for long periods of time.

It would therefore seem worthwhile to attempt to preserve some of the habitat of each of the three subspecies, *before* their populations reach precarious levels. In addition, periodic checks should be made of waters where they are now known to exist, to see the extent of population declines, if any.

References. Bundy, 1970; Cook, 1964; Cook et al., 1966; Evermann and Clark, 1931; Hopkirk, 1962, 1973; Tarp, 1952; Turner, 1966d.

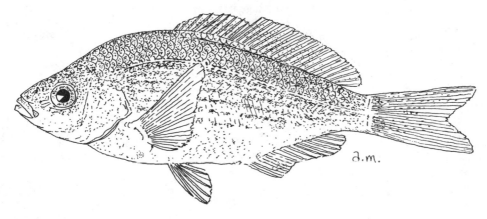

Figure 121. Young-of-the-year shiner perch, 5.0 cm SL, Navarro River, Mendocino County.

Shiner Perch, *Cymatogaster aggregata* Gibbons

Identification. Shiner perch are similar to tule perch in shape and size, but they are not quite as deep bodied. The dorsal fin has only 8 to 9 spines and 18 to 23 rays, but the rayed portion makes up more than 45 percent of the fin. The anal fin has 3 spines and 22 to 25 rays, with a fleshy enlargement of the spiny portion in males. The pectoral fins have 19 to 21 rays, the pelvics have 1 spine and 5 rays each, and the lateral line has 36 to 46 scales. The basic body color ranges from silvery to grey but it is overlain by a series of fine horizontal bars and by three yellow vertical bars. Breeding males may turn nearly black, obscuring the bars with dark speckles.

Names. Cymato-gaster is derived from the Greek words for foetus and belly referring to their viviparity, while *aggregata* means crowded together, an apt description of their schooling habits.

Distribution. Shiner perch range along the Pacific coast from Baja California to Port Wrangell, Alaska (Miller and Lea, 1972). They can be expected in the lower reaches of streams anywhere along the California coast.

Life History. Shiner perch are one of the most common fishes living in the shallow marine waters, bays, and estuaries of California. They are tolerant of low salinities so will often move up into the tidal zone of coastal streams. In the Navarro River, August, 1973, an occasional individual could be found at salinities as low as 1 to 3 ppt, but large schools were noticeable only in regions where the salinity seldom dropped below 9 to 10 ppt. The further downstream and the higher the salinity, the more numerous the shiner perch. Most of the perch found at low salinities are young of the year (4 to 6 cm SL) although, adults (8 to 14 cm SL) are commonly taken in San Pablo Bay when salinities drop to 9 to 14 ppt (Gannsle, 1966). Peak populations occur in the summer months, presumably because the young are mostly born from May through August. Pregnant females may seek out shallow water when giving birth, to give the young some measure of protection from ocean-going predators.

Small (41 to 55 mm SL) shiner perch in the Navarro River taken in August, 1973, were bottom feeding, mostly (95 percent by volume) on small euryhaline amphipods but freshwater tipulid and chironomid midge larvae were also taken.

Status. Shiner perch are abundant and widely distributed. They are an interesting if minor component of the tidal zone of coastal streams.

References. Clemens and Wilby, 1961; Ganssle, 1966; Tarp, 1952.

Mullet Family, Mugilidae

Mullets are primarily tropical and temperate marine fishes but many of the species move readily into fresh and brackish water. Their distribution is worldwide. Since they school in shallow water and estuaries, feeding largely on detritus they stir up from the bottom, they are popular food fish wherever they are abundant. Only the striped mullet, *Mugil cephalus*, enters fresh water in California.

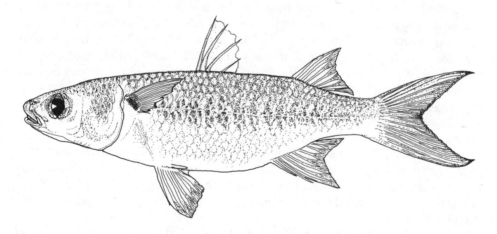

Figure 122. Striped mullet, 19 cm SL, Mexico.

Striped Mullet, *Mugil cephalus* Linnaeus

Identification. Striped mullet have thick bodies, broad, flat heads, small terminal mouths (the maxillary is hidden when the mouth is closed), large eyes (width greater than length of snout), deeply forked tails, widely separated spiny and soft dorsal fins, and translucent adipose eyelids that nearly cover the eyes, leaving only a narrow slit over the pupil. There are 4 spines in the first dorsal fin, 1 spine and 8 rays in the second, 3 spines and 8 rays in the anal fin, 16 to 17 pectoral rays, and 38 to 42 cycloid scales in the lateral line. In fish less than 5 cm TL the adipose eyelid is not evident. The anal fin usually has only 2 spines and 9 rays. The intestine is long with a large gizzard and the gill rakers are long and slender. The backs of living fish are bluegreen, and the sides and belly are silvery with narrow, horizontal black stripes on the upper half of the body.

Names. Striped mullet are known as grey mullet or sea mullet in most of the English-speaking world outside of North America. A complete synonomy of common and scientific names is given in Thomson (1963). *Mugil* is derived from the Latin verb

341

meaning "to suck," referring to their feeding habits, while *cephalus* is apparently derived from the Greek word for head, although the ancient Roman word for mullet was *cefalus*.

   Distribution. Striped mullet are found in tropical and subtropical coastal areas over the world, and around a number of oceanic islands. They are found along the California coast north as far as Monterey Bay, occasionally entering some of the more southern coastal streams. They are common in the lower Colorado River from its mouth to Imperial Dam, about 190 km upstream. They were once the most abundant fish in the Salton Sea but are now extinct or very rare there.

   Life History. Unless otherwise noted, the information in this summary is from Thomson (1963). Striped mullet are primarily dwellers in shallow estuaries and so have been found living in water ranging from 0 to 75 ppt salinity. They cannot tolerate temperatures much below 16°C for extended periods of time and are thus confined to waters that are warm all year around. They regularly ascend sluggish rivers and may be able to complete their entire life cycle in fresh water (Johnson and McClendon, 1970), although they rarely do so. In the Colorado River, most adult mullet migrate out to the Gulf of California to spawn in the winter months and the young gradually move back upstream during the summer of the following year. Thus, most juvenile mullet in the lower reaches of the river are two to four years old (21 to 37 cm SL), while those just below Imperial Dam are three to five years old (29 to 46 cm SL) (Johnson and McClendon, 1970). However, postlarval mullet (28 to 40 mm SL), too weak to swim upstream, have been found 120 miles from the mouth, indicating that some freshwater spawning occurs (Johnson and McClendon, 1970). It is interesting to note that mullet were unable to spawn in the Salton Sea in the 1950s, even though its salinity was close to that of sea water, presumably because the ionic composition was different (Hendricks, 1961). The large populations that once existed there were recruited from young mullet moving up canals from the Colorado River. When the canal system was altered, making access to the sea more difficult, the mullet gradually died out. Some spawning in the sea may have taken place earlier in its history, when salinities were lower (Dill, 1944).

   Mullet are basically schooling fish, especially when young. The schools break up during feeding and frequently adults seem to act more like members of a loosely knit aggregation than of an organized school. Spawning takes place in schools but has not been observed in great detail.

   Feeding takes place on muddy bottoms in shallow water, in areas where the sediment particle size is very small and hence high in organic matter (Odum, 1968). Mullet swim at an angle, scooping up the soft surface material with their stiff lower jaws. Coarse material is ejected through the mouth and gills after a mouthful of the bottom mud has been ground between the pharyngeal plates. Some sand is retained to help the gizzard grind up the organic matter. Nutrition seems to be derived from organic detritus, diatoms, bacteria, and microinvertebrates (Odum, 1968). Occasionally mullet will feed on bits of algae floating close to the water surface (Dill, 1944).

   Age and growth in striped mullet is highly variable. They have not been studied in much detail in the lower Colorado River, but Johnson and McClendon (1970) infer that fish 7 to 13 cm SL were approaching one year old; those 17 to 20 cm SL were one to two years old; those 21 to 28 cm SL, two years old; those 29 to 37 cm SL, four to five years old. The oldest and largest mullet known were from the nonreproducing Salton Sea population; a female 62 cm SL and a male 60 cm SL were probably at least fourteen years old (Hendricks, 1961). Mullet usually become mature at two to three years of age, 23 to 35 cm SL. Females tend to be slightly larger than males.

Status. Striped mullet are still common in the lower Colorado River despite the deterioration of water flow and quality. In fact, prior to man-related changes in water quality, they may have been uncommin in the river (Miller, 1961a). They are of minor importance as sport fish because they can only be taken on small baited hooks sitting on the bottom or with small fry flies (Dill, 1944). They supported a larger commercial fishery in the Salton Sea from 1915 to 1921, and again from 1943 to 1953, when it was forbidden in favor of the sport fishery for other species.

References. Dill, 1944; Hendricks, 1961; Johnson and McClendon, 1970; Odum, 1968; Thomson, 1963.

Goby Family, Gobiidae

Gobies are primarily marine fishes adapted for bottom living in shallow and intertidal waters. Their most distinctive feature is the ventral cone-shaped suction cup formed by the complete union of the pelvic fins. This cup can be used for clinging to rocks in the face of backwash from waves or strong tidal currents. Their bodies are long and ventrally flattened, the heads blunt, the mouths terminal, and the eyes close to the top of the head. These features reflect fishes that live by actively capturing small invertebrates in unlikely places on the bottom.

Although there are more than 700 species in the family, most of them tropical, only a few species of goby have invaded fresh water and can spend all or part of their life cycle there. A number of species, however, are tolerant of low salinities and so will occasionally be found in the lower reaches of coastal streams. Of the five species likely to be found in fresh water in California, only two, the tidewater goby and the yellowfin goby, will spend a significant part of their lives there. The other three species are primarily marine forms, although the longjaw mudsucker occurs often enough in low-salinity regions to justify separate treatment here. The arrow goby (*Clevelandia ios*) is a tidal mudflat dweller that only occasionally enters low-salinity environments, while the chameleon goby (*Tridentiger trigonocephalos*) is a shallow-water form that has not yet been collected in fresh water in California but can be expected there, since it occurs in brackish Lake Merritt in Oakland and in the lower reaches of streams in its native Asia. It was recently accidentally introduced from the Orient into San Francisco Bay and Los Angeles Harbor (Miller and Lea, 1972). Because of their tolerance for fluctuating conditions, it would not be surprising to find occasional representatives of other species of gobies in low-salinity areas as well. Thus, the identification of gobies collected in tidal stretches of stream should be checked in Miller and Lea (1972) or Macdonald (1972).

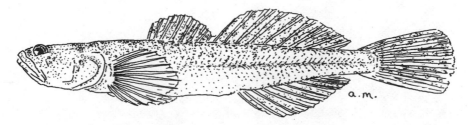

Figure 123. Tidewater goby, 4.5 cm SL, San Luis Obispo Creek, San Luis Obispo County.

Tidewater Goby, *Eucyclogobius newberryi* (Girard)

Identification. Tidewater gobies are small (seldom larger than 50 mm SL), with elongate blunt tails and pelvic fins united to form a sucker. The mouth is large and oblique, the maxillary reaching to the posterior margin of the eye. The scales are small (66 to 70 in the lateral line), cycloid, and absent from the head. There are 6 to 7 slender spines in the first dorsal fin, 9 to 13 elements in the second dorsal fin, 9 to 12 elements in the anal fin, and 8 to 10 gill rakers. Their bodies are dark olive in color with dark mottling on the sides and back. Living fish are nearly translucent. The dorsal fins are mottled, the pelvic fins are yellow or dusky, and the anal fin is dusky.

Names. *Eu-cyclo-gobius* translates as true-cycloid-goby, referring to the cycloid scales (many gobies have ctenoid scales); *newberryi* is after J. S. Newberry, a professor at Columbia University and advisor to the U.S. Geological Survey team that collected the first tidewater gobies, about 1854. A more appropriate name for the tidewater goby is lagoon goby (C. Swift, pers. comm.).

Distribution. Tidewater gobies are found in shallow, marine areas and in the lower reaches of streams from San Diego County north to Humboldt County (Miller and Lea, 1972). They seem to be particularly common in San Luis Obispo County streams. They are uncommon from San Francisco Bay to Humboldt Bay and probably less than forty populations exist throughout their range (C. Swift, pers. comm.).

Life History. Little seems to be known about the life history of this interesting little fish in either fresh or salt water, although studies are being conducted by Dr. Camm Swift of the Los Angeles County Museum. In coastal streams they are usually found in the lower reaches in water ranging from completely fresh to brackish (Jordan, 1894; Hubbs, 1947; Shapovalov and Taft, 1954; Fierstine et al., 1973). They are most abundant in the upper ends of lagoons created by small coastal streams (C. Swift, pers. comm.). The lagoons are usually blocked from the ocean by sand bars, and are seldom subject to tidal fluctuations. In the streams themselves, the gobies inhabit mostly slow-moving areas or pools away from the main current, among emergent and submerged vegetation. Thus, they can be associated with completely freshwater fishes (speckled dace, green sunfish, mosquitofish, riffle sculpin), anadromous fishes (rainbow trout, chinook salmon, threespine stickleback), and euryhaline fishes (staghorn sculpin, starry flounder).

Apparently they can complete most of their life cycle in fresh water, since G. R. Garmen (unpublished data) has collected gravid females in fresh water. Spawning takes place in April and May in southern California (C. Swift, pers. comm.), although Garmen collected gravid females in January and February. They spawn on bottoms of coarse sand (C. Swift, pers. comm.).

Status. Tidewater gobies probably should be managed as a rare or threatened species. Their populations are depleted due to the lowering or elimination of flows in the lower reaches of coastal streams, pollution, especially by sewage, and the filling in, channelization, or other physical alterations of their habitats (C. Swift, pers. comm.). For example, they are apparently absent from the mouth of Corte Madera Creek, Marin County, where they were reported by Hubbs and Miller (1965). This area is now a concrete channel and contains few estuarine fishes. Similarily, C. Swift (pers. comm.) estimates that since 1900 they have disappeared from 74 percent of the coastal lagoons in southern California, from Morro Bay southward. Many, if not most, of the disappearances of goby populations have occurred since 1950. An additional potential threat to the tidewater goby is the recently introduced and spreading yellowfin goby, which can also live in fresh water. It might eliminate tidewater goby populations through competition and predation.

The small size and restricted habitat of tidewater gobies makes them easy to overlook, so they could disappear unnoticed. Their disappearance, however, would signify the deterioration of the fascinating lagoon habitat of coastal streams. Thus, a detailed study of their biology and distribution is needed not only to find ways to preserve this species, but also to preserve a unique habitat.

References. Fierstine et al., 1973; Hubbs, 1947; Hubbs and Miller, 1965; Jordan, 1894; Miller and Lea, 1966; Shapovalov and Taft, 1954.

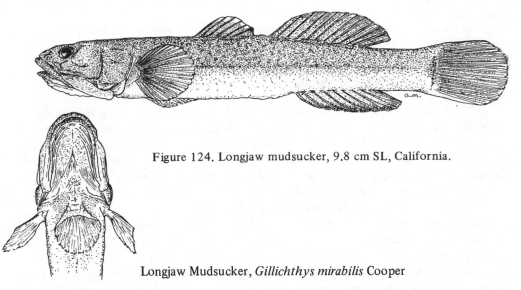

Figure 124. Longjaw mudsucker, 9.8 cm SL, California.

Longjaw Mudsucker, *Gillichthys mirabilis* Cooper

Identification. Longjaw mudsuckers are heavy-bodied gobies with exceedingly long upper jaw bones that nearly reach the opercular opening. The first dorsal is small and low (4 to 8 spines), while the second dorsal is well developed (10 to 17 elements). Anal elements are 9 to 17, pectoral fin rays are 15 to 23, and gill rakers are 10 to 16. Scales are small, cycloid, and imbedded in irregular rows, with 60 to 100 in the lateral series. The scales are largest on the caudal peduncle, becoming smaller towards the head. The anterior portion of the belly is usually without scales. Mudsuckers are dark brown olive in color with yellow bellies and, frequently, a row of faint vertical bars on the sides. Morphological variation in the species is discussed by Barlow (1963).

Names. Gill-ichthys means Gill's fish, named for Theodore Gill, a nineteenth century ichthyologist who worked on gobies. *Mirabilis* means wonderful, perhaps reflecting J. G. Cooper's admiration for their strange appearance and ability to live in mudflats. A complete synonymy is given in Barlow (1961a).

Distribution. Longjaw mudsuckers occur from Bahia Magdalena in Baja California, north to Tomales Bay, and in the northern end of the Gulf of California. Their occurrence in Tomales Bay is apparently unusual, so San Francisco Bay probably contains the northernmost reproducing population (Barlow, 1961a). The population now present in the Salton Sea was started with 500 fish planted in 1950 by the California Department of Fish and Game (Walker et al., 1961).

Life History. Longjaw mudsuckers are not true freshwater fishes. The longest they usually survive in fresh water is three to seven days. Nevertheless, their presence in the Salton Sea, their occasional, if temporary, occurrence in low-salinity intertidal areas, and their use as bait fish in fresh water, particularly in the Colorado River, justifies their inclusion among the inland fishes of California. They typically live on the mudflats of coastal sloughs, retreating into burrows or tidal channels when the tide is low. They can survive temporary strandings on tide flats and low oxygen levels in their burrows by gulping air into their highly vascularized buccopharyngeal chamber (Todd and Ebeling, 1966). They can also wriggle on their bellies for short distances across exposed mudflats to reach water after being stranded (Todd, 1968). In the Salton Sea, mudsuckers seem to be abundant only in a few quiet, shallow areas, although they are widely distributed in the sea and have been taken as deep as 12 m (Walker et al., 1961). They can live in water as saline as 82.5 ppt (Barlow, 1963) and as low as 12 ppt (Courtois, 1973). They can survive temperatures of at least 35°C (Walker et al., 1961), although they prefer temperatures between 9 and 23°C (de Vlaming, 1971).

Longjaw mudsuckers feed on whatever invertebrates and small fish are available. In the Salton Sea, adults eat mostly pile worms (*Neanthus*), with lesser amounts of barnacles, aquatic insect larvae, and fish, including young mudsuckers. Large juveniles (25 to 90 mm SL), which concentrate in shallow areas, feed mostly on brinefly larvae (*Ephydra*), waterboatmen (Corixidae), and pile worms. Small juveniles (15 to 25 mm SL) eat copepods, punkyfly larvae (Heleidae), and freeliving nematodes (Walker et al., 1961). Larval mudsuckers smaller than 15 mm SL are pelagic and so presumably feed mostly on zooplankton. Although Walker et al. (1961) could detect no strong diurnal feeding patterns, Weisel (1947) noted that mudsuckers seem to be most active at night.

Growth is rapid in the Salton Sea. Spring-hatched fish may reach 60 to 80 mm and maturity by late August. Growth slows in the winter but by the start of their second spring most mudsuckers are 80 to 120 mm SL. They live about two years, reaching 135 to 140 mm SL (Walker et al., 1961).

Breeding takes place from January to June in California. Each female spawns more than once, usually in response to changes in temperature (Barlow and de Vlaming, 1972). Breeding ceases during the summer, which is a period of rapid growth and fat storage for mudsuckers. Male mudsuckers construct burrows for breeding and defend them from other mudsuckers. The defense displays in response to an intruder are spectacular: the mouth is opened wide and the long maxillary bones flare the loose buccopharyngeal skin outward, exposing a large expanse of reddish, highly vascularized interior (Weisel, 1947).

The eggs are club shaped and attached in clusters to the side of the burrow by adhesive threads. The male guards the nest until the young hatch, usually in ten to twelve days. The larvae are quite different in appearance from the adults, having short jaws and large eyes. These differences are apparently adaptations for surviving the short period they spend living pelagically, actively feeding on zooplankton.

Status. Longjaw mudsuckers are common throughout their range, although they may be locally depleted by collecting for use as bait. They have considerable value as bait fish because they can be kept for short periods of time in moist algae, are long lived on the hook, and will not reproduce in fresh water (Barlow and de Vlaming, 1972).

References. Barlow, 1961a, 1963; Barlow and de Vlaming, 1972; de Vlaming, 1971; Miller, 1952; Todd, 1968; Todd and Ebeling, 1966; Walker et al., 1961; Weisel, 1947.

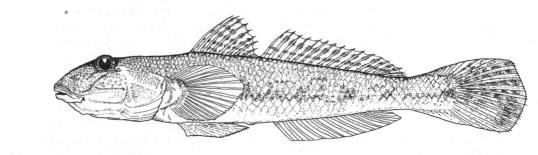

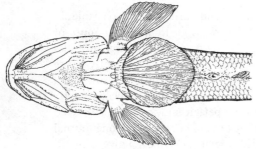

Figure 125. Yellowfin goby, 12 cm SL, Sacramento-San Joaquin Delta.

Yellowfin Goby, *Acanthogobius flavimanus* (Temminck and Schlegel)

Identification. Yellowfin gobies are elongated (to 25 cm SL), bluntheaded fishes, with pelvic fins united to form a sucker. There are 8 spines in the first dorsal fin, 14 rays in the second dorsal, 11 to 12 rays in the anal, and 46 to 56 scales in the lateral line. The maxillaries do not extend beyond the center of the eyes, which are closely spaced on top of the head. The color pattern is as follows: "about eight diffuse dusky spots, each somewhat larger than the eye diameter, arranged in a nearly evenly-spaced series down each side, the first three being concealed beneath the pectoral fin, the last forming a more prominent spot at the base of the caudal fin; the sides and back being indistinctly mottled; the upper two-thirds of the caudal fin with about 10 narrow vertical dusky, zigzag bands, the lower third plain dusky" (Brittan et al., 1963, p. 302).

Names. Acanthogobius means spiny goby, referring to the large number of spines, for a goby, on the first dorsal fin. *Flavimanus* means yellow hand (fin). Goby is apparently derived from *Gobio*, the Latin word for gudgeon, a freshwater gobylike cyprinid of Europe. Yellowfin gobies are also called oriental gobies and *mahaze* (Japanese).

Distribution. Yellowfin gobies are common in shallow coastal waters of Japan, Korea, and China. They were first collected in the Sacramento-San Joaquin Delta in 1963, where they presumably had become accidentally established after being transported across the Pacific in the seawater system of a ship (Brittan et al., 1963). They are now common throughout the Delta and have been collected along the coast from Elkhorn Slough to Tomales Bay (Miller and Lea, 1972). They are also present in the Delta-Mendota Canal and San Luis Reservoir, Merced County. They seem to be spreading rapidly up and down the coast, so they can probably be expected in fresh waters close to the sea anywhere in the state.

Life History. Yellowfin gobies are found in shallow, muddy littoral areas in fresh, brackish, and salt water. They are well adapted for estuarine living because they are capable of withstanding abrupt changes between fresh and salt water, and can survive water temperatures greater than 28°C (Brittan et al., 1970). Since large numbers have been found in San Luis Reservoir, they can probably complete their entire life cycle in fresh water, although usually at least the larval stages are spent in salt water. Not much is known about the biology of yellowfin gobies in California, but some work has been done in Japan where they are a prized food fish (Okada, 1960; Dotu and Mito, 1955).

They usually feed on a wide variety of crustaceans and small fishes associated with the bottom, although algae may be ingested as well. Yellowfin gobies presumably take most of their prey from ambush or by carefully searching the substrate, since they only swim short distances in a jerky manner.

Yellowfin gobies in Japan become mature after one year (about 10 cm TL) and breed from January to March. Usually, Y-shaped tunnels with two entrances are constructed for breeding in bottoms that are a mixture of mud and coarse sand. Pieces of pipe and other artificial materials may also be used, provided water can flow through. The eggs are teardrop shaped and attached by adhesive filaments to the roof of the burrow. They may be guarded by the male until they hatch (twenty-eight days at 13°C), but frequently they are left unattended.

The larvae leave the nest soon after hatching at about 4 to 5 mm TL and assume a pelagic existence for an undetermined period of time. While pelagic they feed on zooplankton, especially copepods. At a length of 15 to 20 mm they settle down to the bottom (Dotu and Mito, 1955).

Status. Yellowfin goby populations in California have exploded since they were first noticed in 1963. They are now one of the most abundant bottom fishes in San Francisco Bay and the Delta, and are still increasing their range. What effect this population explosion will have on native freshwater and estuarine fishes is not known, but freshwater populations of the small tidewater goby might be in some danger of being eliminated through competition. Brittan et al. (1970) noted that in at least one saltwater area, yellowfin gobies may have partially displaced staghorn sculpins. On the positive side, yellowfin gobies have some potential as sport, commercial, or bait fish, at least in salt water. They are considered to be a delicacy in Japan.

References. Brittan et al., 1963, 1970; Dotu and Mito, 1955; Okada, 1960.

Sculpin Family, Cottidae

Perhaps no group of fishes occurring in the fresh waters of California has given biologists (including the author) more identification headaches than the sculpins, genus *Cottus*. In addition to being highly variable in structure and color patterns, most species are widely distributed. Similar species frequently occur together, making careful examination of each specimen necessary. Even competent ichthyologists have had problems identifying these fish, as the confusing literature attests. Only in recent years has enough attention been paid to the variation within individual species so that most of them can be characterized with a reasonable degree of certainty. However, much work still needs to be done on sculpin systematics, as should be obvious to anyone who has tried to identify them.

Freshwater sculpins are small bottom fishes with large flattened heads, fanlike pectoral fins and smooth, scaleless, but occasionally prickly, bodies. These features, combined with the lack of an air bladder, enable sculpins to stay on the bottom, even in fast-flowing streams. A further adaptation for bottom living is the dark mottled coloration which blends in with the rocky areas they prefer, concealing them from predators and prey alike. The large mouth with numerous small teeth and the short gut with its muscular stomach reflect the sculpin's voracious feeding habits. Sculpins are also characterized by the two short dorsal fins, the first composed of soft spines, the second of rays, and by the small pelvic fins located between the pectoral fins.

Although sculpins are generally found in abundance in salmon and trout streams, they usually have little effect on salmonid populations. Occasionally they feed on eggs and fry but this is likely to be a problem mostly in artificial spawning channels where uniform gravel size allows sculpins to burrow down after living eggs. Eggs found in sculpin stomachs are usually loose eggs that the salmon or trout failed to bury. In some lakes and streams, sculpins are important forage for gamefishes.

Freshwater sculpins are actually a small branch of a large family of marine bottom fishes. Their marine ancestry is reflected in the fact that a number of species will enter salt water, especially as larvae. As a result of this salinity tolerance, the genus *Cottus* has been able to colonize coastal and inland streams throughout North America and Eurasia. As many as three *Cottus* species may occur in some of the larger coastal streams, although how they subdivide the habitat is poorly known. In addition to the freshwater sculpins, coastal streams may support true marine sculpins, since a number of them will spend part of their life cycle in fresh water. The freshwater stage, however, is not obligatory. Of two such species recorded for California, the sharpnose sculpin (*Clinocottus acuticeps*) is a rare visitor to fresh water, while the Pacific staghorn sculpin (*Leptocottus armatus*) regularly spends the juvenile portion of its life cycle in coastal streams.

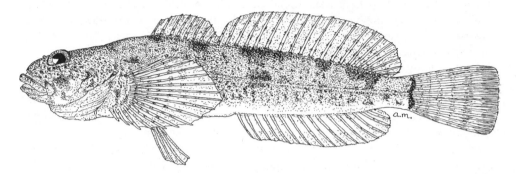

Figure 126. Prickly sculpin, 8.8 cm SL, Suisun Creek, Solano County.

Prickly Sculpin, *Cottus asper* Richardson

Identification. Prickly sculpins are distinguished by their long anal fin (17 to 18 rays, rarely 15 or 16), well-developed palatine teeth that are usually visible without magnification or dissection, and the single pore on the chin (occasionally two). The pelvic fins have 1 spine and 4 rays (rarely 3 or 5); the first dorsal fin has 7 to 10 soft spines; the second dorsal, 19 to 23 rays; the pectoral fin, 15 to 18 rays. Gill rakers are 5 to 6; branchiostegal rays, 6 on each side; prepercular spines, 2 to 3 (usually only one is conspicuous, the lower one(s) being under the skin). The lateral line is complete with 28 to 43 pores. The extent of visible prickling on the body ranges from nearly complete coverage to coverage of only a very small area behind the pectoral fins. Maximum size is about 20 cm SL in California. The caudal peduncle is relatively narrow and rounded. Coloring is highly variable but the back and sides are usually mottled reddish brown to dark brown while the belly is white to yellow. The fins are generally barred and the first dorsal usually has a dark oval spot on the posterior end. Both sexes develop an orange edge on the first dorsal during the breeding season and the body color of the males turns very dark. Out of their breeding colors, males can be told from females by their long, V-shaped genital papilla.

Names. Cottus is apparently the old Latin name for European sculpins, which was derived from the Greek word for head. Both the trivial name *asper*, meaning rough, and official common name reflect the forms upon which Richardson based his original description. He apparently was unaware of the superficially smooth forms typical of the Central Valley. A complete synonomy of the scientific nomenclature is given in Kresja (1970). Sculpins are frequently referred to as bullheads, miller's thumbs, or muddlers. The name sculpin seems to be a corruption of the ancient Greek name (*Scorpaena*) for various marine cottids (Oxford English Dictionary, 1971).

Distribution. Prickly sculpins are found in coastal streams from the Kenai Peninsula, Alaska, down to the Ventura River, southern California. In California they are widespread throughout streams of the Central Valley, mostly at low elevations. They are absent from the upper Pit River.

Life History. Few fishes occupy the wide range of bottom habitats occupied by prickly sculpin populations. They live in waters ranging from fresh to salt, in streams ranging from small, cold, and clear to large, warm, and turbid, and in lakes and reservoirs ranging from small to large, eutrophic to oligotrophic. In one small area near Friant, Fresno County, prickly sculpins are abundant in a cool trout stream (San Joaquin River), a large, warmwater reservoir (Millerton Lake), and a small, shallow lake with bottom temperatures that exceed 26°C in the summer (Lost Lake). In the Tuolumne River they have been found in water up to 28°C (Bond, 1963). Most typically, however, they are found in pools and quiet water of moderate-sized, clear, low-elevation streams, with bottoms of sand, silt, and scattered rocks. They are also the most abundant sculpin in many coastal streams.

As their body shape and cryptic coloration indicate, they spend most of their time quietly lying on the bottom. During the day they hide underneath or in submerged objects, such as rocks, logs, beer cans, and other pieces of trash. At night they come out to actively forage for food. Cook (1964) noted that prickly sculpins were commonly taken in night plankton tows in Clear Lake, Lake County.

Prickly sculpins are usually not gregarious, but neither do they appear to be territorial outside the breeding season, a behavior pattern that might be expected of sedentary bottom fish. Apparent schooling behavior, however, was observed among large numbers of prickly sculpins moving along the shore of a British Columbia lake (Northcote and Hartman, 1959). Downstream migration of adults and upstream migration of young-of-the-year sculpins is typical of many (but not all) populations. Shapovalov and Taft (1954) noted a pronounced downstream movement of adult prickly sculpins in Waddell Creek, Santa Cruz County, during the winter months, especially January and February. The function of the downstream movement is not clear, but it seems to be related to spawning.

As might be expected, prickly sculpins feed mostly on large benthic invertebrates, particularly blackfly, midge, mayfly, stonefly, and caddisfly larvae. Other aquatic insects, molluscs, isopods, amphipods, and small fish are also eaten. In Clear Lake, Lake County, 74 percent of their summer diet is chironomid midge larvae and pupae (Cook, 1964). Their food, however, varies with the size of the fish. Thus, those less than 30 mm TL feed to a great extent on planktonic crustaceans while those greater than 70 mm TL often take small fish, including other sculpins. While trout and salmon are spawning, sculpins may feed on their eggs (Reed, 1967). Most of those eaten are presumably loose eggs that did not get buried during spawning. Several studies have also indicated that sculpins prey heavily on salmon and trout fry (Munro and Clemens, 1937; Shapovalov and Taft, 1954). However, these studies are based on stomach analyses of sculpins caught in traps set for salmonid fry, where the fry are very easy for sculpins to catch. Under normal stream conditions, it seems unlikely that sculpins are very effective predators on healthy active fry.

Growth in prickly sculpins is subject to much individual variation and is thus similar to that of other sculpin species. In the San Joaquin River, they reach 51 to 71 mm SL in their second year, 51 to 85 mm SL in their third, 64 to 90 mm SL in their fourth, and 75 to 90 mm SL in their fifth (Kottcamp, 1973). The oldest fish encountered by Kottcamp was seven years old (105 mm SL), although much larger (up to 160 mm SL) and older fish have been collected elsewhere.

Prickly sculpins become mature during their second, third, or fourth year, depending on the population (Patten, 1971), at 4 to 7 cm SL. Spawning can occur from late February through June, although most spawning in California probably takes place in March and April. Natural spawning usually requires temperatures of 8 to 13°C (Kresja, 1965).

Prior to spawning, prickly sculpins move into areas, in either a freshwater or intertidal zone, that contain large flat rocks and moderate current. The males are ready for spawning before the females and select nest sites underneath the rocks (or in beer cans, auto bodies, or other trash), while the females congregate upstream from the spawning area (Kresja, 1965). Each male then prepares a nest by digging a small hollow underneath the rock and cleaning off the ceiling of the nest. When a female is ready to spawn she moves down into the spawning area and is courted by a male, who lures her into his nest. Further courtship and spawning take place within the nest, mostly at night (Kresja, 1965). During spawning the eggs are attached to the ceiling of the nest in a cluster. The male then chases the female from the nest and guards the eggs until they hatch. Movements of the male help to keep water circulating over the eggs, assuring normal development. Mechanical agitation of fully developed eggs by the male seems to be necessary for hatching (R. J. Kresja, pers. comm.).

Males frequently spawn with more than one female, so as many as 25,000 to 30,000 eggs have been found in one nest (Kresja, 1965). The number of eggs in a nest is usually much smaller. Individual females produce anywhere from 280 to 11,000 eggs, the number depending on both the size and age of the female (Patten, 1971).

The fry when hatched are 5 to 7 mm TL. They start swimming fairly soon after hatching. As a result, they are swept downstream to large pools, lakes, and estuaries where they assume a planktonic existence for three to five weeks. Such larvae are common in the Sacramento-San Joaquin Delta in the spring (Turner, 1966d). Soon after settling down to the bottom, at lengths of 20 to 30 mm, they start a general upstream movement (McLarney, 1968).

Status. Prickly sculpins are abundant where found, and have managed to adapt to man-caused alterations of their environment. In Millerton Lake, they are the only native fish still in abundance and are important forage for largemouth bass. Elsewhere, especially as larvae, they may provide forage for salmon and trout, as well as for fish-eating birds. They occasionally prey on salmon eggs and fry, sometimes feeding in redds while the salmon are spawning (Reed, 1967). However, it is unlikely that they have much affect on salmon populations.

References. Bond, 1963; Cook, 1964; Hopkirk, 1973; Kottcamp, 1973; Kottcamp and Moyle, 1972; Kresja, 1965, 1970; McLarney, 1968; McPhail and Lindsey, 1970; Millikan, 1968; Munro and Clemens, 1937; Northcote, 1954; Northcote and Hartman, 1959; Patten, 1971; Reed, 1967; Robins and Miller, 1957; Shapovalov and Taft, 1954; Turner, 1966d.

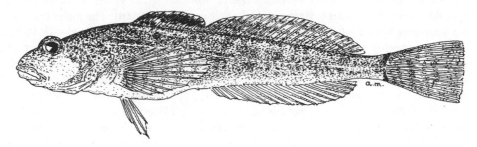

Figure 127. Riffle sculpin, 5.3 cm SL, Bodfish Creek, Santa Clara County.

Riffle Sculpin, *Cottus gulosus* (Girard)

Identification. Riffle sculpins are highly variable but are defined by the following combination of characteristics: four pelvic "elements;" 7 to 8 soft spines on the first dorsal fin; 16 to 19 rays in the second dorsal; 15 to 16 rays in each pectoral fin, some of which may be branched; 14 to 16 rays in the anal fin; palatine teeth usually present; 22 to 36 lateral line pores; prickles present only behind the pectoral fin (axillary patch); 2 to 3 preopercular spines; lateral line complete or incomplete; and dorsal fins usually joined. The mouth is large, so the maxillary reaches as far as the rear edge of the eye. Pelvic fins usually do not reach the vent when depressed. There is usually one one median chin pore. They have the typical sculpin mottled body color, with a large black blotch on the rear of the first dorsal fin.

Names. Gulosus means big-mouthed (literally, full of gullet) or, alternatively, gluttonous. Other names are as for prickly sculpins. Many of the early records for this species may be in fact *C. asper, C. klamathensis, C. pitensis,* or *C. perplexus.*

Distribution. Riffle sculpins have a disjunct distributional pattern. They are found throughout the Sacramento-San Joaquin system (except the upper Pit River) and in coastal streams from Morro Bay, San Luis Obispo County, north to the Noyo River. They are the most abundant sculpin in the Salinas and Pajaro rivers. They also occur in coastal streams from the Coquille River, Oregon, north to Puget Sound, Washington (Bond, 1973). They are absent from the Trinity, Klamath, and Rogue rivers, where they are apparently replaced ecologically by marbled and reticulate sculpins.

Life History. Riffle sculpins are well named, for they are most common in California in headwater streams where riffles predominate. In coastal streams they are found in a variety of habitats, but they seem to prefer cool water and gravel bottoms, avoiding the swifter riffles. The spectrum of habitats they occupy in a stream is broadest when other sculpin species are absent. In the Central Valley, riffle sculpins typically occupy the cool, upper reaches of streams, while prickly sculpins occupy the warm, lower reaches.

Riffle sculpins are opportunistic bottom feeders. In a small Washington stream, they fed on isopods, amphipods, chironomid larvae, snails, and a wide variety of aquatic insects (Millikan, 1968). Isopods and amphipods were most important in the diet of small (less than 45 mm SL) sculpins. Small fish and fish eggs are eaten only rarely.

Age and growth of riffle sculpins is similar to that of other sculpins (Bond, 1963; Millikan, 1968). Most growth occurs in the spring and summer. During their first summer, they grow about 6 mm per month, reaching a length of 25 to 45 mm SL by the end of the growing season. Two-year-old fish average 40 to 50 mm SL, and three-year-old fish, 50 to 60 mm SL, although the largest riffle sculpin on record, 90 mm SL, was only two years old (Millikan, 1968). Riffle sculpins seldom live longer than four years.

Maturity sets in at the end of the second year of life and culminates in spawning in late February, March, and April. Riffle sculpins spawn either on the underside of rocks in swift riffles or inside cavities of submerged, rotting logs. Egg counts in females range from 104 to 449, depending on the size of the fish (Bond, 1963; Millikan, 1968). However, since egg counts in nests range from 462 to well over 1,000, more than one female must spawn in each nest. The males stay in the nest guarding the eggs and fry. Millikan noted that males on nests were generally emaciated, suggesting that they do not feed while guarding the nest.

The eggs hatch in eleven (at 15°C) to twenty-four (at 10°C) days. After absorbing the yolk sac, at about 6 mm TL, the fry assume a benthic existence (Millikan, 1968).

Status. The status of riffle sculpins is difficult to determine since they are so frequently confused with other species. However, they appear to be widely distributed and abundant where found.

References. Bond, 1963, 1973; Fierstine et al., 1973; Hubbs and Wallis, 1948; Millikan, 1968.

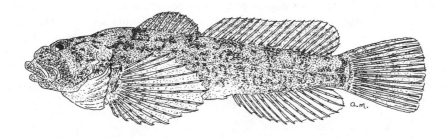

Figure 128. Pit sculpin, 10.0 cm SL, Rush Creek, Modoc County.

Pit Sculpin, *Cottus pitensis* Bailey and Bond

Identification. Pit sculpins closely resemble riffle sculpins but differ in the following ways: palatine teeth are absent; there are usually only 2 preopercular spines but occasionally 3; the lateral line in fish 5 cm TL or larger is usually complete, with 31 to 39 pores (usually 33 to 37); pectoral rays are 12 to 16, usually 13 to 15, and mostly unbranched; and dorsal spines are 8 to 9, occasionally 7 or 10. Anal fin rays are 12 to 15 and the median chin pore is usually absent. There are patches of prickles just behind and slightly above the bases of the pectoral fins. Color patterns are variable but usually 5 to 6 faint dark "saddles" are present on the back, 2 beneath the first dorsal and 3 to 4 beneath the second dorsal. A dark band often encircles the end of the caudal peduncle. Pectoral, caudal, and second dorsal fins are usually banded and the first dorsal usually has a large blotch on the posterior end. The belly is light colored.

Names. Pitensis is after the Pit River. Other names are as for the prickly sculpin.

Distribution. Pit sculpins are common throughout the Pit River system, from the tributaries of Goose Lake in Oregon down to the Sacramento River in Shasta County.

Life History. Pit sculpins were identified as riffle sculpins until Bailey and Bond (1963) described them as a distinct species. Apparently they evolved from riffle sculpin populations isolated in the upper Pit River. As a consequence of their going unrecognized for so long, little is known about their life history except for some brief studies by the author summarized here.

Pit sculpins are most abundant in the smaller streams of the Pit River system. They have a strong preference for riffles, so they will rapidly colonize channelized sections of stream once invertebrate populations have built up again.

Like other sculpins, they feed primarily on aquatic insect larvae. They are highly selective in their feeding. When their stomach contents (N=350+) were compared to the composition of the bottom insect fauna of Ash Creek, Lassen County, it was found that they selected *for* the rounded baetid mayfly larvae and large stonefly nymphs but against the flattened heptageneid mayfly larvae. They showed no preference for, or selected against, two species of web-spinning, caseless caddisfly larvae, which were the most abundant invertebrates in the stream. Yet web-spinning mouth larvae (Pyralidae) were obviously sought out by the sculpins because they were rare in the bottom samples but common in the stomachs. The sculpins also selected against caddisfly larvae with cases, snails, and other hard-shelled invertebrates. One large sculpin had eaten a smaller one. They will feed throughout the day and night, but most intense feeding takes place in the early morning.

Growth in the Ash Creek population appears to be similar to that of other sculpin species living in small, cold streams. In June, 1973, Pit sculpins starting their third summer of life (II+ age class) were 57 to 72 mm SL (mean, 62 mm), while III+ fish were 59 to 89 mm SL (mean, 80 mm), and IV+ fish were 75 to 104 mm SL (mean, 82 mm).

In Rush Creek, Modoc County, dark colored males guarding nests of eggs were collected in April and May. The eggs are laid on the underside of rocks and submerged logs.

Status. In Oregon, Pit sculpins have been listed as a threatened species, since none have been collected in recent years in the Oregon tributaries to Goose Lake (Bond, 1966). In the Pit River of California, they are widely distributed and abundant. Studies are in progress on their ecology and relationships to the much less common rough and marbled sculpins by the author, R. Daniels, and H. Li.

References. Bailey and Bond, 1963; Bond, 1966.

Reticulate Sculpin,* *Cottus perplexus* Gilbert and Evermann

Identification. Reticulate sculpins resemble riffle and marbled sculpins but are identified by the following complex of characters: palatine teeth absent; dorsal fins usually broadly joined, with 7 to 8 spines in the first dorsal and 18 to 20 rays in the second; pectoral fin rays 13 to 16, but usually 14 to 15, and unbranched; anal rays 13 to 16; lateral line complete or incomplete, with 22 to 32 pores; 1 to 2 median chin pores; 1 to 4 preopercular spines but usually only 2 visible; body prickling highly variable but axillary patch always present; and maxilla extends to just below the anterior portion of the eye and the mouth is narrower than the body width behind the pectoral fins. The body is usually patterned with faint vermiculations and small patches of dark pigment. The pectoral fins frequently have a checkerboard pattern like that of marbled sculpins. The first dorsal has a dark blotch on the posterior portion.

Names. *Perplexus* translates as perplexing, reflecting the difficulty in defining the species, although Gilbert and Evermann may have had the reticulated appearance in mind when assigning the name. Other names are as for the prickly sculpin. Reticulate sculpins have been frequently lumped taxonomically with riffle sculpins. Patten (1971), for example, treats the two species as one.

Distribution. Reticulate sculpins occur in coastal streams from the lower Columbia River, Washington, down to the Rogue River, Oregon. In California, they are found only in the few creeks that drain north into the Rogue River. I have examined sculpins assigned to this species only from Elliot Creek. Bond (1973) reported them from the Applegate River as well. Occasional individuals may be expected from the lower Klamath River. Their distribution seems to be limited in part by the presence of other sculpins, especially riffle sculpins, with which they are rarely sympatric (Bond, 1963).

Life History. Most of our information on reticulate sculpins is from Bond (1963), as they are one of the commonest species in coastal Oregon. They live primarily in the slower portions of small coastal and headwater streams, but will occupy a wide variety of stream habitats. When they occur by themselves, they seem to seek out rubble or gravel bottoms in moving water. They tend to live in pools or along the stream edge on sandy or silty bottoms when other sculpins are present. They may be adapted in part for living in streams where other sculpins cannot, especially streams with high or fluctuating temperatures. Experiments by Bond (1963) suggest that they can withstand temperatures up to 30°C and salinities up to 18 ppt.

Reticulate sculpins feed mostly on aquatic insect larvae, especially those of mayflies, stoneflies, chironomid midges, beetles, and caddisflies. Fish are only rarely taken. Under experimental conditions (uniform gravel size in small tanks), reticulate sculpins have been shown to prey on trout eggs and fry, even those buried in gravel (Phillips and Claire, 1966). However, the applicability of these results to natural conditions is questionable.

Growth is slower in reticulate sculpins than for most other species. Bond (1963) found age I fish averaged only 27 mm SL; age II, 42 mm SL; age III, 56 mm SL; and age IV, 64 mm SL. The oldest reticulate sculpin he examined was age VI but only 66 mm SL. Maximum size is about 85 mm SL. Despite their small size, they mature early. Bond recorded females maturing at 30 to 39 mm SL. Fecundity ranges from 35 to 315 eggs per female, depending on size.

*Not pictured.

Spawning occurs in March through May, when stream temperatures exceed 6 to 7°C. The eggs are laid on the underside of rocks 10 to 45 cm in diameter, although various types of trash can also be used. Usually more than one female contributes eggs to each nest. When other species of sculpin are absent or rare, reticulate sculpins spawn in riffles. They spawn in slower-flowing areas when other species are abundant. The males guard the nest from egg predators, probably until the fry are past the yolk sac state and can fend for themselves. The fry assume a benthic existence immediately after leaving the nest and tend to stay in quiet water at the stream edge (Bond, 1963).

Status. Reticulate sculpins are uncommon in California, but abundant in Oregon and Washington.

References. Bailey and Bond, 1963; Bond, 1963, 1973; Patten, 1971; Phillips and Claire, 1966; Robins and Miller, 1957.

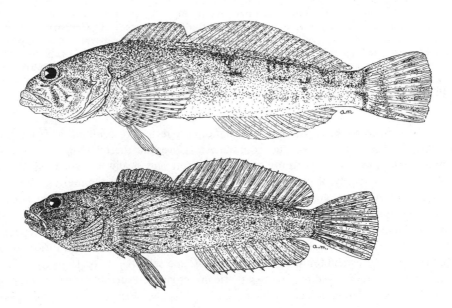

Figure 129. Marbled sculpin, Klamath drainage form (upper), 8.5 cm SL, Scott River, Siskiyou County; Pit River form (lower), 8.5 cm SL, Hat Creek, Shasta County.

Marbled Sculpin, *Cottus klamathensis* Gilbert

Identification. Marbled sculpins are similar to riffle sculpins but can be distinguished from them by the following characteristics: palatine teeth absent; lateral line pores 14 to 22; only one well-developed preopercular spine, although one or two inconspicuous protuberences may be present below it; maxilla usually does not reach posterior edge of eye; and usually no conspicuous dark patch on rear portion of first dorsal, although a band may run across most of the fin. The two dorsal fins are usually broadly joined, with 16 to 18 spines in the first and 18 to 19 rays in the second. Pectoral fins have four "elements" and may or may not reach the vent when depressed. Usually only one median chin pore is present. Prickling may be well developed on young fish but is confined to a small region behind the pectoral fins in adults or is absent. The lateral line may or may not reach the caudal fin, but usually does not. Fish from the Klamath drainage system have a strikingly marbled appearance and barred fins. The pectoral fins often appear checkered with alternating dark and light spots on the rays. Fish from the Pit River are usually darker and less strikingly marked.

Names. Klamathensis is after the Klamath River, while the common name reflects the color pattern of the Klamath River populations. The darker form of the Pit River was originally described by Rutter (1908) as a distinct species, *C. macrops*, but it is considered by Robins and Miller (1957) to be worthy only of subspecies status.

Distribution. Marbled sculpins are widely distributed in the Klamath and Lost River systems. They are also found in scattered tributaries (e.g., Hat Creek) to the Pit River. Most of these tributaries are above the falls at Burney, but occasionally marbled sculpins may be found below the falls.

Life History. Marbled sculpins are found in a wide variety of habitats, from small, cold streams to large, sluggish rivers and to mud-bottomed sloughs of Klamath Lake, Oregon (Bond, 1963). They have been collected in water ranging from 8 to 24°C and on bottoms from mud to cobbles. In the Pit River they are largely confined to muddy bottomed areas in large, clear, tributary streams including the Fall River. Little is known about their life history, except that they spawn in the spring and that females have a high fecundity for sculpins; females 7 to 9 cm TL contain 738 to 1,184 eggs (Bond, 1963). Presumably their life history resembles that of other species of *Cottus*, especially *C. asper* and *C. beldingi*.

Status. Abundant and widely distributed throughout the Klamath system, marbled sculpins presumably play an important role as predators on bottom invertebrates and small fish, and as prey for large fish. However, the Pit River form is only locally abundant and seems to have rather specialized habitat requirements. It may deserve special protection in the future. Certainly its taxonomic position needs to be reevaluated.

References. Bond, 1963; Robins and Miller, 1957; Rutter, 1908.

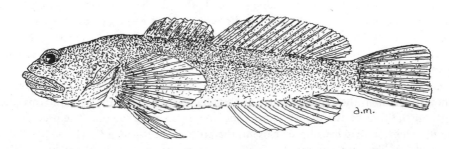

Figure 130. Piute sculpin, 7.5 cm SL, Sagehen Creek, Placer County.

Piute Sculpin, *Cottus beldingi* Eigenmann and Eigenmann

Identification. Similar to marbled and riffle sculpins, Piute sculpins differ from them by having the following combination of characteristics: anal fin rays 11 to 13; palatine teeth absent; prickling completely absent; pectoral rays all unbranched; dorsal fins only weakly united or separated completely; upper preopercular spine usually long and slender, lower spine inconspicuous; more than 23 pores present on lateral line; and median chin pores usually 2, rarely 1. Pelvic "elements" are 4, first dorsal spines are 6 to 8, and second dorsal fin rays are 15 to 18. The maxilla is long, often reaching past the middle of the eye. The lateral line may or may not reach the caudal fin. Pelvic fins occasionally will reach the vent, and the caudal fin is rounded. Coloration is highly variable, although 4 to 5 vertical bands are frequently discernible on the sides. The fins are barred or mottled.

Males can be told from females by their long anal papillae (2 to 3 mm in mature fish) and their larger mouths. In males the width of the mouth is greater than the distance from the pelvic fins to the anus, while in females it is less (Miller, 1951).

Names. Beldingi is after C. Belding, who collected specimens used by Carl and Rosa Eigenmann to describe the species. The common name is after the Piute Indians who lived in portions of the Lahontan Basin where the sculpins are abundant. They have also been called Lahontan and Belding sculpins (La Rivers, 1962). For other names, see prickly sculpin.

Distribution. Piute sculpins are the only sculpins found in the Lahontan system in California and Nevada, including Lake Tahoe and tributaries. They also occur in portions of the Columbia River system in Oregon and Washington, in the Bear River of the Bonneville system in Utah and Idaho, and in the upper Colorado River system in Colorado (Sigler and Miller, 1963).

Life History. The life history of Piute sculpins is perhaps better known than that of any other California sculpin, thanks to studies in Lake Tahoe by Miller (1951), Ebert and Summerfelt (1969), and Baker and Cordone (1969), and in Sagehen Creek by Dietsch (1959), Sheldon (1968), and Jones (1972). In both situations Piute sculpins prefer bottoms of rubble and gravel, although it is not unusual to find them living on other substrates as well. In Lake Tahoe, they also seem to be abundant in aquatic weed beds in deep water. They have been collected as deep as 210 m in Lake Tahoe but the largest numbers live in water less than 60 m deep (Baker and Cordone, 1969). In streams, they are largely absent from high-gradient headwaters, as well as from warm, low-gradient stretches. Their typical stream habitat is the rocky riffle sections of clear, cold mountain streams, where they are almost always associated with trout.

Like other sculpins, Piute sculpins spend the daylight hours in comparative inactivity, hidden among rocks and aquatic weeds. They come out to forage at night. There is no evidence of territoriality connected with feeding, nor of schooling behavior. Baker and Cordone (1969) were also unable to detect any seasonal movements in Lake Tahoe.

Prey is taken on the bottom from ambush. When a prey organism approaches a concealed sculpin, the fish will lunge out suddenly and engulf it. The numerous small teeth on the roof of the mouth prevent the prey from wriggling out. The prey may be any invertebrate that lives on or close to the bottom. In Sagehen Creek, 63 percent of the sculpins' diet, by volume, is aquatic insect larvae, especially those of mayflies, stoneflies, and caddisflies. The remainder of the diet consists of miscellaneous bottom organisms, such as snails, water mites, aquatic beetles, and algae, as well as detritus accidentally ingested with more substantial prey (Ebert and Summerfelt, 1969). Sixty-five percent of the diet of sculpins in the shallower waters of Lake Tahoe is also bottom organisms, especially chironomid midge larvae (41 percent). The remainder is mostly planktonic crustaceans (14 percent) which are generally found close to the bottom and algae (Miller, 1951). Surprisingly, in sculpins taken from deep water (greater than 30 m), detritus (50 percent) and filamentous algae (14 percent) make up the bulk of the stomach contents. Snails, amphipods (scuds), aquatic insect larvae, and other sculpins are the most important animal foods. Snails are most abundant in sculpins taken at 30 to 60 m, while oligochaetes and deep-water amphipods (*Stygobromus*) are most abundant in fish taken at 60 to 90 m (Ebert and Summerfelt, 1969). Piute sculpins usually occur in trout spawning areas but the presence of trout eggs in their stomachs is unusual.

The diet of Piute sculpins varies with the seasonal availability of prey. The sculpins feed year-round, but feeding activity diminishes in the fall and winter. In Sagehen Creek, chironomid midge larvae and caddisfly larvae are most important in the fall diet; mayfly larvae gradually assume importance in the winter. As spring approaches, the sculpins concentrate more and more on the mayfly *Heptagenia* (Dietsch, 1959). In Lake Tahoe shallow-water populations, aquatic insect larvae are consumed in fairly consistent amounts from May through September, but planktonic forms vary in abundance, presumably reflecting seasonal succession in the lake (Miller, 1951). In deep-water populations, snails are eaten mostly in the summer and fall, while amphipods are eaten in the spring and summer. Interestingly enough, other sculpins, which make up 8 to 13 percent of the diet during summer, fall, and winter, are totally absent from the diet in the spring (Ebert and Summerfelt, 1969), indicating that perhaps reproductive activity inhibits cannibalism.

Diet also varies with size of the fish. Sagehen Creek sculpins less than 59 mm TL feed mostly on chironomid larvae, while those greater than 80 mm TL feed mostly on large aquatic insect larvae such as those of caddisflies and mayflies (Deitsch, 1959). In Lake Tahoe, fish greater than 41 mm TL feed on a bigger variety of invertebrates than do smaller fish, which tend to concentrate on ostracods, chironomid larvae, and amphipods. Cannibalism is found only in sculpins larger than 82 mm TL (Ebert and Summerfelt, 1969).

Studying age and growth in sculpins is somewhat difficult because they lack scales, and length-frequency analyses give a poor picture of age-length relationships. In order to get an accurate measurement, otoliths (ear stones) must be removed and examined for annual rings. Growth rates, as determined by otolith examination, are similar for both Lake Tahoe and Sagehen Creek populations. By the end of the first summer (age 0), they are 26 to 36 mm TL; age I fish, at the end of the summer, average 54 mm TL; age II fish, 68 mm TL; age III fish, 83 to 84 mm TL; age IV fish, 93 to 97 mm TL (Ebert and Summerfelt, 1969). A few age V fish are present in Sagehen Creek. Most growth takes place from May to October, although it does continue during the winter months. The largest sculpin on record from Lake Tahoe was 127 mm TL, while the largest from Sagehen Creek was 110 mm TL. Such large Piute sculpins are rare, and are usually males.

Maturity generally sets in by age II and spawning occurs mostly in May and June. Jones (1972) noted that most spawning in his Sagehen Creek study areas took place during a one-week period in early June but that the exact time and length of the spawning period probably depends on when and how rapidly the water warms up. In Lake Tahoe the spawning season is long. Ripe females have been collected from May 2 to August 28 (Miller, 1951). Egg clusters, however, have only been found in shallow water from May to July 4, indicating that peak spawning takes place during that period. As in the case of other sculpins, Piute sculpin eggs are laid in clusters on the underside of a rock and the nest is tended by a male. Spawning males may be territorial, defending the nest from other males, since sculpin eggs have been found in the stomachs of sculpins. Although there seems to be little actual preparation of the spawning site, its selection is careful. The sculpins select crevices under rocks that are located on gravel bottoms, apparently avoiding otherwise suitable sites on bedrock or mud bottoms (Miller, 1951). Most spawning sites in Lake Tahoe seem to be located in wave-swept littoral areas or just off the mouths of streams, yet some spawning must take place in deeper water since no dramatic inshore movements of sculpins have been observed during the spawning season. In streams, most spawning sites are located in riffles.

The number of eggs in each nest is usually 100 to 200. This range is similar to the fecundity range of females, indicating that multiple spawnings in one nest are uncommon, unless each female only lays a small number of eggs at one time. The mean number of eggs from Lake Tahoe sculpins is 123, with a range of 11 to 387 (Ebert and Summerfelt, 1969). Fecundity of Sagehen Creek fish is similar. The number of eggs increases with age and size of the fish. The mean number of eggs in age II fish is 73, while in age III fish it is 130 (Patten, 1971). The length-fecundity relationships are given in Patten (1971) and Jones (1972).

After the fry hatch, at a length of about 10 mm, they drop down among the gravel on the floor of the nest. There they remain for one to two weeks until they absorb the yolk sac. They then assume a benthic existence, consuming small bottom invertebrates and gradually wandering away from the nest site. In Sagehen Creek, however, young sculpins may swim up off the bottom, to be caught by the current and washed downstream. Most of the drift occurs at night (Sheldon, 1968). There are two peaks in the numbers of drifting sculpins, one immediately following yolk absorption and another, of slightly larger individuals, about two weeks later. The initial urge of young sculpins to forsake their sedentary bottom-living habits for a few hours is presumably a mechanism which assures wide dispersal of young sculpins and keeps populations at reasonable levels in spawning areas. The later peak in drifting may be the result of interactions among individuals, the losers of aggressive encounters over food and space being forced to drift downstream (Sheldon, 1968).

Status. Piute sculpins are one of the most abundant fish in the Lahontan system and are certainly the most abundant bottom fish in its colder waters. In Sagehen Creek they may dominate fish production in sections where the habitat is ideal for them with populations as dense as six adults per square meter of bottom (Jones, 1972). Because of their large numbers and carnivorous reputation, the relationship of Piute sculpins to trout has been intensively studied. The results indicate that sculpins have a mostly positive effect on trout populations. No evidence of egg predation has been found in Lake Tahoe and trout eggs are found only rarely in the stomachs of Sagehen Creek sculpins. Competition in streams between sculpins and trout is minimal since trout tend to concentrate on drift organisms while the sculpins concentrate on bottom forms. Thus, in Sagehen Creek the diet of sculpins only overlaps that of trout by 20 percent (Deitsch, 1959). In Lake Tahoe, the overlap is even less and sculpins form a large part of the diet of both lake trout and rainbow trout. Similarly, in Sagehen Creek 20 percent of the diet of brook trout is sculpins. Since brook trout can also be cannibalistic, sculpins may serve as a "buffer" prey, their availability preventing extensive cannibalism by trout (Deitsch, 1959). Their most important role, however, in both lakes and streams, is in the conversion of bottom organisms into a form (sculpins) more available to trout.

References. Baker and Cordone, 1969; Dietsch, 1959; Ebert and Summerfelt, 1969; Jones, 1972; La Rivers, 1962; R. G. Miller, 1951; Patten, 1971; Sheldon, 1968; Sigler and Miller, 1963.

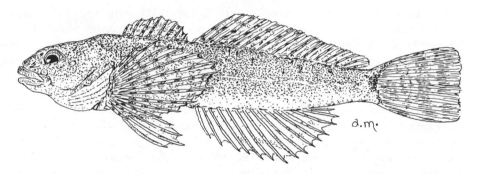

Figure 131. Coastrange sculpin, 7.5 cm SL, Navarro River, Mendocino County.

Coastrange Sculpin, *Cottus aleuticus* Gilbert

Identification. Coastrange sculpins can usually be recognized by the long pelvic fins that reach the vent, the large size of the posterior pair of nostrils, the lack of palatine teeth, the complete lateral line (34 to 44), and the single chin pore. The pelvic fins have 1 spine and 4 rays (4 "elements"); the first dorsal fin, 8 to 10 weak spines; the second dorsal, 17 to 20 rays; and the pectoral fin, 13 to 16 rays. Gill rakers are 5 to 7, branchiostegal rays are 6 on each side. There is only one sharp preopercular spine. Prickling is confined to a small area behind the pectoral fins. Maximum size is about 12 cm. Body coloration is typical of sculpins: dark mottling on the back and white on the belly. Usually there are 2 to 3 more or less distinct vertical bands below the second dorsal fin. Most fins are barred except on juvenile fish. Males have a long genital papilla and develop an orange band on the edge of the first dorsal fin during the breeding season (McPhail and Lindsey, 1970).

Names. Coastrange aptly describes the wide distribution of this species, while *aleuticus*, referring to the Aleutian Islands, does not. They are sometimes called Aleutian sculpins. Other names are as for prickly sculpins.

Distribution. Coastrange sculpins are found in coastal streams from the Aleutian Islands and Bristol Bay, Alaska, down to northern San Luis Obispo County, California (Robins and Miller, 1957).

Life History. In California, coastrange sculpins are seldom the most abundant sculpin in the streams they inhabit. Prickly sculpins tend to be more common in the same streams. Typically, coastrange sculpins are found in swift gravel riffles in the lower reaches of the larger coastal streams but they can also inhabit the brackish quiet water of stream mouths, on bottoms ranging from mud to sand to coarse gravel. Occasional collections have been made from estuaries or freshwater lakes.

Coastrange sculpins are most active at night and, except during the breeding season, usually exhibit little social behavior. Large daytime aggregations, however, have been observed in an Alaskan lake (Greenbank, 1957). Like prickly sculpins, California populations of coastrange sculpins may migrate downstream in January, February, and March (Shapovalov and Taft, 1954), presumably so the eggs will be laid closer to the estuary where the larvae live.

Feeding is primarily on aquatic insect larvae and other bottom invertebrates, especially clams and snails. Like other sculpins, they may take salmon eggs and fry when readily available, especially loose eggs. It is doubtful that this predation has much effect on salmon populations.

No work has been done on age and growth in coastrange sculpins in California, but Bond (1963) noted a maximum length of 77 cm TL and a maximum age of IV in Oregon. Oregon sculpins average 46 mm at age I but only grow 10 to 11 mm per year in following years. Ricker (1960) described a dwarf population of coastrange sculpins living in the deep waters of a British Columbia lake, in which age IV fish reached a maximum length of 49 mm.

Coastrange sculpins mature during their second or third year and usually spawn in early spring. Some females may have two separate spawning periods (Patten, 1971). In California, spawning presumably takes place early since Shapovalov and Taft (1954) noted large numbers of young-of-the-year sculpins moving upstream in March, April, and May. The usual spawning site is the underside of a flat rock in swift water, to which clusters of orange eggs are attached. The number of eggs laid by a single female varies with size and age. Patten (1971) found a range of 100 to 1,764 eggs produced by females ranging in size from 5 to 10 cm TL.

Immediately after hatching, coastrange sculpin larvae are carried by current into estuaries, lakes, or large pools where they live on and among the plankton for three to five weeks (Heard, 1965). These planktonic larvae may serve as forage for trout and salmon. Once they assume a bottom existence they gradually move upstream, although strong movements usually do not occur until after the fish have exceeded 6 cm TL (McPhail and Lindsey, 1970).

Status. Coastrange sculpins are still widespread, even though pollution and reduced flows may have eliminated them from some streams, such as the Pajaro River. At times they eat salmon eggs and larvae but at other times they are eaten by salmon in turn, balancing their value to man (Heard, 1965).

References. Bond, 1963; Greenbank, 1957; Heard, 1965; McLarney, 1968; McPhail and Lindsey, 1970; Patten, 1971; Ricker, 1960; Robins and Miller, 1957; Shapovalov and Taft, 1954.

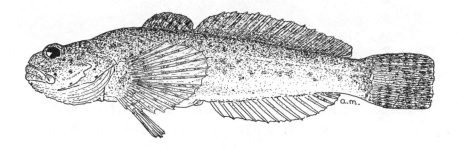

Figure 132. Rough sculpin, 7.2 cm SL, Hat Creek, Shasta County.

Rough Sculpin, *Cottus asperrimus* Rutter

Identification. Rough sculpins are the only California sculpins that consistantly have 1 spine and 3 rays in the pelvic fins (3 "elements"). Palatine teeth are absent and the lateral line does not extend past the end of the second dorsal fin. The sides are covered with prickles, making them rough to the touch. There are 5 to 7 spines in the first dorsal fin, 17 to 19 rays in the second dorsal, 13 to 17 anal fin rays, 14 to 16 rays in each pectoral fin (many of them branched), and 19 to 29 lateral line pores. The upper preopercular spine is well developed, the lower a blunt nob. In life, they are olive brown to purplish brown on the back, dusky on the sides with 4 to 5 irregular blotches, and speckled on the belly. The dorsal fins are brown to reddish, with light streaks.

Names. Asperrimus means very rough, referring to the prickling on the sides. Other names are as for the prickly sculpin.

Distribution. Rough sculpins are restricted to the Pit River immediately above and below the falls at Burney, as well as to Hat Creek and the Fall River and its tributaries.

Life History. Rough sculpins are found mostly on muddy bottoms of large streams, including the Pit River itself. Otherwise, little is known about the habits of this rare fish. Collections taken in the spring have contained ripe females so they are more than likely spring spawners (Robins and Miller, 1957). It is not known why they have such a restricted distribution.

Status. Because of their restricted distribution, rough sculpins are classified as a depleted species by the California Department of Fish and Game and are fully protected under state law (Fisk, 1972). A survey of their populations and habitat requirements is underway by R. Daniels, a graduate student of the author. Initial observations indicate that they are quite abundant where found. Once their distribution is determined, a monitoring program will be needed to make sure their populations are not threatened by further development of the Pit River and its tributaries.

References. Fisk, 1972; Robins and Miller, 1957; Rutter, 1908.

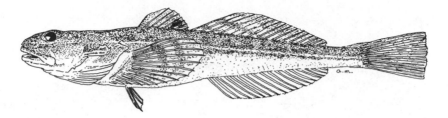

Figure 133. Staghorn sculpin, 9.1 cm SL, Navarro River, Mendocino County.

Pacific Staghorn Sculpin, *Leptocottus armatus* Girard

Identification. Pacific staghorn sculpins can be readily recognized by the conspicuous, antlerlike upper preopercular spine on each side which bears 3 to 4 small, sharp spines. The head is large and flat with small eyes. When they are disturbed, the head is flattened and the spines erected. The maxilla reaches past the eye. Teeth, including palatines, are well developed. The pelvic fins have 4 "elements"; the first dorsal, 7 spines; the second dorsal, 17 rays; the anal fin, 17 rays. The skin is smooth (no prickling), the lateral line is complete, and the caudal peduncle is narrow. Unlike members of the genus *Cottus*, they are greyish olive on the back, creamy yellow on the sides, and abruptly white on the belly. The first dorsal fin usually has a dark spot on the posterior half, while the other fins tend to be barred.

Names. Lepto-cottus means slender-sculpin, presumably after the narrow caudal peduncle, while *armatus* means armed.

Distribution. Pacific staghorn sculpins are found in shallow coastal waters, especially bays and inlets, from Kodiak Island, Alaska, to San Quentin Bay, Baja California. They seem to commonly inhabit fresh water only in the southern half of their range.

Life History. Although these sculpins are primarily marine, their frequent occurrence in the lower reaches of coastal streams justifies their inclusion among freshwater fishes. Even in streams, however, they are seldom more than a mile or two removed from salt water. Their life history in both salt and fresh water has been investigated by Jones (1962), so most information in this summary is derived from his excellent study.

Staghorn sculpins are truly euryhaline. Not only are they found in water that ranges in salinity from fresh to salt (34 ppt and probably higher), but they often move freely between waters of varying salinities. In fresh water almost all staghorn sculpins are juveniles or newly mature adults, ranging from 2 to 14 cm TL, with a few as large as 22 cm TL. Most of them are less than two years old. Jones (1962) demonstrated that the probable reason for the predominance of juveniles is that they are more tolerant of low salinities than are adults or larvae.

Staghorn sculpins can be found in coastal streams at almost any time of the year, but they are most numerous in the spring when newly hatched juveniles move into fresh water. Once there, they gradually move upstream and more, usually younger, juveniles move in from salt water to take the place of the upstream migrants. The net effect of these movements is that the largest fish are found farthest upstream. At the upstream end of their distribution, staghorn sculpins tend to be associated with a combination of true freshwater fishes such as California roach and hitch, euryhaline freshwater fishes such as threespine stickleback and prickly sculpin, and anadromous species such as steelhead rainbow trout and Pacific lamprey. In the lower reaches, their most common fish associates are other euryhaline marine species, especially starry flounder and shiner perch.

The dominant food of staghorn sculpins living in fresh water is bottom-dwelling euryhaline amphipods (*Corophium* spp.). Nereid worms (*Neanthus* sp.), and aquatic insect larvae are of secondary importance (Jones, 1962; Porter, 1964). Aquatic insects are most important during times when high stream flows lower the salinities of their habitat. Amphipods also dominate the diet of juveniles in salt water, although adults (up to 31 cm TL) feed more on crabs, shrimp, and fish.

Jones (1962) found that there were three age classes of staghorn sculpin in Walker Creek, Marin County: young of the year, yearlings, and two-year-olds. Most young-of-the-year fish entered the stream at less than 4 cm TL. Few remain longer than a year, the largest fish encountered being 22 cm TL and two years old. In salt water, they seldom live longer than three years or exceed lengths of 31 cm TL.

Staghorn sculpins mature when they are one year old, so mature sculpins have been collected in fresh water. However, it is unlikely that any spawning takes place in streams since the optimum salinity for the normal development of eggs is 26 ppt. Spawning can take place from October to March, but mostly in January and February, in bay areas of stable salinity. Depending on their size, females lay anywhere from 2,000 to 11,000 eggs, with 5,000 being an average figure. Development of the eggs and larvae is described by Jones (1962).

Larval sculpins are presumably pelagic for a short period of time before settling down to the bottom in estuaries.

Status. Common in both salt and fresh water, staghorn sculpins have a minor importance as a bait fish. There is no evidence that they prey on young salmon or salmon eggs.

References. Jones, 1962; Porter, 1964.

Righteye Flounder Family, Pleuronectidae

Righteye flounders are part of a large group of marine bony fishes highly adapted for bottom living. In order to be as flat as possible, and thus blend with the bottom, flounders spend most of their lives with one side of the body close to the bottom. This has required some rather drastic morphological changes: the jaws become twisted, the dorsal and anal fins become long and nearly identical to each other, and one eye migrates during development from the bottom side of the head to the top side. Flounders swim about like normal fish fry for the first few weeks after hatching, so the changes take place when they start settling down to the bottom. Flounders are colored on their top sides to match the bottom and most of them can change their color pattern to a remarkable degree. They can match substrate patterns closely, hiding themselves from both predator and prey.

The occurrence of flounders in fresh water is rather unusual and there are apparently no exclusively freshwater species. In North America north of Mexico, only three species regularly occur in fresh water: the hogchoker, *Trinectes maculatus* (Soleidae), on the Atlantic coast; the arctic flounder, *Liopsetta glacialis* on the Arctic Sea coast; and the starry flounder on the Pacific coast.

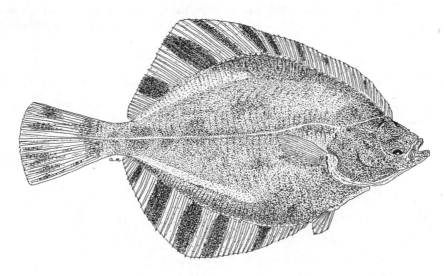

Figure 134. Starry flounder, 10.5 cm SL, Sacramento-San Joaquin Delta.

Starry Flounder, *Platichthys stellatus* (Pallas)

Identification. Starry flounders are the only flatfish likely to be found in fresh water: both eyes on the upper side of the head, white "belly" with a single pectoral fin in the middle, pelvic fins on the dorsoventral ridge behind the operculum, and dorsal and anal fins that extend around the body on each side. They can be distinguished from other flounders that might occur in brackish water by the distinctive, alternating white to orange and black bands on the dorsal and anal fins. There are 52 to 64 rays in the dorsal fins, 38 to 47 in the anal, 10 in each pectoral, and 6 to 11 gill rakers. Although they belong to the right-eyed flounder family, the eyes may be either on the right or the left side. For comparative purposes descriptions of other species of flounders can be found in Miller and Lea (1972).

Names. Plat-ichthys means flat-fish, while *stellatus* means starry, after the distinctive star-shaped spiny plates on the dorsal surface. They are sometimes called rough jackets, diamond flounders, and, in Japan, swamp flounders.

Distribution. Starry flounders are found along the coast of the Pacific Ocean, and in the lower reaches of coastal streams, from the Santa Ynez River, Santa Barbara County, north along the Alaskan coast and the Arctic seacoast of Canada, to Bathurst Inlet. A more detailed world-range description can be found in Orcutt (1950). In California, they are particularly common in the Sacramento-San Joaquin Delta and in the lower parts of small coastal streams. Recently they have appeared in San Luis Reservoir and O'Neill Forebay, Merced County, transported there by the California Aqueduct.

Life History. Starry flounders are primarily marine or estuarine fish but they also commonly live in coastal streams, as far as 75 miles from salt water (Gunter, 1942). In streams, they are generally found in low-gradient areas that are influenced by the tide and have sandy or muddy bottoms. There seems to be some seasonal movement in and out of fresh water, since they are common in the Delta during the summer but uncommon in the winter (Ganssle, 1966).

Although starry flounders are capable of short, swift bursts of swimming propelled by thrusts of the tail, they normally move by gliding slowly over the bottom, propelled by waves of the dorsal and anal fins (Orcutt, 1950). They rest on the edges of these same fins, with the belly slightly off the bottom. When startled, they flip sand or mud over the body with their fins, burying nearly everything except the eyes.

In salt water, starry flounders feed on a wide variety of bottom invertebrates, the type changing with their size. Prior to metamorphosis, they feed first on planktonic algae, then on planktonic crustaceans. Small flounders (to 20 cm TL) feed mostly on amphipods and copepods, while large fish feed more on crabs, polychaete worms, and molluscs (Orcutt, 1950). In estuaries, the diet is similar (Porter, 1964; Ganssle, 1966), but in fresh water they may switch to insect larvae that live in soft bottoms, such as cranefly larvae, Tipulidae (Porter, 1964).

Feeding in fresh water may initially put the flounder under some osmotic stress, since digestion rates are two to three times faster in salt water than they are in fresh water (Porter, 1964). It is not unusual to find starry flounders in fresh water in somewhat emaciated condition. The starry flounders that inhabit fresh water are mostly immature fish less than two years old and 15 cm TL. In the Delta, the smallest fish are generally found the highest upstream (Ganssle, 1966). Young-of-the-year fish, mostly those 3 to 20 cm TL, grow at rates comparable to those living in salt water (Radtke, 1966). The large flounders (over 20 cm TL) encountered in fresh water seem to be mostly migrants from salt water and it is not known if they spawn in fresh or brackish water. However, very small juveniles (8 to 15 mm TL) have been collected in plankton nets in the lower San Joaquin River (Radtke, 1966), indicating that some reproduction may occur in the Delta.

In salt water, males become mature at the end of the second year at about 30 cm SL, breeding at the end of the third year at about 35 cm SL. Spawning occurs in shallow water from November through February (Orcutt, 1950).

Status. Starry flounders are a minor commercial fish but a major sport fish in salt water. They are a minor element of the freshwater fauna so are taken mostly by fishermen trying to catch something else. There is no evidence that they prey on small migrating salmon or trout, although they will do so in the confined conditions of aquaria (Porter, 1964).

References. Ganssle, 1966; Gunter, 1942; Miller and Lea, 1972; Orcutt, 1950; Porter, 1964; Radtke, 1966.

References

Aceituno, M. E. 1974. An annotated bibliography of the Sacramento perch, *Archoplites interruptus* (Girard). Calif. Dept. Fish, Game Inland Fish Admin. Rept. 74-3: 10 pp.

Allanson, B. R., and R. G. Noble. 1964. The tolerance of *Tilapia mossambica* (Peters) to high temperatures. Trans. Amer. Fish. Soc. 93(4):323-332.

Allen, K. O., and K. Strawn. 1968. Heat tolerance of channel catfish, *Ictalurus punctatus*. Proc. 21st Ann. Conf. SE Assoc. Game, Fish Comm.: 399-411.

Anderson, C. A. 1936. Volcanic history of the Clear Lake area, California. Bull. Geol. Soc. Amer. 97:629-664.

Andrusak, H., and T. G. Northcote. 1971. Segregation between adult cutthroat trout (*Salmo clarki*) and Dolly Varden (*Salvelinus malma*) in small coastal British Columbia lakes. J. Fish. Res. Bd. Canada 28(9):1259-1268.

Anonymous. 1964. Trout of California. Calif. Dept. Fish, Game, 56 pp.

———. 1967. A new salmonlike fish. Outdoor California May/June:18.

———. 1968. Where to find California's golden trout. Calif. Dept. Fish, Game, Mimeo, 2 pp.

Applegate, R. L., and J. W. Mullan. 1967. Food of the black bullhead (*Ictalurus melas*) in a new reservoir. Proc. 20th Ann. Conf. SE Assoc. Game, Fish Comm.: 288-292.

———, ———, and D. L. Morais. 1967. Food and growth of six centrarchids from shoreline areas of Bull Shoals Reservoir. Proc. 20th Ann. Conf. SE Assoc. Game, Fish Comm: 469-82.

Armstrong, R. H., and W. M. Morton. 1969. Revised annotated bibliography on the Dolly Varden char. Alaska Dept. Fish, Game Res. Report 7: 108 pp.

Avault, J. W., R. O. Smitherman, and E. W. Shell. 1966. Evaluation of eight species of fish for aquatic weed control. FAO World Symposium on Warmwater Pond Fish Culture. FR VII, E-3:1-14.

Baerends, G. P., and J. M. Baerends-Van Roon. 1950. An introduction to the ethology of cichlid fishes. Behaviour Supp. 11:1-292.

Baggerman, B. 1957. An experimental study of the timing of breeding and migration in the three-spined stickleback. Arch. Nees. Zool. 12:103-307.

Bailey, R. M., and C. E. Bond. 1963. Four new species of freshwater sculpins, genus *Cottus*, from western North America. Occ. Pap. Mus. Zool. Univ. Mich. 634: 25 pp.

———, and T. Uyeno. 1964. Nomenclature of the blue chub and the tui chub, cyprinid fishes from western United States. Copeia 1964(1):238-239.

Baker, P. H. 1967. Distribution, size composition and relative abundance of the Lahontan speckled dace, *Rhinichthys osculus robustus* (Rutter), in Lake Tahoe. Calif. Fish, Game 53(3):165-173.

———, and A. J. Cordone. 1969. Distribution, size composition, and relative abundance of Piute sculpin, *Cottus beldingii* Eigenmann and Eigenmann, in Lake Tahoe. Calif. Fish, Game 55(4):285-297.

Barlow, G. W. 1958a. High salinity mortality of desert pupfish *Cyprinodon macularius*. Copeia 1958(2):231-232.

———. 1958b. Daily movements of desert pupfish, *Cyprinodon macularius*, in shore pools of the Salton Sea, California. Ecology 39(3):580-87.

. 1961a. Gobies of the genus *Gillichthys*, with comments on the sensory canals as a taxonomic tool. Copeia 1961(4):423-437.

. 1961b. Social behavior of the desert pupfish, *Cyprinodon macularius*, in the field and in the aquarium. Am. Midl. Nat. 65(2):330-359.

. 1963. Species structure of the gobiid fish *Gillichthys mirabilis* from coastal sloughs of the eastern Pacific. Pacific Sci. 17:47-72.

, and V. deVlaming. 1972. Ovarian cycling in longjaw gobies, *Gillichthys mirabilis*, from the Salton Sea. Calif. Fish, Game 58(1):50-57.

Barnes, R. N. 1957. A study of the life history of the western roach, *Hesperoleucus symmetricus*. M. A. Thesis, Univ. Calif. Davis, 25 pp.

Barraclough, W. E. 1964. Contribution to the marine life history of the eulachon, *Thaleichthys pacificus*. J. Fish. Res. Bd. Canada 21:1333-1337.

Bartholomew, J. P. 1966. The effects of threadfin shad on white crappie growth in Isabella Reservoir, Kern County, California. Calif. Dept. Fish, Game Inland Fish. Admin. Rept. 66-6: 11 pp.

Bay, E. C. 1966. Adaptation studies with the Argentine pearl fish, *Cynolebias belottii*, for its introduction into California. Copeia 1966(4):839-46.

Beck, W. R., and W. H. Massmann. 1951. Migratory behavior of the rainwater killifish, *Lucania parva*, in the York River, Virginia. Copeia 1951(2):176.

Behnke, R. J. 1972. The systematics of salmonid fishes in recently glaciated lakes. J. Fish. Res. Bd. Canada 29(6):639-671.

Beland, R. O. 1953a. The effect of channelization on the fishery of the lower Colorado River. Calif. Fish, Game 39(1):137-139.

. 1953b. Occurrence of two additional centrarchids in the lower Colorado River. Calif. Fish, Game 39(1):149-151.

Bell, R. R. 1960. Propagation of bait minnows in California. Calif. Dept. Fish, Game Inland Fish Admin. Rpt. 56-11: 20 pp.

. 1971. California marine fish landings for 1970. Calif. Dept. Fish, Game Fish. Bull 194: 50 pp.

Benson, S. B., and R. J. Behnke. 1961. *Salmo evermanni*, a synonym of *Salmo clarki henshawi*. Calif. Fish, Game 37(3):257-259.

Beukema, J. 1963. Experiments on the effects of the hunger state on the risk of prey of the three-spined stickleback. Arch. Nees. Zool. 15:358-61.

Bohn, A., and W. S. Hoar. 1965. The effect of salinity on the iodine metabolism of coastal and inland prickly sculpins, *Cottus asper* Richardson. Can. J. Zool. 43:997-985.

Bond, C. E. 1948. Fish management problems of Lake of the Woods, Oregon. M. S. Thesis, Oregon State Univ., 109 pp.

. 1961. Keys to Oregon freshwater fishes. Ore. State Univ. Ag. Expt. Stat. Tech. Bull. 58: 42 pp.

. 1963. Distribution and ecology of freshwater sculpins, genus *Cottus*, in Oregon. Ph. D. Thesis, Univ. Mich., 198 pp.

. 1966. Endangered plants and animals of Oregon. Oregon State Univ. Ag. Expt. Sta. Spec. Rpt. 205: 8 pp.

. 1973. Occurrence of the reticulate sculpin, *Cottus perplexus*, in California, with distributional notes on *Cottus gulosus* in Oregon and Washington. Calif. Fish, Game 59(1):93-94.

, and T. T. Kahn. 1973. *Lampetra (Entosphenus) minima* n. sp., a dwarfed parasitic lamprey from Oregon. Copeia 1973(3):568-574.

Borgeson, D., and G. W. McCammon. 1967. White catfish, *Ictalurus catus*, of the Sacramento-San Joaquin Delta. Calif. Fish, Game 53(4):254-263.

Botroff, L. J., J. A. St. Amant, and W. Parker, 1969. Addition of *Pylodictis olivaris* to the California fauna. Calif. Fish, Game 55(1):90.

Branner, J. C. 1907. A drainage peculiarity of the Santa Clara Valley affecting fresh-water faunas. J. Geol. 15(1):1-10.

Brauer, C. O. 1971. A study of the western sucker *Catostomus occidentalis* Ayres in lower Hat Creek, California. M. S. Thesis, Calif. State University, Humboldt, 41 pp.

Breder, C. M., and D. E. Rosen. 1966. Modes of reproduction in fishes. Am. Mus. Nat. Hist., N.Y., 941 pp.

Brett, J. R. 1952. Temperature tolerances of young Pacific salmon, *Oncorhynchus*. J. Fish. Res. Bd. Canada 9(6):264-323.

Brice, J. C. 1953. Geology of Lower Lake Quadrangle, California. Calif. Div. Mines Bull. 166: 72 pp.

Briggs, J. O. 1953. The behavior and reproduction of salmonid fishes in a small coastal stream. Calif. Dept. Fish, Game Fish. Bull. 94:1-62.

Brittan, M., A. Albrecht, and J. Hopkirk. 1963. An oriental goby collected in the San Joaquin River delta near Stockton, California. Calif. Dept. Fish, Game 49(4):302-304.

——, J. Hopkirk, J. Connors, and M. Martin. 1970. Explosive spread of the oriental goby, *Acanthogobius flavimanus* in the San Francisco Bay-Delta region of California. Proc. Calif. Acad. Sci. 38(11):207-214.

Brock, V. E., and M. Takata. 1954. A note on spawning of *Tilapia mossambica* in seawater. Copeia 1954(1):72.

Brooks, J. L., and S. Dodson. 1965. Predation, body size, and composition of plankton. Science 150(3692):28-35.

Brown, B. E., and J. S. Dendy. 1961. Observations on the food habits of flathead and blue catfish in Arkansas. Proc. 15th Ann. Conf. SE Assoc. Game, Fish Comm.: 210-222.

Brown, C. J. D. 1971. Fishes of Montana. Big Sky Books, Bozeman, Montana, 207 pp.

Brown, J. H. 1971. The desert pupfish. Sci. Amer. 225(5):104-110.

——, and C. R. Feldmeth. 1971. Evolution in constant and fluctuating environments: thermal tolerances of desert pupfish, *Cyprinodon*. Evolution 25(2):390-398.

Brown, M. W. 1939. A brief history and identification of the three species of black bass now occurring in California. Calif. Fish, Game 25(4):310-312.

Brunson, R. B. 1952. Egg counts of *Salvelinus malma* from the Clark's Fork River, Montana. Copeia 1952(3):196-197.

Bryan, J. E., and P. A. Larkin. 1972. Food specialization by individual trout. J. Fish. Res. Bd. Canada 29(11):1615-1624.

Bundy, D. S. 1970. Reproduction and growth of the tule perch, *Hysterocarpus traskii* (Gibbons), with notes on its ecology. M. S. Thesis, Univ. of Pacific, Stockton, California, 52 pp.

Burns, J. W. 1966. Threadfin shad, 481-488; Hardhead, 518-519. *In* A. Calhoun, ed., Inland Fisheries Management, Calif. Dept. Fish, Game.

——. 1972. Some effects of logging and associated road construction on northern California streams. Trans. Amer. Fish Soc. 101(1):1-17.

Burton, G. W., and E. P. Odum. 1945. The distribution of stream fish in the vicinity of Mountain Lake, Virginia. Ecology 26(2):182-194.

Bury, R. B. 1972. The effects of diesel fuel on a stream fauna. Calif. Fish, Game 58(4):291-295.

Busbee, R. L. 1968. Piscivorous activities on the channel catfish. Prog. Fish. Cult. 30(1):32-38.

Butler, R. L., and D. P. Borgeson. 1965. California "catchable" trout fisheries. Calif. Dept. Fish, Game Fish Bull. 127: 47 pp.

Calhoun, A. J. 1940. Note on a hybrid minnow, *Apocope* x *Richardsonius*. Copeia 1940(2):142-143.

——. 1944. The food of the black-spotted trout (*Salmo clarki henshawi* in two Sierra-Nevada lakes. Calif. Fish, Game 30(2):80-85.

Campbell, J. B. 1882. Notes on the McCloud River, California, and some of its fishes. Bull. U. S. Fish. Comm. 1(1):44-46.

Carl, G. C., and Clemens. 1953. The Freshwater Fishes of British Columbia. 2nd ed. B. C. Prov. Mus. Handb. 5: 136 pp.

Carlander, K. D. 1950. Handbook of Freshwater Fishery Biology. Wm. C. Brown Co., Dubuque, Iowa, 281 pp.

——. 1969. Handbook of Freshwater Fishery Biology. Vol. 1. Iowa State Univ. Press, Ames, Iowa, 752 pp.

Casteel, R. W., and J. H. Hutchison. 1973. *Orthodon* (Actinopterygii, Cyprinidae) from the Pliocene and Pleistocene of California. Copeia 1973(2):358-361.

Chadwick, H. E., C. E. von Geldern, and M. L. Johnson. 1966. White bass, 412-422. *In* A. Calhoun, ed., Inland Fisheries Management, Calif. Dept. Fish, Game.

Chapman, D. W. 1962. Aggressive behavior in juvenile coho salmon as a cause of emigration. J. Fish. Res. Bd. Canada 19(5):1047-1080.

——, and T. C. Bjornn. 1969. Distribution of salmonids in streams, with special reference to food and feeding, 153-176. *In* T. G. Northcote, ed., Symposium on salmon and trout in streams, H. R. MacMillan Lectures in Fisheries, Univ. British Columbia, Vancouver.

Chaston, I. 1969. Seasonal activity and feeding patterns of brown trout (*Salmo trutta*) in a Dartmoor stream in relation to availability of food. J. Fish. Res. Bd. Canada 26(8):2165-2171.

Clemens, H. P., and K. F. Sneed. 1957. The spawning behavior of the channel catfish, *Ictalurus punctatus*. U. S. Fish, Wildlife Serv. Spec. Sci. Rept., Fish. 29:1-11.

Clemens, W. A., and G. V. Wilby. 1961. Fishes of the Pacific Coast of Canada. Fish. Res. Bd. Canada Bull. 68: 443 pp.

Coleman, G. A. 1929. A biological survey of the Salton Sea. Calif. Fish, Game 15(3):218-227.

——. 1930. A biological survey of Clear Lake, Lake County. Calif. Fish, Game 16(3):221-227.

Contreras, G. P. 1973. Distribution of the fishes of the Lost River System, California-Oregon, with a key to the species present. M. S. Thesis, Univ. Nevada, Reno, 61 pp.

Cook, S. F., Jr. 1964. The potential of two native California fish in the biological control of chironomid midges (Diptera: Chironomidae). Mosquito News 24(3):332-333.

——. 1968. The potential role of fishery management in the reduction of chaoborid midge populations and water quality enhancement. Calif. Vect. Views 15(7):63-70.

——, J. D. Connors, and R. L. Moore. 1964. The impact of the fishery on the midges of Clear Lake, Lake County, California. Ann. Ent. Soc. Amer. 57(6):701-707.

——, and R. L. Moore. 1970. Mississippi silversides, *Menidia audens* (Atherinidae), established in California. Trans. Amer. Fish. Soc. 99(1):70-73.

——, ——, and J. D. Connors. 1966. The status of the native fishes of Clear Lake, Lake County, California. Wassman J. Biol. 24(2):141-160.

Coots, M. 1955. The Pacific lamprey, *Entosphenus tridentatus*, above Copco Dam, Siskiyou County, California. Calif. Fish, Game 41(1):118-119.

——. 1956. The yellow perch, *Perca flavescens* (Mitchill), in the Klamath River. Calif. Fish, Game 42(7):219-228.

——. 1965. Occurrences of the Lost River sucker, *Deltistes luxatus* (Cope), and shortnose sucker, *Chasmistes brevirostris* (Cope), in northern California. Calif. Fish, Game 51(2):68-73.

Cope, E. D. 1879. The fishes of Klamath Lake, Oregon. Amer. Nat. 13:784-785.

Cope, O. B. 1964. Revised bibliography on the cutthroat trout. U. S. Fish, Wildlife Serv. Res. Rept. 65: 43 pp.

Cordone, A., and T. C. Frantz. 1966. The Lake Tahoe sport fishery. Calif. Fish, Game 52(4):240-274.

―――, S. Nicola, P. Baker, and T. Frantz. 1971. The kokanee salmon in Lake Tahoe. Calif. Fish, Game 57(1):28-43.

Cornelius, R. H. 1969. The systematics and zoogeography of *Rhinichthys osculus* (Girard) in Southern California. M. A. Thesis, Calif. State University, Fullerton, 194 pp.

Courtois, L. A. 1973. The effects of temperature, availability of oxygen, and salinity upon the metabolism of the longjaw mudsucker, *Gillichthys mirabilis*. M. A. Thesis, Calif. State Univ., Hayward, 32 pp.

Cowles, R. B. 1934. Notes on the ecology and breeding habits of the desert minnow, *Cyprinodon macularius* Baird and Girard. *Copeia* 1934(1):40-42.

Cox, T. J. 1966. A behavioral and ecological study of the desert pupfish (*Cyprinodon macularius*) in Quitobaquito Springs, Organ Pipe Cactus National Monument, Arizona. Ph.D. Thesis, Univ. Arizona, Tucson, 102 pp.

―――. 1972. The food habits of the desert pupfish (*Cyprinodon macularius*) in the Quitobaquito Springs, Organ Pipe National Monument, Arizona. J. Ariz. Acad. Sci. 7(1):25-27.

Crear, D., and I. Haydock. 1970. Laboratory rearing of the desert pupfish, *Cyprinodon macularius*. Fishery Bull. 69(1):151-156.

Cross, Frank B. 1967. Handbook of Fishes of Kansas. Univ. Kansas Mus. Nat. Hist. Misc. Pub. 45: 357 pp.

Culver, G. B., and C. L. Hubbs. 1917. The fishes of the Santa Ana System streams in southern California. Lorquina 1(2):82-83.

Curtis, B. 1934. The golden trout of Cottonwood Lakes (*Salmo aqua-bonita* Jordan). Trans. Amer. Fish. Soc. 64:259-265.

―――. 1942. The general situation and the biological effects of the introduction of alien fishes into California waters. Calif. Fish, Game 28(1):2-8.

―――. 1949. The warmwater game fishes of California. Calif. Fish, Game 35(4):255-273.

Danielsen, T. L. 1968. Differential predation on *Culex pipiens* and *Anopheles albimanus* mosquito larvae by two species of fish (*Gambusia affinis* and *Cyprinodon nevadensis*) and the effects of simulated reeds on predation. Ph.D. Thesis, Univ. Calif., Riverside.

Darnell, R. M., and R. R. Meierotto. 1965. Diurnal periodicity in the black bullhead, *Ictalurus melas* (Rafinesque). Trans. Amer. Fish. Soc. 94(1):1-8.

Davis, S. P. 1963. Commercial freshwater fisheries of California. Calif. Fish, Game 49(2):84-94.

Deacon, J. E., and W. G. Bradley. 1972. Ecological distribution of fishes of Moapa (Muddy) River in Clark County, Nevada. Trans. Amer. Fish. Soc. 101(3):408-412.

Dennison, S. G., and R. V. Bulkley. 1972. Reproductive potential of the black bullhead, *Ictalurus melas*, in Clear Lake, Iowa. Trans. Amer. Fish. Soc. 101(3):483-487.

deVlaming, V. L. 1971. Thermal selection behavior in the estuarine goby, *Gillichthys mirabilis* Cooper. J. Fish. Biol. 1971(3):277-286.

DeWitt, J. W. 1954. A survey of the coast cutthroat trout, *Salmo clarki clarki* Richardson in California. Calif. Fish, Game 40(3):329-335.

Dietsch, E. L. 1959. The ecology and food habits of the sculpin (*Cottus beldingi*) in relation to the eastern brook trout (*Salvelinus fontinalis*). M. A. Thesis, Univ. Calif., Berkeley.

Dill, W. A. 1944. The fishery of the lower Colorado River. Calif. Fish, Game 30(3):109-211.

―――. 1946. A preliminary report on the fishery of Millerton Lake, California. Calif. Fish, Game 32(1):49-70.

, M. Coots, and P. A. Douglas. 1955. The status of the pumpkinseed, *Lepomis gibbosus* (Linne) in California. Calif. Dept. Fish, Game 41(2):157-159.

Dobie, J., O. L. Meecham, S. F. Snieszko, and G. N. Washburn. 1956. Raising bait fishes. U. S. Fish. Wildlife Circ. 35: 124 pp.

Dotu, Y., and S. Mito. 1955. On the breeding habits, larvae, and young of a goby, *Acanthogobius flavimanus* (Temminck and Schlegal). Japan. J. Ichthyol. 4:153-161.

Douglas, P. A. 1952. Notes·on the spawning of the humpback sucker, *Xyrauchen texanus* (Abbott). Calif. Fish, Game 38(2):149-155.

Dryfoos, R. L. 1965. The life history and ecology of the longfin smelt in Lake Washington. Ph.D. Thesis, Univ. Washington, 229 pp.

Ebert, V. W., and R. C. Summerfelt. 1969. Contributions to the life history of the Piute sculpin, *Cottus beldingii* Eigenmann and Eigenmann, in Lake Tahoe. Calif. Fish, Game 55(2):100-120.

Eddy, S., and J. C. Underhill. 1974. Northern Fishes, with Special Reference to the Upper Mississippi Valley. Minneapolis, Univ. Minn. Press, 414 pp.

Eigenmann, C. L., and R. S. Eigenmann. 1893. Additions to the fauna of San Diego. Proc. Calif. Acad. Sci. 3(1890-1892):1-24.

Elliott, G. V., and T. M. Jenkins. 1972. Winter food of trout in three high elevation Sierra Nevada lakes. Calif. Fish, Game 58(3):231-237.

Emig, J. W. 1966. Largemouth bass, 332-353; smallmouth bass, 354-365; red-ear sunfish, 392-398; brown bullhead, 463-475. *In* A. Calhoun, ed., Inland Fisheries Management, Calif. Dept. Fish, Game.

. 1969. The arctic grayling. Calif. Dept. Fish, Game Inland Fish. Admin. Dept. 69-5: 31 pp.

Erkkila, L. F., J. W. Moffett, O. B. Cope, B. R. Smith, and R. S. Nelson. 1950. Sacramento-San Joaquin Delta fishery resources: effects of Tracy pumping plant and delta cross channel. USFWS Spec. Sci. Rept. Fish 56: 109 pp.

Etnier, D. A. 1968. Reproductive success of natural populations of hybrid sunfish in three Minnesota lakes. Trans. Amer. Fish. Soc. 97(4):466-472.

Evans, D. H. 1969. Life history studies of the Lahontan redside, *Richardsonius egregius*, in Lake Tahoe. Calif. Fish, Game 55(3):197-222.

Evans, W. A. 1950. Notes on the occurrence of the bigmouth buffalo in southern California. Calif. Fish, Game 36(3):332-333.

Everest, F. H., and D. W. Chapman. 1972. Habitat selection and spatial interaction by juvenile chinook salmon and steelhead trout in two Idaho streams. J. Fish. Res. Bd. Canada 29(1):91-100.

Evermann, B. W. 1905. The golden trout of the southern high Sierras. Bull. U. S. Bur. Fish. 25:1-51.

. 1916. Fishes of the Salton Sea. Copeia 34:61-63.

, and A. C. Bryant. 1919. California trout. Calif. Fish, Game 5(3):105-135.

, and H. W. Clark. 1931. A distributional list of the species of freshwater fishes known to occur in California. Calif. Dept. Fish, Game Fish. Bull. 35: 67 pp.

, and S. E. Meek. 1897. A report upon salmon investigations in the Columbia River basin and elsewhere on the Pacific coast in 1896. Bull. U. S. Fish. Comm. 17:15-84.

, and C. Rutter. 1894. The fishes of the Colorado basin. Bull. U. S. Fish. Comm. 14:473-486.

Faber, D. J. 1967. Limnetic larval fish in northern Wisconsin lakes. J. Fish. Res. Bd. Canada 24(5):927-937.

Farley, D. 1972. A range extension of the logperch. Calif. Fish, Game 58(3):248.

Feldmeth, C. R., and J. P. Waggoner. 1972. Field measurements of tolerance to extreme hypersalinity in the California killifish, *Fundulus parvipinnis*. Copeia 1972(3):592-594.

Fierstine, H. L., K. F. Kline, and G. R. Garmen. 1973. Fishes collected in Morro Bay, California, between January 1968 and December, 1970. Calif. Fish, Game 59(1):73-88.

Fisher, F. W. 1973. Observations on the spawning of Mississippi silversides, *Menidia audens* Hay. Calif. Fish, Game 59(4):315-316.

Fisk, L. O. 1972. Status of certain depleted inland fishes. Calif. Dept. Fish, Game Inland Fish. Admin. Rept. 72-1: 13 pp.

Fite, K. R. 1973. Feeding overlap between roach and juvenile steelhead in the Eel River. M. S. Thesis, Calif. State Univ., Humboldt, 38 pp.

Flittner, G. A. 1953. The composition and distribution of the fish populations in Sagehen Creek, Nevada-Sierra County, California. M. A. Thesis, Univ. Calif., Berkeley.

Foerster, R. E. 1968. The sockeye salmon, *Oncorhynchus nerka*. Fish. Res. Bd. Canada Bull. 162: 422 pp.

———, and W. E. Ricker, 1942. The effect of reduction of predaceous fish on survival of young sockeye salmon at Cultus Lake. J. Fish Res. Bd. Canada 51(1):315-336.

Follett, W. I. 1928. A note on the squawfish and one of its relatives. Calif. Fish, Game 14(4):282-285.

Forney, J. L. 1961. Growth, movements, and survival of smallmouth bass (*Micropterus dolomieui*) in Oneida Lake, New York. N. Y. Fish, Game J. 8(2):88-105.

Foster, N. R. 1967a. Comparative studies on the biology of killifishes. Ph.D. Thesis, Cornell Univ., Ithaca, 369 pp.

———. 1967b. Trends in the evolution of reproductive behavior in killifishes. Stud. Trop. Oceanogr. 5:549-566.

Fowler, H. W. 1913. Notes on catostomid fishes. Proc. Acad. Nat. Sci. Phila. 65:45-71.

Frantz, T. C., and A. J. Cordone. 1965. Introduction of the Bonneville cisco (*Prosopium gemmiferum* Snyder) in Lake Tahoe, California and Nevada. Calif. Fish, Game 51(4):270-275.

———, and ———. 1967. Observations on deepwater plants in Lake Tahoe, California and Nevada. Ecology 48(5):709-714.

———, and ———. 1970. Food of lake trout in Lake Tahoe. Calif. Fish, Game 56(1):21-35.

Frey, H. W., ed. 1971. California's Living Marine Resources and Their Utilization. Calif. Dept. Fish, Game, 148 pp.

Frost, W. E., and M. E. Brown. 1967. The Trout. Collins, London. 286 pp.

Fry, D. H. 1936. Life history of *Hesperoleucas venustus* Snyder. Calif. Fish, Game 22(2):65-98.

———. 1967. A 1955 record of pink salmon, *Oncorhynchus gorbuscha*, spawning in the Russian River. Calif. Fish, Game 53(3):210-211.

———. 1973. Anadromous fishes of California. Calif. Dept. Fish, Game, 111 pp.

Fryer, G., and T. D. Iles. 1972. The Cichlid Fishes of the Great Lakes of Africa. TFH Publ., Hong Kong, 610 pp.

Ganssle, D. 1966. Fishes and decapods of San Pablo and Suisun Bay, 64-94. *In* D. W. Kelley, ed., Ecological Studies of the Sacramento-San Joaquin Estuary. Part 1. Calif. Dept. Fish, Game Bull. 133.

Gard, R., and G. A. Flittner. 1974. Distribution and abundance of fishes in Sagehen Creek, California. J. Wildl. Mgmt. 38(2):347-358.

Gerald, J. W. 1971. Sound production during courtship in six species of sunfish (*Centrarchidae*). Evolution 25(1):75-87.

Gerking, S. D. 1953. Evidence for the concepts of home range and territory in stream fishes. Ecology 34(3):347-365.

Gerstung, E. R. 1972. A progress report on grayling management in California. Calif. Dept. Fish, Game Mimeo, 9 pp.

Giger, R. D. 1972. Ecology and management of coastal cutthroat trout in Oregon. Oregon State Game Comm. Fish. Res. Rept. 6: 61 pp.

Gilbert, C. H. 1897. The fishes of the Klamath Basin. Bull. U. S. Fish. Comm. 17:1-13.

——, and N. B. Scofield. 1898. Notes on a collection of fishes from the Colorado Basin in Arizona. Proc. U. S. Nat. Mus. 20(1131):487-499.

Gold, J. R., and G. A. E. Gall. In press. The taxonomic structure of six California high Sierra golden trout (*Salmo aguabonita*) populations. Proc. Calif. Acad. Sci.

Gomez, R., and H. L. Lindsay. 1972. Occurrence of Mississippi silversides, *Menidia audens* (Hay), in Keystone Reservoir and the Arkansas River. Proc. Okla. Acad. Sci. 52:16-18.

Goodson, L. F. 1965. Diets of four warmwater game fishes in a fluctuating, steep-sided California reservoir. Calif. Fish, Game 51(4):259-269.

——. 1966. Landlocked striped bass, 402-411. *In* A. Calhoun, ed., Inland Fisheries Management, Calif. Dept. Fish, Game.

Goodyear, C. P., C. E. Boyd, and R. J. Beyers. 1972. Relationships between primary productivity and mosquitofish (*Gambusia affinis*) production in large microcosms. Limn. and Ocean. 17(3):445-450.

Gosline, W. A. 1966. The limits of the fish family Serranidae, with notes on other lower percoids. Proc. Calif. Acad. Sci. 33(6):91-112.

Greenback, J. 1957. Aggregational behavior in a freshwater sculpin. Copeia 1957(1):157.

Greenfield, D. W., and G. D. Deckert. 1973. Introgressive hybridization between *Gila orcutti* and *Hesperoleucus symmetricus* (Pisces: Cyprinidae) in the Cuyama River basin, California. II. Ecological Aspects. Copeia 1973(3):417-427.

——, and T. Greenfield. 1972. Introgressive hybridization between *Gila orcutti* and *Hesperoleucus symmetricus* (Pisces:Cyprinidae) in the Cuyama River Basin, California. I. Meristics, morphometrics and breeding. Copeia 1972(9):849-859.

——, S. T. Ross, and G. D. Deckert. 1970. Some aspects of the life history of the Santa Ana sucker, *Catostomus (Pantosteus) santaanae* (Snyder). Calif. Fish, Game 56(3):166-179.

Greenway, P. 1965. Body form and behavioral types in fish. Experientia 21(489):1-9.

Grinstead, B. G. 1969. The vertical distribution of the white crappie in the Buncombe Creek arm of Lake Texoma. Univ. Okla. Fish. Res. Lab. Bull. 3: 37 pp.

Groves, A. B., G. B. Collins, and P. S. Trefethen. 1968. Roles of olfaction and vision in choice of spawning site by homing adult chinook salmon (*Oncorhynchus tshawytscha*). J. Fish. Res. Bd. Canada 25(5):867-876.

Gunter, G. 1942. A list of the fishes of the mainland of North and South America recorded from both freshwater and seawater. Amer. Midl. Nat. 28(2):305-356.

Hagen, D. W. 1967. Isolating mechanisms in three-spine sticklebacks (*Gasterosteus*). J. Fish. Res. Bd. Canada 24(8):1637-1692.

——, and L. G. Gilbertson. 1972. Geographic variation and environmental selection in *Gasterosteus aculeatus* L. in the Pacific Northwest, America. Evolution 26(1):32-51.

Hale, J. G., and D. A. Hilden. 1969. Spawning and some aspects of early life history of brook trout, *Salvelinus fontinalis* (Mitchill), in the laboratory. Trans. Amer. Fish. Soc. 98(3):973-977.

Hallock, R. J., R. T. Elwell, and D. H. Fry. 1970. Migrations of adult king salmon (*Oncorhynchus tshawytscha*) in the San Joaquin Delta, as demonstrated by the use of sonic tags. Calif. Dept. Fish, Game Fish Bull. 151: 92 pp.

——, and D. H. Fry. 1967. Five species of salmon, *Oncorhynchus*, in the Sacramento River, California. Calif. Fish, Game 53(1):5-22.

Hamada, K. 1961. Taxonomic and ecological studies of the genus *Hypomesus* of Japan. Mem. Fac. Fish. Hokkaido Univ. 9(1):1-56.

Hansen, D. F. 1951. Biology of the white crappie in Illinois. Ill. Nat. Hist. Surv. Bull. 25(4):211-265.

———. 1965. Further observations on nesting of white crappie. Trans. Amer. Fish. Soc. 94(2):182-184.

Hanson, J. A., and A. J. Cordone. 1967. Age and growth of lake trout, *Salvelinus namaycush* (Walbaum), in Lake Tahoe. Calif. Fish, Game 53(2):68-87.

———, and R. H. Wickwire. 1967. Fecundity and age at maturity of lake trout, *Salvelinus namaycush* (Walbaum), in Lake Tahoe. Calif. Fish, Game 53(3):154-164.

Hardisty, M. W., and I. C. Potter, eds. 1971. The Biology of Lampreys, Vol. 1. Academic Press, London, 423 pp.

Harrington, R. W., and E. S. Harrington. 1961. Food selection among fishes invading a high subtropical salt marsh from onset of flooding through the progress of a mosquito brood. Ecology 42(4):646-656.

Harry, R. R. 1951. The embryonic and early larval stages of the tui chub, *Siphatales bicolor* (Girard) from Eagle Lake, California. Calif. Fish, Game 37(2):129-132.

Hart, J. L. 1973. Pacific Fishes of Canada. Fish. Res. Bd. Canada Bull. 180: 740 pp.

Hartman, G. F. 1965. The role of behavior in the ecology and interaction of underyearling coho salmon (*Oncorhynchus kisutch*) and steelhead trout (*Salmo gairdneri*). J. Fish. Res. Bed. Canada 22(4):1035-1081.

———, and C. A. Gill. 1968. Distribution of juvenile steelhead and cutthroat trout (*Salmo gairdneri* and *S. clarki clarki*) within streams of southwestern British Columbia. J. Fish. Res. Bd. Canada 25(1):33-48.

Harwood, R. H. 1972. Diurnal feeding rhythm of *Notropis lutrensis* Baird and Girard. Texas J. Sci. 24(1):97-99.

Hauser, W. J. 1969. Life history of the mountain sucker, *Catostomus platyrhynchus*, in Montana. Trans. Amer. Fish. Soc. 98(2):209-224.

Heard, W. R. 1965. Limnetic cottid larvae and their utilization as food by juvenile sockeye salmon. Trans. Amer. Fish Soc. 99:191-193.

Heman, M. L., R. S. Campbell, and L. C. Redmond. 1969. Manipulation of fish populations through reservoir drawdowns. Trans. Amer. Fish. Soc. 98(2):293-304.

Hendricks, L. J. 1961. The threadfin shad, *Dorosoma petenense* (Gunther), 93-94; the striped mullet, *Mugil cephalus* Linnaeus, 95-103. *In* B. D. Walker, ed., The Ecology of the Salton Sea, California, in Relation to the Sport Fishery. Calif. Fish, Game Fish. Bull. No. 113.

Herald, E. S. 1941. A systematic analysis of variation in the western American pipefish, *Syngnathus californiensis*. Stanford Ich. Bull. 2(3):49-73.

Hergenrader, G. L. 1969. Spawning behavior of *Perca flavescens* in aquaria. Copeia 1969(4):839-841.

Hinds, N. E. A. 1952. Evolution of the California Landscape. Calif. Div. Mines Bull. 158: 240 pp.

Hodges, C. A. 1966. Geomorphic history of Clear Lake, California. Ph.D. Thesis, Stanford Univ.

Holden, P. B., and C. B. Stalnaker. 1970. Systematic studies of the cyprinid genus *Gila* in the upper Colorado River basin. Copeia 1970(3):490-420.

———, and ———. 1975. Distribution of fishes in the Dolores and Yampa River systems of the upper Colorado basin. Southwest Nat. 19(4):403-412.

Holway, R. S. 1907. Physiographic changes bearing on the faunal relationships of the Russian and Sacramento rivers, California. Science, n. s. 26:382-383.

Hoogland, R., D. Morris, and N. Tinbergen. 1956. The spines of sticklebacks (*Gasterosteus* and *Pygosteus*) as means of defense against predators (*Perca* and *Esox*). Behaviour 10:205-236.

Hoopaugh, D. A. 1974. Status of redband trout (*Salmo* sp.) in California. Calif. Dept. Fish, Game Inland Fish Admin. Dept. 74-7: 11 pp.

Hoover, F. G. 1971. Status report on *Tilapia mossambica* (Peters) in southern California. Calif. Dept. Fish, Game Inland Fish. Admin. Rept. 71-16: 31 pp.

————, and J. A. St. Amant. 1970. Establishment of *Tilapia mossambica* (Peters) in Bard Valley, Imperial County, California. Calif. Fish, Game 56(1):70-71.

Hopkirk, J. D. 1973. Endemism in Fishes of the Clear Lake Region. Univ. Calif. Pub. Zool. 96: 160 pp.

————. 1962. Morphological variation in the freshwater embiotocid *Hysterocarpus traskii* Gibbons. M. A. Thesis, Univ. Calif., Berkeley, 159 pp.

————, and R. J. Behnke. 1966. Additions to the known native fish fauna of Nevada. Copeia 1966(1):134-136.

Horne, A. J., and C. R. Goldman. 1972. Nitrogen fixation in Clear Lake, California. I. Seasonal variation and the role of heterocysts. Limnol. Oceanog. 17(5):678-692.

Houde, E. D. 1969. Distribution of larval walleyes and yellow perch in a bay of Oneida Lake and its relation to water currents and zooplankton. N. Y. Fish, Game J. 16(2):184-205.

Howard, A. O. 1967. Evolution of the Landscape of the San Francisco Bay Region. University of California Press, Berkeley, 72 pp.

Howland, J. W. 1931. Studies on the Kentucky black bass (*Micropterus pseudaplites* Hubbs). Trans. Amer. Fish. Soc. 61:89-94.

Hoy, J. B., E. E. Kaufmann, and A. G. O'Berg. 1972. A large-scale field test of *Gambusia affinis* and Chlorpurifos for mosquito control. Mosquito News 32(2):163-171.

Hsai, C., and G. R. Gibson, Jr. 1971. Fecundity of the yellow perch, *Perca flavescens* Mitchill, in the Patuxent River, Maryland. Chesapeake Sci. 12(4):270-284.

Hubbell, P. M. 1966. Pumpkinseed sunfish, 402-404; warmouth, 405-407. *In* A. Calhoun, ed., Inland Fisheries Management, Calif. Dept. Fish, Game.

Hubbs, C. L. 1946. Wandering of pink salmon and other salmonid fishes into southern California. Calif. Fish, Game 32(2):81-86.

————. 1953. *Eleotris picta* added to the fish fauna of California. Calif. Fish, Game 39(1):69-76.

————. 1954. Establishment of a forage fish, the red shiner (*Notropis lutrensis*), in the lower Colorado River system. Calif. Fish, Game 40(3):287-294.

————. 1961. Isolating mechanisms in the speciation of fishes, 537-560. *In* F. Blair, ed., Vertebrate Speciation, University of Texas Press, Austin.

————. 1967. Occurrence of the Pacific lamprey, *Entosphenus tridentatus*, off Baja California and in streams of southern California, with remarks on its nomenclature. Trans. San Diego Nat. Hist. Soc. 14(21):301-312.

————. 1971. *Lampetra* (*Entosphenus*) *lethophaga*, new species, the nonparasitic derivative of the Pacific lamprey. Trans San Diego Nat. Hist. Soc. 16(6):125-164.

————, and R. M. Bailey. 1940. A revision of the black basses, (*Micropterus* and *Huro*), with descriptions of four new forms. Univ. of Mich. Mus. Zool. Misc. Pub. 48:1-51.

————, L. C. Hubbs, and R. E. Johnson. 1943. Hybridization in nature between species of catostomid fishes. Contr. Lab. Vert. Biol., Univ. Mich. 22: 76 pp.

————, and K. Lagler. 1958. Fishes of the Great Lakes Region. University of Michigan Press, Ann Arbor, 213 pp.

————, and I. C. Potter. 1971. Distribution, phylogeny and taxonomy, 1-65. *In* M. W. Hardisty and I. C. Potter, eds., The Biology of Lampreys, Vol. 1, Academic Press, London.

————, and R. R. Miller. 1942. Mass hybridization between two genera of cyprinid fishes in the Mohave Desert, California. Papers Mich. Acad. Sci., Arts, Letters 28:343-378.

————, and ————. 1948. The Great Basin, with emphasis on glacial and postglacial times. II. The zoological evidence: correlation between fish distribution and hydrographic history in the desert basins of western United States. Bull. Univ. Utah 38(2):18-166.

, and   . 1951. *Catostomus arenarius*, a Great Basin fish, synonymized with *C. tahoensis*. Copeia 1951(4):299-300.

, and   . 1952. Hybridization in nature between the fish genera *Catostomus* and *Xyrauchen*. Papers Mich. Acad. Sci., Arts, Letters 38:207-233.

, and   . 1965. Studies of cyprinodont fishes. XXII. Variation in *Lucania parva*, its establishment in western United States, and description of a new species from an interior basin in Coahuila, Mexico. Univ. Mich. Mus. Zool. Misc. Pub. 127: 104 pp.

,   , and L. C. Hubbs. 1974. Hydrographic history and relict fishes of the northcentral Great Basin. Mem. Calif. Acad. Sci. 7: 259 pp.

, and O. L. Wallis. 1948. The native fish fauna of Yosemite National Park and its preservation. Yosemite Nat. Notes 27(12):131-144.

Hubbs, Clark. 1947. Mixture of marine and freshwater fishes in the lower Salinas River, Calif. Copeia 1947(2):147-149.

. 1968. An opinion on the effects of cichlid releases in North America. Trans. Amer. Fish. Soc. 97(2):197-198.

. 1974. Review of J. D. Hopkirk. Endemism in Fishes of the Clear Lake Region. Copeia 1974(3):808-809.

, H. B. Sharp, and J. F. Schneider. 1971. Developmental rates of *Menida audens* with notes on salt tolerance. Trans. Amer. Fish. Soc. 100(4):603-610.

Huet, M. 1959. Profiles and biology of Western European streams as related to fish management. Trans. Amer. Fish. Soc. 88:155-163.

Hunter, J. R. 1963. The reproductive behavior of the green sunfish, *Lepomis cyanellus*. Zoologica 48(2):13-24.

Hurlbert, S. H., J. Zedler, and D. Fairbanks. 1972. Ecosystem alteration by mosquitofish (*Gambusia affinis*) predation. Science 175:639-641.

Hutchinson, G. E. 1966. The Ecological Theatre and the Evolutionary Play. Yale University Press, New Haven, 139 pp.

Hynes, H. B. N. 1950. The food of freshwater sticklebacks (*Gasterosteus aculeatus* and *Pygosteus pungitius*), with a review of methods used in studies of the food of fishes. J. An. Ecol. 19(1):36-58.

Itzkowitz, M. 1971. Preliminary study of the social behavior of male *Gambusia affinis* (Baird and Girard) (Pisces: Poeciliidae) in aquaria. Ches. Sci. 12(4):219-224.

Jerald, A., and B. E. Brown. 1971. Food of the channel catfish (*Ictalurus punctatus*) in a southern Great Plains reservoir. Amer. Midl. Nat. 86(1):110-115.

Jenkins, T. M. 1969. Social structure, position choice and microdistribution of two trout species (*Salmo trutta* and *Salmo gairdneri*) resident in mountain streams. An. Behav. Mono. 2(2):57-123.

Jensen, P. T. 1957. An extension of the range of the long-finned smelt, *Spirinchus dilatus*. Calif. Fish, Game 43:99.

. 1972. King salmon, 44-51. *In* J. Skinner, ed., Ecological Studies of the Sacramento-San Joaquin Estuary, Delta Fish and Wildl. Prot. Study Rept. No. 8.

Jhingran, V. G. 1948. A contribution to the biology of the Klamath black dace, *Rhinichthys osculus klamathensis*. (Evermann and Meek). Ph.D. Thesis, Stanford Univ., 94 pp.

Johannes, R. E., and P. A. Larkin. 1961. Competition for food between redside shiners (*Richardsonius balteatus*) and rainbow trout (*Salmo gairdneri*) in two British Columbia lakes. J. Fish Res. Bd. Canada 18(2):203-220.

John, K. R. 1963. The effect of torrential rains on the reproductive cycle of *Rhinichthys osculus* in the Chiricahua Mountains, Arizona. Copeia 1963(2):286-291.

. 1964. Survival of fish in intermittent streams of the Chiricahua Mountains, Arizona. Ecology 45(1):112-119.

Johnson, D. W., and E. L. McClendon. 1970. Differential distribution of the striped mullet, *Mugil cephalus* Linnaeus. Calif. Fish, Game 56(2):138-139.

Johnson, J. E. 1970. Age, growth, and population dynamics of threadfin shad, *Dorosoma petenense* (Günther), in Central Arizona reservoirs. Trans. Amer. Fish Soc. 99(4):739-753.

⸻. 1971. Maturity and fecundity of threadfin shad, *Dorosoma petenense* (Günther), in Central Arizona reservoirs. Trans. Amer. Fish Soc. 100(1):74-85.

Johnson, R. P. 1963. Studies on the life history and ecology of the bigmouth buffalo, *Ictiobus cyprinellus* (Valenciennes). J. Fish Res. Bd. Canada 20(6):1397-1430.

Jones, A. C. 1962. The biology of the euryhaline fish *Leptocottus armatus* Girard (Cottidae). Univ. Calif. Pub. Zool. 67(4):321-367.

⸻. 1972. Contributions to the life history of the Piute sculpin in Sagehen Creek, California. Calif. Fish, Game 58(4):285-290.

Jonez, A., and R. C. Sumner. 1954. Lakes Mead and Mohave investigations. Nevada Fish and Game Comm. Wildl. Restor. Div. Mimeo, 174 pp.

Jordan, D. S. 1894. Notes on the fresh-water species of San Luis Obispo County, California. Bull. U. S. Fish. Comm. 19:191-192.

⸻, and B. W. Evermann. 1896. Fishes of North and Middle America. Bull. U. S. Nat. Mus. 47(1-4): 3705 pp.

⸻, and   . 1923. American Food and Game Fishes. Doubleday and Company, New York, 573 pp.

⸻, and C. H. Gilbert. 1894. List of the fishes inhabiting Clear Lake, California. Bull. U. S. Fish Comm. 14:139-140.

Jubb, R. A. 1967. Freshwater Fishes of Southern Africa. A. A. Balkema, Capetown, pp. 159-163.

Keast, A. 1966. Trophic interrelationships in the fish fauna of a small stream. Univ. Mich. Great Lakes Res. Div. Pub. 15:51-79.

⸻. 1968a. Feeding biology of the black crappie, *Pomoxis nigromaculatus*. J. Fish. Res. Bd. Canada 24(1):285-297.

⸻. 1968b. Feeding of some Great Lakes fishes at low temperatures. J. Fish. Res. Bd. Canada 24(6):1199-1218.

⸻, and D. Webb. 1966. Mouth and body form relative to feeding ecology in the fish fauna of a small lake, Lake Opinicon, Ontario. J. Fish. Res. Bd. Canada 23(12):1845-1874.

⸻, and L. Welsh. 1968. Daily feeding periodicities, food uptake rates, and dietary changes with hour of day in some lake fishes. J. Fish. Res. Bd. Canada 25(6):1133-1149.

Kelly, H. D. 1957. Preliminary studies on *Tilapia mossambica* Peters relative to experimental pond culture. Proc. 10th Ann. Conf. SE Assoc., Fish Comm.: 139-149.

Kendall, A. W., and F. J. Schwartz. 1968. Lethal temperature and salinity tolerances of the white catfish, *Ictalurus catus*, from the Patuxent River, Maryland, Ches. Sci. 9(2):103-108.

Kennedy, C. H. 1916. A possible enemy of the mosquito. Calif. Fish, Game 2(4):179-182.

Keys, A. B. 1931. A study of the selective action of decreased salinity and of asphyxiation on the Pacific killifish, *Fundulus parvipinnis*. Bull. Scripps Inst. Ocean. 2:417-490.

Kimsey, J. B. 1950. Some Lahontan fishes in the Sacramento River Drainage, California. Calif. Fish, Game 36(4):438-439.

⸻. 1954a. The introduction of the redeye black bass and the threadfin shad into California. Calif. Fish, Game 40(2):203-204.

⸻. 1954b. The life history of the tui chub, *Siphateles bicolor* (Girard), from Eagle Lake, California. Calif. Fish, Game 40(4):395-410.

. 1957. The status of the redeye bass in California. Calif. Dept. Fish, Game 43(1):99-100.

. 1960. Observations on the spawning of Sacramento hitch in a lacustrine environment. Calif. Fish, Game 46(2):211-215.

, and R. R. Bell. 1955. Observations on the ecology of the largemouth black bass and the tui chub in Big Sage Reservoir, Modoc County. Calif. Dept. Fish, Game Inland Fish Admin. Rpt. 55-75: 17 pp.

, and . 1956. Notes on the status of the pumpkinseed sunfish, *Lepomis gibbosus*, in the Susan River, Lassen County, California. Calif. Dept. Fish, Game Inland Fish Admin. Rpt. 56-1: 20 pp.

, and L. O. Fisk. 1960. Keys to the freshwater and anadromous fishes of California. Calif. Fish, Game 46(4):453-479.

, and . 1964. Freshwater Nongame Fishes of California. Calif. Dept. Fish, Game, 54 pp.

, R. H. Hagy, and G. W. McCammon. 1957. Progress report on the Mississippi threadfin shad, *Dorosoma petenensis atchafaylae* in the Colorado River for 1956. Calif. Dept. Fish, Game Inland Fish Admin. Rpt. 57-23: 48 pp.

, D. W. Kelley, R. Hagy, and G. McCammon. 1956. A survey of the fish populations of Pardee Reservoir, Amador/Calaveras counties. Calif. Dept. Fish, Game Inland Fish Admin. Rpt. 56-18: 13 pp.

Kinne, O. 1960. Growth, food intake, and food conversion in a euryplastic fish exposed to different temperatures and salinities. Physiol. Zool. 33:288-317.

Kitchell, J. F., and J. T. Windell. 1970. Nutritional value of algae to bluegill sunfish, *Lepomis macrochirus*. Copeia 1970(1):186-190.

Kjelson, M. A. 1971. Selective predation by a freshwater planktivore, the threadfin shad, *Dorosoma petenense*. Ph.D. thesis, Zoology, Univ. Calif., Davis, 123 pp.

Koch, D. L. 1973. Reproductive characteristics of the cui-ui lakesucker (*Chasmistes cujus* Cope) and its spawning behavior in Pyramid Lake, Nevada. Trans. Amer. Fish Soc. 102(1):145-149.

, and G. P. Contreras. 1973a. Hatching technique for the cui-ui sucker. Prog. Fish. Cult. 35(1):61-63.

, and . 1973b. Preliminary survey of the fishes of the Lost River System. Desert Res. Inst. Cent. for Water Resources Res., Prog. Rept. 23: 45 pp.

Koehn, R. 1965. Development and ecological significance of nuptial tubercles of the red shiner, *Notropis lutrensis*. Copeia 1965(4):462-467.

Kornblatt, B. J. 1974. The genetic status of six high sierra golden trout (*Salmo aguabonita*) populations. M. S. Thesis, Univ. Calif., Davis, 74 pp.

Kottcamp, G. 1973. Variation, behavior and ecology of the prickly sculpin (*Cottus asper* Richardson) from the San Joaquin River, California. M. A. Thesis, Calif. State Univ., Fresno, 56 pp.

, and P. B. Moyle. 1972. Use of disposable beverage cans by fish in the San Joaquin Valley. Trans. Amer. Fish. Soc. 101(3):566.

Kottlowski, F. E., N. E. Collery, and R. V. Ruhe. 1965. The quaternary of the Pacific mountain system in California. *In* H. E. Wright and D. G. Frey, eds., The Quarternary of the United States, Princeton University Press, Princeton.

Kramer, R. H., and L. L. Smith. 1960. Utilization of the nests of largemouth bass, *Micropterus salmoides*, by golden shiner, *Notemigonus crysoleucas*. Copeia 1960(1):73-74.

Kresja, R. J. 1965. The systematics of the prickly sculpin, *Cottus asper*: an investigation of genetic and non-genetic variation within a polytypic species. Ph.D. Thesis, Univ. Brit. Columbia, 109 pp.

. 1970. The systematics of the prickly sculpin *Cottus asper* Richardson, a polytypic species. Part I. Synonomy, nomenclatural history and distribution. Pac. Sci. 21:241-251.

Kroeber, A. L., and S. A. Barrett. 1960. Fishing among the Indians of Northwestern California. Anthro. Records 21(1): 270 pp.

Krumholz, L. A. 1948. Reproduction in the western mosquitofish *Gambusia affinis affinis* (Baird and Girard) and its use in mosquito control. Ecol. Monographs 18:1-43.

Kukowski, G. E. 1972. A checklist of the fishes of the Monterey Bay area including Elkhorn Slough, the San Lorenzo, Pajaro, and Salinas rivers. Moss Landing Marine Lab Tech. Pub. 72-2: 69 pp.

La Bounty, J. F., and J. E. Deacon. 1972. *Cyprinodon milleri*, a new species of pupfish (family Cyprinodontidae) from Death Valley, California. Copeia 1972(4):769-780.

La Rivers, I. 1962. Fishes and Fisheries of Nevada. Nev. Fish, Game. Comm., 782 pp.

Lambou, V. W. 1965. Observations on the size distribution and spawning behavior of threadfin shad. Trans. Amer. Fish. Soc. 94(4):385-386.

Lanse, R. 1965. The occurrence of warmouth, *Chaenobryttus gulosus* (Cuvier), in the lower Colorado River. Calif. Fish, Game 51(2):123.

Larimore, R. W. 1957. Ecological life history of the warmouth (Centrarchidae). Bull. Ill. Nat. Hist. Surv. 27(1): 83 pp.

Latta, W. C. 1963. The life history of the smallmouth bass, *Micropterus d. dolomieui* at Waugoshance Point, Lake Michigan. Mich. Dept. Const. Inst. for Fish. Res. Bull. 5: 56 pp.

Leach, H. R., J. M. Brode, and S. J. Nicola. 1974. At the Crossroads, 1974. Calif. Dept. Fish, Game, 112 pp.

———, and L. O. Fisk. 1972. At the Crossroads. Calif. Dept. Fish, Game, 99 pp.

Legendre, P., C. B. Schreck, and R. J. Behnke. 1972. Taximetric analysis of selected groups of western North American *Salmo* with respect to phylogenetic divergences. Syst. Zool. 21(3):292-307.

Leggett, W. C. 1973. The migrations of the shad. Sci. Amer. 228(3):92-100.

Legner, E. F., T. W. Fisher, and R. A. Medved. 1973. Biological control of aquatic weeds in the lower Colorado River basin. Proc. Ann. Conf. Calif. Mosq. Contr. Assoc. 41:115-117.

———, and W. J. Hauser. 1973. Biological control of aquatic weeds in the lower Colorado River basin. Ann. Rpt. Univ. Calif., Davis, 22 pp.

———, and R. A. Medved. 1973. Predation of mosquitoes and chironomid midges in ponds by *Tilapia zillii* and *T. mossambica* (Teleostei: Cichlidae). Proc. Ann. Conf. Calif. Mosq. Contr. Assoc. 41:119-121.

Levesque, R. C., and R. J. Reed. 1972. Food availability and consumption by young Connecticut River shad, *Alosa sapidissima*. J. Fish. Res. Bd. Canada 29(10):1495-1499.

Lewis, S. L. 1969. Physical factors influencing fish populations in pools of a trout stream. Trans. Amer. Fish Soc. 98(1):14-19.

Lewis, W. M., and S. Flickinger. 1967. Home range tendency of the largemouth bass (*Micropterus salmoides*). Ecology 48(6):1020-1023.

———, G. E. Gunning, E. Lyles, and W. L. Bridges. 1961. Food choice of largemouth bass as a function of availability and vulnerability of food items. Trans. Amer. Fish Soc. 90(3):277-280.

Lewis, W. M., Jr. 1970. Morphological adaptations of cyprinodontoids for inhabiting oxygen deficient waters. Copeia 1970(2):319-326.

Lindquist, A. W., C. D. Deonier, and J. E. Hanley. 1943. The relationship to fish of the Clear Lake gnat, Clear Lake, California. Calif. Fish and Game 29(4):196-202.

Liu, R. K. 1969. The comparative behavior of allopatric species (Teleostei-Cyprinodontidae: *Cyprinodon*). Ph.D. Thesis, UCLA, 185 pp.

Lockington, W. N. 1878. Report upon the food fishes of San Francisco. Rpt. Calif. Fish. Comm. 1878-78:17-58.

Loeb, H. A. 1964. Submergence of brown bullheads in bottom sediment. N. Y. Fish Game J. 11(2):119-124.

Lollock, D. L. 1968. An evaluation of the fishery resources of the Pajaro River Basin. Calif. Dept. Fish, Game Mimeo, 60 pp.

Long, C. W. 1968. Diel movement and vertical distribution of juvenile anadromous fish in turbine intakes. Fishery Bull. U. S. Fish, Wild. Serv. 66:599-609.

Lorz, H. W., and T. G. Northcote. 1965. Factors affecting stream location, and timing and intensity of entry by spawning kokanee (*Oncorhynchus nerka*) into an inlet of Nicola Lake, British Columbia. J. Fish Res. Bd. Canada 22(3):665-687.

Loud, L. L. 1929. Notes on the northern Piute. Univ. Calif. Pub. Arch., Ethnol. 25(1):152-164.

Lowe, C. H., and W. G. Heath. 1969. Behavioral and physiological responses to temperature in the desert pupfish, *Cyprinodon macularius* Physiol. Zool. 42(1):53-59.

——, D. S. Hinds, and E. A. Halpern. 1967. Experimental catostrophic selection and tolerances to low oxygen concentrations in native Arizona freshwater fishes. Ecology 48(4):1013-1017.

Lowe, R. N. 1955. Species of *Tilapia* in East African Dams, with a key for their identification. E. Afr. Ag. J. 20(4):256-262.

Lowenstein, O. 1957. The acoustico-lateralis system, 155-186. *In* M. E. Brown, ed., The Physiology of Fishes, Vol. II, Academic Press, New York.

Lowry, G. R. 1965. Movement of cutthroat trout, *Salmo clarki clarki* (Richardson) in three Oregon coastal streams. Trans. Amer. Fish Soc. 94(4):334-338.

——. 1966. Production and food of cutthroat trout in three Oregon coastal streams. J. Wildl. Mgmt. 30(4):754-767.

MacCrimmon, H. R. 1971. World distribution of rainbow trout (*Salmo gairdneri*). J. Fish. Res. Bd. Canada 28(5):663-704.

——, and J. S. Campbell. 1969. World distribution of brook trout, *Salvelinus fontinalis*. J. Fish. Res. Bd. Canada 26(7):1699-1725.

——, T. C. Marshall, and B. L. Gots. 1970. World distribution of brown trout, *Salmo trutta*: further observations. J. Fish. Res. Bd. Canada 27(4):811-818.

MacPhee, C. L. 1960. Postlarval development of the largescale sucker, *Catostomus macrocheilus*, in Idaho. Copeia 1960(2):119-125.

McAfee, W. B. 1966. Rainbow trout, 192-215; golden trout, 216-224; Eagle Lake rainbow trout; 221-225; Lahontan cutthroat trout, 225-230; Piute cutthroat trout, 231-233; eastern brook trout, 242-260; lake trout, 260-271; Dolly Varden trout, 271-274; landlocked king salmon, 294-295; mountain whitefish, 299-304. *In* A. Calhoun, ed., Inland Fisheries Management, Calif. Dept. Fish, Game.

McAllister, D. E. 1963. A revision of the smelt family, Osmeridae. Bull. Natl. Mus. Canada 191: 53 pp.

McCammon, G. W., D. L. Faunce, and C. M. Seeley. 1964. Observations on the food of fingerling largemouth bass in Clear Lake, Lake County, California. Calif. Fish, Game 50(3):158-169.

——, and C. M. Seeley. 1961. Survival, mortality, and movements of white catfish and brown bullheads in Clear Lake, California. Calif. Fish, Game 47(3):237-255.

McCarraher, D. B. 1972. Survival of some freshwater fishes in the alkaline eutrophic waters of Nebraska. J. Fish. Res. Bd. Canada 28(6):1811-1814.

——, and R. W. Gregory. 1970. Adaptability and status of introductions of Sacramento perch, *Archoplites interruptus*, in North America. Trans. Amer. Fish Soc. 99(4):700-707.

McCart, P., and N. Aspinwall. 1970. Spawning habits of the largescale sucker, *Catostomus macrocheilus*, at Slave Lake, British Columbia. J. Fish Res. Bd. Canada 27(6):1154-1158.

McComita, T. S. 1967. Food habits of bigmouth and smallmouth buffalo in Lewis and Clark Lake and the Missouri River. Trans. Amer. Fish. Soc. 96:70-74.

McConnell, R. J., and G. R. Snyder. 1972. Key to field identification of anadromous juvenile salmonids in the Pacific Northwest. NOAA Tech. Rept. NMFS Circ. 366: 6 pp.

McConnell, W. J. 1966. Preliminary report on the Malacca *Tilapia* hybrid as a sport fish in Arizona. Prog. Fish. Cult. 28:40-46.

McCrimmon, H. R. 1968. Carp in Canada. Fish. Res. Bd. Canada, Bull. 165: 93 pp.

McDonald, C. K. 1972. A key to the fishes of the family Gobii dae (Telestomi) of California. Bull. S. Calif. Acad. Sci. 71(2):108-112.

McKechnie, R. J. 1966. Spotted bass, 366-370; golden shiner, 488-492; logperch, 530-531. *In* A. Calhoun, ed., Inland Fisheries Management, Calif. Dept. Fish, Game.

——, and R. B. Fenner, 1971. Food habits of white sturgeon, *Acipenser transmontanus*, in San Pablo and Suisun bays, California. Calif. Fish, Game 57(3):209-212.

——, and R. C. Tharratt. 1966. Green sunfish, 399-402. *In* A. Calhoun, ed., Inland Fisheries Management. Calif. Dept. Fish, Game.

McLarney, W. O. 1968. Spawning habits and morphological variation in the coast range sculpin, *Cottus aleuticus* and the prickly sculpin, *Cottus asper*. Trans. Amer. Fish. Soc. 97(1):46-48.

McPhail, J. O., and C. C. Lindsey. 1970. Freshwater Fishes of Northwestern Canada Alaska. Fish. Res. Bd. Canada Bull. 173: 381 pp.

Markley, M. H. 1940. Notes on the food habits and parasites of the stickleback *Gasterosteus aculeatus* (Linnaeus) in the Sacramento River, California. Copeia 1940(4):223-225.

Martin, M. 1967. The distribution and morphology of the North American catostomid fishes of the Pit River system, California. M. A. Thesis, Sacramento State College.

——. 1972. Morphology and variation of the Modoc sucker, *Catostomus microps* Rutter, with notes on feeding adaptations. Calif. Fish, Game 58(4):277-284.

Mason, J. C. 1974. Behavioral ecology of chum salmon fry (*Oncorhynchus keta*) in a small estuary. J. Fish. Res. Bd. Canada 31(1):83-92.

Mathews, S. B. 1962. The ecology of the Sacramento perch, *Archoplites interruptus*, from selected areas of California and Nevada. M. A. Thesis, Univ. Calif., Berkeley, 93 pp.

——. 1965. Reproductive behavior of the Sacramento perch, *Archoplites interruptus*. Copeia 1965(2):224-228.

Mathur, D. 1972. Seasonal food habits of adult white crappie, *Pomoxis annularis* Rafinesque in Conowingo Reservoir. Amer. Midl. Nat. 87(1):236-241.

——, and T. W. Robbins. 1971. Food habits and feeding chronology of young white crappie, *Pomoxis annularis* Rafinesque in Conowingo Reservoir. Trans. Amer. Fish Soc. 100(2):307-311.

Mayr, E. 1966. Animal Species and Evolution. Harvard University Press, Cambridge, 797 pp.

Mense, J. B. 1967. Ecology of the Mississippi silversides, *Menidia audens* Hay in Lake Texoma. Bull. Okla. Fish. Res. Lab. 6:1-32.

Messersmith, J. D. 1965. Southern range extension for chum and silver salmon. Calif. Fish, Game 51(3):220.

——. 1966. Fishes collected in Carquinez Strait in 1961-1962, 57-62. *In* D. W. Kelly, ed., Ecological Studies of the Sacramento-San Joaquin Estuary, Part 1, Calif. Dept. Fish, Game Fish Bull. 133.

Miller, D. J., and R. N. Lea. 1972. Guide to the coastal marine fishes of California. Calif. Dept. Fish, Game Fish Bull. 157: 235 pp.

Miller, E. E. 1966. White catfish, 430-440; channel catfish, 440-463; black bullhead, 476-479; yellow bullhead, 479-480. *In* A. Calhoun, ed., Inland Fisheries Management, Calif. Dept. Fish, Game.

———. 1970. The age and growth of centrarchid fishes in Millerton and Pine Flat reservoirs, California. Calif. Dept. Fish, Game Inland Fish. Admin. Rpt. 71-4: 17 pp.

Miller, K. D., and R. H. Kramer. 1971. Spawning and early life history of largemouth bass (*Micropterus salmoides*) in Lake Powell, 73-83. *In* G. E. Hall, ed., Reservoir Fisheries and Limnology. Amer. Fish. Soc. Spec. Pub. 8.

Miller, L. W. 1965. A growth and blood protein analysis of two subspecies of largemouth bass; the Florida bass *Micropterus salmoides floridanus* (LeSueur), and the northern bass, *Micropterus salmoides salmoides* (Lacépède), in San Diego County, California. Calif. Dept. Fish, Game Inland Fish Admin. Rpt. 65-15: 18 pp.

———. 1972a. White sturgeon population characteristics in the Sacramento-San Joaquin estuary as measured by tagging. Calif. Fish, Game 58(2):94-101.

———. 1972b. Migrations of sturgeon tagged in the Sacramento-San Joaquin estuary. Calif. Fish, Game 58(2):102-106.

———. 1972c. White sturgeon, 54-56. *In* Ecological Studies of the Sacramento-San Joaquin Estuary. Calif. Dept. Fish, Game Delta Fish and Wildlife Protection Study, Rpt. 8.

———, and R. J. McKechnie. 1968. Observation of striped bass spawning in the Sacramento River. Calif. Fish, Game 54(4):306-307.

Miller, R. B. 1957. Permanence and size of home territory in stream-dwelling cutthroat trout. J. Fish. Res. Bd. Canada 14(3):687-691.

Miller, R. G. 1951. The natural history of Lake Tahoe fishes. Ph.D. Thesis, Stanford Univ., 160 pp.

Miller, R. R. 1939. Occurrence of the cyprinodont fish *Fundulus parvipinnis* in freshwater in San Juan Creek, southern California. Copeia 1939(3):168.

———. 1943a. Further data on freshwater populations of the Pacific killifish, *Fundulus parvipinnis*. Copeia 1943(1):51-52.

———. 1943b. *Cyprinodon salinus*, a new species of fish from Death Valley, California. Copeia 1943(2):69-78.

———. 1943c. The status of *Cyprinodon macularius* and *Cyprinodon nevadensis*, two desert fishes of western North America. Univ. Mich. Mus. Zool. Occ. Paper 473: 25 pp.

———. 1945. The status of *Lavinia ardesiaca*, a cyprinid fish from the Pajaro-Salinas Basin, California. Copeia 1945(4):197-204.

———. 1946. *Gila cypha*, a remarkable new species of fish from the Colorado River in Grand Canyon, Arizona. Wash. Acad. Sci. J. 36(12):403-415.

———. 1948. The cyprinodont fishes of the Death Valley System of eastern California and southwestern Nevada. Univ. Mich. Mus. Zool. Misc. Publ. 68: 155 pp.

———. 1952. Bait fishes of the lower Colorado River from Lake Mead, Nevada, to Yuma, Arizona with a key for their identification. Calif. Fish, Game 38(1):7-42.

———. 1958. Origin and affinities of the freshwater fish fauna of western North America, 187-222. *In* C. L. Hubbs, ed., Zoogeography, AAAS, Washington, D. C.

———. 1961a. Man and the changing fish fauna of the American Southwest. Papers Mich. Acad. Sci., Arts, Letters 46:365-404.

———. 1961b. Speciation rates in some freshwater fishes of western North America, 537-560. *In* F. Blair, ed., Vertebrate Speciation. University of Texas Press, Austin.

———. 1963. Synonymy, characters, and variation of *Gila crassicauda*, a rare Californian minnow, with an account of its hybridization with *Lavinia exilicauda*. Calif. Fish, Game 49(1):20-29.

. 1965. Quaternary freshwater fishes in western North America, 569-581. *In* H. E. Wright and D. G. Frey, eds., The Quaternary of the United States, Princeton University Press, Princeton.

. 1968. Records of some native freshwater fishes transplanted into various waters of California, Baja California, and Nevada. Calif. Fish and Game 54(3):170-179.

. 1972. Classification of the native trouts of Arizona with the description of a new species, *Salmo apache*. Copeia 1972(3):401-422.

. 1973. Two new fishes, *Gila bicolor snyderi* and *Catostomus fumeiventris*, from the Owens River Basin, California. Occ. Pap. Mus. Zool. Univ. Mich. 667: 119 pp.

, and C. L. Hubbs. 1969. Systematics of *Gasterosteus aculeatus* with particular reference to intergradation and introgression along the Pacific Coast of North America: a commentary on a recent contribution. Copeia 1969(1):52-69.

, and C. H. Lowe. 1964. An annotated checklist of the fishes of Arizona, 133-151. *In* C. H. Lowe, ed., The Vertebrates of Arizona, University of Arizona Press, Tucson.

, and E. P. Pister. 1971. Management of the Owens pupfish, *Cyprinodon radiosus*, in Mono County, California. Trans. Amer. Fish Soc. 100(3):502-509.

, and G. R. Smith. 1967. New fossil fishes from Plio-Pleistocene Lake Idaho. Occ. Pap. Mus. Zool. Univ. Mich. 654:1-24.

Miller, R. V. 1967. Food of the threadfin shad, *Dorosoma petenense*, in Lake Chicot, Arkansas. Trans. Amer. Fish Soc. 96(3):243-246.

Millikan, A. E. 1968. The life history and ecology of *Cottus asper* Richardson and *Cottus gulosus* (Girard) in Conner Creek, Washington. M. S. Thesis, Univ. Wash., 81 pp.

Minckley, W. L. 1959. Fishes of the Blue River Basin, Kansas. Univ. Kansas Publ. Mus. Nat. Hist. 11(7):401-402.

. 1973. Fishes of Arizona. Ariz. Dept. Fish, Game, 292 pp.

, and J. E. Deacon. 1959. Biology of flathead catfish in Kansas. Trans. Amer. Fish Soc. 88:344-355.

, and . 1968. Southwestern fishes and the enigma of "endangered species." Science 159:1424-1431.

, J. E. Johnson, J. N. Rinne, and S. E. Willoughby. 1970. Foods of buffalofishes, genus *Ictiobus*, in central Arizona reservoirs. Trans. Amer. Fish Soc. 99(2):333-342.

Moffett, J. W., and S. H. Smith. 1950. Biological investigations of the fishery resources of Trinity River, California. USFWS Spec. Sci. Rpt. Fisheries 12: 71 pp.

Moodie, G. E. E. 1972. Morphology, life history, and the ecology of an unusual stickleback (*Gasterosteus aculeatus*) in the Queen Charlotte Island, Canada. Can. J. Zool. 50(6):721-732.

Moore, G. A. 1968. Fishes, 21-168. *In* W. F. Blair, ed., Vertebrates of the United States. McGraw-Hill Book Company, New York.

Moyle, J. B., and J. Kuehn. 1964. Carp, a sometimes villain, 635-642. *In* J. P. Linduska, ed., Waterfowl Tomorrow. U.S. Dept. Interior, Washington, D.C.

Moyle, P. B. 1969a. Ecology of the fishes of a Minnesota lake, with special reference to the Cyprinidae. Ph.D. Thesis, Univ. Minnesota, 169 pp.

. 1969b. Comparative behavior of young brook trout of domestic and wild origin. Prog. Fish. Cult. 31(1):51-56.

. 1970. Occurence of king (chinook) salmon in the Kings River, Fresno County. Calif. Fish, Game 56(4):314-315.

. 1973. Recent changes in the fish fauna of the San Joaquin River system. Cal. Neva. Wildl. 1973:60-63.

. 1974. Status of the Modoc sucker, *Catostomus microps* (Pisces: Catostomidae). Cal. Neva. Wildl. 1974:35-38.

. In press. Some effects of channelization on the fishes and invertebrates of Rush Creek, Modoc County, California. Calif. Fish, Game.

. In press. California trout streams: the way they were, probably *in* P. Moyle and D. Koch, eds., Trout-Nongame Fish Relationships in Streams. Publ. Cent. Water Resources Res., Univ. Nev.

, F. W. Fisher, and H. Li. 1974. Mississippi silversides and log perch in the Sacramento-San Joaquin River system. Calif. Dept. Fish, Game 60(2):145-147.

, and A. Marciochi. In press. Biology of the Modoc sucker, *Catostomus microps* (Pisces: Catostomidae) in northeastern California. Copeia.

, S. B. Mathews, and N. Bonderson. 1974. Feeding habits of the Sacramento perch, *Archoplites interruptus*. Trans. Amer. Fish Soc. 103(2):399-402.

, and R. Nichols. 1973. Ecology of some native and introduced fishes of the Sierra-Nevada foothills in central California. Copeia 1973(3):478-490.

, and   . 1974. Decline of the native fish fauna of the Sierra-Nevada foothills, central California. Amer. Midl. Nat. 92(1):72-83.

Mullan, J. W., and R. L. Applegate. 1968. Centrarchid food habits in a new and old reservoir during the following bass spawning. Proc. 21 Ann. Conf. SE Assoc. Game, Fish. Comm.: 332-242.

, and   . 1970. Food habits of five centrarchids during the filling of Beaver Reservoir 1965-1966. U.S. Bur. Sport Fish., Wildl. Tech. Paper 50: 16 pp.

,   , and W. C. Rainwater. 1968. Food of logperch (*Percina caprodes*) and brook silverside (*Labidesthes sicculus*), in a new and old Ozark reservoir. Trans. Amer. Fish Soc. 97(3):300-305.

Munro, J. A., and W. A. Clemens. 1937. The American merganser in British Columbia and its relation to the fish population. Biol. Bd. Canada Bull. 6(2):1-50.

Murphy, G. I. 1943. Sexual dimorphism in the minnows *Hesperoleucus* and *Rhinichthys*. Copeia 1943(3):187-188.

. 1948a. A contribution to the life history of the Sacramento perch (*Archoplites interruptus*) in Clear Lake, Lake County, California. Calif. Fish, Game 34(3):93-100.

. 1948b. Notes on the biology of the Sacramento hitch (*Lavinia e. exilicauda*) of Clear Lake, California. Calif. Fish, Game 34(3):101-110.

. 1948c. Distribution and variation of the roach (*Hesperoleucus*) in the coastal region of California. M. A. Thesis, Univ. Calif., Berkeley.

. 1949. The food of young largemouth bass (*Micropterus salmoides*) in Clear Lake, California. Calif. Fish, Game 35(3):159-163.

. 1950. The life history of the greaser blackfish (*Orthodon microlepidotus*) of Clear Lake, Lake County, California. Calif. Fish, Game 36(2):119-133.

. 1951. The fishery of Clear Lake, Lake County, California. Calif. Fish, Game 37(4):439-484.

. 1963. Trout survival in Taylor Creek, a tributary of Lake Tahoe, California. Calif. Fish, Game 49(1):16-19.

Myers, G. S. 1965. *Gambusia*, the fish destroyer. Aust. Zool. 13(2):102.

Naiman, R. J., S. D. Gerking, and T. D. Ratcliffe. 1973. Thermal environment of a Death Valley pupfish. Copeia 1973(2):366-369.

, and E. P. Pister. 1974. Occurrence of the tiger barb, *Barbus razone*, in the Owens Valley, California. Calif. Fish, Game 60(47):100-101.

Needham, P. R., and R. Gard. 1959. Rainbow trout in Mexico and California, with notes on the cutthroat series. Univ. Calif. Publ. Zool. 67(1): 123 pp.

, and A. A. Hanson. 1935. A stream survey of the waters of Sierra National Forest, California, 1934. U.S. Bur. Fish. Mimeo, 55 pp.

, and A. C. Jones. 1959. Flow, temperature, solar radiation and ice in relation to activities of fishes in Sagehen Creek, California. Ecology 40(3):465-474.

, and T. M. Vaughan. 1952. Spawning of the Dolly Varden, *Salvelinus malma*, in Twin Creek, Idaho. Copeia 1952(3):197-199.

, and E. H. Vestal. 1938. Notes on growth of golden trout (*Salmo agua-bonita*) in two high Sierra lakes. Calif. Fish, Game 24(3):273-279.

Northcote, T. G. 1954. Observations on the comparative ecology of two species of fish, *Cottus asper* and *Cottus rhotheus* in British Columbia. Copeia 1954(1):25-28.

——— (ed.). 1969. Symposium on Salmon and Trout in Streams. H. R. MacMillan Lectures in Fisheries. Inst. Fish. Univ. B. C., Vancouver, 388 pp.

———, and G. F. Hartman. 1959. A case of "schooling" behavior in the prickly sculpin, *Cottus asper* Richardson. Copeia 1959(1):158-159.

Oakeshott, G. B. 1971. California's Changing Landscapes. McGraw-Hill Book Company, New York. 388 pp.

Odemar, M. W. 1964. Southern range extension of the eulachon, *Thaleichthys pacificus*. Calif. Fish, Game 50(4):304-307.

Odum, W. E. 1968. The ecological significance of fine particle selection by the striped mullet, *Mugil cephalus*. Limn., Ocean. 13(1):92-98.

Okada, Y. 1961. Studies on the freshwater fishes of Japan. Prefect. Univ. Mie, Tsu, Mie Prefect., Japan 9: 860 pp.

Orcutt, H. G. 1950. The life history of the starry flounder *Platichthys stellatus* (Pallas). Calif. Dept. Fish, Game Fish Bull. 78: 64 pp.

Parker, R. R. 1971. Size selective predation among juvenile salmonid fishes in a British Columbia inlet. J. Fish. Res. Bd. Canada 28(10):1503-1510.

Parsons, J. W. 1953. Growth and habits of the redeye bass. Trans. Amer. Fish. Soc. 83:202-211.

———, and E. Crittenden. 1959. Growth of the redeye bass in Chipola River, Florida. Trans. Amer. Fish. Soc. 88(3):191-192.

Patten, B. G. 1971. Spawning and fecundity of seven species of northwest American *Cottus*. Am. Midl. Nat. 85(2):493-506.

———, and D. T. Rodman. 1969. Reproductive behavior of the northern squawfish, *Ptychocheilus oregonensis*. Trans. Amer. Fish. Soc. 98(1):108-111.

Pease, R. W. 1965. Modoc County, a Geographic Time Continuum on the California Volcanic Tableland. Univ. Calif. Publ. Geog. 17: 304 pp.

Peden, A. 1972. The function of gonopodial parts and behavioral pattern during copulation by *Gambusia* (Poeciliidae). Can. J. Zool. 50(7):955-968.

Pelzman, R. J. 1971. The blue catfish. Calif. Dept. Fish, Game Admin. Rept. 71-11: 7 pp.

——— 1972. Evaluation of introduction of *Tilapia sparrmanii* into California. Calif. Dept. Fish, Game Inland Fish Admin. Rpt. 72-3: 7 pp.

——— 1973. A review of the life history of *Tilapia zillii* with a reassessment of its desirability in California. Calif. Dept. Fish, Game Inland Fish. Rpt. 74-1: 9 pp.

Perry, W. G. 1968. Distribution and relative abundance of blue catfish, *Ictalurus furcatus*, and channel catfish with relation to salinity. Proc. 21st Ann. Conf. SE Assoc. Game, Fish Comm.: 436-444.

———, and J. W. Avault. 1969. Culture of blue, channel, and white catfish in brackish water ponds. Proc. 23rd Ann. Conf. SE Assoc. Game, Fish Comm.: 1-15.

Phillips, R. W., and E. W. Claire. 1966. Intragravel movement of the reticulate sculpin, *Cottus perplexus*, and its potential as a predator on salmonid embryos. Trans. Amer. Fish Soc. 95(2):210-212.

Pintler, H. E., and W. C. Johnson. 1958. Chemical control of rough fish in the Russian River drainage, California. Calif. Fish, Game 44(2):91-124.

Pister, E. P. 1971. The Rare and Endangered Fishes of the Death Valley System. Desert Fishes Council, Bishop, Calif., 26 pp.

——— 1974. Desert fishes and their habitats. Trans. Amer. Fish Soc. 103(3):531-540.

Pontius, R. W., and M. Parker. 1973. Food habits of the mountain whitefish, *Prosopium williamsoni* (Girard). Trans. Amer. Fish Soc. 102(4):764-773.

Porter, R. G. 1964. Food and feeding of staghorn sculpin (*Leptocottus armatus* Girard) and starry flounders (*Platichthys stellatus* Pallas) in euryhaline environments. M. S. Thesis, Humboldt State College, 84 pp.

Prather, E. E. 1957. Preliminary experiments on winter feeding small fathead minnows. Proc. 11th Ann. Conf. SE Assoc. Game, Fish Comm.: 249-253.

Priegel, G. R. 1970. Food of the white bass, *Roccus chrysops*, in Lake Winnebago, Wisconsin. Trans. Amer. Fish. Soc. 99(2):440-443.

———. 1971. Age and rate of growth of the white bass in Lake Winnebago, Wisconsin. Trans. Amer. Fish Soc. 100(3):567-590.

Pycha, R. L. 1956. Progress report on white sturgeon studies. Calif. Fish, Game 42(1):23-35.

Radtke, L. D. 1966. Distribution of smelt, juvenile sturgeon and starry flounder in the Sacramento-San Joaquin Delta, 115-119. *In* S. L. Turner and D. W. Kelley, eds., Ecological Studies of the Sacramento-San Joaquin Delta, Part II, Calif. Fish, Game Fish Bull. 136.

Raney, E. 1952. The life history of the striped bass, *Roccus saxatilis* (Walbaum). Bull. Bingham Ocean. Coll. 14(1):5-97.

Rawstron, R. R. 1964. Spawning of the threadfin shad, *Dorosoma petenense*, at low water temperatures. Calif. Fish, Game 50(1):58.

———. 1967. Harvest, mortality, and movement of selected warmwater fishes in Folsom Lake, California. Calif. Fish, Game 53(1):40-48.

Reed, R. J. 1967. Observation of fishes associated with spawning salmon. Trans. Amer. Fish. Soc. 96(1):62-66.

Rees, B. 1958. Attributes of the mosquitofish in relation to mosquito control. Proc. 26th Ann. Conf. Calif. Mosq. Contr. Assoc.: 71-75.

Reeves, J. E. 1964. Age and growth of hardhead minnow, *Mylopharodon conocephalus* (Baird and Girard), in the American River basin of California, with notes on its ecology. M. S. Thesis, Univ. Calif., Berkeley, 90 pp.

Reimers, N. 1958. Conditions of existence, growth and longevity of brook trout in a small high-altitude lake of the eastern Sierra Nevada. Calif. Dept. Fish, Game 44(4):319-333.

Reimers, P. E. 1973. The length of residence of juvenile fall Chinook salmon in Sixes River, Oregon. Res. Rpts. Ore. Fish Comm. 4(2):1-43.

Renfro, W. C. 1960. Salinity relations of some fishes in the Arkansas River, Texas. Tulane St. Zool. 8:83-91.

Richardson, W. M., J. A. St. Amant, L. J. Bottroff, and L. Parker. 1970. Introduction of blue catfish into California. Calif. Fish, Game 56(4):311-312.

Ricker, W. E. 1960. A population of dwarf coastrange sculpins (*Cottus aleuticus*). J. Fish. Res. Bd. Canada 17(3):929-932.

Riggs, C. C. 1955. Reproduction of the white bass, *Morone chrysops*. Invest. Ind. Lakes, Streams 4(3):87-110.

Robins, C. R., and R. R. Miller. 1957. Classification, variation, and distribution of the sculpins, genus *Cottus*, inhabiting pacific slope waters in California and southern Oregon, with a key to the species. Calif. Fish, Game 43(31):213-233.

Rogers, D. W. 1974. Chum salmon observations in four north coast streams. Calif. Fish, Game 60(3):148.

Roos, J. F., P. Gilhousen, S. R. Killick, and E. R. Zyblut. 1973. Parasitism on juvenile Pacific salmon (*Oncorhynchus*) and Pacific herring (*Clupea harengeus pallasi*) in the Strait of Georgia by the river lamprey (*Lampetra ayresi*). J. Fish. Res. Bd. Canada 30(4):565-568.

Rosato, P., and D. Ferguson. 1968. The toxicity of endrin-resistant mosquitofish to eleven species of vertebrates. BioScience 18(8):783-784.

Rosen, D. E., and R. M. Bailey. 1963. The poeciliid fishes (Cyprinodontiformes), their structure, zoogeography, and systematics. Bull. Am. Mus. Nat. Hist. 126(1):1-126.

Rudd, R. L., and S. G. Herman. 1972. Ecosystemic transferal of pesticide residues in an aquatic environment, 471-485. *In* Environmental Toxicology of Pesticides, Academy Press, New York.

Rutter, C. 1908. The fishes of the Sacramento-San Joaquin basin, with a study of their distribution and variation. Bull. U.S. Bur. Fish. 27(637):103-152.

St. Amant, J. A. 1966a. Addition of *Tilapia mossambica* Peters to the California fauna. Calif. Fish, Game 52(1):54-55.

———. 1966b. Progress report of the culture of *Tilapia mossambica* Peters hybrids in southern California. Calif. Fish, Game Admin. Rpt. 66-9: 25 pp.

———. 1970. Addition of Hart's rivulus, *Rivulus harti* (Boulenger) to the California fauna. Calif. Fish, Game 56(2):138.

———, and F. G. Hoover. 1969. Addition of *Misgurnus anguillicaudatus* (Cantor) to the fish fauna of California. Calif. Fish, Game 55(4):330-331.

———, and S. Sasaki. 1971. Progress report on reestablishment of the Mohave chub, *Gila mohavensis* (Snyder) – an endangered species. Calif. Fish, Game 57(4):307-308.

———, and I. Sharp. 1971. Addition of *Xiphophorus variatus* (Meek) to the California fauna. Calif. Fish, Game 57(2):128-129.

Sasaki, S. 1966. Distribution and food habits of king salmon, *Oncorhynchus tshawytscha*, and steelhead rainbow trout, *Salmo gairdnerii*, in the Sacramento-San Joaquin Delta, 108-114. *In* J. L. Turner and D. W. Kelley, eds., Ecological Studies of the Sacramento-San Joaquin Delta, Part II, Fishes of the Delta. Calif. Dept. Fish, Game Fish Bull. 136.

Saunders, R. P. 1959. A study of the food of the Mississippi silversides, *Menidia audens* Hay, in Lake Texoma. M. S. Thesis, Univ. Okla., Norman.

Schneider, C. P. 1971. Scuba observations on spawning smallmouth bass. N. Y. Fish, Game J. 18(2):112-116.

Schreck, C. B., and R. J. Behnke. 1971. Trouts of the upper Kern River Basin, California, with reference to systematics and evolution of western North American *Salmo*. J. Fish. Res. Bd. Canada 28(7):987-998.

Schultz, L. P. 1930. The life history of *Lampetra planeri* Bloch, with a statistical analysis of the rate of growth of the larvae from western Washington. Occ. Papers. Mus. Zool. Univ. Mich. 221:1-39.

Schulz, P. D., and D. D. Simons. 1973. Fish species diversity in a prehistoric central California Indian midden. Calif. Fish, Game 59(2):107-113.

Scofield, N. B. 1916. The humpback and dog salmon taken in San Lorenzo River. Calif. Fish, Game 2(1):41.

Scott, W. B. 1967. Freshwater Fishes of Eastern Canada. University of Toronto Press, Toronto, 137 pp.

———, and E. J. Crossman. 1973. Freshwater Fishes of Canada. Fish. Res. Bd. Canada Bull. 184: 966 pp.

Seaburg, K. G., and J. B. Moyle. 1964. Feeding habits, digestion rates, and growth of some Minnesota warmwater fishes. Trans. Amer. Fish. Soc. 93(3):269-285.

Seeley, C. M., and G. W. McCammon. 1966. Kokanee, 274-294. *In* A. Calhoun, ed., Inland Fisheries Management. Calif. Dept. Fish, Game.

Shapovalov, L. 1941. The freshwater fish fauna of California. Proc. Sixth Pac. Sci, Congress 3:441-446.

———. 1944. The tench in California. Calif. Fish, Game 30(1):54-57.

———, W. A. Dill, and A. J. Cordone. 1959. A revised checklist of the freshwater and anadromous fishes of California. Calif. Dept. Fish, Game 45(3):155-180.

———, and A. C. Taft. 1954. The life histories of the steelhead rainbow trout (*Salmo gairdneri gairdneri*) and silver salmon (*Oncorhynhus kisutch*). Calif. Dept. Fish, Game Fish Bull. 98: 575 pp.

Shelby, W. H. 1917. History of the introduction of food and game fishes into the waters of California. Calif. Fish, Game 3(1):3-12.

Sheldon, A. L. 1968. Drift, growth, and mortality of juvenile sculpins in Sagehen Creek, California. Trans. Amer. Fish. Soc. 97(4):495-496.

Sigler, W. F. 1958. The ecology and use of carp in Utah. Utah State Univ. Ag. Expt. St. Bull. 405: 63 pp.

———, and R. R. Miller. 1963. Fishes of Utah. Utah Dept. Fish, Game, 203 pp.

Sisk, M. E., and R. R. Stephens. 1964. *Menidia audens* (Pisces: Atherinidae) in Boomer Lake, Oklahoma, and its possible spread in the Arkansas River system. Proc. Okla. Acad. Sci. 44:71-73.

Skillman, R. A. 1969. The population, organization, and dispersal of redear sunfish in Lake Berryessa. Ph.D. Thesis, Univ. Calif., Davis, 101 pp.

Skinner, J. E. 1962. An historical view of the fish and wildlife resources of the San Francisco Bay area. Calif. Dept. Fish, Game Water Projects Branch Rpt. 1: 225 pp.

———. 1971. *Anguilla* recorded from California. Calif. Fish, Game 57(1):75-79.

———. 1972. Ecological studies of the Sacramento-San Joaquin Estuary. Calif. Delt. of Fish, Game, Delta Fish Wildlife Prot. Study Rpt. 8: 94 pp.

Smith, G. R. 1966. Distribution and evolution of the North American catostomid fishes of the subgenus *Pantosteus*, genus *Catostomus*. Univ. Mich. Mus. Zool. Misc. Pub. 129:1-33.

Smith, P. W., and L. M. Page. 1969. The food of spotted bass in streams of the Wabash River Drainage. Trans. Amer. Fish. Soc. 98(4):647-651.

Snyder, J. O. 1905. Notes on the fishes of the streams flowing into San Francisco Bay. Rpt. Bur. Fish. App. 5:327-338.

———. 1908a. Relationships of the fish fauna of the lakes of southeastern Oregon. Bull. Bureau Fish 27:69-102.

———. 1908b. Description of *Pantosteus santa-anae*, a new species of fish from the Santa Ana River, California. Proc. U.S. Nat. Mus. 34:33-34.

———. 1908c. The fishes of the coastal streams of Oregon and northern California. Bull. U.S. Bur. Fish 27:153-189.

———. 1908d. The fauna of the Russian River, California, and its relation to that of the Sacramento. Science n.s. 27:269-271.

———. 1913. The fishes of the streams tributary to Monterey Bay, California. Bull. U.S. Bur. Fish. 32:49-72.

———. 1918. The fishes of the Lahontan system of Nevada and northeastern California. Bull. U.S. Bur. Fish. 35:31-86.

———. 1919a. An account of some fishes from the Owens River, California. Proc. U.S. Nat. Mus. 54(2333):201-205.

———. 1919b. The fishes of Mohave River, California. Proc. U.S. Nat. Mus. 54(2236):297-299.

———. 1931. Salmon of the Klamath River, California. Calif. Div. Fish, Game Fish Bull. 34: 129 pp.

———. 1933. California trout. Calif. Fish, Game 19(2):81-112.

Staley, J. 1966. Brown trout, 233-242. *In* A. Calhoun, ed., Inland Fisheries Management, Calif. Dept. Fish, Game.

Starostka, V. J., and R. L. Applegate. 1970. Food selectivity of bigmouth buffalo, *Ictiobus cyprinellus*, in Lake Poinsett, South Dakota. Trans. Amer. Fish. Soc. 99(3):571-576.

Stein, R. A., P. E. Reimers, and J. D. Hall. 1972. Social interaction between juvenile coho (*Oncorhynchus kisutch*) and fall chinook salmon (*O. tshawytscha*) in Sixes River, Oregon. J. Rish Res. Bd. Canada 29(12):1737-1748.

Sterba, G. 1959. Freshwater Fishes of the World. Vista Books, London, 878 pp.

Stevens, D. E. 1966. Distribution and food habits of the American shad, *Alosa sapidissima*, in the Sacramento-San Joaquin Estuary, 97-107. *In* J. L. Turner and D. W. Kelley, eds., Ecological Studies of the Sacramento-San Joaquin Estuary, Part II, Fishes of the Delta. Calif. Dept. of Fish, Game Fish Bull. 136.

. 1972. American shad, 52-54. *In* J. E. Skinner, ed., Ecological Studies of the Sacramento-San Joaquin Estuary. Calif. Dept. Fish, Game Delta Fish and Wildlife Prot. Study 8.

, and L. W. Miller. 1970. Distribution and abundance of sturgeon larvae in the Sacramento-San Joaquin River system. Calif. Fish, Game 56(2):80-86.

Stevenson, M. M. 1971. *Percina macrolepida* (Pisces, Percidae, Etheostomatinea), a new percid fish of the subgenus *Percina* from Texas. SW Nat. 16(1):65-83.

Swe, W., and W. R. Dickinson. 1970. Sedimentation and thrusting of late Mesozoic rocks in the coast ranges near Clear Lake, California. Geol. Soc. Amer. Bull. 81(1):165-187.

Swift, C. 1965. Early development of the hitch, *Lavinia exilcauda*, of Clear Lake, California. Calif. Fish, Game 51(2):74-80.

Taft, A. C., and G. I. Murphy. 1950. Life history of the Sacramento squawfish (*Ptychocheilus grandis*). Calif. Fish, Game 36(2):197-164.

Talbot, G. B. 1966. Estuarine and environmental requirements for striped bass, 37-42. *In* R. F. Smith, A. H. Swartz, and W. H. Massmann, eds., A Symposium on Estuarine Fisheries. Amer. Fish. Soc. Spec. Pub. 3.

, and J. E. Sykes. 1958. Atlantic coast migrations of American shad. Fish. Bull. 58:473-490.

Tarp, F. H. 1952. A revision of the family Embiotocidae (the surfperches). Calif. Dept. Fish, Game Bull. 88: 99 pp.

Thomas, J. L. 1967. The diet of juvenile and adult striped bass, *Roccus saxatilis*, in the Sacramento-San Joaquin river system. Calif. Fish, Game 53(1):49-62.

Thompson, R. B. 1959. Food of the squawfish, *Ptychocheilus oregonensis* (Richardson) of the lower Columbia River. U.S. Fish, Wildl. Serv. Fish Bull. 60(158):1-58.

Thomson, J. M. 1963. Synopsis of biological data on the grey mullet, *Mugil cephalus* Linneaus, 1758. CSIRO Fish. Synopsis 1: 65 pp.

Tinbergen, N. 1953. Social Behavior in Animals. Methuen and Company, Limited, London, 150 pp.

Todd, E. S. 1968. Terrestrial sojourns of the longjaw mudsucker, *Gillichthys mirabilis*. Copeia 1968(1):192-199.

, and W. Ebeling. 1966. Aerial respiration in the longjaw mudsucker *Gillichthys mirabilis* (Teleostei: Gobiidae). Biol. Lab. Woods Hole 130:265-288.

Trautman, M. B. 1942. Fish distribution and abundance correlated with stream gradients as a consideration in stocking programs. Trans. 7th N. Am. Wildl. Conf.: 211-223.

. 1957. Fishes of Ohio. Ohio State University Press, Columbus, 683 pp.

Turner, J. L. 1966a. Distribution and food habits of ictalurid fishes in the Sacramento-San Joaquin Delta, 130-143. *In* J. L. Turner and D. W. Kelley, eds., Ecological Studies of the Sacramento-San Joaquin Delta, Part II. Calif. Dept. Fish, Game Fish Bull. 136.

. 1966b. Distribution and food habits of centrarchid fishes in the Sacramento-San Joaquin Delta, 144-151. *In* J. L. Turner and D. W. Kelley, eds., Ecological Studies of the Sacramento-San Joaquin Delta, Part II. Calif. Dept. Fish, Game Fish Bull. 136.

. 1966c. Distribution of cyprinid fishes in the Sacramento-San Joaquin Delta, 154-159. *In* J. L. Turner and D. W. Kelley, eds., Ecological Studies of the Sacramento-San Joaquin Delta, Part II. Calif. Dept. Fish, Game Fish Bull. 136.

. 1966d. Distribution of threadfin shad, *Dorosoma petenense*, tule perch, *Hysterocarpus traskii*, and crayfish spp. in the Sacramento-San Joaquin Delta, 160-168. *In* J. L. Turner and D. W. Kelley, eds., Ecological Studies of the Sacramento-San Joaquin Delta, Part II. Calif. Dept. Fish, Game Fish Bull. 136.

. 1972. Striped bass, 36-43. *In* J. E. Skinner, ed., Ecological Studies of the Sacramento-San Joaquin Estuary. Calif. Dept. Fish, Game Delta Fish, Wildlife Prot. Study Rpt. 8.

Turner, P. R. and R. C. Summerfelt. 1971. Reproductive biology of the flathead catfish, *Pylodictis olivaris* (Rafinesque), in a turbid Oklahoma reservoir, 107-119. *In* G. E. Hall, ed., Reservoir Fisheries and Limnology. Amer. Fish. Soc. Spec. Publ. 8.

U.S. Department of the Interior. 1971. Status of the desert pupfish. Pupfish Task Force Report, Washington, D.C.: 13 pp.

Uyeno, T. 1966. Osteology and phylogeny of the American cyprinid fishes, allied to the genus *Gila*. Ph.D. Thesis, Univ. Mich.

Vanicek, C. D. 1970. Distribution of Green River fishes in Utah and Colorado following closure of Flaming George Dam. S. W. Nat. 19(3):297-315.

———, and H. Kramer. 1969. Life history of the Colorado squawfish, *Ptychocheilus lucius*, and the Colorado chub, *Gila robusta*, in the Green River in Dinosaur National Monument, 1964-1966. Trans. Amer. Fish. Soc. 98(2):192-208.

Varley, M. E. 1967. British Freshwater Fishes. Fishing News Limited, London, 198 pp.

Vestal, E. H. 1942. Rough fish control in Gull Lake, Mono County, California. Calif. Fish, Game 28(1):34-61.

———. 1943. Creel returns from hatchery trout in June Lake, California. Calif. Fish, Game 29(2):51-63.

Vicker, C. E. 1973. Aspects of the life history of the Mojave chub, *Gila bicolor mohavensis* (Snyder) from Soda Lake, California. M. A. Thesis, Calif. State Univ., Fullerton, 27 pp.

Vincent, D. T. 1968. The influence of some environmental factors on the distribution of fishes in upper Klamath Lake. M.S. Thesis, Ore. State Univ.

Vincent, R. E. and W. H. Miller. 1969. Altitudinal distribution of brown trout and other fishes in a headwater tributary of the south Platte River, Colorado. Ecol. 50(3):464-466.

Vladykov, V. D. 1973. *Lampetra pacifica*, a new nonparasitic species of lamprey (Petromyzontidae) from Oregon and California. J. Fish Res. Bd. Canada 30(2):205-213.

———, and W. I. Follett. 1958. Redescription of *Lampetra ayersii* (Gunther) of western North America, a species of lamprey (Petromyzontidae) distinct from *Lampetra fluviatilis* (Linnaeus) of Europe. J. Fish Res. Bd. Canada 15(1):47-77.

———, and ———. 1962. The teeth of lampreys (Petromyzonidae): their terminology and use in a key to the holarctic genera. J. Fish Res. Bd. Canada 24(5):1067-1075.

von Geldern, C. E. 1964. Distribution of white catfish, *Ictalurus catus*, and *Salmo gairdneri*, in Folsom Lake, California as determined by gill netting from February through November, 1961. Calif. Dept. Fish, Game Inland Fish. Admin. Rpt. 64-15: 9 pp.

———. 1965. Evidence of American shad reproduction in a landlocked environment. Calif. Fish, Game 51(3):212-213.

———. 1966. The introduction of white bass (*Roccus chrysops*) into California. Calif. Fish, Game 52(4):303.

———. 1971. Abundance and distribution of fingerling largemouth bass, *Micropterus salmoides*, as determined by electrofishing, at Lake Nacimiento, California. Calif. Fish, Game 57(4):228-245.

———. 1974. Black bass: what does the future hold in store for these fine game fish in California? Outdoor Calif. 35(1):13-16.

Vrat, V. 1949. Reproductive behavior and development of eggs of the three spined stickleback (*Gasterosteus aculeatus*) of California. Copeia (4):252-260.

Wahrshaftig, C., and J. H. Birman. 1965. The quaternary of the Pacific mountain system in California, 299-338. *In* H. E. Wright and D. G. Frey, eds., The Quaternary of the United States, Princeton University Press, Princeton.

Wales, J. H. 1939. General report of investigations on the McCloud River drainage in 1938. Calif. Dept. Fish, Game 25(4):272-309.

——. 1946. The hardhead problem in the Sacramento River above Shasta Lake. Calif. Dept. Fish, Game Inland Fish. Admin. Rpt. 46-1: 4 pp.

——. 1962. Introduction of pond smelt from Japan into California. Calif. Fish, Game 48(2):141-142.

Walker, B. W., ed. 1961. The Ecology of the Salton Sea, California, in Relation to the Sportfishery. Calif. Dept. Fish, Game Fish Bull. 113: 204 pp.

——, R. R. Whitney, and G. W. Barlow. 1961. The fishes of the Salton Sea, 77-92. *In* B. W. Walker, ed., The Ecology of the Salton Sea, California, in Relation to the Sportfishery. Calif. Dept. Fish, Game Fish Bull. 113.

Wallace, C. R. 1967. Observations on the reproductive behavior of black bullhead (*Ictalurus melas*). Copeia 1967(4):852-853.

Walton, I. 1653. The Compleat Angler. Collier Books, New York, 191 pp. (reprint, 1965).

Weatherley, A. H. 1959. Some features of the biology of the tench, *Tinca tinca* (Linnaeus) in Tasmania. J. Animal Ecol. 28:73-87.

Webster, D. W. 1954. Smallmouth bass, *Micropterus dolomieui*, in Cayuga Lake. Part I. Life history and environment. Cornell Univ. Ag. Expt. St. Mem. 327: 38 pp.

Weisel, G. F. 1947. Breeding behavior and early development of the mudsucker, a gobiid fish of California. Copeia 1947(1):77-85.

Werner, R. G. 1967. Intralacustrine movements of bluegill fry in Crane Lake, Indiana. Trans. Am. Fish Soc. 96(4):416-420.

——. 1969. Ecology of limnetic bluegill (*Lepomis macrochirus*) in Crane Lake, Indiana. Am. Midl. Nat. 81(1):164-181.

Wheeler, A. 1969. The Fishes of the British Isles and Northwest Europe. Michigan State University Press, East Lansing, 613 pp.

White H. C., J. C. Medcof, and L. R. Day. 1965. Are killifish poisonous? J. Fish Res. Bd. Canada 22(2):635-638.

Wigglesworth, K. A., and R. R. Rawstron. 1974. Exploitation, survival, growth and cost of stocked silver salmon in Lake Berryessa, California. Calif. Fish, Game 60(1):36-43.

Wilbur, R. L. 1969. The redear sunfish in Florida. Fla. Game, Freshw. Fish. Comm. Fish. Bull. 5: 64 pp.

Willsrud, T. 1971. A study of the Tahoe sucker, *Catostomus tahoensis* Gill and Jordan. M. S. Thesis, San Jose State Coll., 96 pp.

Winn, H. E. 1958a. Comparative reproductive behavior and ecology of fourteen species of darters (Pisces-Percidae). Ecol. Monogr. 28:155-191.

——. 1958b. Observations on the reproductive habits of darters (Pisces-Percidae). Am. Midl. Nat. 59(1):190-212.

——, and R. R. Miller. 1954. Native post-larval fishes of the lower Colorado River Basin with a key to their identification. Calif. Fish, Game 40(3):273-285.

Wynne-Edwards, V. C. 1932. The breeding habits of the blackheaded minnow (*Pimephales promelas* Raf.). Trans. Amer. Fish Soc. 62:382-383.

Index